BRITAIN-USA NOW: A survey in key words

On behalf of the
Institut für Fremdsprachen und Auslandskunde
bei der Universität Erlangen-Nürnberg

Edited by

ISOLDE FRIEBEL and

VERLAG MORITZ DIESTERWEG
Frankfurt am Main · Berlin · München
6654

CIP-Kurztitelaufnahme der Deutschen Bibliothek

Britain, USA now:
a survey in key words / on behalf of the Inst. für Fremdsprachen
u. Auslandskunde bei d. Univ. Erlangen-Nürnberg.
Ed. by Isolde Friebel and Heinrich Händel.
– 4. Aufl. –
Frankfurt am Main, Berlin, München: Diesterweg, 1979.
ISBN 3-425-06654-4

NE: Friebel, Isolde (Hrsg.)

ISBN 3-425-06654-4

4. Auflage 1979

Satz und Druck: Graphoprint, Koblenz
Bindearbeit: A. Hiort, Wiesbaden

Contributors

Godfrey R. Carr, Ph. D. (GRC)

Heinz Fiebiger
Institut für Fremdsprachen und Auslandskunde bei der Universität Erlangen-Nürnberg (HF)

John L. Flood, M.A.
King's College, University of London (JLF)

Dr. rer. pol. Isolde Friebel
Institut für Fremdsprachen und Auslandskunde bei der Universität Erlangen-Nürnberg (IFr)

Heinrich Händel
Universität Erlangen-Nürnberg (HH)

Dr. phil. Paul Hartig
Freie Universität Berlin (PH)

David Heath, M.A.
Universität Erlangen-Nürnberg (DH)

H. C. Hillman, M.A.
University of Leeds (HCH)

Eva Hohenner-Voigt (EV)

Daniel P. Huden, Ph.D.
University of Maryland (DPH)

Collin C. Randlesome, M.A.
Cranfield Institute of Technology (CCR)

Marion Schreiber *(Index)*
Institut für Fremdsprachen und Auslandskunde bei der Universität Erlangen-Nürnberg

Roger L. Snook, M.A.
Universität Stuttgart (RLS)

Hans-Joachim Specht
Oberlandesgericht Nürnberg-Fürth (HJS)

Samuel R. Spencer Jr., Ph.D.
Davidson College, N.C. (SRSp)

Dr. phil. Helga Steininger (HSt)

Dr. theol. Paul v. Tucher (PvT)

Geoffrey Williams, B.A., M.Ph.

In memoriam

Dr. Karl Friebel

Preface to the first edition

The original plan of this book, the arrangement of the material and the method of its presentation are the work of Dr. Karl Friebel, the founder and first director of the Institut für Fremdsprachen und Auslandskunde bei der Universität Erlangen-Nürnberg. After Dr. Friebel's death in September 1962 the main task of completing the book, conceived and begun by him, was undertaken by the members of the staff of this Institute. The editors and contributors hope that they have provided a useful work of reference for translators, interpreters, philologists and all those who in the course of their studies or profession are concerned with the political institutions, social structures, educational systems, churches, economic policies or social services of Great Britain and the U.S.A.

The key words cover important non-literary areas, that is, government and society, law, education, religion, economy and social services. It is hoped that the definition and explanation of the key words will open up for the reader central areas of political, cultural and economic life in present-day Britain and U.S.A. To each key word is appended, where relevant, a short etymology, and a definition of the word's principal current usages. Etymologies and definitions are in most cases based on those of the Shorter Oxford English Dictionary or Merriam-Webster's New Collegiate Dictionary. The subsequent main part of each article consists of a detailed explanation of the key word. Although primary stress is laid on current affairs, some historical background has been sketched in where it contributes to a better understanding of the present. The meanings of many additional technical terms connected with the key words evolve from the wider context. These terms are listed with their page references in a comprehensive index.

The comparative study of British and American institutions stresses the differences in meaning of many key words used in both countries.

The Editors and contributors have the pleasant task of thanking all those who have helped them in their work: Mr. Edward R. Brandt, director of the Deutsch-Amerikanisches Institut, Nürnberg, for providing valuable source material on the U.S.A.; Herr Dr. Paul Hartig, first chairman of the Allgemeiner Deutscher Neuphilologen-Verband, for the assistance he kindly rendered the editors; Herr Diplom-Volkswirt Dr. H. Pfuhlmann, assistant in the Staatswissenschaftliches Seminar der Universität Erlangen-Nürnberg, for his advice and the supplying of bibliographical material for the chapter "Economy and Social Services", Mr. Mark Gibbs, member of the Directors' Association of Laymen's Colleges in Europe, for advice and suggestions in connection with the chapter "Religion"; and Frau Gerda Hieronymus, Staatlich geprüfte Dolmetscherin und Übersetzerin, for unfailing help in preparing the manuscripts for print. Thanks are also extended to Mr. Roger L. Snook, M.A., and Mr. Collin C. Randlesome, B.A., M.A., for the stylistic revision of the articles and to Frau Marion Schreiber, Staatlich geprüfte Übersetzerin, for doing a very thorough job in compiling the subject index.

The Editors

Erlangen, September 1st, 1967

Preface to the second edition

In the present revised and enlarged edition we have made considerable amendments to the original text, especially in chapters I and V. With the passage of time some alterations were inevitable, but we have also gratefully accepted some of the advice offered by reviewers after the book first appeared. Five new key words have been added in this edition: Black Power, Common Market, Open University, Orange and Green, and Self-Assessment.

With regard to the method of selection of the key words we should like to emphasize the fact that our choice was ultimately determined by pragmatic considerations. We are not concerned to delimit areas of meaning by applying theoretical, deductive methods. We aimed, rather, to give detailed explanation of those concepts with which, for example, the reader of a newspaper is most likely to be confronted and which are "keys" to a better understanding of British and American institutions. There is no necessary contradiction if some key words appear to be merely terms otherwise listed in the index, as long as they fulfil their key word function as mentioned above, that is, to provide the reader with sign-posts which will point the way through the complex structure of British and American institutions. Word definitions are given at the beginning of each entry. The cross references within the body of the text serve as connecting links between the key words.

Warm thanks are due to the publishers Diesterweg-Salle, Frankfurt/Main, and Longman Group Limited, London, who made it possible for this second edition to appear both in Britain and in Germany. It is also our pleasant task to thank Mrs. U. Owens who helped us in revising Chapter V, and Mrs. G. Hieronymus for her untiring help in preparing the manuscript for press.

The Editors

Erlangen, December 31st, 1972

Preface to the fourth edition

Many things have changed in the United Kingdom and the United States since the last revised edition appeared in 1972. This has led to a complete revision of the book, with the content of some articles being incorporated into others. Some articles have been added on the following subjects: Devolution (I), Union Jack (I), Impeachment (II), Industrial Democracy (III), Lutheran (V), Mormon (V), and Social Gospel (V).

We should like to thank reviewers from both West and East European countries and the many friends of this book for their criticisms of the second and third editions. Their helpful suggestions have been, wherever possible, taken into account in this edition. We also wish to thank all those institutions which have helped provide us with the necessary documentary material, especially the British Council in Cologne and in Munich, as well as the Amerikahaus in Munich and in Nürnberg. We further wish to thank Mr. Geoffrey Williams, M. A., for examining the new contributions from a stylistic point of view, and Frau Gerda Hieronymus for her valuable assistance in the preparation of the manuscript.

The Editors

Erlangen, September 1978

Note for the User

The following symbols are used in the margin of the book to indicate whether the article refers to Great Britain or the U.S.A.:

● Great Britain
■ U.S.A.

If the article refers to both countries, the symbol for the country chiefly concerned is placed first. Words in italics followed by an asterisk refer the reader to a key word.

Terms treated in this book, but not included among the key words, will be found listed in the index. Readers may well prefer to consult the index first when seeking information. References in the index printed in italics are key words. Page references in bold type indicate major definitions of items.

For the sake of uniformity British spelling has been used in all the articles, except when American quotations and American names are concerned.

All information given in this book was correct on February 1st, 1978.

Contents

PART I

Government and Society

Abolitionist
Aristocracy
Bill
Bill of Rights
Black Power
Broadcasting, Sound and Television
Cabinet
Celtic Fringe
Census
Checks and Balances
Chief Executive
City
Civil Rights
Civil Service
Club
Cockney
Committee
Commons
Commonwealth
Congress
Conservative Party
Constituency
Constitution
County
Declaration of Independence
Deep South
Democratic Party
Department
Devolution
District
District of Columbia
Dixie
Doctrine
Dominion
Empire
Establishment
Filibustering
Four Freedoms
Frontier
Greater London
Home Rule
Immigration
Independent Agency
Indian
Isolationism
Labour Party
Liberal Party
Lobby
Local Government
Lords
Louisiana Purchase
Mayflower Compact
Melting Pot
Missouri Compromise
New England
Opposition
Orange and Green
Parish
Parliament
Parties
Poll
Press
Prohibition
Received Pronunciation
Reconstruction
Republican Party
Royal Prerogative
Speaker
Spoils System
Stars and Stripes
States' Rights
Suffrage
Territory
Town and Township
Union Jack
Whip

Abolitionist: One who aims at abolition, esp. of Negro slavery. 1788.

■ The problems concerning the position of Negroes in the United States must be considered in two fundamental aspects - abolition of slavery (up to 1865) and realization of *Civil Rights** (from 1865). The prohibition of Negro slavery owed much to the activities of the abolitionists, who were motivated not by political but by humanitarian considerations.

As early as 1624, only five years after the first Negro slaves had been landed at Jamestown, some Americans began to protest against the institution of human slavery. For two centuries this protest was feeble but between 1830 and 1860 those who wanted to abolish slavery became an increasingly strong and vocal minority.

Much of the early opposition to slavery in America came from the *Quakers**, members of the Society of Friends; the monthly meeting of the Friends of Germantown, Pennsylvania, passed the first recorded anti-slavery resolution in 1688.

The strength of this sentiment during the early decades of the nation's history was shown not only by the abolition of slavery in the northern states and its prohibition in the northwest territory, but also by the existence of many local anti-slavery societies in both North and South. The effectiveness of these societies was diminished by the invention of the cotton gin, which made the production of short-staple upland cotton profitable. As a result, cotton culture and the plantation system spread rapidly along the Gulf coast, fastening the slave system on much of the South *(Industrial Revolution*)*. Stronger in organization and leadership than the local societies was another manifestation of anti-slavery sentiment: the American Colonization Society. Founded in 1817, the Society conceived the idea of establishing a national home for former slaves in Africa. With the aid of the United States Government, a vast tract on the West African coast was bought, and the first colonists sailed in 1820 to found a new republic which was christened Liberia. Though the Colonization Society numbered among its leaders men as distinguished as Henry Clay, it succeeded in transporting only a few thousand Negroes to Africa. Thus, the anti-slavery movement in the United States after 1830 swung away from colonization and gradualism to "immediacy". This uncompromising and, to most, extreme position characterized the movement from thattime on.

In the South "abolitionist" became a fighting word. Abolitionist literature - newspapers, journals, narratives of runaway slaves, addresses - was considered dangerous. Fearful of repeated incidents like Nat Turner's Rebellion of 1831, when a group of slaves revolted and murdered 57 whites before being subdued, southern states passed laws prohibiting masters from teaching their slaves to read. Leading abolitionists were occasionally tried in absentia by southern courts.

While it was understandable that abolitionists should be detested in the South, they were hardly more popular in the northern states. A Boston mob dragged William Lloyd Garrison, best known of the abolitionists today, through the streets with a rope around his waist; New Yorkers hurled eggs and stones at the homes of leading abolitionists there. Even churches were often closed to them until, as time went on, more and more prominent ministers became sympathetic to their cause.

As an organized movement, abolitionism was at its height in the 1830s and 1840s. Though Garrison was the most articulate and widely publicized abolitionist, he was by no means the only important leader. More effective in the organizational work was the self-effacing but indefatigable Theodore Weld, the leading spirit of the more moderate wing which stretched through New York State and Ohio. Backed financially by a group in New York City of which the philanthropists Arthur and Lewis Tappan were the leaders, Weld and the organizers he recruited succeeded in building up a substantial body of anti-slavery sentiment in hundreds of New York and Ohio towns.

Beginning in 1833 there existed a national organization, the American Anti-Slavery Society. It held annual meetings, encouraged its more than 1,000 local subsidiary groups, published periodicals and other literature, and bombarded *Congress** with anti-slavery petitions. Tension existed within the organization from the first, however. When the Garrisonians gained control at the annual meeting of 1840, the New York-Ohio representatives withdrew and organized the rival American and Foreign Anti-Slavery Society.

One of the points at issue in the movement was that of participation in politics. A small group which advocated a political approach organized the Liberty Party in 1840 and nominated its own presidential candidate. In 1844, the Party polled more than 60,000 votes.

During the 1840s and 1850s it was through articulate individuals such as Henry Ward Beecher, Wendell Phillips, Ralph Waldo Emerson, Theodore Parker, Joshua Giddings, and the Negro abolitionist Frederick Douglass rather than through organized movements that the abolitionist cause was furthered. As time went on, abolitionists made common cause with those who were motivated primarily by opposition to extension of slavery in the territories *(Territory, Missouri Compromise*)*. The Fugitive Slave Act (1850) which abolitionists regarded as especially prejudicial, the novel "Uncle Tom's Cabin" (1852) by Harriet Beecher Stowe, which had been inspired by the Fugitive Slave Act, "Bleeding Kansas", a term used in connection with the civil war in Kansas (1856) resulting from the Kansas-Nebraska Act of 1854, and the Dred Scott Decision of 1857 *(Judicial Review*)*, the raid on Harper's Ferry by the fanatical abolitionist John Brown, all were emotionally charged issues which heightened bitterness between North and South.

Though the new Republican Party of the late 1850s was not an abolitionist party, the moral impulse of the anti-slavery movement contributed to its strength. The election of Lincoln in 1860 was the signal for Southern withdrawal from the Union. It also cast the die for the future abolition of slavery.
S R Sp

● In 1772, Lord Mansfield, Lord Chief Justice, pronounced in the case of the runaway negro slave Somersett the historic decision that any slave on setting foot on British soil was automatically free. Although this decision did not abolish slavery in the whole Empire, much less the extensive slave trade in which British traders played a leading part at that time, it gave a fresh impetus to abolitionists in Britain.

The eventual abolition of the slave trade and of slavery, however, was due to the untiring idealism of William Wilberforce (1759-1833), one of the greatest English philanthropists and reformers, and his Anti-slave-trade Committee. Through his propagandist agitation he at last succeeded in converting the great majority of his fellow-countrymen to his cause. His important supporters were the Dissenters, among whom the Society of Friends *(Quaker*)* were the most active, and the great Whig politician Charles Fox (1749-1806). In 1807, during the brief ministry of Lord Grenville (1759-1834), the slave trade was abolished throughout the Empire. In 1833, under the Liberal Lord Grey (1764-1845), an Act abolishing slavery throughout the Empire was passed by Parliament. On the eve of an age of imperialism during which Britain acquired a large part of Africa the Union Jack thus became especially associated with the individual freedom of the Negro. H H

Aristocracy

Government by the best citizens. More commonly government or state in which the nobility or privileged upper class rule. The patrician class. The nobility and gentry. 1561.

● A distinction should be made between "peerage" and "aristocracy". The former refers to the members of the political institution of the House of Lords, the latter consists of the bearers of titles conferred upon them by the monarch; these titles are part of their names and are either hereditary or non-hereditary. The nobility comprises only the higher and hereditary degrees of the aristocracy, whereas the two lowest degrees (frequently referred to as "gentry", although this designation may include the influential landowning county families) do not belong to the nobility and their bearers do not sit in the House of Lords. The holders of life peerages are not counted among the nobility, their right to sit in the House of Lords being no social privilege but a personal distinction *(Lords*)*, nor are the *Law Lords** and the archbishops and bishops of the Church of England, who are lords in official function, although it may happen that members of these two categories are holders of hereditary titles. There are also members of the nobility who have no right to sit in the Lords' Chamber.

Order of rank: Duke (Duchess) of . . ., Marquess (Marchioness) of . . ., Earl (Countess) of . . ., Viscount (Viscountess), Baron (Baroness). They are addressed as "Your Lordship" or "Your Ladyship", except Dukes and Duchesses, who are formally addressed as "Your Grace". These are the five titles of hereditary nobility which enable their male bearers and the Peeresses in their own right (i.e., those who have inherited the title because there was no male heir to it, and do not have their titles merely by marriage) to sit in the House of Lords. There is an exception to this: as Dukes, Marquesses and Earls have a second title, this inferior title is given to their eldest sons as a "courtesy title", which does not qualify for a seat in the House of Lords. Since 1610, it has been customary to confer the title Prince of Wales upon the eldest son of the sovereign (the title itself was created in 1301); the eldest (or only) daughter bears the title Princess Royal. These titles have no political significance.

The Baronets and the Knights do not belong to the nobility. The former title is hereditary, the latter is not. They have the title "Sir" before their Christian names (which can be used without surnames, never vice versa; e.g. Sir Winston, or Sir Winston Churchill, but not Sir Churchill). Baronets add "Bart". after their names. The wives of Knights and Baronets have the formal title "Dame". This title also indicates that its bearer is a woman who has been awarded the first or second class of one of the Orders of Knighthood. Many Knights belong to one of the Orders of Knighthood; the higher among them are the Garter, the Thistle, St. Patrick (all three with limited membership), the Bath, St. Michael and St. George, the Royal Victoria Order, the Order of the British Empire.

Each Order has different classes. Those Knights who do not belong to an order are called "Knights bachelor".

The nomenclature of the British aristocracy is fairly simple, but it is always difficult to discern what a title signifies. Thus, the title "Lord" can designate (1) a Marquess, Earl, Viscount, or Baron, (2) the eldest son of a Duke, Marquess, or Earl, (3) any of the younger sons of a Duke or a Marquess, discernible by the Christian name following the title (the younger sons of Earls and all the sons and daughters of Viscounts and Barons bear the title "the Honourable" before their full names), (4) a life peer. The title "Lady" can designate (1) a Marchioness, Countess, Viscountess, or Baroness both by marriage and in her own right, e.g. Lady Woodstock (the word Woodstock cannot be a surname here, but is a name conferred with the title), (2) the wife of a Knight or a Baronet by the name of Woodstock, (3) the daughter of a Duke, Marquess, or Earl (e.g. Lady Mary Woodstock), (4) the wife of a younger son of a Duke, Marquess, or Earl (e.g. Lady Henry Woodstock). There are such splendid names as Lyulph Ydwallo Odin Nestor Egbert Lyonel Toedmaz Hugh Erchenwyne Saxon Exa Cromwell Orma Nevill Dysart Plantagenet Tollemache-Tollemache.

The importance of the aristocracy is small now. To be a nobleman is sometimes an obstacle rather than a recommendation for a political career. Nevertheless, the aristocracy has remained involved in the political, economic and cultural life of Britain. The Lords' Chamber persists, no matter how few of the Lords are taking an active part in its work. Some political functions of the state are still linked with membership in the Lords. The award of Knighthood (rather than Peerage) is still a common device to honour a person for his merits as a soldier, scientist, artist, football player, etc. Moreover, the circumstance that only one person, usually the eldest son, can inherit the title tends to keep the number of noblemen down and prevents exclusiveness, because all other sons and daughters become commoners. The influence of the aristocracy declined when it ceased to be representative of the political and economic forces in the country. As a social class it no longer has any real task. But there have been attempts to give the aristocracy in Britain a function beyond that of being a mere ornament of the Crown, especially in connection with endeavours to reform the second chamber. *(Lords, Commons, Parliament*.)* There is a tacit understanding between the two leading parties that no further hereditary titles should be created outside the scope of the Royal Family. H H

Bill

The draft of an Act of Parliament submitted to the legislature for discussion and adoption as an "Act". 1512.

In parliamentary procedure, a bill is a law in the making. The term "bill" is a technical designation of a measure introduced in either house (G.B.: House of Commons or House of Lords; U.S.A.: House of Representatives or Senate). The term "act" is used in referring to a legislative measure which has been finally passed by both houses and become law after the signature of the English monarch or the President of the U.S.A. (exceptions *Chief Executive**). In strictly formal usage, the bill becomes an act (viz. of one of the two branches of the legislature) as soon as it has been passed by the house where it was introduced. A bill normally passes through the following stages before it becomes a law:

● First reading, including introduction (or tabling = putting on the table of the house) of the bill by a member of either of the two houses (in reality only a sheet of paper bearing the title of the bill and the names of those who sponsor it) and reading of the title by the Clerk of the House.

Second reading: debate on the bill (the decisive stage).

Committee: further debate and amendment of the bill by the members of the *Committee**.

Report of the committee to the house; further amendments may be made at this stage.

Third reading and final vote.

If adopted in the third reading, the bill is sent up to the House of Lords (or sent down to the House of Commons if introduced by the Lords) where the same procedure is repeated.

After that the Royal Assent is given through Royal Commissioners in the House of Lords. Though law-French was abolished by Act of Parliament in 1731 (English was first introduced as the language of pleading and judgement in 1362; at schools in 1375; in Parliament 1399), French was used in the Royal Assent till 1967. Under the Royal Assent Act 1967 the House can simply be notified that the Royal Assent to a bill has been granted.

■ Introduction of the bill in either of the two houses (where it is placed into a basket known as the "hopper") and first reading by the Clerk.

Assignment of the bill to committee, where it may be amended, revised or even rewritten completely, often upon recommendations of a spezialized subcommittee.

Report of the committee to the House (or Senate).

Filing and placing of the bill on Calendar (if the committee reported favourably). The powerful Rules Committee can push the bill ahead of other bills already on file *(Committee*)*.

Second reading and debate; at this stage the bill may be amended or returned to the committee for revision before a vote is taken.

Third reading and vote; signature yf the *Speaker** (House of Representatives) or the Vice President (Senate).

If adopted, the bill is introduced in the other chamber where about the same procedure is repeated (there is no Senate Rules Committee). If the other chamber cannot accept the bill, it generally asks for a conference, and the Speaker (or Vice President) appoints five or seven "managers" from each house to form a "conference" *(Committee*)*.

Then the President gives his signature to the bill *(Chief Executive*)* and the bill takes effect as an Act of Congress.

Death of a Bill: in Britain a bill is dead as soon as Parliament is prorogued (normally at the end of each annual session), whereas in the U.S.A. a bill can be considered during the entire duration of a *Congress** without regard to the end of the session.

The influence of the Committees upon law-making is vastly greater in the U.S.A. than in the United Kingdom, which becomes obvious from the above-mentioned sequence of stages.

The most important types of bill:

Public Bill: In Britain this is a bill which affects the public at large. There are two classes of Public Bill: (a) Finance or Money Bills, (b) bills other than Finance or Money Bills. Today the overwhelming majority of these two classes of Public Bill are introduced or sponsored by the government and are therefore referred to as Government Bills. If a private Member of Parliament succeeds in introducing a Public Bill upon his own initiative, this bill is called a Private Member's Bill. Such bills have little chance of becoming law. In the U.S.A. a Public Bill is a bill dealing with classes or groups of people (in contradistinction to Private Bills). They are printed in part 1 (public laws) of the U.S. Statute at Large (bound volume of laws passed in each session).

Private Bill: In Britain this is a bill conferring some particular right (e.g. to expropriate land, to levy taxes, to hold a monopoly) on a particular person or body. It usually deals with matters of internal administration. It is introduced in Parliament by way of petition of some authority, body or individual. Private Bills are there treated like Public Bills, although the committee stage is more important. In the U.S.A. the equivalent of the British Private Bill is the "Request Bill"; whereas a "Private Bill" is a bill for the benefit of individuals and is printed in part 2 (private laws) of the U.S. Statute at Large. In Britain there is a tendency today to replace Private Bills by Provisional Order Bills, which confirm Provisional Orders *(Royal Prerogative*)*.

Finance or Money Bill: In Britain this is a bill primarily concerned with the raising or spending of money. In 1911 (Parliament Act) the House of Lords lost its right to veto such bills, after the Lords had rejected Lloyd George's Finance Bill. In the U.S.A its equivalent is the Revenue Bill. It must always originate in the House of Representatives. This practice is based on the British custom that taxes must be levied and spent by the house directly responsible to the people. This was the House of Representatives, because up to 1913 senators were not elected by the people but by the State legislatures (Amendment XVII).

H H

Bill of Rights

A formal statement of the fundamental rights of the people of a nation. - A bill declaring the rights and liberties of England, and the succession to the throne, passed in 1689. The first ten amendments to the American Constitution. 1799.

● The term is loosely used today in connection with basic rights in general (the football-players' Bill of Rights), but especially the civil liberties of the individual, the erosion of his customary rights and the amplifying of rights not to be interfered with. This modern usage is derived from the historical Bill of Rights, by which the English constitution was decisively changed.

This Bill of Rights is an Act of Parliament of 1689 which implemented the Declaration of Rights of 1689. Among other things it affirmed: that the suspension of execution of laws by regal authority without a consent of Parliament was illegal; that Parliament should have the power to grant money (the control of finance is still considered to be the noblest right of the British Parliament); that everybody should have the right to petition the king; that the raising or keeping of a standing army in time of peace should be unlawful without consent of Parliament; that everybody should have the right of free speech in Parliament, in court and everywhere else; that excessive bail and excessive fines must not be imposed; that cruel and unusual punishment must not be inflicted; that Parliament ought to be held frequently; that Roman Catholics could not henceforth retain the throne (this last provision was added to the Declaration of Rights when it was legalized as a bill in 1689).

The Bill of Rights was a direct consequence of the defects of James II's (1685-1688) policy *(Parliament*)*. Furthermore there was the religious issue:

James II became a convert to the Roman Catholic religion. He openly defied the Test Act *(Religious Test*)* by making scores of appointments of Roman Catholics to army commissions and civil posts. He was determined to make England a Catholic country without delay. After the birth of a son - an event which would have meant a Catholic successor to the throne - the Glorious Revolution broke out (called "glorious" because no blood was shed). Parliament offered the throne to the Prince and Princess of Orange upon the condition that they both signed the Declaration of Rights (1689). Thus, at a time when on the continent Absolutism was at its height a constitutional monarchy was established in England.

The Bill of Rights is the last among the four great documents which established the rule of law in England, the others being Magna Carta (1215), The Petition of Right (1628), and the *Habeas Corpus** Act (1679). *(Constitution*).*

Today, not a few British politicians believe that it is necessary to have a new Bill of Rights to emphasize the ultimate value of the individual in a complex plural society and his rights against the state, to preserve the freedom of the mass media, to prevent collectivism and the corporate state, and, last but not least, to conform with the Universal Declaration of Human Rights of the United Nations and the European Convention on Human Rights.

■ The first ten amendments to the American Constitution are commonly referred to as the Bills of Rights.

As the federal constitution of 1789 was strictly one of governmental powers only, several States (Massachusetts, South Carolina, New Hampshire, Virginia, New York, North Carolina and Rhode Island) felt it necessary to introduce some limitations to these powers in a Bill of Rights. The first eight amendments set out the personal rights of the American citizen such as freedom of religion, freedom of speech, press and assembly and the right to petition the Government for a redress of grievances (Amendment I); protection against unreasonable searches and seizures (Amendment IV); protection against imprisonment without specific charges (Amendment V); the right to a speedy and public trial by an impartial jury (Amendment VI); protection against excessive bails, fines or cruel or unusual punishment (Amendment VII). Most of the enumerated rights go back to the English Petition of Right (Amendments IV and VI) and to the English Bill of Rights (Amendment I, and Amendment VIII).

While the first eight amendments to the American Constitution deal with the protection of the individual citizen Amendments IX and X are general rules of interpretation of the relation between the States and the Ferderal Government. They reserve all powers not expressly delegated by the Constitution to the Federal Government, nor expressly prohibited to the States, to the States or the people. Curiously enough three of the American States (Connecticut, Georgia, and Massachusetts) did not ratify the Bill of Rights until 1937, although the Constitution (which all amendments are part of) had been in force for 148 years.

H H

Black Power

■ Since 1967 a considerable radicalization of the civil rights problem has taken place. On July 1st-4th of that year, the Congress of Racial Equality *(Civil Rights*)* held its national convention. It was there that a "black power" concept was first formulated: withdrawal of U.S. troops from Vietnam (the relative proportion of Negroes fighting at the front line was much greater than that of whites), resistance to the military draft. Stockely Carmichael *(Civil Rights*)*, guest speaker, said he would not discuss nonviolence with whites as long as "the U.S.A. continues to commit violence in Vietnam". This and the idea of self-defence (also present in the name of the Black Panther Party for Self-Defense, founded in 1966) dominated the convention. Immediately afterwards, at its convention in Los Angeles from July 4th-9th, the National Association for the Advancement of Colored People *(Civil Rights*)* rejected the black power concept. The civil rights movement was split, and its radical offspring, black power, is no longer interested in civil rights.

This secession was the decisive step towards the full psychological emancipation of the American Negro from white supremacy. The new self-confidence is great. Blacks have begun to see that "black is beautiful"; many wear traditional African attire and they grow bushy hair supposedly in keeping with African culture; their heroes are no longer Jefferson or even Lincoln, but W.E.B. Du Bois, Marcus Garvey and Malcolm X; there has been an explosion of "black studies"; in fact, black studies have become a leading course at almost all American universities and colleges; it is the study of African and Afro-American history and politics, sometimes set in revolutionary ideology. Since the late sixties the drive by black Americans to identify with Africa has been overwhelming, and many insist that they are not Americans but Afro-Americans who want segregation, not integration, and there is plenty of evidence of this attitude. In 1968, at a black power convention, the "Republic of New Africa" was called into paper-existence; in 1969 land was purchased in Warren County, S. C., for the future site of Soul City; and in 1971, in the State of Mississippi, a group of black separatists founded the capital of the new black republic, which is supposed to be established on part of the territory of Mississippi, Louisiana, Alabama, Georgia, and South Carolina. In Chicago, which has over 1.1 million blacks, the so-called United Front of Black Community Organizations attempted to introduce a curfew for whites between 6 p.m. and 6 a.m. (1969). From June, 1972, broadcasts from a National Black Network (N.B.N.) were on the air. Black power is also to be found on Capitol Hill in Washington, D.C.: the black members of the House of Representatives, all Democrats, have organized themselves to form the "Black Caucus"; their political weight, e.g. in the nomination of a Democratic presidential candidate, is not to be underrated.

Black Power is directly related to Marcus Garvey's (1887-1940) separatist ideas. Through his Universal Negro Improvement Association (1914) he wanted to promote the spirit of race pride, foster worldwide unity among all blacks and establish the greatness of the African heritage. To improve the black man's living conditions he demanded the foundation of independent Negro states and communities (in Africa, as he believed) and of Negro businesses and commercial enterprises. His theory, of course, represents only one attitude among several.

By 1915, there existed four clearly distinguishable models concerning the social interaction with the American whites and the attitude toward their values: 1) the model of "assimilation", advocated by Frederick Douglass (1817-1895), amounting to the acceptance of white values; 2) the model of "accomodation", expounded by Booker T. Washington, who advised his fellow blacks to concentrate on economic gains, which alone could lead to respect by the whites and would ultimately lead to equality with regard to political and social rights; to achieve this he was prepared to accept temporary discrimination until those aims were attained; 3) the model of "integration", advocated by W.E.B. Du Bois (1868-1963), who recommended the preservation of the black's dual nature, i.e. that of being black and of being American; he was against any form of assimilation or accommodation of the black race, two concepts which, in fact, have become completely eliminated today; 4) Marcus Garvey's model of "separation", the most radical theory among all, the extreme self-confidence of which has been adopted by Black Power.

This new self-confidence of the black community in the U.S.A. also led to hatred and the readiness to answer racial discrimination and insults by retaliation. This aspect of black power becomes relevant whenever the claims of the blacks to transform the U.S.A. into an egalitarian society coincide with radical socialist revolutionary ideologies of some kind or other. The leader of black power in Britain *(Immigration*)*, Obi Egbuna, has expressed the views of this type of black power as follows *(The Times,* August 7th, 1971): "Black Power is anti-exploitation and therefore committed to socialism . . . It must bring about an all-out socialist revolution that will smash the system". He then defines black power as an international concept. One of his conclusions is that the black man "must organize on a basis of colour . . . and fight off that oppression." The para-military Black panthers in the U.S.A. have been associated with this kind of militant revolutionary socialism, although it should be made clear that they have almost always acted in defence. The release of official documents in 1977 has revealed the efforts made by the F.B.I. to discredit both Martin Luther King and the Black Panthers by spreading fabricated information (The Times, Nov. 23, 1977). But even the ideal of revolutionary socialism has faded since about 1971, when the party broke apart in two factions, the New York-based Eldridge Cleaver group and the Oakland (California)-based group led by Huey Newton and Bobby Seale. Both groups openly denounced the use of force in 1970 and 1971. Cleaver and Newton spent several years in voluntary exile. Both have returned to the United States, Cleaver in 1975, disillusioned with Marxism and disappointed with the racism in Cuba and Algeria (interview in "Rolling Stone", Sept. 11, 1975), Newton in 1977, strengthened in his belief in socialism and determined to devote himself to the Black Panther Party and to social welfare among the American blacks. He and his followers initiate programmes aimed at creating conditions for the survival of America's black poor, like "People's Free Clothing Program", "Angela Davis Free Food Program" and a dozen more. The occasional shotgun attacks and bomb outrages are committed by small, reckless groups like the "Black Liberation Army" or the black separatist "Death Angels". H H

Broadcasting, Sound and Television

The process of disseminating (audible and visible matter) from a transmitting station. 1921.

■ In the United States broadcasting is regulated under the Communications Act of 1934 which established the Federal Communications Commission "for the regulation of interstate and foreign communications by telegraph, cable, and radio". (The Act also imposed new regulations designed to control broadcasting.) Television is private and hitherto the great majority of

Americans, and, of course, the powerful *Lobby** of the T.V. companies, do not seem to be willing to give up free commercial television in exchange for state control or pay television, although proposals to introduce the latter have repeatedly been made.

The public Broadcasting Act of 1967 can hardly be regarded as an attempt on the part of the Government to change this state of affairs. The Act set up the Corporation for Public Broadcasting to dispense federal and private funds for educational and cultural programme production and networking. An initial budget of $ 9 million was authorized, with long-term financing to be worked out. Operations actually began with private grants. In 1977, the Public Broadcasting Service (P.B.S.) served 266 non-commerical television stations and about 60 million viewers. Thanks to P.B.S. distribution, small public companies all over the U.S.A. have been able to broadcast valuable programmes including "Sesame Street", "The Electric Company" and "The Advocates". The P.B.S. also regularly distributes programmes such as "Black Journal", designed especially for audiences within the Black Community. The Public Broadcast Laboratory was also recently created. It is supposed to do research and experimenting work in the field of educational television (E.T.V.).

Seventy-five million American households have at least one television set; one out of every three has more than that. Adults spend an average of two to three hours a day watching T.V., school children about three to four hours, and pre-school children more than a third of their waking time. T.V. has become an important instrument of instruction on all levels of education. Indeed it is quite customary for teachers to assign a particular T.V. programme as homework. Historical films and the "Western" - its share is still very great in T.V. programmes - do more than anything else to preserve the "American Dream" and the *Frontier** ideals of the past and to demonstrate violence.

America's consumer goods industries virtually live from the persuasive power exerted by the "Plug-in-Drug". This is the reason why American T.V. viewers do not have to pay any fees for television. The television companies, however, live comfortably from the proceeds of "commercials", which business firms intersperse among the programmes and for which they buy time. It frequently happens that a business corporation buys a whole year's programme, actors and staff included.

There are three big T.V. networks: the American Broadcasting Company (A.B.C.), the Columbia Broadcasting System (C.B.S.), and the National Broadcasting Company (N.B.C.). Approximately 700 local networks are affiliated to them, and every fairly large city in the U.S.A. has its T.V. station and local programmes.

One of America's greatest industries, the motion picture industry, has suffered severe losses through T.V. and thousands of cinemas have had to close down.

In the face of the triumph of T.V. it is remarkable that the production of radio sets still increases. This can be explained partly by the change in quality which sound broadcasting has undergone. In contrast to T.V. there are many stations which excel in first-class musical, educational, and generally cultural programmes. Some of these stations have even cancelled any kind of "commercials".

Sound broadcasting is private. The transmission station only needs a licence from the Federal Communications Commission, but through this *Independent*

*Agency** the government exerts a certain control, if only because the licence can be annulled should the broadcasting company violate the "public interest".

In the United Kingdom, broadcasting is regulated by the Wireless Telegraphy Acts of 1949-67, which made the right to broadcast and receive radio communications dependent on a licence, and by the Television Acts of 1954, 1963 and 1964 and the Sound Broadcasting Act of 1972.

Britain is among the world's biggest "consumers" of television, which has affected nearly every sphere of its life. There are two different systems:

(1) The British Broadcasting Corporation (B.B.C.) was first incorporated under Royal Charter in 1927. Its present Charter came into force in 1964 and will expire in 1979. It had the televising monopoly until 1954. For a long time it was characterized by general reverence towards British institutions but this attitude has changed to some extent now, probably as a consequence of the competition of commercial T.V. The absence of "commercials" in B.B.C. transmissions is considered by many people as advantageous; others believe that B.B.C. programmes are culturally better than independent ones. There are two programmes, one of which is transmitted on ultra high frequency.

(2) Independent Television began in 1955 under the auspices of the Independent Television Authority (I.T.A.), established in 1954 and based on the Television Act of 1954 (continued by the Independent Broadcasting Authority Acts 1973 and 1974 and its 1973 Licence, extended in 1974) and renamed Independent Broadcasting Authority (I.B.A.) in 1972, with enlarged responsibilities to include the control of local commercial radio stations in the future. The Authority consists of a chairman, a deputy chairman and a varying number of sundry members, some of whom are in charge of the regional interests of Scotland, Northern Ireland, Wales, and Monmouthshire. The I.B.A. has certain controlling powers, especially with regard to the good taste and decency of programmes but is ultimately responsible to the Minister of Posts and Telecommunications. It operates and owns the T.V. stations, but studios, equipment, and programmes are in the hands of 15 programme companies who have the legal status of limited companies. The I.B.A. does not collect any licence fees, but draws annual rental payments from the programme companies. The programme companies, since they are business enterprises, depend financially on private industry to which they sell time for commercial advertisements.

Educational institutions are increasingly making use of television (over 80 per cent. of all schools in the U.K. are viewing schools), and the *Open University**, which emerged from the "university of the air" scheme of the University of Nottingham, has been a great success.

Up to 1973, sound broadcasting was provided exclusively by the B.B.C. In October of that year the first two independent (i.e. commercial) local radio stations began broadcasting. Their emergence introduced an element of competition into the broadcasting scene. They are financed solely by advertising revenue. There are 19 commercial stations on the air (this is the upper limit now, the original plan of 1971 had envisaged 60), broadcasting on V.H.F. and medium wavebands.

The Annan Report of 1977 suggests the creation of two new broadcasting authorities, one to administer the fourth channel of the B.B.C. ("Open Broadcasting Authority"), the other to run local radio ("Local Broadcasting Authority"). The latter would add 26 local B.B.C. stations to the existing 20 (plus four "community stations" run from Aberdeen, Inverness, Orkney, and

Shetland) and the 19 independent stations. (In July 1978, the Government endorsed the Annan committee's recommendation that the fourth television channel should be operated by an open Broadcasting Authority).

The B.B.C., owing to its extensive external services, is one of the most diversified and efficient broadcasting systems in the world. It is legally defined as an "independent public corporation". It is organized in the following manner: Board of Governors (appointed by the Queen), Director-General (the chief executive), Board of Management consisting of Chief Assistant, Chief Assistant designate, Directors of sound broadcasting, television broadcasting, external broadcasting, engineering, administration. The Government, however, retains ultimate control in questions of general policy. The services of the B.B.C. are financed from an annual budget voted by Parliament, an annual grant-in-aid voted by Parliament for External Services (the European Services, Overseas Services, Monitoring Service) and the net profits from B.B.C. publications and licences. Technically, sound broadcasting is operated on lines common to most other countries. The domestic sound services consist of Radio 1 (pop music), Radio 2 (music and sports), Radio 3 (classical music and artistic and intellectual subjects), and Radio 4 (home service with regional variations, main speech programme). There are broadcasts in 39 foreign languages for over a hundred hours every day. These broadcasts are made up especially of language courses, news, political commentaries, science, music, and drama. H H

Cabinet

In politics: the private room in which the chief ministers meet. 1607. Those who meet in the cabinet (formerly called the Cabinet Council as opposed to the Privy Council). 1644.

● About 20 Ministers (25 in 1977) out of a far greater number holding ministerial rank *(Department*)* are members of an "inner circle" of the government which is called the Cabinet. The Prime Minister alone decides about Cabinet membership, but it invariably includes the Chancellor of the Exchequer, the Foreign Secretary, the Home Secretary, the Secretary of State for Defence, and the Lord Chancellor. Recently it has become customary to confer Cabinet rank upon the Lord President of the Council (see below), the Lord Privy Seal, and the Chancellor of the Duchy of Lancaster - all Ministers without portfolio. The others are chosen by the Prime Minister. Special issues are often deliberated upon by Cabinet Committees. Ministers not in the Cabinet may be members of such committees or summoned to attend Cabinet meetings which are also called "cabinets".

During Mr. Wilson's premiership an additional "Inner Cabinet" was formed, then called the Parliamentary Committee of the Cabinet, which included 10 of the most senior and influential Cabinet Ministers. This concentration of power within the "inner circle" of government has logically continued in the steady growth in the influence of the Prime Minister's private office since 1970 and in the enlargement of the Cabinet Office in the same year through the foundation of a government "think tank" called the Central Policy Review Staff, a brains trust whose task it is to advise the ministers and, above all, the Prime Minister. In addition, there is a complicated system of more or less secret "cabinet committees", whose members are appointed by the Prime Minister. These are indications of a development which may eventually lead to a system of counsels, aides and advisers similar to that of the White House Office in the United States *(Chief Executive*)*, but also of a tendency for the Cabinet to become a façade for one-man rule.

All past and present Cabinet Ministers are members of the Privy Council, which probably developed from the Curia Regis, or Curia Ducis of the Norman dukes, and was the forerunner of the Cabinet. In the 16th and 17th centuries it was the chief instrument by which the government of the Crown was carried out. Today it still performs a few functions, the most important of which are the court function of the Judicial Committee of the Privy Council - it deals with final appeals in ecclesiastical cases, with appeals from the Isle of Man, and the Channel Islands (which are not part of the United Kingdom but are still Crown dependencies), with admiralty prize cases within the United Kingdom, and with appeals from the Colonies and the *Commonwealth**. Its members, approximately 300 in number, are styled "Right Honourable". Among them are also the two English archbishops, the Lord Chief Justice, the Lords Justices of Appeal, the *Law Lords**. The Privy Council is presided over by the Queen or, in her absence, by the Lord President of the Council, who is also a member of the Cabinet.

It was Henry VIII who, in 1526, created a forerunner of the Cabinet: he selected some of the Privy Councillors and ordered them to attend meetings with the king every day from 10 a.m. to 2 p.m. and to advise him in state matters.

The name Cabinet came to be applied regularly between 1630 and 1640 under Charles I, and the sovereign presided at its meetings until 1717. From 1717 onwards it became the practice for one of the Ministers, later called the Prime Minister, to preside, because the Hanoverian George I could not speak English. The Whig Junta of 1697 was the first example of a one-Party Cabinet, although the principle was firmly established only in the early 18th century when it became the rule for the whole Cabinet to be either Whig or Tory and to be responsible to Parliament.

Today, however, "parliamentary government" has ceased to mean "government by Parliament". As a consequence of the emergence of party organizations and party discipline *(Parliament*)* the position of the Prime Minister, who almost invariably is also the leader of his party, has been strengthened enormously. This has resulted in a reversal of the relationship between Commons and Government. Formally the Prime Minister and his Cabinet are still responsible to the House of Commons, but the Cabinet responsibility - collective and individual responsibility - has become meaningless, because those who, as Members of the House of Commons, should control the Government, are controlled in fact by the Government and especially by the Prime Minister. But the Cabinet itself has become involved in this shift of power, for its members are also members of the party of the Prime Minister who has long ceased to be primus inter pares as far as the Cabinet is concerned. He alone now determines the course of government policy; the Cabinet merely assists him in "policy decision", and the non-Cabinet Ministers are practically confined to the task of "policy execution" and administration. It is worth while to recognize the singularity of the Prime Minister's position and the decline of the power of the Cabinet since the beginning of the 20th century. He is undeposable like the President of the U.S.A., and like him he controls the Cabinet. But whereas the American President can never be sure of the support of his own party in Congress, the British Prime Minister, if he is competent and capable of firm leadership, controls Parliament. The Commons and the Cabinet, which in the 19th century could make or break governments, are now, more often than not, merely instruments. The resignation of Neville Chamberlain (1940) and of Harold Macmillan (1963) are only exceptions to the rule. Harold Wilson, while he was Prime Minister (1964-1970, 1974-1976) appointed or reshuffled 403 ministers and secretaries of state, 25 chairmen of nationalized industries, and 18 chairmen of public corporations, not to speak of the judges and bishops which he appointed. In not one of these appointments was he obliged to consult anyone or required to get even the confirmation of the House of Commons. Over 700 Peers have been appointed since the end of World War II, each with a vote in Parliament, upon the sole recommendation of the Prime Minister.

■ All heads of U.S. *Departments** are members of the Cabinet. There are 12 in number. There is no Cabinet responsibility to Congress, neither formally nor in practice, but the Secretaries are individually responsible to the President. The members of the U.S. Cabinet are appointed by the President with the approval of the Senate. He may, however, remove them at will (the impeachment of President Andrew Johnson and the trial against him in the Senate in 1868 decided the question of removal in favour of the President, in spite of the fact that Johnson only narrowly escaped conviction). The U.S. Cabinet is not a unified body like the British Cabinet. It is the President who makes policy, not the Cabinet. The individual members he may, but is not bound to, consult *(Chief Executive*)*.

In October, 1789, George Washington consulted the heads of his Departments on the advisability of making a tour of the U.S.A. and he continued to consult them individually. In 1792, three Cabinet meetings took place. By the time Adams became President in 1797 the practice of Cabinet meetings was well established. I Fr/H H

Celtic Fringe

● Celtic Fringe denotes (a) the inhabitants of the British Isles who are descended mainly from peoples speaking Celtic languages; or (b) the regions of the British Isles inhabited by this section of the population, namely, Wales, Ireland, Scotland, Cornwall, and the Isle of Man.

The Celtic languages of the British Isles are, together with the Breton dialect of Brittany, the last survivors of an Indo-European language which at the time of Alexander the Great was spoken in Britain, most of present-day France and the Iberian Peninsula, Northern Italy, Southern Germany, and the valley of the Danube down to the Black Sea. Despite efforts of those interested in national tradition Celtic is still on the wane, its place as a majority language having been long ago usurped by English in most parts of the Celtic Fringe. As they now exist, the Celtic dialects of the British Isles fall into two well-marked groups: the Goidelic or Gaelic which comprises Irish (sometimes called Erse), Scottish Gaelic and Manx (the Celtic dialect of the Isle of Man), each with several sub-dialects; and the Brythonic consisting of Welsh (or Cymric) and Cornish. In Wales approximately 26,223 of a total population of 2,644,023 (including Monmouthshire) spoke only Welsh in 1961; a further 656,000 knew both Welsh and English. For the same year the Gaelic-speaking population of Scotland (total population then 5,179,344) was 76,587, Gaelic speakers being practically confined, however, to the Western Isles and the fringes of the north and west. In Eire the number of Irish speakers in 1946 was given as 588,725, i.e. 21.2 per cent. of the population, a figure which apparently includes large numbers whose first language is English (the present Republic of Ireland is officially bilingual). In Northern Ireland a few families still use Irish Gaelic. On the Isle of Man 355 persons are reported to have spoken Manx in 1951; this tongue is also used besides English for certain official pronouncements. Cornish ceased to be an effectively living language in the 19th century or earlier. 1

The small dark-haired strain inhabiting much of the Celtic Fringe and also found sporadically in England, though no doubt descended directly from pre-Germanic, Iron Age inhabitants of Britain, is probably not of the same ethnic stock as the Celts described by Greek and Roman authors, the latter people being predominantly tall and fair and not easily distinguishable from Germans. It seems likely that Celtic-speaking people of the latter ethnic type established overlordships in areas they occupied, later becoming submerged in the indigenous populations which had meanwhile adopted the Celtic tongue and customs of their conquerors. Properly speaking, therefore, the peoples of the present-day Celtic Fringe and their ancestors can only be described as Celts if the term is taken in a linguistic, and not an ethnical sense.

Perhaps the best-known cultural event taking place in the Celtic Fringe is the Eisteddfod [ais'teðvɔd], a great musical and poetical festival held each August in one or other of the Welsh towns to promote the use of the Welsh language and to encourage Welsh national tradition in verse, singing, harp-playing, etc. Eisteddfodau are said to have been held as early as the 7th century. A similar festival held in Scotland for much the same purpose is known as the Gaelic Mod. - A Welsh Language Act, designed to promote the equality of English and Welsh in Welsh courts of law, was passed by the British Parliament.

R L S

Census

In the modern sense, census is the official numbering of people, houses, firms etc. Usually the term refers to people. 1634.

■ The American Constitution provided for a census of the population every ten years (from 1790) for two purposes:

(1) It gives a basis for the apportionment of Representatives among the States, because the number of members of each State in the House of Representatives is determined by the State's population. Originally, the *Constitution** had provided that "the number of Representatives shall not exceed one for every thirty thousand, but each State shall have at least one Representative" (Art. I, section 2,3). The latter provision has remained, but the former would now give the House a membership of over 6,800 (in 1790 *Congress** had 65 Representatives), so that after new apportionments following each decennial census (except 1920) a final settlement had to be made. In 1912 Congress fixed the total membership of the House at 435; an act of 1941 provided for a method of finding equal proportions. Between 1958 and 1960 the number rose to 437 owing to the admission of Alaska and Hawaii to the Union. After the census of 1960 and the new apportionment the number reverted to 435. On the basis of the 1970 census, there was one Representative for 467,207 Americans.

(2) It determines how many electoral votes are allotted to each State in

presidential election. As the Chief Executive of the United States is not elected directly by the people, but by electors, the census again is of the greatest importance because, on the basis of the number of people inhabiting each State, it determines (by a principle which is identical with that applied in the apportionment of Representatives) the numerical weight of each State in presidential elections. In the elections of 1976 California had 45, New York 41, Nevada 3 electors.

The Census Bureau, an agency continuously engaged in statistical studies of all kinds, is entrusted with the conduct of the census and its evaluation. Perhaps the most famous announcement it has made was that of closing the *Frontier** in 1890.

● In Britain also a census is held at regular intervals organized by the Government Office of Population Censuses and Surveys. Until 1971 it took place every ten years and is now held quinquennially. It does not have the political significance of the census in the United States. The function of re-apportionment given to the American census can perhaps best be compared to that of the Redistribution of Seats Acts in Britain which have in a similar way influenced the shifting of political weight in the House of Commons.

The first census in Britain was held in 1801, based on an Act of Parliament. Its returns were not very precise, for there was no enumeration procedure, and answers were collected orally. In the 1841 census ages were documented and in 1851 also marital status. The forerunner of the modern census was the Domesday Book of 1086, a special purpose count to tell William the Conqueror whom he had conquered. H H

Checks and Balances

■ The term is used to describe the balance of powers of the three branches of U.S. government. 1787. There are a number of checks and balances in every democratic state because of the free play of political forces there. Only in the U.S.A., however, have checks and balances been laid down in the Constitution as a political principle.

The American *Constitution** contains two apparently conflicting principles: separation of powers into three branches (the legislative, the executive, the judicative) and checks and balances. The essence of the latter principle is that it gives each of these three branches certain authority over the others. Thus, for example, the President can veto a Bill of Congress, but Congress can override the President's veto by a two-thirds majority; Bi-cameralism gives each of the two chambers the power to check the actions of the other; Congressional committees *(Committee*)* can check the powers of both *Congress** and the *Chief Executive**, the President's right to appoint "Officers of the United States" (judges, heads of Departments, ambassadors, etc.) is checked by the right of the Senate to confirm these appointments; the President may negotiate treaties, but the Senate has to assent with a two-thirds majority; the modes of congressional elections, the length of terms of Senators (six years), Congressmen (two years), and President (four years) are perhaps the most typical examples of checks and balances *(Congress*)*.

The difficulty of the system of checks and balances lies in the contradiction that on the one hand the powers of government are clearly divided among the legislature, the executive, and the judiciary by the Constitution, but on the other hand each of them is permitted to encroach upon the spheres of the others. Theoretically one might think that such a system could not work at all. That it does function is perhaps due to two factors: the prevalence of a general consensus in America with regard to the conditions under which people wish to live together, and the egotism of separate groups. This "group utilitarianism" assumes that each group (e.g. labour, bankers, teachers, Negroes, Baptists, birdwatchers, the House of Representatives, the Presidency, etc.) believes that it knows what is best for itself or for its purposes; and that all these individual subdivisions, although on different levels of importance, ultimately check and balance one another. This fact explains the great importance of interest groups and pressure groups in the U.S.A. *(Lobby*)*.

● In Britain the term is used loosely to signify that no one, especially no member of the executive, can set himself up above the law and the Constitution.

H H

Chief Executive

■ The chief executive is the head of the executive branch of the government in accordance with the theory of the separation of power. It is represented by the mayors (local level), the governors (state level), and the President and the Vice-President of the U.S.A. (federal level). The term (spelt Chief Executive) is usually applied to the latter. 1787.

President and Vice-President. The *Constitution** deals with the Executive in rather vague general terms. It states that "The executive power shall be vested in a President of the United States of America. He shall hold his office during the Term of four years and together with the Vice-President, chosen for the same Term, be elected as follows . . ." (Art. II, sec. 1). He is given the power to appoint officials with the advice and consent of the Senate; is charged with the faithful execution of the laws and with informing the legislature as to the State of the Union; he can call Congress into special session; he can veto legislation, can conclude treaties with the consent of two-thirds of the Senate; he is commander-in-chief of the armed forces (a professional army since January 1973) and can pardon offenders against federal laws (except in cases of impeachment). Although authority in the field of foreign relations is divided among three organs - the President, Congress as a whole, and, for the approval of treaties and diplomatic appointments, the Senate - the President's claim to take precedence is but rarely disputed.

From 1789 to 1977, the Vice-President possessed almost no power, except for the little influence he had in his capacity as chairman of the Senate and the right to cast his vote in case of a tie. This waste of the resources of a potential successor in office by practically all American Presidents since George Washington was ended by President Carter in 1977. He made Vice President Walter Mondale his closest adviser, "Assistant President" so to speak, gave him full insight into Chief Executive matters, entrusted him with important tasks both foreign and domestic, particularly with the handling of the difficult relationship between the White House and Capitol Hill, and gave him an office in the White House itself. President Carter has certainly broken new institutional ground, but it is too early to decide if his interpretation of the Chief Executive has set a precedent for the future. The Constitution and the Law of the Land still give the President alone the right to handle the executive power of the U.S.A.

The office of President has emerged today as a power much stronger than the founders of the Constitution intended. This accumulation of power in the hands of the Executive is due to several reasons: (1) The adaptation of the Constitution to new social forces which demanded a stronger central authority, (2) the defeat of the South in the Civil War (1861-65), which was also a defeat of the theory that the *States' Rights** were supreme as against the rights of the central government, (3) the ability and excellence of some Presidents.

This development is marked by the following stages. In the so-called Whisky Insurrection, 1794 (local rebellion against the excise tax), Washington acted alone and thus created a precedent for the sole responsibility of the Chief Executive for the suppression of domestic disorder (this precedent has often been followed, more recently in the President's actions in civil rights disturbances). Jefferson acquired Louisiana, 1803, and the Senate did not approve the treaty until later; by this act the President established himself as the sole instrument of communication with foreign governments *(Congress*)*. Under Jackson (1829-37) the Chief Executive became independent of the State Legislatures because, owing to the extension of suffrage, electors in most States were now chosen by popular vote. The *Spoils System**, although Jackson made little use of it, was firmly established by that time and gave the President the opportunity of building up personal loyalties and power. Lincoln strengthened the position of the Chief Executive still further by making extensive use of his power of commander-in-chief; without prior Congressional action he suspended *Habeas Corpus**, limited the freedom of the *Press**, summoned the State militia, blockaded ports, etc. Theodore Roosevelt and Wilson added further responsibilities to the President's office: Roosevelt's "New Nationalism" demanded government regulation of economic activity, and Wilson's "New Freedom", though presented in the lofty phrases of economic liberalism, was no less interventionist. The doctrine of crisis leadership, associated with F.D. Roosevelt, by which government was transformed into a series of action programmes, and the Second World War with the subsequent crisis still further expanded the power of the Chief Executive; examples are: the secret agreement of Yalta and the Lend-Lease agreement (F.D. Roosevelt); the Korean War (Truman), which largely remained outside the Senate's sphere of influence because the war had never been officially declared; Kennedy's action in the Cuban crisis; and L.B. Johnson's and Nixon's measures in the conflict in Vietnam. (Between 1789 and 1971 U.S. forces participated in military action overseas on more than 150 occasions, but Congress declared war only five times.) It must be noted, however, that this development would have been impossible if the *Supreme Court** and Congress had not tolerated it. Moreover, there are many *Checks and Balances** in the American system to preclude dictatorship.

There are obvious parallels between the growth in power of the President of the U.S.A. and that of the Prime Minister of the U.K., *(Parliament, Cabinet*)*. Today, most bills introduced in Congress and in Parliament are Executive bills (the term "government bill" as used in Britain is inappropriate in the U.S.A., because there the "government" comprises Chief Executive and Congress, and sometimes also the Supreme Court). But whereas the Prime Minister's legislative measures can always be sure of acceptance, the President occasionally finds one of his bills thrown out by Congress; on the other hand, by using his veto, he can, as a rule, prevent the passing of any bill which he does not like *(Checks and Balances*)*. If the President refuses to sign a bill it goes back to that house where it originated, together with his reasons (the so-called veto message), to be reconsidered; if a two-thirds majority approves the bill, it goes to the other chamber where the same procedure is followed; if a two-thirds majority can be obtained here, too, the bill becomes an Act of Congress over the President's veto. Although this rarely happens, there are famous cases of overruling the presidential veto, e.g. Truman's veto of the Taft-Hartley Omnibus Bill. A particular type of veto is the "pocket veto". By the Constitution the President is allowed ten days from the date of receiving the bill (exclusive of Sundays) to give it his approval. If, within this period of time Congress adjourns without the President having returned it, the bill does not become law. Many Presidents have resorted to this device.

The expansion of power and jurisdiction of the Chief Executive has brought with it the development of an apparatus surrounding it. This apparatus is sometimes fittingly called "the Presidency". It comprises those agencies directly attached to the President to assist him in the fulfilment of increasingly specialized tasks. President Nixon ("King Richard") was, at one time, surrounded by 20 Presidential Offices. Under him the Cabinet, with rare exceptions, was reduced to a mere instrument of White House policy. President Carter has made it clear that he would depend more on his Cabinet than on his staff. Nonetheless, the institution of a "brain trust" (a term often used since F.D. Roosevelt to designate the inner circle of the President's staff) has been preserved even under Carter.

The most important unit of the Presidency is the White House Office, a staff of personal Counsels, Secretaries, Special Assistants, Aides, and Advisers (since F. D. Roosevelt, the inner circle of this staff has tended to be a "brain trust"). Second in importance is the Office of Management and Budget. Under the direct authority of the President it controls and co-ordinates the estimates, which then emerge as the Annual Budget. It is, in fact, responsible for expenditure, while the Treasury is responsible for revenues. Its director, together with the chairman of the President's Council of Economic Advisers, the chairman of the Federal Reserve Board, and the Secretary of State for the Treasury has a most decisive influence on American economic policy. Through this office, the President can best obtain an overall picture of the government.

In addition to these there are Offices like the National Security Council, the Central Intelligence Agency (CIA), the Domestic Council, the Council of Environmental Quality, the Office of Telecommunications Policy, the Office of Intergovernmental Relations, the Energy Resources Council, the Special Action Office for Drug Abuse Prevention, the Council of International Economic Policy, the Office of the Special Representative for Trade Negotations, the Federal Property Council, the Council of Wage and Price Stability and the Presidential Clemency Board. Within the Presidency there are also created from time to time certain commissions (comparable to the Royal Commissions in Britain, *Committee*)* to study particular problems (e.g. Price Commission, Commission on Civil Rights). The characteristic feature of the Presidency is that its various units are associated with the Chief Executive in overall planning and control; it is one aspect of the American Executive. The other aspect is the bureaucracy, which includes the *Departments** and the *Independent Agencies** The President has an official residence in the Executive Mansion (White House) in Washington, District of Columbia. He is elected on the first Tuesday after the first Monday in November of a leap-year and is inaugurated on January 20th of the following year (Amendment XX, 1933; up to that year the inauguration took place on March 4th). The Vice President is elected on the same day as the President. (For procedure, see *Poll*.)* In case of the death of the President, the succession (established by an Act of Congress, 1947) is: Vice-President, the Speaker of the House of Representatives, the Secretaries *(Department*)*. In 1965, Congress passed Amendment XXV to the Constitution (ratified in 1967 *(Constitution*)* enabling the President to choose, with the approval of Congress, a Vice-President in case this office should be vacant. The problem arose after J. F. Kennedy's assassination, when the vice-presidency remained vacant for a year.

Moreover, Amendment XXV provides that the Vice-President, as Acting President, can temporarily conduct the affairs of the President as long as the latter requires him to do so. A complicated system of safeguards has been connected with this provision: the Vice-President and the majority of Cabinet members may declare to the President *pro tempore* and the Speaker that the President is unable to discharge his duties; the President may, thereupon, lodge his protest; Vice-President and Cabinet may then restate their former declaration; finally Congress shall decide the issue.

The Governor. He is elected by popular vote. His powers are outlined in the State constitutions, but are generally more confined than those of the U.S. President, because (a) his right of appointment is limited; several high State officials are elected together with the governor; (b) most State legislatures have reserved for themselves a larger measure of administrative control than has the federal Congress; (c) in most States his veto (if any) is limited to individual items; (d) in some States the governor's term of office is still only two years, although the tendency has been towards a four-year term in recent years.

The Mayor *(City, Town and Township*.)* H H

City

Orig. a town or other inhabited place. 1611. In the U.S.A., a town or collective body of inhabitants incorporated and governed by a mayor and aldermen. 1843. In Great Britain and Ireland, a title ranking above that of "town" and associated with episcopal seats and ancient royal burghs, and in recent times conferred by royal authority on important boroughs, such as Birmingham.

■ In America the city is one of the subdivisions of the county. The others are *Town and Township** and village, which is rarely called a borough. In England the city would be called county borough or municipal borough. The separation of metropolitan and non-metropolitan county, however, does not exist in the U.S.A., with three exceptions: Virginia is divided into 96 counties and 38 "independent cities" - the equivalent of the British metropolitan counties; Maryland consists of 23 counties and one independent city (viz. Baltimore, city population approximately 905,000, county population approximately 620,000); and Missouri has 114 counties and one independent city (viz. St. Louis, city population approximately 623,000, county population approximately 952,000). (N.B. The five administrative units of the City of New York are commonly called "boroughs", but are officially designated as "counties": Bronx County = the Bronx, New York County = Manhattan, Queens County = Queens, Kings County = Brooklyn, and Richmond County = Richmond.) These and all other cities are governed under what are normally called their charters. But whereas in England a charter bestows privileges of local administration, in America the city charter is something like a local constitution. It can be obtained by special act of the State legislature, by general laws passed by the State legislature, by option for one of several charters offered by the State, or under "municipal home rule" - a city may frame as well as adopt its own charters. There are today three main types of city charter (or city government):

(1) The mayor-council charter is the oldest type and reflects the pattern of Federal and State governments. The mayor is the chief executive and is independently elected. He usually appoints the heads of the city departments. There is an independently elected school board and a mostly uni-cameral city council, which passes judgement upon the city ordinances. This system tends to make for a vigorous leadership and a dynamic city life, but it can also easily be dominated by party politics. The largest American cities and altogether approximately 50 per cent. of the cities with populations of over 10,000 are governed under this type of charter. In recent years, many of these cities (among them Boston, New York City, Newark, Philadelphia, New Orleans, Los Angeles and San Francisco) have adopted a "strong mayor-general manager plan". It grants the mayor greater powers of budget preparation, administration, personnel management and managerial supervision over city agencies, and it provides for a general manager, appointed and removable by the mayor.

(2) The commission charter was first introduced in Galveston, Texas, in 1912 and was for some time expected to solve all the problems of city government. It provides for an elected commission of three, five, or seven members who are frequently businessmen rather than trained administrators. They divide up the function of the city into departments but are collectively responsible for the city government. The disadvantage of this type of government is that it tends to create uncoordinated, self-contained units instead of strong leadership. The *District of Columbia**, for instance, is administered by this type of commission government.

(3) The city-manager charter has steadily gained adherents since it was first adopted in Dayton, Ohio, shortly before World War I. Today, about one-third of American cities are governed under city manager charters. The system provides for a council which has three important functions: to pass judgement on ordinances (including such providing for functions), to adopt a budget, and to choose a city manager. The manager, who is usually not a resident of the city and in most cases a professionally trained administrator, takes the sole initiative in city affairs and makes his suggestions on policy to the council. The city manager plan represents a further development of the so-called "council-manager plan" in so far as it provides for proportional representation in the council and tends to break the power of the one-party machine.

The village, in England not a technical term in local government *(Parish*)*, can be a unit of local self-government in the U.S.A. There it appears as the "incorporated village" and has its own charter. Its government consists of a legislative branch made up of a board of trustees or a similar body; an executive with a village president, treasurer, public engineer, street commissioner, marshal (chief of police) etc., and a judiciary in the form of a police magistrate who is a State official.

Whereas American cities with a population up to approx. 250,000 are usually healthy communities, the aging metropolises of the Northeast and Middle West (New York, Detroit, St. Louis, Cleveland, Buffalo, Boston, Philadelphia, and others), but also some long-established Southern and

Western cities (including New Orleans, San Francisco, and Los Angeles) are in a deep "urban crisis". High- and middle-income households have migrated into "dormitory suburbs" and "bedroom communities", taxpaying industries have moved to places out of the cities where land is abundant and cheap and where storage and transport facilities are easily available. Low-income and minority populations (especially blacks, Puerto Ricans and Chicanos) have moved into the inner cities. This has led to a drastic reduction of the revenue of the old cities, while, at the same time, costs have been rising tremendously (in some cases, like in New York City, to the point of insolvency) because of the high social service burden, the high crime rate, higher maintenance costs for an obsolete infrastructure, special facilities for thousands of school children who cannot speak English, etc.

But bigness alone does not explain the plight. There are several cities of more than a half million people (like Houston, San Diego, Phoenix, and Memphis) that are growing and prospering. But these growing cities, almost all in the South and West, have a hinterland of their own, so that their suburbs, with their enormous tax potential, are part of the city proper.

It may be noted here that London's (the British capital's) problems are, to some extent, similar to those of the City of New York: it has a large drifting population of immigrants, jobseekers and the poor. But otherwise London has its own problems of "urban renewal" *(Greater London*)*.

● In Britain "city" is not a unit of local government and bears no relation to municipal functions, although the term often appears in official language (e.g. city council, City of London Police Force). "City" is a title of honour by traditional usage, by royal charter, or by statute. Nowadays the designation has nothing to do with whether the place has a cathedral or not, nor with its size or population.

But "the City" is also a term for the business district of London, that half square mile within the City of London *(Greater London*)* which is Britain's financial centre. The City's principal areas of activity consist of insurance, banking, merchanting *(Merchant Bankers*)* and brokerage, and the supply of financial services. There is also a wide range of ancillary professions, e.g. Britain's leading legal and accountancy firms. The most important business institutions in the City are the Stock Exchange, Lloyd's, the insurance companies, and the banks. Each of these sectors breaks down further; the banks for example into the clearing banks, the merchant banks, the banks for the British-based banks operating overseas, and about 180 overseas banks which are now represented in London. - The City of London, taken as a financial centre, has been by far the most successful industry in Britain since the end of World War II. Insurance, banking, and finance companies are earning about half as much as the whole of Britain's manufacturing industry, four times as much as the British chemical industry and about eight times as much as the automobile manufacturers of Britain put together. This success has been due to several reasons. Most important among them is probably the fact that in Britain joint-stock companies and banking developed early and, in contradistinction to developments in the U.S.A. and in Europe, side-by-side with legal and accountancy skills. Even today, in the face of Britain's comparatively weak economic position and New York's efforts to rival London as an international financial centre, its supremacy in the international capital markets remains fundamentally unchallenged. Other reasons for the City's continued im-

portance after the war have been its substantial capture of the Eurodollar market and its role as the banker of the Commonwealth and, with some qualifications, of the world.
H H

Civil Rights

■ Civil rights are the rights which a State's inhabitants enjoy under its constitution and laws, and in which they are protected by the courts. 1866. The term is broader than "political" rights (e.g. the right to vote). It is also distinguished from "natural rights". Typical examples of civil rights are the right to obtain employment, the right to use public facilities like restaurants, trams, toilets, on equal terms with all other persons. In the ultimate analysis, civil rights are social rights.

The select *Committee** on Civil Rights appointed by President Truman in 1946 gave a certain definition of the matter in so far as it named four classes of rights to be studied: (1) the right to safety and security of the person; (2) the right to citizenship and its privileges; (3) the right to freedom of conscience and its expression; (4) the right to equality of opportunity.

The civil rights problem is closely linked with the status of the minority and coloured, especially Negro, citizen of the U.S.A. and, since the early sixties, of the United Kingdom *(Immigration*)*.

It first emerged with the Emancipation Proclamation, January 1st, 1863, by Abraham Lincoln, which must be considered as a war measure to undermine the strength of the Confederacy. It was through Amendments XIII, XIV, and XV that the legal basis was created for the liberation of the blacks and their formal recognition as citizens of the United States.

Several Civil Rights Acts have been passed by the U.S. Congress, the last in 1964. It provides the legal framework within which black Americans can claim their rights and seek to ensure that they obtain them. The Civil Rights Act of 1964 had three forerunners:

The first Civil Rights Act of 1866 gave citizenship to the Negro. It had become necessary because of the famous Dred Scott Decision of the U.S. Supreme Court in 1857 *(Judicial Review*)* in which Dred Scott, a Negro slave, had been denied the civil rights of a citizen of the U.S.A. (that decision widened the cleavage between the North and South and strengthened the case of the *Abolitionists*)*. The Act was passed over President Johnson's veto; he condemned the Act as an invasion of *States' Rights** (it was declared unconstitutional by the Supreme Court in 1883), which led to Amendment XIV being passed.

The second Civil Rights Act of 1870, with provisions similar to those of 1866, was passed after the ratification of Amendment XIV.

The third Civil Rights Act of 1875 guaranteed to the Negroes equal rights in public places (inns, public conveyances, theatres, etc.) and expressly admitted them as jurymen. Its principal sections were declared unconstitutional in the chief of the so-called civil rights cases of 1883 on the ground that these were not civil rights but social rights. This ruling of the Supreme Court was of great importance in the development of civil rights in the U.S.A. because it virtually ended federal attempts to protect the Negro against discrimination by private persons for the following 80 years. The court decision in Plessy v. Ferguson of 1896 was a further setback in the development of civil rights. In it the Supreme Court sustained the validity of the segregation practices of the southern States.

The Court held that a Louisiana statute requiring railroads to "provide equal but separate accomodations for the white and colored races" did not constitute a denial of the equal protection of the laws in violation of the 14th Amendment.

If one leaves aside the Civil Rights Act of 1957, which merely empowered a new division of the Justice Department to get court injunctions to protect voting rights, it was not until 1963 that another decisive attempt at the solution of the civil rights problem was made by President John F. Kennedy. His Civil Rights Bill became the Civil Rights Act of 1964 under President L. B. Johnson's administration. It guarantees to the Negro equal status in every political and social respect and is intended to bring about complete desegregation of the races. The act met with fierce opposition in the South (Virginia, Kentucky, Oklahoma, Arkansas, Tennessee, North Carolina, South Carolina, Georgia, Alabama, Mississippi, Louisiana, Texas, Florida), especially in the *Deep South** (South Carolina, Georgia, Alabama, Mississippi, Louisiana). Not only did southern Senators try to frustrate the civil rights legislation of 1964 by *filibustering**, but after the law had been passed a "white backlash" set in, especially in the South, though to some extent also in those parts of the North where the percentage of Negroes among the population is high (white backlash = retaliation of whites upon Negro demonstrations or acts of violence). Moreover, never since 1860 had the civil rights question played such a role in an election campaign as in 1964 when it produced the somersault of the Republican Party, which had been founded on anti-slavery principles, into an anti-civil-rights party under Barry Goldwater, the Republican presidential candidate (from Arizona). In the same year, Congress ratified Amendment XXIV abolishing poll tax in some States of the South.

Before 1964, decisive steps towards the integration of coloured people had prepared for these legislative measures *(Dixie*)*. The C.I.O. (Committee for Industrial Organization, renamed Congress of Industrial Organizations in 1938 *(Trade (Labor) Unions*))* admitted Negroes. The A.F.L. (American Federation of Labor) had to follow. Today only few unions exclude Negroes. Three wars in which the U.S.A. was involved in the 20th century contributed much to the integration of the Negro. During World War I, Negro units were, for the first time, led by white and coloured officers. In 1941 the Fair Employment Practice Committee was established to end racial discrimination in war industries and armed services but suffered delay because of repeated obstruction in the Senate. (Race riots in Detroit, 1943; Philadelphia, 1944.) By the end of 1946 only five states (N.Y., N.J., Mass., Conn., and Wash.) had enacted Fair Employment Practice Acts of their own. In World War II in the Battle of Bastogne (or Battle of the Bulge or Rundstedt-Offensive), 1944, the American military command was compelled to form mixed units to counter the German attack. It was, however, not until the Korean War (1950-53) that integrated units were officially formed. In 1952 American troops in Germany were integrated. In 1954 the Supreme Court invalidated segregation at school (Brown vs. Board of Education).

13 years after the enactment of the Civil Rights Bill of 1964, the state of affairs is the following:

General

The social, economic, and political condition of America's black population has improved considerably over the past 25 years. For example, Mississippi (one of the 11 Southern States which still house more than half of the black

Americans) black voter registration leaped from 6.7 per cent. in 1964 to 63.3 per cent. in 1975. Nevertheless, the general condition of America's blacks is still quite appalling. The Bureau of Census figures of 1977 show that out of a total population of 215.2 million there are 24.8 million black Americans. Roughly 35 per cent. of these live today in considerable poverty. In the rural South the condition of blacks does not seem to be much better than 100 years ago, and in many Southern small towns racial prejudices have remained very strong. It seems that black migrant workers often live in squalor and work under conditions little better than slaves (N.Y. Times, Aug. 29, 1977, The Times, Sept. 1, 1977). It is generally accepted that there is a strong link between the high crime level in America and the deprivation of the black American. For example, some 55 per cent. of all those who were arrested for looting shops when New York had its power failure in July 1977 were unemployed, most of them blacks.

Education

School integration has made rapid progress in the south (see below) but has remained virtually unchanged in the rest of the country. In the large cities of the north and west, however, segregation is growing. In 1972, in 31 states of the north and west 11 per cent. of black pupils attended all-black schools, 24 per cent. in the border states (including Maryland and the District of Columbia), while in the 11 southern states the figure was 9 per cent. Since 1967 the percentage of black ghetto males who drop out of high school has fallen from 24 per cent. to 18 per cent. (1976).

The most divisive of all issues emanating from Brown vs. Board of Education has been the busing of school children in order to obtain more racial mixing and to foster racial integration at schools. In 1971 the Supreme Court ordered that busing was legal. Opposition to this court order has been especially great in the North, and in 1974 Boston and Denver were forced to carry out desegregation schemes involving busing. But the progress of desegration was adversely affected when Congress legislated against it in the Education Amendments of 1972 in order to correct racial imbalance, and when the Supreme Court turned down cross-county busing in 1974 *(Judicial Review*).*

Public office

An increasing proportion of blacks have been appointed into top positions in the federal government, the universities, the labor unions, the armed forces, etc. In 1974, about 3000 blacks (against about 500 in 1965) were holding elective office (including one U.S. Senator and 16 Representatives, and about 108 mayors representing such big cities as Los Angeles, Detroit, Atlanta, Newark, Cleveland, Gary, and Washington D.C.). But the figure represents only 0.6 per cent. of all elective offices in the U.S.A., compared with approximately 11.5 per cent. blacks in the total population of the country. This misproportion is supposed to be improved by "affirmative action".

Affirmative Action

Based on the Equal Employment Opportunities Act, 1964, an employment quota system has been developed in order to realize equal opportunities for the minorities. This scheme is called "affirmative action". It is a huge federal government programme to coerce all sectors of American business, government, and public life, including colleges and universities to increase their intake of employees and students from the minorities - blacks, Indians, hispanic Americans and Orientals and women. It is an expression of the American government's determination to abide by the promises implied in all the civil rights legislation. It is enforced by a very simple means: the government refuses to award any contract to an enterprise that practises discrimination by refusing to subscribe to the principle of proportional racial employment. Reluctant colleges and universities can be similarly "encouraged", because they are heavily dependent on the government for research contracts, and if they discriminate they get no money. There have also been cases of overcompensation of the principle: some universities and public institutions deliberately discriminate in favour of women and blacks, even if they are less qualified than male or white applicants, in order to show progress towards meeting the goal. Between 59 and 70 per cent. of the blacks now in graduate school would possibly not be there except for special admissions under "affirmative action"; for medical and law schools specifically the figures run close to 80 per cent. (1977). This system of favouring particular social groups on grounds of race has provoked reaction against "reverse discrimination" and raised constitutional and social issues of major importance for the future of America. In June, 1978, the Supreme Court of the United States ordered the University of California's Davis Medical School to admit Allan Bakke, a white American, who had twice been rejected while black students with lesser qualifications had been accepted. He had sued the University claiming that he been denied admission solely because he was white. Though the court's opinion is unlikely to precipitate a widespread cancellation of "affirmative action" programmes, it certainly constitutes a setback in the cause of civil rights in America.

Housing

Plans to integrate residential neighbourhoods ("scatter-site housing") have practically failed. Public housing projects are being undertaken mainly in the poor areas themselves, so that the ghetto situation is being perpetuated. The black population of inner cities, where often slum conditions prevail, rose sharply in the 1960s, while more whites moved to the suburbs. In fact, a black population that was three-quarters southern rural in 1910 is three-quarters urban today and northward migration spilled most of them into the black ghettos. New York has 1.67 million blacks, Chicago 1.1 million, Detroit and Philadelphia 660,000 each. Three cities of more than 200,000 - Washington, D.C., Newark and Atlanta - and 13 other American cities have black majorities. 25 big cities are expected to be mainly black by 1982. - The Civil Rights Act of 1968 formally barred discrimination against blacks in the sale or rental of most housing.

Employment

Historically, the ratio of black unemployment to white unemployment has been 2 to 1. The Equal Opportunity Commission, an agency created in 1964 to end discrimination based on race, colour, religion, sex, or national origin, is expected to end these inequalities. The commission receives charges of discrimination and has repeatedly brought suits in the federal courts, especially in recent years. It has taken steps towards the integration of minorities (including women) into regular employment. A number of court decisions have contributed to bringing about equal, i.e. proportional, employment (see "affirmative action"). - The employment situation is still aggravated by the fact that just over 50 per cent. of the black workers are unskilled or semiskilled, and

need for them is declining as technology advances, so that there are great opportunities for educated blacks, but narrow opportunities for the lower class. 1
This may account for the great number of unemployed blacks; about five million out of 24 receive some form of public welfare payments. - The unemployment figures of 1977 show that some 40 per cent. of black teenagers are without work, but black organizations suggest that 60 per cent. is nearer the truth. The black in many cases remains the last to be hired and the first to be fired in American business.

Income

The 24 million blacks are split into three groups of roughly equal size. Almost one third have family incomes of $ 10,000 or more and enjoy many of the amenities of middle class status. Another one-third, earning between $ 5,500 and $ 10,000, are either on the lower edges of the middle class or stand a fair chance of lifting themselves into it. Beneath them lies the group of black Americans who earn less than $ 5,500 and makes up the troubled lower class. Measured by the Government's official classification just over half of the blacks were below the poverty line in the early 1960s. The figure declined to about one-third of all blacks in 1969 and has remained there ever since (as against approximately 9 per cent. among the whites). In 1974, of all black female heads of households (30 to 40 per cent.) 52.8 per cent. were below the poverty line (in 1977, the poverty line was an income of $ 5,500 for a non-farm family of four). The income situation is aggravated by the circumstance that 30 to 40 per cent. of the black families are single women families. In most cases the men have deserted them.

Social rights

Title II of the Civil Rights Act of 1964, provides that "All persons shall be entitled to the full and equal enjoyment of the goods, services, facilities, privileges, advantages and accommodations of any place of public accommodation . . . without discrimination or segregation on the ground of race, color, religion, or national origin". Compliance with this order has been slow, and *de facto* segregation is still, though decreasingly, practised in all parts of the U.S.A. But social understanding is making progress, especially among the young. In 1950, mixed marriage was illegal in 30 of 48 States. In 1967, State Laws prohibiting mixed marriage were declared unconstitutional by the Supreme Court of the U.S., and since then, the number of marriages between blacks and whites has steadily increased. Especially in the large universities racial barriers are disappearing. On the other hand it must be assumed that the "silent majority" of white Americans, about identical with "middle America", is reluctant to accept integration, and a large minority of black Americans, especially those who identify themselves with *Black Power**, today reject desegregation. In 1972, Aryeh Neier, executive director of the American Civil Liberties Union, was concerned that black people were increasingly being seen by whites as their enemies and hostility against the whites on the part of the black community was similarly on the upsurge.

Today, the 23 million blacks in the U.S.A. are split in two camps: those who regard the present Civil Rights Act as the least that can be done, and those who feel that all white men are their enemies. The National Association for the Advancement of Colored People (N.A.A.C.P.) is representative of the former group, *Black Power** of the latter.

Main organizations

Southern Christian Leadership Conference

It consists principally of southern Negro Protestant ministers who still follow Dr. King's teachings. It is not a mass membership organization. It aims at securing better jobs and housing for Negroes.

National Association for the Advancement of Colored People

Largest and oldest (founded in 1909) civil rights organization in the country. It led the fight which resulted in the 1964 civil rights act and the 1964 law guaranteeing Negroes the right to vote in the deep south. It is now beeing challenged by numerous civil rights organizations as too middle-class and too conservative, as well as being out of touch with the low income and unemployed Negroes living in the ghettos of the large cities.

National Urban League

Founded in 1910 as a bi-racial service organization to help rural Negroes from the south adjust to northern city life. Today it operates with all urban Negroes, offers job training as well as educational projects. It does not operate as a mass membership protest movement. Its staff consists of social workers, job counsellors and educators.

Congress of Racial Equality

CORE was founded in 1942 by a group of mostly white divinity students from the University of Chicago. The organization became nationally prominent during the freedom rides of the 1960s, in which it played a leading role under the direction of James Farmer. Since 1965 CORE has placed emphasis on the slogan "black power" as meaning the development of the Negro's economic and political power through his own business enterprises. It was a direct move away from integration. CORE rejects the word Negro, using the word black instead. In 1967, CORE denounced non-violence as a dying philosophy.

Student Non-violent Coordinating Committee

Commonly called "Snick", evolved out of the sit-in demonstrations conducted by Negro college students in the early 1960s. Originally it was non-violent. "Snick" mobilized hundreds of students, including large numbers of whites, to work in the deep south helping Negroes to register and vote, and to desegregate public facilities. In 1966, with the election of Stokely Carmichael as chairman, "Snick" changed direction. Carmichael and his successor, H. Rap Brown, developed the slogan *Black Power**. It has made an impact among young Negroes.

In the U.S.A. the civil rights problem has not been limited to the Negroes. Three other groups have in recent years become active in fighting for their civil rights: (a) women (b) Hispanic Americans (c) American Indians.

Women

The substance of American women's claims is not just equal pay, but also equal opportunity. Like other civil rights groups they cite the Civil Rights Act of 1964, which forbids discrimination. Their demands have been complied with only in part and on paper so far. In 1972, Congress passed the Equal Rights Amendment Bill intended to become Amendment XXVII one day *(Constitution*)*, but ratification by the States is uncertain and may take up to nine years even if successful. The Equal Pay Act of 1970 came into force in successive stages by 1975.

The new American feminist movement, which began about 1966, attacks all forms of social, economic, educational and job discrimination against women. At first, small consciousness-raising groups were formed throughout the country to encourage independent thinking among women and to spread feminist concepts. Then several national organizations were founded, most important among them the National Organization for Women (NOW, 1966), the Women's Equity Action League (WEAL, 1968), the National Women's Political Caucus (NWPC, 1971), and the Coalition of Labor Union Women (1974); they have put their emphasis on producing change rather than theory. With the leadership of Bella Abzug, Betty Friedan, Shirley Chisholm, Gloria Steinem and others the movement successfully influenced Congress to pass the Equal Rights Amendment Bill in 1972 and has pressed for such changes as abortion reform, equal pay for women, federally supported child care centres, the choice for women to keep their maiden names when they marry, the removal of legal inequities in marriage etc. A number of other organizations, including the American Civil Liberties Union, Common Cause (a nationwide citizens' lobby organization), the American Home Economics Association, and the rather traditional American Association of University Women have adopted feminist positions. Many universities have introduced "Women's Studies" courses. 1

Some landmarks: 108 women ran for election to the. U.S. Congress in 1974 (a figure up by 74 per cent. against 1970), 18 of whom won seats in the House of Representatives, but none in the Senate which is still a male preserve; in 1974 Ella Grasso was elected Governor of Connecticut on her own merits (the other three women governors had merely succeeded their husbands); 42 mayors in the 1,000 largest cities in the U.S.A. are women (1975); the enrolment of women in colleges and universities tripled between 1955 and 1975; in 1976 female cadets were admitted to the Military Academy at West Point. - In business, however, women still rarely rise to the top management level (men-women ratio 600 to 1), they hold less than 5 per cent. of all elective offices and less than 10 per cent. of the full professors on American campuses are women.

Very few avowed anti-feminists have so far organized any opposition to the movement. One organized group is Stop E.R.A. (i.e. Equal Rights Amendment); there are about 10,000 members of a group called Happiness of Womanhood, whose objective it is to emphasize expressions of womanhood and the art of feminity.

● The aims of the women's civil rights movement in Britain are basically the same as in America. It is largely due to its insistence that two Acts were passed by Parliament intended to improve the situation of women: the Sex Discrimination Act 1975 (and a similar Act of 1976 for Northern Ireland) and the Equal Pay Act 1970, effective in 1975 (with corresponding legislation in Northern Ireland). Dr. Shirley Summerskill, Undersecretary of State in the Home Office, is considered main architect of the former, while Barbara Castle, then Secretary of State for Social Services, is given credit for the Equal Pay Act.

The British Government claims that the Sex Discrimination Act is "one of the most comprehensive in the world" (Britain 1977, An Official Handbook). It makes discrimination on the basis of sex unlawful in employment, education, provision of housing, goods, facilities and services, and advertising. The Equal Pay Act entitles women to equal pay with men when doing work that is the same or broadly similar.

But British feminists doubt the effectiveness of the two Acts. Radical feminists are not interested in a few more women in top positions; they argue that true liberation means challenging the principles of present-day society in Britain, especially the widely-held idea that men are basically breadwinners, women their dependants.

New feminism dates back to the end of the sixties when a number of women began to get together to discuss the liberation movement in the U.S.A. Today, there are thought to be more than 1,500 groups of women around the United Kingdom meeting fairly regularly to raise women's consciousness and to discuss, among other things, four main demands: equal pay, equal job and education opportunities, free contraception and abortion on demand, and twenty-four-hour nurseries for children under five, the latter probably being the most important of all, because until women have somewhere to leave their children, the Sex Discrimination Act is little more than a piece of paper for mothers of small children. Similarly, the Equal Pay Act remains meaningless, at least in part, as long as the vast number of women are doing jobs that cannot be compared with men's. The shipbuilding industry, for example, is a male-dominated province, whose average weekly earnings are twice as high as those in the textile industry, which is dominated by women, who, in many cases, are doing even more highly skilled jobs.

Women's organizations in Britain have evolved into an intricate overlapping network ranging from the national level where policies are recommended (Women's National Commission) through second-tier umbrella groups (for example the National Council of Women and the Women's Group on Public Welfare) to the grass-roots level of sub-groups including committees, standing conferences, guilds, and workshops. The following is a selection of names of such organizations and groups: Women's National Commission, National Council of Women, British Federation of University Women, T.U.C. Women's Conference, Women's Liberation Workshop, Women in Media, Women's Rights Campaign, Women's Co-operative Guild, Working Women's Charter Group, Fawcett Society (Dame Millicent Garret Fawcett, 1847-1929, was a noted English feminist), Women's Action Group; to some extent even the Women's Institute *(Club*)* has joined the trend. A battered wives' movement has been called into existence, which is growing fast. There are dozens of women's aid centres, many of them providing temporary refuge for women who have been beaten by their husbands.

In recent years, there has been a distinct growth in women's studies in the universities. - Some of the new women's magazines are feminist, like "Spare Rib", "Shrew", and "Socialist Woman".

■ *Hispanic Americans*

The second group, the Hispanic Americans, about 15.5 million in number, although it is extremely difficult to obtain reliable figures because of the heavy influx of illegal immigrants, are the second largest minority in the U.S.A. Approximately 12 million (nearly 80 per cent.) are Mexican Americans, often referred to as "Chicanos"; about 1.5 million of the group are of Puerto Rican origin; about 580,000 have come from Cuba or other South or Central American countries; the remaining Hispanic Americans (about 1.5 million) are designated by the authorities as "other Spanish". It was a mass emigration after World War II that brought millions of Spanish speaking people to the U.S.A. Most of the Cuban immigrants stayed in the south-east, the Mexicans in the five south-western States (Arizona, California, Colorado, New Mexico, and

Texas). Most of the Puerto Ricans live in New York City (well over a million) and other big northern cities. Like the blacks most of them are underprivileged. Their situation had, until recently, roused little attention although it is just as bad as that of the Negroes, and perhaps worse in one respect: English is a foreign language to them. The reason probably is that they cared little to voice their claims through mass organizations. It was not until 1970 that a militant group of young Puerto Ricans set a first example of violent protest in New York: the "Young Lords", a revolutionary group and a Latin equivalent of the Black Panthers. It was dissolved in the mid-seventies. In October 1971 a first conference of Spanish-speaking activists took place in Washington, D.C., and a political attempt was made to organize in order to press for legislation to end discrimination against Hispanic Americans. Their civil rights demands are hardly less justified than those of the Negroes. A solution of their problems, however, is not yet in sight because of the rising flood of illegal immigrants from Mexico or Central America. It is estimated that at least 200,000 (there are estimates up to 400,000) "wetbacks" swim across the Rio Grande every month to enter the United States illegally. Practically all of them are impoverished. Many go north to work in farms all the way to the Canadian border, but most of them stay in the Southwest. There are 2.5 million Chicanos in Texas (pop. 11.2 million); San Antonio, Texas, has a Chicano majority of its 750,000 population). In November 1974, two Spanish-Americans were elected governors, Raul Castro in Arizona and Jerry Apodoca in New Mexico. This was an important turning-point for Chicanos all over the Southwest, a sign that a long era of discrimination, of economic and political oppression is at last coming to an end. Like the black members of the House of Representatives, the five Hispanic Congressmen have formed the Hispanic Caucus, organized in Dezember 1976 to increase the influence of the "Latinos" on legislation.

American Indians

So long a silent minority, the American Indians, too, are now putting forward their claims with great vigour *(Indian*)*.

There has been a general resurgence of ethnic consciousness ("ethnicity") since the sixties which continues into the present time. All ethnic groups participate in it: blacks, Indians, Chicanos, Chinese-Americans (between 1882 and 1924 discriminated against as "non-Americans"), Japanese-Americans (oppressed and interned in camps during World War II), and, sometimes with racist elements to set themselves apart from other ethnic groups the "white ethnics", i.e. Irish-, Italian-, Armenian-, Greek- and Slavic-Americans, and the Jews. This resurgence has been labelled "New Tribalism", but "New Pluralism" seems to be the more fitting designation. H H

Civil Service

That part of the service of the East India Company carried on by the covenanted servants who did not belong to the Army or Navy; now, all the non-warlike departments of the public administrative service of the state. Also the body of servants of the state employed in the service. 1785.

● In contrast to most administrative bodies the British Civil Service is regulated by no statute of Parliament (with the exception of pensions), but its management has always been considered a function of the Crown and of the Ministers of the Crown. Originally the service was the small personal body of officials maintained by the sovereign, which explains why a civil servant is still considered to be a servant of the Crown. Positions in the service were in the gift of ministers of the Crown, and no qualifying tests were applied. As a result patronage, nepotism, and corruption were rife, in the 18th century in particular.

The Civil Service as it existed until 1968 was the result of the reforms suggested in the report of Sir Stafford Northcote and Sir Charles Trevelyan on the Civil Service published in 1855. They took as their model the civil service of the highly successful British East India Company (the name was also taken over) which had recently instituted competitive examinations and had thus replaced well-connected dilettanti and adventurers with intelligent young men willing to make the service their career.

As a result of the Northcote and Trevelyan report open competition for Civil Service places was introduced and the Civil Service Commission established (1859) as an independent body intended to improve and standardize the methods of recruitment.

Administratively, however, the Civil Service was anything but unified. It had never had a central body and was built up, like the old universities of Oxford and Cambridge, on a collegiate or federal basis. Such unity as existed was provided by the power of the Treasury which grew naturally from its control of the purse.

The official Head of the Civil Service was, by virtue of a minute of 1919, the senior Joint Permanent Secretary to the Treasury.

Each department of the Civil Service contained representatives of each of the four main classes of officers. These were as follows: (1) Administrative Class - recruited largely from university graduates - its function was to prepare legislation and to carry out government decisions. (2) Executive Class - responsible for day-to-day conduct of government business. Entrance qualifications were at least G.C.E. *(General Certificate of Education*)* "A" level. (3) Clerical Class - dealt with routine clerical work. Entrance requirements were G.C.E. "O" level. (4) General Grades - cleaners, messengers, typists, etc. In addition to the classes mentioned there were specialist classes, including lawyers, doctors, scientists, etc.

Because the civil servant is legally a servant of the Crown his position is theoretically very insecure. The Crown has no enforceable obligations to its employees and can dismiss them at will. Pensions are indeed controlled by statute but the civil servant has no legal right to one. In practice, however, a Civil Service position represents a life-time of security and stability. It carries with it the odd and little-known compensation that a servant of the Crown cannot be sued for debt!

Although legally responsible only to the Crown, the civil servant in practice serves the minister at the head of his department. However, his position is unaffected by political changes and it is his duty to serve the government of the day whatever his own political opinions may be. In fact the executive, professional, scientific, and top administration groups are debarred from taking part in national political activities. Before standing for Parliament a civil servant from one of the lower groups must first resign his appointment. Should he fail to be elected, however, he is reinstated in his old job within a week of the election.

Strictly speaking the 360,000 Government industrial employees, working in armaments factories or naval dockyards for example, must also be called civil servants. If they are included the total number of people employed by the Service in Britain is over a million. Normally, however, by Civil Service is understood the non-industrial staffs of government departments at home or abroad.

Major changes in the organization of the Civil Service took place in and after 1968 following the publication of the Report of the Committee on the Civil Service ("Fulton Report") in July 1968. The annual reports of the Joint Committee of the National Whitley Council, which was set up in Juli 1968 following the publication of the Fulton Report, show that a clear indication of the shape and substance of the post-Fulton Civil Service is emerging. The new system involves the following changes:

(1) The integration of the Civil Service Commission (the powerful recruitment and selection authority) into the new Civil Service Department in 1968. Thus the Civil Service was withdrawn from the Treasury and is now autonomous. The Commission has retained its former independence in selection.

(2) The abolition of the three-class structure (leaving out of consideration cleaners, messengers, typists. etc.) and the introduction (January 1st, 1972) of a unified system of pay and grading (i.e. the formal system of grades available to organize work in the most efficient manner) down to and including clerical level. Thus at the highest levels in Departments all the special sections and disciplines will come together in an "open structure". At the start of 1971 there was the merger of the Administrative, Executive and Clerical grades into one single "Administration Group of the General Category". This was followed in September 1971 by the creation of the "Science Category" and in January 1972 by the merger of the Works Group and associated classes into the "Professional and Technology Category". The possibility of combining categories is also being considered. Further streamlining will aim at the complete abolition of any horizontal or vertical class system. It should be noted, however, that the quality at the highest levels of the Service can, so it seems, only be guaranteed by the selection of what one might call the two tiers of (a) the Administration group, and (b) the grades above Assistant Secretary, the latter group still being highly selective. In fact, the Civil Service Commission can still prevent the infiltration of this group by mediocre people from below.

(3) Adoption of new recruitment and selection policies, as graduates and in-Service candidates are now to be selected under the same procedure for appointment as Administration Trainees. There is one examination for both groups of applicants comprising three stages: a written qualifying examination, tests and interviews by the Civil Service Selection Board (C.S.S.B.), and interview by the Final Selection Board (F.S.B.). The abolition of classes appears to be a success, for there is an increasing number of in-Service candidates applying for higher middle management qualifications.

(4) Reshaping of personnel and training policies. Increased attention is being paid to personnel management and individual career planning. A common system of annual reports is being adopted throughout the Service, and systems are being introduced for job appraisal reviews and for career development interviews. Another important innovation is the Civil Service College which opened at its headquarters at Sunningdale Park, Berkshire,

on June 26th, 1970; the remaining two centres - in Edinburgh and London - were also opened in 1970. The college has a full-time research staff working in the fields of economics and administration. The courses are graded for Executive Officer, Administration Trainee, Principal, Middle Management, etc. levels.

A new plan is under consideration by the government again to link the Treasury with the Civil Service Department in a "condominium". Under it the Treasury could become responsible for overall management of the economy, that is to say for the control of manpower and civil service efficiency, while the Civil Service Department's role would be confined to running the civil service and to making appointments. There would also be a greater exchange of staff between the two departments.

■ The American constitution of 1789 did not prescribe the forms which government should take, and the American civil service is more or less the personal creation of George Washington, who founded the first three departments, i.e. Foreign (later State), Finance and War. As a result the service lacks the vast body of precedent and tradition accumulated by the more famous European services.

The history of the American civil service has been shaped by the national dread of a permanent bureaucracy, the changing degree of political patronage used in filling civil service positions, and the uneasy balance of power existing between the federal and state authorities.

Three main stages mark the development of the service. In the first, from its foundation until the presidency of Andrew Jackson in 1829, the Federal service enjoyed a high reputation for fairness and efficiency, largely because civil service positions carried with them security of tenure. The states however were less fortunate in that posts in their administrations were filled by the *Spoils System**.

In the second stage, President Jackson, considering the spoils system to be more democratic, extended it to the Federal system and actively furthered political patronage. Efficiency at once declined and the next sixty years brought increasing pressure for a reform of the service.

After some improvements under Presidents Grant and Hayes, especially upon the initiative of Carl Schurz, the Pendleton Act of 1883 represented the beginning of the third stage in the history of the service. As a result of the Act the President was enabled to appoint three Civil Service Commissioners (of whom not more than two were to be of the same political party) to aid him in introducing "an open competitive examination for testing the fitness of applicants for the public service". This meant the introduction of the "merit system" which has since spread to the entire Federal system and has been adopted by many of the states.

The service was further reformed in 1939 under the presidency of Franklin Roosevelt, when the "Hatch Act" prohibited "pernicious political activities on the part of government employees and struck at the extravagance of political parties".

After World War II America was swept by a wave of militant anti-communism, and to stem wild fears of communist infiltration "regional loyalty boards" were set up in 1947 to check the political sympathies of federal employees. Appeals could be directed to a "Loyalty Review Board". In the same year the "Taft-Hartley Act" was passed, prohibiting strikes by federal employees and similar legislation was introduced by some states to cover their administrations.

The American Civil Service Commission has a staff of some 3,000 only, and its function is to control recruitment, to formulate legislation, to investigate the loyalty of employees and to hear appeals and reviews. The service itself is divided up into a vast number of committees, boards, and commissions whose spheres of authority often overlap, so that there is keen rivalry between them. Some 65 of these amorphous bodies may be considered to be ministries, and characteristic of the American system is the Bureau, a small body of civil servants and politicians existing almost autonomously within a ministry.

The American civil service bureaucracy, with its 2.8 millionen civil servants and civil service employees, is often called "the fourth power of government", which may be true especially of such large departments as those of Health, Education, and Welfare and of Housing and Urban Development. President Jimmy Carter is planning a radical reform of the American civil service in order to end over-bureaucratization, which, to a considerable extent, has resulted from the "merit system" based on job security. If his plans are realized, the most important innovation will be the creation of a Senior Executive Service below Cabinet level, consisting of about 9,000 top managers who will replace the present three top classes of the civil service. Below the Senior Executive Service there will be a second category of about 70,000 higher civil servants. Both groups will enjoy no or only limited job security and their payment will depend on their efficiency. This reform will, to some extent, revive the old spoils system, though the Civil Service Commission, an *Independent Agency**, should be able to control abuses.
In contrast to the British system, which examines a candidate on what he happens to know, civil service examinations in America are strictly practical. Attempts have been made to introduce academic qualifications as a pre-condition for entering the civil service examinations, but such a step has always been rejected as undemocratic. A further feature of the examination system is the favouring of war veterans. H H G R C

Club

An association of persons meeting periodically (under certain regulations), 1670; an association of persons formed mainly for social purposes, and having buildings for exclusive use of their members, and always open to them as a place of resort, or, in some cases, of temporary residence, 1776; the buildings occupied by such a society. 1837.

- London clubs are among the most distinctively English of English institutions. The true precursors of the London club appear to have been the gatherings held regularly in coffee-houses and taverns of the 17th and 18th centuries. It was in the second half of the 17th century that the term "club" in its present meaning gained currency. In 1660 Samuel Pepys, for instance, made a note in his diary that he went "for clubbing" to Wood's tavern. During the 19th century clubs began to move into permanent headquarters of their own and tended to become more specialized in interests and aims.

Most of the older English clubs are thronged in more or less imposing Georgian edifices around the St. James and Pall Mall area in the heart of London. Some of the oldest and more famous London clubs are: White's (a

Tory stronghold), founded in 1693; Boodles (originally known as the "Savoir Vivre", now with a Ladies' Annexe), 1763; Brooks's (formerly a leading Whig stronghold, now politically neutral), 1764; the Portland (cards), 1816; the Travellers (diplomats, the lunch-room being known as "the Foreign Office Canteen"), 1819; the Athenaeum (literary and artistic, the most august of the big clubs), 1823; the Garrick (actors, lawyers, editors, businessmen), 1831; the Carlton (meeting place of Conservative politicians), 1831; the Reform (haunt of the Treasury), 1834; the Savage (artists and actors), 1857; the Savile (publishers, authors, actors, and broadcasters), 1868; the Press, 1882.

Clubs are usually men's associations which admit women merely as guests. There are, however, a few clubs such as the Pilot (1949) and the Lansdowne (1935) which count men and women among their members. Recently the Press Club admitted Queen Elizabeth, the Queen Mother, as the first woman member. There are also a few exclusively ladies' clubs such as the Alexandria founded in 1883, the University Women's Club founded in 1887, and the Pioneer founded in 1892.

The most popular types of club are the Working Men's Clubs and Institutes and the Townswomen's Guilds. The former (approximately 4,000 with about 3.6 million members, mostly men) are affiliated to the Working Men's Club and Institute's Union. The latter (over 2,800 with about 250,000 members) are affiliated to the National Union of Townswomen's Guilds. These clubs are social, recreational and educational in nature.

In connection with club life mention should also be made of the Women's Institutes (England and Wales) and the Women's Rural Institutes (Scotland and Northern Ireland). They number approximately 10,000, and their objectives are mainly educational. R L S

■ The members of the American upper classes, who are mainly of Anglo-Saxon stock and of Protestant denomination *(Establishment*)*, inherited from their English forefathers a special disposition for social intercourse and a distinct capacity for creating voluntary organizations formed for various purposes such as entertainment, sport, and general social activities. This associational tradition attracted the attention of Alexis de Tocqueville in the first half of the 19th century when he pointed out in his book "De la Démocratie en Amérique" (1838) that "Wherever at the head of some new undertaking you see the government in France, or a man of rank in England, in the United States you will be sure to find an association".

Among these voluntary social organizations are the distinguished American country clubs, a characteristic institution, established for the purpose of open-air recreation and outdoor sporting activities. They came into existence with the foundation of the Country Club at Brookline, Mass., in 1882. The country club movement flourished when the suburban trend of the American middle and upper classes was on the upsurge during the twenties. Admission to upper class clubs is dependent upon various qualifications:

(1) The upper class clubs such as the Somerset club of Boston, Mass., the Pacific Union club of San Francisco, Calif., the Brook of New York and the Duquesne of Pittsburgh, Pa. - to mention only a few - are highly selective and admit only gentlemen of high social and financial standing.

(2) All renowned clubs maintain certain racial barriers. When the ethnic heterogeneity of the American population increased with the immigration

waves from Eastern Europe and the Far East *(Immigration*)* the exclusive clubs greatly served to protect the racial and cultural integrity of the American Establishment.

(3) Nowadays some clubs such as the Springfield Country Club, Springfield, Mass., also admit Roman Catholics, but they still constitute a minority. The majority of the leading clubs have a Protestant membership. There are, however, clubs of all large denominations. As far as Jews are concerned, the Metropolitan Club of New York is an exception, for it has a number of distinguished Jews - mostly of German origin like the Lehmanns, Warburgs, Lippmanns, etc. *(Jew*)* - among its members.

(4) Wives and daughters of clubmen, it is true, are welcome guests at the clubs' parties - the debutante balls, for instance, play an important part in club life - but ladies are not members of gentlemen's clubs. There are, however, a considerable number of ladies' clubs which are a typical feature of American club life. The New England Women's Club of Boston and the Sororis of New York, for instance, were both founded in 1868 and women's clubs of all kinds are spreading rapidly over the country. In 1889 the General Federation of Women's Clubs was established.

Other important metropolitan clubs are: the Union League, the Century Association, the Brook, the Scarsdale Golf Club, the Links and many others.

The Union League was founded in 1862 in order to support the idea of the Union and to counter and rebuke all disloyalty to the Federal Government. The idea of the Union League soon spread over the whole nation with branches in New York, Boston, Washington, San Francisco and many smaller towns.

The Century Association was founded in 1847 by a group of artists and authors for the purpose of promoting their cultural and professional interests. There are also Jews among the members of this club. The Brook is sometimes considered to be one of the most aristocratic clubs and it counted the late President John F. Kennedy among its members (it was the only club to which J. F. Kennedy belonged). The Links, one of the youngest clubs, was founded only in 1921 in order "to promote and conserve throughout the United States the best interest and true spirit of the game of golf".

In addition to clubs in which the emphasis is on the social element there are a number of clublike organizations founded for various purposes such as the promotion of professional (e.g. university clubs), commercial philanthropic or religious activities. They are open to all individuals sharing a mutual interest. Like the Union League there are also clubs predominantly political in character which are affiliated to the political parties.

Just as in Britain, children's and youth clubs are flourishing in the U.S., for instance the Boy Scouts and Girl Scouts (in Britain called Girl Guides) as well as the Y.M.C.A. and the Y.W.C.A.

Finally the American Service Clubs are to be noted. Originally used to denote the Service clubs of the Army, Navy, and Air Force the term came also to designate the international Service Clubs - such as the Rotary, the Exchange, the Lions and the Soroptimist Club, the latter being an international ladies' club - which were founded in the United States in order to promote worthwhile programmes of community welfare and mutual understanding between the members of the various nations.

I Fr

Cockney

- Probably from Middle English "cokeney" literally "cock's egg" (c. 1362), later a child overlong nursed by its mother, an effeminate person, a townsman, a Londoner. 1600.

The noun Cockney denotes (a) a Londoner from the lower classes; (b) dialects spoken mainly by the lower classes in the London area. By the early 17th century the name Cockney was already being applied specifically to Londoners born within the sound of the bells of St. Mary-le-Bow Church in Cheapside.

Most vowel sounds of Cockney deviate noticeably from their RP *(Received Pronunciation*)* equivalents. Thus the RP diphthong [ei] is replaced in Cockney by a much wider variant, the word "make", for instance, often being pronounced [mæik] by Cockneys. The diphthong spelt ou, ow is often monophthongized to give the typical cockney pronunciation [taːn] for RP [taun] [town]. A frequent consonantal variation from RP is the substitution of [v] and [f] for the th-sounds [ð] and [θ], as in (wiv) (with) and [fiŋ] (thing).

Cockney dialect is marked off no less by vocabulary and idiom than by its sound features. It has been aptly described as "an almost inextricable tangle of slang and idiom, often of a raciness and expressiveness that put Standard English into the shade" (Eric Partridge, "Slang To-day and Yesterday", London 1950). Rhyming slang, back slang, and centre slang are hall-marks of Cockney. In rhyming slang a word of standard speech is usually replaced by two or three words the last of which rhymes with the word substituted. Thus "corner" becomes "Johnny Horner", "heart" is "raspberry tart", "shirt" is "Dicky Dirt", "bed" gives "Uncle Ned", "to half-inch" means "to pinch", i.e. "to steal", and a Cockney's wife is his "trouble and strife". Asked to take his "plates of meat" off the "Cain and Abel", a compliant Cockney will respond by removing his feet from the table. Very frequently the rhyming word is suppressed so that "hat", originally "tit for tat", becomes "titfer", while "daisy roots" for "boots" gives "daisies". A word is rendered in back slang by spelling it in reverse and, if necessary, rearranging or adding sounds for the sake of pronounceability and euphony. Thus "tekram" is "market", "mur" is "rum", "money" becomes "yenom", and "Cool ta the elrig" is "Kacab Genals" for "Look at the girl". In centre or medial slang a vowel and following consonant within a word become the first syllable of the new word, the remainder of the word being formed rather arbitrarily, often with the addition of one or two syllables, e.g. -er, -es, -erfer. Examples are "eetswe" for "sweet", "oolerfer" for "fool", "operpro" for "proper".

Cockney is both a regional and a class dialect. It is spoken by Londoners from the humbler walks of life and is generally regarded as a mark of inferior education and low social status. The Cockney who aspires to rise in the social hierarchy of England will usually try to adapt his speech to the norms of Received Pronunciation (RP). R L S

Committee

In modern usage a body of persons appointed or elected for some special business or function. 1621. Originally, each person in it was called a committee in the sense of a person to whom some charge, trust, or function is committed. 1495.

Parliamentary committees constitute an important factor in the political life of a democratic country. They are concerned with particular aspects of laws and legislation and are frequently entrusted with the task of investigation. With the exception of the so-called Committees of the Whole House they are in fact miniature parliaments. They are a peculiarly Anglo-American institution which has been adopted by many other countries. Parliamentary committees probably existed as early as 1340, but were firmly established during the reign of Queen Elizabeth I (1558-1603).

The legislatures of Britain and of the United States have established four types of committee: (1) standing committees (they are permanent institutions of the legislature), (2) select committees (they are established for a limited period), (3) committees of the whole house (they have a membership which is identical with that of the house), (4) joint committees (they combine committee members of both houses). But although the same names are applied in both countries, there is a sharp contrast regarding the function and importance of committees in Britain and in the United States. Practically the only thing they have in common is that they are indispensable stages in the process of lawmaking *(Bill*)*.

The most important contrasts between the British and the American practice are: (1) English committees are not specialized except for a few; (e.g. the committees on Accounts and Expenditure), but they are specialized with regard to function and expert knowledge of the members. American committees are specialized, with the exception of the committees of the whole house (see below). This specialization is carried even further in the numerous subcommittees to which the committees entrust part of their work. (2) English committees are generally not allowed to prepare legislation (such work is usually done by Royal Commissions, who submit their findings to Parliament in the form of reports). American committees, however, play an eminent role in the preparation of laws. Committees of the House of Representatives can even originate bills (a practice quite unthinkable in Britain), e.g. if a member presents a petition and refers it to the appropriate committee the latter has authority to draw a bill. The same thing is true when communications addressed to the House from the President or from executive departments are referred to the appropriate committees.

● Standing Committees: Such committees are appointed in every session by either house; but there rarely exist more than five simultaneously. They receive all public bills which have not been sent to a committee of the whole house, a select committee, or a joint committee; standing committees like the two Scottish Standing Committees and the Scottish Grand Committee (comprising all Scottish members and 10 to 15 others), the Welsh Grand Committee (comprising all Welsh members and up to five others), and the Northern Ireland Committee receive such bills as are concerned with these regions. The composition of the English (like the American) standing committee must approximate to that of the whole house. Apart from the above-mentioned ones, English standing committees do not even bear names but merely capital letters (A, B, etc.).

Select Committees: British (like American) select committees are concerned with one particular subject. They are investigating committees and are expected to report their opinion to the house. The Chief *Whips** of the parties have the last word in the selection of the members. Like the American committee (of any kind) the British select committee is usually given the power to summon witnesses and to collect evidence. But the analogy cannot be pushed too far. American Committees can command the presence and the sworn answers of the Executive Branch of Government, including the heads of departments. In this respect they are the equivalent of "question time" in the *Commons** and of the ministerial presence in debates. British select committees include the committees on Expenditure, Public Accounts, Standing Orders, Privileges, Nationalized Industries, European Community Secondary Legislation, the Parliamentary Commissioner for Administration *(Parliament*)*, etc.

Committees of the Whole House: Sometimes the House of Commons is temporarily turned into a committee. This is done to make debates more informal and to enable important members to speak more than once. The Speaker leaves the Chair, the Mace is put under the Table, and the Chairman of Committees takes over. Important Committees of the Whole House were the committees of Ways and Means and of Supply, both abolished in 1967.

Joint Committees: The proposal to commit a matter to a joint committee can come from either house. They are usually composed of an equal number of members of each house. Joint committee reports are presented to both houses simultaneously.

In 1978, a study group set up by the National Executive Committee of the Labour Party approved a plan designed to shift power to remodelled select committees, which would shadow individual departments of state. The proposal is part of a plan for reform of the House of Commons.

■ Standing Committees: In 1946 the Legislative Reorganization Act took effect. Its chief problem was the reorganization of the committee structure. It drastically reduced the number of committees in the Senate from 33 to 15, in the House from 48 to 19. But it also meant to do away with the numerous select committees (a purpose which it did not achieve). The standing committees as they are listed in the Act, have become institutions; only their members must be newly appointed every year, and they are recommended by the political parties and then adopted by the two houses of *Congress**. The Legislative Reorganization Act also made the jurisdiction of the standing committees in a large measure correspond to the existing departments and agencies of the executive. New standing committees have been needed since 1946; and there are some committees which have no equivalent in the executive, because they are "watch-dog" committees (i.e. they are just there to keep a watchful eye on a particular problem). These are the American standing committees (1976):

Senate	*House*
Agriculture, Nutrition and Forestry	Agriculture
Appropriations	Appropriations
Armed Services	Armed Services
Banking, Housing and Urban Affairs	Banking, Finance and Urban Affairs
Budget	Budget
Commerce, Science and Transportation	District of Columbia
Energy and Natural Resources	Education and Labor
Environment and Public Works	Government Operations
Finance	House Administration
Foreign Relations	Interior and Insular Affairs
Governmental Affairs	International Relations
Human Resources	Interstate and Foreign Commerce
Judiciary	Judiciary

Rules and Administration
Veterans' Affairs

Merchant Marine and Fisheries
Post Office and Civil Service
Public Work and Transportation
Rules
Science and Technology
Small Business
Standards of Official Conduct
Veterans' Affairs
Ways and Means

Standing committees were introduced in the U.S.A. as early as 1803; up to then bills were discussed in "committee of the whole" and then referred to a select committee. They were established to avoid prolonged debate before the whole house.

Four standing committees have the task of considering the budget which is submitted to Congress by the President for each fiscal year: the Appropriations and the Finance Committee of the Senate, and the Appropriations and the Ways and Means Committee of the House. They meet in a joint conference.

Select Committees: They have functions similar to those of British select committees, but they are more numerous (between 10 and 15). Like those in Britain they are established by each house for a temporary and special purpose (for example, Nutrition and Human Needs, Indian Affairs). They expire as soon as their special function has been carried out.

Committees of the Whole House: Membership and purpose are the same as in the British Parliament. In the House of Representatives the Speaker gives way to a chairman, and the Mace is moved to a lower pedestal. Speeches are limited to five minutes here, but the "previous question", which is a device to cut off all debate and enforce a division (if supported by the majority of members), cannot be put. (In the House of Commons there is a similar device for the members to enforce a division in the form of the "Closure", i.e. any member may move "that the question be now put", *Filibustering*)*. Technically, there are two such committees: the Committee of the Whole House which considers business on the Private Calendar (listing private bills) and the Committee of the Whole House on the State of the Union which considers business on the Union Calendar (listing all public bills raising revenue or involving a charge against the government; this is not to be confounded with the House Calendar listing all public bills which have nothing to do with money or property, and the Consent Calendar containing bills reported out unanimously). The Senate in 1930 discontinued the practice of the committee of the whole except in considering treaties with foreign countries. In connection with Calendars of the House the most powerful committee of Congress deserves special mention - the House Rules Committee.

All important bills, on having passed their own committees, are sent to the Rules Committee for a "rule" which determines the date and the nature of the following debate. In other words, this committee can speed or delay consideration of a bill before the whole house; it has a sifting and amending function. Only a petition of the whole house can force the Rules Committee to allow a bill out. In the Senate the Steering Committee of the Majority Party plays a similar procedural role.

Joint Committees: American joint committees are established by statute or by resolution of the two houses of Congress. One of the most notable joint committees was the Committee on Organization working on the Legislative

Reorganization Act. An American speciality are the joint standing committees; there are seven: on Atomic Energy, Defense Production, Congressional Operations, Taxation, the Library, the Joint Economic Committee, Printing.

The conference committee is a peculiar, but very important form of joint committee: as in the United States (in contradistinction to Britain) both houses possess fairly equal power, deadlocks are possible and have repeatedly occurred. To decrease the frequency of such difficulties the Speaker (for the House) and the Vice-President (for the Senate) may appoint a joint conference committee made up of 10 to 14 members called "managers". If they do not reach complete accord, the bill fails.

Since 1973, committees have been required to admit the public and the press to their sessions, unless a majority (in open session) has voted to keep it closed.

In 1977, the Senate approved (89-1) a resolution to reorganize the Senate by cutting committees (standing, select, and joint committees) to 25 from 31 and by restricting senatorial committee assignments. The resolution embodies the most sweeping overhaul of the Senate committee system since the Legislative Reorganization Act of 1946. H H

Commons

● The lower order as distinct from those of noble or knightly or gentle rank; the Commons: the members of Parliament constituting one of the two bodies composing the legislature of the United Kingdom. 1546.

The House of Commons (also called the Lower House or simply the Commons) is the legislative chamber which represents the whole population entitled to vote *(Suffrage*)*. Today, therefore, the supremacy of the legislature, though formally in the hands of both chambers, rests more or less exclusively with the House of Commons as representative of the whole nation.

The number of members of the House of Commons, now 635, is identical with the number of constituencies *(Constituency*)*. Members are elected directly and by means of a relative majority. According to the Representation of the People Act (1949) and the House of Commons Disqualification Act (1975) any British subject of 21 years of age may be elected with the exception of peers (but not Irish peers, see *Home Rule*)* clergy of the *Established Churches**, Roman Catholic priests, undischarged bankrupts, lunatics, holders of certain high judicial offices, members of the regular armed forces or the police, high civil servants *(Civil Service*)* (the latter two until they retire from office) and others.

The commons are elected for a period of five years as laid down in the Parliament Act of 1911. The Prime Minister, however, can at any time advise the sovereign to dissolve Parliament before the end of this period, which is the rule rather than the exception. This may be expedient if the majority of the Government is so slim that it must be in constant fear of being defeated in a division. The former tradition, however, that the resignation of a Prime Minister automatically entails the dissolution of *Parliament** has repeatedly been broken (Churchill/Eden, 1955; Eden/Macmillan, 1957; Macmillan/Douglas-Home, 1963; Wilson/Callaghan, 1976).

If the numerical proportion of parliamentary representation determined by the outcome of general (national) elections changes between two elections because members die, receive peerages, or resign their seats (by applying for and being granted the office of Steward or Bailiff or Her Majesty's Chiltern

Hundreds or of the Manor of Northstead, which, because they are technically offices of profit under the Crown, bar their holders from membership of the Commons), the Prime Minister may order a by-election to be held. By-elections are considered to be instructive opinion polls on the popularity of the government.

Parliament is opened, prorogued, and if necessary dissolved by the monarch. The opening of Parliament and its adjournment take place in the House of Lords. On both occasions the Commoners are invited to come to the Lords by the Queen's messenger, called "Black Rod" (so called after his symbol of office) who belongs to the Lord Chamberlain's department of the Royal Household.

The "Speech from the Throne", delivered by the monarch at the opening of Parliament, is a highly political one and therefore does not (and must not) reflect the views of the Crown. It is composed by the *Cabinet** and contains the programme of the Government.

A Parliament, roughly speaking, is the period between two elections, which may consist of several sessions lasting from autumn to summer. Each session consists of a varying number of sittings. At the end of the session Parliament is prorogued by the monarch. Prorogation entails that a bill not completed in one session must be reintroduced in the next.

A typical sitting of the Commons begins with the *Speaker's** Procession and three short prayers read by the Chaplain of the House. After several minutes devoted to technicalities, "question time" follows on the first four days of the week, which owing to the close contact between M.P.s and their constituents is an effective instrument of direct democracy. Thus, a member putting a question to the Government is not infrequently the direct spokesman of the people. After "question time" the "order paper" determines the course of events. In addition there are "standing orders" by which parliamentary business is regulated. From time to time the Opposition "asks for a day", viz. a day to bring in a resolution, usually amounting to a vote of censure criticizing the Government; it is invariably granted. At the end of a sitting the House is adjourned by the Speaker.

There are many rules governing debates and they are much the same in either house (the most conspicuous differences: the Lords do not address their Speaker, i.e. the Lord Chancellor, but the House; and they record their votes by saying "content" or "not content"). In both houses members rise if they want to speak, but they speak from their places. In the Commons, they have to "catch the Speaker's eye" although it has become customary for the Speaker to fix the order of speakers beforehand in accordance with lists handed in by the *Whips**. The Speaker (unlike the Lord Chancellor in the House of Lords) has sufficient power to prevent obstruction and prolonged speaking *(Filibustering*)*. Members speak of other members in the third person because they address the Speaker, but do not call them by their names but by their constituencies (e.g. "the Honourable Member for Roxborough", etc.). Scholars and members holding a military rank are referred to as "the Learned Member" or "the Gallant Member" respectively; Cabinet Ministers and members of the Privy Council are referred to as "the Right Honourable Member" or by their official titles; Irish Lords are styled "the Noble Lord". In spite of these strict rules of order, disorderly incidents occur not infrequently, ranging from rude remarks or the mere throwing of coins or books to physical attacks on Cabinet Ministers.

No member may speak twice on the same issue, though in *Committee** he may. At the end of the debate, the Speaker, of his own accord, may state that he is of opinion that "the ayes (or noes) have it". If any member is not satisfied with this decision, a division takes place; members who wish to vote in favour of the decision leave the House through a door right of the Speaker, those who want to vote against it go out through a door on the Speaker's left; they do not cast ballots but are counted by two M.P.s called "tellers".

A member may unofficially stay away from a sitting if he can find a member of the opposing party who also stays away. This kind of agreement is called "pairing". It reduces the number of members present, but ensures that the proportion of votes in a division remains the same. The quorum (i. e. a sufficient number to form a resolution) in the House of Commons is 40 members. If the quorum is not achieved the Speaker leaves the Chair.

Members of the House of Commons are seated in four tiers rising on either side of the House. Thus the parliamentary parties of the Government and the Opposition face each other instead of being seated in a semi-circle. The leading members occupy the front benches next to the Speaker's chair on either side of the Table of the House. The red lines on the floor along the front benches on either side are said to have been drawn to keep hotheads apart over a length of two swords (a member who chances to trespass over the line while speaking still receives an order call). The less prominent members, or "back-benchers", fill the back benches, i.e. those remotest from the Speaker's chair. The Government is seated on the so-called "Treasury Bench" on the Speaker's right, the Prime Minister and the Leader of the Opposition sitting next to the Mace. Seating "within" the House is available for only 347 members, the others (i.e. those who come latest) have to stand or accommodate themselves on the Members' Side Galleries. The Bar near the south entrance (today a line on the floor) marks the inside and the out. Thus, technically inside the House are: the *Speaker** and his deputies, the other members, either seated or standing, in the lower section of the room, the clerks seated before the Speaker's chair (they are high civil servants appointed by the Crown, who assist the Speaker in procedural matters). Technically outside the House are the civil servants in attendance, the Serjeant-at-Arms (another high official who attends the Speaker with the Mace and is responsible for the maintenance of order), the Members' Side Galleries (it is unusual for M.P.s seated there to take part in the debate), the Hansard and Press Gallery (from 1803 to 1888, the printer Luke Hansard and his sons printed the reports of proceedings of Parliament, briefly called "Hansard"; today this is done by Her Majesty's Stationery Office, but the name has lasted), the Special Galleries for Peers, distinguished visitors, diplomats, etc., and the Public Gallery.

It is still to be noted that one of the ancient and sacred traditions both of the Commons and of the Lords is "parliamentary privilege". It includes the freedom from arrest in civil suits for Peers permanently and for M.P.s during sessions of Parliament and for forty days before or after a session (it is still debatable whether a member from either House is privileged from arrest for summary offences, and, if so, whether the police can arrest him or her outside the House). It further includes freedom of speech in all debates, and access by the Speaker (and each of the Lords individually) to the sovereign. By the Common Law, Parliament has the right to punish any breach of privilege after investigation by the Committee of Privileges, by which it exerts a certain measure of censorhip over the press. Journalists have repeatedly been forced to apologize at the Bar of the House for contempt and, in the 19th century, were even sent to prison for disclosing parliamentary secrets. In 1975, the Committee of Privileges recommended that two free-lance writers for the "Economist" be banned from the precincts of Parliament for disclosing details of a draft report of a parliamentary Committee, an unprecedented measure of censure. Since 1967, the public can lodge complaints arising in connection with actions taken by or on behalf of Government departments to a parliamentary "ombudsman", officially called Parliamentary Commissioner for Administration. He is required to report the results of investigation to the respective member of the House of Commons. He is also required to report to Parliament on the performance of his functions and he may make special reports to Parliament. Every year he completes about 300 investigations. In 1969, the institution was expanded to include Northern Ireland, in 1973 the Health Service, and in 1974 local government. 1

The place of meeting has always been Westminster (named after "the minster west of London", i.e. Westminster Abbey). In 1834 the old Palace of Westminster, dating back to at least 1052 (Edward the Confessor), burnt down. In 1852, the Commons moved into their present lodgings, the north wing of the new Palace of Westminster. In 1941 the House of Commons was destroyed in an air raid, but, upon the initiative of Sir Winston Churchill, rebuilt almost in its old form in 1943. H H

Commonwealth

Community of independent states consisting of Britain and a number of her former colonies; the phrase "British Commonwealth of Nations" was used in the treaty by which Ireland became a Dominion in 1921; since about 1950 "British" has tended to be omitted, leaving "Commonwealth" or "Commonwealth of Nations". Sometimes the term is used more loosely to include the non-self-governing territories, which technically still constitute the British *Empire**. The Republican government in England in the 17th century.

● The Commonwealth of Nations is the free association of states which, before they became independent, had a colonial or protectorate status within the British *Empire**. The association is based on a status of equality. All members are completely independent. As soon as a former colony, protectorate, or trust territory *(Empire*)* becomes independent, it can decide for itself whether it wants to be a member of the Commonwealth or not (e.g. Burma became independent in 1948 but did not stay within the Commonwealth); but admission also requires the approval of all members. Any member can, at any time, leave the Commonwealth as did Pakistan in 1972, over the recognition of Bangladesh by Britain and other Commonwealth countries. The Commonwealth Conference (formerly called Colonial Conference, then Imperial Conference), an assembly of the Commonwealth prime ministers meeting in London or, since 1966, in other Commonwealth capitals at intervals (as a rule every year), can also expel a member by unanimous vote. (South Africa only escaped expulsion by quitting voluntarily in 1961.)

The title "Head of the Commonwealth" replaced "Emperor of India" in the royal title after India changed her constitution in 1950. It does not mean "head of state" and has therefore no bearing on whether any of the members of the Commonwealth has a republican or monarchical constitution.

In our days, the Commonwealth has faced numerous crises: two members waged war against each other (India and Pakistan, 1965, 1971), two members broke off diplomatic relations with Britain (Tanzania and, temporarily, Ghana, 1965, over the Rhodesian question); two others (Malaysia and Pakistan, 1965) broke off diplomatic relations with each other; these two member states broke apart (Malaysia, when Singapore declared its independence in 1965, and Pakistan in 1972); in 1976 Britain severed diplomatic relations with Uganda; in 1968 Zambia and Tanzania gave diplomatic recognition to Nigeria's rebellious Eastern Region "Biafra"; the monetary union within the East African Common Services Organization was repealed in 1965; and the threat that Canada may disintegrate into a French and an English part is still there. Naturally, many people have come to ask what the Commonwealth is, not ideally but in reality.

It is not a federation of states and can never be an alliance, because many of its members are "non-aligned" or pretend to be. There is no common foreign policy. The Crown has ceased to be the link with Britain *(Dominion*)*. The often-repeated "racial equality" should be regarded with caution, as there is much racial discrimination; Britain is no longer ready to accept an unlimited influx of coloured people from the Commonwealth *(Immigration*)*, the African nations resent the presence of their former colonial masters, and where Negroes and Indians have to live together in the Commonwealth the situation is often nearer to war than peace. The idea that British political institutions, especially the "Mother of Parliaments" and the rule of law, have brought lasting benefit to the Commonwealth can only be applied to a few of the 34 member states, and all African and, except India and Malaysia, all Asian members have given up the political system they inherited from Britain in favour of either autocratic one-party systems or military dictatorship. What remains are mutual economic interests: the system of preferential tariffs *(Preferences*)*, the London capital market, and the British aid for the developing countries. For the latter purpose the Commonwealth Development Corporation was set up in 1948 by Act of Parliament. Its finance comes from the British Government not as a grant, but as a loan below market terms. Today it is one of the most experienced development agencies. In the case of Canada, Australia, and New Zealand considerations of kinship are probably more important than economic considerations, as Canada looks to the U.S.A. rather than to Britain, and for Australia and New Zealand, the U.S.A. and Japan are important trading partners now *(Preferences*)*. However, Britain's entry into the Common Market is likely to loosen the bonds even between the "White Commonwealth" and the mother country: Australia promptly reacted by declaring (October 25th, 1972) that she regarded Britain as a foreign country.

An impartial observer may regard the Commonwealth as nothing more than a group of states guided by their own interests. But one may also justly assume that for the dissolution of the Empire there could have been no better and more responsible instrument than that of its gradual conversion into the Commonwealth. And, of course, it is also difficult to tell how many conflicts there would have been, had there not always existed the safety-valve of the Commonwealth Conferences. In 1965, the Commonwealth Secretariat (located in London) was established. Up to the present day many Commonwealth countries have retained the right of appeal up to the Judicial Committee of the Privy Council in London as a final appellate instance: Barbados, Fiji, Jamaica, Mauritius, Australia, New Zealand, Trinidad and Tobago, Malaysia, Singapore, the Gambia, Botswana, Guyana (furthermore, a number of territories with less than total independence like Brunei, the West

Indies Associated States, the Channel Islands, the Isle of Man, Gibraltar, and Hong Kong). Britain's entry into the European Common Market raised great problems for the Commonwealth. Canada's, Australia's, and even New Zealand's anxieties were alleviated, but many among the developing nations of the Commonwealth feared that, in particular, Britain's withdrawal from the Commonwealth system of preferential tariffs might cause them severe economic disadvantages. In 1975, the trade provisions of the Convention of Lomé (capital of Togo) came into effect. They replaced the special trading relations between Britain and the Commonwealth and Empire under the Ottawa Agreement of 1932 *(Preferences*)*, giving 23 developing Commonwealth countries in Africa, the Caribbean, and the Pacific (these ACP-countries are marked with an asterisk in the following list) together with 24 non-Commonwealth ACP-countries the status of Associated members of the *Common Market**. Special commercial co-operative agreements between the Community and India, Sri Lanka, and Pakistan were signed in 1974, 1975 and 1976 respectively.

Member States (May, 1978):
United Kingdom (England, Scotland, Wales, Northern Ireland).
Canada: Dominion 1867 (including New Foundland: Dominion 1855-1933; under British rule till 1949; since then Canada's tenth province).
Commonwealth of Australia: Dominion 1901.
New Zealand: Dominion 1907.
India: Dominion 1947, republic 1950.
Sri Lanka (formerly Ceylon): Dominion 1948, republic 1972; The Democratic Socialist Republic of . . ., 1978.
Ghana: Dominion 1957, republic 1960.
*Nigeria: Dominion 1960, republic 1963.
Cyprus: republic 1961 (independent 1960).
*Sierra Leone: Dominion 1961, republic 1971.
*Tanzania: Union of Tanganyika and Zanzibar, republic 1964 (Tanganyika: Dominion 1961, republic 1962; Zanzibar: Dominion 1963).
*Jamaica: Dominion 1962.
*Trinidad and Tobago: Dominion 1962.
*Uganda: Dominion 1962, republic 1966.
Federation of Malaysia: Dominion (Federation of Malaya) 1957, constitutional monarchy 1963 (including Sabah, Sarawak, and until 1965, Singapore).
Singapore: Republic 1965 (left the Federation of Malaysia in 1965 and became an independent member of the Commonwealth).
*Kenya: Dominion 1963, republic 1964.
Malta: Dominion 1964, republic 1974.
*Malawi (formerly Nyasaland): Dominion 1964, republic 1966.
*Zambia (formerly Northern Rhodesia): republic 1964.
*The Gambia: Dominion 1965, republic 1970.
*Botswana (formerly Bechuanaland): republic 1966.
*Guyana: Dominion 1966, republic 1970.
*Lesotho (formerly Basutoland): Dominion 1966.
*Barbados: Dominion 1966.
*Swaziland (Ngwane): Dominion 1968.
*Mauritius: Dominion 1968.

Nauru: republic 1968 (upon the request of its government a "limited form of membership in the Commonwealth" was devised).
*Fiji Islands: Dominion 1970.
*Tonga: Dominion 1970.
*Western Samoa: Dominion 1970 (it had been treated as a Commonwealth country pending its decision whether it wanted to become a member; in 1970 it was formally admitted).
Bangladesh (formerly East Pakistan): republic 1972.
*Bahamas: Dominion 1973.
*Grenada: Dominion 1974.
*Papua New Guinea; Dominion 1975
Seychelles: republic 1976.

Countries which have left the Commonwealth:
Irish Free State (now Republic of Eire), 1949.
Egypt, 1958.
Republic of South Africa, 1961.
Pakistan, 1972.

Countries which, after independence, did not join the Commonwealth:
Burma, 1948; Palestine, 1948; Sudan, 1956, British Somaliland, 1960 (joined the Somali Republic); Southern Cameroons, 1961 (joined the Cameroon Republic); Maldive Islands, 1963; Aden (later called Yemen P.D.R.), 1967; Bahrain, 1971.

Within the Commonwealth there are several inter-territorial associations, whose members have common economic and, at times, political aims. (1) The Association of South East Asian Nations (A.S.E.A.N.) founded in 1967. Malaysia and Singapore are members (besides Thailand, Indonesia, and the Philippines). They plan to establish a common free trade area. (2) The East African Community, consisting of the Common Market, the East African corporations (air, rail, harbours and posts and telecommunications, various small common service organizations and the community bureaucracy). It was formally set up by the East African Treaty of 1967. About the time of the achievement of independence the three present member states Kenya, Uganda, and Tanzania hoped to form an economic and political union, but as a result of differences between the three states it collapsed in 1977.

Southern Rhodesia's future is still uncertain. Since 1895 it had been a British colony, but in 1965 it declared its independence, which amounted to rebellion against the mother country. In 1970 it became a republic. The British government was willing to grant independence only on condition of general elections in which the coloured population enjoys the same rights as the whites. From the viewpoint of the British Government, however, its constitutional status has remained unchanged since the days before her unilateral declaration of independence, in spite of the internal settlement pact of March, 1978, between Ian Smith, the white Rhodesian prime minister, and three black nationalist leaders, intended to bring about black majority rule to Rhodesia by December 31, 1978.

The term "Commonwealth" is also applied to the 17th century republic during which the "Lord Protector" Oliver Cromwell and his republican successors exercised the power of government.

■ The term "commonwealth" is officially applied to four American states: Kentucky, Virginia, Pennsylvania, and Massachusetts, since 1950 (Act of

Congress) also to the island of Puerto Rico (constitution adopted by Puerto Ricans in 1952).
H H

Congress

The national legislative body of the United States of America, as a permanent institution, and as a body elected for two years; also the session of this body: 1775.

■ The Congress of the United States is the legislative branch of the national government: It consists of two houses, the Senate and the House of Representatives. Article I of the *Constitution** provides its existence and authority. The Senate is frequently referred to as the "Upper House", the House of Representatives as the "Lower House", obviously following the English example. In actual fact, however, (in contradistinction to the United Kingdom) the two branches of the national legislature have completely equal rights, but the social rank of a Senator is incomparably higher than that of a Representative (he ranks behind President and Vice-President and before the State Governor, the most populous States excepted) although Senators and Representatives receive the same salaries.

A Congress commences on January 3rd of each odd-numbered year and continues for two years (Amendment XX, ratified 1933).

Congress gives a perfect illustration of the principle of *Checks and Balances**. Senators are elected for a term of six years, one-third of the Senate being newly elected every two years; whereas members of the House of Representatives are elected for the term of two years only; consequently, a President (term of office four years) may during his administration be confronted with entirely new parliamentary constellations after the lapse of two years. (In this century Presidents Hoover, Truman, Eisenhower and Nixon had to work with majorities in opposition in one house or both houses of Congress.) In addition, party voting has become less important in Congress than it used to be before World War II.

Elections take place on every first Tuesday after the first Monday in November in the even-numbered years (except in Maine, where Congressmen, i.e. Senators and members of the House of Representatives, are elected in September, which has made Maine the barometer of national elections). Members of Congress are elected directly by the people of the individual States. (Before Amendment XVII had been ratified in 1913, Senators were elected by the State legislatures and not by the people.) The leader of the Senate is the Vice-President, his deputy, a President *pro tempore;* the leader of the House of Representatives is the *Speaker**. At the beginning of a new Congress (every two years) the parties elect a Floor Leader each. Both houses have equal power in that

(1) each house has power to start consideration of any proposed law (except laws for raising revenue, the introduction of which is a privilege of the House of Representatives);
(2) each house has power to vote for or against any proposed law which is sent to it for approval after being passed by the other house.

The two houses do not have equal power in that
(1) the Senate alone has the power, by refusing its consent, to block the President's choice of officials;

(2) the Senate must give its consent (by a favourable vote of two-thirds of the Senators present) to any treaty of the U.S. before such treaty can take effect;
(3) the Senate has the right to elect a Vice-President if no candidate has a majority of the electoral votes;
(4) the Senate (with the Chief Justice presiding) alone has the power to try an impeachment;
(5) the House of Representatives has the sole right to impeach (more than half the number of votes are required to start the process);
(6) the House of Representatives is given by the constitution the very important power of raising money: all revenue bills must be passed by the House before the Senate can act on them. The Senate, of course, can make amendments to a revenue bill. This privilege of the House of Representatives stems from the English constitutional principle that the control of the raising and spending of money should primarily rest with that branch of the legislature which is elected directly by the people (see above, Amendment XVII);
(7) the House of Representatives has the right to elect a President if no candidate has a majority of the electoral votes. This happened in 1824 when John Quincy Adams was elected by the House after he had received fewer electoral votes (84) than Andrew Jackson (99). The procedure follows the "unit rule", i.e. the vote of the majority of each State delegation is reported as the State's vote, on the basis of one vote for each State.

Among these enumerated rights the two-thirds requirement for Senate approval of treaties can be the most embarrassing source of conflict between Congress and President. The failure of the Senate to ratify the treaty providing for U.S. membership in the League of Nations in 1919 is a dramatic example of this conflict inherent in the American Constitution. A considerable number of treaties were never even negotiated for fear that the required majority could not be obtained. In some cases, especially after World War II, business with other nations was done in the form of "executive agreements" requiring only simple majorities in either chamber. The Senate confirmed the three treaties that constituted the Louisiana Purchase *(Chief Executive*)* only after the purchase had been effected by Jefferson (Disraeli's purchase of the Suez Canal shares on behalf of the British Government, without waiting for the sanction of Parliament in 1875 is an example on the British side circumventing the constitution); in 1844, the Senate defeated the treaty to annex Texas, but in the end it was annexed by simple majorities, which was an unconstitutional evasion of the treaty power; in 1869, it rejected a treaty negotiated by President Grant to annex the Dominican Republic. It took the excesses of Vietnam, Watergate and presidential foreign policy under President Nixon to make Congress conscious of its treaty-making and other constitutional powers and of the necessity to keep the White House more in check.

In contrast with Britain, the U.S.A. has a genuine bi-cameral system in that powers of the two chambers are fairly equal; although, in actual fact, the House of Representatives is the more important of the two. Its preponderance is accentuated not only by its special powers concerning revenue bills, but also by the fact that the majority of laws originate here. From its rostrum the President reads his State of the Union address and other special messages to the assembled Congress. Declarations of war are requested by the President before the house, and it is in the lower house that foreign statesmen are occasionally allowed to speak, this being, however, an exceptional honour.

The ways in which Congress differs from the House of Commons may be summed up as follows: (1) No member of Congress (except the Vice-President in his capacity of chairman of the Senate) may hold executive office, and there is no executive in Congress exerting pressure on members on pain of expulsion from the party. (2) The art of speech-making or repartee is not in high esteem in Congress, and entries can be made in the Congressional Record (the American "Hansard") which have never been spoken in debate, and the Record can be corrected. (3) There is no "party discipline", and members of the Congress cannot be disciplined for voting against their party; local, regional, minority etc. interests (for example oil, farming, busing problems) determine voting more than party membership does. (4) Congress does not necessarily work with the White House, but very often and quite irrespective of party allegiance works in opposition to it.

The present Congress as provided by the U.S. Constitution had two forerunners: the First and the Second Continental Congress. The First Continental Congress (1774) was a measure of colonial protest, resulting from many public calls (especially from Providence, Philadelphia, and New York City). It passed several resolutions which actually prepared the American revolt against England:

(1) It declared the coercive acts (Acts of Parliament meant as a punishment of Boston for the tea disorders, e.g. the so-called Boston Tea Party or Tea Plot, virtually depriving Massachusetts of its internal self-government) to be void *(Declaration of Independence*)*.
(2) It urged the people of Massachusetts to form a government, to collect taxes and withhold them from the Royal Government until the repeal of the coercive acts.
(3) It advised the people to arm and form militias.
(4) It recommended economic sanctions against Britain.

The Second Continental Congress (1775) resolved to put the colonies in a state of defence and adopted an address to the people of Canada asking them to join the twelve colonies (Georgia was not yet represented at the Congress officially) in their opposition against England. Canada did not follow this invitation. The Second Continental Congress, the members of which included Benjamin Franklin, John Hancock, James Wilson, and Thomas Jefferson, drew up the so-called Articles of Confederation *(Constitution*)*.

The 50 states of the U.S.A. have set up congresses and governments largely modelled on that provided in the federal constitution. Except for Nebraska, which has a unicameral legislature, all States have a bi-cameral system. The referendum is widely used in the U.S.A. This direct form of legislation is known in 43 States.

H H

Conservative Party

● One of the two major parties in Britain. It is the direct descendant of the Tory Party. But the Conservatives of 1830 were in fact a new party, because the political issues of the time were new. The name is believed to have been generally adopted about the time of the passing of the Reform Act in 1832.

Like the American parties, the British parties no longer have a clear-cut profile. Whereas Disraeli's Conservative party could be described as the

Empire party and as the one that was least disposed to welcome domestic reform, the Conservatives of today are as open-minded towards reform as the other parties. Still, there are principles which have never disappeared from the Conservative platform: private enterprise, capitalism, no further *nationalization** (but acceptance of the status quo). A Conservative government would also eliminate a number of Socialist policies like the Community Land Act; the Education Act 1976 (designed to hasten progress towards a fully comprehensive system of secondary education including the phasing out of the direct-grant system); the closed shop *(Trade/Labor Unions*)* unless supported by a massive ballot majority for it; the Industry Act with its disclosure provisions and planning agreements.

It would support radical changes in the National Health Service, including payment for hospital care and increased prescription charges; the freedom of the Local Education Authorities to choose the type of secondary school organization they wish; it would restore direct-grant schools *(Statutory System*)*, reduce immigration and bring in a new Nationality Act.

Of the main objectives of the Conservatives during the early seventies, one has been realized: in 1973, under the leadership of Edward Heath (Prime Minister 1970-1974), Britain joined the European (Economic) Community *(Common Market*)*; another, the reform of the Trade Unions *(Trade/Labor Unions*)*, was not achieved.

Since 1974, the Conservatives have certainly become more searching and radical than they used to be. The Conservative Trade Unionists (CTU) were set up in 1975, and in the same year, the Conservative Party's Community Affairs Department was founded to establish better communication with such important sections of the population as trade unionists, immigrants, small businessmen, and students. 1976 saw the establishment of an Anglo-Asian Conservative and an Anglo-West-Indian Conservative Society and of the Small Business Bureau. The Federation of Conservative Students (FCS, founded in 1920) has been reactivated to involve itself in student politics and to take part in the National Union of Students (NUS); its membership trebled between 1973 and 1977.

The Young Conservatives on the left are the most "progressive" element in the party. The Bow Group (founded in 1951, when it held its first meeting in Bow) represents the more intellectual among younger Conservatives; their organ is "Crossbow"). The Tory Reform Group ("The Reformer") represent another section of the party's left; whereas the Monday Club, although cautiously moving towards a more moderate middle way since the mid-seventies, is still a bastion of right-wing conservatism.

The party (the official name since 1912 has been Conservative and Unionist Party) consists of the Conservative and Constitutional Associations of the constituencies. In 1867, an effective Conservative party organization was called into existence (it is certain that it won the elections of 1874 for the Conservatives); it was then called National Union of Conservative and Constitutional Associations. After the Liberal Unionists *(Liberal Party*)* had officially merged with the Conservatives, the name was changed into National Union of Conservative and Unionist Associations, representing the party in the country as a whole. The four sections of the party are (1) the National Union, (2) the Conservative Peers, (3) the 1922 Committee, and (4) the Cabinet (or Shadow Cabinet). - The national organization is grouped in 12 areas with separate bodies for Scotland and Northern Ireland. The smallest units are the local (i.e. constituency) organizations. In Northern Ireland, or Ulster the party is called the Unionist Party, which, up to 1972, was the ruling party since the beginning of Ulster's separate existence, but now bears little resemblance with the Conservatives of Great Britain *(Orange and Green*)*.

Candidates for national elections are normally chosen in the following way: the local party association (run by an executive committee elected annually) selects the candidates, interviews them, and recommends them to a local general meeting for final choice. Recommendations of the national party headquarters may, but need not, be considered *(Labour Party*)*.

The political course and general policy of the party is laid down at annual party conferences. Resolutions are based on the reports of the National Council, which is guided by an executive committee (chairman, treasurer, and paid staff). They are mere recommendations and not binding for the leader of the party (generally the Prime Minister or the Leader of the Opposition). In 1965, the then leader of the party, Sir Alec Douglas-Home, introduced an innovation, which was considered a revolutionary measure since it meant the beginning of party reform. The party leader is now elected by the parliamentary party; before, he was practically appointed by his predecessor as Prime Minister; and the political parliamentary party, the Cabinet, the Conservative Lords, and the chairmen of the constituencies were merely consulted. - The leader alone is responsible for the policy of the party. He appoints the chairman of the party and through him controls the party organization; through the *Whips** he controls the parliamentary party which falls into two groups: the "front bench" (either Treasury Bench or Opposition Bench) and the Conservative and Unionist Committee popularly known as the "1922 Committee", an association of all other Conservative private members (also called "backbenchers"). The Committee was born out of a backbench revolt in October 1922 led by Sir Gervaise Rentoul against the Lloyd George coalition.

H H

Constituency

A body of constituents (or voters) within a defined political area, who elect a representative for the legislature; it is also used for the residents in that area generally, and for the place or district represented. 1831.

● It is not unimportant to note that in 1831 when the term "constituency" was first used, the struggle over the Reform Bill *(Suffrage*)* was already at its height, and one of the foremost demands of the liberal reformers was the reorganization of the system of electoral districts.

Until the middle of the 18th century, Parliament was fairly representative of the landed interest in the nation. But with the growth of industrial towns in the North and West of England and in the Clyde Valley the accumulation of people in these areas, and the development of new towns there, the old system of representation had become obsolete. A redistribution of seats in the House of Commons had become imperative. Under the old system

(a) every *County**, irrespective of its size and population, was represented by two members;
(b) towns were not represented on a population basis: a town (if represented at all) returned two members irrespective of size (only five towns had one member, London four). This state of affairs was extremely unjust because some towns had developed into really important places (London 1.5

million inhabitants, Birmingham 115,000), whereas others had declined into insignificance, and some had even ceased to exist altogether or existed only in name (the town of Dunwich had been destroyed by the sea, the "town" of Old Sarum consisted of a grass-covered mound, for instance). These decayed boroughs came to be called "rotten boroughs";

(c) many of the small towns were either under the control of the government, or of the great nobles and landowners. Before 1832, the Treasury controlled approximately 30 boroughs. A far greater number were "owned" by noble families (according to contemporaries around 276 out of a total of 513 boroughs in England and Wales). These boroughs came to be called "pocket boroughs"; the phenomenon itself is called the "patronage system";

(d) of the 558 seats in the Commons, 432 fell to the boroughs, 122 to the counties, although the counties generally were more populous than the boroughs, and two each to the universities of Oxford and Cambridge;

(e) the composition of the House of Commons was based on no logical plan or principle whatsoever.

In 1832 the reform of the constituencies began (Representation of the People Act, known more commonly as the Reform Act of 1832). It was passed under Grey's coalition cabinet of Whigs and supporters of Canning and was the first practical step in this direction. It disfranchised 56 pocket boroughs and rotten boroughs (pop. under 2000). 32 small boroughs were deprived of one member each. 143 seats became available and were redistributed. 22 large towns (pop. over 4000) were given two members, 21 towns (pop. 2000 to 4000) one member each. County membership was increased from 94 to 159. The 13 remaining seats went to Scotland (eight) and Ireland (five).

The second Reform Act of 1867, which was passed under Derby's Conservative government, brought with it a further redistribution of seats. Boroughs with a population of less than 10,000 lost their second seats in the House of Commons, while a number of populous towns were given a third seat. Several new constituencies were called into existence.

The third Reform Act of 1884 was passed during the Liberal Gladstone's second administration and was followed by a special Redistribution of Seats Act (1885). These measures abolished the parliamentary representation of all boroughs with less than 15,000 inhabitants, combining them with neighbouring boroughs. The most important innovation, however, was that the numerical principle superseded the historical system of borough and county representation. Each constituency (the term now fully asserted itself) was henceforth represented by one member. An average constituency at that time consisted of 54,000 people.

Permanent boundary commissions for England, Scotland, Wales and Northern Ireland were established in 1944, with the task of ensuring that constituencies are made up of a fairly equal number of people. (A redistribution of seats was made five years later under the Redistribution of Seats Act, 1949.)

The Representation of the People Acts of 1949 and of 1969, gave final shape to the present electoral system. The former Act finally abolished the remains of plural voting left over from the Act of 1884 (a businessman might have two votes if his residence and the seat of his business were in different constituencies; the universities had an extra vote with 12 seats in the Commons:

Oxford two, Cambridge two, London one, the University of Wales one, Queen's University of Ulster one, the other English universities formed a constituency with two, those of Scotland one with three members). The latter abolished all previous qualification for owners of property not based upon residence in the area. *(Orange and Green*.)*

At present, there are 635 constituencies with an average of 62,000 constituents each, 516 of them in England, 71 in Scotland, 36 in Wales, and 12 in Northern Ireland. In spite of the efforts of the Boundary Commission to achieve fairly equal-sized constituencies, local and regional deviations from the "ideal" figures are great (average number of constituents in England: 64,000, Scotland: 51,000, Wales: 55,000, Northern Ireland: 87,000). Each member represents his constituency with its entire population. He does not, however, necessarily have a mandate of the majority of the constituents. This oddity is due to the peculiarity of the British electoral system. Its principal rules are: (1) the ballot is secret (Ballot Act, 1872); (2) members are elected by direct vote; (3) each constituent may cast one vote for one candidate only; (4) the candidate who wins more votes than any of his rivals is returned to Parliament.

The major disadvantage of this electoral system is that it distorts popular opinion. For example: a member may have been elected by 35 per cent. of voters, whereas 34 per cent. voted for another candidate, and 31 per cent. for a third candidate; still, only the first among the three is returned to Parliament. In 1970, 122 of 630 members (19.3 per cent.) were "minority members"; the figures for 1945 are even more striking (203 = 32.5 per cent.).

This electoral procedure also makes it possible for a party to win a majority of the total votes cast, but not a majority of seats in Parliament. This was the case in 1951, for instance, when the Labour Party obtained a quarter of a million votes more than the Conservatives, but 26 seats less and in 1974 (February elections), when the Conservatives polled over 300,000 votes more than the Labour Party but five seats less. At the October elections of the same year, the Labour Party obtained an absolute majority with 39.3 per cent. of the aggregate popular vote, the lowest proportion for any in this century with an overall majority.

The British electoral system also entails a misrepresentation of smaller parties. At the same October elections of 1974 the Labour Party obtained 319 seats compared to 250 to which they were proportionately entitled; the Conservatives won 277 against 227; the Liberals 13 against 116; the Scottish and Welsh Nationalists 14 against 22; the other parties and individuals 12 against 19. This electoral system makes it possible that 5.3 million electors return 13 members of Parliament while 11.5 million electors return 319 members of Parliament. In 1974, 49 per cent. of British voters said they were for electoral reform, 26 per cent. against, 26 per cent. did not know (Research Surveys of Great Britain). In 1977, the House of Commons voted against proportional representation for both Scotland and the European Assembly (with the exception of Ulster: in 1978 the Commons decided that the people of Ulster, alone in the United Kingdom, shall elect three members of the European Assembly by a method of proportional representation to give Roman Catholics a fair chance of returning one of their community).

■ In the U.S.A. the terms "constituency" and "district" are both in use. Each State is divided into a number of electoral districts for the election of the members of the House of Representatives. These districts are single-member constituencies averaging about 450,000. In practice, districts often vary considerably in size in certain States and are sometimes "gerrymandered", i.e. arranged in such a way that one party is enabled to gain more representatives than it could on an equitable system. (This was done in 1812 in Massachusetts by the party of Governor Elbridge Gerry; whence the name.) From time to time the States are "redistributed" to avoid gross inequalities of representation *(Census*)*. H H

Constitution

The system or body of fundamental principles according to which a nation, state or body politic is constituted and governed. 1735.

● The British Constitution is the oldest constitution still in force. It is not embodied in a single document, but consists of various individual documents and a number of resolutions and acts of Parliament. In its essence, it is founded on constitutional conventions which are in a manner unwritten rules tacitly acknowledged by everyone. As there is neither *judicial review** of legislation nor a special court to watch over the Constitution, a normal Act of Parliament suffices to change it; and if Parliament can in such a way grant a new Constitution there is no reason why a successor Parliament should not withdraw it, modify it, or proceed to legislate in terms inconsistent with it. The Constitution is in fact in a state of perpetual change and evolution because each single act of Parliament is part of the Constitution. It is therefore no exaggeration to say that the history of England is largely coextensive with the history of the English Constitution. Cromwell's England had for five years (1653-58) a written constitution known as the "Instrument of Government". It provided (1) the "Lord Protector" and a cooperative council of 21 (executive), (2) Parliament, consisting of the 460 members of the House of Commons. The "Instrument" gave Cromwell authoritarian, but by no means dictatorial powers. This, the first written constitution in Europe (only the "Fundamental Orders" of Connecticut, 1639, preceded it), was abolished after Cromwell's death in 1658.

The first document of the Constitution brought with it the first decisive limitation of the king's powers; and the more the Constitution grew, the more the powers of the Crown shrank. The development of the Constitution was the result of a constant struggle between the central authority and that section of the nation which happened to be fighting for its rights or political emancipation (13th to 17th century: the barons; 17th century: the Puritan gentry; 18th and 19th centuries: the middle classes grown wealthy through the *Industrial Revolution*;* 19th and 20th centuries: the working classes and the women).

The most important documents of the English Constitution are:

The Magna Carta, 1215: Constitutionally relevant are articles 12: 'no scutage or aid shall be levied in our realm unless by common council of our kingdom . . ."; 14, which declares that the common council shall consist of the barons and the church dignitaries; 39, according to which no free man shall be taken, imprisoned, disseized, outlawed, banished or in any way destroyed, nor proceeded against or prosecuted "except by the lawful judgement of his peers or by the law of the land". Articles 12 and 14 pertain to the gradual division of power, article 39 to the rule of law. The barons had compelled King John I (1199-1216) to sign Magna Carta as a confirmation of ancient rights and liberties. It is not a "democratic" document, for it guarantees only feudal rights; but it contains principles which could later be applied without difficulty to all people.

The Confirmation of Charters, 1297: This document is almost as important as the Magna Carta. It was extorted from the monarch by a coalition of the barons and the middle classes. In effect, the Confirmation contained the Magna Carta (and other charters) with the added provision that no non-feudal levy could be laid by the Crown without a parliamentary grant. Edward II, 1272-1307, left the granting of this concession to his son Edward, later Edward III, 1307-28.

Petition of Right, 1628: A series of disastrous military expeditions conducted by Charles I brought the Crown into conflict with the House of Commons. These expeditions, which had led to unparliamentary taxation, billeting, arbitrary imprisonment, and martial law over civilians, were declared illegal in the Petition of Right. The king gave his assent in return for a grant of five subsidies. The Petition of Right prohibited benevolences (= forced loans), all forms of taxation without consent of parliament, the billeting of soldiers in private houses, the execution of martial law in time of peace, the imprisonment of persons unless upon specific charge.

The Habeas Corpus Act of 1679 *(Habeas Corpus Act*)*.
The Bill of Rights of 1689 *(Bill of Rights*)*.
The Reform Acts of 1832, 1867, and 1884, the Representation of the People Acts of 1918, 1928 and 1969 *(Suffrage*)*.
The Parliament Acts of 1911 and 1949 *(Lords*)*.

■ The American Constitution, which took effect 1789 and was ratified by all States in 1790, is the oldest written constitution applying to a nation as a whole. The U.S. Constitution is contained in one document which consists of a Preamble, seven Articles (Articles I to IV are subdivided into a number of Sections), and 26 constitutional amendments. In 1972, Congress approved the women's equal rights constitutional amendment. If ratified by the States, it will go into effect two years after ratification as Amendment XXVII. The Constitution is based on the following principles:

(1) All States are equal. The federal government cannot give special privileges to one State.
(2) There are three branches of government: one to make the laws, another to execute them, and a third to settle questions of law.
(3) All persons are equal before the law, and anyone can demand the protection of the law in the exercise of his rights.
(4) The government is a government of laws, not of men. No one is above the law *(Royal Prerogative*)*. No official of the government can use authority unless the Constitution or the law permits it.
(5) The people can change the authority of the government by changing the Constitution.
(6) The Constitution, the acts of Congress, and the treaties of the United States are the highest law in the land. A State constitution or State law conflicting with them cannot be enforced in the federal courts. The national government is a government of the people and not of the States alone.

With regard to group life the following ideas are laid down in the Constitution:

(1) The Preamble says that the people wanted to form "a more perfect union"; thus the Constitution outlines the purposes of a national government.

(2) The people have delegated some of their authority to the national government; thus final authority belongs to the people. The authority of the national government is divided among President, Congress and the federal courts.
(3) The Constitution describes how the national government is organized; how legislators, the *Chief Executive**, and federal judges are chosen.
(4) The Constitution provides for the settlement of disputes between States. It provides for a functioning of the national government and the State government but makes it impossible for the one to end the other.

The Constitution can be formally changed by amendments to the Constitution. The most prominent among them are amendments I to X, comprising the so-called *Bill of Rights** (1791), Amendment XIII (1865, abolition of slavery), Amendments XIV (1868) and XV (1870) (definition of citizenship and protection of rights thereof), Amendment XVII (1913, senators to be elected by the people of the individual States instead of by the State legislatures), Amendment XXIV (passed by Congress in 1964, abolition of every kind of poll tax). Article V of the Constitution provides two different ways in which changes can be proposed to the States and two different ways in which States can approve such changes and make them part of the Constitution:
(1) Proposal of amendment by favourable vote of two-thirds of those voting in both houses of Congress and subsequent ratification by three-fourths of all the States (or special State Conventions in three-fourths of all the States) "within reasonable time", i.e. usually seven years today.
(2) Proposal of amendment by National Convention called by Congress upon request of two-thirds of the State legislatures and subsequent ratification by the legislatures of three-fourths of all the States (or special State Conventions in three-fourths of all the States).

The President of the U.S.A. cannot influence the passage of an amendment.

It is sometimes overlooked that quite important parts of the U.S. Constitution are not incorporated in the document itself, but are contained in general laws passed by Congress. For example, the present organization of the federal government has resulted from several laws creating the executive departments and many bureaux and commissions; and the important question of who should become President of the United States if the President and the Vice-President should die while in office is not contained in the Constitution but in a general law.

The *Supreme Court** watches over the Constitution. Since its creation it has declared over 100 laws or parts of laws unconstitutional.

The development leading to the ratification of the American Constitution began in 1776 when the Continental Congress, forerunner of the present Congress, authorized a committee of thirteen to draft articles of a more permanent union of the former colonies. The result was the Articles of Confederation (not ratified by all States until 1781). These articles, however, did not call into existence a federal state but a federation of states. There was no president, no judiciary, no authority on the part of Congress to levy taxes, no central control over foreign policy, nor even sufficient means to enforce measures of the Continental Congress; they did not provide for a uniform currency nor for effective interstate commerce. The title "United States of America" first appeared officially in Article I of the Articles of the Confederation: "The Stile of this Confederacy shall be The United States of America".

From May to September, 1787, the so-called Philadelphia Convention met to consider the defects of the existing system. The Continental Congress gave its approval to it with the express purpose of revising the Articles of Confederation. That the Fathers of the Constitution exceeded this purpose and wrote instead a fundamentally new constitution was one of the main objections to the latter until 1790. It was by no means welcomed enthusiastically by the 13 States. Five months after its completion only five States had ratified the document; by June 1788 there were nine States, a sufficient number (two-thirds) for its taking effect. Virginia, New York, North Carolina followed in 1789, Rhode Island in 1790. An important problem that divided the Constitutional convention dealt with the method of representation in the legislature. Virginia's plan proposed a two-house legislature based on size of population, whereas New Jersey's plan proposed equal representation of the States in a single-house legislature. "The Great Compromise" (also of 1787) brought about the present system: representation based on size of population in the House of Representatives (favouring the more populous States) and equal representation of the States, irrespective of size of population, in the Senate. 1

The campaign for the adoption of the Constitution in New York brought forth a literary by-product, "The Federalist", a collection of articles by Alexander Hamilton (afterwards first Secretary of the Treasury), John Jay (afterwards first Chief Justice of the Supreme Court), and James Madison (fourth President of the United States).

Each of the 50 States has its own written constitution. By 1776 New Hampshire, South Carolina, and Virginia had already adopted new constitutions. Soon the other original States, with the exception of New Jersey, which has had a State constitution only since 1947, had set up new constitutions, which were in fact mere revisions of the colonial charters. They generally stressed the "natural rights" philosophy of that time, contained a "Bill of Rights", and provided for a separation of powers. These ideas were included in the federal constitution, too. H H

County

One of the territorial divisions of Great Britain and Ireland, forming an important unit for administrative, judicial, and political purposes. In the U.S.A., the political and administrative division next below the State. 1683.

● There are two units representing the first and highest level of *Local Government** in Britain: the county and the county borough.

The county: The administrative county is the most important unit of local government. There are 58 counties in England and Wales outside Greater London, and six in Northern Ireland. By the County Councils Act of 1888 some of the ancient counties, or shires, were subdivided into smaller counties (e.g. Yorkshire into East, North, and West Riding; Suffolk into East and West Suffolk; Lincolnshire into Holland, Kesteven, Lindsey). But most of the historic counties remained intact. The counties are subdivided into rural districts, urban districts, and municipal districts. Their size and population varies considerably (Lancashire, 2,000,000; Rutland, 20,000). The county council, the governing body of the county, is elected every three years and meets at least quarterly in the county capital. Its members elect a chairman, who like the chairman of the municipal borough is *Justice of the Peace** for the time he is in office. The council is made up of aldermen and councillors (proportion 1:3). The county councils levy their rates indirectly through the municipal boroughs and the urban and rural districts. Their principal spheres of activity are education (through the L.E.A.s), roads, housing, town and country planning, slum clearance, police, sanitation. In Scotland there are 33 counties, two pairs of which (Perth and Kinross, Moray and Nairn) are combined.

The county borough: The county (or city) borough is an urban area within a county, but independent of the latter. It usually has a great density of population. There are 82 in England and Wales outside Greater London, and two in Northern Ireland. By the Local Government Act of 1958 a minimum population of 100,000 was fixed for new county boroughs; but some older ones, like Canterbury, have populations far below this figure. The county (or city) borough council is organized on much the same lines as the county council: it is elected every three years and holds regular meetings at short intervals. Its members elect a chairman (called the mayor), who is Justice of the Peace *ex officio*. Today the council consists of councillors only (the office of alderman was abolished by the 1972 Act, except for the City of London, whose aldermen are appointed for life). Otherwise the pattern follows that of the municipal borough corporation. Rates are levied indirectly through the municipal boroughs and the urban and rural districts. Most important among the council's spheres of activity are education (L.E.A.s), roads, housing, town and country planning, slum clearance, police, sanitation. In Scotland, the equivalent of the county boroughs are the "counties of cities", of which there are four, Edinburgh, Glasgow, Dundee, Aberdeen.

The Local Government Act of 1972 created 54 new counties in England and Wales. The county borough (urban area within a county) was abolished by the Act, but the traditional differentiation between the rural or small urban area and the populous town is perpetuated in the distinction between a metropolitan county and a non-metropolitan county (see *Local Government**). There are six metropolitan and 39 non-metropolitan counties in England (outside Greater London) and nine (non-metropolitan) counties in Wales. The office of alderman went out of existence.

The counties of Scotland were renamed "regions" in 1975. There are nine regions containing 53 districts. Like their English counterparts they are responsible for services such as broad economic and physical planning of the area, road and transport, education, social work, police, and fire.

■ In the U.S.A. counties are the administrative units immediately below State level. There are 3096 including 64 parishes in Louisiana and 29 divisions in Alaska which have the function of counties. The counties are responsible not to the Federal Government but to the State governments. The size of counties averages 1,000 square miles, their population 50,000, although the latter may vary considerably (an unorganized county in North Dakota, for instance, has only 100 inhabitants, while Cook County (Chicago) has over 3.3 million). In most States the form of county government is simple, consisting of a board (or council), which may be of two types, either (1) a small board of commissioners elected by the county, or (2) a large board elected by the townships and cities within the counties. In America, the county is the only unit of administration which both follows the *Chief Executive** system and is based on representation. County functions are most highly developed in the South, where health and education are often primarily a county responsibility. There and in other regions of the U.S.A., their functions usually include the judiciary and law enforcement, welfare, roads, elections, all of them being duties which they share with the State governments. In the North and most of the Middle West the counties are still further subdivided. In New England, the *Town**, is the more important unit and the county merely a convenient instrument for direct State administration. 1

For the American equivalent of the English county borough (or metropolitan county) see *City**.

H H

Declaration of Independence

■ Public Act by which the Continental Congress declared the 13 colonies to be free and independent of Great Britain. 1776.

The Declaration of Independence of July 4th, 1776, was not the cause of the War of Independence, but testimony that the idea of complete independence was beginning to assert itself in the American colonies. This change of opinion was hastened by the unwillingness of the British authorities to make concessions, and by the publication, in January, 1776, of the pamphlet "Common Sense" written by the English emigrant Thomas Paine. However, it should be noted that public opinion remained divided with regard to independence for a long time. The number of loyalists was still substantial in the British-American War of 1812-14; and Nova Scotia, Quebec and Florida remained entirely loyal to Britain. When the Declaration of Independence was proclaimed, the revolutionary war had been on for 14½ months. Its causes were manifold: the attempt of the British Parliament to regulate colonial trade; the Stamp Act of 1765 providing taxation of newspapers, legal documents, playing-cards, etc. (repealed in 1766); the Townshend Acts of 1767 providing a system of import taxes; and the "Intolerable Acts" of 1774, a series of Acts designed to punish Boston for the Tea Party and to show the colonies that Parliament was the wellspring of law and order (Boston's port was closed, Massachusetts lost its charter, accused persons could be sent to England for trial and the much-hated quartering of soldiers was introduced). Three additional factors which aided in building up resistance to the mother country were the Proclamation Line of 1763 marking the southern and western limits of the colonies beyond which settlement was forbidden; the Quebec Act of 1774 extending Canada's boundaries to the Ohio River, an area in which Virginia, Massachusetts, and Connecticut had claims, and aiming to cut off the western extension of the northern colonies; and the continuing religious difference between the mother country and the colonies, especially Puritan New England.

The War of Independence itself lasted from 1775 to 1783, with preliminary hostilities in 1770 ("Battle of Golden Hill" in New York, and the "Boston Massacre"), 1773 ("Boston Tea Party", or, in the British version, "Boston Tea Plot", and other "tea-disorders" in the following year). The first shots between American and British troops were fired in 1775 (skirmishes at Lexington and Concord, Battle of Bunker Hill). In 1781, the war had practically been decided in favour of the Americans, largely owing to the Franco-American Alliance concluded in 1778 (a strong French fleet prevented the British army from retreating by sea in 1781 which meant that the British were forced to surrender at Yorktown). The Treaty of Paris, 1783, declared the U.S.A. to be an independent country with an area extending from Canada and the Great Lakes to Florida and from the Atlantic to the Mississippi River.

The Declaration of Independence certainly had an important share in the victory. It was an advantage that it did not have the force of law but was a statement of moral principles by which political actions can be judged. Jefferson's (the author's) task had been to give expression to political sentiments held by many Americans; but in doing so, he summarized the political doctrine and philosophy characteristic of the Enlightenment: the belief that all men were endowed with inalienable rights, that governments were instituted in order to protect these rights, and that men could alter or abolish any government which became destructive of such rights. This theory was clearly derived from John Locke (1632-1704), but Jefferson made one interesting change in Locke's list of natural rights: he made no mention of the "right of property" but spoke instead of the "pursuit of happiness". It is also important that no reference is made to Parliament but only to King George III; this was because the Continental *Congress** had adopted the theory that the English Parliament had never had any legitimate authority over the colonies, their only legal tie with Britain being their allegiance to the Crown (the "dominion theory", first formulated by James Wilson and Thomas Jefferson in 1774, which is an interesting view in so far as the present relations between Britain and the Commonwealth are regulated by roughly the same conception). The last of Jefferson's charges against the King was the philippic against negro slavery: "He has waged cruel war against human nature itself, violating its most sacred rights of life and liberty in captivating and carrying them into slavery in another hemisphere, or to incur miserable death in their transportation thither . . .". The Continental Congress omitted this passage altogether. Indeed, the discrepancy between fact and rhetoric was too flagrant. Jefferson himself never owned fewer than 100 slaves and sold those he did not want any more rather than freeing them. H H

Deep South

■ From South Carolina and Georgia west along the Gulf coast to Texas stretches an area known as the Deep South. It has no precise limits, being determined more by common characteristics than by geographical boundaries, but it is commonly understood to include all or a part of South Carolina, Georgia, Texas, Alabama, Mississippi, and Louisiana. The term Deep South distinguishes this area from the Upper South, another imprecise term which usually refers to Virginia, North Carolina, Tennessee, and Arkansas, and from the Border States such as Maryland, West Virginia, and Kentucky. Florida, though adjacent to and south of Georgia and Alabama, is not ordinarily considered a part of the Deep South. 1938.

During the era preceding the Civil War, the Deep South states constituted the heart of what became the Confederacy. These were the cotton states, characteristic of which were the plantation system and a massive Negro slave population outnumbering whites in a solid chain of counties extending through the region.

From the Deep South came the most ardent defence of slavery and the strongest insistence upon the rights of the states as against those of the federal government. Consistent with this tradition, the Deep South has continued in the 20th century to be the stronghold of those who championed *States Rights** and "white supremacy". From this area came the most vociferous opposition to recent *Civil Rights** legislation enacted by the federal government. The principal strength of such lingering anti-Negro groups as the Ku Klux Klan is centered there. Consequently, Deep South communities were the scene not only of many civil rights demonstrations, but also of much of the violence accompanying the Negro's effort during the 1950s and 1960s to achieve full equality.

Recent elections have shown that the winds of change are having their effect, however. In 1972, six hundred blacks were elected to office in the 11 Southern States. By 1976, their number had risen to more than 1,300.

During recent years, there has been a dramatic transformation in most of the Southern States, both in social values and economic opportunities. The racial integration campaigns are now scarcely mentioned in just those places where the most dramatic confrontations occurred, although the problems of black Americans are still formidable, as in the upper South and in the North. But American and foreign businessmen have in the past few years come to recognize the immense investment opportunities in the Deep South and the South generally. Atlanta, Ga., has become the business capital of the region, and spectacular architecture is perhaps the best symbol of the new wealth.

S R Sp

Democratic Party

■ One of the two great political parties in the U.S.A. The direct descendant of Thomas Jefferson's Republican Party, it adopted its new name in 1828.

Like the Republican Party, it has undergone radical changes in outlook during this century. Its image today is progress, a touch of youthfulness, liberalism. It is characteristic that all black members of Congress are Democrats.

In 1976, the party pledged itself to a fairer distribution of wealth, income, and power; to the reduction of unemployment by using federal funds; it promised tax reform to ease the burden of the poor and increase it for the rich, and continued efforts to abolish racial inequality; a comprehensive national health insurance system; and a liberal stand in the question of abortion.

In foreign affairs, the Democratic platform differs from that of the Republicans only in that it considers normalizing relations with Communist China to be more important than continuing commitment to Taiwan. *(Republican Party*).*

In the great depression *(Great Crash*)* of the 1930s, basic changes took place in the conflict between parties. Under F. D. Roosevelt's New Deal a wide-reaching policy for economic recovery was introduced. An era of ideological conflict began in the U.S.A., liberal versus conservative, and the Democratic Party became the party of liberal reform. Up to that time, the Democrats had been a party of small towns, rural areas and *States' Rights**, and the white "solid South". Now, under Roosevelt, the Democratic Party emphasized the necessity of centralized government power in order to realize nation-wide economic and social reform, favouring underprivileged groups like the Labor Unions, the new immigrants, the Catholics, Jews, blacks, and those who had become poor by the depression. This "New Deal coalition" in the Democratic Party lasted, more or less, into the 1970s *(Parties*).* Over the civil rights question the Democrats first lost the support of the white South, then that of the urban Catholics, especially in the North East. But in 1972, a new "ideological" coalition of intellectuals, young people, emancipated women, blacks, and "progressives" of various shades came into existence and started a "populist" wave against big government and the established political organizations, in the interests of "the little guy who can't really get a handle on the government" (Senator McGovern, 1972). They demanded social and economic reform, income guarantees, a better tax and health insurance system, etc., and, under the Democratic Party's Reform guide-lines of 1972, they introduced the proportional representation of women, blacks, and young people in State delegations to the national party convention.

They could not possibly win the election in 1972, but they have remained the "ideological" basis of the Democratic Party which had to be broadened considerably towards the centre by Jimmy Carter, because polarised political ideas and "ideologies" hardly find the support of an issue-oriented majority of American voters today.

The party organization is simple, because it conforms to the structure of the U.S. government (local, county, state, national level). The party hierarchy comprises (1) a national committee, (2) State central committees, (3) county committees, (4) city committees, (5) ward committeemen (or election district agents), (6) precinct captains. In contrast to the organization of British parties, the local units are the centre of party power. The national party organization is merely a rather loose federation of state and local party machines, exerts comparatively little power, and becomes active only before elections. There is a national chairman of the party; his role is that of an organizer rather than that of a figure of political weight. The party also has a leader in both houses of Congress elected by the party caucus; however, in the absence of effective party discipline, he has little power. The presidential candidate of the party is nominated in a National Convention of approximately 1,000 party delegates chosen by the State party conventions or by way of direct primary. The National Convention also fixes the party platforms and planks.

The Democratic emblem is the donkey which was adopted in the first place to help illiterate voters to identify the candidates.

Democratic Presidents: Jefferson, 1801-09; Madison, 1809-17; Monroe, 1817-25; Jackson, 1829-37; Van Buren, 1837-41; Polk, 1845-49; Pierce, 1853-57; Buchanan, 1857-61; Cleveland, 1885-89 and 1893-97; Wilson, 1913-21; F. D. Roosevelt, 1933-45; Truman, 1945-53; Kennedy, 1961-63; L. B. Johnson, 1963-69; Carter, 1977. H H

Department

One of the separate divisions or branches of state or municipal administration. 1769.

- In Britain, the Departments are the instruments for the execution of the policy of the Government when Parliament has passed the necessary legislation. The political heads of the Departments make final decisions and act on their own account in all matters relating to the spheres of their responsibilities, unless the matter is of such importance as to require the sanction of the *Cabinet**. In everything they do in their official capacity they are directly responsible to Parliament.

There are normally about 100 persons holding ministerial rank in the British Government. Their number occasionally changes, especially when the Prime Minister reshuffles his Cabinet and Government. There is virtually a five-tier system of Ministers today: (a) Cabinet Ministers including the Prime Minister, the Lord Chancellor, the Lord Privy Seal, the Chancellor of the Duchy of Lancaster and the Lord President of the Council; (b) Departmental Ministers including the Chancellor of the Exchequer; usually with Cabinet salaries; (c) Ministers who are heads of Departments but under the instructions of a Secretary of State, and the Law Officers (see below); (d) Ministers of State, who are civil servants and mostly additional ministers in large departments; (e) Parliamentary Secretaries (or Junior Ministers), whose task it is to relieve their senior Ministers. Moreover, there is a great number of under-secretaries, deputy secretaries and deputy under-secretaries of state, parliamentary under-secretaries, private secretaries of various kinds, and special advisers. There are also several officers of Her Majesty's Household with ministerial rank *(Whip*)*. The Prime Minister alone decides which Departments he wishes to have represented in the Cabinet.

The following is a list of British Departments (Nov. 1977) with titles of their heads where it appears desirable, the usual designation being "Secretary of State for . . .": Lord Chancellor's Office (Lord Chancellor); the Treasury (Chancellor of the Exchequer); Foreign and Commonwealth Office (...Foreign and Commonwealth Affairs); Home Office (...for the Home Department); Department of Education and Science (...and Paymaster General); Department of Energy; Department of Industry; Department for the Environment; Scottish Office; Northern Ireland Office; Welsh Office; Ministry of Defence; Department of Employment; Department of Health and Social Security (...for Social Services); Department of Trade; Ministry of Agriculture, Fisheries and Food (Minister of...); Department of Prices and Consumer Protection; Department of Transport; Law Officers' Department (Attorney General); Ministry of Overseas Development (Minister of State); (for the Ministers without a Department see below). The Colonial Office was abolished in 1966; the Post Office was converted into a public corporation in 1969.

There are some Departments of strictly regional jurisdiction: the Department of Education and Science and the Ministry of Health are responsible only for England and Wales; the Welsh Office, the Northern Ireland Office, and the Scottish Office have executive responsibilities only for Wales, Northern Ireland, and Scotland respectively. They include the Department of Agriculture and Fisheries for Scotland, the Scottish Development Department, the Scottish Education Department, the Scottish Home and Health Department, the Scottish Economic Planning Department, the Scottish Law Officers, and some other administrative Departments, all of them responsible to the Scottish Office; others are responsible to the Northern Ireland Office, such as the Northern Ireland Departments of Agriculture, Civil Service, Commerce, Education, Environment, Finance, Manpower Services, and Health and Social Services.

Many of the names of ministers are self-explanatory, but some may need elucidation: The Lord Privy Seal (originally the keeper of the Sovereign's Private Seal) is the leader of the House of Lords, and thus holds a party office. The Chancellor of the Duchy of Lancaster (since 1399 Lancaster has been separately administered for the Crown by a Chancellor) holds a Ministry without portfolio and can thus be entrusted with special tasks, e.g. that of co-ordinator in the Cabinet for the social services or, as was the case in 1972, with the task of representing Britain in the negotiations with the European Economic Community. The Lord President of the Council (i.e. Privy Council) is the leader of the Commons. The Lord Chancellor holds important positions in all three branches of power: he is the highest judicial officer and invariably in the Cabinet, *Speaker** of the Lords, and highest judge in the country. The Paymaster-General fulfils the function of a banker for the Government *(Treasury*)*. For Chancellor of the Exchequer see *Treasury**; for Prime Minister see *Cabinet**.

■ The American Departments are the instruments of the Chief Executive. But their heads do not act without the sanction of the President. They are not responsible to Congress, but to the President. Like the *Independent Agencies** they are part of the bureaucracy, not of the "Presidency" *(Chief Executive*)*; i.e. they are concerned with the specific aspects of the life of the nation, and not with overall planning and control. Congress has some influence on the Departments in that their chiefs are appointed "with the advice and consent of the Senate" and can be summoned as witnesses by Congress *(Committee*)*.

There are 12 Departments, surprisingly few in comparison with Britain. But some of the Departments are virtually "holding companies" of many sub-departments (e.g. the Department of State comprises over 20 bureaux, agencies, institutes, and other divisions dealing with particular aspects of foreign affairs, e.g. African Affairs, Peace Corps, International Scientific and Technological Affairs). The Department of Defense is a kind of superstructure on top of four other Departments. Moreover, many an *Independent Agency** has acquired the importance of a Department.

The following is a list of American Departments, with titles of their heads, year of establishment, tasks (if not obvious from the name); the order indicates their rank in the succession to the President.

Department of state (Secretary of . . .), 1789, foreign affairs and policy, cultural exchange, Peace Corps. Department of the Treasury (Secretary of . . .), 1789, internal revenue, customs, custody of the currency, Mint, savings bonds, coast guard, narcotics, accounts, public debt, engraving and printing. Department of Defense (Secretary of . . .), 1947, Joint Chiefs of Staff, the different commands (including SAC = Strategic Air Command), weapons evaluation, co-ordination of procurement, research and development, psychological warfare, harbour installations, etc; under the supervision of this Department are the four co-ordinated Departments of the Army (Secretary of . . .), the Navy (Secretary of . . .), and the Air Force (Secretary of . . .), and the Defense Agencies and Joint Service Schools (Director of . . .). Department of Justice (Attorney General), 1794, prosecutions, Federal Bureau of Investigation (F.B.I.), prisons, U.S. marshals, attorneys, immigration and naturalization, alien property. Department of the Interior (Secretary of . . .), 1849, fish and wildlife, mineral resources, public lands, Indian affairs, national parks, outdoor recreation, *Territories**, water and power, reclamation, etc. Department of Agriculture (Secretary of . . .), 1889, soil conservation development, forests, rural electrification, cooperatives, marketing, credits, crop insurance, agricultural research. Department of Commerce (Secretary of . . .), 1903, science and technology, economic affairs, *transportation**, business, Patent Office, Weather Bureau, *Census** Bureau, etc. Department of Labor (Secretary of . . .), 1913. Department of Health, Education and Welfare (Secretary of . . .), 1953, Public Health Service, Office of Education, Vocational Rehabilitation Administration, St. Elizabeth's Hospital, Food and Drug Administration, Social Security Administration, Welfare Administration. Department of Housing and Urban Development (Secretary of . . .),

1965, co-ordination in matters of urban, suburban and metropolitan development, encouragement of private homebuilding. Department of Transportation (Secretary of . . .), 1966, development of national transportation policies and programmes. The Post Office Department (Postmaster General) founded in 1789, was converted into an independent government agency *(Independent Agency*)* in 1972. The title Postmaster General for the head of the new U.S. Postal Service remains the same. Department of Energy (Secretary of . . .), 1977, energy conservation, coal development, energy data programmes, jurisdiction over the naval petroleum and oil shale reserves etc.

The Secretaries are assisted by a staff consisting of assistant secretaries, assistants, under-secretaries, inspectors, directors, advisors, administrators, counsels, etc. H H

Devolution

The delegation of power or authority to subordinate officers, committees, or assemblies; decentralization. 1780 (Thomas Jefferson).

● In December 1977, the Labour Government introduced two separate bills in the House of Commons to establish elected Scottish and Welsh Assemblies in Edinburgh and Cardiff. These bills received their Royal Assent, thus became law, on July 31, 1978. They are based on the Report of the Royal Commission on the Constitution, chaired by Lord Kilbrandon, of 1973. The Commission was established in 1968 to take account of the demand of many parts of Britain, including some regions of England, for a greater share in decision-making. The Report was also, between 1974 and 1976, the basis for two Government White Papers, one supplementary statement, and the Scotland and Wales Bill published in December 1976 and defeated in the Commons. The two Bills reject the idea of separate federal states within Britain, but propose to set up Scottish and Welsh Assemblies directly elected by the people of Scotland and Wales. They also acknowledge the special position of Northern Ireland with its Protestant and Catholic communities. In this connection it should not be overlooked, however, that the Scottish Office (founded in 1885, transferred to Edinburgh in 1939) and the Welsh Office (founded in 1965) have been very successful forerunners of devolution. The creation of the Northern Ireland Office in 1972 was tantamount to the abolition of self-government in Northern Ireland; on the other hand, it created the basis for future devolution in Ulster on equal terms with Scotland and Wales.

It may well be that the devolution of powers from Westminster to the national Assemblies is the most far-reaching reform of the constitution since the Act of Union in 1707 *(Union Jack*)*.

Britain is a country of many nations - the people of England, Scotland, Wales, and Northern Ireland (the latter, though predominantly Celtic, are not a homogeneous ethnic group). These four nations constitute the "United Kingdom of Great Britain and Northern Ireland". Besides these, there are the people of the Isle of Man and of the Channel Islands, both dependencies of the Crown but not part of the United Kingdom. Since the early seventies, there has also been a certain revival of national feeling in Cornwall, the Isle of Wight, and the Shetland Islands *(Union Jack*, Celtic Fringe*)*.

Whereas the dependencies have always enjoyed a large and rarely disputed measure of autonomy, Wales, Scotland, and Ireland were more or less forced into the union with England; Wales and Ireland were conquered, and the union between England and Scotland (1707), preceded by mutual threats of extortion, was a marriage of convenience. Scotland and Ireland lost their parliaments; Wales had never had one. The United Kingdom, as it existed when the Act of Union with Ireland (1801) took effect, was a unitary state in which legislative power rested exclusively with the central parliament at Westminster. Inevitably, centralization provoked its own reaction in a state that included so many different nations. A more or less powerful nationalistic feeling has existed ever since in the three Celtic nations of Britain, ranging from reluctant acceptance to open rebellion.

It was in connection with the struggle for Irish Home Rule that the question of devolution came into prominence. Since Gladstone advocated home rule all round, devolution as an objective of major constitutional reform has been on the political agenda. It was realized only in Northern Ireland, though under very unfortunate auspices *(Home Rule*, Orange and Green*)*. It was probably due to the decline of the Liberal Party, always the champion of devolution, after World War I that no further steps were taken to satisfy the demands of Scotland and Wales. In 1920, J. Ramsay MacDonald (first Labour Prime Minister 1924, 1929/35) still believed that "the overwhelming influence of England on Scottish and Welsh affairs is destroying the native political instincts of these nations" (in "Parliament and Revolution"), and on June 3, 1919, a resolution was adopted in the House of Commons by a vote of 187 to 34 stating "that, with a view to enabling the Imperial Parliament to devote more attention to the general interest of the United Kingdom . . . this House is of opinion that the time has come for the creation of subordinate legislatures within the United Kingdom." One year later, Parliament granted devolution to Northern Ireland. But it took nearly fifty years until the first serious move was made towards the devolution of authority to Scotland and Wales.

Under the Government's devolution proposals of 1977 the Scottish Assembly would consist of about 150 members, the Welsh of about 80. As a proportional representation system for the election of Assembly members has been rejected, they would be elected by simple majority as in parliamentary elections. Assembly members would be elected two for each existing constituency, with larger constituencies electing a third member where their electorates are more than a quarter larger than the average for their countries. Eventually, parliamentary constituencies are intended to be divided into single-member Assembly constituencies. Peers and ministers of any religious denomination would be permitted to stand for election. A member of Parliament would also be eligible for Assembly membership. Election to the Assemblies would take place every four years. By-elections would have to be held within three months of the resignation or death of an Assembly member.

The Assemblies would have power over (1) most aspects of local government administration; (2) the structure and operation of the National Health Service; (3) personal social services, such as the care and support of children, the handicapped, and the elderly; (4) the Statutory school system, policy for private schools and nursery education, further and higher education (but not the universities or the research councils), adult education, youth and community services, national and local libraries and museums, the arts, and sport; (5) the provision of public housing; (6) physical planning and the environment, for example protection of the environment, land use, development, *conservation of land**, river management, water policy, refuse collection, and *New Towns**; (7) roads, bridges, inland waterways, public passenger transport unless provided by national institutions, etc. (the Welsh Assembly's authority in this area would be more restricted than that of the Scottish Assembly); (8) law functions: the Scottish Assembly's authority would extend to the regulation of the courts, the general criminal law, Scottish private law, the legal profession, legal aid, and the treatment of offenders.

The Parliament at Westminster could, however, intervene if the Assemblies overstepped their powers or if proposed laws conflicted with Government policy. - North Sea oil revenue would continue to go to the Exchequer, and the national Government would maintain control over national law and order, regional trade, and economic and financial policy. - The Assemblies would get block grants from the Westminster Parliament, but they would have power to raise extra revenue by a surcharge on local authorities. - The representation of the people of Scotland and Wales at Westminster would continue as at present. *(Commons*)* - Scotland and Wales would not have their own voices in the European Community.

It is intended to give Scotland a Cabinet-type government and a chief executive, who will normally be the leader of the majority party. The government of Wales would work through a system of committees each headed by an executive member. In fact, this would not constitute a particular novelty because Wales already has an elaborate committee system covering the public utilities (like electricity and water), the health services, tourism, some aspects of industrial development, broadcasting, and cultural and environmental interests. Before the Wales Bill was introduced, there were about 70 important non-elected public bodies of this kind so that Wales already had a lot of devolution. What it lacks is democratic control of it.

Eight English regions were suggested in the Kilbrandon Report, but, as yet, the Government has not proposed to initiate any major constitutional change in England. At present, the English, who account for about 84 per cent. of the United Kingdom's population are not specially interested in nationalism and most of them tend to regard the term "English" and "British" as synonymous. Nevertheless, support for devolution is growing in England, too, because of the growing dissatisfaction with centralist tendencies of post-war British governments and the erosion of local rights.

Concerning Ulster it is intended to devolve back to Northern Ireland real powers, not necessarily legislative. There would be an assembly based on proportional representation which would have a consultative role regarding legislation. The devolved powers would, as in Wales, go to committees.

Devolution is likely to remain controversial long after its introduction in the United Kingdom. Most important, perhaps, is the consideration that devolution implies a mere delegation of power from a superior political body to an inferior. In this sense power devolved would mean power retained. The devolution in Northern Ireland under the Government of Ireland Act 1920 *(Home Rule*)* proved to be disastrous, although Westminster had reserved a whole catalogue of rights. While the laws of Scotland and of England have drawn closer over the past 100 years, those of England and Northern Ireland diverged between 1920 and direct rule *(Orange and Green*)*. Moreover, a provincial system of government is likely to mean provincialism in the standards of that government. Then, there is always the danger of one-party rule over a long period of time; the Conservative Party, for example, may soon become an exclusively English party, considering that of its present (1978) seats in the Commons only 24 are based on constituencies outside England. Last but not least, the threat of separatism is always present in Britain, unlike the often-cited Federal Republic of Germany, where separatist ambitions do not exist.

(Referendums were held in Scotland and Wales on March 1st, 1979, in which the Government's Devolution scheme was turned down by the Scottish and Welsh voters.)

■ The devolution of authority to the States is one of the basic principles of the *Constitution** of the United States. The *States' Rights** are anchored in Amendment X of the American *Bill of Rights**, guaranteeing that "the powers not delegated to the United States by the Constitution nor prohibited by it to the States, are reserved to the States respectively, or to the people". About the middle of the nineteenth century the Southern States derived for themselves the right to secede from the union. Their secession in 1860/61 started the Civil War (1861-1865). The victory of the Union forces settled the States' Rights question insofar as it denied to the States the right to declare their independence, but the idea of devolution contained in Amendment X has remained undisputed. The United States is the model of a federal state.

H H

District

A portion of territory marked off or defined for some special administrative or official purpose. A subdivision of a county. 1895.

● The Local Government Act of 1972 introduced a radical change also on the district level of *local government**. In the new two-tier system the districts represent the secound tier. The Act provides for 296 metropolitan and non-metropolitan districts, the main difference lying in the more numerous responsibilities of the former because the problems of an urban, populous, industrial community tend to be more differentiated.

Populations of under 40,000 have been accepted in some cases, so that sparsely populated areas will not have units too large for local government. But a total of 14 below 40,000 under the new arrangements contrasts with 768 of that size under the old system. The average population of a district is about 90,000 (as against the former 28,000). This has added much to the strength of the districts. They are no more sub-divisions of the counties but autonomous local government units. The Act abolished the office of alderman. Councillors are elected every fourth year.

Their functions include: local planning, housing, high-ways, building regulations, refuse collection, etc.

The burghs in Scotland went out of existence in 1975 (see *Local Government**) and have been superseded by 53 districts similar to those in England and Wales, its functions including housing, local planning, environmental health, licensing and amenity services.

■ With the exception of the *District of Columbia**, the 29 "divisions", which are another name for *County** in Alaska, and the term "subdistrict" used in some parts of the Southwest in the absence of "towns" or "townships", the "district" is not a unit of local government in the U.S.A. H H

District of Columbia

■ The capital area of the U.S.A. It is also known as the City of Washington, D.C. Under the U.S. Constitution, it is divorced from the territory of any State, and the responsibility for its government is entrusted to Congress. It is neither a State nor a self-governing municipality. 1790.

The district is situated on the NE bank of the Potomac River, at the confluence of this river with the Anacostia River. It has an area of 61.4 square miles. The population of the city is approximately 726,000, that of the whole district (= standard metropolitan area) is over three million, more than 74 per cent. of them Negroes. Washington has little industry; its manufacturing is for local consumption.

The District of Columbia was the first carefully planned capital in the world. The immediate occasion for its foundation was the inability of Congress in 1783 to pay the soldiers who had served to the end of the War of Independence. Troops from Pennsylvania marched to the State House in Philadelphia, the then seat of Congress and demanded justice. When neither the State government nor the city offered protection, James Madison suggested removing it to another place. Before 1800 Congress sat in eight cities: Philadelphia/Pa., Baltimore/Md., Lancaster/Pa., York/Pa., Princeton/N.J., Annapolis/Md., Trenton/N.J., and New York/N.Y. In 1790 an Act of Congress specified the site of the new capital; George Washington entrusted Major Pierre Charles L'Enfant, a French engineer, who had fought in the War of Independence, with its plan. The Irishman James Hoban designed the Executive Mansion. This was built of white Virginia freestone, which led to its being called the "White House" as early as 1811. The alternative explanation for this name is the coat of white paint which it received after having been burnt down by British troops in 1814 (Second War with Britain, 1812-1814). The plan accepted, and partly followed, for the Capitol was that of William Thornton. When, in 1800, Congress convened there for the first time and John Adams moved into the White House, the city had 2,464 free inhabitants and 623 slaves. In 1840 it was still a "city of magnificent intentions" (Dickens, "American Notes").

The Constitution of the U.S.A., which was drawn up in 1787, had settled the question of the jurisdiction over a future capital (Art. I, sec 8/17), but said nothing about the political rights of the citizens who were to live there. Up to the present day, therefore, the question of self-government has remained unanswered. Under the provisions of the Organic Act of Congress of 1878, the District of Columbia was, until 1967, governed by a commission consisting of two civilians and one officer of the Corps of Engineers. They were appointed by the President, who, together with the commissioners and the judges of the *District Court**, appointed most other officers and boards. The Reorganization Plan of 1967 substituted a single Commissioner (also called Mayor), an assistant and a City Council consisting of 9 members, all appointed by the President. In 1970, Congress passed an Act giving the District one delegate to the House of Representatives. He may vote in committee but not on the House floor. In 1974, the inhabitants of the District approved a charter giving them the right to elect their own mayor and a 13-member City Council, who took office in 1975. The District also obtained the right to levy its own taxes. Both the first Mayor and the first Representative to be elected were blacks. Already, in 1961, Amendment XXIII had given the citizens of the capital the right to vote in an election for President and Vice-President, with 3 electoral votes *(Poll*)*.

H H

Dixie

■ The origin of the word is uncertain. Three theories exist: (1) It may have been derived from the name of one Dixie, a kind-hearted slave-owner on Manhattan Island in the latter part of the 18th century. (2) It may have its origin in the money issued by a bank in New Orleans before the War between the States (1861-1865); the ten-dollar bill bore the French word "dix" (ten) on its back and thus Louisiana, and soon the South in general, came to be called "the land of dixies", Dixie Land, or Dixie. (3) The word is most likely derived from "Mason and Dixon's Line" which was surveyed in 1763 and 1767 by Charles Mason and Jeremiah Dixon after a border dispute between the proprietors of Pennsylvania and Maryland. Before the Civil War "Mason and Dixon's Line" had come to be synonymous with the dividing line between free and slave states east of the Ohio River or, more generally, between the North and the South. As soon as a Negro crossed the line from Maryland to Pennsylvania he was free. *(Deep South*.)*

Up to the abolition of slavery Dixie was a nickname applied to those states where slavery was particularly rife. Today it is frequently used to designate all the Southern States. "Dixie" is also a song which was composed in 1859 by the Negro Daniel Decatur Emmett (1815-1904) and which became very popular among the coloured population of the South, although the Confederates used it as their favourite song during the Civil War. Indeed, there exist one Northern and two Southern versions. The word also characterizes a particular style of American Jazz.

Since 1948 Dixie has acquired a new importance and a new political content through its inclusion in "Dixiecrat". In 1948 President Truman proposed to Congress legislation which would put into effect the recommendations of the Commission on *Civil Rights**. This included: (1) Federal legislation to abolish the poll tax. (2) A new Fair Employment Practices Commission. (3) Abolition of segregation in interstate travel. (4) A federal law against lynching. The reaction was the secession of a Southern faction of the *Democratic Party** who called themselves "States' Rights Democrats" and were called "Dixiecrats". In 1948 they nominated their own presidential candidate, J. Strom Thurmond of South Carolina, who, in the national election, received 1,169,000 popular votes and the 39 electoral votes of Louisiana, Mississippi, Alabama, and South Carolina. The name persists today and "Dixiecrat" now describes any Southern politician who stands up resolutely for the *States' Rights**. H H

Doctrine

That which is laid down as true concerning a particular department of knowledge, as religion, politics, science, etc. A belief, theoretical opinion, dogma. A body or system of principles, a theory. Middle English.

■ The main course of American policy has, on the whole, been determined by four political doctrines: the Loose Constructionist Doctrine, the Strict Constructionist Doctrine, the Monroe Doctrine, and the Truman Doctrine. This is quite in accordance with the constitutional system of the U.S.A. Whereas the British system is highly ideological, and important decisions are made on party lines (however much the "presidential" position of the Prime Minister may have come to the fore recently) the American President is hardly restrained by party considerations *(Chief Executive*)*, which gives him the freedom to promulgate his personal political conception. That such conceptions are sometimes set into the frame of "doctrines" is in the tradition of the Declaration of Independence, which itself contains the political doctrine of the Enlightenment.

The Loose Constructionist Doctrine and the Strict Constructionist Doctrine (1790) are associated with the names of Thomas Jefferson and Alexander Hamilton. The latter had submitted to the House his report on a national bank (1790). Jefferson maintained that the bill was unconstitutional and referred to the strict wording of Amendment X which did not delegate to Congress the power to establish a bank (strict constructionist view). Hamilton interpreted the Constitution more loosely and spoke of powers "implied" in the *Constitution**. Simplifying matters we may say: Jefferson believed that everything the Constitution did not allow was forbidden, whereas Hamilton contended that everything that was not expressly forbidden by the Constitution might be permitted by implication. From such small beginnings, these two doctrines eventually became the basic programmes of the first two parties in the U.S.A. *(Parties*)*. They split the nation into advocates of centralism and advocates of the *States' Rights**, and led to a dispute which was one of the issues of the Civil War (1861-65) and which is still present as an undercurrent in American politics of today.

The Monroe Doctrine (1823) is the most famous of American doctrines. In its essence, it is a check against "any new European colonial establishments" (John Quincy Adams) in the Americas. In 1821, the Czar had extended Russian claims along the Pacific coast to an area north of the 51st parallel which included part of the Oregon country, then jointly occupied by the U.S.A. and Britain. In 1822, at the Congress of Verona, Russia, France, Austria, and Prussia agreed to restore the former Spanish American colonies to King Ferdinand VII. This was against the interest of both the U.S.A. and Britain. For a time, there was far-reaching agreement between President Monroe and Prime Minister Canning; even joint Anglo-U.S. military action was considered, which, however, did not become necessary. While England reached agreement with France, the Russians, under the treaty of 1824, withdrew to a line 54° 40' north. On December 2nd, 1823, in his annual message to Congress, President James Monroe explained the attitude of the U.S.A. towards European interference with American affairs. This doctrine contained four major points: (1) the American continents were no longer subjects of European colonization, (2) the political system of the Americas was essentially different from that of Europe, (3) the U.S.A. would not tolerate any attempt on the part of European powers to establish their system in any part of the Western Hemisphere, (4) the U.S.A. would not interfere with existing European dependencies in the New World, would not interfere in European internal affairs, and would not take part in European wars of solely foreign interest. The consequences of this proclamation were of great importance, although its effects became felt only in the second half of the century: it inaugurated the isolationist policy of the U.S.A. and it focused her attention on Latin America. It was extended and adapted several times. President Polk elaborated it in 1845 in more aggressive tones during the dispute over Oregon *(Louisiana Purchase*)*, whereas President Th. Roosevelt interpreted it more generously in 1904 (when Britain and Germany blockaded Venezuela to enforce payments), saying that the U.S.A. did not "guarantee any state against punishment if it misconducts itself", but he excluded any form of acquisition of American territory. The

Monroe Doctrine was also the model of two other doctrines, the Paramount Interest Doctrine of Secretary of State James G. Blaine in 1881, an interpretation in favour of U.S. interests in connection with the construction of an Isthmean canal in Central America; and the Drago Doctrine of 1902 (formulated by Luis M. Drago, Foreign Minister of Argentina, during the dispute over the collection of Venezuelan debts), its essence being that armed force must not be employed by a European power to collect national debts owed by American nations to foreign creditors. The Monroe Doctrine was not the first official declaration of an isolationist American policy: George Washington's farewell address of 1796 contains his famous Doctrine of Isolationism ("Tis our true policy to steer clear of permanent alliances, with any portion of the foreign world.").

The Truman Doctrine (1947) ended the official isolationism of the U.S.A. caused by the Monroe Doctrine when, in that year, President Harry S. Truman called for the "containment" of Soviet expansion, for resistance to aggression and, more specifically, pledged the employment of U.S. military and economic help to aid Greece and Turkey. (The Eisenhower Doctrine of 1957 was an extension of this doctrine attempting - with only partial success - to give military and economic aid to the countries of the Near East.) The Truman Doctrine marked the beginning of America's anti-communist commitment through various military, economic, and other organizations. Under the Monroe Doctrine, the U.S.A. withdrew in 1919 from the international stage; under the Truman Doctrine it became the reluctant leader of the West. Embodied for the first time in a bill, it declared, "It must be the policy of the United States to support free peoples who are resisting attempted subjugation by armed minorities or by outside pressures". Under the Truman Doctrine the U.S.A. became something like the policeman of the world, and, at least potentially, the doctrine was the basis for an interventionist policy. "Containment" was possible only by means of military strength; and, from 1947, the U.S.A. built up a worldwide system of military pacts:

Organization of American States (OAS, Rio Treaty – 1947: reciprocal assistance in the event of aggression); North Atlantic Treaty Organization (NATO – 1949; its members regard an attack on one as an attack on all); ANZUS Treaty (1951: its members, Australia, New Zealand, U.S.A., acknowledge that an attack in the Pacific against any will involve all); South East Asia Treaty Organization (SEATO – 1954: it covers the general area of South-east Asia and the western Pacific; its members pledge mutual assistance in the event of any aggression in the whole area); Central Treaty Organization of the Middle East (CENTO – 1959: mutual security and economic development; the U.S.A. is not directly a member of the pact, but has pledged to co-operate in mutual defence and, moreover, signed bilateral defence agreements with the three Middle Eastern members); other bilateral defence treaties were concluded with Japan, the Philippines, South Korea and Taiwan; the U.S.A. also controls a dense network of military bases in many parts of the world.

Certainly the Nixon Doctrine (Guam Doctrine), first formulated by President Richard M. Nixon in Guam in 1969, marked a turning point in American foreign policy. Its aim has been to disengage the U.S.A. from its military involvement in Asia; it denounces future interventions of the U.S.A. like that in Vietnam and demands of other nations to assume greater responsibility for their own defence and well-being. In essence the doctrine means the abandonment of the policy of "containment" expressed in the Truman Doctrine and a more conciliatory attitude towards Red China. The Nixon Doctrine was extended by President G. Ford in 1975 ("Pacific Doctrine") who announced that it was the declared aim of the U.S.A. not to stop at mere non-intervention, but, basing on the Shanghai Communique of 1972, to normalize relations with the Chinese and, beyond this, the States of Indo-China and those between the two Korean States.

President Carter has so far renounced any commitments to doctrines, either of domestic or foreign policy, as he believes that the world of today is too complex to be strait-jacketted in such a way, though even in pursuing his international human-rights campaign he has been compelled to use selectivity to comply with America's security interests. H H

Dominion

Name used for some of the self-governing territories of the British Commonwealth of Nations. 1867.

● From 1867 the term "dominion" acquired a specific meaning in connection with the granting of responsible self-government to the Dominion of Canada (= united Canadian colonies). July 1st is celebrated as Dominion Day there. Of outstanding importance in defining the position of the Dominions within the Empire (which had remained undefined during the 64 years between 1867 and 1931) were the Imperial Conferences of 1926 and 1930. Their attempts to clarify the matter of the status of the Dominions resulted in the Statute of Westminster of 1931. This document contained four main provisions:

(1) It established the independence of law-making in each Dominion (". . . that no law hereafter made by the Parliament of the United Kingdom shall extend to any of the said Dominions as part of the law of that Dominion . . .");

(2) It named the countries given Dominion status (at that time "the Dominion of Canada, the Commonwealth of Australia, the Dominion of New Zealand, the Union of South Africa, the Irish Free State, and Newfoundland");

(3) It defined the Dominion status (". . . inasmuch as the Crown is the symbol of the free association of the members of the British Commonwealth of Nations, and as they are united by a common allegiance to the Crown . . .");

(4) It pronounced the right of the Dominions to conduct their own foreign policy, which, together with the control over the armed forces, is the criterion of true self-government ("It is hereby declared and enacted that the Parliament of a Dominion has full power to make laws having extra-territorial operation.").

This definition of Dominion status was an important step in the evolution of the Empire towards the present *Commonwealth**.

Not only the term *Empire** but also the term Dominion are rapidly passing into desuetude, being now applied almost solely in official language.

Con-Dominion (Condominium). Examples of this form of joint control over areas with virtually colonial status are: the Anglo-Egyptian Sudan (Great Britain and Egypt 1899-1953), the New Hebrides, or Nouvelles Hébrides, in the Pacific Ocean (Great Britain and France, since 1887), the Canton and Enderbury Islands (Great Britain and the U.S.A., since 1938).

■ The Dominion of New England (1685-1688). Under the reign of Charles II and even more so under that of James II friction between the Crown and Puritan

New England was for various reasons (abrogation of the Massachusetts Charter by England; refusal of the oath of allegiance by many Puritans; taxation without representation, etc.) on the increase. By order of James II the centralized Dominion of New England was organized, which, under the unpopular governor Sir Edmund Andros, included by 1687 all the New England Colonies, besides New York, New Jersey, and Pennsylvania. The Dominion of New England was brought to an end by the Glorious Revolution of 1688.

The Old Dominion is a popular name in the U.S.A. for Virginia. H H

Empire

An extensive territory (especially an aggregate of many states and territories) ruled over by a sovereign or government. Middle English.

● The term refers to the relationship between Great Britain and the overseas colonies and dependencies which were to a larger or lesser extent under the economic control and administrative jurisdiction of the British Crown.

Historians distinguish between the First Empire, the development of which - roughly speaking - began at the turn of the 16th century (America and India) and came to an end with the loss of the 13 North American colonies in 1783 *(Declaration of Independence*),* and the Second Empire which reached the culmination of its power in the period between Queen Victoria's Jubilee (1897) and the First World War. Then it was gradually transformed into the *Commonwealth*;* the turning point being the Westminster Statute of 1931. *(Dominion*.)*

The colonial government of the Second Empire which flourished in the course of the 19th century and was completed at the end of World War I comprised four different types of British overseas dependencies: (1) Crown colonies: conquered, ceded or annexed territories under the administrative jurisdiction of the mother country with regard to external and domestic affairs. (2) Protectorates: non-self-governing areas which accepted British protection, especially during the second half of the 19th century, usually under pressure, e.g. Uganda, the Rhodesias. (3) Protected states: territories which by treaties accepted British protection and control over their foreign relations but retained a large measure of domestic control, e.g. Tonga until 1970. (4) Trustee territories (formerly called mandates): territories which after World War I were mandated to Britain under the Covenant of the League of Nations (1921) and are still held by Britain in trusteeship for the United Nations Organization.

Although the Second Empire has rapidly disintegrated from 1947 (independence of India and Pakistan) there are still remnants of the former imperial system. They consist of a small number of British colonial territories with a certain measure of self-government which continue to be dependencies of the Crown until the British Government is convinced that their inhabitants are capable of governing themselves, and that the economies of their countries can sustain them.

In 1977, there were 16 remaining dependent territories of the United Kingdom with a total population of 5 million, ranging from 4 million in Hong Kong to 80 people on Pitcairn Island. They are: Gibraltar, Ascension, St. Helena, the Bermuda Islands, Tristan da Cunha, Belize (former British Honduras) which would be independent now but for Guatemala's threat of annexation), the Solomon Islands (to be independent in 1978), the Falkland

Islands, Hong Kong, Brunei (to be independent in 1983), the British Virgin Islands (to be independent in 1978), Gilbert Islands, Ellice Islands (to be independent by the name of Tuvalu in 1978), and other Pacific Islands, Rhodesia, the Cayman Islands, the Turks and Caicos Islands, the New Hebrides, and the Pitcairn Island.

The Caribbean Islands, Antigua, Domenica, St. Kitts-Nevis-Anguilla, and St. Lucia (all 1967), and St. Vincent (1969) were given the status of "non-dependent" states, the official designation of this group of former colonies being West Indies Associated States. Legal effect was given to this special status by the Government of the West Indies Act, 1967. They are responsible for their internal affairs and constitution, but not for external relations and defence. They can sever the association by unilateral declaration. Domenica is to become independent in 1978.

The British colonial government is distinguished by two main features: (1) The power of government is concentrated in the hands of the Governor and his Council, the Governor being responsible for his actions to the Foreign and Commonwealth Office (formerly to the Colonial Office) *(Department*)*. (2) The colony government can increase or decrease at will native participation in the administration of the colony, i.e. without much legislation the degree of self-government can be decreased or, if need be, the supremacy of the Governor can be restored (as was the case in British Guiana, Malta, and, at least formally, in Southern Rhodesia).

The British Empire, on which the sun never set, has practically ceased to exist; the Colonial Office, once the centre of Imperial power, was abolished in 1966. In the place of the former Empire there are now independent or semi-dependent nations, most of them speaking English for convenience if not by right of birth, practising their own versions of British institutions. The remnants of the Empire are today a liability for Britain rather than an asset, and it costs the British taxpayer not a little to finance Britain's development aid *(Commonwealth*)* and defence commitments in the Empire past and present. These commitments are, above all, the reason why Great Britain is a member of the most important defence organizations in many parts of the world: the North Atlantic Treaty Organization (NATO), the South East Asia Treaty Organization (SEATO), the Central Treaty Organization (CENTO) *(Doctrine*)*, and the ANZUK-Agreement of 1971, which is a military pact between Australia, New Zealand and the United Kingdom, with Malaysia and Singapore as associated members.

Today, it is difficult to arrive at a just assessment of the British Empire and to weigh the enormous colonizational achievements of the British in their Empire against the injustice, suppression, and loss of cultural values connected with 19th century imperialism, in which, it must be noted, many nations, including Russia and the United States, participated.

Development of the British Empire (selected facts and figures)

Europe

1171/72, the "Lordship of *Ireland*" established by Henry II; 1494, acts of the Irish Parliament had to receive approval from the English Privy Council (forced upon the Irish by Henry VII through Sir Edward Poynings, thus *Poynings' Law);* 1534, Henry VIII asserted kingship over Ireland; 1534-1537, abolition of monasteries, confiscation of lands; 1537, establishment of the (Anglican) "Church of Ireland" (disestablished in 1869); 1588, defeat of the *Spanish Armada;* 1607, Protestant "settlements and plantations" in *Ulster;* 1649/50, complete subjugation of Ireland by Cromwell; 1651, Cromwell's *Navigation Act;* 1704, *Gibraltar* occupied (recognized at Utrecht in 1713); 1782, repeal of Poynings' Law, formal termination of Ireland's quasi colonial status; 1800, *Malta* occupied (recognized at Vienna in 1815); 1807, *Heligoland,* captured from Denmark (exchanged for the German Zanzibar in 1890); 1878, *Cyprus* under British administration (annexed in 1914).

Asia

1600, *East India Company* chartered: 1640, English settlement at *Madras;* 1661, acquisition of *Bombay;* 1691, foundation of Calcutta; 1757, Robert Clive's victory over the French at Plassey, beginning of the *British Empire in India* (recognized in the Treaty of Paris in 1763); 1784, India Act (dual control of India by East India Company and Crown, 1784-1858); 1795, occupation of *Malacca* and *Ceylon;* 1819, acquisition by the East India Company of the island on which *Singapore* was founded; 1826, acquisition of *Assam;* 1839, capture of *Aden;* 1841, occupation of *Hong Kong* (recognized in the Treaty of Nanking, 1842, enlarged by peninsula of Kowloon, 1860, by treaty of 1898 leased to Britain for 99 years); 1849, annexation of the *Punjab* (Sikh Wars); 1852, capture of *Rangoon,* capital of Burma; 1857/58, *Sepoy Mutiny* against British rule; 1858, East India Company loses most of its functions, direct rule by the British Crown; 1867, *Straits Settlements* (Singapore, Pinang, Malacca, later also Labuan and the Cocos Islands) crown colony; 1877, Queen Victoria crowned *Empress of India;* 1887, *Maldive Islands* self-governing protectorate (now Maldives); 1888, *North Borneo* and *Sarawak* annexed; 1919, *Palestine, Trans-Jordan,* and *Iraq* mandates under the League of Nations.

Africa

1588, British trading rights in *the Gambia* (separate crown colony 1843); 1659, *Saint Helena* occupied and annexed (crown colony 1843); 1713, Britain and Spain sign the *"Asiento",* an agreement giving Britain the sole right to the *slave trade* with Spanish America, the greatest incentive for British colonial activities in Africa during the 18th century *(Abolitionist*);* 1794, *Seychelles* (recognized 1814 at Paris; 1795 and 1806, occupation of Dutch *Cape Colony* (recognized at Vienna in 1814, crown colony in 1833); 1808, acquisition of *Sierra Leone* (used for anti-slavery patrols, 1896, protectorate); 1814, *Mauritius* (Vienna Congress); 1842, annexation of *Natal* (1843, crown colony subject to governor of Cape Colony); 1848, annexation of *Orange Free State* (independent again in 1854); 1861, annexation of *Lagos* (1884/85, at the Berlin Conference, Britain successfully claimed the whole of *Nigeria,* 1914, colony and protectorate); 1867 and 1870, discovery of *diamonds* along the Vaal and Orange Rivers and at Kimberley, 1886 of *gold* on the Witwatersrand; 1868, *Basutoland* protectorate (now Lesotho); 1871, annexation of the diamond-mining region of *Griqualand* in Orange Free State; 1877 to 1881, first annexation of the *Transvaal;* 1882, occupation of *Egypt* (1914 protectorate, partly renounced in 1922); 1884, protectorate of *British Somaliland;* 1884/85, *Bechuanaland,* protectorate (now Botswana); 1888, the *British East Africa Company* obtained a charter to colonize and develop parts of East Africa; 1889, *Shire Highlands* annexed (in 1891 extended and renamed *British*

Central African Protectorate, in 1907 again renamed *Nyasaland,* now Malawi); 1889, the *British South Africa Company,* organized by Cecil Rhodes, obtained a charter giving it rights over enormous territories to the north of the Transvaal, a region from 1895 known as *Rhodesia* (in 1923, when the charter had expired, divided into the semi-autonomous region of Southern Rhodesia and the crown colony of Northern Rhodesia, now Zambia); 1890, *Zanzibar,* protectorate (exchanged for Heligoland); 1894, *Uganda,* protectorate; 1895, *East Africa* protectorate (in 1920 renamed and divided into protectorate of *Kenya* and colony of Kenya); in 1919/20 a number of *German colonies* in Africa became mandates under the covenant of the League of Nations: German East Africa (renamed *Tanganyika,* now Tanzania), *German Southwest Africa* (now Namibia, assigned to the then South African Union), part of *Togo,* and part of *Cameroon.*

Australasia

1768-1779, Capt. James Cook discovered, explored the southeast coast of *Australia* and claimed it for Britain; 1783, settlement considered by the British government; 1788, settlement of British convicts in *New South Wales;* 1803, *Tasmania,* settlement; 1829, *Western Australia,* settlement; 1836, *South Australia,* settlement; 1851, *Victoria,* separated from New South Wales; 1859, *Queensland,* separated from New South Wales; 1817, *New Zealand,* earliest British settlements, 1840, establishment of British sovereignty, 1841, crown colony; 1900, *Tonga,* self-governing protectorate; 1919/20, *Nauru* (German colony), mandate under the covenant of the League of Nations; 1965, *British Indian Ocean Territory* (uninhabited islands).

North America *(Stars and Stripes*)*

1497, John Cabot (Giovanni Caboto) discovered the coast of *Newfoundland,* never doubting that he had reached northeast Asia (the British claim to North America was based on his voyages; in 1583, Sir Humphrey Gilbert took possession of Newfoundland); 1607, *Jamestown* (first permanent English settlement in North America made by the *London Company),* 1619, first shipload of *Negro slaves* brought to Jamestown; 1620, first *Puritan* settlement at *Plymouth (Plymouth Company);* 1630, *Boston* (Puritan settlement, *Massachusetts Bay Company);* 1633, *Connecticut* (Puritan settlement of members of the Plymouth Colony and the Massachusetts Bay Company); 1636, *Rhode Island* (settlement of exiles from Massachusetts Bay); 1663, *Carolina* (proprietary colony owned by "true and absolute Lords Proprietors"; 1711, separated into North and South Carolina; 1729, royal colony); 1664, *New York* (formerly New Amsterdam), captured from the Dutch; 1670, *Hudson Bay Company,* chartered and given practically sovereign rights in the region drained by rivers flowing into the Hudson Bay; 1681, *Pennsylvania,* proprietary Quaker colony; 1704, *Delaware,* quasi-autonomous colony captured from the Dutch in 1664, who had captured it from the Swedes in 1655, before that it had been part of New Sweden, founded in 1638; 1710, *Acadia* (now Nova Scotia, New Brunswick, Prince Edward Island, part of Maine), captured from France (recognized at Utrecht, 1713; the further history of Acadia constitutes a very sad chapter of English imperial policy); 1732, *Georgia,* planned as a refuge for debtors in England; 1738, *New Jersey,* separate colony, captured from the Dutch in 1664, who had captured it from the

Swedes in 1655, before that it had been part of New Sweden, like Delaware; 1763, acquisition of *New France* as far as the Mississippi (1st Treaty of Paris).

Central and South America and the Caribbean Sea

1605, *Barbados,* settlement; 1609, *Bermuda,* settlement (crown colony in 1684); 1628, *Nevis* (Leeward Islands), settlement; 1629, *Turks and Caicos Islands,* settlement; 1632, *Antigua* (Leeward Islands), settlement; 1632, *Montserrat* (Leeward Islands), settlement; 1650, *St. Christopher* or *St. Kitts* (Leeward Islands), settlement; 1655, *Jamaica,* captured from Spain; 1665, *Virgin Islands,* settlement; 1670, *British Honduras* (now Belize), settlement founded by British buccaneers; 1670, *Bahama Islands* (now Commonwealth of the Bahamas), possession of the "Lords Proprietors" of Carolina (cf. above), 1717-1973 crown colony; 1763, *Domenica* (Leeward Islands), occupied (recognized in 1815); 1763, *Grenada,* acquired in the 1st Treaty of Paris; 1763, *Tobago,* occupied (now Trinidad and Tobago); 1763, *St. Vincent* (Windward Islands), occupied; 1797, *Trinidad* (now Trinidad and Tobago), captured (recognized in 1802); 1803, *British Guiana* (now Guyana), captured (recognized in 1815); 1803, *St. Lucia* (Windward Islands), captured; 1833, *Falkland Islands* (including the South Georgia, South Orkney, South Shetland and South Sandwich Islands and Grahamland), occupied. H H

Establishment

The ecclesiastical system established by law; the Church Establishment. 1731.

● Some time ago "Establishment" meant only the *Established Church**, the head of which was the monarch as "Defender of the Faith". The term Establishment, however, has also acquired a special sociological meaning. It nowadays denotes the ruling or upper classes and such institutions surrounded by ancient ceremonials and glamorous traditions as the Crown, the Church of England, the *Public Schools**, the *Colleges** of *Oxford and Cambridge**, the *Lords,* the *Clubs**, the *Treasury**, and the *Bank of England**. The term is also applied to people or groups of people - mainly members of leading old families - who have played a significant part in the life of the nation. These people have often kept out of the limelight, influencing political and economic affairs through private connections. Thus their influence is often beyond democratic control.

During the Victorian period the core of those privileged persons forming the Establishment and centring in the Crown was aristocratic and to a certain extent it is aristocratic even today.

Nevertheless, it has always been a special feature of the British Establishment to be open to promising people from outside not qualified by family background. Access was rendered available by generous scholarships - often "closed" scholarship *(Scholarship*)* awarded by the Public Schools or the colleges of Oxford and Cambridge to specially gifted children from all classes.

In 1923 the Tory Establishment was challenged for the first time by a Labour Government. At that time, however, the Establishment was able to retain its position mainly through the educational system, for pupils of the famous Public Schools and subsequent graduates of Oxford or Cambridge still had the best opportunities of assuming leading positions.

It was World War II and its consequences which changed things fundamentally. There was no longer any room for an Establishment monopoly, for Britain had to make the best use of all its brainpower and resources in order to adjust its economy to postwar conditions. With the growing need for technologists, scientists, and business-school-trained managers *(Management Education*)* the days of the gentleman amateur are definitely past. Expertise and efficiency as characteristic features of the new "meritocracy" are increasingly ousting such previously hallowed factors as family background and social status.

■ Although there is no Crown and no hereditary *Aristocracy** in the United States the ruling upper classes are characterized by the essential features of a genuine Establishment. They comprise those families whose ancestors have belonged to the élite for one generation or more. They enjoy special privileges as to social prestige and leading positions. They are conservative in attitude and convinced of their superiority as bearers of famous names and fine cultural traditions. They are educated in excellent schools and universities, the latter mainly belonging to the Eastern group of the *Ivy League**. As E. Digby Baltzell has shown in "The Protestant Establishment", there are still some additional criteria, however, which are originally American: the members of the American Establishment are all white, they are mainly of Anglo-Saxon descent, and they belong to a Protestant denomination. The "White-Anglo-Saxon-Protestant Establishment" sits atop the social pyramid in the United States. There are, however, some distinctions within this group. The most aristocratic of all are those who can trace their ancestry from the first English settlers who landed at Jamestown/Va. in 1607 or from the "Mayflower" passengers later called the Pilgrim Fathers *(Mayflower Compact*)*. The Pilgrim Fathers landed on the American continent in 1620. In order to emphasize their distinguished ancestry the descendants of the latter founded an exclusive society, the "Mayflower Descendants". The second group comprises the old families whose pedigree can be proved to date from before the Civil War. They form for the most part the society of the "Four Hundred". The name goes back to the number of guests invited to a highly distinguished party by Mrs. Astor in 1892. Further societies symbolizing the American Establishment are, e.g. "the Harvard Man", the "Sons of the Revolution", and the "Daughters of the American Revolution". There is also a "Social Register" - a genealogical handbook, a kind of democratic "Almanach de Gotha" - which today comprises 38,000 families from the whole of the United States. A typical member of the *New England** Establishment was described by Cleveland Amory in his book "The Proper Bostonians".

The American Establishment continued to assimilate new members of the élite, whether they were multimillionaires, entrepreneurs, bankers or financiers, provided they belonged to the Anglo-Saxon-Protestant stock. A new problem, however, arose with the millions of immigrants, especially from Eastern and Asiatic countries which make the United States the most heterogeneous nation in both ethnical and denominational stratification *(Immigrants, Melting Pot*)*. In the course of time some of the hyphenated-Americans (e.g. German-Americans, Italian-Americans, etc.) succeeded in acquiring wealth and influence. A concomitant of this development was the attempt on the part of these immigrants to break into the Establishment. Such attempts were frequently resisted by the old Anglo-Saxon-Protestant core of the Establishment. It has, for instance, been said that the wealthy father of the President John F. Kennedy was refused admittance to the exclusive Boston clubs for no other reason than that he was an Irish Catholic. At that time he was already numbered among America's millionaires. It was not until the Catholic John F. Kennedy was elected President of the United States that the Roman Catholics, a large proportion of whom are Irish, succeeded in gaining admittance to the inner circle of the American Establishment.

It cannot be denied, however, that in most of the large cities which have a population neither of protestant denomination nor of Anglo-Saxon descent, the predominance of the WASP establishment is gradually declining and partly balanced by the influence of large political groups which overcome the established class structure. I Fr

Filibustering

Gerund of verb filibuster, from substantive filibuster, earlier flibutor, adaptation of Dutch vrijbuiter, freebooter, one of a class of piratical adventurers who pillaged the Spanish colonies in the West Indies in the 17th century; now also: one who practises obstruction in a legislative assembly. Filibustering: the obstruction of the business of a legislative assembly, particularly when this is done by making prolonged speeches. 1889.

Mostly used to achieve destructive rather than constructive political ends, it is a grotesque perversion of the idea of freedom of speech. - In order to prevent filibustering, both the American and the British legislatures have introduced rules limiting the time accorded to speakers.

■ In the House of Representatives no member may speak longer than one hour except by unanimous consent of the House. In the Senate it is still most difficult to limit the length of debate; here filibustering is still a device greatly feared by Presidents, particularly in the case of controversial bills. If a determined minority in the Senate, however small, does not want to accept a bill which a majority is prepared to vote for it can talk the bill to death by prolonged speeches, delivered perhaps in relays. It is curious to note that the Senate rules do not prescribe that these speeches must refer to the subject under discussion; thus a Senator may very well read Mark Twain's *Huckleberry Finn* or Webster's Dictionary to his audience. In 1917, the Senate adopted what is called a "cloture rule", which, in its amended form of 1949, provides that the Senate may end debate, but only by a two-thirds vote of the entire body, which, of course, is not easy to obtain (see below); if it is obtained, however, no senator may speak longer than one hour, and "relay-talking" is impossible.

Filibustering was successfully applied during the Civil Rights debate of 1960 by Southern senators; unsuccessfully in 1964 when cloture (or closure) was invoked so that the bill could pass. Until 1964 cloture had never been applied to a debate on *Civil Rights**. The record individual filibuster was established in 1957 by Senator Strom Thurmond of South Carolina with over 24 hours of continuous talk.

● In the House of Commons there exist three devices limiting the discussion of a bill. Under the "kangaroo rule" the Speaker may select certain proposed amendments for discussion. By the application of the "guillotine" a bill is cut up into sections for each of which a limited time is set apart. The most important device is the "closure", according to which any member may move that the "question be now put", i.e. a division take place. If a hundred members or more carry this motion, a division on the point under discussion takes place at once. A degree of filibustering can again be observed in the British Parliament today in that bills are occasionally slowed in their progress by Members making the same speeches at different readings. In the House of Commons one of the Irish Home Rule debates of the second half of the 19th century lasted 42 hours owing to the obstruction of the Irish members. H H

Four Freedoms

■ "Essential human freedoms" enunciated by F. D. Roosevelt. 1941.

On January 6th, 1941, President Franklin D. Roosevelt, in his annual State-of-the-Union Message to *Congress**, stressed the dangers arising from dictatorship for democracy all over the world and asked the U.S. to become the great arsenal of democracy, supplying the free nations with war equipment. In order to ensure freedom and democracy for future times he demanded a world founded upon four essential human freedoms: the freedom of speech and expression, the freedom of every person to worship God in his own way, the freedom from want, and the freedom from fear.

In order effectively to guarantee freedom from fear the American President wanted "a world-wide reduction of armaments to such a point and in such a thorough fashion that no nation will be in a position to commit an act of physical aggression against any neighbour - anywhere in the world".

Those principles were considered as rather vague, more vague than Woodrow Wilson's Fourteen Points. They had to be modified quickly. Within the Atlantic Charter, the first public statement of Anglo-American war aims (August 14th, 1941), only freedom of want was referred to, whereas freedom of worship was not mentioned at all, and freedom of speech was dealt with only inferentially. In any case the Four Freedoms were used as a wartime slogan within the United States. In face of wartime and after-wartime realities they became more and more meaningless. But it is to be expected and hoped that the United Nations will finally become the instrument with the help of which the Four Freedoms might be achieved step by step. P H

Frontier

The part of a country which fronts, faces, or borders on another country. U.S.A.: that part of a country which forms the border of its settled or inhabited regions. 1870. - U.S.A.: owing to the contact of British and French colonial traders and settlers in the 17th and 18th centuries on American soil (Canadian-Great Lakes-Ohio frontier), the pronunciation of "frontier" (French "frontière"), which in Britain had been adapted to the English stress and pronunciation system, was probably refrenchified.

■ "Frontier" connotes westward expansion, confrontation with the forces of nature, fights against the Indians, and generally describes the regions in which white Americans contended with the wilderness. The frontier was one of the great factors in the shaping of a distinct American nationality. It has ceased to be an active factor in American life now since in 1890 the *Census** Bureau of the U.S.A. commented: "Up to and including 1880, the country had a frontier of settlement, but at present the unsettled area has been so broken into by isolated bodies of settlement that there can hardly be said to be a frontier line." But frontier has persisted as a myth. Few authors have not been influenced by it and in the works of many American writers the frontier is a central theme (W. Whitman, Mark Twain, J. F. Cooper, Bret Harte, W. Cather, Madison Jones, J. G. Baldwin, J. J. Hooper, and others). "Western" films dealing with frontier life are still a most popular genre among American films. The entertainment industry makes ample use of the frontier image as is exemplified by "Frontier Town" in Disney Land, near Los Angeles. Nowadays the word has come to be used as a general term for a challenge, a test, a trial, an enterprising spirit ("new frontier", "space frontier", etc.).

The "first frontier" was that which the immigrants of the "Mayflower" *(Mayflower Compact*)* had to face. But the heyday of the frontier was in the 19th century and especially after the discovery of gold in California in 1848. By 1850 only the land between California, Oregon, Utah and the westward moving frontier - the line from eastern Minnesota south through eastern Nebraska and Kansas through Arkansas to Texas - was calling out for settlers. This area was called "the last frontier". It was closed by 1890. Moreover, the distinction is frequently made between the "mining frontier" (in the mountains of the West), the "ranchers' frontier" (cattle), the "farmers' frontier" (agriculture), and the "urban frontier" (St. Louis).

The word "frontier" will always be associated with the American historian J. F. Turner who in 1893 wrote the essay "The Significance of the Frontier in American History". This was revolutionary in so far as it explained American history as something originally American, and not primarily rooted in the Old World. The frontier rather than the New England tradition could explain the development of the U.S.A. as a nation and people. The theory has been criticized for its one-sidedness and indeed there is a considerable amount of speculation in it. Some characteristics of American history cannot be explained by the frontier, e.g. all the aspects of U.S. foreign policy and most of America's role as an industrial nation, but parts of it are convincing. Moreover, Turner had based his thesis on a predominantly agrarian tradition. The theory prevailing in the East at that time that American history could be explained by European history alone was indeed unjustified. Broadly speaking, Turner argued that

(1) The frontier promoted immigration, and the immigrants a highly composite nationality.

(2) The farther west the frontier moved, the more it increased America's independence of England, except in the South (which economically depended on England) and New England.

(3) It strengthened the authority of the federal government because, after the War of Independence, the States owning land or land claims in the West turned this land over to Congress which then created out of these lands territories and new States.

(4) It contributed to the creation of democratic and individualistic feeling and institutions, for the frontiersmen, or "pioneers", were interested in their personal material prosperity and therefore tolerant with regard to nationality and religion. Indeed they developed a variety of systems of local government.

(5) It weakened provincialism and furthered the national spirit because of the mobility of people (the New England Northeast and the conservative Southeast excepted).

(6) It produced certain traits which can be regarded as typically American - a certain coarseness, strength, acuteness, inquisitiveness, a practical, inventive turn of mind, a grasp of material things, lacking in the artistic, a restless, nervous energy, dominant individualism, and buoyancy and exuberance born of freedom. H H 1

Greater London

Unit of local government administration. 1963.

● London was never planned. It has in the course of time developed around the City of London from a mass of villages, such as Kensington, Paddington, Camberwell and Tottenham. Up to the 18th century even Westminster was a separate entity. Indeed, before 1888 London had no central administration. The Cities of London and Westminster, for example, were parts of Middlesex, whereas Southwark - then called "the borough" - belonged to Surrey. The heterogeneity of London's past is to some extent still visible in the structure of its local government, but much has been done to streamline the administration of the British capital. First, the Local Government Act of 1888 established the County of London under the London County Council (L.C.C.). Second, the London Government Act, 1963, brought into being an entirely new system of government under the Greater London Council (G.L.C.).

Greater London now has a population of approx. 7.1 million - two and a half times as large as that of the old county - and covers an area stretching from Barnet in the north to Orpington in the south, and from Hornchurch in the east to Uxbridge in the west. The entire *County** of Middlesex ceased to exist in 1963, when most of it was incorporated into Greater London. Greater London now consists of 32 boroughs which were formed by amalgamations and divisions of all the local units within its limits. These boroughs comprise between 136,000 and 325,000 people each. The 12 boroughs whose areas, together with that of the City of London, constituted the former County of London, have been designated as "inner London boroughs" and the others are known as "outer London boroughs".

Each borough has its own councillors. Councillors are elected at the same time every third year, aldermen every sixth year - half of them retire every third year. The chairman of each council is the mayor and council meetings take place every six weeks.

The Greater London council has powers of jurisdiction over the whole of Greater London. It consists of 150 councillors and up to 16 aldermen. A chairman, who receives no salary, is elected annually, a vice-chairman and the deputy chairman are appointed annually. Meetings take place at least once a fortnight.

The ancient City of London, the historic centre at the heart of London known as "the square mile" around which the vast metropolis and conurbation has grown over the centuries (pop. approx. 4,200), has retained its unique position. It is normally designated as the "Corporation of the City of London" or the "City Corporation" but its legal definition is more complicated - "Mayor and Commonalty and Citizens of the City of London". The City government acts through the Court of Common Council (Lord Mayor, the 25 aldermen, the 153 councilmen). Aldermen, councilmen and Lord Mayor are elected annually. The office of Lord Mayor is an honorary, ceremonial and extremely expensive one because of the innumerable obligations placed upon him during his term of office which begins with the Lord Mayor's Procession. Among the various honorary offices which he holds are such diverse ones as: temporary member of the Privy Council, Admiral of the Port of London, and trustee of the fabric (building) of St. Paul's.

Like the metropolitan councils of Glasgow and Birmingham, the G.L.C. has to cope with the problem of "urban renewal", i.e. of decaying inner city areas. London's problems are the biggest and, what makes it worse, it has 15 per cent. of the population of Britain, but has to face 21 per cent. of the national costs, so that domestic rates in London are much higher than the average for the rest of England and Wales. Furthermore, the council is confronted with the task of redeveloping "dockland", an area of approx. 5,000 acres east of the Tower and associated with the names of famous docks reminding of Britain's powerful past. It is hoped that the regeneration of this area will not only remedy London's housing shortage but also save the homeland of London's *Cockneys**.

H H

Home Rule

Used especially in British politics with reference to the movement, begun about 1870, to obtain for Ireland self-government through the agency of a national parliament. 1860. Home rule, in a general sense, means the management of the affairs of a political community by its own people, Home rule, therefore, is not synonymous with "independence" but rather with "self-government", particularly with regard to domestic affairs. This is also what "Home Rule" (usually with capitals) came to mean in connection with Ireland, to which country this expression primarily refers.

● Home Rule became a political slogan after 1871. In that year Isaac Butt, a Liberal, founded the Home Rule for Ireland Party. His aims were to secure by peaceful means a separate legislature for Ireland. The dominant figure of the party soon became Charles Stewart Parnell (1846-1891), who was elected to the House of Commons in 1875. He hoped to hasten the granting of Home Rule by the use of obstruction in Parliament, but in contrast with the radical and militant Fenian Brotherhood (a secret Irish and Irish-American organization dedicated to the overthrow of British rule in Ireland), his party attempted to reach its goals not by terror, but by parliamentary means. The history of Anglo-Irish relations was full of injustice, discriminations, persecutions, and massacres in the course of repeated conquest and centuries of occupation of Ireland by the English. Moreover, most of Ireland was *Roman Catholic**.

By the Act of Union of 1801 the Irish *Parliament** was "induced" by extensive bribery to consent to the union between Ireland and Great Britain. William Pitt (1759-1806) seemed to make possible the formation of one country out of Great Britain and Ireland on a basis of absolute equality. Pitt intended that Catholics should be fully emancipated. In the Commons Ireland was to be represented by 100 members, in the Lords by 28 Peers (the other Irish Peers were to be eligible for election to the Commons); there was to be free trade between the two islands and one flag and one army, etc. George III, already at that time no longer in possession of his full mental powers, must be blamed for the failure of Pitt's plan; for, in his capacity as Supreme Governor of the Anglican Church, the king refused to give his consent to Catholic emancipation. In 1801, in the midst of the Napoleonic struggle, William Pitt resigned office over the Irish question. Subjugation of the Irish had been impossible; union between Great Britain and Ireland had proved to be a failure; there remained therefore only the alternatives of Home Rule or independence for Ireland. The Irish had four main grievances (1) religious: the unsolved question of the emancipation of Catholics, and the privileged position of the Church of Ireland (Anglican), resented not only by the Catholics but also by the Presbyterians of Ulster; (2) commercial: the Irish economy suffered from the union because the superiority of England's industry made it impossible for Irish manufactures to develop; (3) agrarian: most of the Irish land was still owned by landlords living in Great Britain; (4) political: Ireland continued to be ruled by English officials. 1

As for the religious grievances, in 1828 the Test and Corporations Acts *(Religious Test*)* were repealed, and in 1829 the Roman Catholic Relief Act was passed which admitted Catholics to Parliament and to most public offices. In 1868, after facing fierce opposition, Gladstone's Bill for the disestablishment of the Irish Church was carried by both Houses. The effect of this act was that the Irish Church ceased to sit in the *Lords**. Little was done during the first half of the century to remedy the commercial, agrarian, and political grievances. The Irish population decreased through famine and emigration (mainly to U.S.A.). Political violence returned, in particular through the Young Ireland Party under William Smith O'Brien in the forties, and through the Fenians in the sixties. In the 1870s and 1880s Gladstone's determination to bring about Home Rule for Ireland began to bear fruit in a series of Acts: the first Irish Land Act (1870), which conceded the principles of secure tenure and compensation for improvements; the second Irish Land Act (1881) which made further concessions and also led to a reduction in rent. In 1886 he tried to pass his (first) Home Rule Bill but was defeated owing to the defection of Joseph Chamberlain's Liberal Unionist faction which comprised Liberals who were against Home Rule and for the preservation of the Union. His second Home Rule Bill was passed in the Commons in 1893 but rejected by the Lords. On the whole the Home Rule plank was a domain of the Liberals. They carried a Home Rule Bill twice in the *Commons** (1912, 1913), but the Lords rejected it, as the Bill provided that Protestant Ulster should be incorporated in the Irish state. The refusal of the House of Lords prevented a civil war between the Irish Protestants and Catholics; 100,000 Ulstermen had already been raised to fight. Nevertheless, the bill became law in 1914, because under the Parliament Act (1911) no further sanction by the Lords was necessary *(Lords*)*, its execution, however, was suspended till after the war. It was finally replaced by the Home Rule Bill of 1920 (Government of Ireland Act), which provided that Northern and Southern Ireland were separated and received their own parliaments, but each part was to retain representatives in the British Parliament. In the elections of 1921, in Southern Ireland the (republican) Sinn Fein Party, whose leader was de Valera, one of the heads of the Easter Rebellion of 1916, won 124 of 128 seats. Against their opposition Ireland became a *Dominion** in 1922 (Irish Free State Agreement Act), but Eastern Ulster ("Northern Ireland") has since then constituted a separate state within the "United Kingdom", a term officially used since 1801. In 1932, relations between Britain and Ireland became strained again over the Land Purchase Annuities (interest on the amount for which the British Government had purchased the land of the old landowners to transfer it to Irish farmers, 1903). In the course of the dispute, de Valera, in 1937, proclaimed that Ireland was a Republic (Free State of Eire) within the Commonwealth. During World War II Eire remained neutral. In 1949 she formally seceded from the *Commonwealth* (Orange and Green*)*. H H

Immigration

■ Entrance into a country for the purpose of settling there. 1623.

Basic to any historical or sociological study of the American people is the study of immigration: the influx, during more than three centuries after the first permanent English settlement at Jamestown in 1607, of all the ancestors of the current American population except the American Indians. In a general sense, all those who came from other countries to the "New World" during those years were immigrants. Most Americans make a distinction, however, between those who came during the colonial period, who are called colonists, and those who came after the American Revolution, who are called immigrants. In common parlance, therefore, immigration usually refers to the constant flow of new arrivals in the years after the United States achieved its independence and became a nation.

Relatively few immigrants came during the first quarter century of the nation's existence. However, with the end of the Napoleonic Wars and of the related War of 1812 between the United States and Britain, the stream began to flow with increasing force. From 1815 to 1860 approximately five million landed; from 1860 to 1890, ten million; and from 1890 to 1920, 15 million. Of the 106 million citizens of the United States in 1920, almost 14 million had been born abroad, and more than 21 million others were children of those who had made the Atlantic journey to the New World. The vast majority of these were from Europe. As a result of the dislocations caused by the combined effects of increasing population and of the industrial and agricultural revolutions *(Industrial Revolution, Agrarian Revolution*)*, millions left the farms and villages of the Old World in response to the lure of cheap land and economic opportunity in the New. During the 19th century more than three million Englishmen and Scots came to reinforce the basic stock which had constituted three-fourths of the American population at the time of the first national census in 1790; almost six million Germans swelled the substantial number of their fellow countrymen already in the United States; from Ireland came four and a half million, hard hit by such economic ills as the potato famines of the 1840s. As the century went on, more than a million Swedes and Norwegians joined the ever-increasing flood. Almost 800,000 came in the single year of 1882.

With the approaching turn of the century came a shift in the ethnic origins of the immigrants. Until this time, most had come from the countries of northern and western Europe; now, the number from central and eastern Europe and from the Mediterranean nations climbed steeply. There was a corresponding decline in the number from the former countries of origin. During the early years of the 20th century, four-fifths were from eastern and southern backgrounds, a complete reversal of the proportions which had characterized the immigration of a generation before.

This change gave rise, in the studies of the early 20th century, to a distinction between what was called the "old" and the "new" immigrations. It was contended that the new immigrants came for different reasons, were from lower economic and social strata, and were politically and culturally less assimilable than the old. Though national backgrounds were undeniably different, other alleged distinctions were not so great as once supposed; both old and new immigrants were generally poor and uneducated, and most came for the same basic reason: to find greater economic advantages than they had at home.

Nevertheless, the sheer volume of immigration, coupled with the increasing 1
difficulty of assimilating the new arrivals, brought a demand for immigration restriction. During most of the 19th century, the United States government remained more or less neutral with regard to immigration. Despite sporadic outbursts of feeling against immigrants by "nativist" groups *(Parties*)*, there was little fundamental change in the policy enunciated by Secretary of State John Quincy Adams in 1819 which stated that immigrants would be neither encouraged nor discouraged. Coastal states had taken action to limit the entry of paupers, diseased persons, and other undesirables as the immigrant tide rose; but it was not until 1882, after the *Supreme Court** had declared immigration policy to be a federal rather than state responsibility, that *Congress** passed the first immigration act. Other legislation followed, but it, too, was designed to bar only undesirable individuals. The general attitude was still one of welcome expressed in Emma Lazarus's verse inscribed on the base of the Statue of Liberty in 1886:

> "Give me your tired, your poor,
> Your huddled masses yearning to breathe free,
> The wretched refuse of your teeming shore.
> Send these, the homeless, the tempest-tost, to me!
> I lift my lamp beside the golden door."

The only significant exception had to do with Oriental immigrants. Though their numbers were small in comparison with those from European countries, Chinese were barred from permanent admission by the Chinese Exclusion Act of 1882. Later, first through the "Gentlemen's Agreement" of 1907 and then in other legislation, Congress also excluded immigrants from Japan.

The demand for more forceful legislation with regard to European immigrants, sponsored chiefly by the Immigration Restriction League, reached a crescendo after the turn of the century. The principal restrictive device recommended was a literacy test for immigrants. Though vetoed by three presidents, the literacy test was finally passed over Wilson's veto in 1917. Even this was not enough to satisfy critics of mass immigration. Consequently, in the Immigration Act of 1924, Congress adopted the "national origins" principle which was to govern American policy for 40 years. Under this principle, developed in further legislation of the 1920s, the number of immigrants admissible annually from any given country was limited to a very small percentage of the persons of that national origin in the United States population of 1890. Total immigration was restricted to approximately 150,000 per year. The practical result of this legislation was to assign relatively large quotas to countries of the old immigration such as Britain and Germany and very small quotas to countries of the new.

In 1965, on the recommendation of President Johnson, Congress passed a new immigration act which, though it does not substantially raise the total of immigrants admitted each year, puts selection on a basis of individual qualifications and potential contribution to the United States rather than upon the accident of birth. It fixed a quota of 120,000 immigrants a year from the Americas, and 170,000 a year from the rest of the world. No more than 20,000 may come from any single country. But even under the Immigration Act of 1924 and subsequent legislation (the total number of permitted immigrants was reduced to 190,000 in 1929, and under the Immigration and Nationality Act 1952, or McCarran-Walter Act, various political restrictions were imposed) the rules were relaxed from time to time for various categories of refugees. The Refugee Relief Act of 1953 provided for the admission of 219,000 refugees from various Communist-dominated countries. After the Hungarian uprising in 1956, 40,000 Hungarians were given a new home in America, and 600,000 Cubans were admitted after 1959. Also after 1965, the United States continued to make exceptions. About 150,000 refugees from Indochina have come to the United States since 1975. Thus, though the door almost closed during the 1920s has not been reopened, the United States has returned to a policy more in keeping with its earlier idealism. S R Sp

● Already in the 18th century Britain had a large Negro population; in 1731, approximately 20,000 Negroes lived in London alone (total population approximately 700,000); by about 1780 their number had increased to approximately 40,000. They were easily absorbed. It was only after World War II that a heavy immigration of coloured people from the Commonwealth to Britain set in. In 1978 they numbered approx. 1.9 million, mostly Negroes from the West Indies (in 1977 some 543,000), Indians, Pakistanis, among them many from East Africa. The Commonwealth Immigrants Act of 1962 still made it possible for every Commonwealth citizen to immigrate if he could produce proof that he had found employment in Britain or had certain qualifications or skills. On the other hand it first brought immigration under control and contained some discrimination against coloured people in that it excepted the Irish from any control. Under the stipulations of the 1971 Act, the citizens of Eire have lost their special position: at some level they are still simply Celtic inhabitants of the British Isles, at others they are now foreigners. By the Commonwealth Immigrants Act of 1968 control was further extended, especially for Kenyan Asians.

The present system of control was established by the Immigration Act of 1971, which came into full operation on January 1st, 1973, when Britain joined the European Community. It introduced two sets: one governs Commonwealth citizens, the other deals with E.E.C. nationals and other foreign nationals. Five categories of people are distinguished in the rules:

(1) Commonwealth citizens who have a parent born in the United Kingdom ("patrials") have an unrestricted right of abode in the U.K.
(2) Commonwealth citizens with a grandparent born in the United Kingdom may come to work and settle in the U.K. as long as they like; they do not have to obtain a work permit and are not subject to any form of supervision; but they may be refused entry, remain liable to deportation and require an initial entry clearance before coming to the U.K.
(3) Commonwealth citizens who marry women resident in the U.K. or with a right to reside there will be admitted for settlement provided they have a grandparent born there.
(4) The maximum period of stay of young Commonwealth citizens coming to the U.K. for a working holiday is five years; the period for which they are initially admitted is normally 12 months.
(5) The maximum initial period for visitors is ordinarily 6 months, which may be extended if the visitor is able to maintain himself and his dependents for a longer period.
(6) United Kingdom passport holders will be admitted through the special voucher scheme. This rule applies especially to the British Asians from Uganda, Kenya and Tanzania, tens of thousands of whom have been

expelled by their governments. The present position is that 5,000 of these special vouchers are made available each year for British Asians coming to Britain directly from East Africa.

The Bill was soon criticised for worsening the racial situation, especially by coloured people themselves and by all those institutions which were expected to take care of them: the Race Relation Board, the Community Relations Commission, the Select Committee on Race Relations and Immigration, and the Institute of Race Relations (magazine "Race Today").

In 1976, a new Race Relations Act took effect. It makes racial discrimination unlawful in the following spheres: employment; training and related matters; education; housing; the provision of goods, facilities, and services. It extends the existing law to cover discrimination by private clubs with 25 or more members. It makes discriminatory advertisements unlawful and gives alleged victims of discrimination direct access to civil courts and industrial tribunals. Amending the Public Order Act 1936, it strengthens the criminal law against incitement to racial hatred.

A new Commission for Racial Equality has been called into existence by the Act to replace the Race Relations Board and the Community Relations Commission. The former was established under the Race Relations Act 1965. Its task was to secure compliance with this Act. The latter was set up under the Race Relations Act 1968 to deal with problems of "newness" - for example cultural, religious, dietary, and linguistic difficulties; to deal with the consequences of prejudices and discrimination; to attempt to change hostile attitudes among the indigenous population; to develop and maintain contact with ethnic minority groups; to press the government and other institutions to meet the needs of these groups; etc.

There are a number of tenets and principles underlying the Government's policy regarding race relations and immigrants. Among these are (1) the assumption that the vast majority of the coloured population will remain permanently in Britain; (2) the recognition that members of Britain's minorities are entitled to full and equal treatment regardless of their colour, race, or national origin, and that racial discrimination was morally repugnant to a civilized and democratic society; (3) that the character of Britain's coloured population has altered fundamentally since the introduction of the first Race Relations Bill in 1965, when less than one-quarter of the coloured population was born in Britain, whereas in 1977 it was about 40 per cent., and that soon the majority will be British-born; (4) the necessity of a clear limit to the amount of immigration which Britain can absorb, and of its being in the interests of the racial minorities themselves to maintain a strict control over immigration; (5) that only two substantial sources of Commonwealth immigration remain - the close dependants of immigrants settled in Britain, and the United Kingdom passport holders from East Africa.

The fact remains that reality still lags far behind the measures and expectations of both Parliament and Government. A disproportionately large number of coloured peopble live in areas of housing stress; hundreds of racial attacks and acts of violence against coloured people occur every year; ethnic minorities are grossly under-represented in the new and expanding towns; between 1974 and 1977, there has been a 450 per cent. rise in unemployed young coloured workers (15-25 age group) compared with 130 per cent. in the population as a whole; there are "tens of thousands" of cases of direct discrimination in job recruitment every year, and an unskilled West Indian and

Asian candidate faces a one in two chance of discrimination, white collar applicants a one in three chance, and skilled applicants a one in five chance (Political and Economic Planning study 1974).

The relationship between white and coloured people in Britain is difficult also for psychological reasons. Although (according to a Gallup poll of 1977) two-thirds of the whites are willing to regard non-whites born in Britain as British, about half of them believe that the immigrants have harmed the country economically. The poll also found that most British people have no accurate idea of how many non-white immigrants are in Britain; 14 per cent. think there are six times more than there are. On the other hand it seems difficult to improve relationships while many non-whites, certainly most blacks, see themselves exclusively as victims of racism, discrimination, and rejection and as an underclass with no hope. The gap is broadened by the "widely held myth" among whites that the coloured minorities enjoy special advantages and benefits not available to whites (D. J. Smith: The Facts of Racial Disadvantage etc., 1976). - Some of the non-white activists have joined in organizations like the Carribbean Association, the West Indian Standing Conference, the Black Power Party, the Harambee Association, the Indian Workers' Association. There is also an umbrella organization called the National Organization of African, Asian and Carribean People.

History of parliamentary controls on immigration:

1905 Aliens Act. First recognisable modern attempt to limit immigration. It was introduced to control the number of Jews fleeing from Russia and Central Europe.

1914 Aliens Restriction Act. It replaced the Act of 1905. The powers restricting immigration under the Act were to be renewed annually in the form of Orders.

1948 British Nationality Act. Next major piece of legislation crucial to the immigration situation today. It declared that every citizen of every Commonwealth country was also a British subject. Commonwealth citizens who were entitled to come to Britain to settle could automatically acquire United Kingdom citizenship by registering after a given period of residence. The interchangeability of the terms "British citizen" and "Commonwealth citizen"introduced an element of ambiguity and confusion.

1962 Commonwealth Immigrants Act. It was passed after the favourable employment conditions of the 1950s had begun to deteriorate. The Act required Commonwealth citizens, both coloured and white, to obtain a Ministry of Labour employment voucher before coming to Britain. For the first time categories were created: (1) those who had a job to come to; (2) those who had a skill or qualification that was needed in Britain; (3) those who had neither of these; (4) wives and children were given the right to join the head of the household in Britain.

1968 Commonwealth Immigrants Act. The Act was passed within a few days after it had become known that Kenya would urge its Asian citizens to leave the country in order to further "Africanization". The Act introduced an annual voucher system which drastically limited the immigration of East African Asians to 1,500 a year. The statutory right of wives and children to join the head of the household was modified in that it applied to children under 16 and to parents if they were over 65 and entirely dependent of the son or daughter already in Britain.

1971 Immigration Act. It for the first time introduced a concept of "patriality" (see above).

There is currently (1978) a net outflow of people from Britain. Especially the number of West Indians departing outnumbers those coming into Britain. Two schemes assist immigrants wishing to leave. One is run by the International Social Service under the Immigration Act, 1971; it can pay fares of people who wish to return home. The other, founded in 1973, is run by the Department of Health and Social Security; it helps those immigrants who have no prospect of making a success of their lives in Britain to return home, on condition that payment of the fare can ultimately save public funds. H H

Independent Agency

The term includes organizational units called agencies, administrations, corporations, authorities, board, and commissions. It was first applied to the Civil Service Commission in 1883.

■ Independent Agencies of the U.S.A. comprise almost all Federal executive offices not included under the executive departments. Several - such as the National Labor Relations Board and the Civil Aeronautics Board - have reached or even exceeded the magnitude of some departments but they do not have departmental rank. Nevertheless, the heads of some of them sit in the Cabinet by invitation of the President. These agencies were set up by Congress as offices free from partisanship and presidential influence. Indeed, the President's influence on them is far smaller than his influence on the departments. Their heads are usually members of the President's party and appointed by him subject to Senate confirmation. However, appointments are for a stated number of years and the power of the President to remove them is more or less limited. They are part of the "bureaucracy" (the "fourth power") and exercise quasi-legislative, quasi-executive, and quasi-judicial functions. The authority of these agencies is therefore great. Independent Agencies may undertake investigations and make reports at the request of the President, or either branch of Congress, or a congress committee.

The following Independent Agencies rank among the most important and best known: Interstate Commerce Commission, I.C.C., 1887 *(Interstate Commerce*);* National Aeronautics and Space Administration, N.A.S.A., 1958 *(Aviation*);* Smithsonian Institution, 1846; Tennessee Valley Authority, T.V.A., 1933 *(New Deal*);* Cicil Aeronautics Board, 1938 *(Aviation*);* Farm Credit Administration, F.C.A., 1933 *(Agricultural Relief*);* National Labor Relations Board, N.L.R.B., 1935 *(Trade (Labor) Unions*);* Securities and Exchange Commission, S.E.C., 1934 *(New Deal*),* United States Postal Service, 1972 (formerly the Post Office Department).

It is characteristic that many of the Independent Agencies came into existence during the New Deal, when the Federal Government had to assume many new social and economic responsibilities. From time to time new Agencies are created and others abolished. In 1976 there were 87. H H

Indian

Pertaining to the race embracing the aborigines of America, from the usage of Columbus and the people of his day, who believed that the lands he had discovered were a part of India or the East Indies. 1553.

■ Wherever in North America white settlers moved in, they were confronted with the Red Indians, who were of varied linguistic stocks, of which there were at least 55 north of the Rio Grande alone, and who developed different cultures. For nearly 300 years, the relations between whites and Indians were a succession of misunderstandings, broken treaties and massacres. Finally, the whites took possession of almost the whole country, and the surviving Indians were herded on to reservations. Until the 20th century these reservations resembled vast ghettos, and it is only since 1934 that they have developed into a means for the preservation of half-shattered cultures.

(1) Southwestern culture area: Most of this area was inhabited by Pueblos, who were town-dwelling and farming Indian peoples. The Pueblos have never been warlike, yet through their town organizations they managed to survive against nomadic and warlike tribes, like the Apache. Their neighbours, the Navaho, originally nomads and now the most populous tribe in the U.S.A., were probably induced by Pueblos and whites to settle down and become farming and sheep-herding people. The Indians on the southwestern reservations have developed some crafts and arts, like pottery, jewellery-making, blanket-weaving (Navahos).

(2) Intermediate culture area: This area comprises the arid Great Basin, the northern Plateau region, and Central California. The nomadic tribes of this area were among the last to feel the impact of American westward expansion. Their culture was primitive, their religion shamanistic (shaman = medicine man). Their political organization was based on small bands of family units. Tribal life has ceased since the *Frontier** moved across this area.

(3) Northwest culture area: The area of British Columbia and Alaska. Originally it was one of the most unique Indian cultures, sustained without agriculture, dependent entirely on fishing, hunting, and gathering. This area once had the greatest population density in native North America, with relatively high forms of culture. The Northwestern Indians have developed a peculiar art style; their totem poles are famous. After the Russians (1741), the Spanish (1774) and the Anglo-Americans (1786) had arrived, tribal life was gradually destroyed. But there is still a decimated population in this area, occupying mouldering villages.

(4) The Arctic Coast Culture: A relatively small group of Indians, the Eskimo-Aleut, occupied the long northern coast from the Aleutian Islands to Labrador and Greenland. These Indians have the same basic Mongoloid characteristics as the other Indian populations, though with a few distinctive features. They are chiefly hunters and fishermen. They settle in villages, often very large ones, composed of family groups. Their religion is mostly shamanistic; the medicine man establishes their contact with the supernatural universe. Today, a mixed Eskimo population survives, but this has been more influenced by Euro-American culture than has any other Indian stock, although much of the native language, culture, and economy persists.

(5) The Eastern-Northern culture areas: This is a vast area extending from east of the Rocky Mountains to the Atlantic Ocean. It included the famous "Five Civilized Nations" (see below); the Dakotas (or Sioux) were the greatest

tribe there. In this region the buffalo (American bison) was important for food, clothing, tools and weapons. The Indians there were warlike nomads.

The political organization of the Indians was stronger in the southern than in the northern regions. The smallest unit was the family or the clan, with the "moiety" following, then the tribe, and, finally, the "confederacy", a loose grouping of tribes, with certain concepts of the "state". An important confederacy was that of the Creek (1836-1840) in the South, which included tribes speaking six entirely different languages. The most famous was the League of the Iroquois (founded possibly as early as 1570) in the region of New York State; it included the great tribes of the Mohawks, Onondaga, Oneida, Cayuga, Seneca, and, later, Tuscarora Indians. Their historic hero was Hiawatha (cf. Longfellow's "The Song of Hiawatha"). In the French and Red Indian Wars of the 18th century this confederacy was an important ally of the British against the Hurons who sided with the French.

The introduction of the European horse and of firearms made the Indians a dangerous enemy for the white settlers, particularly during the American westward migration in the 19th century when the Indians had reached their greatest military strength. Altogether, most of the 371 Indian treaties were broken by the whites, and over 40 wars were waged against the Indians in the U.S.A., the two earliest being the Pequot War in New England (1636-37) and King Philip's War (1675-77). After 1828 Alabama, Mississippi, Georgia, and Tennessee likewise broke the federal treaties concluded by the U.S. Government since 1791, guaranteeing the Indians their lands. For the Indians a time of suffering and fierce resistance began. It was decided to evacuate the tribes of the Southeast. A Bureau of Indian Affairs was established in 1836, more or less for this purpose. Some tribes fought for their rights (Black Hawk War, 1832; Seminole War, 1835-43) until they were practically exterminated. By 1838 the "Five Civilized Nations" (the Cherokee, the Choctaw, the Chickasaw, the Creek and the Seminole) were being moved over the "Trail of Tears" to the Indian Territory of Oklahoma. The time of the herding of Indians in reservations, which then were little better than large prison camps, had begun. Again and again, the Indians rose in open warfare against the whites: in the Cheyenne Arapaho War (1861-64), the Red River War (1874), the Sioux Wars (1865-67), the Nez Percé War (1877), the Apache War (1871-87) and the Ghost Dance Uprising (1890). In 1887 a change for the better seemed to have come with the passing of the Dawes Severalty Act (General Allotment Act), under which each Indian head of a family could be given 160 acres of land with full ownership; but it was easy to persuade them to sell this land to whites. In 1889 a final act of violence occurred, sanctioned by the Federal Government. Up to that year, whites were forbidden to enter Oklahoma territory. Nevertheless, the Indians were exploited by whisky dealers and other rabble who came in illegally. They eventually rose in rebellion. To punish them, about 20,000 white settlers were allowed (at the firing of an opening gun) to rush over the boundary, stake out claims, and leave Indians to starvation. Even the official policy towards the Indians seemed to follow General Ph. Sheridan's maxim (he had been appointed in 1865 to "pacify" a wide section of the frontier): "There are no good Indians but dead Indians."

But their situation improved in the 20th century. In 1924, they were given American citizenship. In 1934 the Indian Reorganization Act reversed the Dawes Act and authorized the tribes (and not individuals) to hold their land as communal property.

The long-range policy of the United States Government favoured assimilation, calculated to bring Indians into the American mainstream by terminating their special federal relationship. In 1954, several Acts were passed by Congress providing for the termination of federal trusteeship over several tribes in Oregon, California, Texas, and Wisconsin. At the heart of this policy was the assumption that through a gradual process of "acculturation" (adoption of white cultural standards), "social integration" (participation in white social life), and "amalgamation" (intermarriage) the Indians would finally be completely absorbed in American society. If realized, this would have led to the extinction of the Indian race in the U.S.A. So it was only natural that the termination policies of the mid-fifties became the American Indians' common enemy.

Many Indians who gave up their tribal allegiance were unable to make a living (in 1973, the unemployment rate on Indian reservations was 37 per cent., with an additional 18 per cent. employed in merely temporary or seasonal jobs; the national unemployment rate at that time was about 5 per cent.). To help them, Employment Assistance Offices (until 1962 they had been called Relocation Offices) were established in larger cities. Indians who stay on the reservations are under the guardianship of the Bureau of Indian Affaires, which is a branch of the Department of the Interior. In 1975, the Bureau disposed of approx. $ 635,000, most of which was spent on Indian forestry, agriculture, schools, hospitals, arts and crafts, etc. Industry (particularly saw-mills) is encouraged on the reservations and provides some tribes with good incomes.

There are even rich tribes, such as the Navaho, who derive a large income from petroleum.

All this sounds quite encouraging. But the fact remains that most Indians are poor. Those in the Southwest and West merely vegetate. The life expectancy among Indians is still far below American average, and the infant mortality rate is about 20 per cent. above the national average (against 240 per cent. in 1955).

Since the late sixties, when self-confidence among ethnic groups in the U.S.A. began to rise generally, the government of the U.S.A., which is directly responsible for the Indians through the Bureau of Indian Affairs, has felt its responsibility and has begun to help the Indians. Official interest in termination policy faded. It was gradually replaced by the philosophy that "American society can allow many different cultures to flourish in harmony" (Richard Nixon in 1968). In the broader context of the civil rights activities of other minorities, the situation of the Red Indians has improved since the late sixties. The *Civil Rights** Act 1968 repealed action allowing States to extend legal jurisdiction over Indian reservations without tribal consent. Since 1969, it has become the Bureau of Indian Affairs' policy to encourage the formation of Indian school boards and to invite Indian leaders to take over the management of their own schools and other programmes. Since 1970, a number of "home rule" experiments have been under way among Indian tribes, and most tribally-owned land is owned by tribal organizations, not by the American Government. With the help of institutions such as the Native American Rights Fund (NARF), started by the Ford Foundation in 1971, the Pine Tree Legal Assistance and others, several Indian tribes have been able to bring legal action against the United States and individual States for violation of treaties and Acts of Congress, in several cases crowned with success: the Menominees of Wisconsin, whose federal status fell prey to termination policies of the mid-fifties, were restored as a reservation; the Supreme Court guaranteed fishing and hunting rights to a number of non-federally recognized tribes in the State of Washington; the Court also ruled that Indian tribes could sue on their own behalf to recover lost land or damages for land; in 1970, 48,000 acres of land and Blue Lake were returned to the Taos Pueblos; and, most spectacular perhaps, the Alaska Native Claims Settlement Act, 1971, provided for the establishment of regional and village corporations among Indians in Alaska and gave Native title to 40 million acres of land, $ 426,500,000 from the United States over a period of 11 years, as well as an income of $ 500,000 in mineral revenues.

About the same time, some Indians began to realize that they, too, were an underprivileged minority. In 1961, the anthropologist Sol Tax organized the "American Indian Chicago Conference", a meeting of more than 200 chiefs of Indian tribes. The most important outcome of this conference was the "Declaration of Indian Purpose" ("We, the majority of the Indian people of the United States, . . . have the inherent right of self-government . . . and the same right of sovereignty. . . . It is the universal desire among all Indians that their treaties and trust-protected lands remain intact and beyond the reach of predatory men . . . to regain in the America of the space age some measure of the adjustment they enjoyed as the original possessors of their native land", quoted from William Meyer). In the same year, the "National Indian Youth Council" was founded, a progressive, rather militant organization demanding self-determination and self-help. "Indianness" became a slogan among activists. The "Fish-ins" in the State of Washington in 1964 were the first real protest action of several tribes against the annulment of guaranteed fishing rights. In 1969, a group of Indians occupied the island of Alcatraz (San Francisco Bay) and, in a proclamation "to the Great White Father and All His People" offered to purchase it "for twenty-four dollars ($ 24) in glass beads and red cloth, a precedent set by the white man's purchase of a similar island about 300 years ago". In 1972, a band of Indians occupied the offices of the Bureau of Indian Affairs in Washington, D.C., causing considerable damage. In 1973, members of A.I.M. (see below) occupied Wounded Knee (originally a little creek in S. Dakota, where, in 1890, about 200 Indians were shot by soldiers). By 1970, "Red Power" had come into existence as a militant Indian movement. Among its aims are "tribal nationalism" and "power over our own lives" (Vine Deloria Jr. in 1966, quoted from Stan Steiner). The American Indian Movement (A.I.M.), supported by about 10 per cent. of American Indians, is the militant arm of Red Power. It was founded in 1968 as a defence organization. Russell Means, its leader, denounces the official policy of the United States towards the Indians as that of a colonial power. A.I.M. has also initiated programmes to train Indians for jobs, to fight alcoholism among them, and to give them legal advice. The movement is a member of the United Farm Workers Union, the Chicanos' union. - There are some other, less militant, pan-Indian organizations in the U.S.A.: the National Council of American Indians (1944), thc American Indian Defense Association, the Indian Welfare Committee of the General Federation of Women's Clubs, and the Indian Rights Association. A number of Indian newspapers, such as "Akwesasne Notes", "Warpath", and "ABC" (i.e. Americans before Columbus) help to voice the American Indians' claims and try to convince the other Americans that Columbus discovered America when it already contained civilized inhabitants.

H H

Isolationism

■ Policy of maintaining a nation's rights and interests without alliances, not allowing any foreign interferences into the national affairs, at the same time, in international relations, the policy of non-involvement in the affairs of other nations, indicated by the abstention or withdrawal of a nation from international agreements, treaties, and commitments. 1899.

Isolationism was the essence of the foreign policy pursued by the U.S. towards Europe from 1800 to 1917 and between World War I and II. It was based on the conception that Europe and the Americas constitute two separate spheres of political activities and should have as little to do with one another as possible; the geographical insularity of the country and its preoccupation with domestic affairs made it possible for the United States to stay out of the entangling alliances prompted by the balance of power politics of the European States.

For the first time this American policy of no interference in European affairs was declared by President Washington on September 19th, 1796, in his "Farewell Address" in which he advised the Americans to steer clear of foreign entanglements. This principle was incorporated into the so-called Monroe Doctrine, proclaimed by President James Monroe on December 2nd, 1823, where it was linked up with the rejection of European interference into American affairs. Recalling the two separate spheres of policy established for the New World and the Old World, he declared: "In the wars of the European powers, in matters relating to themselves, we have never taken part, nor does it comport with our policy to do so. It is only when our rights are invaded, or seriously menaced that we resent injuries, or make preparations for our defence" *(Doctrine*)*.

Throughout the 19th century and still into the 20th, the isolationist policy of the U.S.A. was successfully pursued. Isolation was continued until the U.S.A. felt provoked by the German submarine warfare in 1917, declared war against Germany and entered the first World War, convinced that a German victory would be disastrous for democracy all over the world.

But after the war, when American rights and interests seemed no longer menaced, the U.S., rejecting the Treaty of Versailles of 1919 as incompatible with their ideals and thus not entering the League of Nations, retired into complete diplomatic isolation, stressing this attitude by the neutrality legislation of 1935 to 1937.

In face of the growth of fascism in Europe President Franklin D. Roosevelt tried to overcome this isolationist attitude of the Americans, and again and again he pointed out that the changing geopolitical situation no longer allowed the U.S. to live without allies and to remain in neutrality. But all his attempts remained in vain. Finally the Japanese attack on Pearl Harbour, December 7th, 1941, and the following declaration of war against the U.S.A. by Hitler made the Americans definitely give up isolationism and enter the second World War.

Even after World War II, when the United States came to play a central role in world politics, there was still continuing resistance against such a policy. Those who advocated a more limited, if not an isolationist policy for the United States, feared that the burdens of keeping international peace by security pacts with other nations and the provision of economic and military aid to them might deprive the country of the financial means needed to overcome domestic problems. But in spite of such criticism American foreign policy since World War II has been based on the firm consciousness that another American flight into isolationism has become impossible. PH

Labour Party

● The Labour Party is one of Britain's two major *Parties**. Its history began when the Conservatives and the Liberals were already firmly established. Originally it was a working-class party rooted in trade unionism. The party as a whole, however, has never been Marxist or revolutionary, but evolutionary and "Fabian" (see below). 1906.

The platform of the Labour Party set out in detail in "Labour's Programme for Britain 1976", a party document intended to be of continuing validity, is less doctrinaire than it was when the party was young. It advocates an evolutionary socialism to be achieved through the nationalization of key sectors of the economy and the accumulation of a wide range of equity holdings in industry and the full development of a "mixed economy", the establishment and extension of a national *health service**, of *social security**, of an egalitarian system of education favouring the *comprehensive school** (at the expense of the selective system based on *eleven plus** tests, the *public schools** and the direct-grant schools), limited *devolution** of powers to new assemblies for Scotland and Wales, and the reduction of defence costs. Although the party has officially declared its lasting commitment to the European Community (which it has never considered as being anything beyond an economic cummunity), there is a substantial minority who do not conceal their dislike of Britain's membership.

The left wing of the party is represented by the "Tribune" group and the Young Socialists (members to the age of twenty-five), both with a leaning towards Marxist ideas; it demands further nationalization, for example of the *Big Four** (the leading British private banks), of the seven biggest insurance companies, of all the motor insurance market; some would even like to see the 25 biggest private firms put into the hands of the State. - The right wing of the party is represented by the Social Democratic Alliance, which emphasizes that the Labour Party is rooted in the tradition of radicalism, free co-operation, non-conformity, and Christian socialism and owes nothing to Marx, Engels, Lenin, Stalin, Trotsky, Mao, and Castro.

The organization of the party is much the same as that of the *Conservative Party**. A National Executive Committee controls the Central Office of the party, commonly called Transport House (which is the name of the building in which it is housed). The Trade Unions are the main source of the party's finances. In accordance with the Trade Union Act of 1913 they - as organizations - may become members of the Labour Party, where they have a great preponderance of the votes and can even operate a block vote at the annual Labour Party Conferences. The leader of the party is elected annually by the Parliamentary Labour Party led by the "Parliamentary Committee" consisting of five full-time and 12 elected members of the Commons and one member of the Lords.

Candidates for national elections are chosen in a way differing somewhat from that prevailing in the Conservative Party and the *Liberal Party**. The local Labour executive committee, which runs the local party association, asks affiliated organizations, such as Trade Union branches, the *Co-operative Societies**, and various other socialist bodies, to submit names. It then makes a choice of candidates and recommends them to a local general meeting. The choice of the general meeting requires the approval of the National Executive Committee, this being necessary since the candidate, who is not always a member of the Labour Party, must commit himself to abide by the standing orders of the Parliamentary Labour Party *(Conservative Party*)*. There is an annual party congress.

The Labour Party was a direct consequence of the Reform Act of 1867 *(Suffrage*)*. Workers began to organize in unions *(Trade (Labor) Unions*)*, which tried to get some of their members into the Commons. In 1869 the Labour Representation League was founded. In 1874 the Unions returned their first two members to Parliament. In 1886 the Labour Electoral Committee was founded, renamed in 1887 Labour Electoral Association. An efficient party organization came into being when the Independent Labour Party was founded in 1893. In 1900 the so-called Labour Representation Committee was founded. It was a merger of four Labour groups in Britain: the Trade Unions, the Independent Labour Party, the Social Democratic Federation (similar to the continental Social Democrats), and the Fabian Society.

The Fabian Society, founded in 1883 by a group of intellectuals, still exerts a great influence on the party's policy. Sidney Webb, G. B. Shaw, H. G. Wells and Ramsay MacDonald were among its early members. Prominent members of the Fabian Society today are Denis Healey, Anthony Wedgewood-Benn, and Roy Jenkins. The name derives from Quintus Fabius Cunctator (the "Delayer") and indicates the non-revolutionary strategy of the society. The present Labour party was founded in 1906. In the same year it returned 29 members to the House of Commons, and in 1910 there were already as many as 42. In 1918 the Labour Party, represented by 57 Members of Parliament, became the official Opposition. In 1923 it gained 191 seats and formed its first government under MacDonald. This minority government failed as did his Cabinet of 1929-31, his attempt of that year to create a National Labour Party, and the subsequent coalition government of 1931-35. From 1940 until 1945 Labour formed a wartime coalition government with the Conservatives and Liberals, from which the party emerged as the strongest. It formed the Government from 1945 to 1951 under Attlee; from 1964 to 1970 and 1974 to 1976 under Wilson, and from 1976 under Callaghan. H H

Liberal Party

● The Liberal Party is the descendant of the Whig Party. The change of its name into Liberal Party, used officially by Lord Russell in 1839, implied that the issues of the old Whig Party had become irrelevant (at that time "liberal" still had the meaning of "radical"; in its present connotation it was not used before about 1860) *(Parties*)*.

Today it is difficult for the Liberals to formulate a programme giving the party a face of its own. In general terms their programme follows their great tradition of the 19th century. They put their faith in the development of social services and the value of individual freedom. But it was their sensational rescue of the Labour Government in March 1977 ("Lib-Lab pact") through which they were able to regain a clear-cut profile and to set themselves apart from the two great parties. For the vast majority of their supporters the Conservatives have always been the main enemy and the Labour Party their natural ally. Only once did the Liberals support a Conservative government - that of Mr. Eden's over Suez in 1956.

Today, the party advocates proportional representation in Britain and in direct elections to a European parliament; devolution of powers to Scottish and Welsh assemblies, and a new *Bill of Rights** for the better protection of the citizen. It has always been in favour of Britain's entry into the European Community and was the first to stand up for greater autonomy for Scotland, Wales and Northern Ireland. It attributes the greatest priority to Britain's economic recovery and for that reason it committed itself to the Labour Government in 1977; but it is decidedly against any further nationalization plan. On the whole, the Liberal Party of today attracts many people who cannot persuade themselves to subscribe to the policies of either of the two leading parties. The young Liberals are moving far on the party's left, demanding that the party declare itself unequivocally opposed to the whole mechanism of capitalism.

The Liberal Party's support in the country is much greater than is reflected by its representation in the House of Commons. Since the elections of 1950 the Liberal Party has never had more than 14 members in the House of Commons. The British electoral system places the Liberal Party at a gross disadvantage *(Constituency*)*.

The party holds annual national conferences("Assemblies") to which the local party associations send their delegates. The Parliamentary Liberal Party elects the leader. He presides over the Party Committee which lays down the policies of the party inside and outside Parliament. Candidates for national elections are chosen in a way very similiar to that prevailing in the *Conservative Party**.

The Liberal Party was previously the party of reform and remained so until the Labour Party took its place in the second decade of the 20th century. It was mainly responsible for the important reform measures of the 9th and the early 20th century, for instance the abolition of slavery in 1833, the *Suffrage** reform, the introduction of the ballot *(Poll*)*, the educational reform of 1870 *(Primary Education*)*, the legalization of the Trade Unions of 1871 *(Trade (Labor) Unions*)*, the army reform of 1871, the early reform of the Empire (partial self-government to India, 1882-83, the Morley-Minto reforms of 1908-09, autonomy to South Africa, 1909), and the taxation reform of 1909, which led to the radical parliamentary reform of 1911 *(Lords*)*. The Liberal Party was intimately associated with the cause of Irish *Home Rule** which, however, was never effectively implemented. In 1916, a time when it could look into the future with the greatest pride and confidence, the party broke apart into the Asquith and the Lloyd George factions, and, after the war, it had to cede its place to the Labour Party. After a short reunion in 1926, the party split in 1931 into three groups (Sir John Simon, Sir Herbert Samuel, Lloyd George).

H H

Lobby

A passage or corridor often used as a waiting place or ante-room. 1553. In the House of Commons and other houses of legislature, a large entrance-hall open to the public, and chiefly used for interviews between members and non-members of the House. 1640. The term is now also used for those who frequent parliamentary entrance halls in order to influence members of the legislature to vote for or against impending legislation. 1859. In the U.S.A. this connotation of the term originated in the 1830s.

In countries with representative governments it has long been customary for the public to influence law-making by directly applying to the members of the legislature. Formerly done in secret and often entailing bribery and corruption, modern lobbying is generally conducted openly, and it is now usually highly organized. Lobbying in general is not an evil; it is, in fact, often useful since interest groups are often better informed than legislators about the interest they represent.

■ The political life of the U.S.A. in particular has been increasingly characterized by group politics. In that country there are hundreds of interest groups which determine politics at least as much as do the political parties. Any of these interest groups can turn overnight into a pressure group (i.e. a group which brings its particular interest to bear by exerting pressure upon the Government through its lobby) whenever it feels its interests are being prejudiced. It may use the methods it may deem appropriate for the circumstances within the limits of their resources and ethical outlook. If a group loses a round in Congress, it may continue to fight in the *independent agency** charged with the execution of some piece of legislation, or in the courts. A year or two later it may resume its activity in Congress. this process can continue indefinitely.

The following is a random selection of powerful American interest groups all of which have their particular lobby: the labor unions, the co-operatives, about 200 religious organizations, the public interest lobby groups like Common Cause and the Ralph Nader organization, the U.S. Conference of Mayors/National League of Cities, the petroleum industry, the American Legion, the newspapers, the parents' organizations, the loan companies, the textile industry, the T.V. companies, not forgetting the gun lobby. The lobbying of some groups has considerably influenced the political life in the U.S.A., e.g. the China Lobby, the tariff lobby of the farmers' unions, the temperance organizations *(Prohibition*)*, the National St. Lawrence Project Conference, the American Israel Public Affairs Committee (AIPAC), etc.

Corrupt practices could be stopped only during the first years after the passing of the Regulation of Lobbying Act (included in the Legislative Reorganization Act of 1946 *(Committee*)*. In reporting a bill in 1976, to replace the Act of 1946, the Senate Government Operations Committee stated that only 20 to 40 per cent. of those who should register as lobbyists do so, and that only 1 per cent. of all the money spent on lobbying in Washington is reported. Though hearings have taken place in the House Committee on Standards and Official Conduct and the House Judiciary Subcommittee on Administrative Law and Government Relations between 1971 and 1977, no improved lobbying bill is in sight yet.

● Since the early sixties at least the importance of lobbies has also been on the increase in British politics. Backbenchers of the House of Commons have become the target for hundreds of them. But there are also powerful bodies that can afford virtually to ignore backbenchers simply because they have direct access to ministries and governments. Such bodies are the Trades Union Congress, the National Farmers' Union, and the Confederation of British Industry. But even apart from these, the farming, banking, building, and big business lobbies are powerful enough to influence the government's policy. It should also be noticed that in the House of Commons there are many members with clearly identifiable business interests (in July 1970 there were 18, *The Times*, July 3rd, 1970.)

H H

Local Government 1

The administration of the affairs of a town, city, county, etc., by the inhabitants, as distinct from the state at large. 1688.

- The present system of local government in Britain is ultimately based on the Reform Act of 1832 *(Suffrage*)* and is the result of numerous subsequent Acts of Parliament beginning with the Poor Law of 1834 and the Municipal Corporations Act of 1835. The others are: (1) The Local Government Act of 1888 which set up *County** councils and transferred to them the powers of the *Justices of the Peace** who until then administered the counties. It also established the county boroughs and made them independent of the county councils. (2) The Local Government Act of 1894 which established urban *District** councils, rural district councils, *Parish** councils, and parish meetings. (3) The Local Government Act of 1933 which created a uniform constitutional code for local authorities. (4) The Local Government Act of 1958 which set up Local Government Commissions for England and Wales. (5) The London Government Act of 1963 which came into effect in 1965 and reorganized the government of *Greater London**. (6) The Local Government Act 1972, effective in 1974, introduced some major changes in the organization and the responsibilities of local government units in England and Wales. The old three-tier structure was replaced by two tiers comprising (a) the county, (b) the district. In reality, however, the system is more complicated. There are two types of county: (1) the six metropolitan counties of Greater Manchester (with ten metropolitan districts), Merseyside (five), South Yorkshire (four), Tyne and Wear (five), West Midlands (seven), and West Yorkshire (five), all representing the great conurbations in England. (2) The non-metropolitan counties (England 39, Wales 8) comprising the less densely populated or rural counties.

The districts, too, comprise two categories: (1) the metropolitan districts which lie within the territory of the metropolitan counties, and (2) the non-metropolitan districts.

The Act of 1972 reduced the number of local authorities in England and Wales by two-thirds and provided for larger and more populous units that are financially stronger and capable of enlarged responsibilities, which, e.g. include for the districts: the maintenance of district roads, operation of municipal transport undertakings, environmental health matters, and a greater say in local planning.

The government of Greater London is not affected by the Local Government Act of 1972.

After long parliamentary discussions it was resolved that the parish should survive as a local government unit.

The Local Authority (Scotland) Act of 1973, effective 1975, provided for a two-tier system, like that of England and Wales, comprising (a) 9 regions, (b) 53 districts. Orkney, Shetland, and the Western Isles (i.e. the Hebrides) remain outside the unified structure and have a single, all-purpose authority each. The regions (excluding the island areas) are: Highland, Grampian, Tayside, Fife, Lothian, Central, Borders, Strathclyde, and Dumfries and Galloway.

Like in England and Wales, the first-tier authorities (regions) are to be responsible for the major and strategic services; the second-tier authorities (districts) are to carry out the more local functions (see *County*, District**).

At a more local level than the districts there are the community councils. They represent a form of direct democracy best to be compared with that of the parish meeting in England. Their function is be to co-ordinate and express the views of the community which it represents and, perhaps, to take action in the interest of that community. Any 30 or more electors may claim to have a community council elected for an area. The council has no statutory powers, but it can receive public secretarial and financial assistance *(Parish*)*.

In 1971 the Government indicated that a reform of local government in Northern Ireland would probably follow the English pattern, but no local government bill (Northern Ireland) has yet been introduced in Parliament.

Chart of Local Government in England, Wales and Northern Ireland

1st tier	2nd tier
metropolitan county (council) (6)	metropolitan district (council) (36)
non-metropolitan county (council); In Wales: county (council) } (47)	non-metropolitan district (council); In Wales: district (council) } (296)
Greater London (council) (1)	(council of) Greater London borough (32)
	parish (council)
	parish (meeting)
	In Wales: community meeting

Former system of Local Government in England and Wales (in force till March 31, 1974)

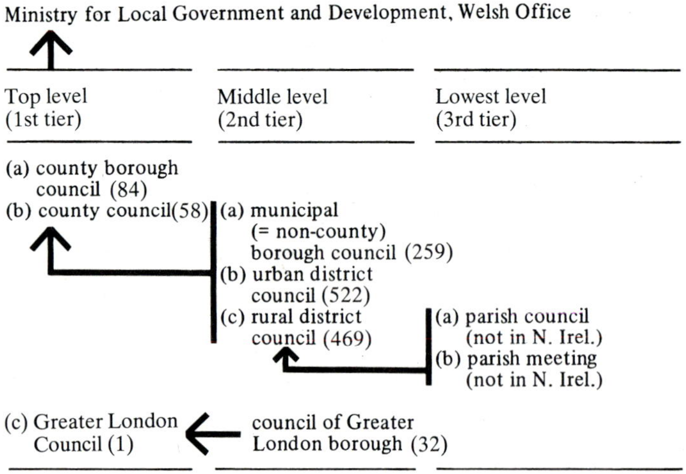

HH

■ The Constitution of the U.S.A. has not vested in the Federal Government any powers which concern local government. Every State, in accordance with Amendment X of the Constitution, has the right to exercise powers of government so far as they are not prevented by the Constitution. Thus *County, Town and Township**, village, and *City** governments form parts of the State system, are created by State constitutions or laws and are subject to change by the forces which made them. The American system of local government is therefore most diversified (see chart). 1

H H

Chart of Local Government in Scotland

1st tier	2nd tier
region (9) (regional council)	district (council) (53)
island areas (3) (islands council)	community council (non-statutory)

System of Local Government in Scotland (in force until May 15, 1975

(Scottish Office)

↑

Top level (1st tier)	Second level (2nd tier)
(a) county of a city council (4) (b) large burgh (town) council (197) (c) county council (33)	
←	(a) small burgh (town) council (b) district council } (198)

Chart of Local Government in the U.S.A.

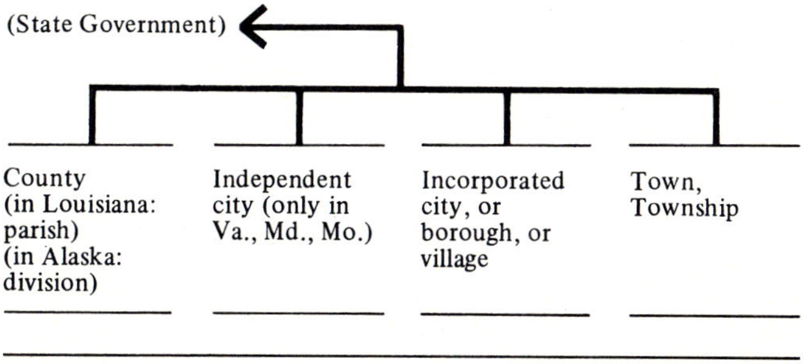

Peers of the realm or those who by courtesy are entitled to the prefix Lord; or some higher title, as a part of their ordinary appellation; the Lords: the Lords of Parliament, as constituting one of the two bodies composing the legislative power of the United Kingdom. 1451.

● The Lords of Parliament constitute the upper chamber of the British Parliament, which is referred to as the "House of Lords", the "Upper House", the "Second Chamber" (formerly the first chamber). The number of members constantly changes; at present it is approx. 1100. They fall into two main groups: (a) The Lords Spiritual: they were originally the great dignitaries of the Church such as the bishops and principal abbots. Their numbers declined after the dissolution of the monasteries (1537-40), and now there are no more than 43, who represent only the *Established Church** of England. They are the Archbishops of Canterbury (Lord Primate of All England) and York (Lord Primate of England), the bishops of Winchester, London and Durham, and 21 other diocesan bishops in order of seniority of appointment. They are "official Lords of Parliament", i.e. they hold neither hereditary nor life peerages, their peerages expiring as soon as they retire from their sees. (b) The Lords Temporal: these are (1) the hereditary Peers who are the heads of noble families with hereditary titles, (2) the Lords of Appeal in Ordinary, up to 11 in number, who hold life peerages and constitute the highest appelate court *(Law Lords*),* (3) Life Peers who are appointed by the monarch, upon advice of the Prime Minister, for life. Their existence is based on the Life Peerages Act of 1958, an attempt to modernize the House of Lords. In 1969 the Lords received their first coloured peer, Lord Constantine, former cricket player and High Commissioner of Trinidad and Tobago.

Among the hereditary peers a distinction is made between (a) the Peers of England (with peerages created before the union of the English and the Scottish Parliaments in 1707); (b) the Peers of Great Britain (with peerages created between 1707 and 1801); (c) the Peers of the United Kingdom (with peerages created from 1801 on, in which year the union with Ireland took place); all Peers of England, Great Britain and the United Kingdom are entitled to a seat in the House of Lords; (d) the Peers of Scotland, who under the Act of Union of 1707 are represented by a maximum of 16 Lords chosen by the Scottish Peers for the duration of each Parliament; (e) the Peers of Ireland, who until 1922 were represented by a maximum of 28 Lords. As no new peerages of Scotland are created now, the number of Scottish Peers is likely to decrease.

Since 1832 when the Lords were first defeated in connection with the Reform Act of that year *(Parliament*)* their political power gradually decreased with every Reform Act (1867, 1884). Nevertheless, they still had the power to veto bills of the Commons as they actually did, for instance in 1906 and 1908 (education bills) and in 1909 (budget of the then Liberal Government). In 1911, therefore, the Commons passed the Parliament Act which the Lords accepted when Asquith (Liberal Prime Minister from 1908 to 1916) threatened a mass creation of (Liberal) Peers which would have shifted the balance in the House of Lords in favour of Liberal policy.

The Parliament Act of 1911 was a milestone in English constitutional history. It provided that (1) the Lords should have no right to veto a money bill *(Bill*);* (2) any other bill should become law after being passed in three successive sessions of the Commons, even if vetoed by the Lords, on condition that two years had elapsed since its first introduction (in another Parliament Act (of 1949) the Labour government reduced this veto to one year); (3) the maximum life of Parliament should be five years instead of seven. Thus, the House of Lords has become a second chamber with very little power. The Lords, however, have received a new impulse through the Life Peerages Act of 1958, which has brought an increasing number of persons of merit and distinction into the upper house. On the other hand the Peerage Act of 1963, which makes it possible for Peers to lay down their hereditary titles and thus become Commoners, has led to a heavy drain on the Lords. 1

The functions appropriate to the Lords may be defined as follows: (1) The examination and revision of bills brought from the Commons, a function much needed, since the *Commons** are under rules limiting debate, while the Lords are not. (2) The initation of bills dealing with subjects of comparatively non-controversial character. (3) The interposition of so much delay in the passing of a bill into law as may be needed to enable the opinion of the nation to be adequately expressed. This delay can be a check against rash actions on the part of the government. (4) Full and free discussion of important questions at moments when the Commons may happen to be so much occupied that they cannot find sufficient time for them. Parliamentary procedure is much the same as in the Commons. The main difference lies in the power of the Lord Chancellor who as *Speaker** of the Lords has no controlling authority and no casting vote. The quorum is three; on questions relating to bills and to delegation of legislative power it is 30. From time to time, and especially when a Labour Government is in power, proposals are made for a more or less radical reform of the House of Lords which has always had a built-in Conservative majority.

H H/J L F

Louisiana Purchase

■ The Louisiana Purchase was the first among the great land acquisitions of the U.S.A. It introduced the territorial expansion towards the Pacific Coast and beyond. 1803.

This westward movement tock place in the following stages: (1) Louisiana Purchase (1803), (2) Florida Purchase (1819), (3) Annexation of Texas (1845), (4) acquisition of Oregon (1846), (5) Mexican Cession (1848), (6) Gadsden Purchase (1853), (7) Alaska Purchase (1867), (8) acquisition of Hawaii and the Philippines (1898).

In 1763 Britain acquired the whole of the French possessions as far as the Mississippi, i.e. New France (St. Lawrence and Great Lakes regions) and eastern Louisiana (the region between the Mississippi and the Appalachians). Britain did not obtain the whole of Louisiana (which would have been an additional area nearly eight times as large as Britain) since in 1762, just before the end of the war, France, by the Treaty of Fontainebleau, had transferred New Orleans and all of Louisiana west of the Mississippi to Spain. In 1783 the U.S.A. became heir to this eastern part of Louisiana, and the Northwest Ordinance of 1787 encouraged settlement there *(Conservation of Land*)*. Since the Mississippi formed the natural outlet for the western section of the U.S.A., the possession of New Orleans by a foreign power could not be looked upon favourable by the U.S.A., the more so as Spain surrendered western

Louisiana to France by the secret Treaty of San Ildefonso in 1800. Fortunately for the U.S.A., Britain declared war on France in 1803. Pressed by the need of money to carry on the war against the British and also fearful that Louisiana might fall into their hands, Napoleon sold the entire territory to the U.S.A. in 1803 for 60 million francs. The purchase of 827,129 square miles of land almost doubled the area of the U.S.A. (888,811 square miles). The treaty, however, did not define the exact boundaries to the north and the west and there was no clear understanding as to whether the cession included West Florida and Texas.

In 1818, the northern boundary of Louisiana was settled by treaty with Britain. The claims to Florida were settled in 1819 by the Adams-Onís Treaty by which Spain ceded East Florida to the U.S.A. and renounced all claims to West Florida (total area of Florida: 58,560 square miles). The latter had been occupied by U.S. troops in 1813 during the British-American War of 1812-14.

The Texas question was settled in 1845. Since 1821, it had been a province of Mexico, but was increasingly settled by people from the southern U.S.A., who, in 1836, established the Republic of Texas by forceful secession from Mexico. In 1845, at the request of these Texans, the U.S.A. annexed the "Lone Star State" (390,144 square miles). The problem of the northwestern boundary of Louisiana became irrelevant owing to the Oregon Treaty of 1846. In the Oregon country and (British) Columbia, Spain, Russia, Britain, and the U.S.A. had had conflicting plans. Spain's claims were eliminated by the treaty of 1819 (see obove); Russia relinquished hers in 1824; by the treaty of 1818 (see above) Britain and the U.S.A. agreed to joint occupation of the territory, and in 1846, the 49th parallel was accepted as the dividing line between the two nations (area gained by the U.S.A.: 285,580 square miles).

The remaining western boundary of the Louisiana area was fixed by the Treaty of Guadalupe Hidalgo, 1848, ending the War with Mexico, 1846-48. The war had been started by the U.S.A. over boundary disputes connected with the annexation of Texas. In the peace treaty of 1848, Mexico ceded New Mexico and California (including the present States of N.M., Calif., parts of Utah, Nev., Ariz., Col.; total area 529,017 square miles). In the Gadsden Purchase of 1853 the present boundary between the U.S.A. and Mexico was fixed (area added: 29,640 square miles).

The later territorial gains bear no direct relation to the Louisiana Purchase; and whereas the acquisitions before the Civil War were somehow connected with the slavery question, those after the war were the result of an increasing involvement of the U.S.A. in world-wide imperialism. *(Missouri Compromise*).*

The purchase of Alaska in 1867 was the work of an ardent expansionist, William H. Seward, Secretary of State under Lincoln and Johnson. Russia considered Alaska as an economic liability and accepted $ 7,2 million as a purchase price. Many Americans regarded this acquisition as a folly (Seward's Folly) and the Russian ambassador was able to secure adoption by Congress only by buying votes.

The Hawaiian island group (or Sandwich Islands) was annexed in 1897 and then used as a military base in the Spanish-American War of 1898. The Philippines fell to the U.S.A. in the Peace Treaty of Paris of the same year for the payment of $ 20 million, and for the first time in history the U.S.A. was faced with the problems of colonial administration. The westward movement, started with the acquisition of eastern Lousiana and the purchase of western Louisiana, had ended in Asia.

It was in connection with the acquisition of Texas that "Manifest Destiny" entered American politics. The phrase was the theme of the expansionists who believed that it was God's will that the U.S.A. should expand its territory and sphere of influence from the Atlantic to the Pacific. It was used by politicians who urged the acquisition of Mexican territory after the war of 1846/48. It was heard in demands for Oregon, the desire for Cuba in the 1850s, the purchase of Alaska, and the annexation of Hawaii. Manifest Destiny combined democratic ideals, pride in Anglo-Saxon achievement, and opposition against European ambitions in the Americas; but it did have imperialist and mercenary overtones. - The term first appeared in the "Democratic Review", July/August 1845, in an article on the annexation of Texas. H H 1

Mayflower Compact

■ A document on the rules of a communal system signed in the cabin of the Mayflower by 41 adults (35 of them "Saints", or "Pilgrim Fathers" as they were called two centuries later in reference to the religious background of their emigration) off Cape Cod, shortly before their landing at the place where they established their first settlement, Plymouth. 1620.

The Mayflower Compact as a solemn written aggreement signed on November 11th, 1620, by 41 English settlers on the American continent, contained a draft for the formation of a democratic community. It represented an early realization of the idea that the relations within any "body politick" should be based on a "compact" (or contract, or covenant). It also anticipated the "contract-theories" of Grotius, Hobbes, Locke, Rousseau and Paine.

Of the 102 Mayflower passengers 35 where separatists (i.e. from the English Established Church) who had emigrated to Holland. When it became evident that it would be difficult for them to preserve their separate community life and their English nationality, they decided to lay a foundation "for the propagating and advancing the gospell of the Kingdom of Christ in those remote parts of the world" and went to America *(Congregationalist*)*.

After having signed their compact aboard the Mayflower, in which they promised each other to combine their efforts towards a "civil Body Politick", to be altered or improved "from time to time" according to any new requirements arising, they started life in the New World under the hardest conditions, in strictest pursuance of their faith. From the very beginning they built up their community according to their Calvinist ideas. Their first administrative measure was the creation of "townships", which were to become the very nucleus of any further constitutional development. These townships with their old political practice of "town-meetings" are still kept up in some northern states of the U.S.A. as a matter of tradition. Some Americans nowadays take pride in tracing their ancestry back to these New England settlers *(Establishment, New England*)*. Societies like the "Mayflower Descendants" (founded in New York in 1894, about six thousand members) uphold their traditions.

The Mayflower Compact was the model for other colonies, especially in New England, to enter into similar contracts. The idea lived on in the recommendation of the Continental *Congress** to the Thirteen Colonies *(Stars and Stripes*)* in 1775 to form governments which were then based on constitutions. The United States *Constitution** of 1789 may be called a descendant of the Mayflower Compact. H H/E V

Melting Pot

A pot in which metals or other substances are melted or fused. Loosely applied to a country in which immigrants of various races are united in citizenship. 1916.

■ The theory of American society as a "melting pot" which fuses persons from many different national and racial backgrounds into a "new breed" entirely different from any of the old dates from colonial times. Referring to "that strange mixture of blood, which you will find in no other country," Hector St. Jean de Crèvecoeur declared in 1782 ("Letters from an American Farmer") that in America "individuals of all nations are melted into a new race of men".

Ralph Waldo Emerson stated the theory in classic terms a half-century later: "As in the old burning of the Temple at Corinth, by the melting and intermixture of silver and gold and other metals a new compound more precious than any, called Corinthian brass, was formed; so in this continent, asylum of all nations, the energy of Irish, Germans, Swedes, Poles, and Cossacks, and all the European tribes, of the African, and of the Polynesians, will construct a new race, a new religion, a new state, a new literature . . .".

A play entitled "The Melting Pot" written in 1908 by Israel Zangwill and produced in the early years of the 20th century when *Immigration** policy was a subject of heated discussion, helped to popularize the phrase. A catchy figure of speech, it has been commonly accepted as a description of the process through which millions of immigrants were assimilated and transformed into Americans by their adopted country. The fact is that the melting pot has worked only imperfectly, though any judgement as to its historical validity depends partly upon definition. While it is not a precise term, it usually implies not merely the fusion of two or more cultural heritages, but the biological mixture of racial and national stocks to such an extent that the originals become indistinguishable one from the other.

Considered in this light, the melting pot functioned only until the middle of the nineteenth century. The predominant national stocks which went to the United States during the 17th, 18th, and early 19th centuries - English, Scottish, Scots-Irish, Dutch, German, and French - did indeed melt together into a mixture indistinguishable both biologically and culturally; but even with these, the process was one in which the non-English cultures for the most part gave way to the English in what has been called by sociologists "Anglo-conformity".

The melting pot ceased to operate, however, when other national groups, first the Irish and later many others, began their migrations to the United States. These groups have accepted basic American values and American institutions, and so have undergone a behavioural assimilation, or acculturation; but they have not all "melted" biologically.

Evidence now indicates, therefore, that American society during the past hundred years cannot be looked upon as a single melting pot. A more accurate modern concept is that of a number of melting pots rather than one. Furthermore, the three principal melting pots are determined not so much by national origins as by religious affiliations. Thus Protestants, *Roman Catholics**, and *Jews** tend to marry within their own communities of faith, submerging former national traits and loyalties only within these invisible boundaries *(Freedom of Religion*)*.

That the melting pot has never operated perfectly, even during the early history of the United States, is demonstrated by the fact that some groups have remained beyond the limits of the melting pot experience, single or multiple. These are such stocks as American Indians, Chinese, Japanese, and Negroes, whose distinct physical characteristics make the loss of identity difficult. Negroes, who now constitute over 10 per cent. of the population, have rarely if ever been popularly considered within the scope of the melting pot theory despite the fact that they have been in America longer than the 19th century immigrant groups, like the majority of Americans are overwhelmingly Protestant, and accept in thoroughgoing fashion American traditions and values. 1

Today the melting pot concept, imperfect as it has been in practice, is also questioned in theory by persons who ask whether equality of opportunity and participation in American life demands that all differences between groups of varying backgrounds disappear. Can we not, asks H. M. Kallen, have "a multiplicity in a unity, an orchestration of mankind?" Such a view implies a society in which members of various subcultures share the values and privileges of the larger common culture on a basis of mutual acceptance and equality without giving up group differences important to them. Increasingly this ideal of "cultural pluralism" is looked upon as a modern alternative to the theory of the melting pot.
S R Sp

Missouri Compromise

■ The Missouri Compromise of 1820 was an attempt to define the geographic boundaries between slave and free territory in the U.S.A. In reality, however, it was one of several postponements of the emancipation of Negro slaves. It was significant because it was the first enactment of Congress which forbade slavery, if only in a certain region.

Slavery in North America had begun before the U.S.A. was founded. A shipload of Negro slaves reached Virginia in 1619, a year before the Mayflower arrived in America. The *Census** of 1790 showed that the Union had 3.9 million inhabitants, of whom approximately 700,000 were Negroes, most of them living in the South. In the course of time many millions of Negroes were transported to America, about three million (a cautious estimate) on British ships alone.

In the early days of the Union, slavery was permitted throughout the country. It was because slavery proved to be economically unprofitable that in the North *Abolitionist** organizations came into existence and laws were passed prohibiting slavery. This went on until, by 1819, there was an equal number of slave and free States, 11 of each (slave: Va., Md., Del., Ky., Tenn., N.C., S.C., Ga., Ala., Miss., and La.; free: Mass., Conn., R.I., Vt., N.H., N.Y., N.J., Pa., Ohio, Ind., and Ill.). By that time the slavery issue had developed into one of considerable magnitude. The population development increasingly favoured the North (population 5,152,000, as against 4,485,000 in the South) and the South was eager to preserve the sectional balance, at least in the Senate. This it achieved in the Missouri Compromise, which provided that Missouri should be admitted to the Union as a slave State, and Maine as a free State. Slavery was prohibited in the rest of the *Louisiana Purchase** territory north of 36° 30' north latitude. (In the old States the Mason-Dixon Line of 1767 remained the dividing line [*Dixie**]). Slavery continued to be defended in the South, whereas agitation against it grew in the North which was against any extension of slavery in America. The Mexican Cession of 1848 reopened the controversy over slavery; but owing to the rapid settlement and political organization of California after the discovery of gold there in 1848, the inhabitants of the newly acquired territory took the slavery question into their own hands and framed a State constitution forbidding slavery. The following dispute over the admission of California led to the Compromise of 1850, which provided that California should be admitted as a free State and that the territories of Utah and New Mexico should be organized without mention of slavery. In 1854 the Kansas-Nebraska Act repealed the Missouri Compromise, which had been thought final and beyond repeal, and left the slavery decision to the people. When, in 1860, the free States had 36 senators and the slave States only 30, and when Lincoln won the presidential election of that year, the situation was beyond remedy. The South seceded from the Union and the War of Secession broke out. But it would be an exaggeration to say that it broke out over the slavery question, which was only one cause among many. The old *States' Rights** question, which had divided Jefferson and Hamilton *(Parties*)*, was still alive. It was characteristic that in the Missouri dispute of 1819-20 Senator Rufus King (N.Y.) maintained that Congress was empowered to forbid slavery in Missouri, whereas Senator William Pinkney (Md.) replied that the Union was composed of equal States and that Congress could not restrict Missouri's freedom of action. The overwhelming superiority of the northern military forces finally swept all compromises away and decided the slavery question and the States' Rights question in a War between the States (1861-65). H H

New England

■ The NE section of the U.S. comprising the States of Maine, New Hampshire, Vermont, Massachusetts, Rhode Island, and Connecticut. The name was first applied to the area by Captain John Smith who explored and mapped it in 1614 and who, in his description of the country, emphasized its resemblance to England.

New England is a clearly defined region of the U.S.A., in contradistinction to such loose geographical expressions as the Middle West or the Southwest.

New England has laid some of the foundations of American civilization in its political, educational, literary, and religious aspects.

The town-meeting of New England became the basis from which the American form of government evolved. Constitutionalism is one of the most notable contributions of New England to American life; it existed in the *Mayflower Compact** (1620), the Charter of Massachusetts Bay (1628), and the Fundamental Orders of Connecticut (1639), which was the first written *Constitution** in the world. And it was the major centre of events leading up to the American Revolution, particularly after 1765, and was the scene of the opening engagements of the War of Independence *(Declaration of Independence*)*.

New England's early educational institutions have played a decisive role in the advancement of learning in the United States and have set basic standards. Harvard, Radcliffe College, Mt. Holyoke College, Smith College, Wellesley College, Amherst College, Williams College (all in Massachusetts), Brown University (Rhode Island), Bowdoin College (Maine), Dartmouth College (New Hampshire), and Yale University (Connecticut) are still some of the most influential educational institutions of the country, and Brandeis University (Massachusetts) and the Massachusetts Institute of Technology (M.I.T.) have added to their fame *(Ivy League*)*.

New England's contribution to American literature and science has been without parallel. New Englanders like Greeley, Longfellow, Hawthorne, Whittier, Lowell, Holmes, Emerson, and Thoreau established the American tradition of writing.

Religion, in the form of Puritanism, was the source from which early American life emanated, and New England attitudes and ethics have continued to exert an influence on American society. Puritanism was brought to New England by the first immigrants in 1620. From there its tenets spread over the U.S.A. *(Puritan*)*. The distinctive features of the New England character were established between 1630 and 1830; they are the heritage of England and of the spiritual influence of Puritanism. They have persisted in spite of fundamental changes in the composition of the population. After 1830 the "new *Immigration*"* into New England led to a heavy influx of Irish, Central Europeans, and especially Southern Europeans. Most of them were Catholics. Today New England has a larger foreign-born population than any other section of the U.S.A., and Boston, once the spiritual centre of Protestant New England, has now become the stronghold of American Catholicism. *(Melting Pot, Immigration*)*. HH/EV

Opposition

A political party opposed to that in office. 1704. Viscount Bolingbroke (1678-1751) was the first to establish a theory of parliamentary opposition. The term "His Majesty's Opposition" was first used by John Hobhouse (1786-1869), radical Member of Parliament, as a witticism in 1826.

● The Opposition in the British Parliament is as much a political institution as the Government itself. Its importance is indicated by the official designation "Her Majesty's Opposition", which attests that it is regarded as legitimate and indispensable. Since 1937 the Leader of the Opposition has been paid a salary to enable him to devote his full energy to the state and to his party. The Leader of the Opposition in the Lords and the Chief *Whips** in both Houses have also received salaries since 1966 (Ministerial Salaries Act).

The Opposition is seated on the Speaker's left. The leading members of the party, who occupy the front bench, form the Shadow Cabinet. The latter is prepared to take over the reins of government at any moment, although since the emergence of party organizations unexpected overthrows of governments have become unlikely *(Parliament, Parties*)*. It is evident that the British two-party system has favoured this polarity of Government and Opposition. Small parties, such as the Liberals and the Scottish and Welsh Nationalists, if they have not formed a coalition with the Government, are not part of Her Majesty's Opposition, but are referred to as "third parties".

The Opposition in the British Parliament was not created; it evolved in the course of the development of distinctive political parties and as the result of the increased power of Parliament relative to the Crown. An Opposition in the modern sense of the term has existed in Britain since after the Glorious Revolution (1688).

■ The United States has a two-party system, but no parliamentary opposition in the usual sense of the term. This is due to several circumstances: the President is not a member of Congress and therefore cannot lead "his party" in the legislature; the Constitution of the U.S.A. does not provide for political parties: the principle of the separation of powers followed in the Constitution and the elaborate system of *Checks and Balances** have led to the confrontation of President and Congress and have not promoted the confrontation of political parties in the legislature *(Parties*)*. To apply the term "Opposition" to American conditions, therefore, would be misleading. H H

Orange and Green

● The term designates the two peoples of Northern Ireland. Orange is the symbol of loyalty to the Protestant king of England, for it was William of Orange who firmly established the Protestant supremacy in Northern Ireland. 1795. Green stands for the green island of Ireland, for the green shamrock and for Catholicism, for, according to tradition, St. Patrick used the trifoliate shamrock to illustrate the doctrine of the Trinity.

On March 30th, 1972, the British Government suspended Stormont (actually a suburb of Belfast, but also synonymous with the parliament and government of Northern Ireland) and imposed direct rule from London on the province. It was the reaction to the events of "Bloody Sunday", January 30, 1972, when a prohibited Catholic civil rights march in Londonderry ended in clashes with British troops, during which 13 civilians were killed.

Thus ended a constitutional experiment which had been born in 1920 under very unfortunate auspices *(Home Rule*)*. In that year Ireland was divided into the Free State of Ireland and Northern Ireland, each with its own parliament. The Government of Ireland Act of 1920 repeatedly mentions the possibility of unification, but it was already obvious at that time (just as it is obvious now) that the Protestant-dominated Northern Irish parliament (i.e. controlled by the Unionist party; *Parties*)* would not agree to such union. Thus, the conflict is rooted in the Act of Parliament that divided Ireland. But the problem is much more complex, and its causes lie in the past and in the present.

The historical causes

The Ulster crisis is usually seen as a religious conflict. But that is not all. One has to go far back in history to understand that it is a relic of a colonial past.

In 1607 the Irish Catholic chieftains, led by Hugh O'Neill, were defeated by the English. Many of them fled to the Continent, many were deported to Scotland. They were dispossessed of their land. About 100,000 Scots Protestants were brought over for the first Plantation of Ulster. In 1609 Derry was given to London, and London companies were given grants of land. During the English Civil War *(Parties*)* the Irish rebelled and decimated the Protestant population. Cromwell subdued the rebellion in 1649, killed 3,000 inhabitants of Drogheda and deported those who survived to America. In 1689 James II, a Catholic himself, brought new hope to the Irish, but in the Battle of the Boyne (1690) he was routed by William of Orange. The Londonderry apprentice boys played an important part in preventing Londonderry from falling in its siege. In 1795 after the French Revolution had inspired an attempt at rebellion (Wolfe Tone), the Orange Order was founded by Protestant extremists to maintain "the Protestant constitution". In 1886, when Gladstone brought in his Home Rule Bill, the Protestants feared for their supremacy. There were riots in Belfast, and the old hostility between Protestants and Catholics broke out again. When the question of Home Rule, meaning a Catholic government for the whole of Ireland, came up again in 1910, the Protestant minority were ready to fight for their leading role *(Home Rule*)*.

Grievances of the minority

Protestant rule was established by the Government of Ireland Act of 1920 and the Irish Free State Agreement Act of 1922. The regional autonomy of Northern Ireland was realized in 1921 and was unique in the constitution of the United Kingdom. It was the only example of a federal structure in Britain and made it practically impossible for Westminster to interfere with the internal affairs of Stormont. (The 1949 Ireland Act established that the United Kingdom could not intervene in Northern Ireland except to control a breakdown of law and order, which happened in 1969.) A series of measures followed that deprived the Catholics of essential constitutional rights, e.g.: (1) in 1929 an Act was passed which abolished proportional representation which the Government of Ireland Act had laid down, and introduced a simple majority system, which gave Catholics little chance of representation in Stormont (only the four Queen's University seats continued to use proportional representation). (2) In 1922, the Civil Authorities (Special Powers) Act was brought in (made permanent in 1933); section 11 allowed arrest without a warrant and internment without trial *(Habeas Corpus Act*)* and it outlawed the Irish Republican Army (I.R.A. - see below). (3) The outcome of local elections was distorted through plural voting *(Constituency*)*, which might give a person up to six votes, the restriction of the franchise to ratepayers, and gerrymandering *(Constituency*)*.

In the autumn of 1968 civil rights agitation began, led by the Civil Rights Association and the People's Democracy (Marxist). They demanded: (1) universal franchise (one man, one vote) in local elections; (2) removal of gerrymandering boundaries; (3) legislation against discrimination in employment at local government level; (4) points system for housing; (5) repeal of the Special Powers Act (see above); (6) disbanding of the B-Specials (Ulster Special Constabulary), a Protestant armed volunteer police reserve, regarded by Catholics as a political instrument.

Determined efforts have been made between 1969 and 1972 to establish equality of treatment in Northern Ireland: (1) Universal adult suffrage for local council elections was introduced in 1969, plural voting for business premises and additional residences abolished. (2) 26 district councils have replaced the 67 previous bodies. About one-third of the new councils is Catholic controlled. (3) Two "ombudsmen" *(Commons*)* were set up in 1969, a Parliamentary Commissioner for Administration and a commissioner to deal with citizens' grievances against local councils and public bodies. (4) A central Housing Organization was established in 1971 with one-third of its members Catholics. (5) The Ulster Special Constabulary (B-Specials) were disbanded in 1970, and replaced by the Ulster Defence Regiment (U.D.R.), a non-sectarian citizens' militia. The Royal Ulster Constabulary (R.U.C.), the only police force in the British Isles which is armed, has become a civilian force under police authority and has ceased to be a paramilitary organization. (6) The British Government assured that the parliamentary system in Ulster would be radically changed giving the Catholics fair representation.

Although all of the civil rights demands have been implemented or are in the process of being fulfilled except for the repeal of the Special Powers Act, there has been increased violence, probably for the following reasons: the measures were taken too late; repeated mass demonstrations on either side escalated hostility; the I.R.A. succeeded in isolating the British troops, who (under the Northern Ireland Act of 1949, see above) had come to protect the Catholics, from both the Catholics and the Protestants; both "republican" (i.e. IRA) and "loyalist" (i.e. radical Protestant) paramilitary groups resort to the most brutal forms of discipline (like "kneecapping", i.e. shooting into the knees, and tarring-and-feathering) within their own ranks to frighten potential defectors or "traitors"; finally, there is an uninterrupted flow of funds into the pockets of the IRA - more than £ 1 million a month turnover pass through the hands of the Belfast brigade alone, generated by robbery, fraud, "protection" money, but also by "legitimate" business: the provisionals are buying up pubs and clubs, butchers, supermarkets, record shops, etc. Another important source of IRA revenue are the Irish-Americans; in 1971, the rhetoric of the North Irish Aid Committee and the Irish National Caucus raised an estimated sum of close to one million dollars for the Provisionals. The amount has dropped to about $ 100,000, probably as a result of an enlightenment campaign of the British Government.

Under the Stormont government Ulster drifted towards civil war. Hundreds of people had been killed, tortured, interned, some shorn and tarred and feathered, before the British Parliament passed the Northern Ireland (Temporary Provisions) Bill, on March 30th, 1972, which suspended the provincial autonomy of Northern Ireland for (at least) one year. Since then, the province has had no tier of representative government between district councils and the House of Commons, though several attempts have been made by the British Government to re-establish some form of self-government or *devolution**. A plebiscite on the future of Northern Ireland was held on March 8, 1973, but was boycotted by the Catholic parties. Shortly after, on March 20, the British Government issued a White Paper stating that (1) direct rule would be continued until agreement on a workable structure of government could be reached; (2) Northern Ireland would remain part of the United Kingdom for as long as this was the wish of the majority of its people; (3) a Northern Ireland assembly of 80 members would be elected soon for a four-year term; (4) Northern Ireland would continue to be represented by 12 elected members in the Parliament at Westminster.

At a meeting at Sunningdale (Berkshire) on December 6-9, 1973, which was attended by members of the governments of the United Kingdom, the Republic of Eire, and the Executive designate of Northern Ireland (Brian Faulkner), agreement was reached on the establishment of a tripartite Council of Ireland intended to oversee changes in the relationship between Northern Ireland and Eire. On January 1, 1974, the British Government terminated direct rule. - Sunningdale could have become the historic turning point. But Brian Faulkner's own Unionist Party *(Parties*)* rejected the agreement, whereupon direct rule was reimposed.

In July 1974, the British Parliament passed the Northern Ireland Act 1974. It provided for the election of a Constitutional Convention to work out proposals for future government institutions, with the provision, however, that any such proposals must provide for the sharing of power between Protestants and

Catholics. At the election held on May 1, 1975, the United Ulster Unionist Council (UUUC, see *Parties*),* a largely anti-Sunningdale coalition of Protestant parties, gained 45 of the 78 Convention seats. It rejected any form of a participation of republicans in a future Cabinet for Northern Ireland. In March 1976, the Convention was dissolved by Order in Council. Northern Ireland, therefore, continues to be governed by direct rule from London.

After years of killing, destruction and economic decay, peace talks have begun and peace groups have been organized, best known among them, though riven with dissent now, the Northern Ireland Peace People movement launched by Betty Williams and Mairead Corrigan, who were awarded the Nobel Peace Prize in 1977.

But there is little hope that the violence will end soon as there is no evidence that the Protestant majority is prepared to give up its links with the United Kingdom nor that the IRA will abandon its utopian aims. The only solution visible in the long run is that the Ulster problem will take care of itself in the supranational association of E.E.C. of which Britain and Ireland are members. Indeed, a new era of economic co-operation between London, Dublin and Belfast was set in motion in September 1977, when a number of joint committees were set up to facilitate regular contact between senior civil servants. *(Home Rule*, Parties).*

Some organizations

Orange Order (founded 1795, fraternity of Protestant extremists).

Irish Republican Army: (a) Official I.R.A., (b) Provisional I.R.A.

The official wing was for many years the only militant arm of Sinn Fein since 1918; through its inactivity in August 1969, when Protestant fanatics burnt down the houses of Catholics, it lost prestige; as a result, the Provisional branch grew up; in December 1970 the ideological split followed; the Officials are Marxist-oriented, proclaiming that the issue should be fought out on class-struggle lines, irrespective of religion or race whereas the Provisionals make clear that terror alone is the key step toward unity. Both wings have committed numerous murders, especially of British soldiers. They fight to control some no-go areas in Belfast and Londonderry (Free Derry). The Officials are also called National Liberation Front. There is a women's branch of the I.R.A.: Cumann n'a Ban.

The Catholic Ex-Servicemen's Association (paramilitary).

Ulster Defence Association (Protestant), since 1972 more and more the Protestant counterpart of the I.R.A.; though sometimes resorting to terrorist activities both against the Catholics and the British Army, the U.D.A. is still legal; it is a predominantly working-class organization.

Ulster Freedom Fighters (U.F.F., Protestant terrorist).

Red Hand Commandos (R.H.C., Protestant terrorist).

(The latter two organizations are associated with the Ulster Defence Association.)

Orange Volunteers.

Ulster Special Constabulary Association.

Down Orange Welfare.

Ulster Volunteer Service Corps.

(The latter five Protestant paramilitary groups and the Ulster Defence

Association are believed to have formed a co-ordinated Ulster loyalist army with a command structure not unlike that of the Provisional I.R.A.)

Ulster Volunteer Force (U.V.F.; a paramilitary working-class organization of Protestant extremists).

Loyalist Association of Workers (L.A.W., Protestant, paramilitary). H H

Parish

Britain: Subdivision of a county. Township (or cluster of townships), having its own church and clergyman. 1839. U.S.A.: see below.

● The rural parishes in England were generally not affected by the local government reform of 1974 except that the powers of the parish councils were increased and a few parishes were divided by the boundaries of new counties and districts. Parishes with 200 or more electors must generally have parish councils. A parish council comprises at least five members. All parishes, irrespective of size and population, have parish meetings, which are the only form of direct democracy in Britain (leaving aside the referendum, which was practised for the first time in 1975, when British membership of the European Community was endorsed by a two-thirds majority). The powers of the parishes include: allotments, arts and crafts, recreational facilities, community halls, cemeteries and crematoria, and many minor functions. Parish councils are to be elected every four years, in the year in which the local district councillor is elected.

In Wales parishes have been replaced by "communities". Community meetings may be convened as and when desired. They have broadly the same powers as English parish councils. Councillors are elected on the same basis as parish councillors in England.

In Scotland local communities have been given the opportunity to form community councils. They are not a third tier of government, nor do they have specific statutory duties or statutory sources of finance.

Before the Local Government Act took effect, the parishes represented the third and lowest level (or tier) of *local government**.

■ In the U.S.A. there are parishes in the State of Louisiana which, however, are in reality *Counties** and are not comparable with parishes in Britain. H H

Parliament

● The Great Council of the nation, which forms, with the sovereign, the supreme legislature of the United Kingdom. Middle English.

The official definition of the legislative power in the United Kingdom is "the Queen in Parliament" that is to say the Queen, the House of Lords (upper house) and the House of Commons (lower house). In reality, however, the legislative power has shifted in the course of centuries from the monarch to Parliament and within the latter from the House of Lords to the House of Commons. Today the majority of bills are introduced by the Cabinet, which indicates a trend towards an increasing sway of *Cabinet** over the legislative power of Parliament. The members of both houses are representative of England, Scotland, Wales, and Northern Ireland. The Isle of Man and the Channel Islands are not represented in Parliament; they are "dependencies of the Crown" and have legislative assemblies of their own.

The roots of the present institution are the Anglo-Saxon Witan or Witenagemot (meeting of wise men), a group of advisers of the king, whose functions appear to have been primarily that of a court, and the Norman feudal system introduced into Britain in 1066 by William I which entitled the king to summon his "tenants-in-chief" for counsel in a Curia Regis (or Common Council, Great Council). The House of Lords and the House of Commons (besides other institutions like the Treasury, the King's Bench, the Privy Council, and the Cabinet) were descendants of the Curia Regis. The present Parliament of England has a continuous history extending over 700 years, which may be divided into five periods. 1

The first period was that of the dependence of Parliament on the Crown (c. 1265-1603). In 1265 Simon de Montfort, leader of the barons against Henry III, defeated the king in battle after the latter had refused to call in the Great Council. In this year Montfort called in a Parliament of his supporters which included barons, knights and burgesses. In 1295 Edward I (1272-1307), the founder of English Statute Law, invited the representatives of all free estates of all England - including the barons, archbishops, bishops (who again invited the lower clergy), and the representatives of the counties and boroughs (Model Parliament).

The early parliaments were still predominantly concerned with cases of law or were summoned by the king because he needed money. It was only after the custom of "petitioning the king" had developed in the middle of the 14th century that Parliament gradually assumed its legislative functions. The middle of the 14th century also brought the separation of Parliament into two chambers, the Commons and the Lords (before 1342), the archbishops and bishops joining the Lords, the lower clergy retiring to their own *Convocations**.

In 1340 Parliament had already appointed auditors to control the royal expenditure (this function has survived in the office of the Comptroller and Auditor General who controls all payments made from the Consolidated Fund). In 1362 Parliament (assembled at Gloucester in that year) for the first time secured a key position in financial matters when Edward III conceded to Parliament "that henceforth no subsidy or other charge shall be levied or granted on wool . . . without the assent of Parliament . . ." In the English Reformation, Parliament for the first time assumed an important function, when it was called by Henry VIII to participate in the most important pieces of Reformation legislation. On the whole, however, the Crown was supreme during the entire period.

The second period was marked by the struggle between Parliament and Crown for supremacy. At its end Parliament emerged as the leading political power in England and had forced the Crown into partnership.

In November 1640 Charles I's attempt to rule in an absolute manner had failed and Parliament had won temporary supremacy (Long Parliament, 1640-60).

When Charles II was called back to England in 1660 (Restoration), he did not find himself in the position of an absolute monarch, for former concessions were still in force. Between 1661 and 1679 (Cavalier Parliament), the conflict between Crown and Parliament remained in moderate bounds. When it broke out over the succession of Charles's Catholic brother James, Parliament was able to force the king to sign the *Habeas Corpus (Act)** (1679), but the king could still afford to rule without Parliament (1681 and 1685). In 1688, however, the Crown finally lost its preponderance owing to James II's religious fanaticism and his lack of political competence.

The third period was marked by the supremacy of Parliament (1688-1832). After the Glorious Revolution of 1688 powers were clearly defined in three Acts of Parliament: the *Bill of Rights** (1689), the Triennial Act (1694; it prescribed that new elections should be held at least every three years), and the Act of Settlement (1701; it settled the question of the succession to the throne; but it also established the independence of the Judiciary). The monarch no longer held his office by the grace of God but by the grace of Parliament. Since 1707 no English monarch has vetoed an Act of Parliament. After 1714, the Cabinet became responsible to Parliament.

The fourth period was marked by the sovereignty of the House of Commons (1832-74). This period began with a sharp attack by the Commons on the Lords: the successful threat by the Liberal Prime Minister, Earl Grey, to create a large number of new (Liberal) Peers to secure a majority in the House of Lords for his Reform Act (Representation of the People Act, 1832; *Suffrage**). The Lords never recovered from this blow; on the contrary: whereas up to 1832 both houses equally represented the aristocracy, the landed gentry, and (to some extent) the commercial class of the country, the picture changed with every new Reform Act (1867, 1884). The House of Commons became increasingly representative of the whole nation, whereas the House of Lords remained what it was, viz. a body representative of a very small section of the society. The Parliament Act of 1911 was merely the formal confirmation of this change *(Lords*)*.

In the present fifth period parliamentary government has been replaced by cabinet government. The beginning of party discipline marked the end of the sovereignty of Parliament. No doubt the development of party organizations caused a considerable change in the functioning of Parliament. The Conservative victory of 1874 can be attributed, for the first time in the political history of the country, to the activity of the Conservative party organization, which was founded in 1868. Consequently, Parliament has ceased to determine the policy of the government. Today it is the Cabinet and the Shadow Cabinet (i.e. practically the Prime Minister and the Leader of the *Opposition*)* who control Parliament.

H H

Parties

The system of taking sides on public questions. 1701.

Modern political parties first developed in England and in the U.S.A. It is worth noting, however, that neither the English nor the American constitution encouraged, or provided for, the creation of political parties.

Britain and the U.S.A. provide classic examples of the two-party system which has its advantages in that there is practically always an absolute majority in the legislature and the parties respect each other because the *Opposition** can always be fairly sure of coming to power sooner or later. Its disadvantages are that the choice provided for the electorate is very small *(Constituency*)* and a tendency towards factionalism exists within the parties. In Britain the two parties alternating in power since 1924 have been the *Conservative Party** and the *Labour Party**. (Of the others only the *Liberal Party** might, under extreme conditions, one day become the balancing factor, as happened in 1924 and in 1977.) In the U.S.A. the two main parties are the *Democratic Party** and the *Republican Party**. 1

• 1641 can be considered, with some caution, as the year of birth of the political parties in England. The cause was religion. Whereas the *Puritan** members of Parliament demanded more thorough reforms of the *Established Church**, the King and the non-Puritan members were decidedly against "root-and-branch" reforms. It was because of this division of opinion that the Cavalier and Roundhead parties were formed in 1641. The former was headed by Lord Falkland and Sir Edward Hyde - both defenders of the Prayer Book - the latter by Oliver Cromwell and John Hampden. After Charles I had tried to arrest six members of Parliament, five of them Puritans, in the House of Commons in person, the two parties prepared for a war which was to last from 1642-46 in its first and from 1648-49 in its second phase (Civil War).

After the Restoration in 1660 neither the religious issue nor the constitutional conflict between King and Parliament had been solved. It is true that in 1661 the Cavaliers dominated Parliament but their adversaries grew stronger. By 1679 when Charles II dissolved Parliament, again two opposing parties were commanding fairly equal support. They called each other Whigs and Tories, both rude names, which they nevertheless readily adopted (Whig: f. whiggam, a word used by certain Scotsmen when driving their horses; Tory: f. Irish, lawless person, Irish Catholic plunderer, viz. of English property in occupied Ireland).

The Whigs were the great landowners and wealthy merchants. They were committed to the idea of Parliament's supremacy over the Crown. They firmly established the principle that a ministry must be supported by the Commons. They stood for religious and political toleration. They abolished press censorship in 1695 and abandoned the strict course of mercantilism. Sir Robert Walpole was their most prominent leader in the 18th century *(Cabinet*)*. The long Whig rule (1688-1761 with only a short interruption) led to corruption inside the party. The Tories represented to a great extent the smaller landowners and the country squires. They were pro-Stuart and pro-Anglican, and although in the end they agreed to call William of Orange and Mary to the throne in 1688, they lost political ascendancy. The Tories would certainly have offered less resistance to the restoration of the Stuarts than the Whigs. George I and George II were therefore suspicious of the Tories and excluded them from government. During George III's reign, however, they were mostly in power again, with William Pitt the Younger as their greatest leader.

Nevertheless the short Whig ministry of the Marquess of Rockingham (1782) was a milestone in English party history. Rockingham enforced a number of institutional reforms which, though superficial, exposed the necessity of greater reform and was the reason for the Whigs becoming the party of social and political reform in the 19th century *(Suffrage*, Constituency*)*. During the years in which the great reform was debated, 1827-32, the two leading parties themselves went through a period of radical reform and adopted new names: *Conservative Party** and *Liberal Party**. The difference between Whigs and Tories was demonstrated by their attitude towards the reigning house; that between Liberals and Conservatives by their attitude towards domestic reform.

The *Conservative Party**, *Liberal Party**, and *Labour Party** are the political parties that have in this century determined the course of political events in

Britain. Owing to the existing electoral system *(Constituency*)*, smaller parties, like the Communist Party (represented in the House of Commons from 1935 to 1950) have always found it difficult to have members returned to Parliament. It is, therefore, remarkable that, since the early seventies, two minor parties have risen to prominence: the Scottish and the Welsh nationalists. The rise of nationalist parties is in conformity with the present rise of nationalistic feeling all over the world. In the case of Scotland, the oil in the Scottish sector of the North Sea has certainly given an additional aspect to the success of the Scottish National Party.

There are now five nationalist political parties: the Scottish Nationalist Party (11 M.Ps in the House of Commons in 1977, against 1 in 1970); Independent Scottish Labour Party (2); Plaid Cymru (Welsh nationalists, 3 in 1977, against none in 1970); Mebyon Kernow (Cornish nationalists); and Vectis National Party (Isle of Wight).

Minor parties of growing influence: United Reform Party (whose leaders demand Britain's withdrawal from the Common Market and the return to a liberal free-trade philosophy); Socialist Workers Party (former International Socialists; the most significant of the various groups on the extreme left); National Front (an amalgamation of five small extreme right-wing parties; it rejects liberalism, socialism, alien cultures like those of Africa and Asia, and openly advocates racism and authoritarian government, and wants Britain to leave the E.E.C., NATO, the United Nations, and to recreate the Commonwealth as an Empire; it has made its name known through a number of acts of street violence; in 1977, Liberal candidates were overtaken at several by-elections by the National Front).

Other minor parties are: Independent Democratic Movement (rightwing); Workers Revolutionary Party (Vanessa Redgrave); International Marxist Group; and exotic groups like the Young Ideas Party and the Fourth World Party.

There is a confusing spectrum of Northern Irish parties: the Official Ulster Unionist Party (6 M.Ps; the great bulk of Ulster Unionists who were opposed to the Sunningdale Agreement *(Orange and Green*)*; it demands *devolution** or complete integration within the United Kingdom); the Democratic Unionist Party (1 M.P.; split from the Ulster Unionists in 1971 in support of a decidedly right-wing and anti-Catholic position; Ian Paisley's party); Vanguard Unionist Party (1 M.P.; split from the Ulster Unionists in 1973; initially one of the most extreme Unionist groupings, it has become increasingly moderate and even ready to form a voluntary coalition with Roman Catholic politicians; it is likely to be disbanded soon); Independent Unionist Party (2 M.Ps; extremist offspring of the Official Unionists); Unionist Party of Northern Ireland (advocates the principle of coalition and power-sharing; the late Lord Faulkner's party); Northern Ireland Labour Party (pro Ulster-Unionist; based on trade-union support; aims at the building of a non-sectarian socialist state along lines advocated by the British Labour Party); Social Democratic and Labour Party (1 M.P.; left-of-centre, non-sectarian, but predominantly Catholic; endorses power-sharing and devolution and eventual re-unification with Ireland); Alliance Party (middle of the road, non-sectarian); Irish Republican Socialist Party (founded by Seamus Costello and Bernadette Devlin-Iliskey; aims at violent revolution; breakaway group of Provisionals and Officials); Volunteer Political Party (founded by Roy Bradford; its members believe that power should lie with working-class rather than with middle-class Protestants); Independent Irish Party (the Latest addition to Northern Ireland's complex political landscape; supports aims scarcely distinguishable from those of Provisional Sinn Fein *(Orange and Green*)*, the foremost being that of forcing immediate British withdrawal from Ulster).

In Britain the Corrupt and Illegal Practices Prevention Act, 1883, and the Representation of the People Act, 1918, make bribery, undue influence, especially with reference to elections, and improper interference with elections punishable acts. Subsequent legislation has modified and further defined corrupt and illegal practices: the Representation of the People Act, 1949, The House of Commons (Redistribution of Seats) Act, 1949, and the Election Commissioners Act, 1949.

Annual financial assistance from public funds is still limited to opposition parties. An opposition party which had at least two members elected at the last general election, or one member elected and a minimum of 150,000 votes cast, receives £ 500 for every member returned and £ 1 for every 200 votes (up to a maximum of £ 150,000). - The Government is considering the report of the Committee on Financial Aid to Political Parties (August 1976). The authors of the report recommend the payment of annual grants to political parties and election candidates for their work outside Parliament, on the basis of each party's electoral support. In addition, there would be some reimbursement of the election expenses of parliamentary and local government election candidates.

■ There were no political parties when the U.S.A. was founded, and the federal constitution does not mention them. George Washington was convinced of the "baleful effects of the spirit of party generally".

Three major issues, however, soon contributed to the formation of political parties: (1) The question of the priority of either the rights of the federal government, or the *States' Rights**. (2) The economic difference between the mercantile and financial interests of the North, and the planters' and slaveholding interests of the South. (3) The question of a friendly or hostile attitude towards England. It is important to note that from the very beginning of the existence of parties in the U.S.A. the regional aspect has been of paramount importance in American party life. Those favouring a strong central authority were led by the northerner Alexander Hamilton and were called Federalists; the others who were in favour of the strengthening of *States' Rights** were led by the southerner Thomas Jefferson and called Anti-Federalists or Republicans (not to be confused with the Republicans of 1854).

In 1796 Washington was followed by the Federalist John Adams who was succeeded by the Republican (or Anti-Federalist) Thomas Jefferson. In that election of 1800 it had become obvious that national parties existed: Jefferson was at the mercy of a Federalist-dominated House of Representatives, which, after the ballot count in the Electoral College resulted in a tie, had to elect the President. The Twelfth Amendment was, in fact, an instrument to adjust the Constitution to the rise of political parties. Jefferson's policy *(Louisiana Purchase*)* was so successful and the Federalists had become so unpopular because of their opposition before 1812 to the War with England that they did not even nominate a candidate in opposition to James Monroe in 1820 and simply ceased to exist. But after the election of John Quincy Adams in 1824 *(Congress*)*, the Republicans split into two factions. The one, under Adams, called itself National Republican Party, the other, under Andrew Jackson, Democratic Republican Party or Jeffersonian Republican Party. In the election of 1828, the Jacksonian, i.e. Jeffersonian, party dropped the "Republican" and called itself Democratic Party, the name that exists today. In 1832, officially in 1834, the National Republicans changed their name to Whigs (they have politically nothing to do with their English namesakes who, incidentally, changed their name to Liberals at about the same time). They lost their identity by becoming a party of all those who were against Andrew Jackson's peculiar form of democracy *(Spoils System*)*. The Whigs succeeded in electing two Presidents, Henry Harrison in 1840 and Zachary Taylor in 1848, but rapidly declined when many of their eminent men joined the new Republican Party which was founded in 1854, one of the two great parties today. In 1856 the Whigs did not even nominate candidates in the presidential and vice-presidential elections. In the elections of 1860 they merged with the American Party and formed together the short-lived Constitutional Union Party. Since 1861 the presidential chair has been occupied alternately by representatives of the *Republican Party** and the *Democratic Party**. No third party has risen to the rank of a major political party in the U.S.A. Numerous minor, or "third parties", however, developed in America on a local, State, or national level and have exerted a remarkable influence on the policies of the major parties and the government. Most of them have been interest groups, as e.g. the Greenback (Labor) Party (1877), which demanded monetary reform; the Populist or People's Party of the U.S.A., the agrarian protest party especially of the South and West; the American Party of 1856; the party of the Know-Nothing Movement, 1852-60, which was generally against foreign immigration; the Prohibition Party, 1872, which is against the drinking of alcoholic beverages; the States' Rights Party of 1948, also called Dixiecrat Party, the Southern anti-civil-rights party *(Dixie*);* and the American Independent Party of 1968, founded by George C. Wallace, "the first successful fascist movement in U.S. history" (Joseph Alsop). There are a number of "third parties", which have repeatedly contended for the offices of President, Senator, or Representative of the United States or for that of state governor:

American Party; American Constitution P.; American Independent P.; Conservative P.; Concerned Citizens P.; Co-Equal Citizens P.; Communist P.; Constitutional P.; Democratic Socialist P.; Free Libertarian P.; George Wallace P.; Human Rights P.; Independent American P.; Independent Conservative P.; Independents for Godly Government P.; Independent P.; Liberal P.; Libertarian P.; Labor P.; La Raza Unida; Liberty Union; Mayflower P.; Nonpartisan P.; National Democratic Party of Alabama; Owl P.; Prohibition P.; Peace and Freedom P.; People's P.; Revolutionary Workers P.; Socialist Labor P.; Socialist Workers P.; United States Labor P.; Workers P.; White Power P.

The two leading American political parties of today can be summarized as follows:

(1) They are "centre" parties, because of the majority of American opinion usually clusters around a centrist position; polar views (in the seventies held by Goldwater, Reagan, and Wallace on the right, McGovern, Humphrey, Church, and Kennedy on the left) attract only minority backing. (2) They no longer permanently represent social classes or groups (e.g., blacks voting Republican; Southern whites, labourers, and new immigrants voting Democratic, etc.). (3) They are non-religious. (4) They have never been strong nationally (few people in America know the names of national party chairmen). (5) They are

issue-directed (voting-rights, urban problems, crime, law-and-order, energy, education, racial and ethnic problems, the Panama Canal, etc.). (6) They are personality-oriented rather than programme- or platform-oriented (by 1972, 62 per cent. of the electorate voted a "split ticket", i.e. for a Republican candidate running for one office, and for a Democratic candidate running for another office; in 1948, the figure had been 38 per cent.).

The two main parties certainly continue to be useful for organizing elections and reducing alternative candidates to a reasonable number, but they have long ceased to be solid blocs of opinion. Even in Congress they furnish a multi-party system with changing alliances between Northern Democrats, Northern Republicans, Southern Democrats, Southern Republicans, hawks and doves, progressives and conservatives, ethnic caucuses, protectionists, etc. In fact, since 1965, the American party system has been in a state of disintegration. Today, few Americans know to what party their candidates belong, Presidential candidates excepted. Party platforms are no longer discussed today. In some parts of the U.S.A., parties have already ceased to exist altogether in county, city, and educational elections, in which the party affiliation of the candidates is no longer mentioned on the ticket.

The cause for this development can, perphaps, be sought in three recent developments: (1) The break-up of group alignments with either of the major parties. (2) The educational explosion in recent years: college enrolment has tripled since 1945, and with it has risen the proportion of voters who take an interest in particular issues and who are able to judge candidates with regard to their ability to deal with these issues, apart from party links. (3) The emergence of television as the principal - in many cases only - source of political information. In 1880, once a party's candidate had been nominated, he stayed at home, and the party conducted his campaigning. Today, candidates come into every sitting-room by T.V., and it is the personality of a candidate that counts, not his party affiliation.

The most important Acts of Congress dealing with corrupt practices are the Corrupt Practices Act, 1925, the Hatch Act, 1939 (revised in 1940), the Labor Management Relations Act, 1947, the Federal Election Campaign Act of 1971, and the Campaign Financing Reform Act of 1974, which, among others contains the following provisions: (1) contribution limits: $ 1,000 per individual for each primary, run-off, and general election, and an aggregate contribution of $ 25,000 to federal candidates annually; $ 5,000 per organization; $ 50,000 for President and Vice President, $ 35,000 for Senator, $ 25,000 for Representative; no foreign contributions, (2) Spending limits: $ 10 million per candidate in Presidential primaries, $ 20 million in Presidential general election campaigns; repeal of the media spending limits imposed by the Act of 1971. (3) Provisions for public financing: Presidential candidates can opt for full public funding, but in this case private contributions are not permitted; all federal money for public funding of campaigns comes from the Presidential Election Campaign Fund; each voter can check off one dollar from the income tax if he contributes to the Fund. (4) Disclosure and reporting dates: each candidate is required to establish a central campaign committee through which all contributions and expenditures must be reported to the newly established Federal Election Commission. (5) Penalties: fines to a maximum of $ 50,000; exclusion of fraudulent candidates from running again for the term of a particular office (plus on year). – In 1977, President Carter proposed legislation to remove some of these rather strict regulations, for example the obligation laid on candidates to report money they spend during an election campaign. It is also planned to increase the funds to cover campaign costs. H H

Poll

The human head. Hence: counting of heads or of voters; voting at an election. 1832. "Poll" describes the procedure, the place and the outcome of the voting at an election. It also designates a survey of public opinion whereby questions are put to a representative selection of people (in U.S.A. and G.B.: American Institute of Public Opinion or Gallup Poll, Louis Harris Organization, Marplan Institute, "Popcorn Poll", Opinion Research Centre, National Opinion Polls, Market and Opinion Research International).

● When the Prime Minister considers it desirable to hold new elections or when the term of five years of a Parliament nears its end he asks the sovereign to dissolve Parliament. On the advice of the Privy Council *(Cabinet*)* a royal proclamation is then read in the House of Lords *(Parliament*)* to the effect that the old Parliament is dissolved. In the name of the monarch writs for a general election are issued to the sheriffs of the counties and the mayors of the towns who act as returning officers in the different constituencies. In theory they select the candidates who in practice are elected by their parties before the dissolution of Parliament.

The next stage is "nomination day", a day on which all the candidates must produce to the returning officer a "nomination paper" signed by a "proposer", a "seconder", and eight voters of the constituency. The candidate must make a deposit of £ 150, which is forfeited if he does not obtain at least one-eighth of the votes polled in his *Constituency**, and is then paid into the Consolidated Fund - the Government's account with the Bank of England. The *Conservative Party** and the *Labour Party** nominate candidates for almost all the constituencies while the *Liberal Party** usually does not. If only one candidate comes forward he is declared elected unopposed and this is called a "walk-over".

Then follows the election campaign.The law requires the Government to give notice of a general election at least 17 days before the poll. Sundays and bank holidays are excluded from the reckoning. In practice, the Prime Minister usually gives a month's notice, or slightly more. As a rule, the election takes place on a Thursday. During the campaign candidates "nurse" their constituencies by holding meetings and sending out letters and photographs, but "canvassing", i. e. making house-to-house calls on the voters, is also a quite frequent practice. Precautions are taken to prevent corruption *(Parties*)*. Should it be ascertained that a member has used corrupt practices he loses his seat, which then goes to the candidate with the second largest number of votes. A whole constituency can be temporarily disfranchised if involved in illegal practices.

The final stage is "polling day". Polling takes place at a number of polling stations in each constituency. Voting is secret *(Suffrage*)*. Voting by mail, in case of a constituent's illness or absence for professional reasons, and by proxy, in case he is resident abroad on official service, are permitted. (For local elections in Britain, see *County*.)*

■ Presidential elections take place at regular intervals and a dissolution of the legislature is neither possible nor necessary *(Chief Executive, Congress*)*.

There is consequently no "nomination day", and election campaigns do not last a few days but several months, from the nomination of the final candidates until polling day. The Constitution does not contain a single word about nominating candidates, but since the firm establishment of political parties about 1830, conventions have become regular institutions. The State party organizations nominate their candidates for President either (a) by petition - a certain number of people of the State demand to have some citizen's name put on the ballot, (b) by primary - a special election is held to give the members of each party a chance to choose their nominees in an internal party election, or (c) by a convention - to which the parties send their appointed delegates. The national party committees decide the time and place of the national conventions. Before they meet each party selects delegates from every State and *Territory**. The final nominee requires a simple majority which may take many ballots. The candidate for Vice-President is next nominated in the same way. President and Vice-President must not come from the same State (Amendment XII). 1

The next stage in the process is the nomination of electors in the individual States. Each State has as many electors as it has U.S. Senators and Representatives combined (Constitution, Art. II, sec. 2, 3). These electors must not be federal office holders. On polling day, the first Tuesday after the first Monday in November in leapyears, the electorate casts its votes for these electors; not for President. On the first Monday after the second Wednesday in the December following their election, the electors cast their votes in their respective State capitals for the candidate to whom they are pledged. The whole system is obsolete. This is obvious from the fact that some States do not even mention the names of the electors but include only the names of the presidential and vice-presidential candidates. The "electoral college" was justified in 1789 in a Constitution which then did not consider the possibility of political parties. Since 1968 the abolition of the Electoral College has been considered. President Carter again suggested its elimination, and in 1977 hearings began in the Senate on reforming the Electoral College.

Immediately after the national conventions have nominated their candidates for polling day each party conducts an election campaign.

Candidates for Congress are also nominated by their parties, and they also conduct campaigns. Illegal practices are prosecuted under various Acts of Congress *(Parties*)*. Offenders lose their seats to their rival candidates.

On polling day American voters may still be confronted with a "blanket ballot" which may include a long list of presidential electors, candidates for Congress, State legislature, county officers, governors. However, voting machines have been in use in many localities. Voting by mail is possible, in case a voter is resident abroad on official duty. By 1888 all States had introduced the ballot in one form or another. (For local elections, see *County*.)* H H

Press

The newspapers, journals, and periodical literature generally. 1797.

- In the United Kingdom the term "national press" is commonly associated with Fleet Street. Most of the important national newspapers have their main offices there or in the neighbourhood. Two prominent exceptions, however, are The Times - offices in New Printing House Square - and The Guardian - offices in Gray's Inn Road. The Press of Great Britain is more national in that sense than that of any other country; the great majority of the better-known newspapers are produced in London and distributed from there throughout the whole country. This is true both of the popular papers (some of them "tabloid" or "yellow", with concentrated, often sensational representation of news mixed with comic strips, etc.) and of those appealing to a more sophisticated reading public. 18 newspapers of a national circulation are published in London.

London, however, is not the only printing and distribution centre in the United Kingdom. Manchester has become the second largest press centre in the British Isles, since many London papers have their northern editions printed there. Further the Glasgow Herald, circulation approximately 85,000, the Scotsman, circulation approximately 70,000, Yorkshire Post, circulation over 100,000, can in a sense be regarded as national newspapers, as their opinions are read all over the country.

The most important British national newspapers are, with year of first appearance, political tendency, approximate circulation, (1976 figures):

Daily newspapers		
The Times (1785) discontinued 1978	Independent	311,200
The Daily Telegraph (1855)	Conservative	1,315,000
The Guardian (1821)	Left of centre	309,000
Daily Express (1900)	Right of centre	2,608,000
Daily Mail (1896)	Conservative	1,739,000
Sun (1964)	Independent	3,638,000
Morning Star (1966)	Communist	41,000
(formerly Daily Worker, 1930)		
Daily Mirror (1903)	Left of centre	3,837,000
Financial Times (1888)	Independent	177,000
Evening News (1881)	Independent	574,000
Evening Standard (1827)	Independent	431,000
Sundays		
The Observer (1791)	Independent	678,000
The Sunday Times (1822)	Conservative	1,375,000
The Sunday Telegraph (1961)	Conservative	733,000
News of the World (1843)	Independent	5,162,000
The Sunday People (1881)	Independent	4,077,000
Sunday Express (1918)	Independent	3,436,000
Sunday Mirror (1963)	Left of centre	4,078,000
Weeklies		
The Economist (1843)	Independent	90,000
New Statesman (1913)	Left of centre	70,000
Spectator (1828)	Right of centre	30,000
Tribune	Left wing	
Punch (1841)	Humorous	98,000

Apart from these national newspapers there are about 100 local dailies and about 1,100 local weeklies in Britain catering for very limited regions (e.g. Northern Echo, Western Telegraph Haverfordwest, Paisley Daily Express, South Wales Echo, Irish News, Isle of Man Examiner). It should be noted that the locals are read by more people than the national papers.

Since 1949, about 20 London and provincial newspapers have had to close down. Among them are the famous Liberal paper News Chronicle (1960), the name of which is associated with Charles Dickens, and the Daily Herald (1964), until then the only important daily paper wholly representing Labour opinion, and the Daily Sketch. All three papers were in financial difficulties although they had a circulation far above a million. This trend is likely to continue. In fact, very few papers are making a profit, the Financial Times being the only English newspaper (1976) not in the red figures, while in the same year The Observer, for example, was running a loss of around £ 500,000. Following the Final Report of the Royal Committee on the Press, 1977, several of the national daily and Sunday newspapers are not likely to survive, whereas the provincial press is generally very profitable.

On the other hand, the leading newspaper groups have increased their share of the total circulation: Reed Publishing Holding Ltd. (part. of Reed International); Associated Newspapers Limited; Beaverbrook Newspapers Limited; the Thomson Organisation Limited; News International Ltd.; the Trafalgar House group; United Newspapers Limited, and Pearson-Longman Limited. The development of newspaper groups continued simultaneously with that of a national press. It began about the turn of this century and is associated with the names of a number of enterprising men generally called the "press lords" (most of them titled). The most outstanding names are:

Alfred Harmsworth, later Lord Northcliffe. Together with his brother Harold he started the Daily Mail as a halfpenny daily. Lord Beaverbrook (William Maxwell Aitken). He obtained control of the Daily Express which was the first English paper to publish its principal news on the front page; this was the beginning of "headlinese", which is the practice of conveying news at a glance. Lord Rothermere (Harold Harmsworth). Lord Astor. His name is associated with The Times, which was founded in 1785 by John Walter (Lord Northcliffe controlled it for some time) and sold in 1966 by the Astor and Walter families to Lord Thomson of Fleet. The Thomson Organization own approximately 80 per cent. of the shares in over 50 interlocking press companies and in all "controls" a hundred newspapers, including The Times. In 1963, Cecil Harmsworth King established the International Publishing Corporation at his time the biggest newspaper group in the world. At present, Rupert Murdoch, the Australian press lord, is building up his empire in Britain (and the U.S.A.). Today, it has become common usage to speak of "the Beaverbrook press", "the Harmsworth papers", etc.

The concentration of such enormous power in the hands of a few has caused anxiety in public and government. Following the recommendations of the two Royal Commissions on the Press of 1949 and 1962 (esp. of the Shawcross Commission of 1962), the Monopolies and Mergers Act, 1965, was passed, by which too great an accumulation of power can be prevented. (No special recommendations have been made for new measures to deal with concentration by the Royal Commission on the Press in 1977.) Moreover, several institutions have come into existence which safeguard the public. The two most important ones are:

(1) The Press Council which resulted from the recommendations of the 1947-49 Royal Commission on the Press *(Committee*)*. It was first set up in 1953 and, following the recommendations of the second Royal Commission - the Shawcross Commission - reinstituted in a revised form in 1963. In it the press organizations and the public - 10 lay members and 20 press members - are represented. It is a voluntary organization which aims at the preservation of the standard of the press and its integrity. By investigating the complaints of the public against the press and by censuring bad journalism whenever it is proven, the Press Council provides

a safety valve and keeps demand for further restrictive legislation at bay. It publishes an annual report on everything relating to the press. The Royal Commission on the Press, 1977, has recommended that the composition of the Council should be changed, so that lay members are in a majority; it should also be given more resources and authority.

(2) The trust system, which some newspapers have adopted. It is intended to secure certain public ends. 51 per cent. of the Beaverbrook press, for example, was to be owned by a trust which Lord Beaverbrook formed in 1954 with the prime intention of ensuring that all its profits go to religious and humanitarian activities (mainly in Canada). The Times trust was founded to see to it that the newspaper did not fall into other hands, commercially and politically (though it turned out to be merely an instrument of control over stockholding when The Times was bought by Lord Thomson in 1966). Likewise, when the American oil group Atlantic Richfield (Arco) won control of The Observer in 1976, the transaction had to be sanctioned by the newspaper's trustees.

In addition the government always has the power to curb too great a concentration of power in the hands of a few through legislation. So far it has followed only the recommendations of the Shawcross Commission to the extent that the self-regulating body, the Press Council, has been strengthened. The commission had also suggested several drastic rules designed to prevent the trend towards larger groupings which have been considered by the government. The reactions of some of the press lords to the new measures have not been altogether friendly.

The numerous general, business, trade and professional periodicals - among which especially the Times Literary Supplement and the Times Higher Education Supplement are internationally known - will not be considered here.

English consumer magazines have never reached the circulation figures common in the U.S.A. Still, well over 3,000 titles are published in Britain every month, including British editions of successful American magazines. They can be classified in several groups: the women's magazines are the largest group (e.g. Woman), the home magazines the second largest (e.g. House and Garden), then follow the romance magazines (e.g. Loving), and last - as a newer sub-group - the young interest magazines (e.g. Honey). Two magazines do not really belong to any of these types: She, a racy news-feature magazine, and The Lady, a weekly with a genteel and old-world touch.

The following is a selection of leading English magazines, with approximate circulation (1976 figures):

Family Circle	881,000	True Magazine	209,000
Honey	180,000	Vogue	123,000
Jackie	660,000	Woman	1,619,000
19	172,000	Woman and Home	680,000
She	313,000	Woman's Own	1,583,000
The Lady	75,000	Woman's Realm	835,000
Living	587,000	Woman's Weekly	1,709,000

■ In the United States there is nothing comparable with "Fleet Street". Most newspapers are based on small neighbourhoods. This makes them dependent on local advertisers, who often exert considerable control over a newspaper. It is symptomatic that the federal capital, Washington, D.C., possesses only one newspaper which receives national and international attention, the Washington Post. Few newspapers in the United States have a circulation much beyond their own immediate regions; in many cases not even beyond a suburb. Only the New York Times, the Chicago Tribune (read in a wide region of the Middle West), the Washington Post, and the Wall Street Journal (printed in six different places) are not local, but regional and, to a small extent, national papers. 1

There are, however, several American newspapers with more than local - and more or less international - appeal. They are included in the following list (with year of first appearance and approximate circulation on weekdays and, in brackets, on Sundays, figures of 1976).

Atlanta Constitution (1868)	205,000	(–)
Baltimore Sun (1837)	373,000	(347,000)
Chicago Tribune (1847)	661,000	(1,120,000)
Christian Science Monitor (1908)	191,000	(-)
Los Angeles Times (1881)	1,005,000	(1,191,000)
New Orleans Times Picayune (1836)	205,000	(305,000)
New York Times (1857)	843,000	(1,419,000)
Philadelphia Inquirer (1934)	427,000	(824,000)
St. Louis Post Dispatch (1875)	289,000	(483,000)
St. Louis Globe-Democrat (1875)	271,000	(-)
Wall Street Journal (1889)	1,367,000	(-)
Washington Post (1877)	521,000	(703,000)

American newspapers are generally non-partisan because American journalism has traditionally been very close to, dependent upon and co-operative with official sources. When issues like Vietnam and Watergate began to divide public opinion and difficulties arose in the relationship between press and government, journalism became more partisan, ideological, Europeanized. Apart from the "free press" (see below) there are papers with a clearly definable right or left image (right: National Review, Human Events; left: National Guardian, New Times, Nation, The New Republic, New York Review of Books, Atlantic Monthly, Harper's Magazine).

American dailies are at present facing a crisis largely owing to the influence of TV, but even more to labour-management disputes. New York alone lost 11 of its 14 dailies between 1954 and 1971, among them in 1966 The New York Herald Tribune and, in 1967, The New York World Journal Tribune, which was an amalgamation of The New York World Telegram and Sun and The New York Journal American. In 1967, the Paris editions of The New York Times and The New York Herald Tribune (now also the Washington Post) were fused into The International Herald Tribune. The crisis has also affected the family magazines: Look died in 1971; Life followed in 1972, but reappeared in 1978. In 1970 alone at least 22 dailies and 16 magazines died, also because of the decline of advertising revenue. In January 1978, New York's latest newspaper, The Trib, was launched with an initial circulation of 250,000. It caters for an educated conservative public.

In contrast to the dailies, American magazines are truly "national" publications. The small number of national dailies is compensated for by the existence of over 100 consumer magazines with circulations of between 20,2 million and 260,000 each. The leading American magazines are (in thousands, 1976):

TV Guide	20,249	Better Homes and Gardens	8,094
Parade	19,537	McCall's	6,512
Reader's Digest	18,165	Ladies Home Journal	6,080
Family Weekly	10,800	Time Worldwide	5,881
Family Circle	8,479	Good Housekeeping	5,312
Woman's Day	8,165		

There are another 46 with circulations over or nearing one million, among them National Geographic (6,869,000), and the famous news magazines Time (4,325,000) and Newsweek (2,928,000). Ebony, which appeals to the black population, has a circulation of 1,288,000, The New Yorker, the humorous magazine for the "caviar sophisticates", but since the early seventies also devoted to sophisticated political criticism, 492,000; Fortune, a high quality magazine with a stress on economics, 627,000; The Advocate, America's first national "gay" newspaper; and, unrivalled in its genre, Playboy, 5,405,000. Monthly magazines like Harper's and Atlantic, which are chiefly devoted to letters, have smaller circulations.

In the U.S.A. as in Britain newspapers have become concentrated in the hands of a few. In 1897 the era of "chain newspapers", or newspaper chains (i.e. not mere affiliation, but common ownership) began with the organization of the Scripps-McRae League of newspapers. Today the most important newspaper chains are: the Hearst Newspapers, the Scripps-Howard Newspapers, the Newhouse Newspapers, Knight Newspapers, and Gannet Newspapers. Further chains today are associated with the names of Norman Chandler, Joseph Pulitzer, Marshall Field jr., Robert R. McCormick, Kenneth Roy Thomson, James and Helen Copley, and Joseph M. Patterson, and - in the magazines sphere - Henry A. Luce.

Along with the modern newspapers there developed the great news agencies like (in America) United Press Association, International News Service, United Press International (merger of both services, 1958); Associated Press (independent non-profit-co-operative); altogether there are about 150 news agencies in the United States; (in Britain) Reuters Ltd. (founded in Aachen in 1850 by Julius Reuter, orig. Israel Beer Josaphat, transferred to London in 1851), Press Association Ltd. (f. in 1868), Exchange Telegraph Company Ltd. (f. in 1872) and the two British subsidiaries of American news agencies, Associated Press Ltd. and United Press International.

In spite of the trend towards the concentration of the press both Britain and the United States have adhered to the principle of the freedom of the press and censorship is absent. The British and American governments do, however, have some degree of control through their Postmasters General. They can withdraw postal privilege from a newspaper, i.e. refuse transportation and delivery by mail - this happened in the case of the New York paper Daily News for 18 months from 1861 when it opposed Lincoln's war policy, and in 1917, when, basing on the Espionage Act, any matter deemed seditious or treasonable was excluded from the mails. In addition, there are many legal restraints on the press, including libel, official secrets, contempt of court, sedition, and racial discrimination.

One more recent phenomenon should be mentioned which is perhaps more characteristic of journalistic activity in Britain and the U.S.A. than in other countries: the underground newspapers, sometimes called "the free press" ("alternative press" in British official language). The final Report of the Royal Commission on the Press included some 500 titles in 1977. Their spectrum

ranges from liberal to revolutionary, more often, however, from revolutionary to more revolutionary still. Many are entirely political, others entirely devoted to erotica. Some are concentrating their attention on religion, the occult, rock music, drugs, worker-student revolution, Women's Lib, or plain muck-raking (like the Daily Planet of New York). In the U.S.A. the underground press today is the most active of all publishing fields, and most large cities have at least one underground newspaper, either weekly, monthly, or sporadic. Two of the best American underground papers are Rat (New York) and Seed (Chicago). Especially San Francisco has made a large contribution to America's underground press with publications like Vile, Fag Rag, Mother Jones, Newsfront International, PL (Progressive Labor), The Black Panther, Guardian, Variety, Industrial Worker, Vector (homosexual or "gay"), it (magazine of personal growth and human effectiveness), Osowatomie (Weather Underground Organization), Pacific Sun, and Barb (sophisticated, Berkeley). Prominent British titles are Gandalf's Garden, Oz, Peace News, Time Out, IT, Gay News, and "ink". In New York there is an underground press news agency, the Liberation News Service (L.N.S.), which distributes articles, photographs, cartoons etc. to some 500 underground, college, and similar papers in the U.S.A.
H H

Prohibition

■ An edict, decree, or order that forbids; a negative command. Spec. the forbidding by law of the manufacture and sale of alcoholic drinks for common consumption. 1851.

Two Amendments to the U.S. *Constitution** are famous for their curiosity: amendments XVIII and XXI, which deal with the prohibition of the manufacture or sale of intoxicating liquors in the U.S.A. This issue affected Federal and State constitutions, was a major issue in presidential elections, provoked the veto of a President of the U.S.A., brought into existence pressure groups feared by Governors and Presidents, and led to the foundation of a national political party with presidential candidates of its own.

The earliest Puritan legislation in the colonies, especially in New England, did, it is true, include acts by various assemblies and local governments regulating the liquor traffic; however, the *Puritans** are often unjustly blamed for things which actually originated in the early 19th century. Whereas dancing, smoking, and drinking were largely tolerated in colonial New England, they were regarded as sinful activities by the leading Protestant churches in the 19th century. "Temperance" in particular became the criterion of a good life, while alcoholism was considered the cause of crime, insanity, and poverty. It was an irony of history that the war against drinking conducted by such movements as the American Society for the Promotion of Temperance (1826), the Temperance Union (1833), the Women's Christian Temperance Union (1879), the Anti-Saloon League (1895), and the Prohibitionist Party (1872) did not lead to abstinence, or even relative sobriety, but to the worst excesses of crime that ever occurred in the U.S.A. Under the pressure of these organizations and with the support of the *Baptist**, *Methodist**, and *Presbyterian** churches one State after another became "dry". Before prohibition became nation-wide in 1920 by Amendment XVIII, absolute prohibition had already been the rule in 32 of 48 States, these 32 including more than one half of the population. On a county basis it is estimated that, before 1920, 95 per cent. of the land area of the U.S.A. was dry, and this area contained about 68 per cent. of the total population. Certainly, prohibition was more than a mere "fit" of Puritanism. It must be seen in the context of religious expansion in the 19th century, when Baptist, Methodist, and Presbyterian preachers followed the frontier line into the West, offering the simplest form of religion founded on emotional experience and morality. The liquor question was profoundly affected in 1917 by the entrance of the U.S.A. into World War I, for Congress came at that time to the conclusion that the sale of liquor would interfere with military efficiency. By Act of *Congress** of November 1918 the manufacture and sale of liquor in the U.S.A. ceased. In 1920, the question was solved constitutionally.

The consequences of prohibition were disastrous. It encouraged millions of citizens to contravene the Constitution by drinking in "speakeasies" (places where intoxicating liquors were sold contrary to the law) liquor smuggled by "bootleggers" (persons concealing liquor flasks in their bootlegs). At the beginning of prohibition there were 200 bars in New York; at the end there were 2,000. And it stimulated crime. Smugglers organized gangs for the protection of their illicit trade, some of these developing into small armies which soon tyrannized whole cities and corrupted many politicians. Chicago became their notorious centre. Theft, bank-robbery, murder in open daylight became everyday occurrences there. Murder statistics exceeded 10,000 a year (Britain approximately 650). The leading gangsters such as Anthony (Mops) Volpe, Jake (Greasy Thumb) Guzik, Machine Gun Jack McGurn, James (King of Bombers) Belcastro, and Public Enemy No. 1 (Scarface) Al Capone reaped enormous incomes from the liquor trade and worse crimes. The local police were powerless, the public (possibly fascinated by this pseudo frontier romanticism) usually tolerant. The Federal Bureau of Investigation (F.B.I.), which possessed certain interstate powers enlarged in the course of the twenties, finally eliminated most of the leading public enemies, and in 1933 Amendment XVIII was repealed by Amendment XXI, which left the question of prohibition to the States. Oklahoma and Mississippi were the last states to abandon prohibition (1959 and 1966) although there are, however, numerous communities under "local option" in other States.

Prohibition was not merely an episode in American life, it was an era of American internal history no less characteristic of a young nation than that of the "rugged individualism" in the second half of the 19th century. But it also marked the beginning of the corporate criminal organization firmly rooted in the social structure and protected by corrupt politicians and high-powered legal advice. So today, as during Prohibition, criminal organizations profit by providing goods and services that are either illicit or, if legal, are handled by people who are vulnerable to underworld pressures. Moreover, changes in American moral attitudes - sexual permissiveness, the drive to legalize gambling, and the relaxed concern over narcotics - have provided a wide field of operation for organized crime.

By far the best organized (and best known) criminal group among many is the Mafia, which was brought to the U.S.A. in the 1860s by Italian immigrants from Sicily, where it had originated in feudal times, when noblemen hired brigands to protect them and their estates. Today, its American offspring dominates gambling, narcotics, pornography, prostitution, cigarette "bootlegging" (from one State to another), loan-sharking, hijacking, and labour-racketeering. It is estimated that the Mafia's 26 families (TIME May 16, 1977) take in at least $ 48,000 million in annual gross revenues and nets about $ 25,000 million in untaxed profits (by comparison: Exxon, the largest industrial corporation in the U.S.A. reported sales of $ 51,000 million and net profits of $ 2,000 million in 1976). 1

Of late, this kind of gangsterism has found imitators in the West of the United States. The new mobsters there are of Mexican origin and model themselves on the traditional Sicilian-based crime syndicate. They have chosen the name Mexican Mafia. Their rivals in the use of violence are the smaller Nuestra Familia (also Mexican), the neo-fascist Aryan Brotherhood, and the militant Black Guerillas.

H H

Received Pronunciation (RP)

- Received: accepted as a standard by tacit agreement.

RP (abbreviation of "Received Pronunciation") is a type of pronunciation which in England is usually accepted as the standard of spoken English. For many Englishmen RP represents the "best" kind of English because it is generally employed by educated and socially influential circles. Others advocate RP as a spoken standard on the ground that it is the pronunciation most widely understood in the British Isles and the one least likely to excite regional prejudice. Although RP originated as a local dialect, it is nowadays restricted to no particular locality of England. It is the kind of English one can hear spoken with little variation throughout the country in *Public Schools**, *Universities**, officers' messes, boardrooms of large companies, and in the law courts. RP has in fact been termed a class dialect, but it is not easy to describe sociologically the class which uses RP. Perhaps RP is best defined negatively as the non-regional dialect of British English, or, more simply, as the kind of British English speech which does not reveal in which part of the country the speaker was brought up. The British Broadcasting Corporation adopted RP for its national service announcers. RP is the pronunciation traditionally taught to foreigners and is the one described in most books on the phonetics of British English.

RP is descended from the dialect spoken in the London region during the early period of New English and more particularly from that variety of it which developed at the King's Court. Remarks of writers in the 16th century leave no doubt that this dialect was already being recognized as the standard of spoken English. Thus in 1589 George Puttenham, or whoever wrote "The Arte of English Poesie", recommends as the best kind of English "the vsuall speach of the Court, and that of London and the shires lying about London within lx. myles and not much aboue". As a marker of position in society this forbear of RP increasingly gained prestige throughout the country. By the 19th century it was being used in the great Public Schools of England, and it is perhaps mainly owing to their influence that this kind of English became firmly established as the dialect of the upper classes. In modern times radio and television have contributed much to the diffusion of RP.

Despite the levelling of British society in recent years the ability to speak RP still has great prestige value. The "wrong accent" can be now as before an impediment to social intercourse and to entry and promotion in certain professions. It is in the large towns of the south of England that the obloquy attaching to non-RP is greatest. There, pronunciations deviating from RP generally strike the RP-speaker as being "vulgar" or "slipshod" – qualities which he will tend to impute to the person using such pronunciations. Genuine rural dialects, however, such as Dorset, Sussex or Somerset, are usually tolerated even in the south. In the Midlands and the north of England, particularly in non-academic circles, speech coloured by regional peculiarities is usually no great social stigma. Nor do the accents of Scots, Irish, and non-British speakers of English generally have adverse social connotations in England.

The term RP is not often used outside the academic world. More usual expressions for this kind of speech among the general public are "public school accent" and "B.B.C. English"; or the RP-speaker may simply be characterized as having a "cultured voice" or a "refined accent". "Received Standard" is occasionally used in the same sense as RP. The term "Oxford English" is frequently employed on the Continent for the kind of English that linguists call RP. This expression, however, is best avoided for it suggests that RP is indigenous to Oxford. "Oxford Accent" has been used in England, often in a derogatory sense, for a pronunciation imagined to be like that of Oxford University men. It is regarded by most who do not use it as affected and pedantic. The expression "Queen's English" is not synonymous with RP; it refers to a standard of English from the point of view of "correct" usage and grammar.

R L S

Reconstruction

■ The action or process of reconstructing; U.S. history: The process by which after the Civil War the States which had seceded were restored to the rights and privileges of the Union. 1865.

The surrender of Lee at Appomattox in April, 1865, ended the Civil War in a triumph for the armies of the federal government. The Union had been preserved; but what was now the status of those 11 "wayward sisters" which had seceded, founded the Confederate States of America, and taken up arms against the United States? For 12 years after the Civil War the federal government wrestled with this problem. The process by which the Confederate States were restored, as well as the period from 1865 to 1887 during which it took place, are referred to as Reconstruction.

One of the initial questions to be decided was that of control. Who was to direct Reconstruction, the executive or the legislative branch of the federal government? Should the process, in other words, be fundamentally presidential or Congressional reconstruction?

President Lincoln, taking the view that the Union was indissoluble and that, constitutionally, secession had never really taken place, announced his Reconstruction plan in December, 1863. Most former Confederates willing to take an oath of loyalty to the United States would receive amnesty; any Confederate state would then be restored when citizens numbering 10 per cent. of its 1860 electorate took the oath and agreed to the emancipation of the slaves.

Vice-President Andrew Johnson assumed that the executive would direct Reconstruction. His Reconstruction Proclamation 1865 followed Lincoln's principles. By December, 1865, every Confederate state except Texas had organized new governments on the President's terms, and when *Congress** convened in January, President Johnson announced the restoration of the Union.

Congress, however, refused to endorse Johnson's actions or to receive Congressional delegates elected by the new southern governments; it set up a Joint Committee of Fifteen to investigate the status of the former slaves and of the governments of the southern states. Dominated by men who considered the Lincoln - Johnson attitude too lenient, the *Committee** proceeded to deal with the former Confederate states as "conquered provinces", to use the words of its most powerful member, Thaddeus Stevens of Pennsylvania. 1

The Joint Committee made its report in June, 1866, asserting the exclusive control of Congress over Reconstruction. Despite Johnson's opposition to the Radicals, as they came to be known, they won a thoroughgoing victory in the Congressional elections that autumn and now cemented into law their own plans. The Reconstruction Act of March, 1867, passed over the President's veto, divided the South into five military districts under martial law. Conventions for the purpose of writing new state constitutions might be called only if elected on the basis of universal manhood suffrage, though most ex-Confederates were disqualified. The new state governments must, as a condition of readmission to the Union, guarantee the ballot to the Negro and ratify the proposed 14th amendment to the *Constitution**, which sought to protect Negro citizenship rights. Thus began a period of "military reconstruction" enforced by 20,000 Federal troops.

In supplementary Reconstruction acts Congress gave the army commanders broad powers and instructed them to put into operation the machinery for creation of new state governments. By 1868 Arkansas, Alabama, Florida, Georgia, Louisiana, North Carolina, and South Carolina, under Radical control, were readmitted; Mississippi, Texas, and Virginia followed in 1870. (Tennessee had returned with Congressional blessing in 1866).

The new state governments in the South were largely conducted by white southerners known as "scalawags" who sympathized with Radical policies, and by northerners called "carpetbaggers" who went south to "aid" in Reconstruction. Many of the former freedmen participated as officials in these governments, some creditably, others not. In a number of southern states the Reconstruction era was marred by corrupt financial and political practices and a steep rise in public debts. On the other hand, the new governments carried out programmes for rebuilding devastated areas, provided more liberal support for social services, and for the first time in the South, guaranteed to all citizens free public education.

Former southern leaders, for the most part disqualified from public office, resented the control by former slaves and the white allies of the Congressional Radicals. As early as November, 1865, before Congress had asserted its authority, Mississippi had passed the first "Black Codes", vagrancy and apprenticeship laws designed to bind Negroes to the land and keep them "in their place". When Congress countered the next year by giving broader powers over protection of *Civil Rights** to officials of the "Freedmen's Bureau", a social welfare agency established to aid Negroes in their adjustment to freedom, Southerners organized such extra-legal societies as the Ku Klux Klan and the Knights of the White Camellia.

Determined to protect Negro civil rights and to maintain the political power which Negro *Suffrage** helped to guarantee, the Congressional Reconstructionists in 1869 pushed through the Amendment XV to the Constitution and the Ku Klux Klan Acts of 1870 and 1871. The amendment provided that no citizen would be deprived of the ballot by reason of race, colour, or previous condition of servitude.

Meanwhile, their feud with Lincoln's successor resulted in the only presidential impeachment trial in American history. In order to circumvent President Johnson, who had unsuccessfully tried to block Reconstruction legislation with the veto, Congress tried to strip him of certain executive powers through such measures as the Tenure of Office and Command of the Army Acts. When the embattled President defied these laws, Congress sought to remove him from office but failed.

Republican success in the elections of November, 1868, which brought General Ulysses S. Grant to the White House with Radical backing, perpetuated Congressional direction of Reconstruction. For eight more years, Congress continued on substantially the same course. One of the final efforts to protect the status of the freedmen came in the Civil Rights Act of 1875.

Reaction against the policies of the Reconstruction Congress, however, set in on both the national and state levels even before Grant's re-election in 1872. Conservative elements regained command in four southern states by that year, and by 1876 only Florida, Louisiana, and South Carolina remained under Radical control. The electoral votes of these three states, awarded to Rutherford B. Hayes by the Republican-controlled electoral commission in the disputed election of that year, made him President over the Democratic candidate Samuel J. Tilden, who had polled a majority of the popular vote. Democrats agreed to raise no further protest about this decision only when Hayes and the Republicans agreed to withdraw the last of the Federal troops stationed in the South. With the departure of these troops in 1877, conservatives recaptured control in the three remaining southern states, and Reconstruction came to an end.

The significance and interpretation of Reconstruction in American history remains in dispute. Well into the 20th century it was looked upon as a "tragic era", to use the title of one of the most popular works on the subject, a period in which small-minded, vindictive, and self-seeking politicians used their position to enforce a harsh peace and perpetuate themselves in power. Later historians have substantially modified this interpretation by emphasizing the constructive achievements of the period and pointing out that Reconstruction Civil Rights legislation, invalidated by the *Supreme Court** of that era, has been re-enacted in much the same form a century later. S R Sp

Republican Party

■ The Republican Party is one of the two great political parties in the U.S.A. It was founded in 1854 with an anti-slavery bias, emerging out of an alliance between parts of the Whig Party (or National Republican Party) and part of the Northern Democrats. The Republican Party came to power in 1861 after Abraham Lincoln had been elected President, an election which led to the War of Secession, 1861-65. - Today it is strong among white petit bourgeois, Southern and middle American voters.

In its platform of 1976, the Republican Party called for less government, less spending, and denounced massive federally-founded programmes to reduce unemployment; it promised tax cuts for the oil industry, for business, for investors and for parents of college students; it rejected busing, a compulsory national health service, and abortion; it demanded greater defence efforts and the development of a new inter-continental missile; in foreign affairs it supports Taiwan as against Communist China. 1

Before the *New Deal**, the Republican Party was considered the party of reform (through business), of industrial progress, of the urban middle class, and - in Lincoln's tradition - the party that guaranteed a strong national government. In the great depression, its politics of business interest received the blame for the failure of the economy, and it moved into the status of a party of the Protestant upper and middle classes, with its strength in the North East and the Middle West. This changed when the Democratic New Deal coalition *(Parties*)* began to dissolve (Dwight D. Eisenhower, 1953/61, was an untypical example of a Republican President; as a "national figure" he had been courted by either party before he made up his mind). In the early 1960s *(Civil Rights*)*, many Americans were concerned over crime and violence, "law and order", changes in American values, the beginning urban crisis *(City*)*, and, especially, the socio-economic revolution of the blacks. Barry Goldwater's nomination as the Republican candidate in 1964 satisfied the expectations of this group of voters. He lost the election (like McGovern in 1972) because his position was too polarised and "ideological" (he had recommended strict sanctions against North Vietnam and an uncompromising anti-civil-rights course). But, like McGovern, he had created the ideological basis from which Richard Nixon operated, however much he had to broaden this basis in order to attract the less uncompromising Republican voters. Especially the attempt of the Democratic Party in the presidential campaign of 1972 to portray itself as the party of radical reform has given the Republicans the opportunity to concede minor points of social reform and to brand the Democrats as dangerously left-wing in comparison with their own middle-of-the-road moderation.

Apart from some slight differences the Republican Party is organized along the same lines as the *Democratic Party**.

The emblem of the Republicans is the elephant (mainly used to help illiterate voters to identify their candidates), and their nickname "Grand Old Party" (G.O.P.).

Republican Presidents: Lincoln, 1861-65; A. Johnson, 1865-69; Grant, 1869-77; Hayes, 1877-81; Garfield, 1881; Arthur, 1881-85; Harrison, 1889-93; McKinley, 1897-1901; Th. Roosevelt, 1901-09; Taft, 1909-13; Harding, 1921-23; Coolidge, 1923-29; Hoover, 1929-33; Eisenhower, 1953-61; Nixon, 1969-74; Ford, 1974-77. H H

Royal Prerogative

- A prior, exclusive, or peculiar right or privilege, esp. in constitutional history: that special pre-eminence which the sovereign, by right of regal dignity, has over all other persons and out of the course of the common law; the Royal Prerogative, a sovereign right (in theory) subject to no restriction or interference. Late M.E.

The constitutional development *(Constitution*, Parliament*, Bill of Rights*)* has deprived the Crown of all its actual political power. Nominally, however, its power is almost as great as it was a thousand years ago. This power, actual or fictitious, has been summed up in the term "Royal Prerogative", which divides into a great number of individual prerogatives. They are all formally still exercised by the Crown. Constitutionally speaking, however, they are in the hands of the *Cabinet**, or the judiciary. The monarch is by name the "Supreme

Governor of the Church" (Act of Supremacy, 1534, and Acts of Uniformity, 1549, 1552, 1559, 1562). He is the supreme landowner who inherits the land of any person who dies, which, of course, is fiction. The "Fountain of Honour" he creates Peers *(Aristocracy*)* and confers knighthoods, but only upon the "advice" of the Prime Minister. He has the "prerogative of mercy", but only on the advice of the Home Secretary. He theoretically appoints and dismisses the "Ministers of the Crown", opens, prorogues, and dissolves *Parliament** - the "Speech from the Throne" at the opening of Parliament is in reality a political speech drawn up by the Cabinet. Only in one case can the monarch dissolve Parliament without "advice": if the Prime Minister has been defeated in the House of Commons on a vote of confidence and refuses to resign. He metes out justice, which is in reality done by the magistrates *(Magistrates' Court*)* and *Judges**, who are independent. He makes the laws (theoretically laws are passed by "the Queen in Parliament"), and, by name, he is the chief commander of the (professional) armed services. All money voted by Parliament is voted "to the Queen" although she is granted only a salary (Civil List, 1978, £ 1.950 million p.a.) by the same Parliament.

This is no contradiction in itself, because the Prerogative no longer pertains to the person of the monarch - although he also has the "natural prerogative" of being exempt from jurisdiction (and from taxation) and thus cannot be sued, as he "can do no wrong" - but to the institution of the Crown (Act of Settlement, 1701), because it has politically no responsibility and cannot do anything at all without the "advice" of the Cabinet. Indeed, the monarch is identified completely with the "state" - a word which does not exist in English constitutional law. There are innumerable cases to illustrate this, e.g. an offence against the state is regarded as having been committed against "the Queen, her Crown and dignity" (therefore "Counsel for the Crown"), in reality, of course, it has been committed against the state.

The practical value of the Prerogative today is that the Government sometimes makes use of it to avoid parliamentary procedure, of course only where the constitution so admits; e.g. when it concludes treaties, or on various other occasions for which a "Provisional Order" or "Order in Council" suffices. An Order in Council is made by the Monarch in Council (i.e. Privy Council). Provisional Orders are made by government departments. Both types of delegated legislation do not normally require parliamentary confirmation.
H H

Speaker

The member of the House of Commons who is chosen by the House itself to act as its representative and to preside over its debates. Late M.E. The presiding officer or chairman of the House of Lords. 1660. The presiding officer of the House of Representatives of the U.S.A.

Each of the two chambers of the legislatures of Britain and of the U.S.A. has a chairman. The chairmen of the House of Lords (G.B.), the House of Commons (G.B.), and the House of Representatives (U.S.A.) are called Speakers; the chairman of the Senate (U.S.A.) is the Vice-President of the U.S.A. *(Chief Executive*)*.

● The term "Speaker" was originally used for the spokesman of Parliament, who submitted the wishes of the members to the monarch. Parliament probably had such spokesmen as early as 1295. By 1376 the office of the Speaker of the

Commons was firmly established. There is a complete list with the names of Speakers from that year on, the first being Peter de la Mare, deputy for Herefordshire.

During the Stuart period the Speaker became increasingly dependent on the Crown. After the Glorious Revolution of 1688, however, he was soon freed from that influence, though this emancipation was not achieved without fierce argument. In 1695 Paul Foley was elected Speaker against the wish of William III.

The Speaker's office did not become free of party influence until 1813. In that year Speaker Abbot was censured by the commoners for interfering with the question of the repeal of the Test Act *(Religious Test*)*.

The Speaker's impartiality could only be guaranteed by making him financially independent. This was done in 1832, from which time on he received an adequate salary from the Consolidated Fund, the Government's account with the Bank of England. Previously he had received five pounds a day from the Treasury deriving the rest of his income from fees and perquisites (five to ten pounds for each bill passed in the Commons).

Since 1835 it has not been permissible for the Speaker to be affiliated to any party.

The English Speaker, also referred to as the First Commoner of the Realm, is chosen by the commoners when a new Parliament first assembles after national elections, but also when a Speaker dies during his term of office (this may cause some embarrassment for the Government if it controls only a small majority as was the case in 1965). The Speaker has his own constituency and is listed separately in the election statistics. His office is one of great distinction. He receives a high salary and is entitled to reside in the Palace of Westminster, the seat of Parliament.

The Speaker always enters the Commons in a procession ("Speaker's Procession"). The Badge Messenger, the Serjeant-at-Arms (a civil servant of high rank, e.g. a retired general) with the Mace walk before him, and a trainbearer, the Secretary, and the Chaplain follow behind. The sitting is opened as soon as he has seated himself in the Chair, and the Mace is on the Table of the House.

He determines the order in which members may speak (usually after consulting the Whips). A member wishing to speak must "catch the Speaker's eye", i.e. obtain his permission to speak. All speeches, questions, remarks, etc., are addressed to him, a circumstance which probably conduces to objectivity and dignity of debates. He presides over divisions, ascertains whether sufficient members are present to form a quorum (40), calls members to order, and decides whether a bill is a Money Bill or not *(Bill*)*. Like the Chairman of Ways and Means (i.e. of Committees) and two deputy chairmen, who act as the three Deputy Speakers, he does not take part in divisions. He may, however, do so in the case of a tie; in this case he can make use of his casting vote. When he retires he is offered a peerage *(Aristocracy*)*.

The function of the *ex officio* Speaker of the House of Lords is now permanently performed by the Lord Chancellor. His chairmanship has derived from his position as the leading law official of the country and the court functions of the Lords. His authority as chairman is much smaller than that of the Speaker of the Commons; he does not control debate, is not addressed by the members during the debate, and has no casting vote. But proceedings cannot commence before he has "taken his seat on the woolsack", a large wool-stuffed cushion once symbolic of England's main source of wealth *(Commons*)*.

■ The American Speaker bears little resemblance to his British counterpart, except that he bears the same title and that he also functions as president of the second chamber of the legislature. He has never been a spokesman of the house who submits wishes of the members to the President. Nor has the historical ritual and pageantry of British feudal tradition ever been attached to his office. Nevertheless, there are a few symbols obviously borrowed from Britain: The Speaker of the House of Representatives has a Mace, and the sitting cannot commence until it has been put down on the pedestal on the Speaker's right. He also has a staff consisting of Clerk, Chaplain, Sergeant-at-Arms, Doorkeeper, Postmaster, and others, and the ceremonial formula permitting a member to speak is "the chair recognizes". The actual power of the American Speaker, however, is much greater than that of his British colleague. He appoints the chairmen presiding over the Committees of the Whole House and appoints all committees. Unlike the British Speaker, he is the representative of his political party, and though he usually tries to be impartial, he need not be so. He can vote, but usually does not do so except in the case of a tie. Together with the leader of the majority (to which he invariably belongs) he may exert a strong influence on the President's policies. He can appoint a Speaker pro tempore to act on his behalf. He himself is elected by the House. The importance of his position is emphasized by the fact that he receives the same salary as the Vice-President of the U.S.A., considerably more than the Cabinet members and the Chief Justice. He is the third man in the state. Should the President and the Vice-President die before the end of their terms, the Speaker becomes President (Presidential Succession Act 1947). He is followed by the President pro tempore of the Senate, the Secretary of State and other members of the Cabinet in order of rank. H H

Spoils System

■ The system or practice of a successful political party giving government or public offices, etc., to its supporters. Spoilsman: one who obtains or seeks to obtain a share of political spoils. 1832.

The spoils system is the use of patronage for party loyalty and party purposes. It was the indirect result of the growth of democracy in the 1820s. Alongside the extension of *Suffrage** developed the principle of rotation in office, and this rotation tended to take place along party lines, i.e. the victorious party organization distributed government offices among its chief supporters as a reward for loyalty. The process was particularly rife in State politics. "To the victor belong the spoils" is a famous remark made in 1832 by Senator William L. Marcy who was a member of the so-called Albany Regency, a powerful group of party politicians controlling New York State after 1828. The rise of the spoils system is linked with that of American political parties. The most unpleasant result of party politics was that it brought into existence a class of professional politicians - the word "politician" has to the present day retained its unsavoury connotation in the U.S.A. - whose main object in life it was to hold public office and who were frequently corrupt.

The spoils system was first used by Th. Jefferson, but firmly established by Andrew Jackson (President 1829-37). He introduced the principle of rotation into Federal civil service, but the system was applied much more in the following years. 1

Spoils politics led to a demand for *Civil Service** reform which was enacted under several Presidents: U.S. Grant, R.B. Hayes (largely upon the advice of Carl Schurz), and especially under C. A. Arthur under whose administration the Pendleton Act (1883) was passed. This Act enabled the Chief Executive to broaden the merit system and limit spoils politics and provided the foundation for the Federal civil service in the present form. In that year, the U.S. Civil Service Commission was created as a permanent "watchdog".

Political patronage in the U.S.A. still plays a much greater part in appointments today than, e.g. in Britain where it is called nowadays "Jobs for the boys", but even there it is less significant than in former times. The merit system is gaining ground and the number of persons included in the so-called "classified service" is increasing whereas the number of those appointed in a spoils system is decreasing. In both Britain and the U.S.A. and certainly anywhere else it is agreed that policy-making positions should be filled by the party in power. But in Britain these positions are very few in number and mostly restricted to Members of Parliament, whereas in the U.S.A. the number is considerably greater. This becomes obvious from the extent to which appointments in America as postmasters, federal judges, federal attorneys, and local administrators of Independent Agencies are made available to local party organizations; and rewarding rich donors, who generously contributed to a candidate's election campaign, with notable foreign posts, and continuing to collect contributions from them, is an old political custom used by many American Presidents up to the present. Nevertheless, in recent years there has been a marked trend towards the creation of an "administrative class" of highly qualified civil servants following the example of Britain and other countries.

H H

Stars and Stripes

■ National flag of the U.S.A. since 1777 by Act of Congress. It contains 13 alternating red and white stripes which represent the original 13 states (which are identical with the 13 original colonies, cf. the list below) and a blue field with 50 white stars representing the present 50 states of the Union.

The legend that Elizabeth (Betsy) Ross of Philadelphia made the first Stars and Stripes upon the request of a "flag-committee" consisting of George Washington, Robert Morris and George Ross is not authentic. No record of it exists.

The Stars and Stripes had several forerunners some of which already displayed 13 stars and 13 stripes:

(a) First Navy Jack, 1775: 13 red and white stripes, a rattlesnake and the words "Don't tread on me";
(b) Grand Union Flag, 1776: 13 red and white stripes and the Union Jack;
(c) Rhode Island Flag, 1776: white with a blue field containing 13 white stars, in the centre a blue anchor with a scroll on top bearing the word "hope".

The territorial development of the U.S.A. can be followed in the change of the Stars and Stripes between 1777 and 1959. The original flag remained unchanged until 1794, when, after the admission of Vermont and Kentucky, two stars and two stripes were added. In 1818, when the Union consisted of 20 states, the present rule was adopted by Congress: the national flag should contain 13 alternating red and white stripes and a new star should be added on July 4th following the admission of a new state.

Number of stars and stripes; name of state with abbreviation and capital; year of ratification of constitution or, from 1796, admission to the Union; probable origin and meaning of name:

13 stars, 13 stripes:	Delaware (Del., Dover)	1787	From Lord de la Warr, first governor of Virginia.
	Pennsylvania (Pa., Harrisburg)	1787	From Latin, meaning "Penn's woods", suggested by Charles II. in honour of Adm. William Penn, father of William Penn, the founder of the state.
	New Jersey (N. J., Trenton)	1787	From the island of Jersey in the English Channel.
	Georgia (Ga., Atlanta)	1788	In honour of King George II of England.
	Connecticut (Conn., Hartford)	1788	From Indian "Quonoktacut", probably meaning "beside the long tidal river".
	Massachusetts (Mass., Boston)	1788	From the Massachuset Indian tribe; meaning "large hill place" or "at or about the Great Hill".
	Maryland (Md., Annapolis)	1788	In honour of Queen Henrietta Maria, wife of Charles I of England.
	South Carolina (S. C., Columbia)	1788	In honour of Charles II of England.
	New Hampshire (N. H., Concord)	1788	From the county of Hampshire (Hants) in England.
	Virginia (Va., Richmond)	1788	From the "Virgin Queen", Elizabeth I.
	New York (N. Y., Albany)	1788	In honour of the Duke of York, later James II of England.
	North Carolina (N. C., Raleigh)	1789	In honour of Charles II of England.
	Rhode Island (R. I., Providence)	1790	From Dutch "Roode Eylanat" = red island; or after the island of Rhodes.
13 original	States		
	Vermont (Vt., Montpelier)	1791	From French, meaning "green mountain".
	Kentucky (Ky., Frankfort)	1792	From the Indian name "kentah-ten", meaning "land of tomorrow".
15 stars, 15 stripes,	by Act of Congress of 1795:		
	Tennessee (Tenn., Nashville)	1796	Indian origin, possibly derived from the name of ancient Cherokee capital.
	Ohio (no abr., Columbus)	1803	From Indian, meaning "beautiful river".
	Lousiana (La., Baton Rouge)	1812	In honour of Louis XIV of France.
	Indiana (Ind., Indianapolis)	1816	Land of Indians.
	Mississippi (Miss., Jackson)	1817	Ojibway Indian "gathering of all the waters" or "great river"; (mis = "great", sipi = "river").

21 stars	Illinois (Ill. Springfield)	1818	Indian tribe, Illini (= "men", with French ending).

Henceforth
13 stripes and according number of stars by Act of Congress of 1818:

22 stars	Alabama (Ala., Montgomery)	1819	From Creek Indian word meaning "place of rest"; or from name of Alibamu Indians.
23 stars	Maine (Me., Augusta)	1820	Perhaps from the name of a province of France (North-west of France); in charter of 1622 styled "Province of Maine".
24 stars	Missouri (Mo., Jefferson City)	1821	Indian word meaning "big muddy stream".
25 stars	Arkansas (Ark., Little Rock)	1836	Indian tribe meaning "downstream people".
26 stars	Michigan (Mich., Lansing)	1837	Indian word meaning "great lake" or "great water".
27 stars	Florida (Fla., Fl., Talahassee	1845	From "pascua florida", Spanish for "flowery feast" – Easter Sunday; named by Ponce de Leon who sighted Florida shortly after Easter 1513.
28 stars	Texas (Tex., Austin)	1845	From Texas tribe of Indians.
29 stars	Iowa (no abr., Des Moines)	1846	Indian name, meaning uncertain; perhaps "beautiful place".
30 stars	Wisconsin (Wis., Madison)	1848	Indian name of uncertain meaning; perhaps "meeting place of the rivers" or "wild rushing river".
31 stars	California (Cal., Sacramento)	1850	From Carci Ordónez de Montalvo's story "Las Sergas de Esplandián", a land close to Terrestrial Paradise, first applied to Lower California; or from "caliente forno" – hot furnace.
32 stars	Minnesota (Minn., St. Paul)	1858	Indian name meaning "clouded water".
33 stars	Oregon (Ore., Salem)	1859	Origin unknown; perhaps mythical river of the west, used by W. C. Bryant in "Thanatopsis".
34 stars	Kansas (Kans., Topeka)	1861	Indian tribe, Kanzas, meaning "wind people".
35 stars	West Virginia (W. Va., Charleston)	1863	see Virginia.
36 stars	Nevada (Nev., Carson City)	1864	Spanish for "snowy".
37 stars	Nebraska (Nebr., Lincoln)	1867	Sioux Indian name meaning "shallow water".
38 stars	Colorado (Colo., Denver)	1876	Spanish, meaning "reddish coloured", first given to the river.
39 stars	North Dakota (N. Dak., Bismarck)	1889	Indian, meaning "allies" (of tribes of the Nadowessioux, i. e. Sioux).
40 stars	South Dakota (S. Dak., Pierre)	1889	see North Dakota.
41 stars	Montana (Mont., Helena)	1889	From Latin for "mountainous region".

42 stars	Washington (Wash., Olympia)	1889	In honour of George Washington.
43 stars	Idaho (no abr., Boise)	1890	Indian word meaning "gem of the mountains".
44 stars	Wyoming (Wyo., Cheyenne)	1890	From Wyoming Valley in Pennsylvania, scene of Indian massacre in 1778.
45 stars	Utah (Ut., Salt Lake City)	1896	From Indian "ute" meaning "high up".
46 stars	Oklahoma (Okla., Oklahoma City)	1907	Choctaw Indian name meaning "red people".
47 stars	New Mexico (N. M., Santa Fe)	1912	From Indian name "Mexitl", an Aztec god.
48 stars	Arizona (Ariz., Phoenix)	1912	Indian name meaning "place of small springs".
49 stars	Alaska (no abr., Juneau; in 1976 it was decided by the citizens of Alaska to build a new capital at Willow South, about 70 miles NW of Anchorage, by 1980)	1959	From Eskimo word "Alakshak", meaning "mainland" or "the great country".
50 stars	Hawaii (no abr., Honolulu)	1959	Origin uncertain.

The "Star-Spangled Banner" is a patriotic song composed by Francis Scott Key in 1814. It was officially made the national anthem in 1931.

The "Stars and Bars" is a name often applied to the flag of the Confederate States of America (1861-65). It consisted of a red field with a white space extending horizontally through the centre. In 1863 it was replaced by another flag with a red field and a blue St. Andrew's cross containing 11 white stars which did not so much resemble that of the United States. These two flags can still frequently be seen in the southern states of the U.S.A., esp. in the *Deep South**.

● For the territorial development of the United Kingdom of Great Britain and Northern Ireland see *Union Jack**. H H

States' Rights

■ Constitutional rights and governmental power of member states of a federal union in face of a central government, especially of the U.S.A., where the principle of States' Rights was adhered to in numerous instances. 1791.

The American War of Secession (1861-65) was in one way the outcome of different interpretations of the American *Constitution** of 1789. Even today the constitutional position of the States in the Union is vividly discussed *(Interstate Commerce*)*.

The American struggle for States' Rights arose immediately after the adoption of the U.S. Constitution in 1789. In 1791 the first ten amendments were added in order to limit strictly the new central government with regard to the States and individuals. In Amendment X it is stipulated that "powers not delegated to the U.S. by the constitution nor prohibited by it to the states, are reserved to the states respectively or to the people". Thus a wide basis was created for the States' Rights. Among others, education, law - as far as not conflicting with federal law, e.g. marriage and divorce, consumption of alcoholic drinks - intrastate commerce, and the right to vote, are subject to the regulations of the individual state.

Whereas at that time Hamilton stood for more power to the Union Jefferson insisted upon strictly limited powers for the federal government. In the 19th century the States again and again protested against the policies of the national government; the defenders of States' Rights continued to oppose governmental centralization and demanded restrictions of central authority. Finally John C. Calhoun in defence of slavery in the southern States stood for the sovereignty of the States and urged that States of a certain region had the power to veto central policy detrimental to their interests, in this case to veto abolition of slavery. Accordingly the southern States concluded their Confederacy and proclaimed secession as their right.

The American Civil War became a turning point in American constitutional history on its way towards governmental centralization. Whereas until that time national powers had been restricted and States' Rights safeguarded no postwar amendment increased State powers. On the whole the States' Rights have been more and more restricted; national authority has consequently increased. So the "due process" and "equal protection" clauses of the 14th amendment, ratified in 1868, have been successfully invoked by racial groups against unpopular State action. By a decision of the Supreme Court in 1954 and 1958 therefore segregation in *Public Schools** was declared unconstitutional for the whole Union. States' Rights now suffer more and more from the financial subsidies of the federal government, for those subsidies entail substantial central control. The result of this subsidy process in the second half of the 20th century has been that the federal government exercises varying degrees of influence in fields that according to the Constitution are clearly States' Rights, e.g. vocational education, airport construction, state and local road construction. But generally the American national government and State governments are succeeding in working together in numerous projects such as in highway development, education, welfare, and civilian defence in a new sense of partnership instead of in a spirit of rivalry between nation and States.

P H

Suffrage

The exercise of a right to vote. Election by voting. The right or privilege of voting as a member of a state, body, etc. 1789.

● Until 1832, suffrage in the English counties was limited to landowners possessing freehold land, i.e. land in absolute ownership, which yielded an annual rental value of 40s. All other persons, however wealthy, were excluded from the right to vote and among them many manufacturers and merchants of the new industrial middle class. The working classes were excluded altogether. In the towns there was a confusing variety of voting qualifications but all of them prevented the majority of the inhabitants from voting. In Bath, for example, only 35 people out of a population of approximately 35,000 were eligible; in the Scottish county of Bute only 21 out of the 14,000 inhabitants were qualified to vote. Moreover, corruption, bribery and blackmail were normal practice before elections. There was no secret ballot.

In 1832 the third reform bill became The First Reform Act. Although it only slightly increased the percentage of people entitled to vote it was the most important among reform laws because it broke the ice. All householders in towns who paid £ 10 annual rental were given the right to vote; in the country leaseholders, copy-holders (i.e. a copy of the manorial court-roll, a very insecure form of tenancy) for 60 years (£ 10), and leaseholders at shorter terms and tenants-at-will (i.e. at the will or pleasure of the lessor) (£ 50). The importance of the First Reform Act lay in the fact that it shifted the power to the industrial and commercial class. But even then only approximately 7.1 per cent. of the population had suffrage *(Constituency*)*.

The workers expressed their discontent in the People's Charter of 1838 (Chartist Movement). In six points they demanded: (1) Vote for every man; (2) Equal electoral districts to lend to every vote the same importance; (3) Payment of members of Parliament because a factory worker returned to Parliament ceased to have an income; (4) Abolition of property qualifications; (5) Voting by ballot; (6) Annual parliaments - i.e. popular elections. Not even the Chartists thought of the women.

In 1867 Disraeli (then leader of the Conservatives in the Commons), adopting a bill originated by Gladstone, who had been defeated on the same issue, persuaded Parliament to pass the Second Reform Act. It gave suffrage to all householders in towns and to those in the counties whose rental was £ 12 or more per annum. Lodgers who paid as much as £10 per annum for unfurnished rooms were also given a vote. A further redistribution of seats of populous towns and counties took place. Separate laws were once more passed for Scotland and Ireland. The most important result of the Act was that through household suffrage great political power was placed in the hands of the workers.

In 1872, the Ballot Act was passed introducing the possibility of casting one's vote secretly.

In 1884, Gladstone's Franchise Act was passed, followed in 1885 by a Redistribution Act *(Commons*)* which granted household suffrage to the counties and thus gave the small farmers the right to vote.

The Representation of the People Act of 1918 extended the franchise to women over 30 who were householders or wives of householders. Women were also made eligible for membership in the House of Commons.

The Representation of the People Act of 1928 finally realized democratic universal suffrage by placing women on an equal basis with men and establishing the voting-age for both as 21.

The Representation of the People Act of 1949, the Representation of the People Act of 1969, and the House of Commons Disqualification Acts of 1957 and 1975, constitute the basis of the present British System of voting *(Constituency*, Commons*)*. The former Act gives the franchise (not the right to stand for election, for which the required age is still 21) to British subjects of at least 18 years of age and restates former qualifications. The latter Acts refer to the right to be elected to the House of Commons. They provide that undischarged bankrupts, clergymen of the *Established Churches** and of the Roman Catholic Church, and certain people holding offices of profit under the Crown are not eligible for the House of Commons. The last category includes high civil servants and some local government officers, holders of judicial office, members of the police and regular armed forces, and members of public corporations and government commissions.

All qualified persons are supposed to be registered for parliamentary and for local elections. (Electoral Registers Acts of 1949 and 1953.)

Several forms of "absentee voting" are permitted, e.g. for "service voters" (citizens in posts outside the United Kingdom). In exceptional cases (e.g. severe illness) voting by post or even by proxy is admissible.

■ Before the revolution of 1776 nothing like universal suffrage existed in any of the 13 colonies, nor was there any uniform suffrage system. In most colonies the picture changed but little even after 1776. Although "the people" were everywhere recognized as sovereign, all the constitutions of the 13 states, except that of Vermont, introduced property qualifications for voting, the underlying idea being to put the control of government in the hands of those who had "a stake in society". Even the democratic Benjamin Franklin declared "as to those who have no landed property . . . the allowing them to vote for legislatures is an impropriety". Georgia, New Hampshire and Pennsylvania gave suffrage to all who paid a poll tax; Delaware, Rhode Island and Virginia to all landholders; other states had various property qualifications. In most States, like in England, there were *Religious Tests** for persons to be elected to an office. South Carolina's constitution of 1778 was especially conservative. Here suffrage was limited to men with a 50 acre freehold and qualifications for the holding of offices were very high: a senator, for example, had to possess an estate worth $ 2,000, a governor one worth $ 10,000.

It is significant that Vermont and Kentucky provided the exeptions among the Eastern states. They did not establish property qualifications for voting and the holding of offices. Vermont upheld religious liberty and prohibited slavery. In many ways it was a *Frontier** state and like all these tended to be more democratic than the old colonies. Wyoming, e.g., was not only the first State to grant full female suffrage in 1869, but it did so 21 years before it was admitted to the Union as a State.

In 1776 the working population of Pennsylvania forced the adoption of a low-tax-paying franchise. In 1809 Maryland granted male suffrage, in 1818 Connecticut followed with a low poll tax, as in 1820 did Massachusetts with a small tax-paying restriction. Virginia abolished freehold qualifications in 1830. Rhode Island, the last to join the United States in 1790, was also the most obdurate in refusing to grant democratic suffrage. Indeed, the suffrage problem is a fair example by which the peculiar federal structure of the United States and the consciousness of the individual States of their "rights" can be illustrated *(States' Rights*)*. When Amendment XIV was ratified in 1868 and attempted to grant *Civil Rights**, including the right to vote, to the Negroes, not only the whole South but also several Northern states, among them Connecticut, Ohio, New Jersey, Pennsylvania, simply refused to do so. Amendment XV remained similarly ineffective. It is obvious that the federal structure and the existence of a civil rights problem have made the suffrage question infinitely more difficult in the U.S.A. Whereas the British Representation of the People Act, 1928, brought about de facto universal suffrage in Britain, neither Amendment XIX, 1920, which granted suffrage to women, nor Amendment XXIV, 1964, which abolished any kind of poll tax, could achieve universality.

The present situation with regard to suffrage in the U.S.A. is the following: each of the 50 States has the right to decide on the voting qualifications of its citizens. The federal courts can interfere with this right only in case of a violation of Amendments XV and XIX which provide that the right of citizens cannot be taken away because of race, colour, previous condition of servitude, or sex. The Voting Rights Act of 1965 limited State residence requirements to

30 days in all elections. Most States require registration; until 1965 some required a literacy test, which, together with other remaining voter tests was abolished in the Voting Rights Act of that year. Until 1964 payment of a poll tax was demanded in Alabama, Arkansas, Mississippi, Texas, and Virginia (see above). Since the abolition of the various measures discriminating against black citizens, registration of negroes before elections had risen to approximately 60 per cent. by 1968 as against 12 per cent. in 1947. The voting age is 18 (Amendment XXVI, 1971). In 1970, the Justice Department published the Voting Rights Act Amendments which stated that the Act of 1965 had enfranchised the estimated 2 million American civilians abroad who until then had been unable to vote because of restrictive State requirements. The inhabitants of the national capital, Washington, D.C., still have limited suffrage *(District of Columbia*)*, and approx. 5.5 million public employees are still forbidden to run for public or party office, under the Hatch Acts of 1939 and 1940. H H

Territory

■ One of certain regions in the West of the U.S.A. belonging to and under the government of the American Republic, and having some degree of self-government, but not yet admitted as a State into the Union. 1799.

In the United States "Territory" means a politically organized geographical region which has not yet attained statehood. Art. V, sec. 3, of the *Constitution** permits the creation of new states. From the beginning of the U.S.A. to the present day the territorial status has been the usual stage on the way to the admission as a State of the Union. Only seven of the 37 States following the 13 original ones were admitted without having been territories. Art. V of the so-called Northwest Ordinance of 1787 made 60,000 inhabitants one of the prerequisites for statehood.

All "continental" Territories of the U.S.A. have become members of the Union. Of the outlying Territories, Alaska (1959) and Hawai (1959) have become States; whereas the Philippines became an independent country in 1946. (Alaska was bought from Russia in 1867 upon the initiative of the then Secretary of State Seward for $ 7.2 million, the purchase was then called "Seward's Folly"; Hawaii was annexed "by treaty" in 1897.) There remain, however, several dependencies of the U.S.A. which have the status of Territories, with appointed governors and a limited measure of self-government:

American Samoa (1899), Canton Islands and Enderbury Island (1939, Condominion U.S.A./Britain), Corn Islands (1914), Guam (1898), Midway Islands (1867), Panama Canal Zone (1904, "leased in perpetuity", but, following the Panama Canal Treaty of 1978, to be returned to Panama in successive stages, by the year 2000), Puerto Rico (1898), Trust Territory of the Pacific Islands (1952, U.N. trusteeship), Virgin Islands of the U.S. (1917), Wake Island (1898), and a number of islands (some of them uninhabited): Caroline, Christmas, Danger, Flint, Funafuti, Kingman Reef, Malden, Manahiki, Navassa, Nukufetau, Nukulailai, Nurakatha, Palmyra, Penrhyn, Rakahanga, Starbuck, Vostok, Phoenix Group (except Canton and Enderbury), Union group, Baker, Howland, and Jarvis Islands; claimed both by the U.S.A. and Columbia: Sueno Bank, Roncador Cay, Serana Bank. In 1976, the northern Mariana Islands formerly part of the Trust Territory of the

Pacific Island were granted commonwealth status (comparable to that of Puerto Rico) after 85 per cent. of their population had voted for it in 1975.

This territorial empire comprises four categories: the territory proper, like Guam, Puerto Rico and the Marianas (their inhabitants are U.S. citizens); governance, like American Samoa (whose inhabitants are only U.S. "nationals"); possession, like Midway or Wake (with practically no population except for military personnel) and trust territory, like Micronesia (which is practically under colonial rule).

From a realistic viewpoint, only Puerto Rico has a fair chance of becoming a State of the Union; curiously, it is the Puerto Ricans, not the Americans, who hesitate, because by giving up their territorial status they would deprive themselves of considerable tax priveleges. But there is also a substantial minority among Puerto Ricans favouring independence. - Puerto Ricans have full freedom to move in the U.S.A. *(Civil Rights*).* H H

Town and Township

An assemblage of buildings, public and private, larger than a village, and having more complete and independent local government. M.E. In the U.S.A., units of local government.

■ In America towns are in general subdivisions of the county and form part of the State system of government. They owe their existence to the constitutions and laws of the States. Towns are characteristic forms of local government in the North, Middle West, and Northeast, but their greatest importance is in New England where the town constitutes the principal unit of local administration. Here the town is usually made up of a village with a large amount of surrounding territory. Its political organization is based on the town meeting - a striking example of direct democracy. At least once a year all the eligible voters meet to choose the Board of Selectmen - i.e. officers to conduct municipal affairs - a school board, and other officials, and to discuss and pass judgement on ordinances, taxes, and expenditures *(Mayflower Compact*).*

In the rural areas west of *New England**, but not in the South and Southwest, towns are called "townships". They are usually more uniform in size, and comprise an area of between 30 and 40 square miles, but sometimes use different names for their local officers. These "civil townships", however, should not be confused with the "congressional townships", which are units created for surveying purposes (6 x 6 miles).

A typical American town or township has the following system of government: (1) Legislative: town meeting; (2) Executive: Board of Selectmen (or supervisors, president, chairman, or mayor); (3) Judiciary: *Justice of the Peace** who forms part of the State system of law. Towns and townships are concerned with local conditions like education - which in America is based on the local community - health, sanitation, traffic regulation, lighting, and recreation.

● British law does not define the term "town". In Britain it is therefore not a technical term in *Local Government**. Nevertheless, the word is used frequently in official and unofficial language, e.g. town development, town and country planning, *New Town**, to denote centres of population larger than a village, especially those places which have not been given the royal charter of a *City**. H H

Union Jack

Originally and properly, a small British flag flown at the jack-staff of a ship (Jack being a familiar appellation for a sailor but also a naval colloquialism for "small"); later extended to any size or adaptation of the union flag. 1674.

- The British Union Flag is a composite emblem. It includes the emblems of England, Scotland, and Ireland: the red Cross of St. George on a white field, the white saltire of St. Andrew on a blue field, and the red saltire of St. Patrick on a white field. It is not clear how the cross of St. George became the symbol of England, but its use has long been traditional. According to legend, St. Andrew's relics, after a shipwreck, were cast up on the coast of Scotland, and a Scottish king named Achaius adopted the diagonal cross as his emblem. Though St. Patrick was the missionary of Ireland, the so-called St. Patrick's Cross has no associations with him, as he was not crucified.

But apart from the emblematic interest which the Union Jack may arouse, it also reflects important stages in the history and territorial development of the United Kingdom: the union of the crowns of *England* and *Scotland* in 1603, when James VI of Scotland, son of Mary Stuart, became king of England as James I; and the union of Great Britain (i.e. England, Scotland, and Wales) and *Ireland* in 1801, by which the United Kingdom of Great Britain and Ireland was formed. *Wales,* whose emblem is the red dragon on a white and green field, is not represented in the Union Jack. It was formally annexed by the Act of Union of 1536 (Henry VIII), which was a measure meant to bring about complete assimilation not admitting for any separate Welsh identity. Although Wales, in contradistinction to Cornwall, managed to preserve a cultural and religious tradition of its own through the centuries, it was, until quite recently, regarded as part of England.

Cornwall is often neglected in historical accounts. In the latter stages of the Anglo-Saxon conquest, the remaining territories of the Welsh (Cymri) were cut into three separate parts - Strathclyde in the north, Wales in the centre, and Cornwall in the south. Geographically isolated from Wales, Cornwall could offer little resistance to invaders, but to this day it has remained Celtic in its character and population. It had its own parliament, the Stannary (f.L. stannum = tin, Cornwall's greatest wealth since Phoenician times), founded in 1201, dissolved in 1752, and revived (though unofficially) in 1974. And up to the eighteenth or nineteenth century it spoke its own Cornish language.

The two dependencies of the crown, the Isle of Man and the Channel (or Norman) Islands, are not a part of the United Kingdom, nor are they included in the Union Jack. They have their own flags and enjoy complete regional autonomy; they print their own money, levy their own taxes, have their own legislative assemblies and systems of law, and even separate arrangements with the European Community.

The symbol of the *Isle of Man* is the Trinacria, three armoured legs, in white and yellow, meeting at the thigh. It is supposed to be of Sicilian origin, introduced into the Isle of Man in the thirteenth century. - The Island has the world's oldest Parliament, the Tynwald, which, with its two constituent branches, the Legislative Council (Upper House) and the House of Keys, originated in the lawmaking assemblies of the Norsemen who governed the Kingdom of Man and the Isles (i.e. Hebrides) from the ninth century until 1266, when it passed to Scotland, then, under Henry IV (1399-1413), to the Stanleys (Earls of Derby). In the eighteenth century it passed to the Dukes of

Atholl (Scottish dukedom). Finally, in 1765, it was purchased by the British Crown. The Queen is the Lord Proprietor of Man, and honoured as "The Queen, Lord of Man".

The *Channel Islands* Jersey and Guernsey still use the ancient emblem of England, three lions in gold, on a red shield, that of Guernsey differing by a sprig of golden leaves at the top of the shield. The flag of Alderney is a St. George's Cross; at its centre there is a gold lion holding a sprig of leaves, surrounded by a green gold-bordered circle. The flag of Sark (or Sercq) is also a St. George's Cross with two gold lions in the canton. - Victor Hugo called the Norman Islands "pieces of France fallen into the sea and gathered up by England" (morceaux de France tombés à la mer et ramassés par l'Angleterre). They are the last vestiges of the Duchy of Normandy, most of which was lost by King John (Lackland) to Philip II of France in 1204. They have jealously guarded their regional independence from England since the Middle Ages. The Queen is their sovereign, and she is represented by a lieutenant-governor. In Jersey and Guernsey the Bailiff presides over the States (i.e. parliament) and is the chief magistrate. Alderney is headed by a president of the States Assembly, Sark by a Seigneur presiding over the Chief Pleas (Sark's parliament). - Laws, which are partly Norman in origin, vary from island to island, Guernsey law students still attend Caen University, in Normandy. French remains the official language of the courts. Many of the principal officers in the islands have French titles - procureur, comptroller, greffier, jurat, séneschal, precôt, vavasour, and so on. The patois is still commonly spoken. It is still possible to buy a fief, though some relics of feudal times have disappeared; women, for example, until 1973 their husbands' chattels, are now free and can own property.

Territorial development of the United Kingdom:

1171/72 "Lordship of Ireland" established by Henry II *(Empire*)*.
1204 The Channel Islands retained by the English Crown.
1282 English conquest of Wales accomplished, confirmed in the Statute of Rhuddlan, 1284.
1301 Edward (later Edward II) first Prince of Wales.
1536 England and Wales united through Act of Union.
1603 Crowns of England and Scotland united through James I's (James VI's of Scotland) succession to the English throne.
1649/50 Complete subjugation of Ireland under Cromwell.
1707 Parliaments of England and Scotland united through Act of Union; abolition of the Scottish parliament.
1765 Isle of Man purchased by the English Parliament from the Duke of Atholl.
1801 Parliaments of England and Ireland united through Act of Union, abolition of the Irish parliament.
1920 Partition of Ireland through the Government of Ireland Act; Northern Ireland remaining part of the United Kingdom *(Home Rule*)*.
1922 Proclamation of the Free State of Ireland, which became a self-governing *Dominion**.

■ For the territorial development of the United States of America see *Stars and Stripes** and *Louisiana Purchase**. H H

Whip

An instrument for flogging or beating. One who wields a driving-whip. A member of a particular party in Parliament whose duty it is to secure the attendance of members of that party. 1853. The action of "whipping up" the members of a party for a parliamentary division, or any body of persons for some united action. 1828.

● The Whips are the organizers of their parliamentary party, i.e. they are not officers of *Parliament**, but party functionaries. Each party has a Chief Whip - in the 18th century he was known as the Patronage Secretary - whose position is one of eminence and considerable influence, and, depending on the strength of the parliamentary party, between nine and twelve Whips, each of whom is responsible for about 30 Members. The Government Chief Whip is Parliamentary Secretary of the *Treasury**, thus, a member of the Government and receives a salary. Some Government Whips receive salaries as Junior Lords of the Treasury, others hold paid positions in the Royal Household. By the Ministerial Salaries and Members' Pensions Act, 1965, the *Opposition** Chief Whips in the Lords and Commons also receive salaries.

Their work is generally inconspicuous for they are active "behind the Speaker's Chair". This means: (1) They are the connecting links between the Government, especially between the Prime Minister and other party members. It is their task to see to it that the members of their party are present on important occasions, especially when divisions take place. They control the system of "pairing", i.e. finding a member of the opposite party who also abstains from voting in a division, and they lend an ear to the grievances of the backbenchers. (2) The Chief Whip of the Government and the Chief Whip of the Opposition are in constant contact with each other. They constitute the "usual channels" through which the programme of the days is arranged. They also suggest to the *Speaker** of the *Commons** the order of speakers of their parties. It is usually the Chief Whip who after question time moves the "motion to adjourn".

The office of the Chief Whip is not a popular one. Edward Heath's election to the position of leader of the Conservative Party was indeed unusual when the fact is taken into consideration that he once was the party's Chief Whip. The Whips should not be confused with the leaders of the parliamentary parties; a Minister, sometimes the Prime Minister, is usually the leader of a party in Parliament and is not normally concerned with questions of organization.

A whip is also a printed note usually sent to members by the Whips on Fridays. It contains the programme of the following week with instructions. It is a serious step not to follow these instructions, because this is tantamount to secession from the party, though lately members on both sides have increasingly refused to accept the dictates of the whips, which is tantamount to relaxed party discipline. This became especially obvious in the debate and division on Britain's entry into E.E.C. Example of a day's schedule contained in a whip: "On Thursday, November 12th" (underlined), "the House will meet at 2.30 p.m. Continuation of the General Debate on Housing. Divisions will take place and your attendance at 4.30 p.m. and throughout the sitting is essential unless you have registered a pair" (the whole last sentence underlined three times, "4.30 p.m." underlined four times; the lines indicate the degree of urgency). The practice has been handed down from England's fox-hunting aristocracy in the 17th century, and the name comes from the fox-hunting term "whipper-in", a phrase which in Dickens's parliamentary sketches was still used in full.

■ Both parties in the House of Representatives have Whips. They have the task of ensuring good attendance and keeping track of all important legislation, especially when a vote is about to take place. Their position, however, is much weaker than that of their British counterparts. They do not control "pairing", which, incidentally, is tolerated in both houses, and they are unpaid. H H

PART II
Law

Attorney
Barrister
Common Law
County Court
Courts of Appeal
Crown Court
District Court
Equity
Habeas Corpus (Act)
High Court of Justice
Impeachment
Inns of Court
Judge
Judicial Review
Jury
Justice of the Peace
Law Lords
Magistrates' Court
Precedent
Rules of Evidence
Sheriff Court
Solicitor
Statute Law
Supreme Court of Judicature
Supreme Court of the U.S.

Attorney 2

One appointed, an agent, deputy. One duly appointed or constituted to act for another in business and legal matters. 1466.

■ In the U.S.A. an attorney at law (or attorney and counsellor at law) is a member of the legal profession. He is qualified and legally appointed to appear in court to prosecute or defend any action on behalf of his client in criminal and civil proceedings. He is authorized to give legal advice, to prepare briefs and to transact business for his clients.

Originally "attorney" designated a lower class of advocate, the higher being "counsellor" (similar to the distinction between *Solicitor** and *Barrister** in Britain). Today the term counsellor as distinct from attorney, continues to exist only in the State of New Jersey.

In the U.S.A. the courts direct the qualification and admission of attorneys and counsellors. Admission to the Bar is regarded as a judicial act. Usually the Supreme Court of the State prescribes the conditions for admission which vary from State to State.

Courses of studies, periods of preparation and legal training are required everywhere. The period of training is spent at a recognized law school. In some States the applicant has to submit to an examination by the court itself or by examiners appointed for this purpose. The method of preparing oneself in an office of a practising attorney or counsellor is today almost obsolete in the U.S.A. The graduates of recognized law schools or of a law department of a university who have obtained the degree of a Bachelor of Laws are admitted to practise at the bar without further examinations.

The Attorney General is the head of the Department of Justice. His staff includes the Solicitor General (second-ranking officer in the department), several assistant attorneys general in Washington, and the assistant attorney general in the Division of Customs in New York City, a pardon attorney, and their assistants. Generally the assistant attorneys general are division heads specializing in antitrust litigation, the custody of alien property, prosecution of criminals, etc. The Attorney General is the chief advocate of the U.S.A. and gives advice and opinion when requested by the President or by the heads of the executive departments. He is involved in the appointment of judges. He supervises and directs the attorneys and marshals of all districts. He advises county officials upon legal matters connected with their official duties and prosecutes in all civil and criminal actions in which the State or county may be interested or involved. He is usually elected by the people for a term of two to four years. Local Prosecuting Attorney, District Attorney, and State Attorney are the different titles of persons in charge of the State's legal business in the particular county or district.

● The title "attorney" was abolished for practising advocates in Britain in 1873. It is still used, however, in the title of Attorney General, who is the senior law officer of the Crown. Like his deputy, the Solicitor General, he is occupied in the Law Officers' *Department** and is always a *barrister**. He takes charge of the legal business of the Government and his opinion is frequently sought in legal matters. He and the Solicitor General may also conduct important prosecutions.

H J S

Barrister

- f. bar (barrier or wooden rail at which prisoners are stationed for trial, etc.). 1532 A student of law who has been called to the bar, and practises as advocate in the superior courts of law. Formally barrister-at-law.

A barrister is a lawyer who has reached a professional standard accepted by the Council of Legal Education. Once he has passed the law examinations of the latter he becomes a member of one of the four *Inns of Court** and is called to the Bar. He has the exclusive right of pleading in higher courts (right of audience). After years of practice he can obtain a patent appointing him Queen's (or King's) Counsel. Members of that group occupy the highest judicial posts in the land.

In Great Britain barristers carry out only specific duties, mainly pleading in the higher courts. Barristers do not generally accept mandates from the client directly. A *Solicitor** prepares the briefs and then asks the barrister to represent the client in court.

The division into the two branches, barristers and solicitors, goes back to 1873 when the Judicature Act stipulated that all lawyers acting formerly as *Attorneys**, proctors or solicitors, thenceforth be called solicitors and thus be distinct from the barristers. In Scotland the term used for the English barrister is "advocate". He usually holds an arts degree. The conditions governing his profession are similar to those in England. Nowadays only in Ireland an advising barrister is called counsellor (at law). In England "advocate" and "counsellor" are no longer used as terms in connection with the legal profession.

H J S

Common Law

The unwritten law of England, administered by the King's courts, based on ancient and universal usage, and embodied in commentaries and reported cases (opposed to statute law); the law administered by the King's ordinary judges (opposed to equity, ecclesiastical and admiralty law, etc.). 1848.

The body of law developed in England primarily from judicial decisions based on custom and precedent, unwritten in statute and code, and constituting the basis of the English legal system and of the system in all of the U.S.A. except Louisiana.

- Common Law, as it is known today, is to a large extent the law made by judges and based on cases of *Precedent**. On the whole the decisions of the judges are directives for subsequent cases, the common law thus being case law. Common law broadly expresses the sound instincts of the people, the common sense in human activity and social life. It therefore covers the whole of constitutional, civil, criminal as well as public law. Judges, however, are not bound hand and foot to precedents. They may deviate from a precedent provided they have sufficient reason for doing so; they are even obliged to do so if parliamentary statutes have given rise to new legal concepts.

The development of the English common law goes back to the Anglo-Saxon period, its principles then being applied in local courts and mainly reflecting the customs of the local community. The development of the English legal system has not much been influenced by the ancient Roman Law; in the 13th century the study of Roman Law was even forbidden.

During the reign of Henry II (1154-1189) a King's Court was installed before which all subjects of the realm could bring their suits. The King sent judges riding through the counties to control the local courts and to hold sessions. The judges decided the cases according to their individual concept of justice. Later the King ordered their decisions to be collected and recorded. From the end of the 13th century onwards the decisions of judges on circuit and in the royal courts were contained in Year Books which, after the middle of the 16th century were to become the Law Reports existing up to the present day. 2

As the power of the Crown decreased from the 15th century onwards the "common" rights of the individual increased, as can be seen from the Petition of Right (1628), the *Habeas Corpus (Act)** (1679) and the *Bill of Rights** (1689) which were milestones in the development of individual rights.

In the course of time the common law courts stuck so firmly to precedents that it was regarded as necessary to compensate for the shortcomings of the system in individual cases. A special tribunal, the Court of Chancery was entrusted with the task of administering justice on the principles of *Equity**. The separation of the jurisdiction of common law and equity proceedings resulting from the establishment of the Court of Chancery was again eliminated by the Judicature Act of 1873 which merged the jurisdiction into one *Supreme Court of Judicature**.

Scottish common law is based on the description of reputed lawyers of the 17th, 18th and 19th centuries who described the legal situation of their times. Jurisdiction developed the principles shown by these lawyers and formed the modern non-statutory law of Scotland. The principles of equity were always respected but a separate system of equity never existed.

■ Although the original 13 states were colonies of Britain they were uncertain for a while whether to adopt the continental or the English law system. Finally they took over common law. Louisiana is an exception because it was for a time French property and favoured the "Code Napoléon".

After the 13 states had declared themselves independent (1776) they drew up the federal *Constitution** in 1789. The Constitution of the United States did not expressly adopt the common law but acknowledged it as the law of the States of the Union. Of course, common law had to be modified so that it complied with the written Constitution. It is obvious, however, that the unity of a system is in danger of being destroyed when it is applied in the federation as well as in each of the states itself. (It may be argued that there are 50 different systems of common law in the United States.) State courts are bound to their own precedents and to the decisions of the federal courts. Thus jurisdiction may differ. The development of common law has often taken different courses in the various states.

There were numerous attemps to unify and codify the substantive law, but they did not enjoy great success. This is due to the Constitution of the United States which prohibits interference with the common law of the states. Consequently the federation cannot enforce a unification.

The supreme law of the Union consists of the U.S. Constitution, the Acts of Congress and the foreign treaties, while the law of the individual states – as long as federal rights are not concerned – is based on the constitution of the state, common law and the statutes of the individual state. H J S

County Court

● The County Courts are local courts of civil jurisdiction. Their origin is in pre-Norman times, their modern form dates from the County Courts Act of 1846.

County Courts are presided over by a paid *Judge** who sits alone in most cases. By a court's decision a *Jury** of eight persons may be ordered at the request of one of the parties. The procedure is comparatively simple, the costs of the proceedings are reasonable. Each County Court employs a registrar and bailiffs, but some of the County Court Judges have to administer more than one court because a circuit may consist of one court or a group of courts. The registrar who is usually a *solicitor** hears the smaller cases.

In 1973, a small claims arbitration service was created. It is expected to give better protection to the consumer. The registrar, acting as judge, has the power to refer any case to arbitration if less than £ 75 are involved. The arbitration procedure settles small claims cheaply and in an unbureaucratic way, without formal hearing. Litigants, even the party who wins the case, have to pay their own counsel. They are thus discouraged from employing lawyers.

The jurisdiction of a County Court generally covers for example civil actions up to an amount of £ 1000, equity jurisdiction up to £ 5,000, etc. Actions assigned to the Queen's (or King's) Bench Division of the *High Court of Justice** may be tried by County Courts regardless of the amount involved, provided the parties give their written consent. Thus the proceedings may include high values of claim. Appeals against the decisions of a County Court are heard by the Court of Appeal *(Courts of Appeal*)*.

Side by side with the County Courts, a few local courts worked with similar jurisdiction until 1972 (London, Liverpool, Lancaster, Durham, Bristol, Salford). Most of them were survivals from the medieval borough courts. It was a general rule that appeals from a local court were heard by the Queen's Bench Division if a statute ordered no other regulation. Appeals from the local courts of the great cities were referred to the Court of Appeal.

■ Less than half of the American States have County Courts as courts of limited jurisdiction within the area of their county. The functions of American County Courts vary considerably from State to State. Civil cases may be tried, ranging in matters of a few dollars up to $ 2,000. Some County Courts try criminal cases from misdemeanours to more severe offences, other ones have no criminal jurisdiction at all. In Kentucky and Tennessee, e.g., County Courts also handle non-judicial matters. Since 1950 there has been a tendency to replace the jurisdiction of the *Justices of the Peace** by the County Court system. H J S

Courts of Appeal

● Since 1972, one single Court of Appeal (Civil and Criminal Division) has been exercising the duties of the former two courts of appeal: the "Court of Appeal" dealing with civil appeals, and the "Court of Criminal Appeal" dealing with criminal appeals.

The "Court of Appeal" was constituted by the Judicature Act of 1925 as part of the *Supreme Court of Judicature**. It was organized into divisions, each sitting with three judges. Its real head was the Master of the Rolls who was one of the permanent members of the court. He was assisted by the Justices of Appeal. Furthermore the Lord Chancellor, the Lord Chief Justice, the Lord

President of the Probate, Divorce and Admiralty Division of the *High Court of Justice** and most of the Lords of Appeal in Ordinary *(Law Lords*)* were members of the Court of Appeal. The court heard appeals from the High Court of Justice, the Assizes, the Local Courts and County Courts. As a result of the procedure in the Court of Appeal the court could order a retrial or a reversal of the judgement of a lower instance. It could increase or reduce the amount of damages. Otherwise it confirmed the first instance decision.

The court usually sat with three judges, except in cases when the appeal was based on an alleged violation of practice or procedure, in which case two judges were present. In case of a decision of great importance the whole court could be summoned by the president of the court. Further appeal to the "High Court of Parliament" (i.e. the House of Lords) was possible.

Courts of Appeal

The English System of Courts and Instances of Criminal and Non-Criminal Appeal

(a) non-criminal

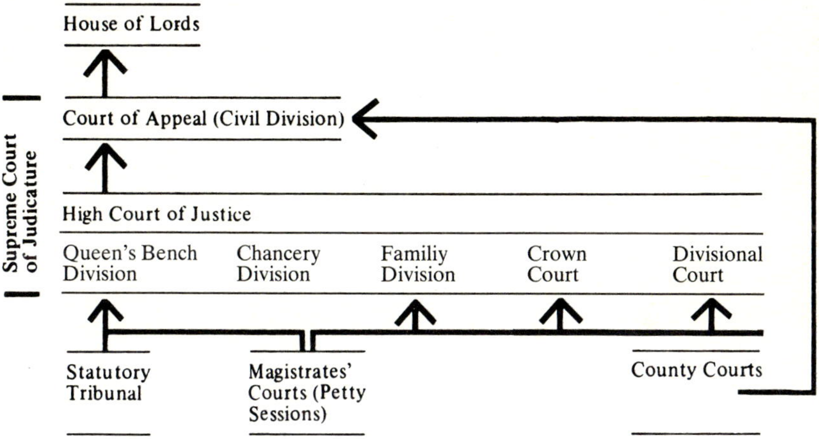

(b) criminal

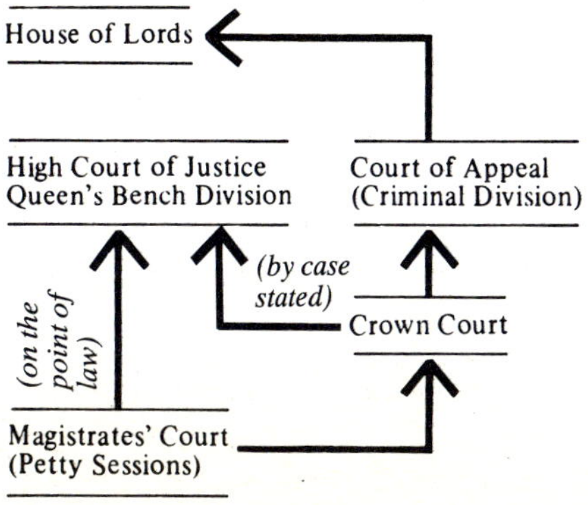

HJS

The U. S. System of Courts and Channels of Criminal and Non-Criminal Appeal

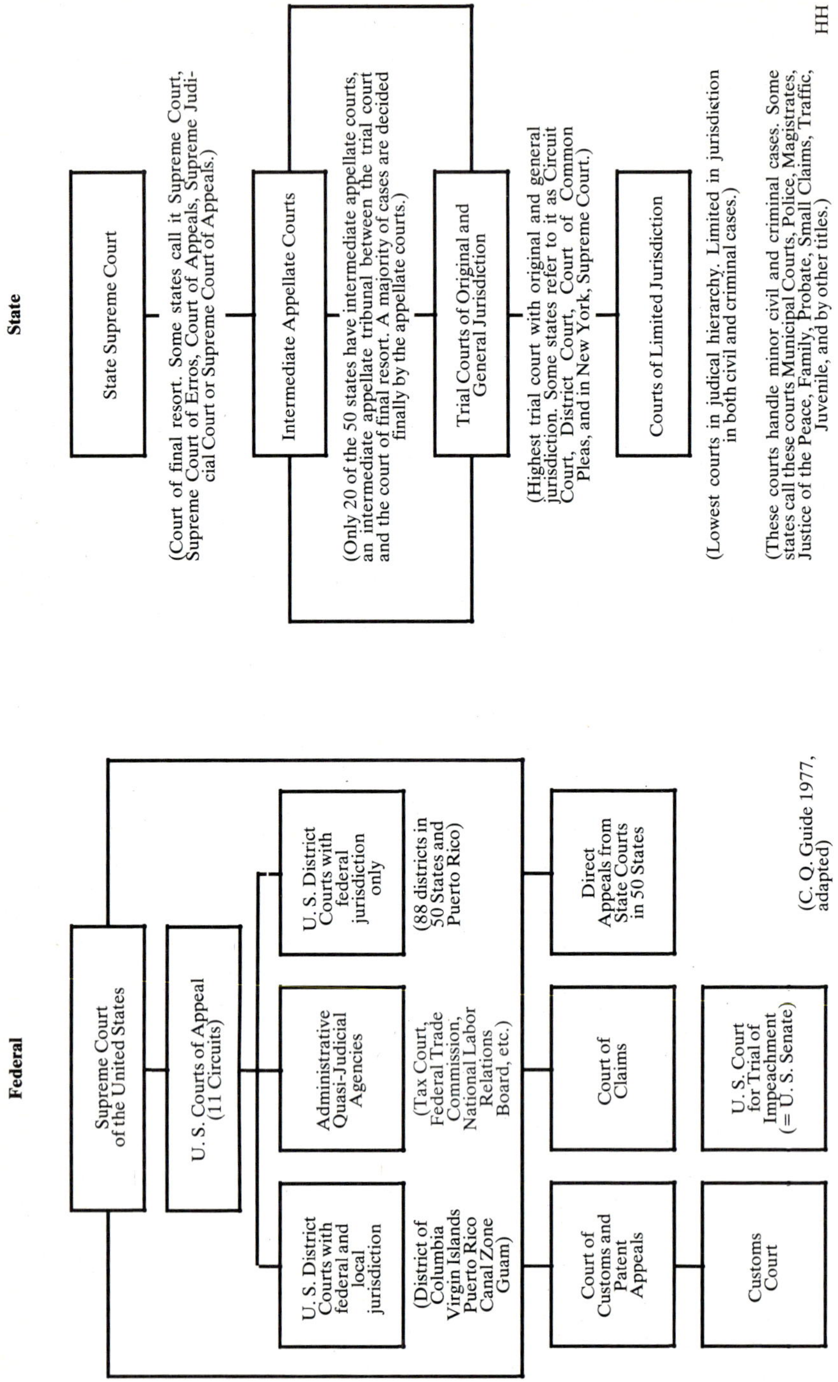

The "Court of Criminal Appeal" was established by the Criminal Appeal Act of 1907. The Lord Chief Justice presided. The court sat with three (in special cases with five) *Judges** of the Queen's Bench Division of the High Court of Justice. It heard appeals against convictions or sentences by courts of Quarter Sessions, Assizes, the Crown Courts, and the Central Criminal Court. It had its seat in London.

The "Court of Criminal Appeal" had the power to order a retrial in case of fresh evidence. It was able to quash the conviction and to acquit the accused. In all other cases it confirmed the first instance decision. The majority of the judges hearing the appeal and sitting usually in an uneven number of not less than three determined the question in court. Appeals to the House of Lords were possible if the court certified that a point of law of general public importance was involved.

In Scotland civil appeals can be heard by the Inner House of the Court of Session. It is possible to appeal to the House of Lords. The last instance for criminal procedures is the High Court of Justiciary which sits with three or more judges. There is no possibility of appeal to the House of Lords.

■ In the U.S.A. the Circuit Courts of Appeal function as appelate courts in matters civil and criminal. They were established in 1891 in order to relieve the *Supreme Court** of the U.S. As the name implies these courts exercise only an appelate jurisdiction. They accept the facts delivered from the lower court and therefore do not need a jury. They only decide questions of law.

The Circuit Courts of Appeal sitting with three or more judges hear appeals from district and other lower courts. The majority of the judges constitutes a quorum. The opinion of the majority of the judges sitting decides the case in dispute. The decision is usually final, yet a hearing by the Supreme Court of the U.S.A. is possible if a legal instruction is requested from the Supreme Court, or a review is ordered by it.

H J S

Crown Court

● Until 1971 Crown Courts continued to exist only in Liverpool and Manchester. Since 1972 the name of a single court for criminal and civil jurisdiction according to the Courts Act of 1971.

In 1972 the Crown Court took over the duties of the Courts of Assize, Quarter Sessions and the Crown Courts of Liverpool and Manchester, and replaced them.

Assizes were the periodic sessions of the Courts of Assize which were branches of the High Court of Justice.

Some of the 68 puisne judges (i.e. judges without special office) of the High Court used to travel to the assize towns which were usually the county towns and some of the other big towns. There they presided over the trials in which a jury decided the questions of fact. The judges were "on circuit" three times a year. Each assize town was visited at least once on each circuit. The courts of assize passed judgement first in criminal and afterwards in civil cases. The jurisdiction of the courts of assize as branches of the High Court of Justice covered all civil and the most serious criminal offences (e.g. murder and manslaughter). In criminal cases they were both a first instance and an appellate court.

The term "assizes" is not used in the United States, but itinerant judges perform the same duties within the circuits of their courts *(Supreme Court of the U.S.*)*.

A Court of Quarter Sessions was a local court of record. It exercised limited criminal and civil jurisdiction. It was a first instance court for most crimes and offences except, e.g., murder, capital felony, offences against the Sovereign or the Parliament; in civil cases it was mostly an appellate court. The trials at the Courts of Quarter Sessions were conducted in the presence of a *Jury**. In the counties the court was usually presided over by a bench of lay magistrates under a legally qualified chairman.

The name "Quarter Sessions" dates back to 1388 when a statute ordered that "justices shall keep their sessions in every quarter of the year at least".

Consequently the Crown Court is now competent for all criminal cases above the level of the *Magistrates' Court**. A limited original civil and appellate civil and criminal jurisdiction, formerly lying with Quarter Sessions, is also vested in it.

The new court is able to sit anywhere in the country independent of any itineraries. It holds session regularly at almost 90 centres.

It is manned with High Court judges, Circuit judges (professional judges) and Recorders (part-time judges).

Criminal offences have been divided into classes. The Lord Chief Justice decides which classes of case have to be presided over by a High Court judge, a Circuit judge or a Recorder.

The office of recorder is open to the *Solicitor**. Recorders having held office for five years may be elected as Circuit judges. Thus the Courts Act enables *Solicitors** to become *Judges**.

According to the Courts Act many centuries-old courts are abolished, e.g. the courts of Bristol, Liverpool, Durham and Lancaster. H J S

District Court

■ The U.S.A. is divided into judicial districts which do not necessarily correspond to a State. In virtue of the Judicial Code of 1911 each district has a District Court where a professional District Judge regularly holds office. The jurisdiction of the District Courts includes *Common Law** and *Equity**, it deals with civil matters as well as with criminal offences, admiralty and bankruptcy cases. Their function is restricted to suits referring to the Federal Constitution, Federal Laws and Treaties *(Supreme Court of the U.S.*)*. The value of claim in civil cases handled by the District Courts must exceed $ 3,000.

The District Courts are instances of the facts. Therefore they usually sit with a *Jury**. Appeals against decisions of District Courts are heard by the Circuit *Courts of Appeal**. *H J S*

Equity

The recourse to general principles of justice (L. naturalis aequitas) to correct or supplement the ordinary law. 1574. In England, Ireland and U.S.A., a system of law existing side by side with the common and statute law (together called "law" in a narrower sense) and superseding these, when they conflict with it. 1591.

● As the system of *Common Law** could not provide a remedy outside the recognized writs (i.e. a limited register of possibilities to address a court as recognized by jurisdiction) a supplementary law was felt to be necessary which made possible the prevention of imminent evil or damages in matters not recognized in common law. The property of married women, for instance, was a case in point; in former times married women were not allowed to own property. In order to enforce rights not recognized in common law, or to give relief or provide a remedy to replace a common law remedy that had been lost, "equity" came into existence during the Middle Ages. In case a plaintiff or defendant regarded himself as treated inequitably by a common law decision it was possible for him to apply to the Sovereign's Grace. This application was first decided by the King's council on the recommendation of the Chancellor, who acted as the "Keeper of the King's Conscience", and later by the Chancellor himself. Gradually it became the custom to address petitions to the Court of Chancery rather than to the King. Thus equity as a supplementary law was administered in the Court of Chancery which worked outside the common law courts and was directed by the Chancellor. Criticism soon arose that decisions were totally dependent on the personality of the Chancellor. Chancellors who were clergymen formed equity on the basis of the canonical law or general moral principles; others who were lawyers made use of ideas from the ancient Roman philosophers. Several decisions were based on the law of nature. The situation changed when the decisions of the successive Chancellors were collected and quoted. It slowly became an unwritten law for each Chancellor to feel bound to the decisions of his predecessors. Thus equity became nearly as fixed as common law. 2

Equity is applied only in civil law where common law and equity exist side by side. Today equity plays a most important role in the rights of property.

A suit in equity is instituted by filing a bill or petition. Equity cases are decided by a *Judge** never by a *Jury**. The procedure is mostly a written one. In urgent cases a decision may be given without the defendant being heard. Usually the procedure is similar to that of common law and the *Rules of Evidence** are generally the same. The decision of the judge is called a decree. It is a decision in respect of the person which widely adapts to the facts and circumstances while a common law decision is a consequence of proven facts. Fairness, therefore, plays an important role in equity. As a consequence of the dualism between common law and equity it could happen that a plaintiff won an action according to the rules of common law, but his opponent addressed an equity court and by a decree of this court prevented the plaintiff from making use of the decision in his favour if the equity court considered this decision unequitable. In order to avoid contradictory decisions regarding one and the same matter the *Supreme Court of Judicature** Act of 1873 provided that equitable defences are admitted legally in the common law courts. Thus all courts nowadays apply both common law and equity. The Act of 1873, however, laid down that equity is to prevail where there is conflict between the rules of common law and equity.

In Scotland a separate system of equity does not exist but equitable principles are to be found in the ordinary rules of the law.

■ The United States took over the British system of common law and equity. Separate equity courts exist in the States of Arkansas, Delaware, Mississippi and Tennessee. Elsewhere equity is included in the jurisdiction of the common law courts. In contrast to the situation in Britain the efficacy of equity is often greater than that of the common law. Offences against equity decisions are regarded as contempt of court in special cases and are punished heavily.

In the United States an abuse of the possibilities offered by equity led to a severe restriction of the right to strike. In 1932, however, the Norris-La Guardia-Anti-Injunction Act restricted this abuse in equity decisions with regard to *Collective Bargaining**. H J S

Habeas Corpus (Act)

Habeas corpus ad subiiciendum, requiring the body of a person restrained of liberty to be brought before the judge or into court, so that the lawfulness of the restraint may be investigated and determined. Transl. app. "thou (shalt) have the body (in court)". A writ directed to some person detaining another, commanding him to bring the body of the person into court or before a judge for the purpose specified on the writ, so that the lawfulness of the restraint may be investigated or determined (writ habeas corpus ad subiiciendum). 1465.

● The Habeas Corpus Act (1679) declared that (1) all persons, except those charged with treason or felony, could demand from one of the judges a writ of habeas corpus, directing the gaoler to bring them before him within three days, so that the legality of their detention might be tested; (2) all persons charged with treason or felony must be tried at the next sessions after commitment, or else be admitted to bail; and, if not tried at the second sessions after commitment, must be discharged; (3) no person could be recommitted (i.e. tried again) for the same offence; (4) no person was to be sent as a prisoner to Scotland, the Channel Islands, or any place beyond the seas within or without the king's dominions.

Today, the stipulations of the Habeas Corpus Act amount to a guarantee whereby nobody can be detained longer than three days without a fair trial, i.e. his detention must be based on a writ of arrest, he must be told why he has been detained, proceedings against him must begin within three days, he must be given the opportunity of providing for his defence, and he cannot be tried twice for the same offence, even if, after his acquittal, it turns out that he is guilty. At the time of its encactment Habeas Corpus was also a safeguard of Parliament against the possibility of absolutism and dictatorship and was felt to be desirable after experiences during the time of Charles I and Cromwell. Together with Magna Carta (1215), the Petition of Right (1628) and the *Bill of Rights** (1689) it is one of the classical landmarks of English constitutional development in respect of the establishment of the rule of law in England. Similar provisions can now be found in the constitutions of most states.

Historically the Habeas Corpus Act must be understood within the context of the struggle between Parliament and Crown and the exclusion of Charles II's Catholic brother James (II) from succeeding to the throne. A series of habeas corpus bills were passed in the Commons between 1668 and 1675 but were rejected by the Lords. In 1679 a new bill was introduced which, this time, passed the Commons and the Lords after the latter had become increasingly liberal. Before its passage (1) only the Court of King's Bench could issue the writ of habeas corpus; but as no single judge could issue the writ during vacation, it frequently happened that prisoners were unduly detained. (2) The law did not apply to imprisonment out of England, so that in order to evade the law prisoners were often sent out of the country, for example to one of the colonies or even the Channel Islands, which are not part of England. (3) Gaolers were not compelled to bring up the prisoner within a specified time. (4) The law applied to criminal charges only.

In Scotland the Act does not apply because it was passed in England before the merger of the two parliaments, but persons unlawfully detained can be released upon order of the High Court of Justiciary.

There have been temporary suspensions of the Habeas Corpus Act in Great Britain: in 1696 when a plot was discovered to assassinate William III; in 1794 when William Pitt decided to prevent the spread of revolutionary principles in Great Britain; in 1817 when Lord Liverpool put a stop to the widespread unrest among workers who demanded an extension of suffrage and social justice (1816 "Spa Field Riots" at Bermondsey; 1817 rebellion in Derbyshire; 1819 "Manchester Massacre" or "Battle of Peterloo"); in 1847 when a series of agrarian crimes had been committed by the radical Young Ireland Party under William Smith O'Brien.

■ The privilege of the use of the writ of Habeas Corpus as a safeguard against arbitrary imprisonment was regarded so highly by the American colonists that after independence had been gained they adopted it in their Constitution (Article I, section 9) and in the so-called *Bill of Rights** (in Amendments IV, V, and VI). Wrongful refusals to issue the writ were one of the grievances leading to the War of Independence. The most prominent example of a temporary suspension of the Habeas Corpus Act occurred in 1861 when President Lincoln as commander-in-chief at the very start of the Civil War authorized its suspension along the military supplies lines between Philadelphia and Washington, because the State legislature of Maryland accepted Southern independence and, at least, wanted Maryland to remain neutral in the conflict.

H H

High Court of Justice

● The High Court of Justice constitutes a part of the *Supreme Court of Judicature**. It is a first instance and an appellate court for civil, and appellate only for criminal matters. As a result of the Judicature Acts of 1873 and 1875 courts such as the Chancery Court, the Court of Common Pleas, the Court of Exchequer, King's (or Queen's) Bench and some others, the roots of which went back to medieval times, merged into the High Court of Justice. London became its seat.

The High Court of Justice, according to the Administration of Justice Act, 1970, comprises three divisions: (a) The Chancery Division consists of the Lord Chancellor who is its president, assistant judges and masters. The latter are directed by the Master of the Rolls who is a nominal member of the division. The Chancery Division, the equivalent of the old Chancery Court, deals with land and company law, trusts, the wardship of minors, etc., and decides on appeals concerning such matters; (b) The Queen's (or King's) Bench Division is presided over by the Lord Chief Justice who is assisted by 70 judges. It performs the duties of the former Courts of Common Pleas, Exchequer, King's Bench and operates as a bankruptcy court, thus it tries civil and criminal cases both in London and in the provinces (Assizes, *Crown Court**, *Supreme Court of Judicature**), and hears appeals in civil matters from the Magistrates' Courts, and heard from the former Local Courts and Courts of Quarter Sessions; in criminal matters it deals with points of law from the *Magistrates' Courts**, and, until 1972, the Quarter Sessions. It may also review the decisions from statutory tribunals (administrative courts deciding specific questions with regard to administrative measures). Admiralty and prize jurisdiction lies with an Admiralty Court of the Queen's Bench Division; (c) The Family (former Probate, Divorce and Admiralty) Division consists of the Lord President and two judges. It exercises jurisdiction in cases of matrimonial, divorce and testamentary matters and, like the Chancery Division, decides on appeals concerning first instance decisions of Magistrates' Courts.

High Court judges sit singly when hearing cases of first instance. Appellate cases are decided by the opinion of a majority of usually three judges. Decisions of the High Court of Justice may be reviewed by the Court of Appeal.
The Commercial Court, the Companies Court, and the Divisional Court operate in special cases. High Court Judges constitute these courts. H J S

Impeachment

● The form of judicial parliamentary procedure against high ranking public officials; its origins date back to the 14th century.

In England the House of Commons has the right to act as prosecutors in case of treason, bribery and other serious crimes and misdemeanors. The charges of impeachment have to be formulated in articles. The accused is authorized to answer in writing.

In the hearing the House of Lords acts as court, presided over by the Lord High Steward or the Lord Chancellor. The accused may be defended by a counsel. The rules of the procedure are the same as in an ordinary trial.

At the end of the hearing it is "put to each peer" whether the accused is guilty or not. It is up to the House of Commons to decide whether he receives a penal sentence and/or is removed from office.

The last impeachment in England took place in the 19th century. Nowadays it is almost obsolete.

■ The concept of impeachment was adopted in the American Constitution. The task of initiating proceedings was vested in the House of Representatives. It is, however, the Senate which decides the impeachment charges.

According to Art. I, sec. 2, cl. 5 "the House of Representatives . . . shall have the sole power of impeachment", which means bringing the charges of impeachment before the Senate. Art. I, sec. 3, cl. 6 provides "the Senate shall have the sole power to try all impeachments". Thus they act as judges.

The President, Vice-President and all civil officers – federal judges included – may be removed from their office after conviction following impeachment proceedings, for which a majority of two thirds of the members present is necessary.

The American Constitution, however, stipulates that there shall be no conviction over and above removal and disqualification from office.

Between 1789 and 1974 only 12 charges of impeachment were brought, one of which was against a President – Andrew Johnson. Only four, all of which were against federal judges, were successful. The last impeachment proceeding was initiated versus Richard Nixon, the former President, but was subsequently dropped on his resignation from office.

The constitutions of the individual States have their own regulations on impeachment. H J S

Inns of Court

- The Inns of Court are those buildings in London occupied by four legal and voluntary societies which have the exclusive right to "admit persons to the bar". This power is exerted by the Benchers, a group of barristers at each Inn, whose members are usually over 70. The four societies are Lincoln's Inn, Gray's Inn, the Inner Temple, and the Middle Temple. The names derive from English noblemen and the Knights Templar from whom the buildings were purchased. In the Middle Ages they were also concerned with legal education. 1396.

Nowadays the Inns of Court are a curious mixture of club, college, fraternity, and trade union. Certain medieval rituals are still performed. A candidate for the bar, for instance, must keep 12 terms of three weeks each - which practically amounts to dining in hall a certain number of nights. Moreover, barristers are still subjected to the exclusive disciplinary power of the Inns of Court. In 1966, the Senate of the Four Inns of Court was established to represent the common views of the Inns, and to exercise jurisdiction in matters of legal education, discipline, professional planning and public relations.

The Inns have lost much of their importance as institutions for the training of barristers, which is now principally achieved during the time of apprenticeship to qualified barristers, but they still organize lectures and mock-trials – so-called "moots" – and provide other facilities, including accommodation for barristers who choose to have offices, "chambers", there.

The Inns of Court developed between 1275 and 1377, after Edward I (1272-1307), the "English Justinian", had mooted his great legal reforms. The founding of these Inns of Court is closely connected with the development of English case law: unofficial reports of cases commenced to be published in annual Year Books. (The first inkling of a future system of English case law may be found in Richard Fitz-Neal's "Dialogus de Scaccario" between 1177 and 1179, or even in the records of the Constitutions of Clarendon, 1164 (cf. *Precedent*).* Although these books were records of court proceedings dealing mainly with procedural points to help practioners rather than reports of case-book law in the modern sense, they did come to serve as an increasingly important source of precedents and contributed to the further development of the principle of "stare decisis" (i.e. stare decisis et non quieta movere = let past decisions stand and do not disturb things at rest), still a fundamental characteristic of the *Common Law**. In fact, the Inns of Court were to become strongholds of the common law, an importance which they have lost, as the predominant position of the common law is now undisputed in England.

Their importance and power was at its peak from the 16th to the 19th centuries. A direct relation between the Inns of Court and the survival of democratic institutions in England may be legitimately inferred. The Tudors attempted to give preference to the codified Roman Law for several reasons. Not only did Henry VIII need to have recourse to it in his various marriage difficulties but international relations were also generally based on it. What was most important, however, was the fact that the theory "princeps legibus solutus", contained in Roman Law, exempted the monarch from jurisdiction. Thus the suppression of Common Law in favour of Roman Law would have resulted in the strengthening of the *Royal Prerogative**. When therefore in 1551 the Oxford and Cambridge law schools were called into existence to teach the Roman Law, the Common-Law jurists of the Inns of Court resisted by means of petitions and publications and finally together with a courageous

House of Commons prevented its adoption during the reign of the first two Stuart monarchs. They deprived them thus of a basis for absolutist rule *(Parliament*)*.

There is a separate Inn of Court of Northern Ireland for barristers in Ulster. The King's Inns in Dublin, the legal school in Ireland, correspond closely to the English Inns of Court with regard to both purpose and organization. In Scotland, where the Roman Law was recognized shortly before the Scottish Reformation – after 1546 – in order to counteract the tyranny of the clergy, the corresponding corporation is the Faculty of Advocates in Edinburgh.

Up into the 19th century the Inns of Chancery were of some importance in England. They were founded by clerks of chancery in the Middle Ages and accepted students for legal training. As the penning of writs and other legal documents was a prominent part of their work, students obtained thereby a good grounding in law. In the course of time the Inns of Court secured control of the Inns of Chancery, supervised their affairs and often bought their buildings.

In the sixteenth and early seventeenth centuries, the Inns of Court and the Inns of Chancery were not only famous for their eminent lawyers, but they were also the frequent scene of theatrical performances and revels. Each Christmas and Shrovetide the students and younger barristers of Gray's Inn, for example, performed a masque. H H

Judge

A public officer appointed to administer the law. One who has authority to hear and try cases in an court of justices. M.E.

● The British legal system makes use of professional judges as well as laymen *(Justice of the Peace*)*. Their duties differ. In general the judge has to preside at trials and to decide the case in dispute. In the latter function he can be assisted by a *Jury**. In criminal cases he fulfils two functions: he has to instruct the jury by determining questions of law and to sum up the evidence for the jury. After the decision of the jury he has to acquit the accused or to pass sentence. He alone decides on the extent of punishment, but he takes no part in the jury's decision as to guilt or innocence. Civil actions are usually tried by a judge without a jury, although one of the parties may in special cases insist on a trial by jury.

In the United Kingdom the Sovereign is responsible for all appointments of the judiciary because the Crown is the historic source of all judicial power. The monarch acts on the recommendation and advice of the Prime Minister, the Lord Chancellor, and the Ministers.

In Scotland the right of recommendation lies with the Prime Minister for a few special cases. Generally the Secretary of State for Scotland proposes able persons for appointment and is also responsible for the *Justices of the Peace**.

Most British judges (N.B. not the justices of the peace) are appointed from experienced practising *Barristers** (in Scotland advocates) especially from Queen's (or King's) Counsels. *Solicitors** may become circuit judges. In order to guarantee the complete independence of the judges they are appointed until statutory retiring age or for life.

Judges of the superior courts have not to answer for judicial actions even if they have acted maliciously or corruptly. The other judges are protected to a smaller extent. However, in cases of misconduct, incapacity, or neglect of duty a judge may be removed by the Lord Chancellor or, in the case of judges of superior courts, by resolution of Parliament and the assent of the Sovereign. In Scotland the Secretary of State initiates the removal of judges by issuing an order of removal which needs the assent of both Houses of Parliament.

The number of judges is steadily increasing since public opinion has criticized the long duration of proceedings, though the number of professional judges is comparatively small because the great majority of criminal cases (not civil cases) are disposed of in *Magistrates' Courts** or *Crown Courts**, the former are generally not presided over by professional judges but by lay magistrates. The judges have therefore to deal with only comparatively small numbers of actions. In addition, the orders of procedure allow quick decisions.

■ Owing to the federal structures of the U.S.A. there are federal courts with federal judges and State (and local) courts with State (and local) judges. Federal judges are appointed by the President of the U.S.A. with the approval of the Senate. Their appointments are for life or during good behaviour; they may retire at the age of 70. A federal judge can, against his will, be removed from office only through *impeachment**.

Many States elect their judges at all levels by popular vote, in others appointment is general, and some States use both methods. In the State systems life appointments are not unknown, but fixed terms, between four and 15 years, are more usual. Where judges are elected, their integrity and impartiality occasionally leave much to be desired. H J S

Judicial Review

A constitutional doctrine that gives to a court system the power to annual legislative or executive acts which the judges declare to be unconstitutional.

■ Judicial review furnishes the courts with the authority to examine and to decide whether action of the legislative, executive, and administrative institutions of the government conform to the U.S. constitution. If they do not they can be declared unconstitutional and are therefore illegal. Judicial review is an important component of the system of *Checks and Balances**. It is not expressly mentioned in the Constitution, and, in fact, the Supreme Court assumed this important authority in 1803 through its own broad interpretation of its vested powers.

Judicial review as it exists in the United States is remarkable in two respects: (1) All courts, federal as well as state and local courts, have the power to declare federal and state actions and statutes unconstitutional; (2) Owing to the vagueness of the U.S. constitution the *Supreme Court of the U.S.** has been able to use it as a means of interpreting the Constitution to an extent which has given this court a decisive active influence upon the political, social, and economic life of the country.

The power whereby the courts exert such influence is nowhere laid down in the Constitution. Chief Justice John Marshall (1801-35) established the Supreme Court's right to review acts of Congress and of State legislatures. He laid down the supremacy of the U.S. Supreme Court over State courts in constitutional cases. "It is a Constitution we are expounding", he proclaimed in 1819. Judicial review, therefore, enables the American judiciary to "create the law" to a remarkable extent.

Such power in the hands of a few men has not invariably been wielded in accordance with the "national consensus".

A change of general attitude of the Supreme Court in the course of the years since 1789 can be observed.

In its first period up to the middle of the 19th century and under John Marshall in particular, judicial review tended to favour the strengthening of central authority. In the second period beginning after the Civil War there was a shift in favour of economic interests. Substantial parts of F. D. Roosevelt's *New Deal** legislation probably fell victim to this attitude (in 1935 and 1936, the court struck down 11 New Deal statutes, the heart of the recovery programme, because they constituted an encroachment on property rights).

In the third period, from about the end of New Deal to the present day, the emphasis has shifted away from business and favoured once more the central authority, especially the social aspect of American life and, above all, the issue of the civil rights of Negroes. Between 1954 and 1968, the Supreme Court frequently based its judicial review on the stipulations of the *Bill of Rights**. It was involved in several cases of judicial review. It forced, for example, the State criminal courts and the police to comply with the strict standards imposed on federal courts and ruled that even if evidence shows the guilt of a person he must be freed if that evidence was illegally obtained. The last instance of this kind of judicial review occurred in 1965 when the Supreme Court ruled that individuals may refuse to register with the government as members of the Communist Party on the grounds that such registration was tantamount to punishment without trial. This period favouring the rights of the individual seemed to have come to an end when Earl Warren, certainly one of the great Chief Justices in the history of the Supreme Court, resigned from his post in 1968. Since then a conservative, "strict constructionist" *(Doctrine*)* trend has been observed in the court's decisions under Chief Justice Warren E. Burger. In 1972 it ruled against the Fifth Amendment when it upheld laws which compel witnesses who are granted limited immunity from prosecution to testify on crimes they themselves may have committed. It was obviously a setback to Civil Rights when, in the same year, it refused to prohibit states from issuing liquor licences to private clubs which practice racial discrimination. Nonetheless, the "Burger Court" also extended the safeguards of civil liberties and civil rights. It elaborated the rights of women to an abortion during the first three months of pregnancy, rejected the Attorney General's claim that he could utilize wiretaps without a court order, curbed the imposition of the death penalty, held that the government could not restrain publication of the "Pentagon Papers" (a detailed examination of Vietnam policy which Daniel Ellsberg, a former Pentagon expert, leaked to the press in 1971), and, in a unanimous decision in 1971, sustained the busing of pupils out of their neighbourhoods in North Carolina in order to foster racial integration. On the other hand, in a 5-4 decision in 1974 it turned down a desegregation plan that called for cross-county busing in Detroit, Michigan, and 53 surrounding and politically separate communities, though, one year later, it upheld the busing of children across city boundaries to the white-dominated schools of the suburbs.

Perhaps the two most famous cases of judicial review are Marbury *v.* Madison, 1803, and Dred Scott *v.* Sandford, 1857. The former concerns the denial of a commission by President Jefferson, through his Secretary of State Madison, to a man who was appointed magistrate by President Adams. This was the first case in which the Supreme Court ruled that an action of the President and a law of Congress (Judiciary Act, 1789) were null and void. It established a precedent which has been followed ever since. In the latter case in

1834, Dred Scott, a slave, was taken by his owner from the slave state of Missouri to the free state of Illinois and from there to the Wisconsin Territory where slavery was forbidden by the Missouri Compronise of 1820. Scott was later brought back to Missouri and in 1846 he sued for his freedom on the ground that he had lived in a free State. Chief Justice Taney ruled that Scott, as a Negro, was not a citizen and had "no rights which the white man is bound to respect". The decision helped to bring about the Civil War.

The incidence of court ruling overturning acts of Congress is not high; only a few more than 100 acts or parts of acts have so far been declared unconstitutional. The significance of judicial review lies primarily in its deterrent effect. – Contrary to popular legend the Supreme Court cannot exert judicial review spontaneously. It must wait for issues to be presented by genuine litigants. Thus an act of Congress may have been in effect for years before it is declared unconstitutional. The court is very cautious in handling cases concerning constitutionality and rejects those not yet "ripe" for decision. Of more than ten million cases tried in U.S. courts each year the Supreme Court eventually receives approximately 2,500 and hands down opinions in approximately 150.

- There is no judicial review of legislation in Britain. Indeed, its absence is a basic principle of English constitutional law. The courts cannot sit in judgement upon the laws which Parliament makes, and the concept of some "higher law" to which parliamentary legislation would have to conform is wholly absent in English constitutional thinking. Since the time when Sir Edward Coke (1552-1634), the champion of common law against the *Royal Prerogative** and prominent in the drafting of the Petition of Right, told James I that the King was subject to God and the law, there has been no great confrontation between the government and the law courts, because the latter have always accepted the ultimate sovereignty of Parliament. When, in 1971, A. R. Blackburn (Blackburn v. Attorney General) asked the courts to prevent Britain from entering the European Community without first having a constitutional referendum, they refused even to consider the case. Blackburn's appeal to the Court of Appeal was likewise dismissed, because it was the sole power of the courts "to decide and enforce what is the law and not what it should be – now or in future", and that it was "no part of this court's function or duty to make declarations in general terms regarding the powers of Parliament" (quoted from F. L. Morrison, Courts and the Political Process in England, London, 1973, p. 98). H H

Jury

A body of laymen officially summoned to render a verdict in a case submitted to them in a court of justice. M.E.

- In England a jury consists of 12 persons (8 in the county courts) and of 15 persons or less in Scotland. Any householder of British nationality between the age of 21 and 60 is liable for jury service and can be exempted from it only under certain conditions. The jurors in modern proceedings are judges of the facts. In criminal cases their verdict is only "guilty" or "not guilty". In Scotland, however, there is a third possibility: "non-proven". They do not decide the amount of punishment, this decision lies with the *Judge** alone. Where the accused himself pleads "guilty" there is no need for a verdict from the jury, because no evidence is given. In civil cases the jury decides questions of fact and fixes the amount of damages which must be paid to the injured party. Since 1972 a majority verdict has been sufficient, provided that in the normal jury of 12 people there are not more than two dissentients.

In criminal cases the decision of the jurors until 1967 had to be unanimous – except in Scotland where a majority verdict of the jury was accepted. Now the jurors must try within two hours to find a unanimous verdict, otherwise the opinion of the majority decides the case, provided that there are not more than two dissenting jurors. They answer under oath and this fact should add to their responsibility, although no juryman has to answer for his decision to anybody.

A jury is completely independent of both the executive and the judiciary, but in criminal cases the accused has the right to reject up to seven jurors and can exchange them without giving any reason. Besides, prosecution and defence can try to have a juror replaced for definite reasons. But as soon as the members of a jury have taken the oath any interference is illegal.

The coroner's jury operates outside the judicial system. It investigates suspicious deaths. The local coroner, who may be a barrister, a solicitor or a doctor, has to summon a jury in cases, e.g. of suspected murder, manslaughter, or infanticide. The same takes place if the circumstances of death are uncertain or if death was caused by using a vehicle on a public highway. If the jury returns a verdict that confirms suspicion the coroner is obliged to commit the case for trial, but he must not disclose the names of suspects.

The origin of the jury as an institution goes back to medieval times. In the beginning the jury was a means of establishing evidence. The riding judges of the Sovereign could not know the variety of local and habitual rights of the communities, nor the personal circumstances of the persons involved and the background of the case to be tried. In order to prove the claimed right or fact the interested person could rely on the evidence given by a certain number of local people of rank who formed the jury. From this source developed the trial by jury as seen at a variety of trials in the High Court (Assizes) and at the *Crown Courts**.

The lack of confidence of the peers with regard to the independence of judges, all of whom were appointed by the Sovereign, influenced the development of the jury. The result of the efforts of the peers was laid down in the Magna Carta (1215): "No freeman shall be taken or imprisoned . . . except by the lawful judgement of his peers" (peers then meaning "equals"). Thus the function of the jury changed in that it was no longer a means of evidence but it helped the judges to decide the questions submitted to them. In recent times juries function only in *Common Law** and not in *Equity** proceedings.

In recent years the jury system was severely criticized in England. Nearly 40 per cent of all persons committed for trial had to be released because the juries were unable to reach a unanimous verdict although it was obvious that several persons were offenders. Jurors have repeatedly been found to be corrupt. Thus the majority verdict had to be introduced.

■ The jury in the U.S.A. has nearly the same duties as that in Britain. This fact may be explained by historical development. In the U.S.A. there are two types of jury for criminal trials: the grand and petit jury. The grand jury decides the initiation of a criminal trial. It consists of 23 or fewer laymen and is called in by a court from time to time. The decision of a grand jury is purely accusatory. If it has found reason to suspect a person of having committed a crime, this person has to stand trial before a petit or trial jury which determines the question of guilt. After having heard the prosecutor's evidence the grand jury decides whether or not the suspicion is well-founded. The defendant is then either discharged or committed for trial.

The method of jury election varies from State to State, but everywhere the jurymen must possess various qualifications among which, however, none concerns education. The accused himself can influence the election of the jury or can do so through his defending counsellor who can reject jurors up to a varying number without further argument.

In accordance with a decision of the Supreme Court of the U.S.A. in 1972, in criminal cases a unanimous verdict is required only in federal courts, and not in State courts.

The coroner's jury in the U.S.A. operates on almost the same lines as in Britain. HJS

Justice of the Peace

An inferior magistrate appointed or elected to preserve the peace in a county, town, or other district, and discharge other local magisterial functions. M.E.

- A Justice of the Peace (J.P.) fulfils the functions of a judge, but he is in fact not a judge, since this term applies only to judges of the *High Court of Justice**, who receive salaries and are of course trained in law. J.P.s, on the other hand, are unpaid, and untrained in law, except for a few Stipendiary Magistrates, professional lawyers, who officiate in the police courts of London and some large provincial cities. J.P.s constitute by far the largest body in the judiciary in England (in 1975, there were 19,454 justices of the peace on the active list, 6,508 were women) and approximately 98 per cent. of criminal cases and practically all minor offences are dealt with by them, but they have also a minor quasi-civil jurisdiction in a few matrimonial cases, in the confiscation of illegal drugs and miscellaneaous matters mostly connected with petty offences. They also regulate the licensing of public houses and similar establishments. J.P.s administer for the most part summary justice at a *Magistrates' Court**. At Petty Sessions, the bench consists of between two and seven J.P.s administering summary justice. The Criminal Justice Act of 1967 has stripped the magistracy of its power of imprisonment. They are advised by the Clerk to the Justices, who is a *Solicitor**. Justices of the Peace are divided among a number of "Commissions of Peace", of which there is one for each administrative county. J.P.s are appointed by the Lord Chancellor upon the recommendations of the Lord Lieutenant of the County – the formal representative of the Crown in each county – who is advised by the Commission of Peace. In Scotland Justices of the Peace Courts and Police Courts deal with petty offences and breaches of the peace. Since 1966, every Justice of the Peace has been required to attend a course of instruction in his duties before he can sit at Court.

The office of the J.P. came into existence during the great medieval law reforms (Edward I, II, III), probably in 1360. At the beginning, J.P.s seem to have been used rather after the manner of high-ranking policemen. They made arrests, cross-examinations, and indictments. But from the late Middle Ages until 1888, their chief responsibility was in *Local Government**. The counties (not the boroughs, which were governed by corporations or councils) were administered by the Justices of the Peace. The system was changed by the Local Government Act of 1888, but has remained unchanged in the Courts Act of 1971.

■ In the United States the Justice of the Peace undertakes all the functions of his English counterpart, but in contradistinction to the latter he also deals with minor civil matters. Furthermore, he certifies affidavits, and marriages are formally concluded in his presence. J.P.s are not appointed as they are in Britain, but elected for a time which varies from place to place. In larger cities there is a tendency to replace untrained J.P.s by police magistrates who are trained in law, and the laymen courts by police courts.

The functions which were in the hands of J.P.s. in England before 1888 are in America performed by the Sheriff, a local officer who has police duties, is guardian of the peace, executive agent of the county, warden of the prison, bailiff of the court. He also opens court sessions and may undertake other functions depending on state or local laws (cf. chart U.S. system of courts).

H H

Law Lords

● Members of the House of Lords qualified to take part in its judicial business.

The eleven Law Lords, or Lords of Appeal in Ordinary, constitute the highest court of appeal in England, Scotland (only in civil cases), Wales, and Northern Ireland. They always include the Lord Chancellor, who is the president, and the former Lord Chancellors. Law Lords are appointed, receive salaries and hold life peerages. Theoretically all members of the House of Lords may participate in the court proceedings, but in practice only those peers holding, or who previously held, high judicial offices are admitted. There must be a quorum of three judges. Court hearings of the House of Lords are not ordinary sittings. They normally take place in a committee room in the morning, and if they take place in the Lords' Chamber the Lord Chancellor does not sit on the Woolsack (a large upholstered seat filled with wool once representing the wealth of Britain). Furthermore the work of the Law Lords does not end when *Parliament** prorogues.

The appellate function of the House of Lords was introduced by the Judicature Act of 1873 which, along with supplementary Acts, consolidated the three Common Law courts, chancery and various other tribunals into one *Supreme Court of Judicature**, with the possibility of further appeal to the House of Lords, which was strengthened by the Appellate Jurisdiction Act of 1876. The latter added three, later increased to four, Law Lords of life tenure.

At that time the House of Lords still served several other judicial functions which have now ceased: the function of a court before which the Commons might impeach a person for political "high crimes and misdemeanours" ceased when impeachment fell into disuse after 1806; the trial of peers for treason and felony by the Lords (Magna Carta, Art. 39, *Bill of Rights**) was abolished by the Criminal Justice Act of 1948; and the right of deciding Peerage claims is now vested in the Committee of Privileges of the House of Lords. H H

Magistrates' Court

● Magistrate: a justice of the peace; also applied to salaried officials having criminal jurisdiction of the first instance. 1688.

The Magistrates' Court, also called Court of Petty Sessions, was defined by the Interpretation Act of 1889 as a "court of summary jurisdiction consisting of two or more justices sitting in a Petty Sessional Court . . .". The Magistrates'

Courts deal with civil and criminal matters. Their great importance lies in the field of criminal jurisdiction because 98 per cent. of all offences in Great Britain are tried by them. They also undertake preliminary investigations in case of more important offences. A Magistrates' Court operates usually with two to seven lay judges *(Justice of the Peace*)*, nearly 20 000 of them hold office unpaid and part-time. A variety of the Magistrates' Courts are the Police Courts where salaried (or stipendiary) magistrates decide criminal cases of minor importance. These courts exist in London and some other big towns in England and Wales.

The equivalent in Scotland are the burgh courts, survivals of medieval times, in big towns (boroughs), where town councillors decide the cases under a summary procedure. Juvenile courts are presided over by not more than three magistrates (usually one of them being a woman) with special qualifications.

If in a criminal case before a Magistrates' Court a grown-up person is expected to be committed to prison for more than three months he or she can claim to be tried by jury.

The majority verdict of the justices present decides the judgement. In case the number of votes is equal a new hearing is ordered before another court. If the same result ensues the case is dismissed.

The Magistrates' Court may fine the accused or commit him or her to the *Crown Court** in order to effect that a sentence of detention in a Borstal or other reformatory institution may be passed. The Magistrates' Court may also convict the accused directly.

The appeal against decisions of the Magistrates' Court is usually heard by the *Crown Court**, but it may lead to the Queen's (or King's) Bench Division of the High Court of Justice directly on points of law or by cases stated.

Magistrates' Courts also exercise a fair amount of civil jurisdiction which is, however, limited to small claims. Yet jurisdiction in cases of disputes between husband and wife is unlimited. Their jurisdiction also covers cases of bastardy and disputes between labour and management.

Appeals in civil procedures are heard by the *Crown Court** in cases of bastardy or on points of law. The latter appeal may also be brought before the Queen's Bench Division of the High Court of Justice. The Chancery Division is the appellate instance for guardianship cases, and the Family Division for matrimonial cases. The Divisional Court operates an appelate jurisdiction in specific cases.

There are Magistrates' Courts in the U.S.A. which are usually called Police Courts there.
HJS

Precedent

Law: A previous judicial decision, method of proceeding, or draft of a document which serves as an authoritative rule or pattern in similar or analogous cases. 1523.

● *Common Law** is law made by judges, therefore case law to a great extent. When he makes the law, however, the English *Judge** is not completely free. He has to follow a strict method. This method of judging is ruled by two principles, expressed in Latin: (1) "res judicata" (decided case) stands for the principle that a court shall not alter its jurisdiction in equal cases; (2) "stare decisis" (to stand to the decided case) sets out the rule that decisions of the superior courts bind the lower ones. Thus a *County Court** is bound by a High Court's decision, and the High Court cannot nullify a decision of the *Court of Appeal**, etc. Each decision is a directive as a precedent for the deciding court itself as well as for all the subordinate ones. In order to realize these principles it was and is necessary to collect the decisions. As early as the Middle Ages the decisions of the judges were collected (Constitution of Clarendon, 1164); these collections were called Year Books and are the forerunners of the Law Reports. Nowadays the Law Reports are edited by private editors. The number of volumes runs into several thousands, the number of decisions, which continues to increase annually, is almost unknown.

In Great Britain the above mentioned principles are strictly observed. The deciding *Judge** looks for one or more precedents to justify his decision. Only if he considers a precedent as plainly unreasonable, does he ovverule it.

This judicial method is embarrassed by the following fact: the sentence of a precedent is a directive only in so far as it was necessary for the former decision. If a part of the sentence was not essential for the former decision, it is an "obiter dictum" (an incidental remark) of the judge, thus unauthoritative and not to be used as a precedent. In this way British jurisdiction achieves continuity by means of precedents.

■ In the U.S.A. precedents have generally the same functions as in Great Britain. But the principles of "stare decisis" and "res judicata" are not so strictly observed. This results from the splitting up of the jurisdiction into a federal and a state system, whereas the jurisdiction in Great Britain holds true as an entity.

The above mentioned principles are applied in the U.S.A. in the following manner: A state court is only bound to its own decisions, and in some respects to federal ones, but it is not obliged to pay attention to any decision of other state courts. A lower court is only bound to the decisions of the state court in its state. There is no obstacle, however, to a court's following precedents of other state courts if there is a reason for doing so. The decisions of highly qualified courts, such as those of the State of New York, are taken as precedents nearly everywhere in the U.S.A.

Owing to the differences in the findings on federal, state and local levels in the huge territory of the U.S.A., the number of American reports exceeds tens of thousands of volumes. Since 1923 they have been collected by the Law Institute of America and edited as restatements. H J S

Rules of Evidence

The rules concerning information that is given in a legal investigation to establish the factor point in question. 1503. Also, the rules concerning statements or proofs admissible as testimony in a court of law. 1817.

● Just as in sports certain rules are formulated, each proceeding needs rules by which it is to be conducted. Any case in law has to deal with facts (e.g. an unnatural death, an unpaid debt), thus the most important problem is how to bring these facts to the knowledge of the court. The term "evidence" includes all facts which may prove or disprove the questions under enquiry, as far as they are admitted to the legal proceeding. The rules applied herein are called "rules of evidence". The law of evidence in its modern form is comparatively young. It is a law made by judges in the last two centuries, completed by statutory enactments and modified for the trial by *Jury**. In any action there are questions to be decided by the judge and others to be decided by the jury. The judge decides on questions of law, the jury on questions of fact; e.g. the judge has to decide whether or not a certain piece of evidence is admissible, the jury must decide whether the evidence is sufficient or a witness is credible. All facts must be proved if they are denied. It is accepted as a general rule that the burden of proof lies with the person who states a fact. This means that the plaintiff or the prosecutor has to prove the facts maintained by him. This rule may also be reversed in civil cases, so that the defendant carries the burden of proof, e.g. if he pleads infancy or fraud. He has also to prove the facts which are exclusively in his knowledge. The rules of evidence are very similar in both civil and criminal cases.

The following are some fundamental rules of evidence of English law: the accused person is innocent until proved guilty, the prosecutor has to collect all facts to convict him, there is no need for evidence if the accused pleads guilty, the testimony of an accomplice is generally not sufficient to convict the accused if other evidence is lacking. The accused himself may be sworn as a witness in his own defence and then be questioned. All facts must be proved to such an extent as to eliminate any reasonable doubt. The rules of evidence are strictly observed in criminal cases whereas in civil cases the parties may give their consent to a deviation from the rules.

In conclusion it can be said that a party not able to prove the facts in its favour within the rules of evidence will lose the case.

■ The above also holds true for the U.S.A. The same rules of evidence are applied in the U.S.A.; but they are laid down to a larger extent by State and federal enactments than in Great Britain.

H J S

Sheriff Court

● In England and Wales, before the Norman conquest, the sheriff was a high officer, who presided in the shire-moot and was responsible for the administration of the royal demesne and the execution of the law. At the present time the sheriff (or high sheriff), appointed for one year by royal patent, is nominally responsible for the keeping of prisoners in custody, preparing the panel of jurors for the assizes, the execution of the sentence of death, etc. The sheriff also acts as presiding officer at parliamentary elections for the county. Ireland (since 1542) and U.S.A. (since 1662): here the sheriff has similar functions (in the U.S.A. he is usually elected). In Scotland formerly the sheriff had functions analogous to those of the English sheriff; since 1747 the sheriff is the chief local judge in a Scottish county.

Scotland is divided into 15 sheriffdoms each comprising a county or a combination of counties. Each sheriffdom is further divided into sheriff court districts. Each sheriffdom has a sheriff and a varying number of sheriff deputies who perform among others judicial duties. They act as Judges of the Sheriff Court. Their duties and rights are laid down in the Sheriff Courts Acts of 1907 and 1913. The Sheriff Courts exercise extensive local jurisdiction in civil as well as criminal matters. A Sheriff Court is both a first instance and an appellate court for civil procedures. It deals with nearly all actions regardless of the value of the claim. An appeal against a decision of a sheriff substitute is heard by the sheriff-principal or by the Court of Session which is composed of an "Outer House" and an "Inner House" and is a court of universal jurisdiction. In criminal cases the Sheriff Court has no general appellate function. A person convicted by a Sheriff Court may appeal to the High Court of Justiciary.

H J S

Solicitor

One properly qualified and formally admitted to practise as a law agent in any court; formerly, one practising in a court of equity as distinct from an attorney. 1577.

● A solicitor in Britain belongs to the profession of lawyers. He is competent to advise and instruct clients in legal matters. He prepares cases and submits them to *Barristers**. He is allowed to plead only in certain lower courts (e.g. *Magistrates' Courts**, coroners' courts, *County Courts**). The Courts Act of 1971 opened a way for solicitors to become circuit judges in the *Crown Court**.

An applicant for the profession of a solicitor must be admitted to training by the professional organization of solicitors, the Law Society. He must work as an articled clerk for at least five years in the employment of a practising solicitor. He is obliged to prepare himself for the prescribed examinations by attending courses at a recognized law school supervised by the Law Society. In this way experience and academic training are combined. Only after passing the final examinations held under the auspices of the Law Society is he allowed to become a member of this organization. The division of the legal profession into two branches, i.e. solicitors and barristers, is the result of a development which began in 1873 with the Judicature Act and was concluded in 1922 by the Solicitors Act which transferred disciplinary powers to the Law Society.

In Scotland the equivalent of a solicitor has been a "law agent" since the Law Agents Act of 1873. His professional rights and duties are practically the same as those of a solicitor.

The Solicitor General in England is a member of the Law Officers' Department. He is second to the *Attorney** General. He is appointed by the government in power which he advises in legal matters. He also reprensents the Crown in the courts.

■ The Solicitor General in the U.S.A. is the second law officer of the Federal Government. He has no cabinet rank and is not in all cases the deputy of the Attorney General. His main task is to represent the government in the courts. In some states a Solicitor General is the chief law officer. He deals principally with the legal matters of the individual State. H J S

Statute Law

Statute: An enactment, containing one or more legislative provisions, made by the legislature of a country at one time, and expressed in a formal document; the document in which such an enactment is expressed. Statute law: the system of law contained in statutes, as distinct from common law. M.E.

● A statute is a written law made by, or by the authority of, the legislature. Nowadays *Parliament** is the supreme legislative body. In the early Middle Ages the legislative body was the king and his council, the Curia Regis, whose ordinances formed the earliest law enactments in England. In the late 13th century the concept of Parliament began to develop and law-making by Parliament slowly commenced. During the 16th century a statute became an enactment by the Sovereign consented to by the *Lords** and *Commons**.

Nowadays statute law may be Acts of Parliament – these being the most important ones - or Orders in Council which are made by virtue of the *Royal Prerogative** or under statutory authority of Parliament, or rules, orders, etc., made by a Minister under the authority of Parliament, or regulations of local government and other authorities. The modern tendency is for Parliament to confer the power of legislation to delegated or subordinate bodies and for these bodies to administer numerous special matters by local orders. Since the Statutory Instruments Act of 1946 these local orders have been called "statutory instruments".

2

Since Great Britain joined the European Community, Community law must be observed. It consists of the law made by the treaties establishing the EC and the instruments made by it. When conflicting, Community law prevails over domestic law.

Statute law played no important part in the English legal system prior to the Reform Act of 1832 *(Suffrage*)*. Since then statute law has steadily increased in importance and today covers a wide range of activities.

On the one hand, statute law is expected to correct the defects of the common law; on the other hand, common law rights cannot be destroyed by a statute unless effected by clear words or plain implication. In a similar way statutes in favour of common law may be altered or varied only by further enactments.

The Interpretation Act of 1889 provided an authentic interpretation of terms and phrases used in statutes in order to ascertain the contents of any particular act. Modern acts often contain an interpretation section which explains particular expressions of that act.

The public general statutes apply also to Scotland provided nothing contradicts their application. The Acts of the old Scottish Parliament, however, refer only of Scotland. On the whole the statute law constitutes the third column of justice beside *Common Law** and *Equity**.

■ The American federal *Constitution** brought about dualism in statutory law. The order of supremacy of the different laws is as follows: the federal constitution is the supreme law; next are the federal acts which are superior to the acts of the States. Both of them have to conform with the Constitution. Should there arise any doubt in this respect, the degree of conformity has to be checked by means of *Judicial Review**. Outside public law the federal power is fairly weak, particularly in common law.

Although the States have a comparatively greater say in the creation of statutes, which may differ from State to State, statutes are of less importance in the U.S.A. than in Britain. Only about two thirds of the States possess written criminal and civil procedure orders, and criminal and civil law is only codified in a few States. Since 1923 attempts have been made to unify the different State laws, but with only small effect. There remain big differences in most spheres especially in marriage and divorce law.

Nevertheless the system has its advantages. The lack of unity in law gives each State a chance to abandon statutes according to the special circumstances of its area. The following example may illustrate the split between federal and State law: in 1965 several accused persons were acquitted by a State court of the charge of murdering three civil rights workers. The same persons were sent to jail for several years by a federal court because they were found guilty of having contravened the *Civil Rights** Act of 1964.

H J S

Supreme Court of Judicature

Judicature: the act of judging; administration of justice; judicial process. 1530. Attrib. 1873.

● The establishment of the Supreme Court of Judicature in 1873 was an attempt to abolish the judicial functions of the *Lords**. As the superlative "supreme" indicates, this court was to be considered as the final instance. The attempt, however, failed and the *Law Lords** are still in existence representing the third (and final) instance of appeal. The Supreme Court comprises two major groups of courts: the *Court of Appeal** which is a court of the second instance, and the *High Court of Justice** which is both a first instance and an instance of appeal.

The aforementioned courts are superior (or higher) courts. They are believed to date back to the Curia Regis (King's Court) of medieval times. In the course of development the system of higher courts branched out, and it was only in 1873 and 1875 (Judicature Acts) that all the higher courts were united in the Supreme Court of Judicature and their organizations merged into one. This status was fixed by the Consolidating Act of 1925, the proceedings were facilitated by the Tribunals and Inquiries Act of 1958. Civil cases arising from bastardy, guardianship and matrimonial causes are heard in Petty Sessions and are appealed through the same channels as criminal cases. As London was not included in the circuit system of Assizes civil cases that would have been sent to the Assizes elsewhere were tried by the Queen's Bench in the Law Courts in the Strand.

In addition to these courts there are a number of courts in England and Wales exercising special functions. Most important among them are the coroners' courts *(Jury*)*, military courts (or courts martial), ecclesiastical courts, the National Industrial Relations Court, and administrative tribunals (e.g. the Rent Tribunals, the Transport Tribunal, the Special Committee of the Law Society).

H J S

Supreme Court of the United States

Highest court of original and appellate jurisdiction in the U.S.A. 1789.

■ The Supreme Court of the United States is the only court provided for by the *Constitution** itself. It is the highest court in the country; its decisions are final. In some cases as defined in Art. III, sect. 2, of the Constitution it has original jurisdiction, i.e. it is a court with general jurisdiction acting as a first and last instance. It is also the highest appellate instance in practically all other cases as is defined in Art III, sect. 2, of the Constitution and in Amendment XI. It is the highest of the federal courts which, in accordance with Art. III, sect. 1, of the *Constitution**, Congress created in the Judiciary Acts of 1789, 1801, and 1802. The "inferior courts", as they are vaguely styled in the Constitution, are the circuit *Courts of Appeal** and the *District Courts**.

The function of the Supreme Court of the United States and its inferior courts is to interpret the law and to guard and interpret the Constitution. To a considerable extent, however, they also make the law. Their principal instrument is the *Judicial Review**.

The decisions of the Supreme Court are not always popular with the executive. In 1935, the Supreme Court voided an important part of F. D. Roosevelt's *New Deal** legislation, such as the National Industrial Recovery Act (N.I.R.A.). In 1965, the Supreme Court voided an act of Congress which prevented members of the Communist Party from holding leading positions in the labor unions *(Judicial Review*)* on the grounds that nobody should be punished without due process of law.

In addition to questions of constitutionality the federal courts handle cases of the following types: offences against federal law or treaties; civil cases arising under federal law or treaties; disputes between States; controversies to which the United States is a party; cases involving maritime or admiralty jurisdiction; cases in which a foreign nation or citizen is a party. Ambassadors, ministers, and consuls are also under federal jurisdiction.

The session of the Supreme Court begins on the second Monday in October and generally extends to July. Ancient rules are followed in the procedure of the court which are reminiscent of English court practices. For example, the Court Crier, a minor official, opens the court session by saying, "Oyez! Oyez! Oyez! The Honorable, the Chief Justice and the Associate Justices of the United States." After the Justices have entered in order of seniority and have taken their seats he continues, "All persons having business before the Honorable, the Supreme Court of the United States, are admonished to draw near and give their attention, for the court is now sitting, God save this United States and this Honorable Court." A quorum of two-thirds of the Justices, that is six, is required for a decision to be made. The Chief Justice does not need to be present. Federal judges are appointed for life. They enjoy high prestige and are well paid.

Not everybody can practise before the Supreme Court. Attorneys wishing to do so must apply to that court for admission. Moreover, they must have been recommended by a fellow lawyer who is already qualified.

The State court systems are modelled on the federal system. There is a supreme court at the top, although it is not in all cases designated as such, and there are one or more layers of inferior courts called district courts, or superior courts, or circuit courts, or common pleas courts, which vary in the individual States. They are generally authorized to handle both civil and criminal cases. The simplest form of State court function is exercised by the *Justice of the Peace** (cf. chart U.S. system of courts).

Apart from the ordinary functions mentioned above, the State supreme court, like the federal courts, possesses the written or unwritten power to declare a law unconstitutional with regard to the respective State constitution. Thus the principle of judicial review is also effective on the State level. H H

PART III

Economy and Social Services

Agrarian Revolution
Agricultural Relief
Appalachia
Assisted Areas
Austerity
Aviation
Balance of Payments
Bank of England
Belt
Big Four
Bretton Woods
Collective Bargaining
Common Market
Conservation of Land
Co-operative Society
Corporate Enterprise
Discount Houses
Dollar
Federal Reserve System
Free Trade
Great Crash
Health Service
Incomes Policy
Industrial Democracy
Industrial Revolution
Interstate Commerce
Legal Tender
Lloyd's
Merchant Bankers
Nationalization
New Deal
New Towns
Preferences
Protectionism
Public Utilities
Rail and Road
Reclamation of Land
Restrictive Trade Practices
Self Assessment
Shipping
Slums
Social Security
Sterling
Trade (Labor) Unions
Treasury
Trust
War on Poverty
Welfare State

● The term "agrarian revolution" refers in England to the change in the rural society caused by the abolition of the open field system and the enclosure of the open fields during the second half of the 18th and the first quarter of the 19th century. During this time the population of Great Britain was increasing rapidly, thus causing a growing demand for food and an increase in the prices of agricultural products. The rising population in the towns resulting from industrialization created new markets for agricultural products. Thus it was not by chance that the agrarian revolution coincided in time with the beginning of the *Industrial Revolution**.

Enclosures - the cutting up of open fields and reallocation of arable land to the landowners for the purpose of creating consolidated farms which could be "enclosed" by hedges, fences or walls - had occasionally been carried out earlier by agreement of the landowners, but what is known as the "Enclosure Movement" did not come into existence as a national policy until the fourth decade of the 18th century, reaching its climax during the reign of George III (1760-1820). The resistance of individual proprietors was overcome by special Acts of Parliament passed for each village and implemented by a Parliamentary Commissioner. The decisions of the Commissioner were law. The enclosures now proceeded on a large scale and also included the so-called "common land" consisting of pasture and woodland which the villagers had used in common for generations. This common land was allocated to the lord of the manor.

An incidental result of the enclosure movement was the chessboard pattern of rectangular fields enclosed by hedges or stone walls so characteristic of the English landscape today. The economic effect of the enclosure movement was an increase in agricultural output resulting from the disappearance of fallows, the cultivation of waste and woodland, capital investment and improved methods of cultivation. The price of this economic gain was a decrease in the number of independent farmers. Many of the smaller landowners, now deprived of the possibility of using the common land for grazing cattle and obtaining fuel,were no longer able to make a living. They were bought out by the big landlords and became landless farm labourers or factory hands. The "great estate" system with its many tenant farms came into existence. A new structure of the rural community was created, consisting of three clearly distinguished classes: the landlords, the tenant farmers (mostly former small squires) and the "labouring poor" working on tenant farms.

The two World Wars having made clear how disadvantageous it is for Britain to be dependent on imports for its food supply, there has been in recent decades a tendency to encourage domestic farming by governmental subsidies (*Agricultural Relief**) and to increase the arable land under cultivation. After World War II the Estate Duty (also called Death Duty because levied on the value of landed property of deceased persons) was introduced. It amounts to 80 per cent. of the estate value even for descendants in the first degree. Frequently, and especially when several heirs to the property have died within a comparatively short period, this heavy death duty may compel the owners to sell their estate, parts of which are bought by former tenants. The number of tenant farmers, therefore, is gradually decreasing and today more than half of the farms in Great Britain are again owner-occupied.

■ Whereas in Britain the Agrarian Revolution is to be considered as an economic prerequisite to industrialization - because it provided for a new class of landless labourers - in the United States it was not a prerequisite but a consequence of industrialization. From the second half of the 19th century onwards the most striking factor of the Agrarian Revolution was the enormous increase of agricultural output per head of the labour force due to the application of machinery and agricultural science to the process of farming *(Land-Grant College*)*. Mechanization of farming required large amounts of capital which led to the gradual disappearance of the traditional self-sufficing farms of 160 acres as established under the Homestead Act of 1862 and their replacement by large-scale enterprises (often managed by corporations) in American agriculture. A further consequence was the increasing mortgage indebtedness of American farmers. Agricultural overproduction caused by the mechanization of farming brought with it a decline of agricultural prices in the domestic market. The farmers found temporary compensation for these losses through exports to Western Europe especially after Britain repealed the Corn Laws in 1846. But soon competition from Argentina, Canada, Russia, etc. arose and agricultural prices declined also in the international market. The American protective tariffs for manufactured goods *(Protectionism*)* meant further hardship for the farmers, who had to pay high prices for their machinery while agricultural prices were declining. In addition the farmers suffered from the discriminatory rate and freight policy of the American railroads *(Interstate Commerce*)*.

In order to help themselves the farmers founded the Patrons of Husbandry in 1867 which by 1875 included 20,000 "granges" or local lodges. The "Patrons" initiated the laws popularly known as "Granger Laws" enacted by various Middle Western States to eliminate railroad discrimination. In the late eighties the granges were succeeded by the "Farmers' Alliances". In the subsequent years the revolution of the farmers concentrated on the American Populist Party.

But the Agrarian Revolution in the United States is still going on today. It is characterized by agricultural overproduction as a consequence of technological advances which entail the trend toward bigness and standardization. Thus big business corporations have begun to penetrate into agriculture and to replace the traditional family farm by corporate farming. To a great extent, for example, the broiler industry has moved into farming; this can be considered as a vertical concentration. The impact of corporate farming on agriculture, however, has led to a consiberable shrinkage in the number of farms and to a corresponding increase in the average size of corporate farms. Finally it has also affected the small rural American towns which have been faced with a gradual depopulation and a deterioration of public facilities. I Fr

Agricultural Relief

● Since the latter part of the 19th century agricultural overproduction in the United States has increasingly affected the British agricultural market, thus rendering some form of Government assistance for agriculture in Britain inevitable. This was especially true in the Great Depression of the 1930s, when the Government began to pay farmers subsidies to protect and assist home production. During the Second World War and the subsequent years of *Austerity** agricultural production was placed under state control, and farm products were purchased and sold by the Government at fixed prices. Postwar support of farming was achieved under the provisions of the Agriculture Act of 1947. A special feature of British agricultural assistance was that of guaranteed prices for a number of agricultural products such as livestock-products, cereals, potatoes, etc. The guaranteed prices for each year were determined in England and Wales by the Minister of Agriculture, Fisheries and Food and the Secretary of State for Wales, in Scotland and Northern Ireland by the Secretary of State for Scotland and the Home Secretary for Northern Ireland after consultation with the Farmers' Unions. If the average market price for products eligible for guarantee was below the guaranteed prices - which usually was the case since agricultural products from overseas, especially from the *Commonwealth** countries, were allowed to enter the British market free from duty - the producers were entitled to obtain deficiency payments (i.e. the differences between market and guaranteed prices) out of government funds. Furthermore, grants-in-aid, known as production grants, are paid for particular kinds of production or farming practices in order to improve land fertility, pasturage, breeding herds, farm buildings, silage, roads, drainage and various equipment. The estimated expenditure for price guarantees, grants and subsidies amounted to £ 230 million in the 1975-76 season. 3

The Agriculture Acts of 1957 and 1970 confirmed the system of guaranteed prices and production grants. In order to improve and facilitate the marketing of agricultural commodities the Agricultural Marketing Act of 1958, which consolidated earlier legislation on the subject, provided for marketing boards, which were producers' organizations regulating the marketing of particular goods.

In January, 1973, Britain's membership in the European Community became effective. In accordance with the Treaty of Accession signed by Britain, Denmark, the Republic of Ireland and the six original member states of the Community in January 1972, Britain had accepted the system of agricultural support under the Common Agricultural Policy (CAP) of the Community. The treaty provided for a transitional period of five years during which CAP should be introduced into Britain by six equal steps. The transitional period ended on December 31, 1977.

The main difference between the support of farmers under CAP and the former British system is as follows:

Britain formerly paid direct subsidies to her farmers to keep them in business while farm products from abroad could enter the country free of duty and were sold in the domestic market at (cheapest) world market prices. The Community, however, levies import duties on agricultural goods from third countries (i.e. countries not belonging to the E.C.), which entails an increase of prices for imported food up to the level which is set in Brussels once a year. These artificially high prices are charged for agricultural goods in the domestic markets of the Community and protect Community farmers against competition from third countries. Therefore, the adoption of CAP by Britain means that food prices are likely to increase in the British home market (see also *Common Market**).

■ During World War I the economic condition of agriculture in the United States improved owing to the increasing demand for agricultural goods. From 1914 to 1918 the wholesale price index rose from 100 (1914) to 208 (1918) and 211 (1920). From 1921, however, agricultural prices began to decline and continued to fall, even during the prosperity period of the 1920s *(Great Crash*)*. With mortgage debts rising from $ 7,857 million to $ 10,785 million in 1923 it became obvious that public assistance was needed to avoid economic collapse in agriculture.

As early as 1916 the Federal Government laid the foundation for a farm credit organization under the Farm Loan Act of 1916. It divided the United States into 12 farm credit districts in accordance with the Federal Reserve Bank districts and provided credit facilities for long- and short-term credits in each district. The *New Deal** legislation was introduced to broaden and coordinate by a number of amendments the measures enacted during the 1920s (Agricultural Credits Act of 1923 and Agricultural Marketing Act of 1929), and to supplement the relief system by the Agricultural Adjustment Act of 1933. Although declared unconstitutional by the Supreme Court in 1936, the A.A.A. was modified and revived in the new Agricultural Adjustment Act of 1938. The major part of the New Deal Farm Relief policy - enlarged and adjusted to changing conditions - has been the legal basis of agricultural assistance until the present day.

Today farm relief in the United States is a very complex system mainly comprising schemes such as:

(1) A farm credit system supervised and coordinated by the Farm Credit Administration, which has been an *Independent Agency** since 1953, and managed by the Farm Credit Board (established by the Farm Credit Act, 1953). The farmers living in the 12 farm credit districts are allowed to obtain long-term mortgage loans from the federal land banks through the federal land bank associations (Farm Loan Act, 1936 and amendments). The federal land banks are co-operative and farmer-owned. Short-term credit may be obtained from the local production credit associations which were originally capitalized by Government-owned corporations *(Corporate Enterprise*)* but have been owned since 1964 by their farmer-members.

(2) A price support system, which is carried out by loans to farmers or direct purchases of agricultural goods by the Agricultural Stabilization and Conservation Service (A.S.C.S.), was established in 1961 by the Secretary of Agriculture.

(3) Production was adjusted in order to bring supply and demand into equilibrium by way of marketing quotas, acreage allotments for commodities in abundant supply (cotton, tobacco, rice, wheat, corn, etc.), and by converting cropland not currently needed for crop use into grass, forests, or wild life development and conservation areas. These measures, which are intended to reduce agricultural production, will comprise about 50 million acres. Farmers agreeing to the changes are entitled to adjustment payments which are expected to amount to $ 1,000 million within the following ten years. The reduction of surplus production calls to mind the first Agricultural Adjustment Act of 1933 *(New Deal*)* which met with strong criticism at that time because it seemed unjustifiable to reduce production when many people were urgently in need of food.

(4) Storage facility programmes are carried out by the Agricultural Stabilization and Conservation Service (A.S.C.S.) and the Commodity Credit Corporation (C.C.C.), the latter being an independent agency established in 1948. The main purpose of the storage programme is to avoid heavy price fluctuations and to store grain and other foodstuffs for cases of emergency, a policy which is also in accordance with the Defense Food Program.

The Food and Agriculture Act of 1965 was in line with previous agricultural support. It provided for direct income payments to farmers as well as production controls on output. The Agricultural Act of 1970, however, moved toward a more market-oriented farm policy. It allowed farmers to select the most profitable mix of crops on their lands and based direct payments on market prices rather than minimum price support levels. Furthermore a ceiling of $ 55,000 per crop on payments to individual producers of cotton, wheat, and feed grains was fixed. The programmes under the Agricultural Act of 1970 were to extend for four years, through December 31, 1973. At the end of 1973, however, most of the programmes were continued under the Agriculture and Consumer Protection Act 1973. The Act of 1973 established a new "target price" payment system under which the Government paid farmers the difference, if any, between the market price they had received for their produce and a target price written into the Act for wheat corn, cotton, etc. Among others, the Act reduced the annual subsidy ceiling to £ 20,000 per farmer compared with £ 55,000 imposed in 1970. Furthermore it extended the Food Stamp Programme *(War on Poverty*)* and other products for the developing countries through the fiscal year 1977. The Agriculture and Consumer Protection Act 1973 expired in 1977. In the meantime a new farm bill has been presented to Congress which at present is still under debate.

Another way to bring supply and demand into equilibrium is to open up or expand foreign markets for American agricultural commodities as had been attempted by tariff cuts for such goods under the agreements of the Kennedy Round and negotiations about increased imports of agricultural produce into the E.E.C. countries.

I Fr

Appalachia

■ Appalachia: Derived from the adj. Appalachian which recalls "Appalachi" the name of a Red Indian tribe belonging to the Creek Indians.

Appalachia is neither an administrative term nor a geographic one. Since about 1959 it has been used to denote the development areas following the Appalachian mountain range. It includes parts of the region of the ten States: Pennsylvania, West Virginia, Ohio, Maryland, Virginia, Kentucky, Tennessee, North Carolina, Georgia and Alabama, the governors of which in 1959 formed a conference to discuss the common economic problems of their depressed areas called by them "Appalachia". It covers 165,000 square miles - an area approximately the size of Japan - and contains approximately 15 million people.

The north of this region - famous for its wealth in bituminous coal and anthracite deposits and including such important industrial towns as Pittsburgh/Pa., Charleston and Huntington/ W.Va. - is one of the oldest industrial centres of the United States. Some of the big industrial towns, of course, are prospering, but on the whole the declining demand for coal, on the one hand, and increasing automation, on the other, has led to structural unemployment (mine employment declining nearly 60 per cent. and factory employment nearly 14 per cent. during the 1950s).

But one of the worst pockets of poverty was the rural part of Appalachia comprising above all the southern Appalachian region and the Appalachian plateau, where the farm land is poor, the hillsides eroded, the valleys narrow and the remote hamlets nearly inaccessible. The inhabitants, however, may boast of being descendants of the early English colonists. But these so-called Southern Highlanders, though of early Anglo-American stock, are today as poor as their ancestors were when they came into the country. Sometimes the soil was exhausted by wasteful exploitation and by the burning down of forests, as was the case in Indian and also in early colonial times. Sometimes the topsoil was impaired or destroyed by erosion. Public services such as roads, flood control, sewage facilities and also schools and hospitals were inadequate by modern standards so that the region's resources in timber and water power could not be exploited successfully. The result was that about one-third of America's poor families lived in Appalachia. Only one-third of its adults finished high school and approximately 200,000 of the Appalachian population migrated annually from the area to seek jobs elsewhere.

John F. Kennedy was the first to draw public attention to the economic problems of chronically poverty-stricken Appalachia. When he was succeeded by Lyndon B. Johnson, the new President took up the recommendations of the ten States concerned which had already been elaborated under Kennedy's presidency. President Johnson visited the area in April and May, 1964 and submitted his Appalachian Aid Program to Congress on April 28th, 1964, which became law as the Appalachian Regional Development Act on March 9th, 1965. Its major items provided for: (1) a new road and highway net "for improved access and communication" of the Appalachian region; (2) flood control to prevent the serious damage caused by floods, especially in Kentucky and Pennsylvania, and the development of water resources; (3) retraining of unemployed persons in order to decrease the structural unemployment of the region; (4) research work` for developing new uses for coal, and (5) improvement of pastures to help the farmers. The plans for Appalachia were part of President Johnson's nation-wide, long-range "War on Poverty".

In the meantime the migration from the Appalachian area has not only been stopped but since about 1973, more people have moved into the region than out of it, which could be attributed mainly to the economic development of the region, especially the provision of roads, public facilities and the creation of jobs, carried out up to now.

The Appalachian Regional Development Act drew public attention to the problems of other economically depressed areas existing in the U.S.A. Thus the Public Works and Economic Development Act of 1965 aimed at helping those areas especially by federal grant-in-aid funds allocated for the improvement of public facilities. Both acts were amended in 1967, 1969 and 1971. In 1972, the definition of economic development areas was broadened so that assistance could be given (under the act) to areas of "substantial" unemployment.

Today, the following areas, or parts of them, are defined as Economic Development Regions:

New England
- Maine
- Vermont
- New Hampshire
- Massachusetts
- Connecticut
- Rhode Island

Upper Great Lakes
- Michigan
- Minnesota
- Wisconsin

Ozarks
- Arkansas
- Kansas
- Missouri
- Oklahoma

Coastal Plains
- North Carolina
- South Carolina
- Georgia

Four Corners
- Arizona
- Colorado
- New Mexico
- Utah

Appalachia
- Alabama
- Georgia
- North Carolina
- Virginia
- Kentucky
- Tennessee
- Maryland
- Pennsylvania
- West Virginia

Ohio
South Carolina
New York
Mississippi

I Fr

Assisted Areas

- Assisted Areas (formerly called Development Areas) are those British districts which need planned development to offset a constant decline of their local industries causing persistent unemployment, poverty and migration of population (into other industrial places) with a consequent shrinkage of the local market, a fall in municipal revenue and decreasing standards of public services (schools, roads, hospitals etc.). Today nearly the whole of Scotland and Northern England, Wales, Northern Ireland as well as parts of the South West and the Midlands regions are designated as assisted areas. See map on p. 209.

Within the assisted areas a distinction has to be made between three categories: first, the special development areas which are in especially urgent need of Government aid, to eliminate structural unemployment in their region; second, the development areas which suffer from similar but not so depressing problems and third, the intermediate areas where only some selective assistance is necessary. Under the provisions of the Industry Act 1972 financial assistance can be granted to meet the cost of buildings and works on premises used for specified activities in manufacturing, construction and mining. Special development and development areas can be granted additional aid for the cost of plant and machinery.

In order to induce industrialists to settle in assisted areas incentives are also given by providing new well-equipped factories for sale or for lease. These factories are built in England by the non-profit making English Industrial Estates Corporation and in Scotland and Wales by the Scottish and Welsh Development Agencies, which are non-profit making, too. Needless to say that all firms willing to set up or expand industry in the assisted areas are granted tax concessions, especially in the form of depreciation allowances on investment at any rate they choose.

All these encouragements are also given to foreign employers who decide to settle in assisted areas, which is of special importance with regard to Britain's membership of the Common Market.

Under the Industry Act 1975 a new statutory body, the National Enterprise Board (NEB) *(Nationalization*)* was established. Its function, among others, is to stimulate and encourage investment projects especially in areas of high unemployment. For this purpose it acts as a channel for selective financial aid under the Industry Acts 1972 and 1975. It is also to be mentioned that as a member of the EC Britain participates in the European Regional Development Fund of the European Community. In 1975, Britain's gross share of the Fund amounted to £ 35 millions, i.e. nearly 28 per cent. of the funds allocated to the European Regional Development Fund.

Similar though not quite so far reaching aids and encouragements are given to industrialists willing to set up or expand industry in Northern Ireland. The corresponding provisions are made under special Northern Ireland legislation especially under the Industries' Development Acts. The Ministry of Commerce (Northern Ireland) is responsible for the administration. It is assisted by the Northern Ireland Economic Council established in 1965 in order to promote economic growth in Northern Ireland.

The fact that there are areas in Britain which are in need of public aid for planned industrial development is partly due to a redistribution of industry and population from the former industrial centers to the southeast corner of the country.

The former mainstays of British prosperity coal mining, wool and cotton textiles, shipbuilding, iron and steel industry seriously declined between the two World Wars owing to a fall in British exports, rising competition in international trade and new technological development (electronics, atomic energy, etc.). While heavy industries were declining, "light industries" – electrical engineering, consumer goods manufacture, silk, rayon and plastics industries – were growing up in the south-eastern corner, chiefly in the London conurbation *(New Towns*).* They attracted a large number of people from depressed areas. The Great Depression of the 1930s – when more than one-third of the industrial population in the depressed areas was "on the dole" – had first drawn public attention to the problem of industrial location and subsequently led to the Special Areas Development and Improvement Act of 1934 (amended in 1936 and 1937). The name Special Area was changed into Development Area by the Distribution of Industry Act of 1945 and into Assisted Area in 1972.

As early as 1940 the Royal Commission on the Distribution of Industrial Population (Barlow Commission) emphasized the social, economic and strategic drawbacks of an industrial overconcentration in the South East accompanied by a serious decline of basic industries in the 19th century's industrial centres. Following the recommendations of the Barlow Report, the Board of Trade, empowered by the Distribution of Industry Act of 1945, effectively intensified the measures for "bringing the work to the workers" in the renamed Development Areas. In the following years the number of the unemployed in the Development Areas was reduced, but it remained still higher than the United Kingdom's average. I Fr

Austerity

- Austere: severe in self-discipline, strict, abstinent; severely simple, without any luxury.

Austerity in an economic sense means doing without. It describes a situation of economic hardship. Hardship accrues when there are shortages and "so long as there are shortages", said Clement Attlee, the British Prime Minister of the Labour government, in September, 1947, "you must have controls". The controls are of two kinds: there are direct physical controls with quantitative allocation and rationing of goods, materials and services and there are financial controls, enforced through fiscal and monetary policies. Throughout World War II and during the post-war period the British government imposed austerity upon the people by rationing and by taxation. Little or no attempt was made to control spending by making money dear or cheap.

As in many country engaged in war, many real resources available in Britain were channelled into the war effort. Consumption had to give way. The

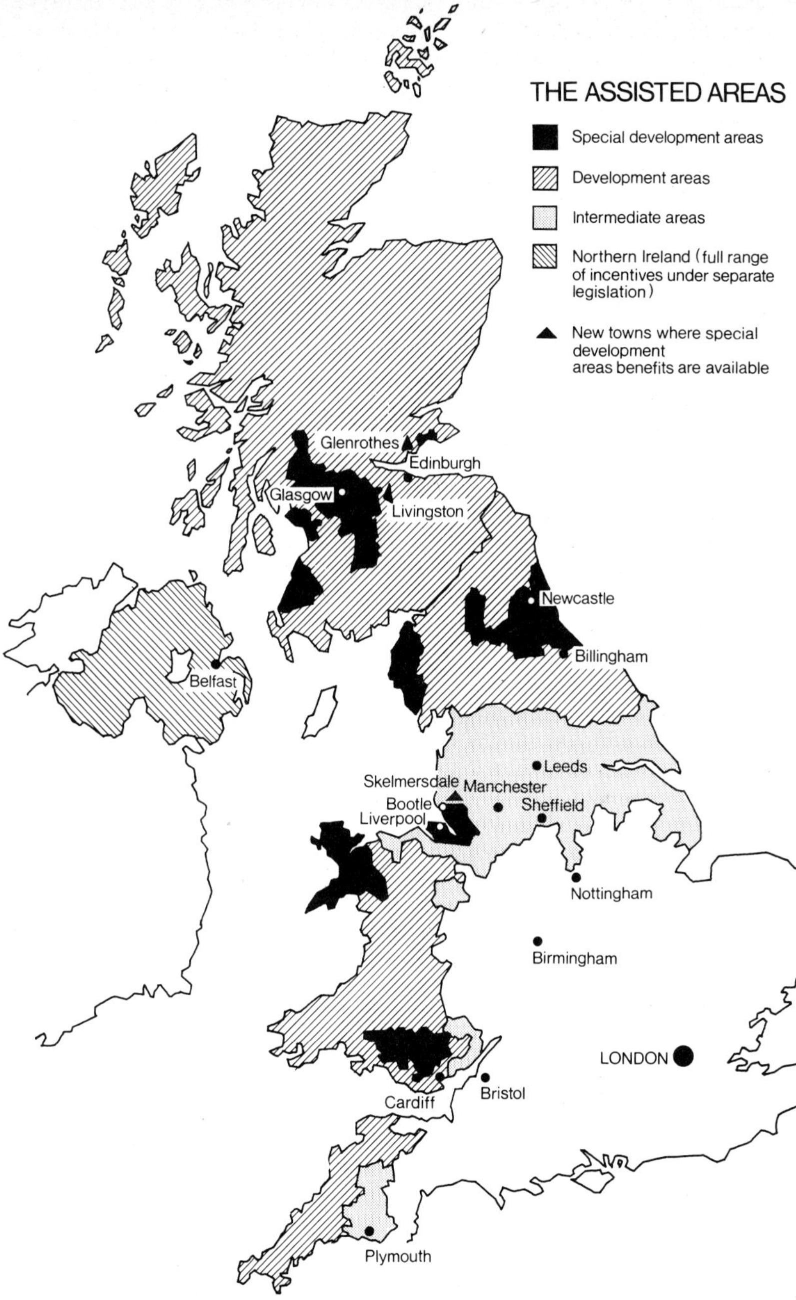
THE ASSISTED AREAS
Special development areas
Development areas
Intermediate areas
Northern Ireland (full range of incentives under separate legislation)
New towns where special development areas benefits are available
Glenrothes
Edinburgh
Glasgow
Livingston
Newcastle
Billingham
Belfast
Leeds
Skelmersdale
Manchester
Bootle
Sheffield
Liverpool
Nottingham
Birmingham
LONDON
Cardiff
Bristol
Plymouth

practical question of how much austerity the public would stand could never be ignored. However severer limitations on the level of real consumption were accepted in Britain for a longer time than in any country of unoccupied Western Europe including Germany. Aggregate consumption expenditure at constant prices fell quickly on food to 80 per cent., on footwear to 70 per cent., on clothing to 60 per cent., on furniture to 20 per cent., on private motoring to 8 per cent. of the 1938 level. At this extremely low level of pre-war consumption, there took place a vast standardisation of consumer goods under the heading of utility standards. These utility schemes for the most part laid down precise manufacturing specifications. The range of specifications was often restricted to a narrow "austerity" selection of possible ways of making an article. The mere fact that for the whole of 1945 aggregate consumption was well below pre-war, although the population had grown by 5 per cent., whilst in the United States consumption was up by 50 per cent., gave rise to the question whether the British public would accept austerity and whether austerity was necessary in peace under a newly elected Labour government.

The necessity for a continuation of restraint on consumption was a logical outcome of the war. Britain was impoverished by it. Whilst two-thirds of the cost of the war was paid for through austerity, the other third was met from the sale of its accumulated wealth ($ 1,118 million), from overseas loans (£ 303 million) and from a net increase in floating indebtedness in the form of sterling balances held abroad (£ 2,576 million). When moreover at the end of the war American Lend-Lease suddenly ended, the British government took steps to negotiate under the leadership of Lord Keynes American and Canadian loans. The sum of £ 1,400 million so raised had to be added to the above-mentioned, war incurred, losses on external account of about £ 4,000 million. Britain, which had been the greatest of creditor nations, became the greatest of debtors after the war.

The new situation posed for the new Labour government a structural problem of vast dimensions. Before the war net service receipts on external account from shipping, from mercantile and financial profits on international trade and, above all, from interest and profits on overseas investments paid for more than one-third of the British volume of imports. In 1945 it paid for less than 2 per cent. Hence the Labour government correctly estimated that "the full restoration of a reliable equilibrium which can persist without measures of restriction or the defensive mechanisms of the type with which it is hoped to dispense may require a volume of exports nearer 75 per cent. than 50 per cent. in excess of the pre-war level". Thus direct controls, and the austerity consequent upon them, were not regarded by the government as an end in itself, but as a means to an end. That end after the war was above all the full restoration, of a reliable equilibrium in the country's *Balance of Payments**.

In 1945 and in several succeeding years the problem of exports was one of production. There was then no difficulty in finding foreign buyers. The wartime policy of austerity was reinforced by an export drive, in pursuance of which manufacturers were persuaded or compelled to reserve a certain portion of their output for exports. The government could put pressure on manufacturers through their control of the importation and allocation of materials. The export drive was successful in the sense that in 1951, when in October of that year the Labour government was replaced by a Conservative government, the volume of exports was 176 of 1938 (= 100). It had risen to that high level from 31 in 1944. On the other hand the volume of imports throughout this period remained well below 1938 and in 1951 reached only 96 of 1938 (= 100). Although the structural problem posed by the external account was solved in the course of the Labour government's tenure of office with toil and determination on the one side and continued austerity on the other, it clearly did not increase the Labour Party's popularity. The citizens cannot always distinguish nicely between the needs of the case and the culpability of the government.

During its term of office the Labour government faced of course many specific problems which were superimposed on the structural one. Thus the granting of the American and Canadian loans was made dependent upon the convertibility of the £ *Sterling**. Owing to sharper increases in the prices of British imports than of British exports, the loans ran out quicker than was expected. Because of the extremely hard winter of 1946-47, British coal production fell and temporarily curtailed industrial production. When according to agreement the £ sterling convertibility came into operation in July 1947, more than one half of the loans had been spent and within six weeks the remainder had gone as foreign holders of sterling converted their balances into dollars. In August convertibility had to be suspended. Dalton, the Chancellor of the Exchequer, was blamed for not foreseeing the foreign exchange crisis and in this crisis Stafford Cripps was made Minister of Economic Affairs. In preparing an autumn budget, Dalton's minor indiscretion to a journalist deprived him of office. Cripps from then on combined the two offices in his person. He became the most influential member of the government. The policy of austerity was in the popular image largely associated with his name. He imposed further restrictions on overseas purchases. Bread rationing was introduced in peace time which had not been necessary in wartime. He persuaded the Trade Unions to accept a policy of wage restraint. The Unions and the public accepted the continuation of austerity willingly because Cripps retained and strengthened the highly redistributive system of taxation and kept a strict control on the price level.

In subsequent years as the level of production under a regime of full employment increased, the shortages of supply eased. Hand in hand with the improvement of supply went what was called the "bonfire of controls". As direct controls slowly disappeared, austerity also diminished. The range of free consumers' choice widened. By the time of election in October 1951, the most stringent restraints on consumers had gone, but not their memories of hardship. In choosing a Conservative government the public voted that a regime of austerity and hardship was no longer necessary. Under the new government the financial controls were retained. Monetary policy which had been dormant for more than a decade was revived. It gradually replaced indirect quantitative controls and complemented fiscal policy. By the twin tools of monetary and fiscal policy the new Conservative government tried to influence and regulate all spending streams. When in subsequent years dear money and taxation became the instruments of austerity, as hardship had to be imposed, the climate and the economic situations were very different from those which faced the Labour government in 1945. It is at least questionable whether the fundamental structural problem on external account which faced them in 1945 could have been tackled without direct controls and the regime of austerity consequent upon them.

H C H

● In 1919 two Englishmen, John Alcock and Arthur W. Brown, pioneered the first flight across the Atlantic from St. John's, Newfoundland, to Clifden, Ireland. This event opened new prospects for the development of high speed passenger and mail transport by air throughout the whole of the British Empire. But at that time air transport was a risky and very expensive enterprise. The British Government therefore agreed to grant a subsidy of £ 1,000,000 to Imperial Airways Ltd. which was established in 1924. In the subsequent years Imperial Airways succeeded in opening regular through services from London to India as well as to Central Africa and to Australia. Shortly before the Second World War the assets and liabilities of Imperial Airways were handed over to British Overseas Airways Corporation (B.O.A.C.) which was established in 1939 to serve the long-distance lines. In 1946 British European Airways (B.E.A.), which mainly links the United Kingdom with the Continent of Europe, was also founded. Both companies are nationalized public corporations (in January 1973, they were renamed British Airways) *(Nationalization*)*. Besides these public corporations, however, there are still 46 independent operators licensed by the Air Transport Licensing Board (A.T.L.B.) which was absorbed by the newly established Civil Aviation Authority in 1972. The independent operators work mainly on a charter basis. The responsible authority for civil air transport is the Department for Trade and Industry. Most of the airports are owned by the municipalities or by the Government itself.

After World War II the competition of air transport had an effect on rail and water transport, first of all with regard to passenger traffic. Although scheduled air freight services were also established at that time, these services could not compete with rail and waterways except where commodities of high value and relatively small size, or perishable goods were concerned. But with light industry (electronics, electrical and chemical products etc.) playing a steadily growing part in British industry *(Development Area*)* it is not surprising that the share of British overseas trade carried by air transport is gradually increasing. In 1975 14 per cent of imports and 17 per cent of exports were carried by air.

■ In the United States the development of civil air transportation was greatly assisted by a system of indirect Government subsidies. They consisted of air mail contracts which the Postmaster General was authorized to make with airline companies under the Air Mail Act of 1925 (Kelly Act). The mail payments were to cover not only the actual cost of carrying mail but also that of enlarging and improving the American airline services. The enactment of the Air Mail was followed by a rapid expansion of domestic airlines which received additional stimulus from the prosperity period of the 1920s and the "easy money policy" of the Federal Reserve which facilitated capital investments *(Great Crash*)*. As early as 1929 the Department of Commerce listed 44 operators of scheduled services on domestic passenger and express air traffic. The increase even continued during the Depression period of the 1930s.

The spectacular one-man, non-stop flight of the American Charles A. Lindbergh from New York to Paris in 1927 showed once more the possibility of intercontinental flights and thus helped to encourage the establishment of transoceanic route services.

In accordance with the American Constitution interstate commerce is under the control of the Federal Government *(Interstate Commerce*)*. As air traffic is more interstate in character than any other means of transportation the Federal Government was authorized to regulate air traffic under the Air Commerce Act of 1926. The "encouragement and development" of United States civil aviation was entrusted to an *Independent Agency** established by the Civil Aeronautics Act of 1938. The agency was named the Civil Aeronautics Board in 1940. Its regulatory functions include the licensing of airports (owned by the municipalities) and of pilots, the jurisdiction of rates and fares charged for air transportation, the payment of subsidies to air carriers "where required by the public convenience and necessity", etc. A further agency, the Federal Aviation Agency, had been created pursuant to the Federal Aviation Act of 1958. It was abolished under President Nixon. U.S. air-borne exports and imports are steadily increasing. 3

I Fr

Balance of Payments

The economic and financial transactions of a country with other countries are summarized in the balance of payments. The most important division within the balance of payments is between the current account and the capital account.

The balance of payment on current account records, above all, the payments and receipts for imported and exported goods. This part is known as the balance of trade or of visible items. A second part on current account reflects payments and receipts for services rendered on foreign order in the domestic market or on domestic order abroad and comprises services such as shipping, freight haulage, insurance, tourism etc. It is especially to be noted that all income earned on investments abroad is also recorded in the balance of services or invisible items as this part of the balance on current account is called.

The capital account, on the other hand, includes all capital transactions into or out of the country such as investments of domestic firms in foreign industries or of foreign firms in domestic industries respectively, purchases or sales of securities, public or private loans as well as short-term liabilities.

If a country imports more goods and services than it exports and if, at the same time, it engages in net foreign investments then more funds flow out of the country than into it: in brief, the "overall" balance of payments records a deficit. Such a deficit can be financed either by payment in gold, convertible currencies or allocated SDR's (Special Drawing Rights see *Bretton Woods**) or by an increase of a country's external debt.

● It has been a notable feature of British economic life for more than a century that the country imports more in food and raw materials than it exports in manufactured goods. Consequently, in terms of payments made and received, the British "visible" balance almost always registers a deficit.

The traditional deficit on "visible" trade has been supportable because of a large surplus which is normally earned on services' account or on "invisible" transactions.

Before the Second World War the value of imports exceeded that of exports by 56.7 per cent. This deficit was almost wholly covered by a corresponding surplus on invisible account. In the whole post-war period, however, the surplus on "invisibles" paid for only about 3 per cent. of the value of imported goods. In view of this war induced structural deterioration in the contribution of invisible earnings to needed imports, it was necessary for exports of goods to rise over the increase of imports by at least 49.6 per cent. This was the export task which confronted the United Kingdom, in order to reach tolerable solvency on external "current" account. In pursuance of it, the British government of the immediate post-war years reinforced its harsh domestic policy *(Austerity*)* by a deliberate drive for the promotion of exports. Between 1946 and 1954 the increase in the value of exports rose over that of imports by no less than 36.1 per cent. and between 1955 and 1964 it rose by 50.5 per cent. Since in all post-war years, except 1962, the "terms of trade", that is the ratio of export prices to import prices, were heavily against the United Kingdom, she had for every unit of imported quantities to offer more units of exported quantities than before the war.

The substitution of a surplus for a deficit on "current" account between the two post-war periods here distinguished was due partly to the effort that went into the provision of exports and partly to the fact that the rate of increase of imports declined in relation to that of the national income. It fell from 2.9 in the first period to 1.4 in the second period. In other words, whilst between 1946 and 1954 a growth of national income at constant prices by one per cent. was accompanied by an increase in the volume of imports by 2.9 per cent., in the period between 1955 and 1964 a one per cent. income growth only called forth an import growth of 1.4 per cent.

At the same time the United Kingdom became a heavy net investor on "long-term capital account". This account reflects not only investment by British firms in overseas industries and by overseas firms in British industry, but also the flow of government loans and repayments and other transactions on the London market in British and overseas securities. In the years between 1955 and 1964 the United Kingdom's net overseas investments averaged £ 157 million a year. As during this period the surplus on "current" account was only £ 23 million a year, it meant that there was a average deficit on "overall" account of £ 134 million a year.

The United Kingdom's gold and convertible currency "reserves", amounting to £ 986 million at the end of 1954, clearly could not have withstood an average drain of £ 134 million per year over a ten year period. Thus the "overall" deficit was financed by a decrease of the "reserves" by £ 16 million per year and by an increase of the United Kingdom's short-term indebtedness by £ 118 million a year.

From the United Kingdom's point of view this increase is somewhat precarious, for a massive withdrawal of short-term funds by foreigners would immediately reduce the reserves and threaten the external value of the £ sterling.

This survey of the British balance of payments over the whole post-war period includes the years of crisis on external account (1946, 1947, 1951, 1955, 1960 and 1964). In these years the rate of growth of imports markedly exceeded the rate of growth of exports on "visible" account. For instance, in 1964, the "visible" balance registered a deficit of £ 534 million, which, with a reduced surplus on "invisibles" of only £ 122 million, turned the "current" account passive to an amount of £ 412 million. Moreover, net foreign investment increased to £ 344 million, thus yielding an unprecedented deficit on "overall" account of £ 756 million, This was financed by a reduction of the "reserves" by £ 122 million and by an increase of £ 634 million in the United Kingdom's short-term liabilities. Of the latter no less than £ 573 million represented direct emergency assistance in the form of loans provided by the world's central banks and by the International Monetary Fund.

This crisis, which the government inherited, has strengthened the conviction of experts in the United Kingdom that, despite all post-war achievements, the competitiveness of the economy is not yet good enough. In the absence of another devaluation, the immediate balance of payments crisis was gradually being overcome by a temporary surcharge on imports, by a small subsidy on exports, by fiscal and other direct discouragements of long-term capital outflows.

But neither the temporary surcharge on imports nor the fiscal measures, mentioned above, could prevent a devaluation of sterling which took place on November 18th, 1967 *(Sterling*)*. As a rule, devaluation is favourable to exports because commodities become cheaper in terms of foreign currencies. But in 1968 the British balance on visibles was still in deficit because exports and imports rose nearly at the same rate. In the subsequent year there was still a deficit on visibles but it was not nearly as high as in 1968. In fact, it decreased by about £ 500 million from £ 643 million in 1968 to £ 141 million in 1969 while the balance of invisibles showed a remarkable improvement from +£ 335 million in 1968 to +£ 581 million in 1969. It was not until 1970 that for the first time in many years there was a small surplus on visibles whereas invisibles remained nearly unchanged (+£ 576 million). In 1971 the terms of trade became favourable for Britain because export prices increased more than import prices. In that year trade surplus amounted to approximately £ 300 million; visibles and invisibles totalled £ 952 million at the same time. The balance on capital account also showed a surplus which was said to be due partly to speculative inflows from abroad.

The balance of payments was improving remarkably from 1969 to 1972. While in 1969 its surplus amounted to only £ 743 million, it increased to L 1,420 million in 1970 and reached a peak with £ 3,351 million in 1971. The realignment of exchange rates in December 1971 *(Sterling*)* led to a revaluation of the pound sterling by about 8.5 per cent. against the dollar. But since competitive currencies like the DM were revalued by a higher percentage the realignment, as a whole, was not as unfavourable to Britain's international trade position as it easily might have been. The temporary improvement of the balance of payments at the beginning of the seventies, however, did not continue during the following years. In June 1972 the Government allowed the pound sterling to float which led to a de-facto devaluation of sterling and which, under normal circumstances, would have been favourable for the promotion of British exports. Nevertheless, there was still a deficit on visibles of £ 683 million in 1972 which increased to 2,295 million in 1973 and still more to £ 5,220 million in 1974. This deterioration in visible trade could be attributed to sharp price rises for goods imported into Britain and, in particular, to the price explosion for oil imported from the OPEC countries (OPEC: Organization of Petroleum exporting Countries).

In 1975, the deficit on visibles could be reduced to £ 3,204 million due to a significant increase in exports while imports remained nearly unchanged, and the deficit on visible trade could partly be offset by a surplus on invisibles which was mainly caused by rising receipts from shipping, air-traffic and tourism, above all from the Continent, the latter obviously being stimulated by the de-facto devaluation of the pound sterling. But at the same time this devaluation unfavourably affected expenditure for much needed imports, so that in spite of growing exports the trade balance again showed a deficit of more than 3,000 million at the end of 1976. Although the trend to increased tourism continued during 1976 and 1977 it could only help to balance part of the deficit on visibles.

In consequence of the balance of payments difficulties the international indebtedness of Britain increased to a large extent in 1976. After having availed herself of the ordinary credit tranches of the International Monetary Fund (IMF) during the first half of 1976, Britain had to borrow a stand-by-credit of US $ 5,300 million from the central banks of the Group of Ten in order to support the sagging exchange rate of sterling in the international exchange markets. In September, 1976, the Government finally entered into negotiations with the IMF which aimed at a further big loan which should help to repay the stand-by-credit of the Group of Ten. After long deliberations in London the IMF eventually granted a further credit of 3,900 million, of which 2,970 million were made available by eight countries of the Group of Ten under the General Agreement to Borrow.

A remarkable credit item in the British balance of payments has become the production of British North Sea oil which first was brought ashore in June 1975. By 1980 the production rate is expected to rise to over 100 million tons from existing fields and latest estimates by the National Institute of Economic and Social research (NIESR) indicate that British off-shore oil will meet or even exceed the country's requirements in the 1980's.

■ From 1888 to 1971, the United States had a surplus of commodity exports over imports, i.e. the balance of trade was favourable. The reasons for the American surplus in visible exports were manifold, the most important being the rich natural resources of the country, its technological efficiency and standardized mass-production, which increased exports on the one hand, and the high protective tariffs *(→ Protectionism*)*, which curtailed imports on the other.

Before World War I, the United States was a debtor nation. Receipts from export surplus, therefore, were required to make payments on U.S. external debts. The situation changed after 1918. The United States then became a creditor nation which used its receipts from surplus on visible current account for making large capital loans to foreign countries, capital investments abroad were restricted only during the Great Depression.

During World War II, 80 per cent. of American exports were on lend-lease, for under the provisions of the Lend-Lease Act of 1941, allied countries were allowed to receive munitions, foodstuffs and other products from the U.S.A. by sale, exchange, or by lease. Total lend-lease aid of the U.S.A. amounted to $ 50,600 million during World War II. American lend-lease, it is true, ended in August 1945, but the United States granted Britain an additional loan of $ 3,700 million payable at 2 per cent. in 50 annual instalments. As a result of the war, Britain became one of the great debtor nations of the world *(→ Austerity*)* and U.S. Government expenditure on capital account for foreign loans and aid, such as Marshall aid and others, accounted for more than one third of total U.S. exports for some years immediately following World War II. In 1950 and subsequent years additional U.S. Government expenditure on current account was required for military purposes during the Korean War. At the same time, the Government had to make current expenditure for troops stationed in Europe. It was not therefore surprising that the overall deficit of the United States averaged $ 1,500 million a year from 1953 to 1956, although exports in visibles and invisibles continued to exceed imports. The year 1958 saw a sharp fall in American exports (from $ 20,862 million in 1957 to

$ 17,896 million in 1958) while imports remained steady. This fall in exports which continued in 1959 was due to the recession of 1958 but also reflected the rising competition especially from Western Europe and Japan. It unfavourably affected the balance of payments, which showed an average overall deficit of $ 3,700 million per year from 1958 to 1960. In 1961, the boom period began. At the same time, the balance of payments improved so that the overall deficit decreased to $ 2,370 million in 1961.

From 1961 onwards, grants and loans to developing countries and areas have caused an increasing drain of U.S. capital. Under the Foreign Assistance Act of 1961, the United States has given economic and technical assistance to more than 80 developing countries. From 1964 to 1973, government expenditure on the Vietnam War was an additional large debit item, which could be partly offset because the balance of trade continued to remain favourable until 1971. The current account on invisibles was adversely affected by increasing expenditure of American tourists abroad.

Private U.S. short-term and long-term capital investment overseas was another factor contributing to the unfavourable American balance of payments during the 1960s. The Johnson administration, which based its economic policy on the recommendations of the President's Council of Economic Advisers, tried selective measures to combat the trend toward capital investment abroad. At first the interest equalization tax was introduced to curtail the purchase of foreign securities. Next a "voluntary" programme of "guidelines" on direct business investment overseas was set up for the purpose of voluntary co-operation between industry and the banks in order to restrict these investments. But the measures did not succeed in offsetting the balance of payments disequilibrium. In 1970, increasing unemployment induced the Government to return to easy money policy. The subsequent difference in the level of U.S. interest rates and those in the international, particularly European, money market led to an increase of capital outflows. Although there was a slight improvement in trade and services in 1970, the balance of payments showed a deficit of nearly $ 10,000 million on the basis of official reserve transactions (the official reserve transactions balance reflects change in official reserves assets against foreign central banks).

Things went from bad to worse in 1971. The dollar repeatedly came under pressure and the trade balance showed a deficit for the first time in nearly 80 years. It amounted to $ 2,700 million and reached a peak of $ 6,900 million in 1972. During 1973, however, the situation improved remarkably mainly as a result of the two devaluations of the US dollar which had been carried through in December, 1971, and February, 1973 (Dollar*). In terms of foreign currencies they reduced the prices of American export goods, thus fostering purchases from the States and resulting in a change on visibles from a deficit in 1972 to a small surplus of $ 0,700 million in 1973. The considerable expansion of agricultural exports also added to this surplus, and the traditionally high level of interest rates favourably affected the balance on capital account, so that the overall balance on the basis of official reserve transactions showed a deficit of only $ 5,300 million, i.e., half the amount of 1972. The US Administration therefore repealed the interest equalization tax as well as the restrictions on American business investments overseas in January, 1974. But already in the course of 1974 the balance of payments worsened again partly as a consequence of steadily increasing capital export in the form of direct and portfolio investments overseas and partly because of an important rise in imports. As a matter of fact the deficit in visible trade which rose to over $ 4,000 million in 1974 also reflected the excessive price increases for oil from OPEC-countries.

If measured against the balance of payments the following year, 1975, was a much better one, for exports rose by nearly 10 per cent. while imports decreased by about 4 per cent. On the basis of official reserve transactions the debit balance reduced to about $ 2,500 million and consequently the exchange value of the US dollar in 1975 was firmer than in the two years before.

A recurrent development became evident in 1976 when imports rose by more than 25 per cent. while exports could obtain a growth of merely 7 per cent. which was to a large degree due to agricultural exports, e.g., delivery of grain to the U.S.S.R. (Union of Socialist Soviet Republics).
For 1977, however, a deficit on visibles up to $ 83,000 million has been expected because of extraordinarily high oil imports. To reduce the contry's dependence on imported oil the President of the United States presented an energy bill to Congress which aimed at energy saving in industry as well as in private and public buildings such as schools, hospitals etc. But the two Houses of Congress have not yet decided on this energy package. The adverse balance of payments which has been expected for 1977 is one of the reasons for the rapid fall of the exchange rate of the US dollar on the international exchange markets. I Fr/H C H

Bank of England

● The Bank of England - very often referred to just as "The Bank" - is the central bank of the English banking system. It is the bankers' bank and the banker to the Government and it has the monopoly of bank note issue in England and Wales. In some sense it is the central bank for the whole United Kingdom of Great Britain and Northern Ireland. It exercises, however, only an indirect control over the banking systems of Scotland and Northern Ireland, which also have their own banks of issue *(Legal Tender*)*.

The Bank of England's nickname, "The Old Lady of Threadneedle Street", refers to the Bank's site in Threadneedle Street and to a cartoon published in 1797 by James Gillray called "Political Ravishment, or the Old Lady of Threadneedle Street in Danger", depicting William Pitt the Younger, who was at that time Prime Minister, attempting to get possession of the Bank's gold by assaulting an aged woman sitting on a trunk labelled "Bank of England". The cartoon is to be seen in the exhibition room of the Bank. The Bank's own house magazine appears under the title of "The Old Lady".

The foundation of the Bank of England dates back to the time of William of Orange. In an endeavour to raise money for the King who, owing to his military engagements, was in financial difficulties, several schemes were proposed. It was William Paterson who finally succeeded in raising a public loan of £ 1.2 million. The Government's creditors were incorporated by Royal Charter and a corporation called "The Governor and Company of the Bank of England" was established on July 27th, 1694. The Bank opened for business on August 1st, 1694, its staff consisting at that time of seventeen clerks and two doorkeepers. The Bank was authorized to issue notes on Government security up to the amount of the sum lent. Although it was a private joint-stock bank, it was soon granted certain privileges. An Act of Parliament passed in 1708 provided that no other corporation consisting of more than six partners should be allowed to issue promissory notes payable on demand. Thus, for over 100 years the Bank of England shared the right of note issue only with small banks - a fact which soon led to its predominance. In 1751 it was entrusted with the administration of the National Debt.

During the second quarter of the 19th century, Bank of England branches were opened in fourteen towns. Eight of these branches still exist today, at Birmingham, Bristol, Leeds, Liverpool, Manchester, Newcastle, Southampton, and one in London. These branches proved a great help in meeting the growing financial demands of the rapidly developing industry and commerce. At the same time it became evident that it was not possible to uphold the right of note issue for the great number of small banks, which were not always able to back the notes issued, and thorough reform was felt to be necessary. It was brought about by the historic Bank Charter Act of 1844 which - among other things - restricted the right of note issue of the other banks in favour of the Bank of England. In 1844 there were still 72 banks of issue in England, in 1913 only 13, and since 1921 the Bank of England has been the sole bank of issue in England and Wales.

Another provision of the Bank Charter Act, which - with some modifications - still very much determines the structure of the Bank of England today, was that the Bank was divided into an Issue Department and a Banking Department. Furthermore it was stipulated that the fiduciary note issue should be limited to approximately £ 14 million, which were backed by Government securities; all notes above this amount were to be backed by gold. *(Sterling*.)* Until the outbreak of World War II, the Bank of England was the keeper of the country's gold reserves. In September, 1939, virtually all the Bank's gold was transferred to the Exchange Equalization Account, which is managed by the Bank of England on behalf of the Treasury, and very little gold is now held by the Bank's Issue Department.

Finally, the Act stipulated that the Bank was to publish weekly statements of its accounts for both the Issue Department and the Banking Department (the so-called Weekly Return).

By the Bank of England Act, which came into force on March 1st, 1946, the Bank of England was nationalized. The whole of the Bank stock was transferred to Treasury which compensated stockholders by an equivalent amount of Government Stock. The former Board of Directors was replaced by the Court of Directors of the Bank consisting of the Governor, the Deputy Governor, and 16 Directors. All of them are appointed by the Crown. The Governor and the Deputy Governor are appointed for five years, while the Directors' term of office is four years. For the practical work of the Bank its nationalization did not mean a great change since it had already been the great central bank for a long time.

Apart from the sole right of note issue for England and Wales the principal functions of the Bank of England include the following: As the bankers' bank it receives deposits from the London clearing banks, which must keep an account with the Bank of England, and from other great banks. Since these balances can be converted into legal tender notes at any time the banks may regard them as cash and they usually keep a large part of their liquid reserves on deposit with the Bank of England. The banks of Scotland and Northern Ireland maintain working balances at the Bank of England enabling them to settle their positions with other banks.

The Bank of England does not exercise any formal control over the clearing banks' operations, although the Bank of England Act of 1946 contains provisions authorizing it to do so. Its relation with the banks is mainly based on mutual trust and personal contact. It is regarded as the channel of communication in matters of finance and monetary policy between the Government and the clearing banks and vice versa.

The Bank of England also maintains relations with the central banks of other countries, which include banking connections as well as - in many cases - an exchange of opinions.

As banker to the Government the Bank of England maintains the account of H.M. Exchequer as well as the accounts of many Government Departments. It receives the revenue, effects all payments authorized by Parliament from the account of the Exchequer, manages the Government Stocks, which form the bulk of the National Debt, keeping the register of stockholders and paying dividends on the due dates. The Bank also provides for the Government's needs for short-term money; it receives the tenders for the weekly issues of Treasury Bills, issues these Bills and redeems them on maturity.

As the central bank it carries out the Government's financial policy. It exerts its influence on the money market by fixing the Bank Rate - the minimum rate at which the Bank of England is ready to discount British Government Treasury Bills or approved bills of exchange for the Discount Market or to make advances to the Discount Market. In the latter case the Bank is acting as "lender of last resort" at a penal rate. *(Discount Houses*)*

With effect from October 13th, 1972, the Bank of England, with the approval of the Chancellor of the Exchequer, replaced Bank rate by "the Bank of England's minimum rate for lending to the market". This new lending rate is determined by the average rate of discount for Treasury Bills established at the most recent tender, plus one half per cent., rounded to the nearest one quarter per cent. above. It, thereby, changes automatically with changes in the Treasury Bill rate thus ensuring a greater flexibility; i.e. the "last resort rate" now normally follows the movements in market rates. The rate is published each Friday afternoon. Provisions have been made allowing the Bank, with the approval of the Chancellor of the Exchequer, to suspend temporarily the above formula in certain cases until market rates have adjusted themselves to the new level.

Another instrument of the Bank's monetary policy is its open market operations. By purchasing securities against cash in the open market it will increase the amount of money in the market or at the disposal of the commercial banks; by selling securities, on the other hand, it can absorb a certain amount of the money. During the years from 1932 until 1951, when the Bank Rate remained unchanged at 2 per cent. (with the exception of a short period in September/October, 1939), the open market operations were the effective means of controlling monetary situation.

Apart from its executive duties to the Government, the Bank also has certain advisory functions. It is the intermediary between the Government and banking circles, and it maintains a close contact with the British Bankers' Association, the Stock Exchange, and other important financial organizations.

H St

■ An area especially suited by its climate, soil, etc. to a particular crop.

The term is used to signify the main agricultural regions of the United States. These regions are:

The HAY AND DAIRY BELT in the north which extends from Minnesota through Michigan and eastern Ohio to Maine. In this area the climatic and soil conditions are most favourable for dairy farming. Furthermore the dairy industry is favoured by its advantageous location near the industrial centres of the East which provide excellent markets for farm products. To the south the Hay and Dairy Belt borders on:

The CORN BELT which stretches from central Ohio to central Nebraska, covering a distance of nearly 900 miles. When the first European settlers landed in Jamestown and Plymouth the cultivation of corn (maize) was still unknown in Europe. The Indians, however, had grown corn for a long time as their only cereal food. Thus corn, cultivated with the simplest tools, became a means to save the early colonists from starvation in the New World. The Corn Belt is an area of mixed farming. Since corn is suitable fodder for animals, cattle raising was stimulated in this region. Livestock is often shipped in for fattening from the dry plains west of the Corn Belt, so that half of the produce of the croplands is fed to livestock.

The WHEAT BELT - a broad strip surrounding the north-western, south-western and southern part of the Corn Belt - stretches from North Dakota and the eastern part of Montana across Nebraska, Kansas, Missouri, Oklahoma and Arkansas to the northern part of Texas. The northern part of the Wheat Belt (the two Dakotas, Montana, Minnesota) contains spring wheat because wheat has to be sown in spring on account of the long cold winters, while in the southern and south-western parts winter wheat is grown. The state of Kansas ranks first in wheat production. To the west wheat yield decreases with the increase of aridity, and west of the so-called precipitation line of the 97th meridian *(Reclamation of Land*)* the cultivation of wheat mostly requires artificial irrigation. Since the 1930s wheat production has been included in the farm relief programmes *(Agricultural Relief*)* in order to compensate for the economic disadvantages caused by surplus production.

To the south the Wheat Belt borders on:

The COTTON BELT which covers the south-eastern states of the U.S.A. from the southern part of Virginia, Kentucky, Illinois and Missouri down to Florida, Alabama, Mississippi, Louisiana and Texas. These humid sub-tropical regions have long been the area of "King Cotton". In recent years, however, cotton cropland has decreased to approximately 40 per cent. of what it was originally. This is partly due to the attempt to overcome the cotton monoculture, which exhausts soil fertility, and partly due to a reduction of the acreage under cultivation which is in accordance with the provisions of the various farm relief programmes *(Agricultural Relief*)*. The centres where cotton is grown as the main crop have become known as the "cotton nuclei". They comprise the Texas High Plains, the Texas Black Waxy Prairies, the Appalachian Piedmont, the Coastal Plains of the Carolinas and Georgia, the Texan Gulf Coast and part of the Mississippi Valley. Today the Cotton Belt is to a large extent an area of mixed farming. Cotton, however, is still the predominant crop in the southern region of the United States.

Since the northern part of the Cotton Belt is also the tobacco- growing district, Virginia, Kentucky and the two Carolinas are called: The TOBACCO BELT. The two greatest tobacco-growing areas are Virginia and Kentucky.

The GRAZING AND IRRIGATED CROPS BELT, covering mainly the Great Plains, belongs to the semi-arid land, the greater part of which is west of the 97th meridian. It is marked by the transition from crop farming, by means of irrigation, to cattle or sheep grazing in the drier areas. Today the open ranch which formerly characterized the cattle-grazing areas has generally been replaced by fenced ranches, a development which deprived the cattle region of the "cowboy", one of its most legendary features. The ranches often cover areas up to several hundred thousand acres.

The CITRUS AND WINTER VEGETABLE BELTS comprise California, especially its southern part, and Florida and the coastal lowlands along the Gulf Coast where subtropical and mediterranean fruits and early vegetables are grown. The sunny slopes of the Californian ranges south of San Francisco are also the main wine producing areas of the United States. Spanish missionaries once brought their seedlings from across the Atlantic Ocean and were the first to grow wine in California. The wine industry increasingly gained commercial importance in the domestic market.

The term "belt" is also applied to the region of the greatest industrial concentration in the United States which has become known as the INDUSTRIAL BELT. It extends from New England to Alabama and from the western shores of Lake Michigan to the great bend of the Mississippi, including the following States entirely or in part: Massachusetts, Rhode Island, Connecticut, New York, Pennsylvania, New Jersey, Delaware, Maryland, West Virginia, Ohio, Michigan, Indiana, Illinois, Wisconsin, Kentucky, Tennessee and Alabama.

With the climate being very rough and cold in winter, the northern part of the Industrial Belt is sometimes called the SNOWBELT. From about 1950 onward it has been noticed that the increase of population in the Snowbelt has been slower than in the Southern States. This remarkable fact is attributed to the climatic conditions in the Southern part of the country, often called the American SUNBELT, running from Georgia West to Texas. The Sunbelt has become attractive also for foreign companies which have established offices and factories in this part of the country, the reason being that land is cheaper and the Labour unions less powerful than in the Northern States.

Furthermore the term "belt" is used to designate the time zones. For a long time the relation of time to longitude produced endless difficulties, especially on the railroads, until in 1883 the present system of time belts was introduced dividing the country into four zones by meridians of longitude, a distance of 15 degrees equalling a time difference of one hour.

The STANDARD TIME BELTS are: Eastern time (75th meridian = 12 o'clock); Central time (90th meridian = 11 o'clock); Mountain time (105th meridian = 10 o'clock); Pacific time (120th meridian = 9 o'clock); Alaska time (150th meridian = 7 o'clock). I Fr

Big Four

● Barclays Bank Ltd., Midland Bank Ltd., Lloyds Bank Ltd. and National Westminster Bank Ltd. are the largest joint-stock banks in England and are often referred to as the "Big Four". Joint-stock banking in England developed strongly during the second half of the 19th century. Amalgamations and affiliations took place, and by now a comparatively small number of large banks have emerged, of which the Big Four are the most important. Up to 1968, when the National Provincial Bank Ltd. and the Westminster Bank Ltd. merged into National Westminster Bank Ltd. there were still five of them. Together with two other joint-stock banks the Big Four are the members of the London 3

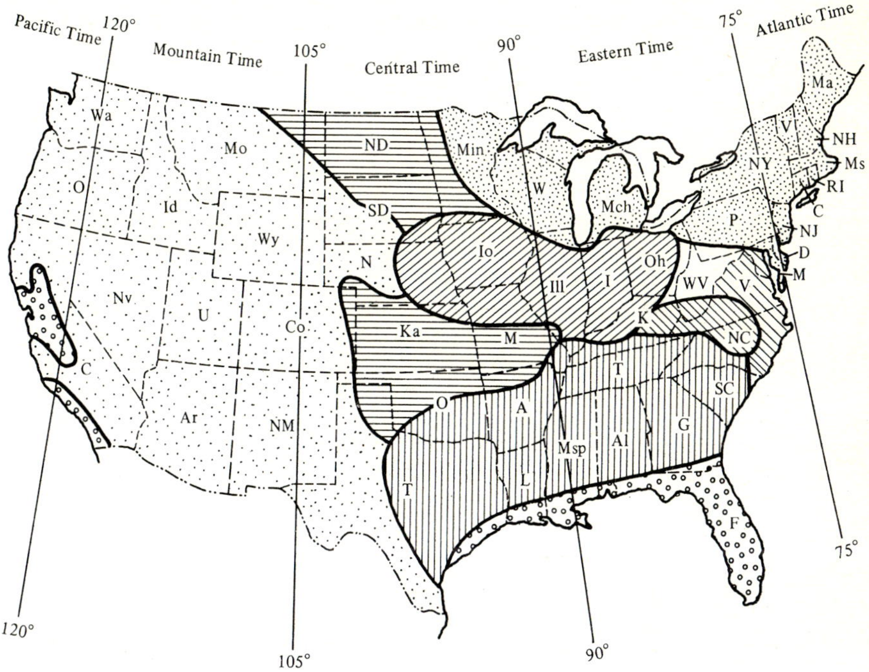

CROP BELTS

- Hay and Dairy
- Corn
- Wheat
- Cotton
- Tobacco
- Grazing and Irrigated crops
- Citrus and Winter vegetables

STATES

Ma	Maine	I	**Indiana**
NH	New Hampshire	Oh	**Ohio**
V	Vermont	WV	**West Virginia**
Ms	**Massachusetts**	V	Virginia
RI	**Rhode Island**	K	**Kentucky**
C	**Connecticut**	M	Missouri
NY	**New York**	Ka	Kansas
NJ	**New Jersey**	Co	Colorado
D	**Delaware**	U	Utah
M	Maryland	Nv	Nevada
P	**Pennsylvania**	C	California
Mch	**Michigan**	Ar	Arizona
Min	Minnesota	NM	New Mexico
W	**Wisconsin**	O	Oklahoma
ND	North Dakota	A	Arkansas
Mo	Montana	T	**Tennessee**
Wa	Washington	NC	North Carolina
O	Oregon	SC	South Carolina
Id	Idaho	G	Georgia
Wy	Wyoming	F	Florida
SD	South Dakota	Msp	Mississippi
Io	Iowa	L	Louisiana
Ill	**Illinois**	T	Texas
Al	**Alabama**	N	Nebraska

Industrial States in **bold lettering**

Bankers' Clearing House. Before 1968 there were eleven clearing banks in London with many branches all over the country, but in the process of amalgamation the number of clearing banks has been reduced from eleven to six, i.e. Barclays, National Westminster, Midland, Lloyds, Williams & Glyn's and Coutts. I Fr

Bretton Woods

Name of a town in New Hampshire, U.S.A.

This name is often used to denote the important Financial and Monetary Conference which took place in Bretton Woods, N.H., in July, 1944. The members of the Conference were the United Nations (the U.S.S.R. was included but did not ratify the agreement). The purpose of the Conference was to avoid the international monetary chaos which was expected to occur after the War.

The Conference had been initiated by the British Treasury and the Treasury of the United States. The British "Proposals for an International Clearing Union" were based on the suggestions of the famous British economist J. M. Keynes (hence Keynes Plan) while the Americans elaborated a "Preliminary Draft Outline of a Proposal for an International Stabilization Fund of the United and Associated Nations" which became known as the "White Plan". The main difference between the two plans was that Keynes recommended not only a Stabilization Fund but an international clearing union as a super-central bank which ought to be capitalized at more than double the amount which White regarded as necessary.

According to the Articles of Agreement signed at Bretton Woods - which were mainly a compromise between the Keynes and the White Plan - the International Bank for Reconstruction and Development commonly known as the "World Bank" and the International Monetary Fund (I.M.F.) came into existence. The World Bank, opened in December, 1945, was established as an international credit agency to facilitate long-term loans to member nations. The Monetary Fund was opened in March 1947, in order "to facilitate the expansion and balanced growth of international trade and to contribute thereby to the promotion and maintenance of high levels of employment and real income and to the development of the productive resources of all members as primary objectives of economic policy".

The Fund implements these objectives by providing liquid resources for short-term credits available for member countries in temporary balance of payments difficulties. 126 nations were members of the I.M.F. in June 1975.

The I.M.F. is supported by subscriptions of the member states. The quota which every country has to pay is fixed according to its particular financial and economic circumstances. 25 per cent. of the subscription quota is to be paid in gold, the remaining 75 per cent. in the country's own currency. In this way the I.M.F. obtains liquid reserves in gold and convertible currencies which enable it to sell the currency of any member to any other member in exchange for the latter's own currency. The member states have the right to draw on the Fund when they are in need of gold or foreign exchange to bring a temporary deficit of their balance of payments into equilibrium.

When the Fund opened in 1947 the exchange rates of the member countries were fixed in relation to the U.S. dollar which was the only currency officially defined in weight of gold (originally one ounce of gold = $ 35) and dollar assets held by foreign central banks could be converted into gold at this official rate. The members agreed not to change the fixed exchange rates without previous consultation with the other members of the Fund and the central banks obliged themselves to intervene as soon as the currency of a member state fluctuated in the domestic exchange market beyond a margin of ±1 per cent. from the par value. The monetary system drawn up at Bretton Woods is based on the gold exchange standard which means that gold and foreign exchange are regarded as reserves for the member currencies. Since there has been an insufficient supply of gold the habit has grown of using dollar and sterling as international "reserve" currencies.

The purchase of gold or foreign currencies in exchange for a country's own currency increases, of course, the Fund's deposit of this currency. In order to limit the drawing rights it was therefore determined that the drawing rights should be limited to 125 per cent. of the quotas of the member states. Furthermore, the deficit countries were obliged to repurchase (in gold or foreign exchange) the surplus of their currency above their quota from the Fund within an agreed period of time.

It was hoped that the mechanism of the Bretton Woods monetary system would moderate a disequilibrium in international payments and help to integrate the domestic monetary policies of the member nations. The system certainly contributed to the restoration of international trading after the War. During the second half of the 1950s, however – especially after the Suez crisis – the question gradually arose whether the Fund's resources in gold and convertible currencies were sufficient to meet all needs when member states came into severe payments difficulties. In order to increase international liquidity, therefore, informal arrangements were made between certain European central banks which were to provide additional resources to hold each other's currencies. In March 1961, the Basle Agreement was signed to foster monetary co-operation. Some other arrangements such as the "Agreements to Borrow" signed in January 1962, by ten central banks, sometimes called the "group of ten" (Belgium, Canada, France, West Germany, Italy, Japan, the Netherlands, Sweden, Great Britain and the U.S.A.) were intended to help each other in international payments difficulties.

The problem of international liquidity became acute when in the beginning of the 1960s sterling increasingly showed weaknesses because of the continual British deficit in its international current account *(Balance of Payments**)*. In November 1964, the sterling crisis was at its height. The I.M.F. being short of gold and convertible currencies could put at Britain's disposal only an insufficient loan of $ 1,000 million. The United Kingdom therefore had to borrow $ 1,000 million and some time later $ 3,000 million from foreign central banks under the provisions of the Basle Agreement.

Since that time the discussion concerning world liquidity has not come to an end. Many proposals have been made to improve the liquid resources of the Fund. Among others, the quotas of the member states were increased several times. Finally a new facility intended to meet the need for a supplement to existing reserve assets was created by the special drawing rights proposed by the Group of Ten in August 1967, and unilaterally approved by the I.M.F. in September 1967, at the Rio de Janeiro Conference. The special drawing rights are intended to serve as a new reserve currency as well as a credit line. Participants in the special drawing rights scheme are expected to repay the convertible currency drawn by them in exchange with their special drawing rights within a period of five years. The special drawing rights scheme became effective in 1970. The large scale dollar crisis of the years 1971 and 1973 finally led to a collapse of the monetary system created in Bretton Woods. When on August 15, 1971, the President of the United States suspended the convertibility of the US dollar into gold *(Dollar*)* one of the fundamental conditions of the Bretton Woods monetary system no longer existed. The final blow, however, came in 1973 when a second devaluation of the dollar was announced, *(Dollar*)* which entailed intense speculative activities against the dollar and consequently a substantial transfer of dollars into hard currencies, especially into German marks and Japanese yens. The excessive inflow of US dollars definitely induced the central banks of EEC member states and other trading partners of the United States to abandon the system of fixed exchange rates and let their currencies float against the dollar, which on principle meant that the exchange rates of the floating currencies against the dollar were furthermore to be determined by supply and demand on the international exchange markets. With the system of fixed rates abandoned, the second fundamental condition of Bretton Woods was gone.

While in this way the monetary system of Bretton Woods came to an end in March 1973, the two important international institutions created in Bretton Woods, i.e., the World Bank (International Bank for Reconstruction and Development) and the I.M.F. (International Monetary Fund) have continued to play an essential role in international financial and credit policy as could be seen, for instance, by the activity of the I.M.F. Committee in London in 1976. After detailed negotiations the I.F.M. then agreed that the United Kingdom should be granted another credit of $ 3,900 million partly with the assistance of central banks belonging to the Group of Ten. I Fr

Collective Bargaining

Bargain: to haggle over terms, negotiate; to arrange terms; collective bargaining: negotiations between an employer and union representatives on wages, hours and working conditions.

● Since 1871 the British Government has recognized "collective bargaining" as the normal means of settling labour disputes and has even fostered voluntary conciliation agreements between the two sides of industry under the provisions of the Conciliation Act of 1896 and the Industrial Courts Act of 1919, which have been in force until this day. The procedure of collective bargaining is voluntary and rests upon the principle of mutual consent. In many industries Joint Industrial Councils have been established consisting of representatives of employers' and employees' associations and dealing with wage claims, working conditions and subjects of general interest for the industry concerned. Collective agreements are not civil contracts between particular employers and employees and not enforceable at law. If voluntary negotiations do not succeed in settling the labour disputes, the matter in question may be referred, at the request of both parties, to independent arbitrators or ad hoc Boards of Arbitration, or to the Industrial Court. The Minister of Labour could assist the industry's negotiation machinery but was not allowed to interfere; nor were the parties obliged to notify the Minister of the dispute before "early warning" was enacted. A breakdown of collective bargaining may lead to strikes and lockouts as the last weapons of the two sides of industry to enforce their demands. In case of national emergency a compulsory arbitration for avoiding stoppages of work may be instituted as was the case during the two World Wars (Munitions of War Act of 1915 and Conditions of Employment and National Arbitration Order of 1940) and after the General Strike of 1926 when the Trade Disputes and Trade Unions Act of 1927 declared strikes and lockouts illegal. In 1946 the prohibition of strikes and lockouts was withdrawn again, and a wave of large-scale strikes ensued.

A special feature of the labour-management relations in Britain has been the relatively large number of unofficial strikes – often also called wildcat strikes – which have taken place largely as a result of unofficial and unconstitutional action by small groups of workers. Sometimes strikes were initiated by the shop stewards at a particular place of work without authorization by union officials. Workers refusing to participate in an unofficial strike have been prevented from entering the plant by pickets or even brought to "trial" by their fellow workers. The unofficial strikes have been encouraged by the large number of smaller British trade unions(*Trade (Labor) Unions**). Wildcat strikes have often impeded economic growth which is so vitally important for the country.

In order to outlaw wildcat strikes a compulsory "early warning" legislation was enacted by Parliament under the provisions of the Prices and Incomes Act of 1966. In accordance with the "early warning" legislation claims for higher wages (or prices) were to be notified to the Government in advance, and fines were imposed for default, thus giving the Government legal authority to interfere in labour disputes. After bitter attacks by the Unions and the Labour Party the Industrial Relations Act became law in August 1971, and came into operation on February 28th, 1972. It created a completely new legal framework for the industrial relations system in Britain, mainly providing for:

collective agreements to be legally binding;
the power of the government to order a secret ballot of workers or to impose a cooling-off-period of 60 days in labour disputes which threaten the national economy;
union closed shops to be outlawed; unfair industrial practices (e.g. unofficial strikes) to be adjudicated and fined by the newly established Industrial Relations Court;
trade unions and employers associations to be registered with the Registrar set up under the Act.

But the Industrial Relations Act, so much rejected by the unions, was only in force for just over two years. Following the general election of February 1974, the Labour Party took office again, after having promised to repeal the Act and to abolish the Industrial Relations Court as well as the registry of trade unions and employers' associations. The Labour Government did so by introducing a bill on Labour Day, May 1, 1974. Among other things it provides that collective agreements shall not be legally binding unless they specifically provide for this. Furthermore the new Act gives protection against unfair dismissal or discrimination because of trade union membership. Protection against dismissal and discrimination was strengthened still further by the Employment Protection Bill introduced in March 1975.

In September 1974 the Secretary of State for Employment had established the Advisory, Conciliation and Arbitration Service (ACAS) as an independent institution, which became statutory under the provisions of the Employment Protection Act 1976.

To support the Labour Government's anti-inflation strategy the Trades Union Congress (TUC) gave recommendations to the unions that pay increases should be kept in line with the "guidelines" of the "social contract", this originally being a joint statement of intent made by the TUC-Labour Party Liaison Committee in February 1973. As a voluntary pay restraint promised by the TUC to the Labour Government the social contract should ensure that wages did not increase faster than the cost of living and that a 12 month interval was observed between pay settlements. In 1975, however, rises in the rate of inflation led to an agreement between the Government, the Confederation of British Industry (CBI) and the TUC according to which a limit of £ 6 per week on pay increases and a limit of 10 per cent. on dividend increases was introduced on 1st August 1975. The end of voluntary pay restraint came when the social contract expired on July 31, 1977. The Government tried to renew the contract and indicated a 10 per cent. guideline for pay increases as compatible with inflation control on the one hand and the rising cost of living on the other. But the unions did not agree. As a consequence there was fear of a future wage explosion. Pay claims which far exceeded the guideline of 10 per cent. could partly be compensated for by productivity agreements, and the 12 month rule for wage settlements helped to gain some time.

■ The Norris-La Guardia Anti-Injunction Act of 1932 prohibited for the first time the use of injunctions, such as were previously issued in labour disputes under *Equity**, and also the use of the "yellow dog" contract, by which an employee promised in writing not to join labour organizations. Although this Act was a considerable achievement on the part of the labor unions, the law of collective bargaining was first properly established by the *New Deal** legislation enacted under the Franklin D. Roosevelt Administration in 1933 and the following years. The National Industrial Recovery Act of 1933 (N.I.R.A.) first gave the workers the right "to organize and bargain collectively through representatives of their own choosing". In 1935 the N.I.R.A. was declared unconstitutional by the Supreme Court, but the National Labor Relations (Wagner-Connery) Act of the same year confirmed anew the legal right of collective bargaining. The Wagner Act is still regarded as the "Magna Carta" of labour. It included a list of "unfair labor practices" which employers must not indulge in. Under the terms of the Wagner Act the National Labor Relations Board was established as an *Independent Agency** and was made responsible for the prosecution and adjudication of all unfair labour practices. The N.L.R.B. thus created the foundation for the whole collective bargaining structure. The year 1938 brought the enactment of the Fair Labor Standards Act which established basic minimum wages and overtime payment requirements for employees engaged in *Interstate Commerce**. During World War II union heads gave a no-strike pledge and the National War Labor Board set up in 1942 was empowered to settle labour disputes. But the close of the war also brought the end of the no-strike pledge, and many large-scale strikes ensued during the subsequent years. Between 1939 and 1947 several States passed restrictive union control laws. In 1947 the trend towards the restriction of collective bargaining reached its peak when Congress enacted the Labor Management Relations Act, popularly known as the Taft-Hartley Act. The Act prohibited "unfair labor practices" on the part of the unions, for instance mass picketing, boycotting of goods of a particular employer, etc. It authorized the States to prohibit the "union (or closed) shop" (a firm in which the employer by agreement with the union hires only union members) within their boundaries by passing "right-to-work" laws (19 States, especially southern States, have passed such "right-to work" laws since 1947). Furthermore, the Taft-Hartley Act authorized the President to enforce a "cooling-off" period of 80 days during which strikes had to be deferred if they would endanger public health or safety. The unions have for long been trying to change the provisions of Taft-Hartley through Federal legislation. In fact, the House of Representatives passed an amendment of the Taft-Hartley Act to abolish the anti-closed-shop laws, but the bill was brought down by the Senate. This defeat was largely a result of the New York transportation strike in January, 1966. Lasting for 12 days, it aroused widespread public resentment and made evident the abuses of the concentration of power in the big unions. The so-called "cooling-off" period could not be enforced because – with civil servants involved in it – the strike was in itself illegal. It was different in the case of the large-scale miners' and dockers' strike, called in 1971. It was halted because President Nixon invoked the Taft-Hartley law (*Trade (Labor) Unions**).

Up to now about 30 stoppages of work have been deferred under the provisions of the Taft-Hartley Act because of danger to public health or safety.

During the election campaign of 1976 the American labor unions fully supported the Democratic Party and thus to a high degree contributed to Mr. Carter's election as President. In return the Carter administration presented the Labor Reform Act 1977 to Congress. This reform package, however, does not provide any structural change in management-labor relationship. Its most important provisions are the following: uninhibited access of union representatives to factories whenever they wish to give information on union measures to the workers, improved protection against illegal sacking of workers because of union activities and sanctions on companies which violate the orders of the National Labor Relations Board. Furthermore, the President agreed to accept an increase of the basic minimum wage from $ 2.30 to $ 2.65 per hour. In accordance with the Fair Labor Standards Act minimum wages have to be set by federal law.

I Fr

Common Market

● When on October 28th, 1971, after a long debate, the House of Commons agreed by 354 to 244 votes to Britain's entry into the Common Market, a decision of historic importance had been made. Moreover the vote put an end to the controversies which had lasted nearly a decade both in Britain and in the member states of the European Economic Community (E.E.C.). On January 1st, 1973, Britain's membership of the E.E.C. became effective. At the same time, Denmark and the Republic of Ireland joined the Community.

Britain had participated from the very beginning in the negotiations which led to the Treaty of Rome in 1957. But she was not prepared to join the Community at that time because she still felt traditionally committed to the Commonwealth for political, economic and traditional reasons. Things changed, however, as time went on. Increasingly the Community succeeded in achieving a rapid growth in productivity. Its average real earnings grew by 75 per cent. between 1958 and 1969 while British average real earnings grew only by about 40 per cent. during the same time. Still more surprising was the fact that from the late fifties on British external trade with the Commonwealth tended to decline whereas trade with Western Europe continued to increase. In 1962 British exports to the E.E.C. exceeded those to the sterling area for the first time. In 1968 they rose by 24 per cent. and increased by another 18 per cent. in the following year. Thus the economic development, undoubtedly, seemed to indicate a turn to Europe as did the political and military situation. Neither the formation of a North Atlantic Free Trade Area (N.A.F.T.A.), which had sometimes been under discussion, nor the Commonwealth were considered to be genuine alternatives. The Government pointed out in its White Paper *The United Kingdom and the European Communities:* "We have grown accustomed to the political and military predominance in the world of two super powers whose strength is based on their great size and economic resources . . . Individually no European country can ensure that its voice is heeded; collectively, as the Six have shown already in the Kennedy Round, the voice of the Communities cannot be ignored".

Upon application of the then Conservative Government Britain and the Six had entered into negotiations about British membership as early as 1961. The negotiations, however, broke down in consequence of the French veto *(Preferences*)*. In 1967 Mr. Wilson's Labour Cabinet renewed the application under the provisions of the Rome Treaty. Negotiations reopened in Luxembourg on June 30th, 1970 and agreements were reached between the Foreign Ministers of the Six and Mr. Rippon, Chancellor of the Duchy of Lancaster (in charge of Common Market Affairs) on June 23rd, 1971.

Consensus was reached on the following issues:

The United Kingdom is represented in the Community's organs (the European Commission, the Council of Ministers, the European Parliament, the European Court of Justice) in the same way as France, Germany and Italy. English, together with French, German, Italian und Dutch, is an official language within the Community. The common external tariff (C.E.T.) is accepted by Britain as is the common agricultural policy (C.A.P.) subject to some transitional arrangements. All internal tariff barriers between Britain and the Six will be eliminated within a period of five years. During this period Britain will gradually phase out her system of agricultural support *(Agricultural Relief*)* and adapt to the Community's system of agricultural policy. (The E.E.C. levies import duties on agricultural produce in order to raise the price of imported goods to the level of the so-called threshold price at which those goods are sold on the domestic market *(Protectionism*.)*

With regard to the percentage of Britain's contribution to the Community budget it was agreed that the British contribution will finally correspond to Britain's share in the total gross national product of the E.E.C. countries. But for the first year her contribution will amount only to 8.64 per cent. of the budget. During the subsequent four years it will increase annually up to 18.92 per cent.

At the outset of the negotiations Mr. Rippon had made it clear that Britain only accepted C.A.P. provided that satisfactory arrangements could be made for the imports to Britain of dairy products from New Zealand and sugar from the Commonwealth countries. Up to the end of 1974 Britain was obliged to purchase agreed quantities of sugar from the Commonwealth countries under the Commonwealth Sugar Agreement (C.S.A.). The negotiators came to the conclusion that the independent Commonwealth countries and the British dependent territories should be invited to become associate members of the Community. The association would entitle these countries to export domestic produce free of duty to the enlarged European Community. *(see Preferences*.)* (In this connection it may be of interest that in February 1975 a five-year agreement, known as the Lomé Convention was reached between the E.C. countries and 46 developing nations, among them most of the former Commonwealth countries. It is mainly concerned with trade, aid, and economic co-operation between the industrialised world and the developing countries. *Commonwealth*.)*

Finally the agreements provided for a harmonization of the taxation system within the Community. On the whole, the British system is similar to that prevailing in the Common Market. Nevertheless there are differences to be adjusted. A taxation reform therefore came into operation in April 1973 in order to bring the British fiscal system into line with that of the E.E.C. countries. The reform is mainly concerned with taxes on personal and corporate incomes. The British system traditionally consists of an income tax, which is mostly deducted at source under the P.A.Y.E. system (pay-as-you-earn) and a surtax on incomes above a certain level. In April 1973 this two-tier system was replaced by a single graduated income tax. A reform of corporation tax is also under discussion. Above all, it aims at making the taxation of companies conform with the respective practices in the Common Market. British estate or death duty, though not different from the continental system on principle, is worth mentioning because it is to be paid at full rate even from descendants in the first degree. Excise duties on tobacco, alcoholic beverages, etc., are customary in E.E.C. countries too. Purchase tax and selective employment tax (S.E.T.) however, which have been special features of the British taxation system for years, were abolished on April 1st, 1973, when V.A.T. (Value Added Tax) came into operation. V.A.T. is modelled after the fiscal system of the Community. Its introduction in Britain was already announced by Mr. Rippon at the Luxembourg negotiations.

During the discussions which preceded the Luxembourg negotiations, the role of sterling as an international reserve currency *(Sterling*)* had been an issue of major concern for the then member countries of the E.E.C. The issue was settled when Mr. Rippon declared: "We (Her Majesty's Government) are prepared to envisage an orderly and gradual run-down of official sterling balances after our accession".

After the general election of February 1974, however, the Labour Party returned to power. Labour had pledged in its manifesto to renegotiate the terms of British membership of the Community and to submit the question of membership to the British people by means of a referendum.

Renegotiations with the Council of Ministers began in April 1974; they led to results which satisfied Britain, especially with regard to British payments to the Community budget and to a more flexible operation of the common agricultural policy (CAP).

The referendum was held on the 5th of June 1975. The question: "Do you think that the United Kingdom should stay in the European Community?" was answered in the affirmative by more than 65 per cent. of those voting. In a following statement the then Prime Minister, Mr. Wilson, said: "The British people in clear and unmistakable terms made their historic decision that Britain shall remain a member of the European Community . . . Their verdict has been given by a vote and by a majority bigger than that achieved by any government in any general election in the history of our democracy." I Fr

▬ Boundaries of Federal Reserve Districts — Boundaries of Federal Reserve Branch Territories

⬤ Board of Governors of the Federal Reserve System

● Federal Reserve Bank Cities • Federal Reserve Branch Cities

Conservation of Land

A careful preservation and protection of something; especially: planned management of a national resource to prevent exploitation, destruction or neglect.

■ When the first settlers began to penetrate westward into the wilderness, land and natural resources seemed to be inexhaustible. Nearly 1,000 million acres were covered by virgin forest. In clearing the land the farmers often burnt down the forests. Other large areas were deforested by careless tree-felling since a considerable amount of logs was needed for building houses and barns. Furthermore, timber provided fuel.

As farmland was limitless, it seemed to be of minor importance that widerspread erosion caused by wind and water (rain, snow, uncontrolled flood) resulted from large-scale deforestation. Once the land was exhausted by erosion it was easy to take up new land. The greedy exploitation of the land and its resources was accelerated by the *Industrial Revolution**, the beginning of which coincided with the expansion westward across the Appalachian highlands where new sources of raw materials (coal and iron) were discovered. Coal was mined by extracting only the most easily accessible deposits, millions of tons being left untouched.

Until 1781 the conflicting claims of the various States to the western regions prevented a general policy of land use. The problem of land disposal, however, was solved by the Articles of Confederation in 1781 when the 13 States agreed to transfer their land claims (granted to them by royal charter in colonial times) to Congress "to be parcelled out by Congress into free, convenient, and independent governments in such manner and at such times as the wisdom of the assembly shall hereafter direct". Consequently, as the frontier pushed westward, the Federal Government gained the right to dispose of vast areas of "public land" or "public domain" – both terms applying to the land owned by the Federal Government. During the first half of the 19th century, a great amount of public land was granted to railroad corporations in order to encourage railroad development *(Interstate Commerce*)*, while further areas were given to the States for the founding of colleges (Morrill Act of 1862; *Land- Grant College*)*, and a considerable portion was granted to settlers under the Homestead Act of 1862. The Homestead Act, designed to attract settlers and immigrants, offered any citizen 160 acres of public domain after 5 years of continuous residence and payment of a small registration fee. As an alternative, land could also be required after 6 months' residence at $ 1.25 per acre. There is, however, no doubt that the generous grants of public land tended to promote speculation and that a large portion of the public domain intended to help the small farmer under the Homestead Act went ultimately to the big corporations. For the land laws were easy to evade and large areas of public land fell into private hands for the smallest fees without fulfilment of the conditions. The Timber and Stone Act of 1887, for instance, allowed the purchase of 160 acres of land rich in timber and minerals at no less than $ 2.50 per acre, enabling corporations interested in mining or lumbering to buy through their agents land which was worth many times the small amount paid for it.

From the very beginning of colonization, far-sighted persons recommended national measures to prevent further land waste. The reckless deforestation, in particular, forced the Americans into the necessity of a national conservation programme. In 1908 the conservation movement received its impetus from the Conservation Commission held under the Theodore Roosevelt Administration. As a result 140 million acres of public domain were set aside as national forest land or reserved for the National Parks and the Indian Reservations. At the same time 80 million acres of mineral land and 1,500,000 acres of water-power sites were withdrawn from public sale. A licensing system was established for the use of water-power on public land and subsequent legislation separated the title to the surface of land from the title of underlying minerals which could be disposed of by lease rather than by sale. Thus an end was put to the depletion of good coal reserves and waste of iron (located mainly in the Lake Superior region), petroleum (Texas, Louisiana, Pennsylvania), and natural gas. A number of States followed the federal example and withdrew State land from public sale. Today National and State Parks serve not only as vast stores of timber but also as wonderful recreation centres. Among the most famous are the Yellowstone National Park (NW. Wyoming, E. Idaho, and S. Montana), including plateau regions notable for numerous geysers and hot springs; the Grand Canyon National Park (Arizona); the Mount Rainier National Park (Washington); the Yosemite National Park (California); the Zion National Park (Utah); the Bryce Canyon National Park (Utah); and the Shenandoah National Park (Virginia).

A great incentive to a conservation policy was also provided by the *New Deal** legislation. In 1933 the Civilian Conservation Corps Reforestation Relief Act, first passed as an unemployment relief programme, established the Civilian Conservation Corps (C.C.C.) intended to provide for reforestation, flood control, and to prevent further soil erosion. In the same year the Tennessee Valley Authority (T.V.A.) was set up to carry out a large programme of hydroelectric power development which also embraced the prevention of further soil erosion by flood control, and reforestation in the Tennessee Valley.

The functions of conservation of natural resources on public lands have been performed under the supervision of the Department of the Interior through certain *Independent Agencies**, such as the Bureau of Land Management, the Office of Mineral and Solid Fuels, the Office of Oil and Gas, and the Bureau of Mines.

● In 1947 the National Parks Commission proposed the conservation of extensive areas of land for the purpose of preserving the characteristic landscape, wild life, and places of architectural interest, and providing facilities for open-air recreation. This report resulted in the National Parks and Access to the Countryside Act of 1949 which provided for the establishment of ten national parks in England and Wales: the Peak District, the Lake District, the Yorkshire Dales and the North York Moors, Northumberland, Snowdonia (North Wales), the Pembrokeshire coast, the Brecon Beacons (South Wales), Dartmoor in Devon and Exmoor in Devon and Somerset. In addition to the national parks seven national forest parks were established in Great Britain (almost half a million acres) which have been opened to the public by the Forestry Commission. Under the Countryside Acts of 1967 (Scotland) and 1968 (England and Wales) the National Parks Commission was replaced by the Countryside Commission (England and Wales). I Fr

Co-operative Society

An enterprise or organization owned by and operated for the benefit of those using its services. 1821.

Co-operative associations constitute a type of business enterprise which differs markedly from the individual enterprise, the partnership, and the corporation. The principal distinguishing feature of the co-operative association is that it is organized not for private profit but for mutual benefit.

There are producers' co-operatives, consumers' co-operatives, marketing co-operatives, credit co-operatives and agricultural co-operatives. Friendly societies (in which the members receive benefits in return for regular contribution) are not usually regarded as forming part of the co-operative movement. 3

Consumers' co-operatives include both retail and wholesale societies. They distribute profits among their members according to purchases made, not according to stock owned. Nor is voting based on the number of shares, as it is in the ordinary business corporation. Each member in a truly co-operative society is entitled to only one vote.

Producers' co-operatives represent the effort of workers to carry on a productive enterprise through group action. They have been less successful and permanent than consumers' co-operatives.

The co-operative movement has also been distinguished by the rise of marketing associations, which have been especially helpful in the distribution of agricultural products. Farmers also co- operate in the purchase and use of machinery and commodities used on the farm.

Credit co-operatives include such organizations as mutual savings banks, credit unions, building and loan associations and mutual life-insurance companies.

● The co-operative movement, in the modern sense, took shape in Great Britain in the 1820s, mainly under the influence of Robert Owen. Its establishment in Britain is usually dated from the foundation of the Rochdale Pioneers' Equitable Society (1844), though there had been earlier ventures and the Pioneers represented only one type of society – the consumers'. From these beginnings co- operation spread also to British colonial territories.

At the end of 1963 there were 871 retail co-operative societies in Britain registered under the Industrial and Provident Societies Act (1852). Amalgamation is slowly diminishing the number of societies, the total having fallen by 84 in three years. More than a quarter of the total membership of the co-operatives - 12,961,000 – was provided by the ten largest societies, each of which has a membership of more than 150,000. One, the London Co-operative Society with just under 1,3 million members and a turnover of over £ 50 million a year, is the largest retail co-operative society in the world. Total sales of the retail co-operative societies in Britain reached £ 1,150 million in 1972. They have about 300,000 employees.

Retail co-operative societies are free to purchase where they wish and to produce their own goods; but in order to secure the advantages of large-scale production and distribution they have collectively established wholesale and production societies. This stage was already reached in 1863 with the foundation of the North of England Co-operative Wholesale Society. In 1872 it dropped the words "North of England" and became generally known as the "C.W.S.". It opened its first factories in 1873 for the manufacture of boots and biscuits and soon expanded into a wide range of productive operations. In 1868 Scottish co-operators had founded their own Scottish C.W.S. Later on the C.W.S.s also developed their own banking departments. The English C.W.S. now has about 54,000 employees and a capital of £ 500 million. It was inevitable that C.W.S. would start to influence the shape of the movement's retail structure. In response to appeals for mergers and as result of financial pressure the 1,000 autonomous retail societies of the early 50s have been reduced by now to a quarter of that number, and more amalgamations are on the way. Mr. Alfred Wilson, the chief executive of the C.W.S., sees big regional societies as the only means to co-ordinate effort and offer keen prices, thus also counterbalancing the competition of supermarkets and chain stores.

After 1900 attempts were made to build up agricultural co-operation in Great Britain. There was a fairly rapid growth of societies both for marketing and for the purchase of farm supplies, the most important of them being the Agricultural Organization Society (A.O.S.). A similar body was formed for Scotland in 1905 and later for Wales after the collapse of the British A.O.S. This collapse was largely due to quarrels with the Irish co-operators. On the whole one can say that agricultural co-operation failed to strike firm roots in England, its most active section being the societies for a collective buying of farm supplies.

■ The earliest U.S. consumer co-operative effort recorded was in 1829, when Philadelphia working men paid 20 cents a month to buy at cost, and when in New York city a former association secretary from England helped to establish a store. The first Rochdale-type co-operative was realized in 1862 in Philadelphia. Deviation from Rochdale techniques, mismanagement and dissention led to failures which alternated with periods of expansion. On the whole one can say that consumers' co-operatives in the United States have lagged behind those in Great Britain and other countries of Europe. A number of reasons have been suggested for this disappointing development. It has been pointed out that Americans are too highly individualistic in nature to associate themselves readily in co-operative enterprises. The relatively high wages prevailing in the United States have also tended to remove from the American wage earner the necessity of resorting to co-operative buying ventures in order to obtain small savings. There has been, however, an awakened interest in consumers' co-operatives in the United States during the last three or four decades. Among the commodities and services which it is now possible to purchase in the United States through consumers' co-operatives are gasoline, groceries, fertilizers, insurance, oil, tools, farm machinery, and burial services.

Wholesale co-operatives have also been established in the United States. Among those which have been most successful are associations composed of independent retail sellers of drugs and groceries.

Marketing co-operatives have developed in the States on a large scale in response to a demand for a more efficient distribution of agricultural products. Lately one-fourth of all farm production, worth more than $ 7,000 million, was marketed by co-operatives which also purchased farm requisites to the value of $ 2,000 million. Farms groups provided their own petroleum products, building materials, paints and sprays and processed cotton and milk. Other operations were freezing, canning, dehydrating and packaging.

One of the most noteworthy examples of co-operative marketing associations is the California Fruit Growers Exchange. It is composed of a number of smaller exchanges and does a tremendous volume of business in the distribution of California fruit throughout the United States, Canada and Europe. The Florida Citrus Exchange is working successfully on similar lines. There are also marketing associations for the distribution of apples, cotton, wheat, potatoes, berries, milk, etc. Middle West dairy farmers have been very efficient co-operators.

In 1929 the U.S. Government recognized the importance of co-operative marketing associations when it attempted through the Agricultural Marketing Act to aid these associations in the distribution of farm products.

Agricultural mutual savings banks have a long tradition in the United States, the first having been founded in the beginning of the 19th century. The co-operative credit associations often have recourse to government credits. Two thousand of 10,000 farm associations borrowed £ 500 million each year from governmentfinanced banks for co-operatives. Nearly 1,000 farm power co-operatives financed by the Rural Electrification Administration with loans totalling £ 3,000 million electrified U.S. farms. Urban co-operatives, except housing, received no public aid. H F

Corporate Enterprise

Enterprise formed into an association and endowed by law with the rights and liabilities of an individual.

Corporate enterprise is carried on by a group of individuals in accordance with the provisions of a charter issued by the state. A Company (G.B.) or Corporation (U.S.) is an entity separate from and in addition to those individuals who associate themselves for its formation. It assumes the legal form of an individual and, as such, is entitled to carry on business activities just as an individual. It may enter into business agreements, buy or sell, make contracts, incur debts, bring lawsuits against individuals or companies, or be sued by others.

Early corporate bodies were incorporated by royal charter, but industrial expansion in the 19th century needed a simpler method of incorporating companies. In 1862 the first of a series of "Companies Acts" was passed elaborating the provisions for incorporation and for regulating a company when incorporated. Following this 1862 act there were until the mid-20th century three major acts, consolidating amendments previously made: viz. the Companies (Consolidation) Act of 1908; the Companies Act of 1929; and the Companies Act of 1948. By the middle of the 20th century the number of companies registered had greatly increased, and a business of any dimension was almost invariably carried on by a company limited by shares.

The legal constitution of a company, as established by the acts named above, determines that any seven or more persons – or for a private company (see below) two or more persons – associated for any lawful purpose may, subject to certain conditions, form an incorporated company, though corporate status does not arise until the necessary formalities of registration with the registrar of companies have been completed and he has issued a certificate of incorporation. The constitution consists of a memorandum – containing name, lieu of office, object, limited liability, amount of capital divided into shares – and the articles of association regulating the internal management.

The capital stock comprises two classes of shares:

(1) Preference shares with the right to a fixed cumulative dividend and priority in a winding-up for repayment of capital and divident arrears;

(2) Ordinary shares with the right to the balance of profits and assets.

Shares are personal property, freely transferable unless restricted by the articles regulating internal management.

Direction and management are generally vested in a board of directors who need not be shareholders unless the articles require, as they generally do, a share qualification. Directors are appointed in the generally meeting.

The general meeting enables the members of a company to express their corporate will. But the shareholders, although nominal owners of their company, have no effective control over its policy. Their capability of intervention is rather limited. It is the absence of controlling owners which makes the corporation such an odd development in Western economic history. Whereas early capitalism *(see Industrial Revolution*)* led to a division between labour and the means of production, late capitalism is characterized by the division between management and capital ownership.

Nevertheless, the corporations behave better and more in the public interest than economists had ever expected. Several explanations have been offered: the development of a managerial class, concerned with prestige as much as profits; the growth of the trade unions' and consumers' countervailing power; finally the emergence of what we might qualify as a "corporate conscience".

The Private Company is a combination of limited liability and personal relationship. The normal limit of membership is 50, the transfer of its shares being restricted. The major part of corporate enterprises belong to the group of private companies.

Britain's largest companies are the imperial Chemical Industries Ltd., founded by the late Lord Melchett (the former Sir Henry Mond) and Sir Harry (later Lord) McGowan, which employs more than 100,000 persons in the United Kingdom; the Royal Dutch/Shell group, an enterprise centred in London and The Hague; and the Unilever group, equally Anglo-Dutch, of London and Rotterdam.

The top 15 companies in the UK and their turnover figures for the last quarter of 1972

B.P. (Transport and Trading)	£ 3,153,000,000
Shell	2,923,000,000
British American Tobacco	1,847,000,000
ICI	1,524,000,000
Unilever	1,357,000,000
Imperial Tobacco	1,276,000,000
Shellmex and B.P.	1,230,000,000
British Leyland	1,177,000,000
General Electric	924,000,000
Courtauld	681,000,000
Esso (UK)	677,000,000
Ford (UK)	588,000,000
Associated British Foods	585,000,000
Dunlop	585,000,000
Shipping Industrial Holdings	578,000,000

The biggest Life Insurance Company is the "Prudential" (Fortis qui prudens), generally referred to as "the Pru". But most insurance companies (e.g. the "Royal Group" and the "Commercial Union Group") handle both Life and non-Life. *"Lloyd's"** which has a constitution of its own is only interested in non-Life insurance.

The public corporations constitute a special group of corporate enterprise. In Britain, they are statutory bodies set up by the government to facilitate the management of public enterprise. They play an important part in the management of nationalized industries such as the National Coal Board, the British Steel Corporation and British Airways (see *Nationalization**).

Among the public corporations the National Coal Board with about 530,000 employees is the most important.

■ What has been said about the history of corporate bodies in Britain applies equally to the American colonial period. Associations called in Great Britain companies became known in the American colonies as corporations. Several of the American colonies were chartered by the king as corporations and these charters were the oldest corporations whose activities related to the American part of the British empire. In 1789 there were only 21 business corporations in the U.S.A.

The effect of the federal and state constitutions adopted after the Revolution was to vest power of corporation in congress and state legislatures, but except in the field of banking, Congress has made limited use of its incorporating power, so that most corporations owe their existence to the statutory law of some state. The attainment of U.S. independence was quickly followed by a great increase in the incorporation of banks, insurance companies, toll bridges, etc. At the beginning of the 19th century most of the north-eastern states added manufacturing to the types of enterprise for which corporate charters were readily granted. In consequence of the many failures among these early manufacturing ventures the usual corporate privilege of limited liability was sometimes denied to the shareholders Until about the middle of the century the laws of most states required persons who desired incorporation to petition the legislature for the enactment of a statute incorporating their enterprise – a system which obviously lent itself to favouritism. Beginning with the Louisiana Constitution of 1845, the power of the legislature to create corporations was either abolished or narrowly restricted. By the end of the 19th century general corporation laws had replaced incorporation by special act in all states. Now the states sought to increase the revenue which they derived from corporate franchise taxes by making their corporation laws attractive to promoters even of business enterprises which carried on their activities in other parts of the Union. The most important bidders for the business of granting corporation charters to out-of-state enterprises were New Jersey and Delaware. Many other states modernized their corporation laws during the second quarter of the 20th century. As a result, the tendency to incorporate under Delaware law rather than under the law of the state in which the organizers of the corporation reside or do their business is now less pronounced than it was before.

The Delaware Act, typical of most similar statutes, specifies that the certificate of incorporation – commonly refferred to as the corporation's charter – should state the corporate name, amount of capital (not less than $ 1,000), the names and residences of the incorporators, etc. Such statutes usually authorize a group of three or more persons – exceptionally also only one or two persons – to form such a corporation. If there are to be several classes of shares, with different dividend or other rights, these rights must be stated in the certificate of incorporation. The same applies to all other special or additional provisions (relating to the powers of the directors or shareholders, to priority subscription of new shares and the like).

There are corporations of many types, each type or class being governed by laws which normally apply only to that class. The more important kinds of corporation are the Aggregate Corporation, the Civil Corporation, the Close Corporation, the Limited-Dividend Corporation, the Private Corporation, the Public Corporation, the Quasi-Public Corporation and the Sole Corporation.

The Aggregate Corporation consists of more than one person.

The Sole Corporation is composed of only one member.

The stock of a Close Corporation is held by relatively few persons and usually is neither bought nor sold in the open market.

The Civil Corporation is created exclusively for business purposes.

A Limited-Dividend Corporation aims at earning just enough to meet the maximum dividend requirements and to maintain reserves. It aims rather to reduce its prices than to accumulate a large surplus.

The Private Corporation is created to conduct enterprises for private profit. The term includes quasi-public and public-service corporations.

Public Corporations are chartered by the government to facilitate the administration of public affairs. (The Public Service Corporation is a private business organization which provides a service of particular importance to the public's welfare, such as production of gas or electric power, telephone system, distribution of water.)

The Quasi-Public Corporation must under regulatory legislation serve all who apply for its goods or services. It frequently operates under a franchise, i.e. a monopoly or partial monopoly.

Another form of partnership, the members of which are issued shares of transferable stock up to the amount of their investment, is the Joint-Stock Company. Although this has a legal personality like a corporation, there are important differences. Unlike a corporation, a joint-stock company can sue and be sued only through some designated officer. Moreover, unlike stockholders of a corporation, who enjoy limited liability, members of a joint-stock company are individually an collectively liable for the debts of the organization.

The largest U.S. corporations are:

1. General Motors, Detroit (which is at the same time the world's largest company)
2. Standard Oil, New York
3. Ford Motor Company, Dearborn (Michigan)
4. General Electric, New York
5.hU.S. Steel Corporation, New York
6. Socony Mobile Oil, New York
7. Chrysler, Detroit
8. Texaco, New York

(The place of Royal Dutch and Unilever would be between Standard Oil (2) and Ford (3), and General Electric (4) and U.S. Steel (5) respectively.)

There are big differences between British and American corporations. In Britain the amalgamation is still continuing. The British managerial revolution is less developed than in America. The nationalized area of British industry is much larger, and all industry has been influenced by the threat of nationalization. British companies are apt to be less ruthless than American corporations and more exposed to administrative hypertrophy. The biggest companies in Britain – notably Shell/Royal Dutch and Unilever – are bigger in proportion to the country than their American counterparts and belong more to an international than to a national economy. After Britain's inclusion into the Common Market, they are likely to become still more supranational.

H F

Discount Houses

- Discount: A deduction made for payment before it is due, or for prompt payment, of a bill or account; any abatement from the nominal value or price, 1690; the interest charged for discounting a bill of exchange or promissory note.

Discount Houses are financial institutions which specialize in the discounting of bills, i.e. buying them at a discount before maturity. Nowadays the Treasury Bill has become far more important than the bill of exchange, but it was the latter that played the significant part in the development of the London Discount Market; and although the use of the bill of exchange as an instrument of financing trade has declined, the Discount Houses still hold a considerable amount of commercial bills.

Today there are twelve Discount Houses. These form the London Discount Market Association and, together with a few smaller firms, actually constitute the London Discount Market, the most important element of the London short-term money market. In its functioning the London Discount Market is unique. Along with the Accepting Houses *(Merchant Bankers*)*, the Discount Houses made London a ready market for bills thereby contributing greatly to the importance of London as a world financial centre.

The Discount Houses are joint-stock companies which finance their operations partly by their own capital and by deposits placed with them, but also to a very large extent by borrowing from the commercial banks. They borrow the money for a very short time, usually "at call" and often even as "overnight money". They re-lend it – in discounting bills – and their profit accrues from difference in the rate of interest at which they borrow and that at which they lend the money.

The work of the Discount Houses makes it possible for the commercial banks to reduce to a minimum the amount of cash required for covering their customers' demands. The commercial banks need not leave their surplus funds unemployed because they always have the opportunity to lend them out at such short notice that no risk is involved. They can "call" their money from the Discount Houses at any time and can adjust their liquidity daily. Usually about half of the Discount Houses' borrowings come from the London clearing banks, and about one-third from other commercial banks in the United Kingdom. If the commercial banks require more cash they withdraw part of the loans made to the Discount Market. If too much of the money loaned to them has been called, the Discount Houses may find themselves obliged to got to the Bank of England, which acts as "lender of last resort", and the market is then said to be "in the Bank". *(Bank of England*.)*

When the commercial banks wish to acquire bills for their bill portfolios they usually make use of the Discount Houses' services. It is more convenient and less expansive for the banks to buy bills through the Discount Houses, which possess expert knowledge and information as to the trustworthiness of a bill, rather than to build up an intelligence department of their own.

In recent decades the importance of the bill of exchange has declined, partly because business firms have been working with more capital of their own, partly because other means of settlement (e.g. overdrafts on current accounts) have become more popular, partly also because of fears of crises, devaluation, etc. At the same time the amount of Treasury Bills has risen, and today the Discount Houses invest by far the largest part of their funds in Treasury Bills. These are issued every week by the Government for short-term finance (usually two or three month). Part of the supply of Treasury Bills goes direct to public departments with funds to invest and also to certain foreign monetary authorities. These issues are called "tap" issues. The rate of discount at which they are offered is not known, and it is of no consequence to the Discount Market. The remaining Treasury Bills are the weekly "tender" for which the market must bid. Each Discount House bids for a certain proportion of the total tender, and usually the Discount Houses form a syndicate and agree beforehand on the rate at which they wish to buy the Treasury Bills. They know how much of the tender each of them can take, and they make their bid dependent on this. "Outside" bidders – foreign banks, etc. – will only get a share out of the tender if their bid is higher than that of the Discount Houses. The clearing banks do not bid for Treasury Bills, except on behalf of their customers. They will, however, acquire Treasury Bills from the Discount Houses after a few weeks, when they are nearer to maturity, and very few of the bills will remain in the Discount Houses' portfolios until their date of maturity. Thanks to the Discount Houses the Government can more or less rely on its Treasury Bills being taken up every week.

In the early nineteen-thirties the volume of bills of exchange in the market shrank, and at the same time there was a decline in earnings from Treasury Bills. This meant that very little profit accrued to the Discount Houses from their bill operations. By way of compensation the Discount Houses took to investing also in short-term Government securities (usually not longer than five years) or such securities as had originally been long-term but had become short as they approached maturity. This was of great importance both for the Discount Houses, which found a new possibility of investing their funds, and for the Government, whose funded debt had grown to such an extent that the market facilities provided by the Stock Exchange now proved inadequate. Since the greater fluctuations in the prices of these securities called for stronger capital resources on the part of the Discount Houses, a number of mergers took place during the nineteen-thirties and the nineteen-forties, eventually reducing the number of Discount Houses to twelve. H St

Dollar

In 16th century daler, daller = High German taler, thaler, in full Joachimstaler, lit. "(gulden) of Joachimsthal" where they were coined in 1519. English name for the German thaler; English name for the peso or Spanish piece of eight (i.e. eight reales), largely used in the British North American Colonies at the time of their revolt; the standard unit of the gold and silver coinage of the United States, containing 100 cents; also a coin of the same value in some British colonies. 1553.

Although the term "dollar" may refer to currencies outside the U.S.A., e.g. the Canadian dollar, the Hong Kong dollar, the Liberian dollar, the Australian dollar and the New Zealand dollar, it is chiefly understood to mean the U.S. dollar, the monetary unit in the United States. The abbreviation $ stands for U(nited) S(tates).

The U.S. dollar widely serves as a means of settlement in international trade. Furthermore, until recently, it played a dominant role as a key reserve currency of the Western World and most of the developing countries. The key position of the U.S. dollar was rooted in the regulations of the *Bretton Woods** Agreement of 1944. Article IV, Section 1 of this agreement stipulated that "The par value of the currency of each member shall be expressed in terms of gold as a common denominator or in terms of the United States dollar of weight and fineness in effect on July 1st, 1944". Thus, by this agreement the exchange rates of all the member states of the International Monetary Fund (I.M.F.) were fixed in relation to the U.S. dollar at a parity of $ 35 per fine ounce of gold.

However, the predominance of the dollar in the international monetary system began to dwindle with the increasing deficit in the American balance of payments during the 1950s and 1960s, and it changed fundamentally when on August 15th, 1971, President Nixon directed the Secretary of the Treasury "to suspend temporarily the convertibility of the dollar into gold or other reserve assets".

After President Nixon's announcement, the question arose whether or not the U.S. dollar could still be considered a key currency. On December 17th-18th, 1971, the Ministerial Meeting of the Group of Ten (i.e. the central banks of Belgium, Canada, France, Germany, Italy, Japan, the Netherlands, Sweden, Great Britain and the U.S.A.) at the Smithsonian Institution in Washington made it clear that the U.S. dollar, though de jure still a key currency had de facto ceased to be the world's dominant currency. For, in accordance with the so-called Smithsonian agreements of December 1971, which provided for a realignment of exchange rates, the United States agreed "to propose to Congress a suitable means for devaluing the dollar in terms of gold to 38 dollars per ounce (instead of 35) as soon as the related set of short-term measures is available for congressional scrutiny". This devaluation of the U.S. dollar by about 8 per cent. became law when President Nixon signed the Par Modification Act on March 31st, 1972. It is worth noting that this was the first devaluation of the dollar since President Franklin D. Roosevelt's currency reform of 1934.

The history of the U.S. dollar shows many changes and ups and downs, thus reflecting the history of American banking and the political and economic history of the United States.

As the original 13 States had been British colonies one might have expected the pound sterling to become the monetary unit in the United States. However, since the Spanish colonies were heavily indebted to the original 13 States and much Spanish money was in the country, the Continental Congress of 1774 authorized dollars to be printed rather than sterling when financing the Revolutionary War.

The Coinage Act of 1792 made the dollar a bimetallic currency. Full-bodied gold and silver coins were minted and were made *Legal Tender**. Everybody was allowed to buy, own, or sell both metals or to have them minted into coins. However, the Act overrated the value of silver on comparison to the value of gold. The result was that Gresham's law ("Bad money drives out good" operated: gold disappeared from circulation, and in practice the United States was on a silver standard.

The so-called Gold Bill of 1834 and its amendment of 1837 was designed to abolish the inadequate ratio between gold and silver. The gold content of the dollar was finally fixed at 23.22 grains whereas the silver content of the silver dollar remained unchanged. The degree of fineness for both gold and silver coins was reduced from 11/12 to 9/10. These changes, however, actually reversed the situation. It was now gold that was overrated, and silver tended to flow out of the country, leaving the United States on a de facto gold standard although the law still provided for a bimetallic standard. Owing to the lack of fractional coins, the Silver Subsidiary Coinage Act was passed in 1853. The silver dollar remained a full-bodied coin, but smaller silver coins were made light-weight and in 1857 foreign coins which had still been in circulation, ceased to be legal tender.

Apart from coins, paper money was in circulation. After 1836 it was restricted to bank-notes issued by the state-chartered banks of which there was at least one in each state by 1800. In general, the bank-notes issued in the eastern states were honoured whereas those of the West tended to be unreliable. The terms "wildcat" money and "wildcat" banking first came into use at that time.

The legislation of the individual states, which aimed at making paper money safe, had little effect, and although the Americans had been used to paper money for quite a long time, the first issue of irredeemable legal-tender bank-notes authorized by Congress came as a shock. These United States notes – commonly called "greenbacks" – were issued early in the Civil War in order to pay for the military and other needs of the government.

By the National Bank Act of 1863 – at first called National Currency Act – a system of National Banks was established, and when a federal tax of 10 per cent. was levied on state bank notes in 1866, the National Banks became the only banks of issue at that time. The effect on the currency was a very wholesome one. In the late sixties, the state bank issues of varying descriptions, values, and designs were being replaced by national bank notes whose security was guaranteed by the United States government. As every National Bank was obliged to accept at par "any and all" notes issued by any other National Bank, national bank notes were never traded at a discount, no matter how far away from their place of origin. Gold and silver having been hoarded during the Civil War, the currency consisted mainly of greenbacks, national bank notes, and some fractional paper money. Although in California, where gold was mined, people refused to accept United States notes as legal tender, they were the standard money for all other states from 1862 to 1879. The issue of gold certificates was authorized by the Act of March 3, 1863. On the other hand, the discovery of silver mines in Nevada caused a strong drive towards the re-introduction of the free coinage of silver. Though this was not realized, several Acts provided for heavy silver purchases on the part of the Treasury, and silver certificates were issued, which were backed by silver dollars.

In 1879 United States notes were made redeemable again, and theoretically the bimetallic standard was re-established. In practice, however, only silver certificates were redeemed in silver; United States notes and gold certificates were redeemed in gold so that the country was practically on a gold standard, sometimes called a "limping" gold standard owing to the large amount of silver on the market. The situation finally became clear when the Gold Standard Act became effective on March 14th, 1900. The gold dollar was made the standard unit of value, and all money issued or coined by the United States was to be kept at parity with it.

After the *Federal Reserve System** had been established by the Federal Reserve Act of December 23rd, 1913, Federal Reserve notes were issued.

Apart from these, there were also so-called Federal Reserve bank notes for which there were no gold reserve requirements as they were secured by certain Government bonds. In fact, the Federal Reserve bank notes were only used on three occasions. In 1918 they were issued to replace silver certificates which had been withdrawn because the silver dollars they represented were melted down and the bullion sold. They were again issued in 1933 during the Great Depression, and in 1942, but then more or less as an economy measure, because more of them had been printed earlier than had actually been needed.

There was a short revival of the issuance of national bank notes after 1932 for three years when the National Banks were authorized to use certain Government securities as a collateral for new issues. However, when this privilege expired, the Government called these securities, which meant that the national bank notes had to be retired, as had been planned when the Federal Reserve Act was passed.

The years of the Great Depression and the monetary crisis of 1933 also affected the dollar, of course *(New Deal*)*. In spite of the critical situation, the price of the dollar on the foreign exchange markets remained nearly at par, and the gold supply in the United States was also satisfactory. Nevertheless, the country was in a situation that called for drastic measures. On April 19th, 1933, the Treasury suspended all gold-export licences for ordinary purposes. All gold was to flow to the Treasury, and all United States coins and paper money were declared full legal tender. At the same time the President and the Secretary of the Treasury declared that the United States was not on a gold standard, a consequence of this announcement being that the dollar price dropped. In radio addresses in May and October, 1933, the President announced his plans to raise commodity prices by raising the price of gold, and soon afterwards the Reconstruction Finance Corporation announced that it would buy all domestic gold at a price of $ 31.36 per ounce (the price until then having been $ 20.67). As these purchases were also extended to foreign markets, the gold price rose. This gold-buying plan was fiercely debated, and it was doubted whether this was the right step. At any rate it prepared the country for the devaluation of the gold dollar, which became effective on January 31st, 1934, and which was one of the measures provided for in the Gold Reserve Act of 1934. On January 30th, 1934, the President issued a proclamation fixing the new weight of the gold dollar at $15\frac{5}{21}$ grains of gold, $\frac{9}{10}$ fine, and fixing the mint price per fine ounce at $ 35. The new weight of the dollar was 59.06 per cent. of the former weight, and the new dollar was sometimes called the "59-cent dollar". Furthermore, the gold stock was transferred from the Federal Reserve Banks to the Government, and a $ 2,000 million Stabilization Fund was created for the stabilization of foreign exchange rates.

In 1944, an agreement was reached at the monetary conference of Bretton Woods that the par value of the dollar in terms of gold should not be changed. This agreement, however, did not prevent the parity of the dollar from being changed from $ 35 to $ 38 per fine ounce in December 1971. In February 1973, the dollar experienced one of its worst crises. After world-wide manoeuvrings, the dollar was devalued on February 12th, 1973, (for the second time in 14 month) by 10 per cent., which corresponded to an official gold price of $ 42.22 per ounce.

The term "Euro-dollar" is used for dollar assets, held by non-American banks outside the U.S. and lent out by them on interest in the international (mainly the European) money market. The American balance of payments deficit which could be settled in U.S. dollars because the dollar was a key reserve currency, gave rise to the accumulation of enormous dollar reserves with international banks (mostly European), thus leading to the development of the so-called Euro-dollar market. I Fr/H St

Federal Reserve System

■ The Federal System is the banking system in the U.S.A. It was created by the Federal Reserve Act of December 23rd, 1913, after the National Banking System had proved inadequate. Owing to the vast extent of the country and the prejudice against too strong a concentration of money power in the U.S.A., a system was created that may be called a decentralized central banking system, comprising twelve central banks instead of just one. Branch banking was little developed in the U.S.A. and most of the commercial banking institutions were of purely local character ("unit bank", "single-office bank"). One of the underlying ideas of the Federal Reserve System, therefore, was to enable banks to co-operate and, by making its facilities accessible to banks throughout the country, to ensure elasticity in the credit system.

Between 1927 and 1929 and during the subsequent depression many defects in the system became evident, and the Banking Acts of 1933 and 1935 as well as other supplementary legislation designed to eliminate these defects made fundamental changes in the system. Today the Federal Reserve System is organized as follows:

The Board of Governors of the Federal Reserve System (until 1935 the "Federal Reserve Board", a name often still used), which has its residence in Washington, D.C., is the central and supervisory body of the whole system. Its seven members are appointed by the President and must be confirmed by the Senate. Each of the Governors holds his office for 14 years, the term of one of the members expiring every other year in order to guarantee continuity in the Board's policy. During his term of office no Governor may have any connection with any bank or trust company as a director, employee, or stockholder. The Board of Governors is responsible for the regulation of the general credit policy. It exercices control over the operations of the Federal Reserve Banks and also has an influence on their internal affairs (appointment of directors, salaries, etc.), and it controls the member banks in various respects. Among the many functions of the Board are the following: it fixes the reserve requirements, determines the margin requirements on securities *(New Deal*)*, fixes the maximum interest rates on time deposits; it controls the issue as well as the retirement of Federal Reserve notes; it appoints three out of the nine directors of each Federal Reserve Bank, and it reviews and determines the discount rates in cooperation with the Federal Reserve Banks.

It also influences open market operations since seven of the twelve members of the Federal Open Market Committee are the members of the Board of Governors. The remaining five are representatives of the Federal Reserve Banks, who are elected annually by the boards of directors of the Federal Reserve Banks. One of them must be a representative of the Federal Reserve Bank of New York. The Federal Open Market Committee, which was established in its present form in 1935, plays a very important part within the Federal Reserve System. It decides on the conditions and the volume of the open market operations (i.e. purchase and sale of securities in the open market) of the Federal Reserve Banks and thereby guarantees a uniform open market policy throughout the Federal Reserve System always, of course, with the view of keeping the credit situation as stable as possible. The meetings of the Federal Open Market Committee take place at least once every three weeks.

The Federal Advisory Council consists of twelve members – one from each Federal Reserve District – who are elected annually by the boards of directors of the Federal Reserve Banks. It holds its meetings at least four times annually in Washington, D.C. The functions of the Council include advice regarding discount rates, minimum reserves, open market policy, note issue, etc.

The Federal Reserve Banks are the most important feature of the system. The whole country is subdivided into twelve Federal Reserve Districts with a Federal Reserve Bank in each of them. In making this subdivision and in choosing the Federal Reserve Cities, many factors were considered, e.g. density of population, economic structure of the area, amount of business done, number of banks eligible for membership, etc. Consequently, the Federal Reserve Districts in the East of the United States are smaller than those in the West. The 24 branches ensure a more even distribution of the Federal Reserve facilities in the country. Federal Reserve Banks and branches are in the following cities: District 1: Boston; District 2: New York, branch in Buffalo; District 3: Philadelphia; District 4: Cleveland, branches in Cincinnati and Pittsburgh; District 5: Richmond, branches in Baltimore and Charlotte; District 6: Atlanta, branches in Birmingham, Jacksonville, Nashville, and New Orleans; District 7: Chicago, branch in Detroit; District 8: St. Louis, branches in Little Rock, Louisville and Memphis; District 9: Minneapolis, branch in Helena; District 10: Kansas City, branches in Denver, Oklahoma City, and Omaha; District 11: Dallas, branches in El Paso, Houston, and San Antonio; District 12: San Francisco, branches in Los Angeles, Portland, Salt Lake City, and Seattle. When Alaska and Hawaii were admitted to the Union (on January 3rd and March 18th, 1959, respectively) they were assigned to Federal Reserve District No. 12. See map on p. 232.

Before 1927 each Federal Reserve Bank was chartered by the Government for 20 years; in 1927, however, these charters were made indefinite. They can only be annulled by an act of Congress or if there is a violation of the law.

Each Federal Reserve Bank is a private corporation, its capital being owned by the member banks in its district. These member banks must subscribe 6 per cent. of their capital and surplus to the stock of their Federal Reserve Bank (special conditions are applied in the case of mutual savings banks, which have no capital stock), and they receive an annual dividend which has been fixed at 6 per cent. A Federal Reserve Bank must have a minimum capital of 4 million dollars. Since Federal Reserve Banks are public institutions, all their earnings – after payment of dividends and current expenses and after a comparatively small percentage has been transferred to the surplus account – will be paid to the Treasury.

All National Banks *(Dollar*)* must be members, whereas membership is optional for state banks *(Dollar*)*, mutual savings banks, trust companies, and industrial banks. Private banks are not admitted. Although the Federal Reserve system comprises only about half of all banks existing in the United States, the percentage of deposits out of the total of commercial deposits is much higher. All member banks are required to keep a certain fixed percentage of their deposits as a reserve with their respective Federal Reserve Bank. These legal reserve requirements are higher for demand deposits than for time deposits, and they also vary in accordance with the location of the member bank (they are, for instance, higher for banks in large cities). The Board of Governors is authorized to change this percentage if necessary. As banks of issue the Federal Reserve Banks issue Federal Reserve notes *(Dollar, Legal Tender*)*.

In their capacity as bankers' banks the Federal Reserve Banks extend loans to their member banks – rarely, however, to non-member banks. Most of the clearing throughout the United States is done by the Federal Reserve Banks or through them . They co-operate closely with the clearing houses.

The Federal Reserve Banks perform other functions besides these. For instance, they act as fiscal agents of the Treasury, i.e. they receive and hold funds for the government (taxes, customs duties, etc.) and they effect payments on behalf of the Treasury (salaries, pensions, interest on government bonds, etc.). They perform all business connected with government securities and also act as fiscal agents for a number of corporations established by the government.

Each Federal Reserve Bank has nine directors who are classified into Class A directors, Class B directors, and Class C directors. The three Class A directors are representatives of the member banks of the particular Federal Reserve Bank; Class B directors are men who take an active part in the commerce, agriculture, or industry of their district, but must not be directors or employees of any bank. Both Class A and Class B directors are elected by the stockholding member banks, whereas the three Class C directors are appointed by the Board of Governors. No director, officer, employee, or stockholder of a bank can become a Class C director. The directors are in office for three years, one out of each group being replaced every year. The Board of Governors designates one of the Class C directors to be the Chairman of the Board of Directors and the Federal Reserve Agent and another to be the Deputy Chairman. The duties of the Board of Directors of a Federal Reserve Bank are comparable to those of the board of directors of any commercial bank. In his capacity as the Federal Reserve Agent the Chairman is the official representative of the Board of Governors at his bank and performs functions connected with the issue of Federal Reserve notes.

The branches have either five or seven directors, the majority of whom are appointed by the parent Federal Reserve Bank, the others by the Board of Governors.

Of the Federal Reserve Banks, the Federal Reserve Bank of New York is by far the most important. Its share in the total business done by all Federal Reserve Banks is far greater than that of any of the others. It performs all foreign exchange transactions as well as purchases and sales of gold for the government and administers the Stabilization Fund *(Dollar*)*. Its foreign exchange department holds accounts for international financial institutions such as the International Monetary Fund, the International Bank for Reconstruction and Development as well as for foreign governments and central banks. H St

Free Trade

- An open and unrestricted trade; trade or commerce left to follow its natural course, i.e. without the interference of customs duties or of bounties.

The policy of free trade as pursued in Britain from 1846 to 1932 stems from the classical doctrine of economic liberalism as described by Adam Smith in his famous book "Inquiry into the Nature and Causes of the Wealth of Nations" of 1776. It implies the conception that division of labour and specialization between individuals and nations ought to be allowed to develop without any governmental intervention because free competition tends to lower prices and cost of production, thus serving best the general welfare. As applied to international trade this doctrine firmly rejects export or import duties – except for public revenue – and requires free international exchange of commodities. Later the doctrine of economic liberalism was used by the so-called Manchester School to support the repeal of the Corn Laws and the transition to free trade.

During the Napoleonic Wars (1803-1814) the price for English wheat rose by as much as 200 per cent. The ensuing increase in the price of bread meant high profits for farmers and landlords but almost unbearable hardship for the labouring poor. After the wars foreign corn was imported again. As a result prices declined and a number of farmers were ruined. The landed gentry, however, who at that time predominated in Parliament succeeded in passing through the Corn Laws – tariffs protecting agriculture – in 1815 against strong opposition from the manufactures and the urban population.

It was mainly due to the political activity of the Anti-Corn-Law League founded in 1839 in Manchester, and to the speeches of its leader Robert Cobden on the floor of the House of Commons that the then Prime Minister Sir Robert Peel was finally persuaded in 1846 to repeal the Corn Laws.

This repeal marked the beginning of the period of free trade which was to last for nearly a century. Free trade helped industry, for it enabled manufacturers to import raw materials and foodstuffs free of duty and, in turn, made it possible for import merchants to buy manufactured goods from Britain. Competition from foreign manufactured goods was not to be feared because Britain was far ahead in industrialization. From 1870 onwards, however, competition from American agricultural products made itself felt in the British market and led to a gradual decline in British wheat acreage. This made it clear enough that free trade favoured industry rather than agriculture. In 1902 small duties were imposed on corn and flour imports for revenue purposes; these, however, were repealed a year later. It was not until the Great Depression that Britain abolished free trade under the Import Duties Act of 1932. The provisions of the Act were intended to protect home markets and to serve as a basis for negotiations with foreign countries aimed at reciprocal tariff concessions. (For trade agreements with the Commonwealth countries see *Preferences*.)* During World War II imports were sharply restricted and continued to be restricted during the *Austerity** period after the war. In 1947, however, considerable efforts were made to modify and reduce protective tariffs by reciprocal agreements. In that year a multi-lateral agreement was reached by the "General Agreement on Tariffs and Trade" (G.A.T.T) signed in Geneva by 23 participating countries in order to increase international trade by reducing tariff barriers and other restrictions. As a member of G.A.T.T. Britain participated among others in the round of tariff negotiations known as the Kennedy Round *(Protectionism*)*. Britain also initiated the European Free Trade Association (E.F.T.A.) set up in 1960 to bring about the elimination of customs tariffs within the area of E.F.T.A. The then member countries were Austria Denmark, Iceland, Norway, Portugal, Sweden, Switzerland and Britain. Finland became an associate member in 1961. In January 1973, Britain (together with Denmark and the Republic of Ireland) joined the European Economic Community. Britain's entry was effectuated after renegotiations about British contributions to the Community budget had taken place and after the referendum of June 5th 1975, had achieved a big majority of those voting in favour of Britain's membership in the Community *(Common Market*). I Fr*

Great Crash

■ The term "great crash" refers to the historic day on which the New York Stock Exchange broke down in 1929. The term "Black Friday" often used instead, is a misnomer probably caused by the six hours' difference between Central European and U.S. Eastern Standard time. In fact, it was Thursday, October 24th, 1929, when the Great Crash of the New York Stock Exchange made it evident that the long period of unprecedented and – apart from minor fluctuations in 1924 and 1926 – uninterrupted prosperity of the twenties had come to an end. The boom period, which started in 1922, was mainly due to technological advances. An increasing demand for electrical power – in both the industrial and the domestic sector – was met by the development of power production, especially in the form of hydro-electricity. The enormous expansion of the automobile industry was first a result of standardization and rationalization such as was introduced by Henry Ford. Standardization made mass production possible at prices within the reach of middle-class people. Moreover, business was boosted by the instalment system which was beginning to gain ground at that time. Another important stimulus to the prosperity of the twenties was the new radio industry, the stocks of which – frequently purchased on speculation – went up by fits and starts during 1928 and 1929. The enormous expansion of the refrigerator industry must also be mentioned. John Kenneth Galbraith has outlined the economic development of those years in his publication "The Great Crash 1929". According to his statements the upward trend continued under normal prosperity conditions until 1927. In that year the turning point from an ordinary prosperity phase to excessive overspeculation came with the easing of credit by the Federal Reserve Board, which cut the rediscount rate of the New York Federal Reserve Bank from 4 to 3.5 per cent., while at the same time ordering purchases of the Government Securities on the open market.

In 1927 the reduction of the New York rediscount rate stopped the slight American recession of 1926. Unfortunately, however, it also fostered the hope – which soon proved illusory – that cyclical fluctuations could be checked once and for all by financial measures of the Federal Reserve Board. Even in December 1928 President Coolidge expressed this feeling of optimism in his last message to Congress: "No Congress of the United States ever assembled surveying the State of the Union has met with a more pleasing prospect than that which appears at the present time"

When in 1927 credit became easily available and stock market rates were expected to rise indefinitely, not only the rich but also the man in the street were encouraged to buy securities. Speculators often bought securitis on margin, which means that they had to pay but a small margin; the remainder was advanced by the broker on loan and the securities were left with the broker as collaterals. Since the buyer had full title to his property purchased with brokers' loans, he had the chance of acquiring capital gains with a rising market; but he also ran the risk of margin calls when prices were on the decline.

Another source of danger was the great number of investment trusts called into being at that time. Investment trusts originated in Scotland and had there proved to be sound enterprises of good standing. Their purpose was to spread

3

the risk of stock business so that the layman could also venture to buy investment units backed by gilt-edged securities. In the twenties, however, investment trusts became highly speculative enterprises in the States. In 1928 no fewer than 186 investment trusts made their appearance; in 1929 the number increased to 265, the stock ownership of which was usually interlocked, the result being that these investment trusts were very prone to crisis as indeed became manifest on October 24th, 1929. Until then, however, prosperity seemed to continue incessantly. The Dow Jones Index of the 30 standard industrials, which quoted 135 in March 1926, reached its peak level of 381 in September 1929. Under the Hoover Administration the Federal Reserve Board tried in vain to get the market under control by increasing the rediscount rate step by step from 3.5 to 6 per cent. Credit restriction, which would possibly have been effective two years previously, now came too late; and so did the order of the Federal Reserve Board to its member banks "to restrain the use, either directly or indirectly, of federal reserve credit facilities in aid of the growth of speculative credit" (Circular of the Federal Reserve Board of February 7th, 1929).

Finally when in the morning of October 24th, 1929, prices at the New York Stock Exchange began to fall slowly people were seized by panic; everybody wanted to sell stocks then dropping in value precipitately. Buyers on loan, unable to respond to margin calls, were compelled to sell at any price. On that day sales totalled 16.4 million stocks and the ticker did not finish recording quotations until approximately 8.30 p.m. Although an organized price support by well-known bankers brought a short recovery in the afternoon, the stock market collapsed. Further "black days" (e.g. October 29th) followed and the outcome was a loss of property and reputation for many well-known people.

The Great Crash, however, though one of the most important landmarks in economic history, was not the beginning of the recession . Speculation had pushed prices up to a level which obviously no longer corresponded to industrial output, which had been lagging behind industrial capacity since June, 1929 (index of industrial output: June 126; October 117). The construction industry – always a criterion for the cyclical situation – had already been declining since 1927. In fact, a recession was already in progress when the Great Crash occurred. Nevertheless, the stock market made a slight recovery in spring 1930, and nobody expected the recession to slide off into a World Crisis as it actually did from autumn 1930 onward. In December 1930, the failure of the Bank of the United States (a medium-sized bank at New York) was attended by many withdrawals of deposit accounts all over the country involving bankruptcies of approximately 1,400 private banks, Confidence in banking institutions and in the general economic situation was seriously weakened. Shrinkage of investment activity and consumer demand further exacerbated the situation. In July 1932, the Dow Jones Index showed 41 (approximately one-tenth of the level of September, 1929). Estimates of the number of unemployed ran from 13 to 17 million and the steel industry made use of only 12 per cent. of its capacity.

(As to further economic development see *New Deal*.) I Fr

Health Service

● Public responsibility for national health conditions began when the Public Health Act was passed in 1848. Though not very effective, the Act laid down minimum standards for sanitary equipment in order to prevent the further spread of the cholera which was raging in the north of Britain at that time *(Slums*)*. Subsequent improvements to the Act (1875) dealt with the provision of pure water, sewerage, refuse disposal, cleaning of the streets etc. Yet a comprehensive national health service available for every citizen did not come into being until 1946 when the Labour Government passed the National Health Service Act (England and Wales), which was followed by the Health Service Act (Scotland), 1947, and the Health Services Act (Northern Ireland), 1948. As part of the Labour Party's welfare legislation *(Welfare State*)* the Acts came into force in July, 1948. The administration of National Health services is the responsibility of the Secretary of State for Social Services, the Secretary of State for Scotland and the Secretary of State for Wales.

The National Health Service was originally designed to provide free medical treatment for every citizen in the United Kingdom. It included treatment in hospitals and in sanatoria, specialist services, blood transfusion, ophthalmic treatment, radiography, rehabilitation, mental health service, maternal care, child welfare, home nursing, vaccination, artificial teeth and limbs and preventive measures. As a matter of course it also included medical research. But under the National Health Service Contributions Act of 1957, the original idea of medical services wholly free of charges had to be given up since prices, salaries, costs of drugs and equipment had risen. The contributions introduced by the Act of 1957 were flat-rate and relatively small, at least in comparison with those for the same purpose required in other European countries. According to the Social Security Act of 1975 contributions to the National Health Service amount to 0,4 per cent. of the earnings of employed persons over minimum school-leaving age.

Furthermore charges were introduced for each item on a prescription form, for dentures, spectacles, and certain other items. The annual expenditure on the National Health Service now amounts to approximately 5 per cent. of the total national income. The major part of the total cost is met by the Exchequer out of taxation. Visitors from abroad are expected to pay for medical services in Britain, except in cases of emergency.

There is no doubt that – in spite of some shortcomings – the National Health Service has helped "to secure improvement in the physical and mental health of the people . . . and the prevention, diagnosis and treatment of illness", as was the object of the Acts. The birth rate has steadily risen since 1955; infant mortality has declined sharply and the expectation of live has been lengthening from about 50 years at birth from 1900 to 1910 to about 70 years at birth now.

■ In 1965 the Congress of the United States passed the law popularly referred to as "medicare". Its official title is the "Health Insurance for the Aged Act", enacted as part of the Social Security Amendments of 1965. Medicare is neither a public health service available for everybody nor a compulsory insurance against sickness which covers all residents of the country.

The medicare programme provides two types of insurance: hospital insurance and medical insurance. Everyone who is entitled to social or railroad retirement benefits will have hospital insurance automatically at the age of 65. However, in order to receive the benefits of the medical insurance plan the individual must enrol and has to pay a special monthly premium. Some 17.3 million have enrolled for this part of medicare.

The basic hospital insurance plan provides protection against the costs of hospital and related care. Benefits from this plan include payment for: (1)

In-patient hospital services for up to 90 days during a spell of illness. (Each spell of illness begins with the first day of hospital confinement and ends after 60 consecutive days of non-confinement); (2) Post-hospital treatment in a skilled nursing home for up to 100 days during a spell of illness; (3) Post-hospital home health services, for up to 100 visits in the year after discharge, by nurses, therapists and certain other health workers associated with qualified home health agencies; (4) Outpatient hospital diagnostic services. 3

The voluntary medical insurance plan provides protection against the costs of medical care by a physician or surgeon, and other medical or health services such as: (1) Home health services for up to 100 visits in each calendar year by nurses, therapists, and certain other health workers from home agencies, but without the need for previous hospitalization; (2) X-rays, diagnostic and laboratory tests: (3) Surgical dressings, splints and casts; (4) Drugs administered as part of a physician's services (prescription drugs are excluded); (5) Rental of wheelchairs, hospital beds, oxygen tents, and other medical equipment; (6) Prosthetic devices, braces and artificial limbs; (7) Limited out-of-hospital psychiatric care.

Medicare has been supplemented by Medicaid, i.e. a medical aid programme for "medically indigent" persons regardless of age. Medicaid programmes have been developed by the individual states and are granted financial assistance by the Department of Health, Education and Welfare I Fr

Incomes Policy

● A British incomes policy was first introduced in 1964 after the Labour Government had come into power. There were three main stages of development:

(1) In December 1964, the Joint Statement of Intent on Productivity, Prices and Incomes was published by the Secretary of State for Economic Affairs after consultation with the Trades Union Congress (T.U.C.), the Confederation of British Industry (C.B.I.), and the Association of the British Chambers of Commerce. It asserted that the major task of a national incomes policy must be: to ensure that British industry is dynamic and that its prices are competitive; to raise productivity and efficiency so that real income can increase, and to keep increases in wages, salaries and other forms of income in line with this increase; to stabilize prices.

(2) In February 1965, a National Board of Prices and Incomes was set up which was charged with the task of investigating any price or group of prices of goods and services in the private and public sector of industry and of investigating claims or settlements relating to wage increases. It was hoped that both sides of industry would comply with the recommendations of the Board as to wages and prices policy.

(3) In April 1965, a White Paper "Prices and Incomes Policy" was presented to Parliament by the Secretary of State for Economic Affairs. In this White Paper the annual growth rate in output per head of the labour force was assumed to range from 3.5 to 4.0 per cent. on average. Against this background the Government laid down a "norm" indicating the average rate of annual increase of money incomes per capita which was consistent with stability in the general level of prices. This figure ranged between 3 and 3.5 per cent. But the National Economic Development Council was expected to re-examine the accuracy of this figure from time to time.

The incomes policy, it is true, succeeded in restraining prices in a few industries but the general upward trend in prices continued as did the increase in wages. In order to curb the inflationary trend and to increase British competitiveness in the international market the Prices and Incomes Act of 1966 gave the Government statutory power to freeze prices as well as incomes for 6 months by parliamentary order. The incomes freeze was followed by a period of "severe restraint" in wages and prices for a further 6 months. The Trades Union Congress (T.U.C.) as well as the Confederation of British Industry (C.B.I.) agreed to support the wage and price freeze.

The Conservative Government came into power again in June 1970. They believed that the Industrial Relations Act *(Collective Bargaining*)* would reduce the loss of working hours caused by strikes. Furthermore they were confident that fiscal measures introduced under the Finance Act of 1971, such as tax allowances for investments, reduction of corporation tax, of selective employment tax and of purchase tax would play their part in the promotion of productivity, thus increasing the growth rate of the economy. Nevertheless the inflationary trend continued and the cost of living increased by about 10 per cent. in 1971. The Government therefore felt obliged to introduce the Counter Inflation (Temporary provisions) Bill in November 1972, imposing a statutory standstill on increases in pay, prices, rents and dividends. Phase One of the new wage and price freeze was to last 150 days. Phase Two, beginning in May 1973, was to provide even stricter controls of prices and incomes if necessary to curb inflation.

In 1973, the Counter Inflation Act became effective. Under its provisions two independent statutory bodies were established, viz., the Pay Board and the Price Commission. Their functions were to enforce a statutory Price and Pay Code presented to Parliament in March 1973. The Price Commission was to avoid price increases not justified on grounds of rising costs while the Pay Code was to keep wage increases in line with productivity rises. The statutory incomes control, however, was cancelled after the Labour Party had taken office again in March 1974. Based on the Social Contract *(Collective Bargaining*)*, free collective bargaining without statutory control was reintroduced. While the Government committed itself to pay subsidies on basic foodstuffs to halt price increases and to control housing rents and grant other social benefits, the unions promised to restrain pay claims within the range of the guidelines recommended by the Social Contract. During 1974-1975 the pay round kept to the guidelines to a certain extent. But, nevertheless, inflation continued to rise and in 1975 the Government – on the recommendation of the TUC – endorsed a wage increase of £ 6 per week for employees earning less than £ 8,500 a year. This new voluntary pay limit was compensated for on the part of the Government by even higher subsidies on foodstuffs and housing to keep these prices in line with wage restraint. Although in 1976 Britain's inflation rate was still about 18 per cent. compared with the previous year, another round of voluntary pay restraint was reached in 1976 with a limit of 5 per cent. pay increase. It was valid until July 31, 1977, when the Social Contract finally came to an end. Since that time the Government has been confronted with excessive pay claims as for instance by the miners' union which demands pay increases up to 90 per cent.

■ In order to counteract inflation and to keep the average price level stable, the Johnson Administration established the anti-inflation wage-price guideposts in

1966. They allowed an annual increase of 3.2 per cent. which was in line with productivity increase. But the President's appeals to both labour and management to show voluntary self-restraint have largely remained ineffective. When the Nixon Administration took office in 1969 it was opposed to any control of prices and wages whatever. But excessive wage claims especially in the construction industry caused the President to review his attitude towards wage-price policy. In order to halt the disastrous wage-price spiral the President announced a price-rent-wage-freeze for 90 days on August 15th, 1971. On October 15th, 1971, the Pay Board and the Price Commission were established within the Cost of Living Council. It consists of representatives of labour, management and public bodies. On November 9th, 1971, the Pay Board set a 5.5 per cent. guideline for wage increases, which was intended to cut inflation by between 2 and 3 per cent. by the end of 1972.

As the Price Commission stated on November 13, 1972, that the anti-inflation policy had been successful, the following Phase Three permitted controls to be voluntary with the Pay Board and the Price Commission acting in a more advisory capacity. Consequently prices began to increase rapidly so that on June 13, 1973, a standstill on prices and wages had to be ordered for 60 days. It was followed by a still harder Phase Four on the 13th of August. Price increases were allowed only if approved by the Price Commission and as far as they were caused by rising production costs. And management and labor were expected to keep wages in pace with productivity.

But all these measures failed to be effective so that the administration abandoned statutory price and wage controls at the end of April 1974. It had become evident that they were more detrimental than advantageous. They led to price distortions and sometimes even to commodity shortage, because businessmen kept commodities on stock instead of selling them at the prices prescribed, Eventually the price and wage stop ended in rapidly rising costs of living and in double digit inflation rates never before experienced in the United States.

I Fr

Industrial Democracy

The term was used as the title of a report "Industrial Democracy" published by the Trades Union Congress (1974-1977). It refers to labour-management relations and especially to employee participation in management policy. Formerly, co-determination was used as a synonym; today, workers (employees) participation or employee representation is the usual synonymous term.

During the seventies, the idea of employee participation in decision-making on the board of directors has increasingly gained momentum in Britain. Fresh impetus to the idea was given when in West Germany the so-called "Mitbestimmungsgesetz" was passed on May 4, 1976. But it has been recognized from the beginning that the German model of "Mitbestimmung" is not appropriate to British conditions, nor were the schemes already in operation in the Netherlands or in Sweden. For in Britain there is no real equivalent to the German "works council" (Betriebsrat) nor is there a supervisory board (Aufsichtsrat) separate from the management as is legally prescribed for German Aktiengesellschaften. In Germany, therefore, employee participation is provided for on the supervisory board and not on the management board.

The majority of employers and shareholders, however, are very critical of worker participation at management board level because, with no supervisory board existing, employee representatives would have a say not only in long-term company strategy but also in day-to-day decisions at board level which is likely to slow down the decision-making machinery. Thus the Confederation of British Industry (CBI) warns against a statutory standard system applied to all companies regardless of structure, size etc. and emphasizes the value of voluntary participation. Moreover, it points to the fact that a well developed "sub-structure" of participation below board level will be essential to the success of representation on the board of directors.

On the other hand, employers and shareholders admit that employee participation may be a suitable means of reducing industrial tension to a certain degree.

But the unions' attitude towards workers participation is also divided. Originally they were opposed to it. Today, however, they consider participation as an instrument to increase trade union power in both the private and public sector of industry. Therefore, in the report "Industrial Democracy", first published in 1974 by the TUC, they require that only union members should sit on the board and that they are to be selected through union machinery. On the other hand, the unions sometimes doubt whether employee representation on the board is compatible with collective bargaining, for employee representatives on the board are expected to take into consideration not only the interests of the employees but also those of the company as a whole, which is likely to entail a conflict of interests.

The majority of employees, however, seem to be not very interested in being represented at board level and a long period of training will probably be necessary to make them willing to take responsibilities.

To investigate the problems relating to workers participation in the private sector of industry a "Committee of Inquiry on Industrial Democracy" was established in August, 1975, under the chairmanship of Sir Alan (now Lord) Bullock, Master of St. Catherine's College, University of Oxford.

The Committee was asked to take "into account in particular the proposals of the Trades Union Congress report on industrial democracy . . ." and to report on the results of its inquiry within twelve months from the first meeting in December 1975. The report was presented to Parliament by the Secretary of Trade in January,1976.

The main proposals of the Bullock Committee are as follows:

1. In accordance with the recommendations of the TUC, only union members should represent the workforce of a company on the management board. Thus non-unionist employees would be excluded from representation.
2. Employees and employers or, where applicable, shareholders should have equal representation on the board.
3. The Committee is opposed to the introduction of a dual board (also called two-tier system), i.e. the introduction by law of a supervisory board separate from the board of directors. Representation should therefore be on the management board as the only decision-making body. Furthermore, the board of directors should take over some responsibilities of the general meeting of shareholders.
4. The Committee is opposed to a statutory introduction of anything like a "works council" though it recognizes the importance of a well developed representation below board level, which they call a sub-structure.

Opponents of the Bullock Committee drew attention to the possible consequences of the participation scheme proposed for investment which is so vitally important to improve the productivity and effectiveness of British industry. With propensity to invest being small in Britain a loss of investors' confidence – especially of foreign investors – in British industry is likely to decrease capital investment in British industry even more. The Committee discussed these arguments but came to the conclusion that participation schemes as proposed in the report will not decrease future capital investment.

The proposals of the report, however, did not meet with the approval of all members of the Committee. Therefore, the main report was supplemented by a minority report signed by three members. They wished to make it clear that they did not agree with fundamental recommendations of the main report, e.g. the selection of employee representatives through union machinery which would exclude non-union members from representation, and the rejection of a two-tier system. According to them the extension of union power would, finally, lead to a "control" (as the TUC itself called it) of the whole private sector of industry.

The Bullock proposals did not satisfy either the employers or the unions. The unions above all criticized the lack of provision for a legally prescribed disclosure of company strategy to union representatives and the lack of parity union representation on the boards of nationalized industries.

Nevertheless, some employee participation scheme is likely to be introduced in Britain in the near future. This will be the case if the trend to "industrial democracy" continues in other member states of the EC. In this connection it is worth mentioning that as early as 1972 the Commission of the European Communities published a draft Fifth Directive on Company Law, the proposals of which were revised in 1975 by the Green Paper "Statute for European Companies. Amended proposal for a regulation". To harmonize company laws in the member states of the EC the Commission proposes the introduction by law of a dual board system consisting of the board of directors and a supervisory board. Furthermore, it recommends employee representation on the supervisory board. But the Commission now leaves it to the member states to devise a system of worker participation which is appropriate to their own economic and social structure. I Fr

Industrial Revolution

● The term refers to the industrialization which took place in Britain from the second half of the 18th century onwards. Its characteristic feature is the change from work done by hand to work done by machine and, closely connected with it, the change from the domestic to the factory system of production. These changes were fundamental, for they divided the worker from the means of production thus creating a cleavage between labour and capital which laid the foundation for the development of industrial capitalism. Textile manufacturing was the first industry to be affected by the process of industrialization. Before the Industrial Revolution started, spinning and weaving were the occupations of country people carried out in their cottages. The implements used were owned by the manufacturer himself. The invention of the spinning-jenny by James Hargreaves in 1764 increased the output of production but the machine was still worked by hand. The fundamental change did not come about until the invention in 1769 of Arkwright's spinning machine, operated by water power, and the invention of the power-loom by Cartwright in 1785. The result was the decline of domestic textile manufacturing which impaired all the more the social condition of farmers brought about by the *Agrarian Revolution**. A new era of industrialization began in 1782 when James Watt patented his steam engine which solved the problem of driving heavy machinery where water was not sufficiently at hand. A further important development in the process of industrialization was achieved when the two Abraham Darbys discovered a method of smelting iron by the use of coal-coke instead of charcoal. The discovery of this method gave rise to the beginning of what was later called the coal and iron age, because the combination of iron and coal led to an immense development of the industry, espcially in regions where coal and iron were found together.

The region west and northwest of Birmingham comprising parts of South Staffordshire and East Worcestershire soon became known as the "Black Country" on account of the coal dust drifting down from the blast furnaces. Today coal mining and iron ore smelting have ceased in this region. The derelict land has partly been reclaimed to provide public parks, playing fields etc. *(Reclamation of Land*)*. Now the main centres of coal mining are Yorkshire, Derbyshire, Nottinghamshire, and South Wales as well as the Clyde Valley; the steel industry is concentrated mainly in the North East, in South Wales and in Scotland.

The rapid growth of industrialization depended largely on capital investment. The system of the money market, which was developed in the City of London, facilitated the lending of money for industrial purposes and was an essential prerequisite for successful industrialization. (See *Merchant Bankers** and *Big Four*.)*

The social conditions, however, which resulted from the Industrial Revolution were extremely bad for the labouring poor. As a consequence of an enormous increase in population during the 18th century and the migration of landless labourers from country to town *(Agrarian Revolution*)* the supply of labour was abundant. Thus wages were lowered nearly to starvation level. The gathering of large numbers of people in the industrial centres created housing conditions which had been unprecedented before the Industrial Revolution. Women and children, forced to earn money to keep the family alive, worked in factories and even in coal-mines. The system of "apprenticeship" as originated from the Poor Law of 1601 gave the employers further opportunity to profit from cheap labour. According to the Poor Law pauper children had to be apprenticed to a trade, thus enabling the employers to hire children as apprentices who had only to be fed, housed and clothed. They worked for 12 to 16 hours a day.

The social conditions of this period, later called early capitalism, inspired the development of utopian socialism. Its most prominent British representative was Robert Owen (1771-1858), who advocated social reforms and founded a model community at New Lanark, Scotland. It was also against the social background of the Industrial Revolution that Karl Marx and Friedrich Engels advanced their doctrine of the class struggle as expounded in the Communist Manifesto in 1848.

■ In the United States, industrialization started about 50 years later than in Britain. American industrialization was somewhat delayed by a lack of domestic capital. Therefore it had to be financed partly with foreign capital – a fact which explains why the United States was to be a debtor nation until World

War I. Moreover the Industrial Revolution in the United States was delayed by a lack of transportation facilities. The latter obstacle was to be overcome by the development of the railroad system during the 1830s and subsequent decades. 3

The Industrial Revolution in the States came first in the manufacturing of textiles when in 1791 Samuel Slater, an English immigrant, established the first spinning mill which was operated by water power at Pawtucket, R. I. It marked the beginning of the factory system. Several years later, Eli Whitney invented the cotton gin (patented in 1794). A daily output of 50 lbs. of cleansed cotton per capita was obtained by the introduction of the cotton gin. The United States became the chief supplier of cleansed cotton, the major part of which was exported to England where the cotton industry flourished during the first half of the 19th century. The invention of the cotton gin, however, led to a large extension of the slavery system in the Southern States *(Abolitionist*)*. Further progress in the textile revolution came in 1814 when Francis Cabot Lowell, a Boston merchant, put a new set of spinning machinery and a power loom into operation at Waltham, Mass.

But the revolution in iron and coal was still more spectacular than that in the textile industry, for the beginning of the American Industrial Revolution almost coincided with the movement of American settlers into the trans-Appalachian region during the last decades of the 18th century. It was there that new sources of raw materials, i.e. coal and iron ore, were discovered. But it took several decades before iron ore could be smelted with anthracite coal. It was not until 1830 that this problem was solved satisfactorily. New impetus was added to the revolution in iron and coal when the American William Kelly independently discovered the Bessemer method of decarbonizing molten metal in 1851. Large-scale development of steel production and mechanical engineering received great impetus from the railroads *(Interstate Commerce*)* A further stimulus to industrialization was given by the Civil War. Pittsburgh, P.A., became one of the largest centres of the American iron and steel industry, the other iron and steel region centring around Chicago on the southern end of Lake Michigan. The 20th century saw new sources of power such as electricity and atomic energy. From the 1920s onwards the appearance of the automobile, the advance in the chemical industry (especially on account of the increasing demand for synthetic materials) and the development of electronics provided extraordinary opportunities for industrial expansion. Moreover the United States which after World War I became one of the greatest creditor nations of the world could afford tremendous capital investment for the application of research and development in industrial processes. It was no wonder, therefore, that after World War II the United States took the lead in industrial progress.

But the dynamic changes ushered in by the Industrial Revolution are still going on. Recently the process of automation has created new problems the results of which cannot be foreseen today. Automation has often been called the "Second Industrial (or Technological) Revolution". I Fr

Interstate Commerce

■ Interstate commerce is a typical phenomenon of the federal structure of the United States. Whereas commerce within the boundaries of the several States is an affair of the State concerned interstate commerce is under the control of the federal authorities; for the American *Constitution**, Article I, Section 8, Clause

3 declares that "the *Congress** shall have power to regulate commerce with foreign Nations, and among the several States, and with the Indian Tribes". In connection with Article I, Section 8, Clause 18, which gives Congress legal authority "to make all Laws which shall be necessary and proper for carrying into execution the foregoing Powers", this regulation of interstate commerce has become a remarkable means to broaden the scope of federal authority in the field of economic affairs. For "commerce" may be interpreted in a wide or in a narrow sense. Whether or not it is up to Congress to regulate economic affairs largely depends on the interpretation of that term. In the course of time economic problems arose which could not have been foreseen by the Fathers of the Constitution. Hence the Supreme Court, in making its decisions, interpreted "commerce" as covering all economic affairs which were of a general or national character and not limited to the several States. This was the case with railroads, especially with trunk lines, and with big business, particularly with business combinations "in the form of trust or otherwise" (Sherman Antitrust Act of 1890) and also with labour and social security legislation.

From the very beginning of railroads in the U.S.A. (the Baltimore and Ohio Railroad was opened in 1830), the Federal Government had been much interested in this new means of transportation since railroads facilitated access to the new land acquired by the westward pushing *Frontier**. They helped to increase settlement in those areas and improved the exchange of industrial goods from the East for agricultural goods from the West. The advance of the Frontier determined the course of railroad development, but the railroad system itself also contributed to the close of the Frontier by encouraging settlement and *Immigration**, especially when the first transcontinental railroad joining the Atlantic and Pacific Oceans was opened in 1869. In order to promote the building of transcontinental lines the Federal Government made vast land grants to railroad corporations. The corporations sold the land to settlers for their own profit and thereby received the necessary funds for the cost of railroad construction. In 1851, the Illinois Central Railroad was the first land-grant railroad of the U.S.A.

But soon the railroads, built for private profit and without any public regulation or planning, proved to be a typical example of economic "laissez faire". During the second half of the 19th century their development was characterized partly by ruthless competition between the several corporations and partly by abuse of existing monopoly conditions. The abuses mostly consisted of discrimination against some groups of shippers who had to pay unjust and excessive freight rates to make up for rebates and other advantages given to other groups of shippers. The system often resulted in bribery of officials and political corruption.

The farmers of the Middle West were among those dependent on railroads for the transportation of their agricultural goods. After the Civil War they suffered severe losses through overproduction and declining prices in consequence of the large areas of fresh agricultural land opened up by the Frontier. They were seriously affected by the high freight rates. But the "Granger Laws" passed by the States of the Middle West from 1869 onward *(Agrarian Revolution*)* failed to solve the problem of trunk lines because they were limited to intrastate commerce. Consequently the federal authorities had to take charge of an effective railroad regulation. They did so in 1887 when Congress referring to Article I, Section 8, Clause 3 of the Constitution, passed

3

the Interstate Commerce Act and the President appointed an Interstate Commerce Commission to supervise the execution of the provisions of this Act. It prohibited pooling, charging of unjust and excessive rates, discrimination, etc. Of course, the Act met with strong opposition on the part of railroads. In fact, the trend towards pooling and railroad consolidations went on, and it was not until the first decade of the 20th century that an effective control over railroads came about. At that time the Federal railroad legislation marked by the Elkins Act (1903), the Hepburn Act (1906), and the Mann-Elkins Act (1910) definitely abolished discrimination and rebating and strengthened the jurisdiction of the Interstate Commerce Commission to such an extent that even today it is one of the most important regulative bodies of the United States *(Rail and Road*)*.

The railroad consolidations were the first powerful monopolies in the country. The Sherman Antitrust Act passed in 1890 *(Trust*)* had given legal authority to the Federal Government, to dissolve such railroad combinations which were established "in restraint of trade or commerce among the several States". This passage from the Sherman Antitrust Act points to the fact that the antitrust legislation also has its legal basis in the power vested by the Constitution in the Federal Government "to regulate Commerce with Foreign Nations, and among the several States, and with the Indian Tribes".

As to labour and social security legislation see *New Deal** and *Social Security**.

I Fr

Legal Tender

Legal tender: Money or other things that may be legally tendered or offered in payment; currency prescribed by law as that in which payment may be made.

Legal tender is any form of money which must be accepted in settlement of a debt, and which the creditor cannot refuse. In the course of history, both in Great Britain and in the United States of America, there have been various kinds of legal tender *(Sterling, Dollar*)*.

● The Decimal Currency Acts of 1967 and 1969 showed that the United Kingdom was going to break with a tradition over a thousand years old. The changeover from the old £ s. d. division to decimal currency - £ 1 = 100 new pence - was effected on February 15th, 1971. Notes of £ 1, £ 5, £ 10 and £ 20 are issued by the Bank of England and are currently in circulation. Of these notes, only that for £ 1 is legal tender for any amount in any part of the United Kingdom, the Isle of Man and the Channel Islands. Notes of £ 5, £ 10 and £ 20 are legal tender for any amount in England, Wales, the Isle of Man and the Channel Islands, but not in Scotland or Northern Ireland.

The coins issued by the Royal Mint are legal tender in any part of the U.K., the Isle of Man and the Channel Islands. 50 new pence and 25 new pence (75 per cent. copper, 25 per cent. nickel) are legal tender up to £ 10; 10 new pence, 6 new pence, 6 (old) pence = 2½ new pence (75 per cent. copper, 25 per cent. nickel) are legal tender up to £ 5 while the new 2 pence coins, the new 1 penny and the new ½ penny (97 per cent. copper, 2.5 per cent. zinc, 0.5 per cent. tin) are legal tender up to 20 new pence. Although legal tender, coins of 25 new pence are not regarded by the Royal Mint as being "in circulation", as they are generally held by collectors.

There are now three note-issuing banks in Scotland: The Bank of Scotland, Clydesdale Bank Limited, and the Royal Bank of Scotland Limited. They issue notes in denominations of £ 1, £ 5, £ 10, £ 20 and £ 100. Although these bank-notes have no legal tender qualities they are accepted without question in Scotland for all purposes. It was during the two World Wars that notes issued by Scottish banks were given legal tender status in Scotland.

There are four banks authorized to issue notes in Northern Ireland: The Northern Bank, The Ulster Bank, the Bank of Ireland and the Provincial Bank of Ireland Limited. The first two have their head offices in Belfast, the latter two in Dublin. Notes issued by these banks are not legal tender in any part of the United Kingdom.

The Government of the Isle of Man issues notes for £ 1, £ 5 and £ 10, and coins of 50 new pence, which are not legal tender outside the Island. Likewise, the States of Jersey and Guernsey issue notes for £ 1 and £ 5 and coins of 50 new pence, which are legal tender only in their respective islands and, in the case of Guernsey, in its dependencies.

■ Before 1933 the various types of money circulating in the United States differed with regard to the degree of their legal-tender qualities. Some of them, including gold coins, gold certificates, and certain bank-notes, were unlimited legal tender, while other bank-notes as well as silver and other coins were limited as to their legal-tender power *(Dollar*)*. By the so-called "Thomas Amendment" of June 5th, 1933, an equal legal-tender power was granted to all forms of money circulating in the U.S.A. Banknotes of the following denominations are in circulation in the United States: $ 1, $ 2, $ 5, $ 10, $ 20, $ 50, $ 100, $ 500, $ 1,000, $ 5,000, $ 10,000. The number of $ 5,000 and $ 10,000 notes in circulation is, however, very small. Most of the bank-notes are Federal Reserve notes, which have been issued in all denominations except $ 2. Although the Federal Reserve Banks have authority to issue $ 2 notes, they have not done so. Few notes of this denomination are used, and for many years all $ 2 notes have been United States notes. The first $ 1 Federal Reserve notes were put into circulation in November, 1963, after the United States Treasury Department discontinued the printing of $ 1 silver certificates under authority granted by the Untited States Congress.

Current coins in circulation are in denominations of 1 cent, 5 cents (nickel), 10 cents (dime), 25 and 50 cents, and the $ 1 silver coin. However, no silver dollars have been coined since 1935 and they are now very rare.

The most widely used means of payment in the United States is the cheque, although it has no legal-tender qualities. H St

Lloyd's

● The Corporation of Lloyd's is a unique institution which, although not an insurance company, is closely connected with insurance, mainly marine insurance.

Its origin and name date back to the end of the 17th century, when people taking an interest in shipping news and insurance used to meet at Mr. Edward Lloyd's coffee house in Tower Street, London. The exact date of its opening is uncertain, but the first known reference made to it is of February 21st, 1688, in the London Gazette. In 1771 the first Committee and Chairman of Lloyd's were elected from among seventy-nine of the leading merchants, underwriters and brokers. During the following hundred years, the original and more or less private character of Lloyd's changed, and this development culminated in an Act of Parliament granting incorporation in 1871. This Act restricted the corporation's activities to marine insurance; however, Lloyd's Act of 1911 eliminated this restriction, and today practically all types of insurance are carried on by Lloyd's (except whole life and financial guarantee cover), although marine insurance still ranks first. Further Lloyd's Acts of 1925 and 1951 contained amendments to meet the requirements of modern development. – Since 1970, Lloyd's earnings have surpassed those of all other British insurance companies combined.

The uniqueness of the institution is that Lloyd's as a corporation does not subscribe policies at all. This is done by the individual Underwriting Members of Lloyd's. On January 1st, 1965, there were 5,827 Underwriting Members of Lloyd's grouped into 277 syndicates. In turn, these syndicates comprised 137 marine, 84 non-marine, 26 motor, 25 aviation, and 5 life.

As in the case of a very exclusive club, it is not easy to become a Member of Lloyd's. Only underwriters who have the recommendation of at least six Lloyd's Members will be admitted. Their names must be approved by the Committee, and they must transact business with unlimited and personal liability. They have to pay a high entrance fee and an annual subscription. Furthermore, they are required to supply security in an approved form to the Corporation up to an amount fixed by the Committee and proportionate to the volume of business to be transacted. For members not previously connected with the Corporation the minimum is £ 15,000 if they are to accept both marine and non-marine insurance. Underwriters who are Lloyd's Members must have their books audited annually; and some further conditions must be fulfilled (e.g. contributions to a Central Fund and furnishing of guarantee policies) – all destined to guarantee that the Members will at all times be in the position to meet their liabilities, and thus to render the security of a Lloyd's policy unimpeachable.

The business of insuring takes place in the "Room" where underwriters and brokers meet. This Underwriting Room is – so to speak – a market where business is conducted in a competitive atmosphere. Lloyd's Underwriters may only do business in the Underwriting Room and trough the 217 firms of Lloyd's Brokers. The Lloyd's Brokers, however, are not restricted to Lloyd's but may also work with the insurance companies. In the course of years, the premises occupied by Lloyd's have changed several times. The present building, in Lime Street, was opened by Her Majesty Queen Elisabeth the Queen Mother in 1957.

While formerly all insurance policies at Lloyd's had to be signed by the individual underwriters who took a share of the risks, today no Lloyd's policy is valid without the seal of Lloyd's Policy Signing Office, a department administered by the Committee of Lloyd's.

The administration of the Corporation is in the hands of the Committee of Lloyd's consisting of twelve Members who are elected for a period of four years by their fellow Members. After that period they have to retire for at least one year before they become eligible again. Election takes place by rotation – three Members being elected every year to take the places of three who have to retire. The Chairman and Deputy Chairman of the Committee are elected annually by the Committee Members.

Lloyd's is also the centre for shipping intelligence. There are today some 1,500 Lloyd's Agents and Sub-Agents throughout the world who collect and transmit shipping, aviation and other news. Lloyd's Agents also give assistance in the case of accidents and act as surveyors in cases of damage or loss of a ship or her cargo, and they are also authorized to settle claims on behalf of Lloyd's underwriters. Their functions do not, however, include the transaction of insurance business.

The shipping intelligence collected by Lloyd's Agents is collated in Lloyd's Intelligence Department and then distributed to newspapers, radio, television, etc., and it is also published by the Lloyd's Editorial Department in a number of Lloyd's own publications the oldest of which is Lloyd's List and Shipping Gazette which first appeared in 1696 and is now published daily. It indicates the movements of all ships in the world that are surveyed by Lloyd's. All Lloyd's publication organs together provide the most comprehensive shipping intelligence service in the world.

Though historically linked with the Corporation of Lloyd's *(Lloyd's*)*, Lloyd's Register of Shipping has since 1834 operated as a seperate organization. It is a classification society of international scope with its head office in London. Its origin, too, dates back to Mr. Lloyd's coffee house. Merchants and underwriters found it desirable and useful to have a register of the ships and cargoes offered for insurance. Thus, the first Lloyd's Register of Shipping was published as early as in 1760. In 1834, for the first time, standard rules for shipbuilding were set by the society, and today its prime functions apply before the ship's maiden voyage, surveying everything from the initial design to the material used, power and refrigeration plant, etc. Lloyd's Register, which is published by the society annually gives information about type, condition, nationality, tonnage, owner, etc. of all ships surveyed by Lloyd's and classifies them into different groups. The highest classification a ship can get is "A1 at Lloyd's", which means that it is in perfect order and condition. ("A1" was first used in 1775 to denote the highest class of a ship. It has found access into English colloquial language as characterizing something absolutely first-class. U.S. usage is: "A No. 1".) A very high percentage of the world's tonnage of merchant shipping is classed with Lloyd's.

In recent years the society has also extended its activities to other spheres beside shipping. It has taken to supervising such land installations as oil refineries, atomic power plants, etc.

Although the Corporation of Lloyd's and Lloyd's Register of Shipping are two separate institutions, there is a close liaison between them, and Members of the Committee of the former also serve on the Committee of the latter.

The society has its headquarters in London and local committees in other important towns of Great Britain. It also has national committees in foreign countries. H St

Merchant Bankers

● The name "Merchant Bankers", which is still in use today, refers to the historical background of some of the banking institutions in the highly specialized British banking system – more precisely in the London Money Market. Most of the Merchant Bankers are today more commonly known as Accepting Houses and some of them, which have taken to assisting would-be raisers of capital in the issue of securities, are also known as Issuing Houses. They are providers of short-term and long-term credit respectively.

The names of the Merchant Bankers reveal that many of them originally came from Germany, e.g. Rothschild, Kleinwort, Erlanger, Baring, Brandt, Schroder. They were important merchants in the 17th and 18th centuries dealing in commodities and chiefly engaged in foreign trade. They had developed a banking side of their business and especially made it their task to accept bills of exchange on behalf of foreign importers against a commission. Today they are no longer engaged in commodity trade. Most of the Merchant Banks are privately controlled and hereditary. Although they are small compared with other British banks they are of great importance. In the 19th century some of the London Merchant Bankers were richer than governments. The Accepting Houses maintain agencies in many foreign trading centres and collect intelligence concerning the credit standing of foreign firms. On the strength of such information they carry on their business of accepting bills of exchange. The Accepting House may negotiate with the foreign firm directly (having made sure that the firm is credit-worthy) by opening an Acceptance Credit. The British exporter will then draw his bill not on the foreign importer but on the Accepting House. The bill will be accepted and thus bear the name of a first-class British banking institution. It will be more readily discounted – and at a lower rate – than a normal acceptance and it will be more easily negotiable. If the Accepting House deals with the importer's bank rather than with the importer directly, i.e. if the foreign bank secures an acceptance credit with one of the Accepting Houses, we speak of a Reimbursement Credit. This business, therefore, is not one of borrowing or lending money directly. The Accepting House with its renowned name only acts as guarantor that the bill of exchange will be duly honoured. A commission is charged by the Accepting House for this service. It is a matter of course that the Accepting House must have ample resources of its own, and a great part of them must be highly liquid so that obligations can be met without fail and punctually. Usually the firms which make use of the Accepting House's services are expected to deposit some money with it.

There are seventeen Accepting Houses, and they submit themselves to a certain informal control by the Bank of England. Since their ordinary banking business is very limited in scale, they are not serious competitors for the clearing banks in this respect. They do, however, compete with one another, and with the clearing banks (which also do some acceptance business now) for the quality of their services.

The Merchant Bankers also act as Issuing Houses for firms that whish to raise capital. Furthermore, they act as trustees and investment advisers for charitable foundations, colleges, corporations, etc. This gives them a very influential position in the economy since the institutions which seek their advice usually have very large sums to invest. For some of the Accepting Houses this latter function has almost become the most important. H St

Nationalization

● The term "nationalization" covers the two aspects: public control and public ownership. In the proper sense of the word "nationalization" includes the transfer of property to the nation. But in the broader sense a company may be considered as partially nationalized if it has been brought under public control though its property is not yet acquired by the nation. Public control is very often the first step to nationalization.

Since the beginning of this century state intervention has become a feature of growing importance in a modern economy. The trend towards public control increased during World War I and the Great Depression of the 1930s and was given further impetus by the economic conditions during and after World War II *(Austerity*)*.

In Britain there were various reasons for this trend towards state intervention, such as the desire to avoid monopolies, the co-ordination of competitive services, the provision for proper distribution of supplies, and the encouragement of research and development. These reasons strengthened the trend towards state participation, especially in communications, transport and public utilities. As a result a number of industries and services concerned in the generation of electricity, broadcasting, London passenger bus and underground services, part of air-transport – to mention the most important – had been brought under public control already before the Labour Party came into power in 1945. While in its former periods of government (1923 and 1929-31) Labour had been dependent on Liberal support, it gained an absolute majority in 1945, which for the first time enabled it to enforce its economic concepts, irrespective of other political parties. The nationalization of further industries and services was the most distinctive manifestation of its socialist platform.

Nationalization as a whole affected the following industries and services:

(1) The basic industries: coal, iron and steel. According to the socialist programme the basic industries ought to be nationalized because 'the whole economy depends on them''. In the case of coal mining there were also weighty economic reasons for nationalization. This industry required large capital investment for modernization and up-to-date equipment; for, with the best seams exhausted, coal had to be extracted from deeper and less productive seams. Moreover, with the change in the economic structure (electricity generated from water-power resources, growing competition from oil, atomic energy, etc.) investments in coal mining became increasingly unprofitable. For this reason the Sankey Commission had recommended the nationalization of the coal mining industry as early as 1919. The coal miners themselves, who had been suffering from great unemployment, vigorously advocated nationalization, which was finally established under the Coal Nationalization Act of 1946. The National Coal Board (N.C.B.) was established to manage the coal industry. Nevertheless, demand for coal continued to decline during the subsequent years and deficits from some coal mining areas (Scotland, South Wales, Lancashire) exceeded the profits from other areas (East Midlands) so that on the whole coal mining proved to be a non-profitable industry.

In contrast to coal mining, iron and steel were efficient industries before they were nationalized under the Iron and Steel Act of 1949. It is not surprising, therefore, that their nationalization was heavily opposed. When the Conservatives succeeded the Labour Government in 1951 they denationalized iron and steel under the Iron and Steel Act of 1953. At the same time the Iron and Steel Board was established for the purpose of supervising the iron and steel industry. When in 1964 the *Labour Party** returned to office, the country was prepared for further nationalization. In fact the Labour Party made steel nationalization an essential issue of its programme for the elections of March

1966. After its victory the Iron and Steel Act was passed by Parliament in January 1967, and took effect on July 28th, 1967. The nationalized iron and steel industry comprises 14 major steel companies which employ about 220,000 people, while some 200 companies accounting for about one-third of the industry's sales are still privately owned. The private sector companies employ some 115,000 people. The state-owned part of the industry is now managed by the British Steel Corporation established under the Iron and Steel Act 1967. It holds the shares of the 14 major companies.

(2) Public utilities: especially gas and electricity. Part of the undertakings for the supply of gas and electricity were under public ownership before 1945. In the North of Scotland Hydro-Electric Board a public corporation was set up as early as 1943 to utilize the water resources of the Highlands for generating electric power. Furthermore, a great number of undertakings for the supply of electricity and gas were owned and managed by local authorities. A certain measure of public control with regard to distribution had been a feature of public utilities from the very beginning. From this point of view nationalization of gas and electricity, as introduced by the Electricity Act of 1947 and the Gas Act of 1948, was more concerned with re-organization and centralization than with the transfer to public ownership *(Public Utilities*.)*

(3) Transport: railways, road haulage, the canals, part of air transport, and London passenger traffic. Since transport performs a public service vitally important for the whole economy, the idea of proper co-ordination between competitive transport services was decisive for nationalizing rail and road haulage services under the Transport Act of 1947. As early as 1933 the London Passenger Transport Board (renamed London Transport Board under the Transport Act of 1962) combined rail and road passenger services, which proved a great success. Yet the inclusion of road haulage in the nationalization programme of the post-war Labour Government met with strong opposition. The Conservative Government which took office in 1951 denationalized road haulage under the Transport Act of 1953.

Nationalization also included part of civil aviation under the Civil Aviation Act of 1946, which established British European Airways (B.E.A.) as a public corporation. (The British Overseas Airways Corporation (B.O.A.C.), a public corporation, had been founded in 1939.) Both public corporations became divisions of British Airways under The Civil Aviation Act 1971. It established the Civil Aviation Authority (CAA) and the British Airways Board (BAB) and became effective in 1972. The Transport Act of 1947 also brought most of the canals under public control *(Rail and Road*, Aviation*)*.

(4) Bank of England. The Bank of England had increasingly gained a key position as the central note issuing authority for England and Wales since the Bank Charter Act of 1844 (Peel's Act). Britain having abandoned the gold standard as well as the fixed rate of exchange for sterling in 1931, the Exchange Equalization Account was established in 1932 as part of the Treasury to prevent undue oscillations of the pound. Thus responsibility for foreign exchange policy was partly transferred to the Exchequer, and this, in fact, turned out to be a partial nationalization of the Bank. After World War II the Labour Government argued that a joint-stock company ought not to be allowed to act as a central note issuing authority. With the Government acquiring its entire capital stock, the Bank of England was nationalized under the Bank of England Act in 1946 *(Bank of England, Sterling*)*.

(5) Communications. In Britain postal and telecommunication services are provided by the Post Office, which was founded as early as 1657. It was a government department until 1969. Under the Post office Act of that year, it became a public corporation under a chairman and a board of directors. They are responsible to the Minister of Posts and Telecommunications.

The nationalized industries are not managed and operated by Government departments, but by special statutory bodies, which were given a certain independence of status. The public corporations *(Corporate Enterprise*)*, as the most important of these statutory bodies, operate the industries or services concerned in the public interest but not as a function of the Crown *(Civil Service*)*. Their employees, therefore, do not rank as civil servants. Their managing boards are appointed by the minister concerned or through him by the Queen (as is the case with the Bank of England and the B.B.C.), and it is they and not the ministers who are responsible for the management of the corporations. The corporations do not work for profit.

In February 1971, the famous Rolls-Royce Company went bankrupt. In view of the special importance of Rolls-Royce as a supplier of aeroengines and marine and industrial gas turbine engines the government felt obliged to nationalize these branches of the Rolls-Royce production although on principle the Conservatives were opposed to state interference in private enterprise.

Under the Industry Act 1975 the National Enterprise Board (NEB) was set up as a statutory body which enables the state to interfere with industry in a far-reaching way. The NEB is intended to act as a kind of holding company as well as a state investment board. As state investment board it grants loans out of Government funds to industrial firms for capital investment programs and sometimes even for assistance in short-term cash difficulties. Yet in return the NEB can take a shareholding in the borrowing firm, which opponents sometimes call a "backdoor nationalization". As a kind of holding company the Board holds the shares acquired on behalf of the Government and thus is able to get a controlling interest in firms which are in need of credit.

In this way, (for example) major shareholding in the famous British Leyland Ltd. was taken by the Government through the NEB. Already at the end of 1974, a Government loan of £ 50 million to Leyland had raised some criticism because the money approved by Parliament for capital investment was in fact needed to pay the wages and to keep the company afloat. With insufficient productivity and an appalling record of strikes, the economic situation of British Leyland Ltd. remained critical so that a big rescue operation by state-financed capital investment for the firm's restructuring became inevitable.

Plans for nationalization have not yet come to an end. Thus the Labour Government is going to take into state ownership four firms of the aerospace industry under the new British Aerospace Corporation, while the participation rights of the Government in the exploitation of British off-shore oil resources are administered by the recently established British National Oil Corporation.

Furthermore, proposals to nationalize the shipbuilding and aircraft industries as well as British banks and insurance companies belong to the major issues of the Labour Party's platform.

Nevertheless, the British economic pattern can still be called a "mixed economy", for in 1977 only about a quarter of the working population was employed in nationalized industries whereas nearly three quarters of them worked for private sector industries. I Fr

New Deal

■ deal sb.: the act of dealing; the distribution of cards to the players for a game; new deal: the supposed resemblance to the situation of freshness and equality of opportunity afforded by a fresh deal in a card game. New Deal (capitalized): the legislative and administrative programme of President Franklin D. Roosevelt designed to promote economic recovery and social reform. 1932.

The term "New Deal" was first used by Franklin D. Roosevelt in his speech accepting the Democratic nomination for President in July 1932. He told the Convention: "I pledge you, I pledge myself to a new deal for the American people". The press took up the expression and it has gradually come into use to designate the period of the Franklin D. Roosevelt Administration aiming at the President's three Rs of Relief, Recovery, and Reform.

The economic situation which the President faced when he took the oath of office in March 1933 was unprecedented in American history. Estimates of the number of unemployed ran from 13 to 17 million (unemployment census of the United States began only in 1937.) In 1932, 1,400 commercial banks had failed and the banking crisis reached its climax with the banking moratoria of a number of American States in March 1933. In order to meet this condition Congress was called by the President on March 9th, 1933, and was held in session until June 16th, a session later to become known as the "Hundred Days". At the end of the Hundred Days, Congress had enacted a whole series of legislative measures, the most important of which were: the Agricultural Adjustment Act and the Farm Credit Act for agricultural relief; the Civilian Conservation Corps Reforestation Relief Act, the Federal Emergency Relief Act, and the Tennessee Valley Authority Act for unemployment relief; the National Industrial Recovery Act (N.I.R.A.) for industrial recovery; the Emergency Banking Relief Act, the Federal Securities Act and the Banking Act (Glass-Steagall Act of 1933) for currency and banking reform.

This reconstruction legislation initiated by the President and shaped by his advisers (known as the "Brain Trust") put an end to economic "laissez faire" and was in effect an approach to "planned economy". It strengthened the federal government's control and its participation in the economic life of the nation. It entailed an increase of federal bureaucracy; for a great number of agencies *(Independent Agency*)* had to be established to carry the New Deal into effect. Furthermore the measures taken were inspired to a certain degree by theories elaborated by the economist John M. Keynes in his publication "General Employment, Interest and Money" (1936). In his book he recommends that decreasing effective demand and investment within the private sector of the economy should be compensated by increasing investments of public authorities, even if resulting in a large deficit of the public budgets.

Since the farmers' distress was mostly due to surplus production *(Agrarian Revolution*)* the Agricultural Adjustment Act was designed to raise prices by reducing agricultural production. In addition, the Farm Credit Act, supplemented by the Farm Mortgage Refinancing Act of 1934, facilitated credit for farmers to refinance farm mortgages on long terms at low interest *(Agricultural Relief*)*

On inauguration day the President had declared "our greatest primary task is to put people to work". Apart from an appropriation of $ 500 million granted to States and municipalities under the Federal Emergency Relief Act, the Civilian Conservation Corps (C.C.C.) was to provide work for unemployed citizens between 18 and 25 years of age in reforestation, road construction, etc. The C.C.C. was placed under the Public Works Administration established under the provisions of the N.I.R.A. It is worth mentioning that the National Job Corps established by President L. B. Johnson *(War on Poverty*)* in 1964 is quite similar to the C.C.C. of the New Deal.

The Tennessee Valley Authority (T.V.A.) was a further measure to provide for employment and, at the same time, for long-term regional planning, embracing flood control, power development, land reclamation, etc. *(Reclamation of Land*)*.

The National Industrial Recovery Act (N.I.R.A.) was to establish industrial self-regulation under federal supervision by a system of voluntary fair competition codes including agreements upon prices, wages, and sales methods. The N.I.R.A. temporarily set aside anti-trust legislation but the *Supreme Court** declared it unconstitutional in 1935. Likewise the Agricultural Adjustment Act was declared unconstitutional in 1936, the latter, however, was revived in a modified form in 1938.

The currency reform of the first Roosevelt Administration was intended to raise prices and reduce debts through inflationary methods such as the abandonment of the gold standard, the issue of fiduciary notes as legal tender up to $ 3,000 million, the devaluation of the dollar to 59,06 cents in relation to its gold content, and a gold embargo *(Dollar*)*. The banking reform established under the Banking Act of 1933 was supposed to "put an end to speculation with other people's money" by eradicating the evils which had contributed to the *Great Crash** of 1929. It curbed speculative bank activities; it enabled the Federal Reserve Board to prevent speculation on credit; it safeguarded depositors by providing for the insurance of member-bank deposits up to $ 5,000 with the Federal Deposits Insurance Corporation. The Securities Act of 1933 also required full disclosure with regard to new security issues to be registered with the Federal Trade Commission. Supplementary legislation provided for the regulation of margins and brokers' credits under the Securities Exchange Act of 1934, which also created the Securities and Exchange Commission (S.E.C.), designed to prevent unfair practices in the security business.

Whereas the first New Deal (1933-35) was outlined to overcome the disastrous consequences of the Great Depression, the second New Deal (1935-39) aimed at a long-term social reform. The most important legislative measures were: the Social Security Act of 1935, which for the first time introduced unemployment compensations, old age and survivors' pensions, and various social services under federal legislation *(Social Security*)* and the National Labor Relations Act (Wagner-Connery Act) which guaranteed the workers the right of collective bargaining through unions of their own choice *(Collective Bargaining*)*. In 1938 the Wagner Act was supplemented by the Fair Labor Standards Act which fixed working hours at 40 per week and provided for minimum wages. It also outlawed child labour in industrial plants. The introduction of graduated income tax under the Revenue Acts of 1935-1937 (see *Self-Assessment**) was of great importance for the social structure; for "Our revenue laws have operated in many ways to the unfair advantage of the few, and they have done little to prevent an unjust concentration of wealth and economic power" declared President Roosevelt in his message to Congress on June 19th, 1935. In order to alleviate housing conditions in low income groups the National Housing Act (commonly known as Wagner-Steagall Act of 1937) established the U.S. Housing Authority (U.S.H.A.) which was designed to grant loans to local public agencies for *Slum** clearance and housing projects. These enactments were very important from a social point of view. Yet, there was still another aspect of economic relevance: the reform measures functioned as anti-depression tools by increasing consumption, thus giving incentive to economic expansion. The public security system and the public works planning, therefore, are also called "built-in cushions" or "built-in stabilizers" for they mitigated economic downswings and helped to stabilize economic fluctuation. In 1941 America's entry into World War II put an end to further social and economic reforms. After the war, the Truman Administration, however, continued the Roosevelt policy under the so-called "Fair Deal" which was much along the same lines as the New Deal.

I Fr

New Towns

● The New Towns of Britain are "established and developed as self-contained and balanced communities for work and living" (Report of the Reith Committee, 1946). They provide housing, employment, social services as well as recreation and leisure facilities within the town's own boundaries. Therefore the New Towns differ essentially from the satellite towns built by large cities outside their boundaries to meet their housing requirements as well as from the garden suburbs which are mere dormitory settlements for people who often have to travel great distances to work.

The new Towns were established under the New Towns Act of 1946 (consolidated in 1965 and 1968). The planning authorities for the New Towns are the Secretary of State for the Environment, the Secretary of State for Scotland, the Secretary of State for Wales and the Minister of Development in Northern Ireland. They determine the site of the planned New Town after consultation with the local authorities concerned while the building of the New Towns is the responsibility of the development corporations or the development commission in Northern Ireland, respectively. The development corporations acquire the necessary land within the designated area by consent or compulsory purchase. The fund provided for the New Towns under the New Towns Act of 1946 and subsequent legislation amounts to £ 2,750 million. The advances are paid by the government on loan and repayable within a period of 60 years. Up to now there are 33 designated New Towns in Britain. Among them 23 in England and Wales, six in Scotland and four in Northern Ireland. Some of them, e.g. Peterborough, Northampton, Warrington, are based on long existing communities which became the nucleus for large-scale expansion under the New Towns concept.

The main purpose of the British New Towns programme is a furtherance of decentralization and a redistribution of population and industry. The uneven distribution of population which is so characteristic of the English landscape can be traced back to the *Industrial Revolution**, which gave rise to a large-scale urbanization of the country. Whilst at the end of the 18th century 78 per cent. of Britain's population lived in the countryside, a hundred years later more than

80 per cent. lived in towns. In the 20th century the mass concentration of population and industry in some of the biggest industrial centres created the problem of the so-called conurbations. The latter are urban areas which increasingly engulf the surrounding areas and even smaller towns already existing. But the most striking change in the distribution of British industry and population came with the spread of industrialization to the south-eastern region *(Development Area*)* which called for a curbing of the further expansion of Greater London on the one hand and for a redistribution of industry and population on the other.

In order to redistribute industry and population within this area eleven of the New Towns (Basildon, Bracknell, Crawley, Harlow, Hatfield, Hemel Hempstead, Milton Keynes, Northampton, Peterborough, Stevenage and Welwyn) were designed to absorb surplus population willing to move from Greater London.

When the development of a New Town is nearly completed its assets and liabilities are transferred from the development corporation to the Commission for the New Towns as was already the case with Crawley, Hatfield, Hemel Hempstead and Welwyn.

The six Scottish New Towns (Cumbernauld, East Kilbride, Glenrothes, Irvine, Livingstone, and Stonehouse (according to a Government decision Stonehouse will not be further developed) were established to relieve overcrowding in Glasgow, whereas Runcorn and Skelmersdale meet the housing problems of Liverpool and north Merseyside as do Telford and Redditch with regard to the population of Birmingham. Warrington took people from Manchester while the rest of the New Towns (Aycliffe, Corby, Cwmbran, Peterlee, Washington, Central Lancashire New Town, Newton in mid-Wales as well as Londonderry, Craigavon, Antrim and Ballymena in Northern Ireland) were to meet the special needs of their areas.

The success of the New Towns experiment was largely dependent on the provision of employment. In order to promote the transfer of industry from Greater London to the New Towns, the Development Corporations built factories with modern equipment which were leased to smaller firms, or they leased land (usually for 99 years) to firms wishing to build factories of their own. Investment allowances and grants to firms moving from London provided a further stimulus for the industrial expansion of the New Towns. The Development Corporations, of course, are very much interested in attracting different types of industry in order to give progressive young people a wide choice of occupation. The firms of the New Towns are usually such as have a large demand for skilled labour – light industry, electrical engineering, woodworking, pharmaceuticals, etc. There are also research laboratories, branches of government departments and administrative offices which chiefly employ white-collar workers. On the whole endeavours to attract industry from congested London have been successful.

With regard to housing, one of the leading principles has been the separation of the industrial from the residential areas – the latter are called neighbourhoods – and the separation of the pedestrian from the motorist. In order to solve this problem pedestrian shopping precincts have been established, which calls to mind the recommendations of the Buchanan Report "Traffic in Towns" of 1963. Within the neighbourhoods there are shops for everyday needs, primary and secondary schools and the church of the denomination predominant in the neighbourhood, while the town centre offers a large shopping area and contains all administrative offices. The Englishman's love of gardening and a house of his own was to a large extent taken into consideration as can be seen from the large number of small terraced houses which are the chief architectural feature of all New Towns. As a matter of fact, it is no easy task for the architects to meet this demand for small houses each with its own garden and to avoid uniformity and monotony in planning the New Towns. Nevertheless a variety in the pattern of design has proved possible. The spaciousness of the New Towns is impressive. On the whole, the New Towns programme can be considered as a successful enterprise, from the economic point of view; the social aspects of it are still under observation.

■ Since the late 1950s some courageous private developers have started to built New Towns across the United States. The hazards for the developers have been and still are immense. Enormous capital investments have to be made while returns may be earned only five years later or more. Today there are 15 New Towns in the States: Irvine Ranch, Calif., California City, Calif., Valencia, Calif., Columbia, Md., Lake Havasu City, Ariz., Clear Lake City, Tex., Litchfield Park, Ariz., Westlake, Calif., El Dorado Hills, Calif., Park Forest South, Ill., Laguna Niguel, Calif., St. Charles Communities, Md., Reston, Va., Rancho Bernardo, Calif., and Jonathan, Minn. Three of them – Park Forest South, St. Charles Communities and Jonathan – have been built with Federal loan guarantee.

I Fr

Preferences

● In political economy: the practical favouring of one customer before others in business relations; spec. the favouring of one country by admitting its products at a lower import duty than that levied on those of others or of foreigners generally, or by levying a duty on the latter while admitting the former free.

With regard to Great Britain the term "preferences" (originally the Imperial Preferences) refers to the Ottawa Agreements between the United Kingdom and its Dominions made at the Imperial Conference of Ottawa in 1932. The countries of the British Empire decided to levy import duties on the goods of each other lower than on goods from outside countries, this policy being based on the principle of "home producers first, empire producers second, foreign producers third".

The Ottawa Conference was held when the Great Depression was making itself most felt. The consequent shrinkage of international trade induced the United Kingdom and its dependencies to provide for "sheltered markets" within the British Empire. For the same reason the United Kingdom, then ruled by a Labour Government, abandoned *Free Trade** and introduced a protective tariff under the Import Duties Act 1932. It marked a radical change in British tariff policy, which from 1846 (repeal of the Corn Laws) to 1932 had been based on the free trade principle. Under the terms of the Import Duties Act the United Kingdom permitted goods from the Dominions to enter the United Kingdom free of duties, so that the Ottawa Agreements turned out to be more favourable for the Dominions than for the United Kingdom. Subsequently the competition of Dominion textiles entering the British market free of duty often aroused great opposition in the British textile industry.

In the ensuing years British trade began to increase, which was attributed to the Imperial Preferences, although there was unquestionably another factor which contributed to the development of British trade. In 1931 Britain had abandoned the gold standard and freed the rate of exchange, and sterling dropped to a level at which supply and demand were in equilibrium. This de facto depreciation encouraged British exports because prices for British commodities now declined (in monetary units of foreign currencies), thus making purchase of British goods more profitable for foreign traders. Moreover, the currency arrangements between the countries of the Sterling bloc (later called Sterling Area) tended to facilitate trade within the Sterling Area.

However, in the course of time, especially after World War II, it became manifest that the Commonwealth preferences were no longer of such vital importance for British trade as previously assumed. For during the 1950s British trade began to shift from the *Commonwealth** countries to Western Europe, especially to the European Economic Community (E.E.C.) and to the countries belonging to E.F.T.A. In 1964 British exports to Western Europe amounted to 37 per cent. of total exports, whereas only 36 per cent. went to the Sterling Area. Imports from Western Europe have also increased (in 1964, 31 per cent. of total imports) while imports from the Commonwealth countries have tended to decline. Considering these facts it is understandable that in 1961 Britain decided to become a member of the E.E.C. The Commonwealth preferences however, became an issue of major importance in the negotiations for Britain's entry. Above all, France objected because she feared competition between the former French colonies and the Commonwealth countries if the latter were granted preferential access to the Common Market. The former French colonies as well as the former dependencies of Italy, Belgium and the Netherlands had become associate members of the E.E.C. under the provisions of the Treaty of Rome. Though not represented in the Communities' organs, they were allowed to import their produce free of duty to all markets of the Community. The problem of Commonwealth preferences was not solved until Britain became a member of the E.E.C. on January 1st, 1973 (see *Common Market**).

Protectionism

■ The theory or system of protecting home industries against foreign competition by imposing duties or the like on foreign production.

The policy of protectionism originates in the theory of mercantilism according to which an excess of exports over imports should be aimed at to collect the highest amount of precious metals within the domestic economy. Early American tariffs (1789-1816) were chiefly designed for raising revenue though its actual effect was also some protection for industrialization. The transition to tariff policy for the main purpose of protection came only after the Napoleonic wars (1803-1814). In 1816 Congress passed the first protective tariff on manufactured goods in order to protect infant home industries from the competition of English commodities. In subsequent years protectionism further increased and by 1828 reached its first peak in the so-called "tariff of abominations". Protectionism aroused severe opposition in the Southern states, the economy of which was based on agriculture rather than on industry. The Southerners suffered from the high prices of manufactured goods, and during the following decades tariff protection of manufactured goods became an important issue which separated the North from the South. The civil War gave new impetus to protectionism. It began with the Morrill Tariff in 1861 and increased under the subsequent revisions which levied ad valorem duties up to an average of 47 per cent. In 1909, it is true, the Payne-Aldrich Tariff brought some moderation of tariff rates, but it was not until the Democratic Party came to power (1912) that the tariff rates were lowered to 30 per cent. and a number of products were put on the free list.

As a result of World War I the United States became a great creditor nation. Although no longer in fear of competition from abroad, the States returned to *Isolationism** and protective tariff policy. Thus the foreign debtors of the States were deprived of the opportunity to settle their war debts, for the high import duties prevented American importers from purchasing commodities from the debtor nations. The Fordney-McCumber Tariff of 1922 and the Smoot-Hawley Tariff of 1931 which raised import duties up to 49 per cent. upon manufactured as well as agricultural goods, were fully in line with isolationism. During the Great Depression the United States, then ruled by a Democratic Administration, inaugurated a new tariff policy under the Trade Agreements Act of 1934. It introduced a reciprocal tariff which authorized the President to negotiate trade agreements with foreign countries for a reduction of specific duties by as much as 50 per cent. Agreements of that kind did not require ratification by Congress and were to be based on the unconditional most-favoured nation principle. By 1951 the United States had concluded reciprocal agreements with 53 nations.

Since World War II there has been a significant trend towards a liberalization of international trade. As a result of the Geneva Trade Conference of 1947 23 nations, including the United States, signed a multilateral agreement known as the General Agreement on Tariffs and Trade (G.A.T.T.) which was intended to reduce preferential duties, import quotas and other trade restrictions (today 72 nations are members or associate members of G.A.T.T.). In 1962, the United States passed the Trade Expansion Act initiated by President John F. Kennedy which aimed at an international linear tariff cut of 50 per cent. In 1963 the Kennedy Round was established to initiate negotiations on this issue. The members of the Kennedy Round were the United States, the E.E.C. countries, the E.F.T.A. countries and Japan. The discussions in Geneva, which is the seat of G.A.T.T., lasted more than three years, the main obstacles being chemical and agricultural products. In view of its agricultural surplus production *(Agrarian Revolution*)* the U.S.A. was especially interested in expanding the international agricultural market which was to be accomplished by the E.E.C. countries cutting their tariffs on U.S. agricultural products. The European Common Market for its part required the repeal of the American Selling Price System (A.S.P.) on chemicals. The A.S.P. is one of the most striking examples of tariff disparities (i.e. different levels of tariffs) between the U.S.A. and the European countries. Under the A.S.P. system tariffs are fixed on the wholesale price of comparable American products instead of on the price paid for the imported chemicals in the European market. In spite of these obstacles a final agreement was reached on May 15th, 1967. The major accomplishments of the Kennedy Round were tariff cuts averaging about 35 per cent. on industrial and agricultural products. Although far below President Kennedy's aim of 50 per cent. across-the-board tariff cuts, the Kennedy Round took a remarkable step towards the liberalization of world trade. But it could not prevent a re-awakening of protectionist tendencies and a neo-isolationist trend during the subsequent years.

In 1970 Senator Mills introduced into Congress the Trade Bill commonly known as Mills Bill. It was mainly designed to protect the American textile industry against import of textiles from Japan. While the House of Representatives approved the Bill the Senate postponed it to the next session. But it has not been discussed in Congress any more.

The American attitude regarding protectionism, however, must be seen against the background of Japanese competition on the one hand and protectionist measures of the E.E.C. against agricultural imports on the other. For to push up import prices for foodstuffs to the level of the so-called threshold price by variable import duties is undoubtedly highly protectionist. *(Common Market*.)* When President Nixon ordered a 10 per cent. surcharge on goods imported from abroad on August 15th, 1971, it was actually meant to improve America's balance of payments position rather than to protect home industry. Although the surcharge on imported goods was repealed on December 18th, 1971, protectionist ideas have been increasingly gaining ground among U.S. politicians. With long lasting recession a trend towards protectionism makes itself felt in nearly all industrial countries of the Western world and calls to mind the tariff barriers erected during the Great Depression of the 1930s which finally led to a breakdown of international trade. Nevertheless the surcharge has become a welcome object for bargaining over in export-import relations with foreign countries.

Americans who are far-sighted enough to see the danger of an international trade war have therefore suggested a new tariff round to be set up in the near future. I Fr

Public Utilities

Public utilities is a designation for those industries which are conducted under the public regulation because their operation is in the public interest. They may be either publicly controlled or publicly owned *(Nationalization*)*. In almost every country a varying number of them are operated by the state or by local authorities. But privately owned or administered as public functions, they invariably sell their services to the general public, and their prices are not fixed in the open market but by the central or local government.

Although economic and technical evolution is continually changing the character of these industries, public utilities may be classified according to the general functions which they perform in economic life. They comprise: power (gas and electricity) and water supply; in a broader sense even transport and communication services.

Since transport and communications are treated in special sections *(Nationalization*)* the term "public utilities" will refer here to water, gas and electricity exclusively. (For transport see *Aviation, Rail and Road, Shipping*.)*

● Unlike other public services in Great Britain, the responsibility for the supply of water remains in the hands of a large number of undertakings of different kinds. But the national water policy rests with the Minister of Housing and Local Government.

It was not until the 19th century that the supply of water became a public service. The dangers of an inadequate supply of water and sanitation led to the Public Health Act of 1848, the first of a long series of similar statutes. From the middle of the 19th century onwards a number of private and municipal water undertakings were set up to provide water for the expanding population.

Under the Water Act of 1945 the Minister of Housing and Local Government has the duty to promote the conservation and proper application of water supplies in the country . There is a statutory Central Advisory Water Committee which advises the Minister. Since the Act was passed some smaller – mostly local – water authorities in England and Wales have been absorbed by larger ones. There are now some 190 statutory water undertakings of which about a third are local authorities, a half joint boards of local authorities and the remainder statutory companies.

The Metropolitan Water Board, which is probably the largest single water undertaking in the world supplies about 385 million gallons daily to approximately 6 million people in the London area. The public water supply in England and Wales reaches over 99 per cent. of the population and totals some 2,900 million gallons a day.

The public supply of gas in Britain dates from 1807. In 1812 the London and Westminster Gas Light and Coke Company received a royal charter to supply gaslight to London. As in the case of other public utilities, the British system of regulation was on the basis of special charters and the granting of franchises. The Gas Regulation Act of 1920 was typical of this kind of law. There was established a standard selling price for gas and a standard maximum rate of dividend.

The Gas Act of 1948 placed the gas industry in Britain, in which about 125,000 persons are at present employed, under public ownership and control. The assets of 991 undertakings are vested in 12 regional Gas Boards. The central Gas Council is appointed by the Minister of Power.

There are about 13 million consumers. The quantity of gas produced exeeds 600,000 million cubic feet annually. Half of this gas is sold for household consumption and the remainder for industrial and commercial purposes.

The public supply of electricity was first provided in Britain in 1881. Public control has been a feature of the industry from its earliest days; indeed there were quite a number of Electricity (Supply) Acts even in the last century. In 1926 a Central Electricity Board was established. Under the 1957 Electricity Act the industry, nationalized ten years before, was modernized and the former administrative authorithies replaced by two new bodies: The Electricity Council and the Central Electricity Generating Board. The new organization does not, however, satisfy everybody and is much criticized.

The present organization of the electricity supply industry occupies more than 213,000 people. The output capacity of the generating stations totalled 56,033 megawatts in 1970; at the same time electricity supplied exceeded 224,000 million kilowatt-hours. An analysis of the generation shows that it is mostly produced in coal-fired steam generating stations. Thus the electricity authorities are the largest consumers of coal in Britain. In 1943 the North of Scotland Hydro-Electric Board (N.S.H.E.B.) was established to develop the water-power resources of the Highlands. In 1970-71, 3,435 million units were generated by that Board, compared with 322 million units in 1949.

■ There are not so many government-owned or government-controlled public utilities in the United States as in Britain or most other countries. This, the Americans say, is in accordance with their traditional policy of individual enterprise. Even rail-roads are still privately owned *(Rail and Road*)*.

Most local utilities are regulated by their respective States. As a public utility expands in size and extends its territory it tends to pass from local to State and finally to federal regulation. Even if the state abstains from direct intervention it has been a principle of American legislation and jurisprudence that "business affected with a public interest has ceased to be 'juris private' only" (Lord Chief Justice Matthew Hale in the famous case of Munn versus Illinois, 1877). Between 1923 and 1934, and particularly during the depression years, a series of cases involving the constitutionality of price regulations was decided by the U.S. Supreme Court. The court often ruled against the regulation of the retail prices.

In recent years the Federal Government has become more active in legislation affecting utilities. As early as 1920 the Water Power Act was enacted which reserved for the Federal Government the authority to dispose of water power under federal jurisdiction. The organization of the Tennessee Valley Authority by the Roosevelt administration in 1933 was another important step in this direction. When many private public utility companies collapsed in the depression following the "Great Crash" Congress finally passed a Public Utility Holding Company Act (1935) which required interstate gas and electricity companies to register with the Federal Securities and Exchange Commission whose permission had to be obtained to buy or sell securities *(New Deal*)*.

The new policy of constant regulation requires an effective agency in order to bring legislative standards and principles into effect. This need has been met by the setting-up of a modern administrative commission acting as an agent of the legislature. With the exception of the above-mentioned Securities and Exchange Commission which is concerned only with financial ownership, these agencies are in general charged with the provision of adequate service at reasonable rates. Their powers vary according to the utility involved but, apart from the regulation of rates, cover mostly such matters as licensing of operations, maintenance of services and safety regulations.

Thus state control is nowadays extensive but the commonest form of organization of public utilities is still the private corporation. The one exception is water supply. In 1957, only 20 per cent. of cities of over 5,000 generated and distributed their own electricity, only five per cent. provided their own gas, compared with 75 per cent. which owned water supply and distribution systems. Indeed, 12,000 of the 16,000 water systems are publicly owned.

H F

Rail and Road

● September 27, 1975, marked the 150th anniversary of the opening of the world's first regular steam-hauled passenger service by the Stockton and Darlington Railway in Britain. In the course of the 19th century British railways, like those of the United States, acquired a position of monopoly, with the consequence that they were soon subject to public restrictions intended to avoid discriminatory passenger and freight charges. (For similar problems in the early history of U.S. railroads see *Interstate Commerce*.)* During World War I and II the British railways were placed entirely under Government control. Although released from governmental control in 1945, the railways finally became nationalized under the Transport Act of 1947 which was passed by a Labour Government. The railways were put under the authority of the British Transport Commission (B.T.C.), established in 1948. To modernize the railways, for instance through the replacement of steam traction by electric or diesel traction, large capital investments were needed. But despite these investments made from public funds, the railways suffered increasingly from the growing competition of road traffic. In the 19th century the turnpike roads – managed by private turnpike trusts who levied tolls on the road users - had declined when railway competition began. In the 20th century, however, the trend was reversed. The decline of the railways was closely connected with the increase in road traffic, especially after the appearance of the motor car which necessitated the development of the road network. In addition to competition from road traffic the railways increasingly have to compete with air traffic, in particular with passenger traffic by air.

In order to redistribute freight transport between rail and road, a system of licensing for road haulage carriers was introduced under the Road and Traffic Act of 1933. The nationalization of hauliers engaged on long-distance haulage (Transport Act of 1947) was a further attempt to obtain better co-ordination between rail and road services. Both attempts failed to stop the further shift of traffic from rail to road. As a result, the deficit of British Railways (renamed "British Rail") amounted to £ 150 million in 1962. In view of this the Beeching Report (Report on the Reshaping of British Railways) of 1963 recommended that little-used passenger services should be withdrawn from about one-third of the railway network while at the same time the Hall Report proposed a rapid enlargement of the motorway and trunk road system. The Buchanan Report of the same year was concerned with traffic congestion in towns. *(New Towns*.)*

Under the Transport Act of 1962 the British Railways Board was set up. It replaced the British Transport Commission and assumed the whole responsibility for the British railway system. In 1968 a new Transport Act was passed, which brought a number of important legislative innovations. First of all the finances of British Rail were put on a healthy basis by cutting down capital debt and introducing grants for unprofitable rail passenger services. Furthermore the National Freight Corporation was set up which manages the nationalized road haulage. At the same time Freightliners Ltd. was established, owned partly by the British Railways Board and partly by the National Freight Corporation. The main purpose of the Transport Act of 1968 was to rehabilitate British Rail financially and to integrate road and rail services as far as possible. Under the Transport Act 1974 a general scheme of government compensation for rail passenger services was introduced and replaced the former specific grants.

■ The private corporations which own and operate U.S. railroads are, like any other corporations, bound to pay taxes to federal, state and local authorities. Between 1950 and 1956 these taxes averaged $ 1,130 million a year or 11 per cent. of the railroads' total income. The railroad companies do not obtain subsidies but are granted loans out of public funds. Although the railroad corporations are business organizations there is no doubt that the services rendered by them are of a public character. For that reason their passenger fares and freight rates are regulated by the Interstate Commerce Commission (I.C.C.) *(Interstate Commerce*)*. During recent decades U.S. railroads have been faced with even more severe problems of competition than those experienced by British railways, for the United States is provided with an outstanding network of intracontinental highways.

The large-scale development of interstate highways began with the Federal Aid Road Act of 1916, when grants-in-aid were given to the States from federal funds for constructing roads mainly interstate in character. Under the Federal Highway Act of 1921 the road building programme was improved and continued during the Depression of the thirties for the New Deal legislation made road construction a relief programme to reduce unemployment. In 1956 the "National System of Interstate and Defense Highways" was started and financed up to 90 per cent. out of federal funds. It was designed to embrace a 41,000 mile (65,981 km) network after its completion in 1975. The American Highway System has been supplemented by excellent turnpikes like the famous Pennsylvania Turnpike, the first of the great modern toll roads opened in 1940. Passenger car fees are levied from the road users for the maintenance of the turnpikes.

Highways, turnpikes, and smaller roads in the United States largely contributed to a further shift of passenger and freight traffic from rail to road. In 1965 75 million passenger cars and 15 million trucks and buses (among them the well-known Greyhound buses providing through passenger services) were registered in the country.

Under the circumstances it was not surprising that the railroads could no longer be considered monopolies, as was the case in the 19th century. In contrast to the former Government policy which had prohibited railroad combinations under the Sherman Antitrust Act of 1890 *(Interstate Commerce*)*, from 1920 onwards the I.C.C. began to recommend railroad consolidations (Transportation Act of 1920) which were intended to bring financial advantages by the elimination of terminals, by improved car use etc.

Since 1959 the I.C.C. has approved more than 30 mergers, one of the most important ones being the merger between the New York Central Rail Road Company and the Pennsylvania Rail Road Company. The combined Rail Road Company was named Penn Central Transportation Company. This merger took place in 1968 and was meant to solve the companies' financial problems. But it could not prevent the Penn Central Transportation Company going bankrupt in June, 1970. This failure was a shock for the U.S. Government as well as for the American people. Therefore the Railpax Act was passed in October 1970, in order to avoid a further decay of the U.S. railroad system. Under this Act a new rail passenger system went into operation in May 1971; the name was changed from Railpax to Amtrak, this being an abbreviation for American Transportation on Track. Amtrak is a kind of holding organization now controlling 16 railroad companies. It is subsidized out of public funds and tries "to get people back on trains" by a number of innovations such as better through passenger services, all-expense-tours, etc. In 1975, a subsidy of $ 1.2 billion out of public funds was granted for these projects. In 1977, Amtrak presented a new five-years' programme. It was intended to make rail services more comfortable for passenger traffic, though emphasis will remain on freight transportation.

Although the rivalry between rail and road is as great as ever, it should not be forgotten that both of them decisively helped to shape the American nation. When the colonial period began, the rivers – as far as they were navigable – and the Indian trails had to be used by trappers, explorers and early settlers when penetrating the wilderness. In the 18th century the turnpike toll roads built with private capital became the main arteries of colonization. In the 19th century the railroads gradually took the place of the early turnpikes, and today the railroads are partly superseded by traffic on highways, modern turnpikes and by airline services.

I Fr

Reclamation of Land

The making of land fit for cultivation. The act or process of reclaiming; restoration to use.

■ The term reclamation of land includes all efforts undertaken by federal, State or local governments to restore the fertility of waste land previously under cultivation or to make barren land fit for cultivation.

Although the United States has been endowed with an abundance of natural resources and arable land, all arable land that could be cultivated easily had been settled by 1900. Since precipitation progressively decreases from the Atlantic in a western direction until – at the Ninety-Seventh Meridian, sometimes referred to as the "precipitation line" – it reaches an annual average of only 10 to 20 inches, the Ninety-seventh Meridian, roughly speaking, marks the line where (with the exception of small coastal regions in Northern California, Oregon and Washington, which do not belong to the dry regions) the arid West of the United States begins. Hence, the 17 States west of the 97th meridian, including the Great Plains area from North Dakota to Texas, are largely dependent on irrigation. Water was first supplied by wells, later by windmills pumping up the groundwater.

Modern irrigation of the arid West began in 1847 when the Mormon pioneers stopped their westward trek in the Valley of the Great Salt Lake and founded Salt Lake City in the midst of desert land. The irrigation project of the Mormons was a great success, and the beginning of modern reclamation of land in the interior West. Other projects in Utah, Colorado and California were likewise successful, and at the beginning of this century irrigation was supplying water to more than 10 million acres of the arid West. This growth of reclamation aroused public interest and brought the economic, social and political problems created by the reclamation of land within the scope of national issues. The Desert Land Act of 1877 authorized settlers to acquire 640 acres at 25 cents each, provided that the land was irrigated by them within three years. The Carney Act of 1894 authorized the President to grant a maximum of a million acres of public land to the western States for the purpose of irrigation, reclamation and settlement. Under the Theodore Roosevelt Administration the trend culminated in the National Reclamation Act (Newlands Act of 1902) which set aside the proceeds of public land sales in the western and south-western States in order to finance irrigation projects in arid States. Examples of such projects are the Boulder Dam on the Colorado River and the Grand Coulee Dam and the Bonneville Dam on the Columbia River. These dams stored water for irrigation and provided for power development, thus meeting the steadily growing demand for power from the new industries in the West.

Eventually voices were raised against reclamation projects. It was pointed out that there was considerable surplus production of agricultural products and that the country was consequently not in need of further farmland. *(Agrarian Revolution*.)*

Apart from land reclamation by irrigation, large parts of the best agricultural land of the United States (approximately one-fifth) have been made arable by artificial drainage. Wet lands subject to drainage for agricultural purposes are located along the Atlantic coast (Carolina, Virginia, New Jersey), in the Great Lakes District (Indiana, Michigan, Minnesota, Ohio, Illinois, Iowa), and above all in the Valley of the Mississippi and its tributaries.

The reclamation programme further includes the restoring of soil fertility by preventing floods, by planting shelter belts of trees, constructing dams, and gradual reforestation, especially on mountains and hillsides. Such measures were also carried out by the C.C.C. (Civilian Conservation Crops) under the *New Deal** legislation.

A great problem is the reclamation of derelict sites resulting from mineral mining and other industries producing large quantities of waste materials. Dumps of blast furnace slag and spoil heaps, which are sometimes mountains of mineral waste, have often produced areas of desolation, as was the case in parts of the Appalachian region *(Appalachia*)*, where formerly spoil and slag, dug out from now derelict collieries, lined the roads. Since the slag contains a residue of coal, it is even apt to catch fire. In 1965 a number of States and local governments have passed legislation required the worked land to be levelled and reclaimed for housing or other purposes. *(Appalachia*.)* Finally, the Surface Mining Control and Reclamation Act of 1977 solved the problem to a certain degree.

● In England and Wales approximately 150,000 acres of derelict land, damaged at some time by industrial development, would remain an eyesore unless the land were reclaimed by special treatment. A concentration of derelict land is to be found in places associated with the industrial revolution of the 18th and 19th centuries. It has often been said that the *Industrial Revolution** spoiled the face of Britain. But since the end of World War II considerable efforts have been made to reclaim derelict land for providing houses, open spaces, schools or playing fields. In 1953 the Lancashire County Council successfully experimented with the reclamation of colliery shale for agriculture. In cases where reclamation for agricultural or other use was not possible, at least improvement in appearance was achieved. The reclamation and improvement schemes have been carried out by the County Councils under the prime responsibility of the Minister of Housing and Local Government (now Minister for Planning and Local Government within the Department of the Environment). Although the local authorities have no statutory duty to reclaim derelict land, they have powers for dealing with reclamation in pursuit of the general well-being of their districts. Derelict land may therefore be acquired for the purpose of development under the Town and Country Planning Act of 1962 or for the purpose of restoration and improvement in appearance of derelict land under the National Parks and Access to the Countryside Act of 1949. In addition, the Mineral Working Act of 1951 set up an Ironstone Restoration Fund – contributions to the Fund are made by operators, landowners and the Exchequer – to assist in financing the restoration of land worked for ironstone by opencast methods. The worked land must be levelled and re-fertilized by owners and occupiers, who may obtain grants from the Restoration Fund to meet the cost of the reclamation.

Good progress has already been made in reclaiming waste and derelict land for agricultural of for recreational or housing programmes. I Fr

Restrictive Trade Practices

● In the British economy big business combinations organized as *Trusts** for the purpose of monopolizing the national (sometimes even the international) market have not played such a predominant part as in the United States. In British usage therefore the term "trust" has largely preserved the original meaning of a body of persons entrusted with the administration and preservation of anything for the benefit of some other person or group of persons; hence, for instance, the "National Trusts" which administer land and places of natural beauty or historic interest for the benefit of the public *(Conservation of Land*)*. For the British newspaper trust system see *Press**.

But there is no doubt that starting in the 19th century, restrictive trade practices under different forms have been gaining ground in both Britain and the United States, as well as in other highly industrialized countries. These practices have mainly taken the form of cartel arrangements regulating the prices, or even the production and purchasing of goods between the member firms. For instance, prior to its *Nationalization** in 1949 the iron and steel industry is said to have made excess profits through prices determined not by supply and demand but by cartel arrangements.

Apart from the *Common Law**, which made "unreasonable" restraints of trade illegal there was previous to 1948 no special legislation prohibiting monopolistic practices. However, the increasing power of restrictive agreements made inevitable detailed regulations for determining what were "unreasonable" restraints. In 1948, therefore, the Monopolies and Restrictive Practices (Inquiry and Control) Act provided for the Monopolies and Restrictive Practices Commission under the Board of Trade. The Commission was intended to investigate industries where "one-third of a particular type of business was controlled by one firm or by arrangements between several firms" and to decide whether or not restrictive trade practices were in accordance with "the public interest". In determining "the public interest", factors in favour of restrictions – such as efficiency, technological advance furthered by capital concentration, etc. – as well as factors against restrictions – such as elimination of competition, monopoly prices, etc. – were to be taken into consideration. Once the restrictive practices were found to be not in accordance with public interest they could be prohibited by parliamentary order. In addition, according to the Restrictive Trade Practices Acts of 1956 (amended 1968) such practices had to be registered in a public register when one-third of the output was controlled by one firm or by arrangements between several firms. Under the Act of 1956 the Restrictive Practices Court was established and vested with legal authority to declare practices illegal if found to be contrary to the public interest. The Act of 1956 (amended by the Resale Prices Act of 1964) also prohibited collective enforcement of resale price maintenance which had previously attracted widespread attention and given rise to intense political discussion. The Restrictive Trade Practices Acts of 1956 and 1968 were amended by the Fair Trading Act 1973. Under the Act the name of the Monopolies and Restrictive Practices Commission was changed into the Monopolies and Mergers Commission, which has the duty of investigating and reporting on mergers and monopoly situations. According to the provisions of the Act a monopoly situation is defined by a market share of one quarter. The Secretary of State for Prices and Consumer Protection may refer a merger to the Commission if, among other things, it results in a monopoly situation. Furthermore, the Act of 1973 extended the range of restrictive agreements to be registered. Above all, agreements on common prices and on the limitation of production are included. The registered agreements have to be notified to the Director General of Fair Trading who brings them – with some exeptions – before the Restrictive Practices Court. The Court is empowered to prohibit the agreements if they are contrary to the public interest. The Monopolies and

Mergers Acts of 1948 and 1965 strengthened the legislation on restrictive trade practices especially with regard to newspaper mergers *(Press*)*. I Fr

Self Assessment

■ Self assessment and voluntary compliance are unique features of the American taxation system. The taxpayer has to file an income tax return on April 15th of each year with the Internal Revenue Department. Every item subject to taxation and the deductions which are allowed from gross income are to be recorded in the tax return. If the taxable income is below $ 750 per year the person concerned is exempted from income tax as is any individual over 65 years of age. In accordance with incomes and deductions recorded in his return the taxpayer himself has to estimate the amount of income tax he is obliged to pay for the preceding year. When preparing his income tax return he can get some information and assistance from Internal Revenue officials, but the main point is that he is fully responsible for the estimate of his actual tax liability. Tax payments can be made in three ways. Total income tax due for the year may be paid at the end of the taxable year (April 15th), or the taxpayer may prefer payment under the pay-as-you-go scheme, introduced by the Current Tax Payment Act of 1943. It means that quarterly instalments of the estimated tax amount have to be paid. Another method of tax collection is "withholding at source". According to this scheme the employer withholds taxes to be paid by the employee from wages and salaries. The amount to be withheld are based on tax liabilities estimated by the employee. The withholding system was introduced for certain groups of people as early as 1862. It was, however, abolished under the Revenue Act of 1917, which replaced "collection at source" by "information at source" It was not until 1942 that Congress definitely returned to withholding.

Self assessment and voluntary compliance is based on the assumption that the individual taxpayer will record his taxable income honestly and completely. Nevertheless the system has some loopholes for evading payments of taxes intentionally or through ignorance. In 1959, for instance, the Treasury Department stated that there was a loss of revenue amounting to $ 800 million because millions of receipts from dividends and interest had not been recorded. Therefore an attempt was made under the Revenue Act of 1962, to extend withholding to dividends and interest. But the proposal, recommended by President John F. Kennedy, met with such strong opposition that the provision had to be dropped from the bill. Though not allowed to withhold dividend and interest payments, corporations and banking institutions are obliged to report such payments to the Internal Revenue Department. Things changed when the automatic data processing went into operation in 1962 at the National Computer Center near Martinsburg/W.Va. Incorrect statements in tax returns can now easily be detected.

Apart of the system of self assessment there are some other peculiarities in American taxation worth mentioning. There is, for instance, taxation on individual and corporate income both at federal and state level, which impressively reflects the federal structure of the United States. While income tax had long been known as a source of revenue in the several states, it was not until 1862 that Congress attempted to introduce a federal income tax to outweigh the financial burden of the Civil War. But federal tax on income caused violent disputes, for the Constitution (Article I, Section 2, Clause 3) provided direct taxes to be apportioned among the several states according to population. The Supreme Court therefore declared federal taxation on income unconstitutional in 1874. Only after the Sixteenth Amendment had been ratified in 1913 was federal taxation on income definitely legalized; the Amendment stated that "Congress shall have power to lay and collect taxes on income from whatever sources derived without apportionment within the several states".

Under the Revenue Act of 1913 a federal flat-rate income tax and a surtax on incomes above a certain level were introduced. Furthermore the Act provided for a flat-rate federal tax on corporate income. In 1935-37, the Revenue Acts of the *New Deal** led to a considerable increase of the surtax rate on individual incomes. They also extended the principle of progression from individual to corporate incomes. Together with estate, gift and excise taxes (the latter on automobiles and telephone services) taxation on income has remained the mainstay of federal revenue until today.

Taxation at state and local level is very complex, because the states are empowered to introduce taxes under their own legislation. As a rule, state revenue is derived from sales taxes on gasoline, alcoholic beverages, tobacco products, etc., from property taxes (mostly on real estate) and from income and corporation taxes, whereas county and city governments are usually dependent on real estate or property taxes as their main sources of revenue.

Considering the special importance of investments in the human resources of society, a number of states have introduced school taxes to provide for better educational facilities and thereby to raise the standards of their school systems. In the budget for the fiscal year 1972 the federal government apportioned more than $ 7,100 million to meet the educational requirements of poorer school districts.

I Fr

Shipping

● Britain developed very early an interest in shipping and overseas trade, which was mainly caused by her geographical position on the ocean highway connecting the north-eastern coast of the United States with the European countries bordering the North Sea and the Baltic. Britain's coasts on the Atlantic and on the North Sea are indented by a number of estuaries, these being the tidal mouths of rivers where the tide meets the current of the river. The estuaries allow seagoing ships to enter deep into the country and are favourable to the location of ports and dockyards. In the south of England the estuaries of the river Thames and the river Severn, in the north of England the estuary of the river Humber and the opposite estuary of the river Mersey play an important part in overseas traffic whereas the Scottish estuaries are of minor importance for international trade. A further geographic advantage is that the industrial centres are not far from the sea. In fact, there is no geographical point of Britain more than 70 miles from the sea.

British shipping, which had gradually expanded after the establishment of the East India Company in 1600 (an incorporated company granted a monopoly of the trade with India and the Far East), gained its predominant position with the expansion of international commerce which followed the *Industrial Revolution**. Since industrialization in England started approximately 50 years earlier than in the United States and in the continental countries, England had an immense advantage over competitive maritime powers in overseas trade. The growth of international commerce coincided with specialization in shipping.

Whereas prior to the Industrial Revolution the merchant was the owner of the ships which carried his goods, from the end of the 18th century onwards shipping as a transport industry distinct from production and trade came into being. Shipping companies now provided only the service of sailing and carrying cargoes and passengers upon payment of charges; a service provided either by regular scheduled liner shipping on certain routes or by tramps chartered for special transports on a contract basis.

An effective system of marine insurance and shipping intelligence such as was established in London *(Lloyd's*)* helped to reduce navigational hazards, thus functioning as an essential element in the development of British shipping.

In 1886 the tonnage owned by Great Britain, Ireland and the British Empire still exceeded the total tonnage of all other nations in the ratio of 53 to 47. Although in the second half of the 19th century British shipping was subject to growing competition from continental mercantile fleets, more than half of the world's maritime trade was still carried by the British merchant fleet. During World War I neutral states began to expand their merchant fleets, while a large part of British tonnage was sunk. The consequences made themselves felt in the growing rivalry after the war. The Great Depression of the thirties *(Great Crash*)* also affected British shipping so that in 1935 voyages of tramp steamers had to be subsidized by the Government to enable them to stand the pressure of competition (British Shipping Act of 1935). During World War II the loss of British merchant ships amounted to the enormous total of 11,677,475 gross tons. Since World War II Britain has considerably increased its merchant fleet again. Today it comprises about 31,600 gross tons making the British merchant fleet the third largest in the world in active employment. Merchant shipping is under the responsibility of the Department of Trade.

■ (a) Coastal Shipping

The continental coastlines of the United States, which offer many favourable locations for harbours, are of great economic value not only for ocean-going but also for coastwise and intercoastal shipping, the latter including the sea route between the Atlantic and the Pacific U.S. coasts via the Panama Canal and the sea route between the continental U.S. area and outlying areas such as Hawaii and the Aleutian Islands. During World War I coastwise and intercoastal shipping was threatened by submarines. The United States therefore began to construct the Intracoastal Waterway. From Boston/Mass. to Brownsville/Tex. on the Rio Grande del Norte it runs parallel with the East Coast and the Gulf Coast. The Intracoastal Waterway, which allows ships to go from *New England** to the South without going out into the Atlantic Ocean, was of particular value during World War II.

(b) Inland Waterways

The two main arteries of intra-continental commerce are the large inland waterways from the Great Lakes region in the North to the Gulf of Mexico in the South and the St. Lawrence Waterway from the Great Lakes to the Atlantic seaboard. The connection between the Great Lakes region and the Gulf is provided by the Mississippi river system with its main tributaries, the Missouri, the Ohio, and the less important tributaries. On the Mississippi river system southbound transportation consists mainly of iron and steel products as well as of grain and grain products from the Great Lakes region whereas the northbound ships mostly transport petroleum from the large mineral oil deposits in Louisiana and Texas.

The St. Lawrence Waterway consists of the St. Lawrence River, which mainly constitutes an extension of the Great Lakes, and its large estuary opening into the St. Lawrence Gulf and the Atlantic Ocean. In order to overcome the International Rapids between Montreal/Quebec and Lake Ontario, which had much impeded navigation on the St. Lawrence, the so-called St. Lawrence Seaway was built and is now being operated jointly by the United States and Canada. From Duluth at the western end of Lake Superior to the Atlantic the St. Lawrence Waterway (not to be confused with the St. Lawrence Seaway meaning only the canalized part of it) covers the enormous distance of 2,342 miles (approximately 3,768 km), thus allowing ocean carriers to enter the Middle West directly from the Atlantic. The huge water supplies of the St. Lawrence are used not only for transportation purposes but also for generating electrical power.

The economic importance of the St. Lawrence Waterway can be gauged from the fact that its region includes approximately 85 per cent. of the iron and steel production area of the U.S.A., a large percentage of the munitions industry, chemical industry, and the major part of the refining capacity (another refining centre is situated in Louisiana and Texas) and from the fact that 80 per cent. of American grain is cultivated within the areas adjoining this region.

When the St. Lawrence Seaway was first projected at the beginning of the 20th century, it met with strong opposition, not only from the railroads but also from Atlantic coast ports and from coal mines. All these opposing groups were brought together into the "National St. Lawrence Project Conference", which came to be one of the most powerful Washington *Lobbies** in United States history. Largely as a result of this lobby's activities the St. Lawrence Seaway did not come into existence before 1959.

(c) Ocean-going Shipping

During the first half of the 19th century the American merchant marine had rapidly increased and by 1860 was next in tonnage to that of the British *Empire**. But the American Civil War to a great extent ruined the merchant marine, which lost its former important position during the decades following the Civil War. In 1886 the United States total of vessels of 100 tons gross and over was only approximately one fifth of that owned by the British Empire. By 1914, it is true, U.S. tonnage had increased, but was not more than approximately 25 per cent. of that owned by the British Empire. During World War I the United States enforced an emergency ship-building programme in order to keep pace with the war losses suffered by the British marine. As a result, the U.S. ocean-going fleet was the largest in the world at the end of the war. In 1922 it totalled 14,738,606 gross tons. This vast tonnage exceeded the demand particularly since international trade declined during the world crisis of the thirties. The high wage level prevailing in the United States further diminished the competitive power of its merchant fleet. Therefore a system of indirect subsidies had to be introduced (Merchant Marine Acts of 1920, 1929 and 1936). The Merchant Marine Act of 1929 also required that government-built ships had to be sold at a fraction of their cost. However, the situation changed fundamentally with the outbreak of World War II. The U.S. Government had to carry out a vast emergency ship-building programme. As a consequence, the tonnage of the U.S. merchant fleet amounted to 36,000,000 tons gross at the end of the war. Confronted with the problem of what to do with the surplus tonnage, the U.S. Government decided once more that ships had to be sold below cost price. Furthermore, an emergency defence reserve fleet was established which comprised 14,000,000 tons gross of mothballed ships. In 1971 the ocean-going merchant fleet of the United States comprised 15,529,000 gross tons while that of the United Kingdom amounted to 24,070,000 gross tons. I Fr

Slums

A highly congested area marked by deteriorated unsanitary buildings, poverty and social disorganization.

● Those overcrowded districts of an industrial town consisting of monotonous ugly rows of unhealthy, mostly "back to back" houses, which have been called "slums" since about 1825, were hurriedly erected at the lowest possible cost by employers for their "labouring poor" during the 19th century. These areas lacked even a minimum standard of sanitation, there usually being no water supply, inside lavatory, refuse collection, drainage, pavement of streets.

The slums first made their appearance when vast masses of people drifted from country to town at the beginning of the Industrial Revolution *(Agrarian** and *Industrial Revolution*)*. The necessity of accommodating masses of people in a small space created the problem of congestion and overcrowding, which had been unknown up to the Industrial Revolution. The new factor of overcrowding, together with the insanitary conditions, contributed to the spread of epidemic diseases among the inhabitants. The first Public Health Act had to be enacted in 1848 as a result of the cholera which in 1830 und 1848 raged in the industrial north of Great Britain. The Act laid down minimum standards of sanitary equipment and was in a way a sanitary self-defence; but the Act was not very effective until its improvement in 1875. The City of Birmingham was the first to make attempts at "slum clearance" – the demolition of deteriorated slum dwellings and the rehousing of inhabitants – under Joseph Chamberlain, Lord Major of Birmingham from 1873 to 1876. Joseph Chamberlain was a man of great importance in social reform. The example set by Birmingham was later followed by the London County Council and by other municipalities, and such projects were finally supported by the central government.

But it was not until 1909 that slum clearance on a nationwide scale was provided for by the first Housing and Town Planning Act. In accordance with this Act county councils were to set up health and housing committees to deal with slum clearance. The Housing Acts of 1919, 1923-24, 1930 and 1933 amended and extended the earlier legislation. The responsibility for the slum clearance activities run by the local authorities was vested in the new Ministry of Health.

Today the Department of the Environment in England, the Secretaries of State for Scotland and Wales, and the head of the Department of Housing, Local Government and Planning in Northern Ireland determine the general housing policy and supervise the housing programmes of the local authorities. In 1955 the number of slum dwellings unfit for human habitation was estimated to amount to approximately one million. Since that time, however, most of them have been cleared and about 3 million people have been rehoused. In addition to the house building programmes of local authorities the government stimulated the establishment of non-profit-making housing associations and societies by a variety of measures such as the granting of loans for house building projects or the provision of subsidies on loans for this purpose. Nevertheless Shelter – a private organization which cares for the homeless – argues that the measures taken by central and local governments to meet housing problems are still inadequate especially in large indutrial towns like Glasgow, Newcastle upon Tyne, Birmingham and others. It must be considered, however, that the housing problem in Britain is aggravated by the influx of large numbers of immigrants from the Commonwealth countries.

■ A distinction must be made between rural and urban slums in the U.S.A. The spreading of rural slums is closely related to the growing industrialization in agriculture during the past decades *(Agrarian Revolution*)*, which has increased the output per capita to approximately four times that of 1940. As a result employment opportunities for the rural population declined to about one-fourth, with the consequence that there has been an outmigration of young people (approximately 50 per cent. during the last decade) looking for jobs in urban and metropolitan areas. They left behind aged persons unable to earn their own living, which meant a sharp decline in public tax revenue entailing a gradual deterioration of public services such as water supply, sewage facilities, roads, etc. *(Appalachia*.)* Among the worst of the rural slums are those where the agricultural migratory labourers live during the harvest period.

The deterioration of urban central districts is a reflection of the outward movement of the well-to-do to the surburban fringes followed by the inflow of the very poor (often non-white people) into the derelict central districts, sometimes called "inner-cities". They are gradually changing into slums because the private owners are not willing to make capital investment in houses inhabited by non-whites, nor can they afford the enormous cost for redeveloping large tracts of central districts. One of the worst urban slum district is East Harlem located on Manhattan Island at a small distance from Wall Street and the Broadway. In an area of less than 1.5 square miles there live more than 200,000 coloured people. In contrast to those districts which deteriorated in consequence of the outward trend of their former inhabitants, East Harlem was built as a slum district. From its very beginning in 1890, it was designed to house as many immigrants as possible. Most of these immigrants moved away after a short time and only those were left behind who had failed to make headway. After World Wars I and II a great number of Negroes and Puerto Ricans crowded into East Harlem.

There are slums to be found, however, in some other large cities of the United States, such as Chicago, Detroit, San Francisco and others. Under the provisions of the Housing Acts of 1954-68 a great variety if programmes for urban renewal has been developed. Urban renewal programmes are designed to provide "a decent home . . . for every American family". It means that people have to be rehoused if their dwellings are no longer fit for human habitation and that every building of a substandard quality has to be rehabilitated. Federal, state and local governments are all involved in these programmes. But an urban reneval scheme must be approved by the Department of Housing and Urban Development (H.U.D.) in order to be financially assisted out of federal funds.

The Housing and Urban Development Act of 1968 provided for the construction or rehabilitation of 26 million homes during the subsequent decade. Six million of them are to be built to house families with low and moderate incomes. I Fr

Social Security

The principle of public provision for economic security and social welfare of the individual and his family.

● The term refers to a wide range of social services covered by the National Insurance Acts of 1946-70, the Family Allowances Acts of 1945-65, the National Insurance (Industrial Injuries) Act of 1948-75 and the Social Security Acts 1966-1975. War pensions also belong to the body of social security services.

For centuries economic insecurity caused by structural or cyclic unemployment or by individual disability was considered inevitable and little was done to prevent the entire burden falling on individual persons or groups of wage-earners. In England the Poor Law was enacted as early as 1601. Often supplemented and adjusted to changing conditions, it remained the only public provision for the relief of needy or disabled persons up to the 20th century. But apart from the Poor Law a great number of charitable socities were established for the purpose of alleviating the disastrous conditions of the "labouring poor". Largely sponsored by the churches *(Quaker** and *Methodist*),* these voluntary organizations provided schools (see *Statutory System*),* hospitals and other forms of relief, thus pioneering the provision of social services.

Yet it was not until the turn of the 20th century that the idea of public responsibility for social welfare gained momentum. In 1897 the workmen's compensation was established. In 1908 non-contributory old age pensions were introduced in Britain. The same year marked the beginning of unemployment insurance. A contributory health insurance was started in 1912. Between the World Wars the scheme was supplemented and extended to cover an increasing number of people. Nevertheless, there remained gaps to be filled, mostly due to its piecemeal development. It became the task of C.R. Attlee's postwar Labour Administration to co-ordinate the scheme of social services and to extend it to the present comprehensive system.

In contrast to the American system, the rates of contributions and benefits were originally flat-rate and unaffected by the level of previous earnings. In 1961, however, a graduated scheme of contributions and benefits was introduced for retirement pensions. The National Insurance Act of 1966 further improved the system of social services by the introduction of earnings-related supplements to flat-rate contributions and benefits for the first six months of illness, unemployment or widowhood. A further improvement was introduced in 1970, when pensions were provided for people who were above pensionable age (65) when the scheme started and for widows between 40 and 50 years of age.

Approximately 45 per cent. of the total contributions are derived from the employers and the persons insured, while the remaining part is covered by the Exchequer. Family allowances are provided for children other than the first child by the Family Allowances Act of 1965. In August 1971, Family Income Supplement was introduced for families and single persons with children if the family's weekly income was below a certain level.

The National Assistance Act of 1948, which abolished the Poor Law, secured additional grants from central and local government funds for people still in need. The scheme was replaced by the provision of supplementary benefits under the Social Security Act of 1966. The benefits are determined by the Supplementary Benefits Commission which was established within the then

Ministry of Social Security (today Department of Health and Social Security). The structure of the Social Security system was changed by the Social Security Acts 1973-1975. The Act of 1973, still passed under the then Conservative Government, considerably increased (up to 29 per cent.) all kinds of benefits (sickness, retirement, unemployment) and also raised allowances for widowed mothers and for attendance of severely disabled or chronically diseased persons. Social Security provision was extended to further groups of disabled people by the Social Security Benefits Act 1975.

The pension system above all was concerned in the Act of 1973. As before, the pension scheme consisted of two components: a flat-rate basic pension similar to that already existing and an additional pension which should no longer be graduated but fully earnings-related (contributions and benefits fixed at a percentage of salaries or previous salaries respectively). The Act was planned to come into force in April 1975. In the meantime (March 1974) the Labour Party came into power. The Labour Government accepted the basic provisions of the 1973 Act with some alterations and supplementary regulations which were authorized by the Social Security Act 1975 (now the principal Act).

In September 1974 the Labour Government had published a White Paper "Better Pensions fully protected against inflation". In view of the British inflation rate – higher than that of other European countries – the promised protection against inflation was of special importance. It was introduced by the Social Securities Pension Act 1975.

To realize the new supplementary fully earnings-related pension scheme for retirement, widowhood and invalidity many preparations had to be made for which time was needed. The replacement of the old graduated scheme by the new earnings-related pension scheme is to become effective in April 1978. It should be mentioned that contributions to national insurance are now collected by the "pay as you earn" system (PAYE), i.e., they are deducted at source. Furthermore, it may be of interest, that, as already provided by the 1973 Act, employers now have to contribute a larger share to the cost of national insurance than the employees.

As Britain is a member of the European community, the Community's Regulations on social security are valid for foreigners from EEC-countries working in Britain as well as for British nationals working in any other member state of the Community. Both of them are entitled to benefits under the social security system of the EEC country in which they are employed. The social security services are administered by the Department of Health and Social Security in Great Britain and by the Ministry of Health and Social Security in Northern Ireland.

■ In the United States today the term social security comprises among others the following programmes mostly carried through by combined action of the Federal Government and the various States:

(1)Retirement insurance
(2)Survivors insurance
(3)Disability insurance
(4)Hospital and medical insurance for the aged (medicare) disabled and persons still in need (medicaid) *(Health Service*)*
(5)Unemployment insurance
(6)Public assistance (including medical assistance and family services)
(7)Services of maternal and child health and child welfare.

In the United States public aid to people in need was first provided under the Poor Laws which the early English settlers adopted from the motherland. As time went by, the individual States began to outline emergency programmes for some groups of needy persons such as the blind, the aged, etc. But the first comprehensive body of legislation for social security was enacted only under the second *New Deal** of the Franklin D. Roosevelt Administration. It was a turning point because the Federal Government was taking responsibility for the social and economic security of its citizens for the first time. Social insurance membership and contributions were made compulsory. The Social Security Act of 1935 established a federal social insurance for the elderly and surviving dependants and provided for a co-operative Federal-State system of unemployment compensation. With regard to the constitutionality of such insurance plans the Supreme Court declared old-age and survivors insurance to belong to the federal government affairs; the States, however, should be free to establish unemployment insurance programmes of their own. In order to finance unemployment insurance the Social Security Act introduced a federal tax on the employers' payrolls which could be offset, within certain limits, by payments of the employers to an approved state unemployment fund. This provision soon induced the States to set up and administer their own unemployment insurance systems. Today there are unemployment insurance plans in all States.

The federal insurance for the aged and survivors, as established by the Social Security Act, was extended by several amendments to cover an increasing number of gainfully employed persons and to include disability of the insured. Since 1963 a comprehensive federal system has embraced old-age, survivors, and disability insurance (O.A.S.D.I. now Retirement, Survivors and Disability Insurance). It is financed by contributions paid by employers, employees and the self-employed, the money being deposited in trust funds which are administered by the Secretaries of Health, Education and Welfare, of Labor, and the Treasury. The whole system is the responsibility of the federal Social Security Administration (S.S.A.), which is a division of the Department of Health, Education and Welfare. In 1973, the federal Government took over the responsibility for the welfare of the needy aged, the blind and the disabled; a supplemental security income (S.S.I.) can be granted to the group of persons concerned.

Despite a few fundamental principles which the British and the American systems have in common, there are a number of important differences between the two schemes of social security:

(1) There is no public insurance against sickness in the United States with the exception of the "medicare" for elderly persons *(Health Service*)* introduced in 1965;
(2) Since unemployment insurance is not federal in character there are great differences in the amount of compensation and in the duration of payments among the individual States;
(3) Unemployment insurance is financed wholly from employers' taxes which are levied on the employer's total payroll, except in Alaska, Alabama and New Jersey, where employees have to contribute.
(4) Retirement, Survivors and Disability Insurance is financed without government grants by contributions (taxes) in relation to earnings. The taxes are paid in equal portions by the worker and his employer.

(5) Benefits which the insured persons receive are always related to their prior earnings.
(6) Benefits which the insured persons receive are sufficient to prevent destitution, but make additional income necessary such as savings, private insurance, home-ownership, and the like. For the most part, benefits replace only a portion of lost income. Today, retirement survivors and disability insurance covers not only wage earners but alomost all self-employed people.
(7) Non-governmental social security through voluntary private organizations has always played an important role in American social life. These charitable, non-profit-making organizations are often promoted by denominations *(Quaker, Methodist, Unitarian*)*, or rely upon funds from large foundations. They mostly work in close co-operation with governmental welfare services.

The non-governmental insurance plans sponsored by employers, employees and the unions are still to be mentioned as so-called "Employee-benefit plans", sometimes also referred to as "group plans". They provide for supplementary insurance in cases of retirement, death, sickness, and unemployment, the combined benefits of which often amount to approximately 50 per cent. of the worker's earnings. Since 1959 employee-benefit plans have to be registered with the U.S. Department of Labor.

On the whole, the social security system in the U.S.A. is not supposed to take the only responsibility for a person's security from "the cradle to the grave", but mainly to serve as a basis upon which persons may build, by their own efforts, the kind and amount of security they want. I Fr

Sterling

- Sterling:originally perhaps steorling "coin with a star", some of the early Norman pennies having on them a small star. The English silver penny of the Norman and subsequent dynasties. Often in "pound of sterlings", orig. a pound weight of silver pennies, afterwards a name for te English pound (240 pence) as a money of account. Money of the quality of the sterling or standard silver penny; genuine English money. 1565 English money as dist. from foreign money. Formerly often in contrast to "currency", i.e. the depreciated pounds, shillings, and pence of certain colonies.

Sterling is the monetary unit in the United Kingdom as well as in the Sterling Area. Together with the U.S. *Dollar**, sterling is a medium of reserve and settlement in many countries of the world, i.e. it is one of the two key reserve currencies.

The pound sterling was subdivided into 20 shillings, one shilling containing 12 pence. The abbreviations were derived from Latin; £ stands for "libra" (= pound); s. (for shilling) is the abbreviation of "solidus", an old Roman gold coin, and d. (for penny, pence) is derived from 'denarius", the principal silver coin in acient Rome. Since February 15th, 1971, the unit of currency has been the new pound sterling which is divided into 100 new pence. *(Legal Tender*.)*

In early times "sterling" was used to denote silver having the same degree of purity as the penny. Later it came to mean "of standard quality". When applied to character, principles, qualities, or persons, "sterling" means "thoroughly excellent, capable of standing every test".

The dominating position of sterling as a world currency – especially until World War I, but also after it – can be attributed to several factors: Its unrestricted convertibility - as reinforced by the Bank Charter Act of 1844 – accounted for the world-wide acceptability of sterling. Furthermore, there was London's importance as an international financial centre, which was based to a large extent on the expert knowledge of British bankers, particularly that of the *Merchant Bankers** and of the *Discount Houses**. Business throughout the world found it most convenient and least expensive to finance their foreign trade in London, which, of course, implied that invoicing and settling were done in sterling. This created what may be called the sterling system. In fact, still today about one-third of the world's trade is conducted in terms of sterling. The growth of the Commonwealth was another factor contributing to the extensive use of sterling in trade and also as a currency for investment.

Until 1914 Great Britain was on a full gold standard, i.e. gold coins were in circulation and bank-notes could be exchanged for gold coins on demand. By 1914 the fiduciary issue which had originally been limited to £ 14 million by the Bank Character Act of 1844, had risen to over £ 18 million. Fears that the *Bank of England** might be deprived of its gold led to the Currency and Bank Notes Act passed on August 6th, 1914, which authorized the Treasury to issue Currency Notes of £ 1 and 10s. without any limit and without gold backing. These were *Legal Tender** and like Bank of England notes, they were convertible into gold on demand. In this respect, therefore, Britain was theoretically still on the gold standard. However, by appealing to the loyalty of the people, the government was gradually able to stop the habit of converting bank-notes into gold-coins. Gold coins were replaced by bank-notes and Currency Notes. Furthermore, under wartime conditions, no gold was to be exported – except under special licence, and thus one of the characteristics of the gold standard, viz. the free movement of gold into and out of a country, was lacking. The Currency and Bank Notes Act of 1928 discontinued the issue of Currency Notes by the Treasury and transferred it to the Bank of England. This Act also set a new limit for the fiduciary issue.

From April 1925, (Gold Standard Act) until September 1931 (Gold Standard Amendment Act) Great Britain was on the gold bullion standard, the central bank being required to convert bank-notes into gold in the form of bullion instead of into gold coins. It is another tribute to the quality of sterling that during these years a number of countries, notably the Commonwealth countries and the Scandinavian countries, fixed their currencies at a parity in relation to sterling rather than to gold. This meant that their central banks would exchange the currency of the country not for gold but for sterling. These countries were then said to be on the Gold Exchange Standard. It implied that their central banks had to keep large reserves of sterling.

After the Wall Street crash of 1929, the United Kingdom suffered as did other countries. Unemployment, a budgetary deficit, and a number of other factors resulted in the abandonment of the gold standard (Gold Standard Amendment Act, September, 1931). However, even after Great Britain had left the gold standard, a number of countries, above all the Commonwealth countries (except Canada) and the Scandinavian countries, decided to make their currencies convertible into sterling. This resulted in the formation of the Sterling Bloc. It was a loose association of countries which made their currencies and monetary policies dependent on Great Britain. The Sterling

Bloc was renamed the Sterling Area in 1939. World War II made a certain amount of exchange control and special regulations necessary for the Sterling Area countries.

Between 1931 and 1939 the pound sterling had been floating freely against gold and the dollar; in 1939 a new parity was fixed at $ 4.03.

During the Second World War international trade was very much restricted. But as exports to Great Britain were protected by British convoys, many countries preferred to export to the United Kingdom for credit rather than have no outlet at all. Thus, at the end of the war, a great sterling debt had accrued. Furthermore, it was not only invisible earnings from shipping that had shrunk *(Shipping*)*, but also invisible receipts in the form of capital interest, since £ 1,000 million of overseas investments had to be sold, almost half of them to North America. This meant a great strain on Britain's *Balance of Payments**.

In 1947 the U.S.A. granted the United Kingdom a very generous loan under the United States Loan Agreement. This agreement re-established convertibility; however, it proved a failure, and sterling had to be dealt with in more or less the same way as before.

Apart from the sterling held by resisdents of the United Kingdom, certain other categories of sterling emerged during the post-war years, for instance "Sterling Area sterling", "sterling in American accounts", "transferable account sterling", "security sterling", etc., the difference consisting mainly in the regulations governing the extent of their convertibility or transferability.

One of the means by which exports were to be boosted after the war was the devulation of the pound sterling in 1949 from $ 4.03 to $ 2.80. This may be regarded as an overdevaluation with respect to exports; however, the authorities wanted to stop speculation against the pound by this measure. Some British economists are of the opinion that it was all too drastic and, perhaps, also untimely.

From 1945 until 1955 there had been something like a "black" market for inconvertible sterling, and it was quite obvious that in the long run such blackmarketeering was bound to be detrimental to British currency. Already in 1952 it had been agreed at a meeting of Commonwealth Finance Ministers that efforts had to be made to make sterling convertible again.

In February, 1955, the Bank of England finally intervened in the black market. Certain black-market practices were stopped, and although there still remained a discount of up to 1 per cent. on the transferable sterling, this step meant the de facto return to convertibility. In December, 1958, the discount on transferable sterling was abolished and full sterling convertibility was restored. Strictly speaking these two steps were unilateral since theoretically they could have been reversed by the British authorities although this was, of course, very unlikely. The last step, which was formally binding, was taken in 1961 when the British authorities accepted the obligations of Article 8 of the International Monetary Fund.

Since 1961 there have been recurrent sterling crises. In the autumn of 1964 the danger of devaluation was avoided by a great credit action; the central banks of over ten nations made $ 3,000 million available in order to support the pound. But it did not take long for sterling to come under pressure again. Insufficient competitiveness of British industry in the international market caused a deterioration of the balance of trade. High expenditure abroad, especially for military purposes, and short-term borrowing abroad increased. The long-lasting strike of dock workers in 1967 added to the fatal development.

By the second half of 1967 the Bank of England had to intervene increasingly on the foreign exchange market in order to support sterling and when in October 1967, the Board of Trade announced that the trade deficit amounted to £ 107 million it was obvious that the balance of payments continued to show a heavy deficit. Now a devaluation of the pound sterling became inevitable. On November 18th, 1967, sterling was devalued by 14.3 per cent.; i.e. the exchange rate of the pound against the U.S. dollar was lowered from $ 2.80 to $ 2.40. In December, 1971, however, the devaluation of the *dollar** and the subsequent realignment of exchange rates caused a revaluation of the pound sterling by 8.5 per cent. against the dollar.

Contrary to all expectations sterling came under pressure again in June 1972. On June 23rd, 1972, the British Government decided to float the pound, i.e. to halt, for the time being, interventions in the foreign exchange markets in order to support sterling.

Over the years the problem connected with the role of sterling as a reserve currency has increasingly gathered momentum. As has long been the custom many countries, especially former Commonwealth countries, hold their official reserves in sterling with the Bank of England. In September 1976 total non-resident official sterling holdings amounted to about $ 3,800 million. It is obvious that an abrupt withdrawal of these sterling holdings must be detrimental to the British balance of payments and would result in a heavy decline of sterling's external value. Such serious consequences became evident above all in 1976, when renewed pressure on sterling was mainly due to considerable fluctuations in non-resident official sterling holdings.

In order to ensure that sterling ceases to be affected by pressures associated with any rundown of official sterling holdings, an agreement was reached at a meeting of Central Bank Governors in Basle in January 1977. It provides for a new credit facility amounting to $ 3,000 million which enables the British Government to achieve an orderly reduction in the role of sterling as a reserve currency. Now the Government is prepared to offer official holders the option of converting their sterling holdings into negotiable medium-term foreign currency bonds to be issued by the Government on market-related terms. The new credit facility aimed at stabilizing the exchange rate of sterling is operated by the Bank for International Settlements (BIS) with the support of central bankers in Austria, Belgium, Canada, Denmark, the Federal Republic of Germany, Japan, the Netherlands, Norway, Sweden, Switzerland, and the United States. I Fr/H St

Trade (Labor) Unions

Trade Unions: (Br.) An association of workers in any trade or in allied trades (trade usu. applied to skilled handicraft as distinct from professional or mercantile occupation on the one hand and from unskilled labour on the other) for the protection and furtherance of their interests in regard to wages, hours and working conditions. 1831. Labor Unions: (Amer.) An organization of workers formed for the purpose of advancing its members' interests in respect to wages and working conditions.

● Although in the 17th and 18th centuries there were already small local trade societies among skilled workers such as carpenters, joiners, etc., a trend to form unions on a larger scale did not appear until the *Industrial Revolution**. The factory system had so much weakened the position of the individual worker in dealing with his employer that only group action could succeed in ameliorating the worker's standard of living. But the "right to organize and bargain collectively" obtained legal recognition only after a long period of bitter conflicts *(Collective Bargaining*)*. The Combinations Act of 1799-1800 declared all trade combinations illegal. Regarding trade unions as conspiracies, the Act reflected the fears of revolutionary movements raised by the French Revolution of 1789. The Combinations Act, it is true, was repealed in 1824, but the legal status of the trade unions remained uncertain. In fact, they were allowed to exist but many restrictions were imposed on their activities.

During the period of the Reform Acts the workers gradually succeeded in improving their conditions. The First Reform Act of 1832 left them disfranchised, which induced them to express their dissatisfaction in the People's Charter of 1838 *(Suffrage*)*. The Second Reform Act of 1867 enfranchised a large number of urban workers and in 1874, for the first time, two miners were elected M.P.s. But the real turning point in the history of British trade unionism came with the Trade Union Act of 1871 which brought about the legal recognition of the trade unions and provisions for regulating strikes and picketing. In the subsequent years (especially after the London dock strike of 1889 had ended in favour of the dockers) the trade unions made large gains in membership. In 1886 the Trades Union Congress (T.U.C.) was founded in Manchester as a central federation of all British trade unions.

From the beginning British trade unions had been engaged in political action. It was therefore largely due to the unions' activities that in 1906 the *Labour Party** was created, which in turn led to an increase of the unions' political and economic power. In the case of W. V. Osborne *v.* Amalgamated Railway Servants (1901) the House of Lords, however, decided that the unions were not allowed to take political action. This decision was reversed under the terms of the Second Trade Union Act of 1913 but the political action was restricted by a provision that gave objectors among unionists the right to vote against a political action ("contracting out").

Since during World War I official trade union activity was restricted under the Munitions of War Act of 1915 *(Collective Bargaining*)*, the shop stewards were able to increase their unofficial influence in the workshop. They often claimed control of the workers in industry (shop stewards' movement). The Great Depression of the 1930s greatly weakened the unions' position. In 1945, however, with the Labour Party coming into power, the unions greatly increased their membership as well as their political and economic influence.

At the end of 1976 there were 462 trade unions in Britain, with approximately 12,4 million members. The relatively large number of unions is accounted for by the fact that British trade unions are, to a large extent, based on the craft principle, the qualification for membership being occupational rather than industrial, while industrial unions in Germany and in the United States, etc., comprise all persons employed in an industry whatever their occupation. *(Collective Bargaining*.)* To avoid competition among British Unions and to prevent them from poaching members from each other, the Bridlington Agreement was embodied in a resolution passed by the Trades Union Congress in 1939.

■ The labor union movement in the United States resulted mainly from the rapid industrialization following the Civil War *(Industrial Revolution*)*. But for a long time the development of the labor unions was hampered by the consequences of *Immigration** which provided cheap labour from the masses of immigrants ready to work under any conditions. The first important labour organization on a national basis was the "Noble Order of the Knights of Labor" founded originally as a secret union in 1869. By 1886 the number of members already amounted to 1,000,000. Nevertheless, the Order was not able to serve the workers' interest well owing to its ambitious but incoherent political and economic programme. This programme was a result of its heterogeneous composition, members being not only skilled and unskilled workers but also professional men and small businessmen. In 1886 the American Federation of Labor (A.F.L.) was established as a federation of approximately 100 national and international unions which were autonomous with regard to their internal affairs. The A.F.L. had no political programme of its own and was strictly non-partisan. Apart from the A.F.L. there were a large number of independent unions, the most important of them being the railroad brotherhoods comprising approximately 500,000 railroad workers of all kinds.

Since the A.F.L. was organized on the craft (or trade) principle, a serious problem arose from the increasing number of unskilled labourers employed in mass production. During the 1930s the demand for organization on an industrial basis became pressing and resulted in a controversy between the craft unionists and the adherents of the industrial principle among the members of the A.F.L. Ultimately the industrial unionists formed the Committee for Industrial Organization "to encourage and promote industrial union organizations of the workers in mass production ...". Since the A.F.L. executive council refused every compromise, the C.I.O. was, in 1938, transformed into an independent federation known as the Congress of Industrial Organizations (C.I.O.). The dispute about the two principles – the craft (or trade) principle represented by A.F.L. and the industrial principle represented by C.I.O. – went on for nearly two decades. During this time, however, mass production and the number of unskilled workers continued to increase. In the end the American Federation of Labor found itself obliged to organize workers on an industrial basis. In 1955 a merger between the two organizations was accomplished. The new federation was named A.F.L.-C.I.O.

On the whole 19,4 million employees are members of American labor unions which means that only about 25 per cent. of the working population are organized in labor unions – an astonishing fact in a highly industrialized country like the United States.

U.S. labour played a major part in the creation of the International Confederation of Free Trade Unions (I.C.F.T.U.), established in 1949 to ensure "collaboration between the free and democratic trade union movements throughout the world". I Fr

Treasury

- The Treasury is a government *Department** whose central function is to prepare the annual budget, to present the Estimates to the House of Commons and to make proposals for balancing revenue and expenditure. Formally the Treasury is headed by the Board of the Treasury which consists of the Lords Commissioners. The Board, however, is no longer of importance. Today the effective head of the Treasury is the Chancellor of the Exchequer who is also called the Second Lord of the Treasury. The first Lord of the Treasury is always the Prime Minister – a fact which emphasizes the Treasury's position of supreme importance. The Treasury enjoys special prestige and is traditionally "first among equals" in Whitehall, the Chancellor being the highest paid civil servant. By virtue of a Minute of 1919 the senior Joint Permanent Secretary to the Treasury *(Civil Service*)* is the official head of the civil servants. A number of departments such as the Royal Mint, the National Debt Office and the Public Works Board are also the responsibility of Treasury ministers. With the exception of the period between 1940 and 1943 the Chancellor of the Exchequer has invariably been a member of the *Cabinet**. The predominant position of the Treasury can be ascribed to the fact that it "controls" all government expenditure. It can cut expenditure down by scrutiny of the Estimates submitted by government departments for the annual budget. Moreover it can keep an indirect check on departmental expenditure through the Exchequer account also known as Consolidated Fund held by the Treasury at the Bank of England, into which and from which all Government moneys flow. Money granted by Parliament through annual appropriation acts or statutory grants is transferred (in such sums as may be required from day to day) from the Consolidated Fund to the Paymaster General's account at the Bank of England. Government departments make their payments by drawing payable orders on the latter's account.

The Treasury has to share its responsibility with other authorities of economic importance – for instance the Bank of England which for centuries has played a significant role in monetary policy. The relationship of the Treasury with the Bank of England can be understood only against the background of long accepted, though undefined traditions which for long have allowed the Treasury to take the lead in the wider issues of economic policies. Until 1932 the Bank was still independent of the Treasury to a considerable extent. In 1932 the Government abandoned the gold standard and set up the Exchange Equalization Account as part of the Treasury. Since then the Bank has operated this account as an "agent" of the Treasury, this giving the Treasury a right to participate in foreign exchange policy and requiring constant consultations between the Governor of the Bank and the Chancellor in matters of external monetary policy *(Bank of England*)*. The year 1946, after Labour had gained power the previous year, saw the *Nationalization** of the Bank of England. The Bank of England Act of 1946 made it clear that the Treasury from that time onward should have not only a traditional but also a statutory right to give directions to the Bank as well as to the clearing banks. Chapter 27, Section 4(1) of the Act stated: "The Treasury may from time to time give such directions to the Bank as, after consultation with the Governor of the Bank, they think necessary in the public interest" and the Bank may "if authorized by the Treasury issue directions to any banker . . .".

The Bank's relationship with the Treasury was, among other matters the subject of long and serious discussions within the "Committee on the Working of the Monetary System" under the chairmanship of Lord Radcliffe. The committee submitted its Report (Radcliffe Report) to Parliament in 1959. It suggested that the power of the Treasury to give directions should be exercised only – to use a common phrase – "in the last resort" and that "subject to any such directions" the "affairs of the Bank" (comprising the fixing of Bank Rate, the management of the money market and the Note Issue Department's portfolio) should be managed under "first" or "direct" responsibility of the Court which consists of the Governor of the Bank, a Deputy Governor and sixteen directors. Other activities such as the management of the Exchange Equalization Account were considered purely "agency" functions. As can be seen from the Minutes of Evidence on which the Report was based some witnesses were of opinion that the central note-issuing bank should be completely independent of political influence as is the case with the American Federal Reserve System; yet the members of the committee dissociated themselves from this view. They even suggested that the Bank Rate should be announced in the name of the Chancellor and not of the Governor in order to make it clear that the final responsibility lies with the Treasury; this suggestion, however, was not implemented.

After the Department of Economic Affairs had been dissolved in 1968, the Treasury partly assumed the responsibilities of the former Department of Economic Affairs. Now the Treasury is the leading department for the framing of overall economic policy based on short-term and medium-term economic forecast. These forecasts are prepared by the National Economy Group which is a division of the Treasury. In order to set up targets for economic growth, the National Economic Development Council was established in 1961 as an independent advisory body.

■ The American Department of the Treasury has no authority - neither by law nor by tradition – to interfere with the activities of the Federal Reserve System. The Department was created by Act of Congress in 1789. Its main function is to superintend and manage the national finances. The Department is headed by the Secretary of the Treasury. Revisions and amendments of the Act of 1789 have broadened the scope of the Treasury Department, now embracing a number of diversified bureaux and offices such as the Coast Guard, the Bureau of Narcotics, and the Secret Service. The Department also controls the coinage and printing of money. Among other functions, the Secretary of the Treasury is U.S. Governor of the International Monetary Fund (I.M.F.). The Federal Reserve System is by law independent of the Treasury. According to the Federal Reserve Act of 1913 *(Federal Reserve System*)* the Board of Governors has the authority to determine general monetary, credit and open market policies and to influence credit conditions within statutory limitations.

The independence of the Federal Reserve Board of political influence becomes obvious when the Board raises the rediscount rate against opposition from the Administration. The Federal Reserve Board can openly contradict the Administration and this has the final word in credit policy. I Fr

Trust

■ Derived from the term "trusteeship" meaning in law: a property held by one person for the benefit of another; a body of persons appointed as trustees; something committed to the charge of trustees, hence "trust funds"; in commerce: a combination of companies with a central governing body of trustees which hold a majority of the whole of the stock of each of the combining firms, thus controlling each.

The term "trust" in the commercial sense was used for the first time for the Standard Oil Company when it combined under its control most of the oil refineries in the United States (1879). The combined firms ceded their stock to the trustees of Standard Oil and received so-called "trust certificates" in exchange, these entitling them to proportional shares of the profit. In this way Standard Oil, which then controlled approximately 90 per cent of the refining capacity of the country, achieved a monopoly by the elimination of competition.

The unfair price manipulations of the early trusts (for railroad consolidations see *Interstate Commerce*),* which resulted in monopoly prices and consumer exploitation soon aroused public disapproval, and the term "trust" came to be popularly used as a synonym for a monopoly of any kind.

In the eighties public opposition against the trusts had already led many States to introduce measures restricting monopolistic policies. These State regulations, however, failed to solve the interstate problem of monopolies because they were limited to trust activities within the boundaries of the individual State *(Interstate Commerce*).* That is why the Federal Government passed the Sherman Antitrust Act in 1890 in accordance with Article I, Section 8, of the *Constitution**. It declared the trust to be an illegal extension of the trusteeship and prohibited "every contract, combination in the form of trust or otherwise, . . . in restraint of trade or commerce among the several states". Furthermore, "every person who shall monopolize any part of trade or commerce between the several states" should be deemed guilty. (As to the question whether the provisions were applicable to labour organizations, which partly resorted to monopolistic pactices see *Collective Bargaining*.)*

Despite the Sherman Antitrust Act the trend towards capital concentration and intercorporate affiliations increased under different forms and types, the most important being:

(a) cartels, first developed in Germany for the purpose of regulating prices and marketing conditions between legally independent business organizations;
(b) holding companies established to hold sufficient capital stock of some other corporation to control the latter's affairs;
(c) mergers intended to purchase all of the capital stock of some other corporation for the purpose of absorbing the latter;
(d) pools established to combine independent business units for some specific and often temporary purpose (mainly profit or patent pooling, etc.).

A common feature of all these different forms of combination (in the U.S.A. sometimes called consolidations, especially in the case of railroad combinations) is that they are formed for the purpose of restricting or eliminating competition. The most important reason for the "combination movement" is that mass production for mass consumption in a modern industrial society needs an enormous capital accumulation, especially for research and development. Combinations, therefore, are usually far ahead of smaller organizations in technological progress thus being able to reduce the cost of production further than smaller firms.

In 1901 the American combination movement culminated in the foundation of the U.S. Steel Corporation. Recognizing that capital concentration can play a constructive role in economic progress, the then President Theodore Roosevelt (1901-09) recommended legislation for the purpose of abolishing the abuses of combinations without destroying the combinations themselves. This recommendation stressed the performance criterion instead of the structural criterion by arguing that economic power embodied in a combination or in a single giant corporation is not in itself bad as long as it is not abused.

In subsequent years the public attitude towards business combinations often varied in accordance with the particular competitive situation of the industry concerned. In 1914 the Clayton Antitrust Act supplemented and strengthened the Sherman Act by prohibiting both price discriminations which tended to create a monopoly, and interlocking directorates for two or more companies capitalized at $ one million or more. At the same time the Clayton Act declared labour organizations not to be illegal under Federal jurisdiction *(Collective Bargaining*)*. In contrast to the antitrust legislation the Transportation Act of 1920 even recommended railroad consolidations previously prohibited under the Sherman Act. This change in attitude towards railroad consolidations was obviously caused by the severe competition from truck and bus services which the railroads suffered. It was obvious that consolidations could compete more effectively than individual railroad companies *(Rail and Road*)*.

In 1937 resale price maintenance was permitted in interstate commerce under the Miller-Tydings Act if such agreements were lawful in the individual States. The Sherman Act of 1890 had declared resale price contracts to be illegal.

After World War II the growing number of mergers raised new problems and led to the Anti-Merger Act passed by Congress in 1950.

The discussion for and against combinations, however, has not come to an end. For the trend to economic concentration – so characteristic for the period of late capitalism – has increased since the sixties to an unprecedented degree. It is not only a matter of the horizontal combinations of firms engaged in the same business activities and the vertical combinations covering the production process from raw materials to the final commodity but more recently also of combinations of firms engaged in totally diverse business activities; the latter combinations are called "conglomerates". Examples are: Procter and Gamble, Ling-Temco-Vought, Inc (L.T.V.) and the International Telephone and Telegraph Company (I.T.T.). There have been strong controversies between the antitrust authorities (i.e. the Antitrust-Division of the Department of Justice and the Federal Trade Commission (F.T.C.) on the one hand and the management of the industries concerned on the other which might lead to a revision of the antitrust legislation in future.

For monopoly restriction in Britain see *Restrictive Trade Practices** I Fr

War on Poverty

■ The term "War on Poverty" usually refers to the programme which was initiated by John F. Kennedy and first realized by President Johnson in 1964, although there had been efforts to overcome the disastrous consequences of poverty long before. The President's programme – embodied in the Economic Opportunity Act popularly known as the Anti-Poverty Act – was presented to *Congress** in March 1964 and passed by Congress on August 20th, 1964.

Whether or not in any particular case "the quality or condition of being poor" exists, depends on the standards by which poverty is measured. Therefore the term "poverty" calls for a definition. According to the definition of the Office of Economic Opportunity (O.E.O.) established in 1965 persons were regarded as poor if their incomes were below the poverty line. The poverty lines were different for farm- and non-farm families and were to be redefined each year. In 1969 the poverty line for a family of four was about $ 3,700 per year. In the same year there were 24,289 million Americans whose incomes were below the official poverty line. Contrary to the general opinion the majority of the poor were white.

In former times – even in the 20th century – poverty was considered inevitable and even necessary for economic progress, this notion being contained, for instance, in the economic theories of David Ricardo (1772-1823) and Thomas Robert Malthus (1766-1834). To alleviate the fate of the poor was considered a private and charitable concern and not one of the responsibilities of public administration. In the U.S.A. the change came during the Great Depression of the 1930s when both Federal and State Governments were confronted with a problem of mass unemployment previously unknown on such a scale. At that time it was realized that the guaranteeing of a minimum subsistence to the poor (especially the unemployed, the aged, the sick and the dependent; see *New Deal*)* is not a private but a national task. Thanks to the New Deal measures the problem of poverty is no longer one of dire need, but the problem of a minority who for reasons beyond their control are unable to fully participate in economic progress and prosperity. The reasons may be manifold, e.g. changes of the economic structure by unfavourable location and limitations in mobility *(Appalachia*)*, etc. But one of the major reasons for this new kind of poverty is poor education and no vocational training. The demand for unskilled labour is shrinking so that under-educated children of poverty-stricken families have only a slight chance of getting jobs. In order to help them to escape the "vicious circle of poverty" which breeds poverty anew from generation to generation, better education and vocational training are necessary. This was provided by the Economic Opportunity Act of 1964 as follows:

(1) A National Job Corps with training centres in cities and conservation camps in rural districts was designed to take up school dropouts and young persons of 16-21 years of age who were out of work and to teach them vocational skills, basic work habits and the responsibilities of citizenship. The idea of the Job Corps goes back to the Civilian Conservation Corps of the Great Depression *(New Deal*)*.
(2) A work-training programme provided part-time jobs for needy high-school and college students to help them to complete their studies.
(3) Local community-action programmes, the cost of which was borne by the federal authorities up to 90 per cent., were intended to educate illiterate adults, particularly migratory agricultural labourers, and to improve living conditions by health and social services, especially in poverty pockets.
(4) The Volunteers in Service to America (Vista) – also called Domestic Peace Corps – were to work on public services in America itself as does the American Peace Corps in developing countries overseas.

Enrolment and participation in all these programmes were completely voluntary.

In early 1973, the then President, Richard M. Nixon tried to abolish the OEO by cutting off funds in the federal budget for the fiscal year 1974 (beginning July 1) allocated to the Office and its major programme, i.e., the aid for local community action. At that time, the dismantling of the OEO and its basic anti-poverty programme was halted. With some programmes expiring, however, the future of the OEO remained uncertain. But the need for poverty programmes became still more pressing as unemployment rates and cost of living were increasing. Therefore, in 1975, the programmes of the OEO were continued and even extended. But the Office of Economic Opportunity itself was replaced by the Community Services Administration within the Health, Education and Welfare Department. This department has now the responsibility for a wide range of poverty programmes, e.g., community food and nutrition assistance, development and repair of housing for lower income families, senior opportunities and services programmes for the aged poor etc. Assistance for migratory labor, job training and work experience programmes, however, were transferred to the Department of Labor.

In addition to the anti-poverty programmes formerly under the responsibility of the OEO, there are further benefits which needy Americans can receive under existing legislation. First of all, the Aid to Families with Dependent Children (AFDC) is worth mentioning as an attempt to help dependent children if the male wage-earner is no longer with the family. AFDC is administered at State level with federal assistance. A few states provide aid even if the father is still living with the family. Another welfare programme for the very poor was introduced in 1968. It consists of food stamps which are to help the poor to get food at a lower cost than usual.

In 1977, President Carter presented a new welfare reform package to Congress. It is called "Better Jobs and Incomes". According to the President it is intended to provide jobs for those who need work, and fairer and more uniform cash benefits for those who are not required to work. Furthermore, the programme should promote family stability and reduce the financial burden of the States for welfare activities by about 10 per cent. One of the most difficult problem seems to be the creation of jobs. For this purpose about $ 30 billion is to be spent out of government funds for creating 1,4 million public service jobs. A still more interesting aspect of the Carter programme is the proposal to do away with AFDC, food stamps and SSI *(Social Security*)* and to replace them by one flat cash benefit paid to families eligible under the proposals. In this way the vast and very complex welfare system of the U.S.A. could possibly be simplified and, perhaps, even the cost of administration reduced. I Fr

Welfare State

● A social system based upon the assumption by a political state of primary responsibility for the individual and social welfare of its citizens.

Social welfare as the main concern of the so-called welfare state is in the first place designed to protect the individual against hazards such as unemployment, accident, illness, old age. Moreover, it comprises social or public assistance for persons in need of special care such as children, mothers, handicapped persons, etc. But the term "social welfare" is also broad enough to include services such as housing, public health service, education, and the provision of employment. In this broad sense of the word economic policies designed to secure full employment belong to a social welfare scheme as do educational services intended to give "equality of opportunity" for all young people. The term welfare state has been primarily applied to the body of social legislation enacted by the first post-war Labour Government (1945-51). This usage, however, is somewhat misleading. For the main social services were not an emanation of socialist ideas but rooted in the legislation enacted between 1906 and 1914 by the then Liberal Government *(Social Security*)*. During the years immediately following World War I, the scope of the compulsory social insurance scheme covering health and unemployment was gradually extended and so was the non-contributory old-age pension which had been introduced as early as 1908. By 1920 unemployment insurance already covered most employees. The great educational reform, which provided "secondary education for all", was initiated in 1944 when Britain was ruled by a coalition government *(Secondary Education*)*.

In 1942 Sir William (later Lord) Beveridge, Liberal member of Parliament and Chairman of the Unemployment Insurance Fund, outlined the principles of a comprehensive social security system designed to care for the aged, the sick, the disabled, and the unemployed and to combat the five "giants" (want, disease, ignorance, squalor, and idleness). It aimed at providing "a job when you can work and an income when you can't". For in accordance with the Beveridge Report "Social security means security of income up to a minimum but the provision of income should be associated with the treatment designed to bring the interruption of earnings to an end as soon as possible." By providing for the maintenance of a minimum demand for consumer goods the social security system was simultaneously intended to function as a kind of "built-in stabilizer" in case of economic depression. 3

After the war the Labour Government adopted the Beveridge principles, which also included a national health service. The latter was embodied as a new contribution to the social security scheme under the National Health Service Act of 1946 *(Health Service*)*. Apart from this innovation, the social legislation after 1945 was mainly designed to co-ordinate, supplement, and universalize the social services already in existence, thus providing a comprehensive system of social security.

One consequence of the war with which the Labour Government was confronted was a great housing shortage requiring a government-subsidized campaign for house building. More than seven million have been built since World War II by local authorities under the supervision of the Ministry of Housing and Local Government (now Department of the Environment) in England and Wales, the secretary of State in Scotland, or the head of the Department of Housing, Local Government and Planning in Northern Ireland (as to housing see *Slums** and *New Towns*)*.

In the United States there has also been social security legislation since 1935 *(New Deal*)*, although it has certainly not been as comprehensive as the British system. Strictly speaking, social legislation in the United States has not moved too far in the direction of a genuine welfare state. The term "welfare state" still preserves a slightly derogatory meaning in American usage. Initiative and self-reliance, increased managerial efficiency, productivity, and economic growth are still considered the decisive factors for the welfare and prosperity of the American nation.

I Fr

PART IV

Education

Accreditation
College
Comprehensive School
Elective System
Elementary School
Eleven-Plus
External Degree
Extra-Curricular Activities
Extra-Mural Work (University Extension)
Fellow
Foundation
Fraternity and Sorority
Further Education
General Certificate of Education
Graduate
Grammar School
Guidance
High School
Ivy League
Land-Grant College
Liberal Arts
London University
Management Education
National Defense Education Act
National Education Association
National Union of Teachers
New University
Open University
Oxford and Cambridge (Oxbridge)
Parent-Teachers' Association
Prefect
Preparatory School
Primary Education
Private University
Progressive Education
Public School
Red-Brick University
Sandwich Courses
Scholarship
Secondary Education
Sixth Form
State University
Statutory System
Streaming
Students' Union
Teacher Training
Tutor
Universities
University Grants Committee

Accreditation

■ The act of recognizing an institution as maintaining standards which qualify the graduates for admission to a higher or more specialized institution or for professional practice.

A feature of higher learning in the United States which ranks as unique is the practice of accreditation. The system accords recognition to those institutions which comply with the standards or the criteria established by a competent agency or association. The accrediting of colleges and universities is carried out largely by non-governmental organizations of various types, but state agencies also participate in accrediting services. There are six regional accrediting associations in the United States providing an almost exhaustive coverage of the country: the New England Association of Colleges and Secondary Schools, the Middle States Association of Colleges and Secondary Schools, the Southern Association of Colleges and Secondary Schools, the North Central Association of Colleges and Secondary Schools, the Northwest Association of Secondary and Higher Schools, and the Western College Association.

Accreditation is felt to be necessary in the United States because of the heterogeneity of educational institutions which the country embraces. Each institution places at the disposal of its students its own programme and sets its own standards in the absence of any state examination or examination approved by the state.

Accreditation does not grade the institutions; it either accredits or refuses to accredit. The effects of accreditation are nevertheless extensive. Accreditation furnishes the separate institutions with a stimulus to improve their programmes and with them their educational standard. The pronouncements of accrediting agencies are often helpful in cases when administrative officers wish to maintain high standards but face local difficulties; political interference in colleges and universities has often been prevented by the agencies calling attention to standards which should be met. Furthermore, accreditation enables the credentials of a student to be evaluated comparatively when transferring from one institution of higher learning to another. (In contrast to Britain, students in the United States are allowed to study at different universities.) Accreditation informs those who intend to employ graduates in professional practice about the quality of the education the graduates have received.

The accrediting procedure carried out by the competent agencies includes four stages: first, academic standards are established; second, the competent authorities inspect the institution to determine whether it meets the established criteria; third, lists of institutions which conform to standard are published; fourth, periodic reviews are made in order to determine whether accredited institutions continue to meet the criteria.

● There is no accreditation system in Britain comparable to that of the United States in the field of higher education. The nearest British equivalent is the practice introduced for independent schools which are visited regularly by Her Majesty's Inspectors. On the basis of favourable reports submitted by the Inspectors these schools are "recognized as efficient" by the Department of Education and Science.

C C R

College

An organized society of persons performing certain common functions and possessing special rights and privileges, a society of scholars incorporated within, or in connexion with, a university, or otherwise formed for purposes of study and instruction. The building or set of buildings occupied by such a society. In U.S. also a preparatory or high school, an independent institution of higher learning offering a course of general studies leading to a bachelor's degree. In U.S.A. and G.B.: An institution offering instruction usually in professional, vocational or technical field (teachers' college); a part of a university offering a specialized group of courses.

● The term "college" was first used in the 13th century to denote the community of scholars living together in college buildings (later called the "Houses", 1536) which provided "hall, chapel and chamber" as well as opportunities for study and research. The colleges possessed a permanent income of their own from large endowments. Although later incorporated within the university, they were autonomous bodies and to a great extent independent of the university with regard to finances as well as to the studies pursued. Therefore it is no wonder that in the course of time (especially during the 17th and 18th centuries) the colleges attracted a large part of the university's activities and temporarily became the principal centres of learning. This situation changed when the *Industrial Revolution** made it necessary for the universities to adopt new subjects and new methods of academic learning especially in the field of science *(Oxford and Cambridge*)*.

Nevertheless, the fundamental features of the medieval colleges have been preserved and the colleges have remained the focuses of academic life at the Universities of Oxford and Cambridge. They still constitute autonomous corporate bodies which dispose of their own property and are governed by their own *Fellows**. Only the great libraries, such as the famous Bodleian Library at Oxford, as well as the laboratories and other facilities for research work especially in the field of pure and applied sciences are owned by the university and placed at the disposal of all students regardless of the college to which they belong. The university is also the only degree-granting body. This history of the colleges of Oxford and Cambridge comprises a period of more than 700 years from the foundation of University College, Oxford, in 1249 until the opening of St. Catherine's College, Oxford, in 1964. (Durham and Newcastle, patterned after Oxford and Cambridge, have also adopted the college system.) Another type of "college" is represented by the constituent, non-residential colleges of the University of London such as King's College and University College *(London University*)*, and by the colleges of the University of Wales which are likewise non-residential. The colleges of the University of St. Andrews, however, are nowadays the names of the buildings where the faculties of the University are housed.

In the field of *Further Education** institutions which are also called "colleges" were established for the purpose of vocational or non-vocational instruction. In the vocational field they offer technological, commercial, and a wide variety of crafts courses. There are also technological courses of a more professional character which lead to national certificates approved by joint committees representative of the education departments and the appropriate professional body *(External Degree*)*. The colleges of further education offering courses for general education or vocational training are sometimes

4

classified on a geographical basis as Local, Area, Regional or National Colleges. Another modern type of college is the training college, especially created for the training of teachers. It is intended to expand training college provisions in order to cope with an increase of 26,000 students. This will roughly double the existing capacity of the training colleges. But these colleges largely are being assimilated into "liberal arts" colleges within the reorganisation of teacher training (*Teacher Training**). In the field of adult education, an important post-war advance was the establishment, mainly by local educational authorities, of about 30 residential colleges which provide room for discussion groups and organize short courses of lectures.

Finally it is to be noted that the term "college" or "university college" has often been applied to denote an institution of higher education which is in the process of acquiring university status. Thus, for instance, the *Red-Brick Universities** were founded as "university colleges" during the 19th and 20th centuries. Only recently the Colleges of Advanced Technology (C.A.T.s) underwent a similar development. Originally founded as "colleges" in the 1950s, they have been granted university status in the meantime. Many of them – as can be seen from their university charters – have changed their names. Battersea College of Advanced Technology, for instance, has become the University of Surrey at Guildford; Birmingham College of Advanced Technology has been renamed University of Aston in Birmingham; Bradford Institute of Advanced Technology is now the University of Bradford; Brunel College, Acton, is now Brunel University; and Bristol College of Science and Technology is now the Bath University of Technology. P H

■ It was in America that the college first appeared exclusively as a separate institution of higher learning characterized by a four-year programme of undergraduate studies beginning at the end of the high school and leading to the bachelor's degree. Nowadays high school graduates may take a choice: either they enter a junior or community college, or a 4-year college, or the undergraduate division of a university, apart from professional or technical schools. A public or private junior or community college normally offers a 2- or 3-year programme of studies beyond the secondary level. Programmes usually include a curriculum leading to a certificate, and students receive credits that may be acceptable toward a bachelor's degree in a 4-year college. Some programmes are terminal in nature and prepare students to become proficient in one of a wide variety of semi-professional and technical occupations. There exist now over 1,100 junior colleges. It is anticipated that junior colleges will continue to grow at a more rapid rate than other kinds of institutions. Two of the more probable projections are 4,430,000 and 3,746,000 enrollees in 1980.

The 4-year college offers a curriculum in the liberal arts and sciences and is authorized to confer the bachelor's degree upon completion of the 4-year programme. In 1975 to 1976, there were 553 public and 1361 private colleges of this type in the United States. They differ from a university in size and scope of curriculum; they may be independent or an undergraduate division of a university. Generally the colleges do not include graduate studies which are the main concern of universities, but there are independent colleges which offer advanced degrees, particularly at the master's level. P H/D P H

Comprehensive School

- The term Comprehensive School is applied to a secondary school which provides education for all children from a given district, regardless of their background, ability or intelligence, who are between the ages of 11 and 19. Since this type of school embraces pupils of widely differing abilities and interests it must offer a correspondingly wide range of courses to cope with each pupil's needs, and in fact includes in its syllabus the type of education offered at *Grammar**, Secondary Technical* and Secondary Modern Schools* respectively. Ca. 1958.

Although the development of comprehensive schools has been largely socialist inspired, it must be noted that it was not the official policy of the Labour Government to promote pioneer work in this field in the years of educational restructuring immediately after the 1944 Education Act. Although it embodies many reforms this Act appears in retrospect a backward-looking document, based as it is on a series of prewar reports which, despite a certain liberality of approach, were not at all scientific in their methodology. There is no educational research for instance which would justify the tripartite system (secondary modern, grammar and secondary technical schools) to which the Labour Party pledged itself in this Act. Many educationalists have pointed out that not only is this three stream system socially divisive and designed to perpetuate and reinforce class differences, but that it also makes little economic sense in terms of the wastage of potential it incurs.

It was in fact from socialist-run local authorities such as London, Middlesex, Anglesey, Coventry, Oldham and the West Riding of Yorkshire that the main stimulus for this new type of school originated in the 1950s. They were quick to realize that a common school on comprehensive lines would be an ideal basis for building a classless community in keeping with socialist ideals. The other powerful argument which they advanced was that the inadequate selection method of the *Eleven-Plus** examination could be abolished. With a widespread system of comprehensive schools a child would no longer be graded at the age of 11 into one of three categories of ability and would no longer have to bear the social and psychological consequences of having been classified at this early age as a success or a failure, which in efect is what the Eleven-Plus implies.

By 1964, however, the Labour Government had realized that the thinking enshrined in the 1944 Education Act was mistaken. The then Secretary for Education and Science, Mr. Michael Steward, revealed in the Commons that 68 local authorities, representing 63 per cent. of the secondary school population, were implementing or examining firm proposals for reorganizing their schools along comprehensive lines. Then, on July 12th, 1965 "Circular 10" was issued, which declared that the restructuring of secondary education on comprehensive lines should be national policy. Local authorities which had not yet done so were invited to submit their plans for comprehensive schools to the Secretary of State.

The accession of a Conservative Government in June 1970, put an end to these short-lived proposed reforms. The Conservative Party, and also some educationalists with no specific political allegiance, were largely opposed to comprehensive schools. They would have preferred to see improvements to the tripartite system. They argued, too, that comprehensive schools could not compete with the standards maintained by the grammar schools, and that in order to serve adequately the needs of all their pupils, they would be far too large to be satisfactorily administered.

Almost immediately upon taking office the new Minister in charge of Education, Mrs. Margaret Thatcher, withdrew "Circular 10" and informed local authorities that schemes for secondary education need no longer proceed in accordance with comprehensive principles. During the years 1950 to 1969 there had been a steady increase in the number of comprehensive schools and in the proportion of secondary school pupils attending them. Ten comprehensive schools in 1950 accounted for 0.47 per cent. of all secondary school pupils. By the end of the school year 1968-69 there were 920 comprehensive schools with 736,000 pupils, or about 26 per cent. of all children in maintained secondary education.

The brake on reorganisation applied by Mrs. Thatcher did not last long. For, the return of a Labour government in 1973 under Prime Minister Harold Wilson saw renewed vigour in the introduction of comprehensive schools, with the result that by 1974 there were 2,273 comprehensive schools in England and Wales, and, by January 1976, there were 2,878.

Comprehensive schools fall into 5 main categories. At the top end of the age-range is a small number (68) of sixth-form colleges, but the largest number of comprehensive schools falls in the category catering for the 11 to 18 age group. Other categories cater for different age groups up to 18, up to 15 or 16, and up to 13 or 14. In 1976 there were 2,878 comprehensive schools in total with 2,753,327 or almost 75 per cent. of all secondary school pupils.

British comprehensives are similar to the large, multipurpose U.S. high school, in which the ability grouping system is known as "tracking". G W

Elective System

An optional study as in a course at college. A study which a student may select from among alternatives. 1825.

■ This system enables above all *College** students to choose the courses they take. It developed in the last decades of the 19th century on account of the increasing number, range and importance of new courses. Previously almost the entire curriculum had been prescribed. One of the ways in which new courses could be given their due significance was to render certain older courses elective. Students have in most cases great freedom of choice except where survey courses are required of all students. On the whole the student in a *Liberal Arts** college enjoys more freedom in this respect than does the student attending a course which will train him for a profession.

The elective system is also applied in high schools, though the student's freedom of choice is usually restricted there. It is meant to help children determine the limits of their professional future by themselves. It is important to note that considerable time in junior high school or middle school is given to *guidance**, which is intended to ensure that children select programmes suited to their abilities and interests.

The typical secondary school curriculum consists of some prescribed subjects and a large number of free or restricted electives. The system varies in the different states and communities, but there is a typical pattern. A senior *High School** (in the 6-3-3 type the final three years) may, for example, offer the following programme in the tenth grade of the College Preparatory Course: English, Gymnastics, Geometry (required subjects); Latin, French, German or

Spanish or Italian, World History, Biology (restricted electives, two of which have to be chosen); Nutrition, Home Nursing, Social Adjustment, Home Management, Typewriting, Clothing, Public Speaking, Mechanical Drawing, Musical Appreciation and Harmony, Choral Singing, General Music, Band, Art (free electives). There are many high schools requiring only one or two academic subjects even in the senior grades, e.g. English plus Gymnastics or History or First Aid.

Thus a senior pupil is normally required to concern himself with only one to four academic subjects, two of which he may drop after one or two years if he finds it convenient to do so. P H/D P H

Elementary School

In the U.S.A. a school generally including the first six or eight grades of the common school system. It has also been called the "grade school" or the "grammar school". 1870

■ The American elementary school fulfils the task of providing a fundamental programme of education for all the children of the nation for a limited number of years. The education is then continued by the *High School**. The task of the elementary school is generally defined as the accumulation of the knowledge which should be possessed by all citizens: i.e. reading, writing, arithmetic, geography and history, social studies, physical education, handicraft and music.

The beginnings of elementary schools in the United States can be traced back to 1642 when the colony of Massachusetts demanded of all parents that their children should be able to read. The Dutch settlers at that time brought with them the tradition of elementary education to New Amsterdam which later became known as New York. In the course of years the *New England** colonies provided for the establishment of elementary schools which were placed more and more under the control of local school boards. The *Constitution** of 1789 does not mention education: the problem therefore was handed over to the states. At that time there were public elementary schools in many towns and settlements of all the 13 original states where children were taught free of charge. With the westward expansion of the U.S.A. public schools of this nature were established everywhere by the local communities. But it was thanks to the initiative of Horace Mann (1796-1859) that the elementary school achieved general recognition as a necessary public institution for all the children of the nation. According to Mann the "common school" ought to be universal and accept children from all layers of society and from all denominations. Thus it became the "great equalizer", "the balance-wheel of the social machinery". His ideals and projects were first realized in Massachusetts and later spread throughout the U.S.A. The elementary school gradually became compulsory by legislation in all the states.

Attendance at the co-educational elementary school generally begins at the age of 6 years (in some states a year later) and encompasses five to eight years, from grade 1 to 5/6 or 8. The eight-year curriculum is being more and more replaced by the five- or six-year curriculum. Either a Middle School (grades 6-8) or a Junior High School (grades 7-9) commonly intervene between elementary and high school, in order to ease the transition from elementary to secondary schools. Before children enter the elementary school they can have attended a public or private nursery school from the age of 3 to 4 or 5, then a public kindergarten. The latter enrolls 4- to 5-year old children for 1 or 2 years,

Organization of Education in England and Wales

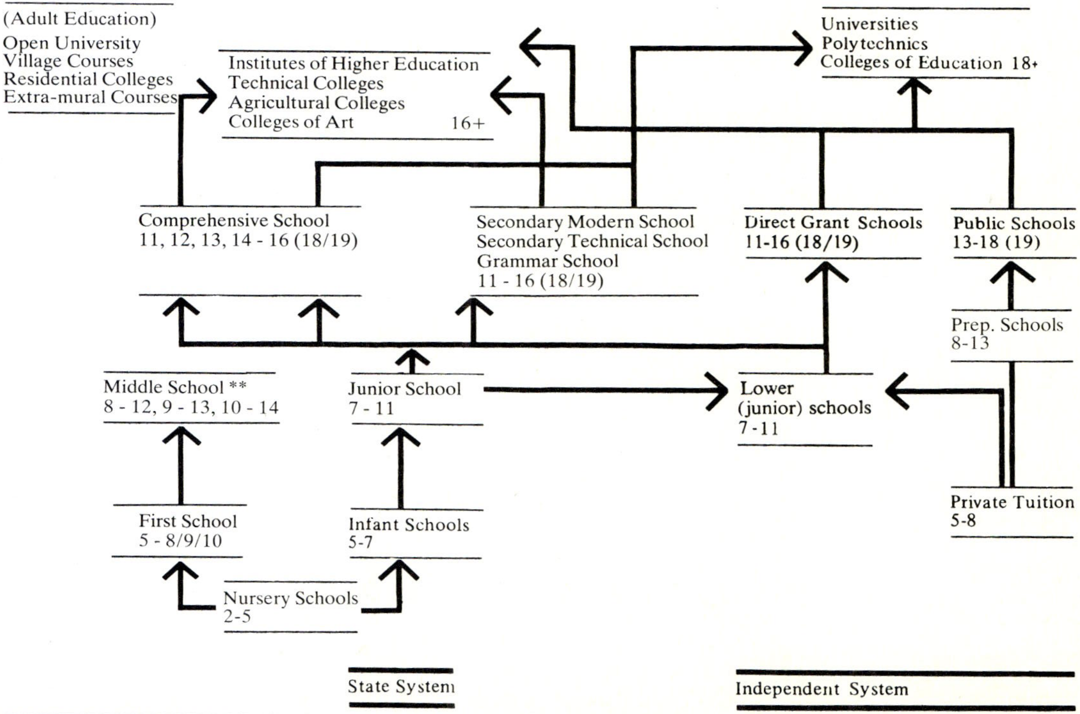

Age 2-5 : nursery school (voluntary)
5-11: primary education (compulsory)
11-18: secondary education
(compulsory to the age of 16)

16 (18)- : further education
18- : higher education

** Middle Schools: –
according to the age-range of pupils Middle Schools are either Junior or Secondary Deemed.

GW

4

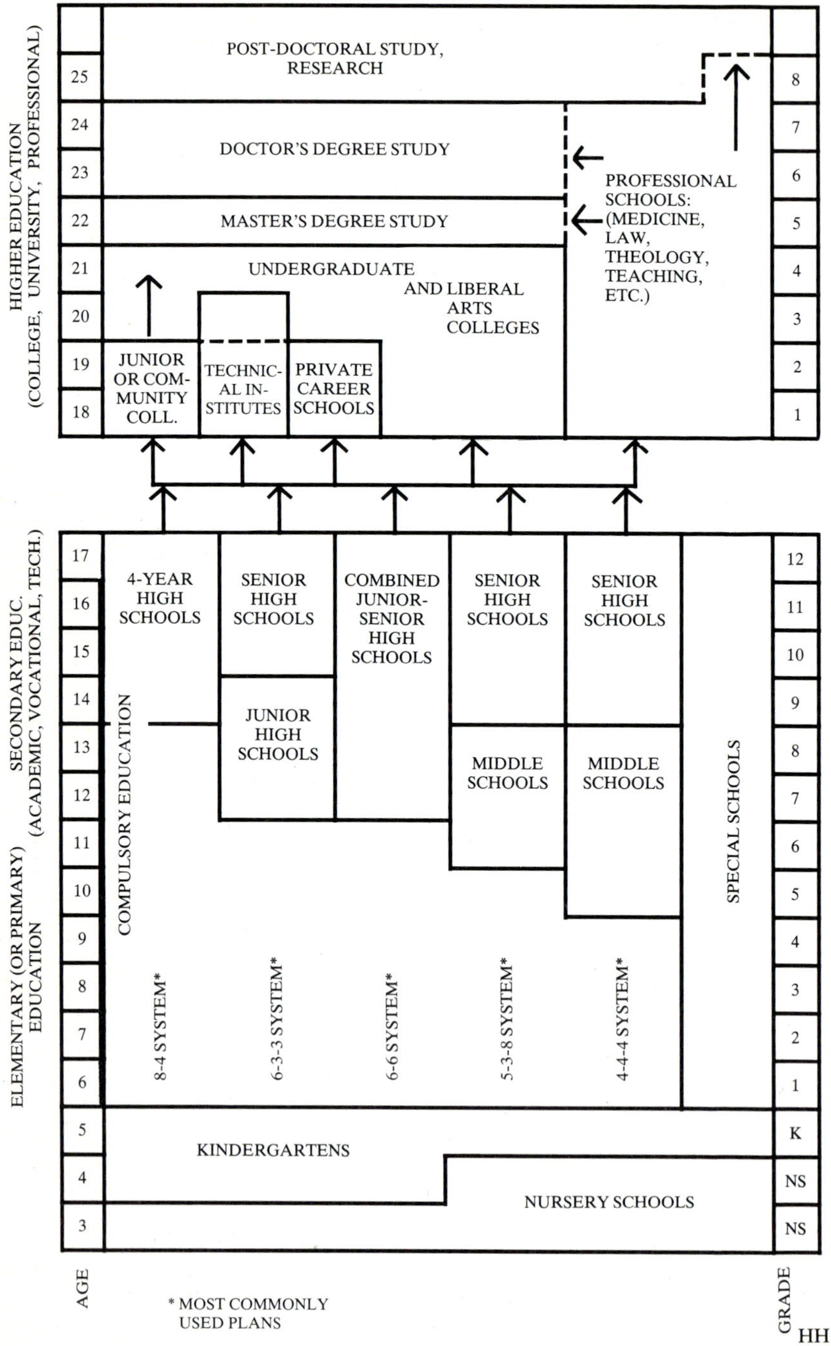
HIGHER EDUCATION
(COLLEGE, UNIVERSITY, PROFESSIONAL)
POST-DOCTORAL STUDY, RESEARCH
DOCTOR'S DEGREE STUDY
MASTER'S DEGREE STUDY
UNDERGRADUATE AND LIBERAL ARTS COLLEGES
PROFESSIONAL SCHOOLS: (MEDICINE, LAW, THEOLOGY, TEACHING, ETC.)
JUNIOR OR COMMUNITY COLL.
TECHNICAL INSTITUTES
PRIVATE CAREER SCHOOLS
SECONDARY EDUC.
(ACADEMIC, VOCATIONAL, TECH.)
ELEMENTARY (OR PRIMARY) EDUCATION
4-YEAR HIGH SCHOOLS
SENIOR HIGH SCHOOLS
COMBINED JUNIOR-SENIOR HIGH SCHOOLS
SENIOR HIGH SCHOOLS
SENIOR HIGH SCHOOLS
JUNIOR HIGH SCHOOLS
MIDDLE SCHOOLS
MIDDLE SCHOOLS
SPECIAL SCHOOLS
COMPULSORY EDUCATION
8-4 SYSTEM*
6-3-3 SYSTEM*
6-6 SYSTEM*
5-3-8 SYSTEM*
4-4-4 SYSTEM*
KINDERGARTENS
NURSERY SCHOOLS
AGE
25 24 23 22 21 20 19 18 17 16 15 14 13 12 11 10 9 8 7 6 5 4 3
GRADE
8 7 6 5 4 3 2 1 12 11 10 9 8 7 6 5 4 3 2 1 K NS NS
* MOST COMMONLY USED PLANS

HH

before they enter the first grade. Approximately 84.1 per cent. of the 5-year olds in the population were enrolled in kindergarten in 1973. Moreover there is a considerable growth in nursery school enrollments; they almost tripled from 1965 to 1973. Close to 20 per cent. of the 3- and 4-year olds were in the pre-kindergarten programmes in 1973. This trend is likely to continue. In 1975 31,547,000 children attended 62,749 elementary public schools taught by 1,171,700 teachers. The elementary school aims at a general development of the child's capacities and abilities within the community and for the community, and thus introduces the child into social life. Gymnastics, physical sport, and health education are given due consideration but the accent is naturally placed upon the teaching of the basic skills – reading, speaking, writing, and arithmetic. In the fifth grade geography and history are introduced, while especially stressed are social studies. Some musical education is also undertaken. The general educational principle which can be observed throughout the elementary school is that the child is encouraged and helped to develop his own activities without any unnecessary constraint or pressure.

Whereas formerly the "little red schoolhouse" in which children of different ages were taught in one room played a great part in the education of the nation, the tendency is to abolish this and to divide the children according to intelligence. In rural districts the so-called "central schools" were founded. Elementary schools with more than 2,000 children are not rare, which necessitates children being conveyed by school buses. There is now a wide-spread movement for the development of optional programmes that allow parents and students to choose from a variety of curriculum offerings and learning environments. For example, many elementary schools provide both an open classroom setting and a more structured setting that emphasizes instruction in basic skills at all grade levels. So far, optional educational programmes have been established mainly within public institutions.

Great attention is now devoted to *Teacher Training**. In the United States special courses are instituted for furthering the teachers' abilities. More than 85 per cent. of the elementary school teachers are women.

Since the turn of this century educators have sought ways of identifying children in their early years. Observation by the teacher of the child's performance and the giving of individual and group intelligence tests have been found helpful in the identification of gifted children. Different methods are naturally applied in the education of gifted children. P H/DPH

Eleven-Plus

● Examination, gradually being phased out, and which taken at about the age of 11 to decide which type of secondary school, under the tripartite system, a child should attend.

The term 11-plus dates back at least to 1926 and the Consultative Committee on the Education of the Adolescent. The ommittee's Report, the Hadow Report, used the term, however, merely to denote the approximate age at which children should transfer from the primary to the post-primary level of education.

Since 1944 the term Eleven-Plus has been used somewhat differently. It is the name given to an examination employed to a decreasing extent to allocate pupils to the different types of secondary schools in existence under then tripartite system: *grammar school**, secondary modern school, secondary technical school. The basis pattern of this examination, common to all Local Education Authorities, is as follows: (1) tests of innate intelligence (2) tests of ability in English and arithmetic (3) records of a child's primary school work and teachers' reports (4) an interview if a child is a borderline case.

The introduction of comprehensive schools in the majority of local education areas has meant a considerable drop in the number of pupils sitting the 11-plus. Nonetheless, of 97 Local Education Authorities including the Inner London Education Authority (ILEA), 68 or 70 per cent. still retain the tripartite system in whole or in part, although under the great majority of authorities any form of selection is being phased out. Of all LEAs, only the London Borough of Kingston-upon-Thames has steadfastly refused to implement any form of comprehensivisation in its schools, and in 1976 retained 10 secondary modern and 2 grammar schools.

Since its introduction the 11-plus has been the subject of criticism levelled principally at its methods of selection which allegedly give an incomplete picture of a child's ability and can be too much influenced by other factors such as parental ambition and the child's home environment. The 1959 Crowther Report ("15 to 18") laid much stress on the fallibility of the 11-plus and influenced many LEAs in their adoption of comprehensive schools, and abandonment of tripartite system.

The secondary modern schools have always been the poor relation of the tripartite system. Although intended under the 1944 Act to give a good all-round education, they have suffered from poor buildings, inadequate facilities and other constraining factors such as higher pupil-teacher ratios and academically less well qualified staff. In recent years there has been some improvement in the level of pupil attainment with the introduction of the General Certificate of Education (GCE) 'O' and, in some cases, 'A'-level courses, and the (CSE) examinations, but on the whole the secondary modern schools have welcomed the change to comprehensive schooling. The extent of this change can be measured by the fact that in 1976 the secondary modern schools catered for only 16 per cent. of the secondary school population as opposed to 41 per cent. in 1970.

The secondary technical schools were intended, in theory at least, for pupils whose talents lie in a practical rather than in an academic direction. In practice, however, and largely because the selection procedure existing under the 11-plus examination cannot determine whether a child's aptitudes are practical or academic, the technical schools have had to be content with pupils who do not fall into the top layer of those passing the 11-plus. The number of secondary technical schools, always small, has been drastically reduced from 82 in 1970 to 23 in 1976. This has also been due to the development of the comprehensive system. As far as pupil numbers are concerned, in 1970 there were 43,700 or 1.5 per cent. of all secondary school pupils at technical schools, compared with 15,000 or 0.4 per cent. in 1976. G W

External Degree

An academic rank conferred by a university or college on a student who has never attended that institution. 1858.

● Since 1858 it has been possible to obtain an academic degree of *London University** without actually having attended courses held in one of the constituent *Colleges** or institutes of the University. Any person adequately (the qualification usually being passes in a certain number of subjects at the G.C.E. examination) may still register with the University as an external student. After the requisite period of time since registration has elapsed and having meanwhile studied privately he may present himself for examination and if successful he will be awarded an external degree. The syllabuses and examinations are substantially similar to those prepared for internal students (that is, students studying at the University itself); the external degree, therefore, represents the same high standard of attainment as is expected of an internal candidate.

Within Britain the London external degree proved a great asset at the time when numerous University Colleges existed which did not have the power to grant their own degrees. Such institutions, all of which now enjoy full university status *(Red-Brick University*)*, prepared students for the London examinations. A similar situation used to be met with in institutions of higher learning throughout the British *Empire** and *Commonwealth**.

Many of the old University Colleges both in Britain and the Commonwealth have in the meantime been empowered to grant their own degree and the London external degree has largely outlived its usefulness. In Britain itself the external degree used to play a particularly important role in the field of *Further Education**. Many students took external degrees at technical colleges where courses were often provided not only in science but also in arts subjects *(Liberal Arts*)*. Most candidates aimed at a B.Sc., B.A. or B.Sc. (Econ.) degree, although some candidates registered for a higher degree (for example: M.A., M.Sc., Ph.D.) which could also be taken externally in certain circumstances.

The high number of registrations under the External System – more than 33,000 in the early 1970s – is now a thing of the past. For the establishment of the Council for national academic Awards (C.N.A.A.) in 1964, a body which makes awards to persons who have successfully completed courses of study at institutions which do not have the power to grant their own degrees, e. g. technical colleges, and, further, the foundation of the *Open University** deprived the scheme of much of its *raison d'être*. Notwithstanding its long and illustrious history it had become a luxury London University could no longer afford to run; it imposed an enormous additional burden on the University's academic and administrative staff and resources. Consequently, since September 1977, no further registrations for External Degrees have been accepted except from candidates studying privately. This means that polytechnics and other colleges that had hitherto availed themselves of the External System have now had to devise their own degree courses for approval by the C.N.A.A. J L F

Extra-Curricular Activities

Extra-curricular: not falling within the scope of a regular curriculum; specifically: of or relating to officially or semi-officially approved and usually organized student activities (e.g. athletics) connected with school and carrying no academic credit.

As far as schools are concerned the line between the normal curriculum and the extra-curricular activities has always been vaguely drawn; indeed many former extra-curricular activities are nowadays part of the regular school programme, e.g. art and music.

Extra-curricular activities should be considered under three headings: (1) Activities taking place largely in classrooms and in classtime, but not first and foremost preparing pupils for an examination or qualifying them for a future career. (2) Games generally taking place on Saturday mornings or afternoons. (3) Clubs, societies, generally meeting after school on weekdays and covering a wide range of interests.

● In accordance with a long and successful tradition extra-curricular activities under headings (2) and (3) are those most favoured in schools.

In higher education it is to be noted that extra-curricular activities play a very important role in the education of the students. Sporting activities the main function of which is to encourage the qualities of team spirit and fair play are of special importance but such matters as debating, drama, music, etc., also fall within the scope of extra-curricular activities. *(Students' Union*.)* P H

■ Participation in extra-curricular activities is encouraged at all levels of education. In schools the extra-curricular activities are mostly under the *Guidance** of the school. These activities should be regarded as an adjunct to the broadened curriculum of the modern school, if not almost a part of the curriculum itself. They are considered as an effort to meet youth needs that are not clearly related to conventional school subjects. They will also enable students to investigate areas of knowledge which they frequently cannot include in their studies. Widespread support is given to the concepts and programmes of career education that have been added at all levels of the elementary and secondary curriculum in thousands of school systems. At the elementary level, it generally takes the form of career awareness programmes. At the secondary level, observation of actual work places, work experience, and apprenticeships have been advocated along with occupational guidance programmes. In high schools there is a growing tendency toward the development of vocational education, e.g. toward preparation in new fields such as airport and airlines operation, nautical occupations, health occupations, and motel-hotel management. Latest development is the introduction of courses in sex education, encouraged by the U.S. Office of Education with federal grants.

In higher education extra-curricular activities - especially sporting activities - are an even more prominent feature of American college and university life than is the case in Britain. Nowhere are sporting activities fostered in institutions of higher education to a greater degree than in the United States.

P H/DPH

Extra-Mural Work, University Extension

Extra-mural: outside the walls or boundaries, as of a city or town or a university.

● The English use the term "extra-mural work" or "extra-mural studies" to designate a variety of ways of extending the educational services of the universities to the general population. These services include correspondence courses and class courses, on or off the university premises, for persons not registered as students. Extra-mural work is sometimes also called university extension. The services of university extension are a part of the much larger field of instruction known as adult education. Education for the adults in organized courses began in the 1870s. It was then that Professor Stuart inspired the University Extension Movement in Cambridge (hence the centre of extra-mural studies in Cambridge is called Stuart House). This was the origin of the valuable extra-mural studies which have now become an important feature of English universities *(Red-Brick University*)*. In their extra-mural departments the universities have always sought to maintain a high standard, the purpose of their tutors and lecturers being to bring the learning of the university to the people. In their extra-mural departments many of the universities now have full-time staff appointed for extra-mural work. The extra-mural (= adult education) departments of the universities in cooperation with the Workers' Educational Association (WEA), the largest of the recognized voluntary bodies, provide extended part time courses of more academic studies. Often the WEA provides the organisation, and the teaching is provided by the extra-mural departments, many of which have full-time staff appointed for this purpose and can also call on the services of other departments of the universities. In 1973-74 about 300,000 students attended such courses. P H

■ Educational services for persons not regularly enrolled as full-time students are made available by most American universities. In broad usage the term "university extension" is applied to any services and programmes of this nature wherever they are located in the university's structure. Many universities have established divisions to carry on such work. The term "university extension" is thus employed sometimes to refer specifically to the work of these organized units. Most cater for adults. The terms "university adult education" and "continuing education" are frequently used as synonyms for "university extension".

Scattered individual and institutional efforts for providing off-campus college level work were made throughout the 19th century. Under the influence of the developments in Cambridge and Oxford, the more organized form of extension work emerged in the middle of the 1880s. William Rainey Harper, first president of the University of Chicago, included extension in the form of off-campus centres and correspondence courses, etc., in his plans for the new institution of higher learning. Strong leadership also came from state universities, notable from the University of Wisconsin under Charles R. van Hise. At his inauguration in 1903 van Hise stated his intention of making the boundaries of the university extend to those of the state. Agricultural extension, through the *Land-Grant Colleges**, and the Co-operative Extension Service have been important features of university extension since 1914. Urban universities in particular have done much in the extension field. The demands of modern social and economic life have substained the vigorous growth and innovations of the university extension programmes. Among other developments, the creation of university level programnmes by industrial concerns, the armed forces, and other organized groups are notable. The National University Extension Association and the Association of University Evening Colleges are two of the most active and well-known professional groups in this field. In the 1970s continuing education and lifelong learning are among the most rapidly growing and highly valued aspects of higher education.

P H/DPH

Fellow

In college or university use: (a) One of the company or corporation who, with their head, constitute a college, and receive emoluments from the corporate revenue. 1449. Hence: (b) One of the holders of certain stipendiary positions (called "Fellowships") tenable for a limited period, on condition of pursuing some specified branch of study. 1888. (c) A member of the governing body, e.g. in the University of London. 1837. (d) A member, or one of certain privileged members, of various learned societies, e.g. the Royal Society, etc. 1664.

● The term refers primarily to the members of the *Colleges** of *Oxford* and *Cambridge** and can be traced back to the early history of these colleges. Throughout the 13th and 14th centuries all members of a college were called "scholar". From about the middle of the 15th century, however, the term scholar came to be applied only to the junior members of the colleges who where still "in statu pupillari" (today they would be called undergraduates) while the graduates who were elected members of the governing body of the college became known as "fellows". (In more colloquial use the fellows or tutors of a college are sometimes also called "dons" which is likely to be derived from the Spanish title of one having authority.)

A fellow at Oxford or Cambridge is entrusted with particular tasks especially those of lecturing at the university or working as a tutor at the college to which he belongs. He is also entitled to certain privileges, especially to the privilege of receiving a fixed emolument out of the college's revenues. Most of the fellows of the colleges are members of the teaching staff of the university and the majority of professors, readers and lecturers of the university are fellows of one of the colleges affiliated.

A fellow may also be a graduate to whom an allowance called a "fellowships" is granted for the pursuance of postgraduate studies or research work. Fellowships are established for a fixed number of years.

The term "fellow" has also been used to designate a privileged member of a learned society.

Finally it is to be mentioned that a "fellow" may also be one of the 36 members of the Senate of the University of London, who are appointed for life by the Crown. P H

■ In some of the older universities *(Ivy League*)* the term "fellow" has retained its British meaning of a graduate sharing in the government of a college and receiving an emolument in return for his activities. In 1650 the term was first mentioned in the Charter of Harvard College which provided for five "fellows" to be members of its governing body.

An American fellow, however, is more commonly the holder of a fellowship, or grant of financial assistance, either from an individual institution or from a *Foundation**. Particularly well known are Woodrow Wilson, Danforth, National Merit, Fulbright and Wenner-Gren fellowships. They carry widely differing financial benefits, and also differ in the activity demanded of the fellow. Fellows may teach, study, do research work, creative writing, compose, paint, travel, or undertake a variety of other activities. The selection of the students for fellowships is based mainly on intellectual and personal attributes, but financial need also may be considered. P H/DPH

Foundation

The establishing of an institution together with provision for its perpetual maintenance. That which is founded or established by endowment. 1513.

■ Foundations are institutions based on endowments. Their legal form is mostly that of a non-profit-making corporation.

When in 1901 the Scotsman Andrew Carnegie sold his steel interest to the U.S. Steel Corporation for $ 250 million he lived up to what he had written in his book "The Gospel of Wealth" a year before: rich men are "trustees" of their wealth and should administer it unselfishly for the good of the public. His benefactions totalled approximately $ 350 million, the greater part of which was used to establish foundations such as the Carnegie Institution of Washington (1902, endowment $ 22 million) "to encourage in the broadest and most liberal manner investigation, research and discovery, and the application of knowledge to the improvement of mankind"; the Carnegie Foundation for the Advancement of Teaching (1906, total endowment $ 27 million); the Carnegie Endowment for International Peace (1910, endowment $ 10 million); the Carnegie Corporation (1911, outright endowment $ 125 million plus Carnegie's residuary estate) which finances libraries, colleges, institutions for fine arts and for sicientific and educational research , and the Carnegie Institute of Pittsburgh concerned with the preservation of works of art. In addition Carnegie spent $ 60 million on Carnegie Libraries in thousands of cities and provided the funds for the erection of Carnegie Hall – a musical centre in New York City.

Carnegie was not the only public benefactor nor was he the first. But his example is characteristic. Enormous sums of private capital have during the past 80 years been invested for the creation of philantropic foundations, most of them being concerned with education or purposes related to education. This fact conforms to the American philosophy of Pragmatism and Instrumentalism, in which the educated mind is the prime instrument for the acquisition of truth and reality, and to the general popular belief in the cash value of education.

There are now about 30,000 foundations in the United States, of which nine-tenths have been founded since the end of World War II. The largest among them (by assets, figures for 1974 except where otherwise stated: Ford Foundation ($ 2,902 million); Robert Wood Johnson Foundation ($ 1,102 million, 1971); Lilly Endowment, Inc. ($ 778 million); Rockefeller Foundation ($ 757 million); Duke Endowment ($ 510 million); Kresge Foundation ($ 433 million); W. R. Kellog Foundation ($ 3,93 million); Charles Steward Mott Foundation ($ 371 million); Pew Memorial Trust ($ 367 million); Alfred P. Sloan Foundation ($ 303 million); Carnegie Corporation of New York ($ 283 million); John A. Hartford Foundation, Inc. (S 277 million); Andrew W. Mellon Foundation ($ 234 million); Longwood Foundation, Inc. ($ 226 million, 1968); Houston Endowment, Inc. ($ 209 million); Rockefeller Brothers Fund ($ 198 million); Emily and Ernest Woodruff Foundation ($ 187 million); Bush Foundation ($ 163 million); Danforth Foundation ($ 162 million); Richard King Mellon Foundation ($ 140 million).

It is one of the most notable features of American education that many of the best institutions of higher learning were founded with private money and have consequently been free of supervision or participation of public authority. From 1885 onwards a rapid expansion of privately endowed colleges and universities took place. It began with Stanford University, California, founded in 1885 with an endowment by Leland Stanford, and was followed by the University of Chicago in 1891 (John D. Rockefeller) and Duke University in 1924 (James B. Duke). Among the eminent endowed universities are, of course, also the *Ivy League's**. The private foundations have especially promoted research on the post-graduate level of studies. They are very much a product of the American ethic. Having amassed a fortune through the free enterprise system, someone endows a foundation, which then dispenses grants to praiseworthy institutions and causes. A special incentive is provided by the fact that both the foundation's income and individual contributions to it are free of tax. Foundations, it is sometimes argued, are often the wealthiest people's method to avoid taxation. Moreover, they lack democratic responsibility, are uncontrolled, and possibly even potentially dangerous concenrations of economic power. The discovery in 1967 of the CIA's involvement in some 39 American foundations cast some doubt upon the integrity of the foundations and the assumption that they provide the funds for disinterested research.

● English philanthropy is rooted in the Middle Ages. The development and present structure of *Oxford and Cambridge** is due to a succession of foundations. As early as in 1249, University College at Oxford was founded and endowed with a permament income. - The Reformation was perhaps the most decisive factor in the development of philanthropy in England. In its course the English welfare system was almost entirely secularized. – The "Statute of Charitable Uses" created under queen Elisabeth I was a further landmark in the development of charitable endowments both in England and in America *(Ivy League*)*.

There are today some 115,000 charitable trusts in the United Kingdom, of which about 5,000 make grants of any size.

The most important among British philanthropic foundations are:
The Rhodes Trust (1902), founded by Cecil Rhodes to provide scholarships to Oxford University for students from the British Empire, the U.S.A. and originally also from Germany, is a British foundation devoted to purely educational purposes. A great number of British colleges and other university institutions, however, receive gifts from private sources (often endowed by their former graduates). The Nuffield Foundation, established in 1943 for the advancement of health, the improvement of social well-being and the care of the aged is the only big philanthropic foundation in Britain. Part of its funds provide for the Dominion Scholarship and for the Nuffield College of Oxford University, and for research in the field of teaching methods. Other philanthropic organizations that provide for research in Britain are the Calouste Gulbenkian Foundation (grants distributed or offered in 1977 totalled £ 737,717), the Leverhulme Trust (income in 1973 approx. £ 1,250,000), the Bernard van Leer Foundation, the Ford Foundation, the Carnegie United Kingdom Trust, the Wolfson Foundation, the Foundation for Management Education, the Carnegie Trust for the Universities of Scotland; Lord Kitchener National Memorial Fund; City Parochial Foundation (income 1973 £ 744,933), and the Winston Curchill Memorial Trust. H H

Fraternity and Sorority

■ A group of people associated for a common purpose, interest, or pleasure: as, for instance, a student organization formed chiefly for social purposes having secret rites and a name consisting of Greek letters.

The fraternities or sororities respectively are mainly social but sometimes also professional organizations the membership of which is drawn from university or college students. The fraternity for male students and the sorority for girl students – sometimes also called Greek-letter societies – trace their origin back to the literary clubs of the 18th and 19th centuries, one of the oldest fraternities being the Phi Beta Kappa established in 1776. The fraternities and sororities grew up gradually during the 19th century and expanded considerably after the Civil War. In the last decades of the 19th century they dominated the social life of the campus first in the Eastern universities from which they spread all over the country.

The main function of the social fraternity is to serve as a kind of "collegiate" home, their houses being the social centres where their members can live, take their meals and participate in student *Extra-Curricular Activities**. The fraternities have sometimes formed a caste system on the campus by rejecting new members on ethnic, racial or religious grounds.

At the *Ivy League** universities and colleges the importance of the fraternities has very much declined and since the beginning of the 1970s their once-dominant role apparently has lost significance even in the social life of smaller campuses. There are various reasons for this development; obviously one of them is the "anti-establishment" attitude of the younger generation of students.

The professional fraternities confine their membership to a specific field of professional education. They are organized for the purpose of furthering professional competence rather than social life. I Fr

Further Eduction

Full-time and part-time education for persons over compulsory school-age and not engaged in higher education. The term has been in official use since 1944.

● In Britain any course of study taken voluntary after attaining the school-leaving age can in general be termed "further education". Strictly speaking, however, a distinction should be made between "further education" and "adult education", the former implying in particular vocational training, while the latter is concerned mainly with instruction in leisure-time pursuits for persons over 18 years of age. Further distinction should be made between the above two categories and the term "higher education" which has come to be used mainly for studies at university or polytechnic level.

Local Education Authorities in Britain are required by *Parliament** to provide or assist in the provision of further education for young people who have completed their period of compulsory schooling. Today students find a wide range of courses and other eductional amenities provided for them. Instruction is available in all subjects of importance in the world of agriculture, business and industry in a large number of agricultural, commercial and technical colleges. In 1974 there were over 340,000 full-time students and over 1,518,000 part-time students attending *Colleges** of further education. By far the largest single group of students at technical colleges are young employees and apprentices released from work by their employers one day a week to enable them to study subjects of value to them in their work. Of particular interest are the so-called *Sandwich Courses**. The various types of college offer a wide range of subjects at all levels; many of the courses (such as the "sandwich courses") lead to the award of a diploma or a university degree.

In the field of adult education the range of subjects which may be studied is even more extensive. Here too it is sometimes possible to gain a diploma or a university degree on successful completion of the course, although this is not the main purpose of this type of education. The principal aim is to give people an opportunity to nurture and develop their talents and leisure-time interests.

Thus the emphasis is on non-vocational subjects such as handicrafts, cookery, literature, music, languages, and photography. In 1974 nearly two million people took part in the classes available at evening institutes and at residential colleges and other centres providing short weekend courses. An increasingly important role is being played by the *Open University**.

It was in 1873 that an experiment was begun, under the auspices of Cambridge University, to extend university teaching to the great manufacturing centres of the North Midlands – Derby, Nottingham and Leicester. These "university extension lectures" were such a success that the universities of London and Oxford also adopted the idea, in 1876 and 1878 respectively. In Sheffield, Nottingham, Reading and Exeter, universities were later to spring up as a direct result of these extension lectures. Today the extra-mural departments of many universities carry on the laudable tradition of adult education. In addition courses are held by Local Eduction Authorities and also by many voluntary organizations such as the Workers' Eductional Associations (W.E.A.), which are recognized by the education departments and receive government grants. Mention should also be made of the nine "village colleges" in Cambridgeshire which combine facilities for both secondary and adult education and which have proved a great success.

■ In The United States adult eduction or further education as it is also called is conducted along lines similar to those in Britain. The universities play a particularly important role, although, of course, the importance attached to this type of work varies from place to place. The British experiment with the Open University has proved to be a stimulus for America, too. Several American universities in fact offer Open University programmes; the University of Maryland, for instance, is already running more than 700 courses in the Washington/Baltimore area. Nine Mid West universities have combined to found something similar to the British institution, called "The University of Midamerica". J L F

General Certificate of Education (G.C.E.)

● A certificate awarded on the successful completion of an exmination taken by British secondary-school students. 1947.

Examinations leading to the award of the C.C.E. or, to give it its full title, the General Certificate of Eduction were first held in 1951. They are confined to England and Wales; Scotland and Ireland having their own examination schemes. The G.C.E. examinations were designated to replace the old School and Higher School Certificate Examinations. They are conducted by eight examining boards which are administered by a number of *Universities**. Since the task of examining does not lie in the hands of the candidates' own teachers a uniform national standard is more readily achieved. In the older School Certificate examinations candidates had to offer a group of subjects all at one time; in the G.C.E. they may take subjects singly or in any combination, for there are no compulsory subjects. The range of subjects in which examinations can be held is wide and comprehensive. In most subjects the examination is held at two levels. The lower, the Ordinary Level ("O" level), is designed for candidates who have not specialized in the subject concerned. This examination is not normally taken until the age of sixteen years; there is no upper age limit. The Advanced Leven ("A" level) is intended for candidates who have specialized in a particular subject. At least two "A" level passes are required for university entrance. Apart from helping the universities in the selection of their students and employers in the selection of their employees the G.C.E. serves another useful purpose in that it gives the schoolchildren a sense of achievement.

For children not of the academic calibre necessary to take the G.C.E. a different examination leading to the award of the Certificate of *Secondary Education**, or C.S.E. was introduced in 1965. There is only one level of C.S.E. examination. A pass at the highest grade is roughly equivalent to a G.C.E. "O" level pass. The examination is conducted by fourteen boards. There is a wide variety of subject syllabuses and examination techniques. Some syllabuses are set by the boards and the examination papers marked by them. Other syllabuses are devised by individual schools or group of schools, and in some cases schools set and mark their own examinations subject to moderation of standards by the boards. Overall control of the C.S.E. examinations lies in the hands of the School Council whose task it is to ensure national comparability.

At the present time a new integrated examination system, to replace the G.C.E. and the C.S.E., is under active consideration. This would require candidates to take a number of subjects at Normal Level ("N" level) and a smaller number at the more advanced Further Level ("F" level).

In Scotland secondary school children present themselves after four years for the Ordinary Grade or after five years for the Higher Grade of the Scottish Certificate of Education. Northern Ireland has an examination similar to the English G.C.E. J L F

Graduate

One who has obtained a degree from a university, college, etc. 1479. In U.S.A. occasionally: a pupil who has completed a secondary school course.

- The British system of higher education is devided into undergraduate and postgraduate studies.

After a course of studies lasting from three to four years which must be pursued at one and the same university the undergraduate student sits for a final examination which, if je passes it, entitles him to a first degree. At English universities the undergraduate courses normally lead to the bachelor's degree. But not all degrees which have the title of "Bachelor" are first degrees. The Oxford B. Litt., e.g. is to be considered as a higher degree. At Scottish universities, however, the Master of Arts (M.A.) is the first degree of the Arts Faculty while in faculties other than the Faculty of Arts the title of bachelor is awarded as a first degree at Scottish universities, too. Throughout the Middle Ages studies in Arts (*Liberal Arts**) were the first stage of university education, and the Faculty of Arts, therefore, was preparatory to the faculties of theology, law, and medicine to which only holders of the B.A. were admitted. Following this tradition, Oxford and Cambridge still call the first degree in most faculties Bachelor of Arts, e.g. B.A. (Law), B.A. (Theol.) etc.

At the end of the 18th century the general education leading to the B.A. could no longer meet the requirements of the Scientific Age which was just beginning (*Industrial Revolution**). In 1782, therefore, the necessity for specialization and intensification of studies led to a distinction between two different types of degrees called Pass (or Ordinary) degrees and Honours degrees. The latter were awarded for higher proficiency in some subject beyond that required by Pass degrees. This distinction has been maintained. Because the Honours degree requires specialization whereas the Pass degree requires a more general education, some universities (e.g. Birmingham, Bristol, Sheffield, Exester, etc.) have introduced the terms "Special degree" (for Honours) and "General degree" (for Pass or Ordinary degree).

After taking a first degree the graduates aiming at a professional career leave the university. Only students who are interested in research work follow the postgraduate or advanced studies. They are accepted for postgraduate studies only if they achieved an exceptional mark in the final examination for the first degree. The number of postgraduates is increasing. In Cambridge, for example, there were 2,121 postgraduates – compared with 8,246 undergraduates – in June, 1970. The postgraduate studies lead to higher degrees most of which are Master's or Doctor's degrees. Postgraduate (also called research) students are expected to carry out independent research and are granted the Master's degree by thesis or examination after a minimum of one or two years of advanced studies. Only at *Oxford and Cambridge** is the Master's degree awarded to graduates some years later without further examination. The doctorate generally requires an outstanding proficiency in some specialized branch of research. It is regarded as the highest degree.

■ In the United States the term "graduate" has taken on a complex meaning. A graduate may be a person who has graduated from *High School** or may also be one who has passed the final examination of a *College** or a university. The high school graduate is entitled to sit for a college entrance examination. After four years of study at a college entrance examination. After four years of study at a college (two years junior and two years senior college) the student takes the examination for the Bachelor's degree and becomes a college graduate. If interested in some spezialized branch of study, the college graduate may enter one of the graduate schools of the university and take the Master's or Doctor's degree. Since approximately 1920 a distinction has been introduced between Honours and Pass degrees similar to British university practice. Swarthmore College, Pa., was one of the first to introduce Honours courses. Frank Aydelotte, President of Swarthmore at that time, described the Honours studies as follows: "The honours student has his work outlined for him not in terms of what he must do but in terms of what he must know. Instead of taking courses he studies a subject. He must find out and strengthen his own weakness, develop his own strong points and, in general, take the responsibility of his own salvation." The level of the academic degrees varies greatly from university to university (*Accreditation**). I Fr

Grammar School

● Originally ancient foundations dating back to the 16th century or earlier and set up for the teaching of Latin grammar, they are now secondary schools of decreasing importance.

As a result of the 1902 Education Act and the resultant expansion of secondary education in the public sector, the number of grammar schools increased greatly. In 1900 less than one child in seventy could expect to enter a grammar school, but by the late 1960s one child in five could find a place. In 1968 23 per cent. of all secondary school pupils attended grammar schools, yet by 1967 this number had dwindled to 8 per cent. This startling decrease is accounted for by the fact that most of these schools have been integrated into the comprehensive system. This applies mainly to the maintained or state grammar schools and not to the Direct Grant schools. Since 1976 a process of phasing out of these schools, previously financed directly from the Department of Education and Science and not from the Local Education Authority, has been implemented by the government. By the end of 1975 fifty-one direct grant schools had said they intended to opt for entry into the state system as comprehensive schools. Many others hoped, finances allowing, to become fully independent of the state.

Where grammar schools still exist as an integral part of the state secondary school system they are reserved for those children who are succesful in the 11-plus examination. Since the introduction of comprehensive schools has got fully under way throughout the country, however, the majority of children approaching secondary education no longer sit for the 11-plus, and those that do so must, if necessary, be prepared to travel outside their local area and at their parents' expense.

Besides the more academic character of the traditional grammar school curriculum, the most outstanding feature of these schools were perhaps the highly specialised courses offered at sixth-form level. Since reorganisation, however, the comprehensive schools, and particularly the small number of sixth-form colleges, offer an ever increasing range of subjects at the Advanced Level of the General Certificate of Education. In 1976 the number of comprehensive schools offering courses at 'At'-level amounted to 1,881 as against 475 grammar schools. It is a logical inference that the majority of university entrants are no longer solely grammar school products.

The relatively small number of grammar schools that remains can look back on a tradition some 1400 years old, for Augustine is credited with the founding of the first grammar school in England at Canterbury in A.D. 598. Today, despite their dwindling numbers and encouraged to some extent by political and educational reaction to the comprehensive system, they pride themselves on offering a curriculum that is unashamedly academic in approach, but which at the same time places more emphasis on extra-curricula activities such as sporting, cultural and club interests than their counterparts in other European countries. GW

Guidance

■ Also called counselling. The process of helping an individual discover his educational, vocational, and psychological potentialities.

One characteristic of American education nowadays is the particular accent placed on guidance which is considered to be one of the vital functions of the American teacher. According to James B. Conant, "Guidance is the keystone of the arch of public education; every effort to improve the guidance services in our schools should be encouraged". In its broadest sense it encompasses all the activities of teachers for helping the child in his school career and in the choice of his vocation. Thus the child is expected to arrive at a better utilization of his abilities to the ultimate good of not only the individual but also society.

Guidance in the present conception as assistance to pupils in understanding and handling their problems and in making intelligent choices at school *(Elective System*)* and with regard to their later vocation is the result of a historical process which has passed through a variety of phases in educational theory and practice. It began about 80 years ago with the work of Jesse Davis in Detroit and Frank Parsons in Boston. Originally it was considered to be a service to prevent mistakes in occupational choices and was therefore termed "vocational guidance". Though vocational guidance goes on playing a most important part it was soon enlarged to encompass "educational guidance". It was recognized that vocational guidance towards the end of the school career demanded a corresponding continual preparation in education, especially when the *Elective System** came more and more into use in schools and colleges. Then arose the urgent need for assisting the pupils and students to make intelligent choices from the items of the curriculum, according to their capacities and abilities. Today guidance profits from various movements:

(a) The testing movement which brings to the schools a wide variety of psychological abilities and aptitudes;
(b) The mental health movement which is intent on achieving and maintaining that emotional adjustment which lies at the basis of a sound personality;
(c) The curriculum study which defines all the different demands inherent in the different subjects in relation to the pupil's capacities;
(d) The progress in psychological studies, especially those concerned with child growth and development, which furnishes educationalists with a sound basis for determining reasonable expectations.

The guidance function is considered to be comprehensive; comprising educational and vocational guidance as well as recreational and moral guidance, etc., those different varieties being considered as phases of a continuous, unitary process. So, e.g. satisfactory occupational activity by effectual vocational guidance involves educational decisions, personal traits, and emotional adjustment. In no case must guidance be dictation; the students is to be "advised" in his attempts to arrive at reasonable decisions. In education, guidance and instruction are now considered to be complementary phases, and guidance is not to be separated from the learning experiences. So on the American school staff everyone has some responsibility for guidance.

But on account of the intrinsie difficulties of guidance many schools have a director of guidance - sometimes called a "counsellor". His function is to co-ordinate the guidance activities of the entire school. Professional study of guidance gives him special competence in dealing with difficult problems of pupils' adjustment and special knowledge in particular areas of pupils' choice.

Since 1969, a major new effort, "Career Education", has gained federal support. It aims to acqaint all young people with the world of work, and to make them ready to earn living after secodary school PH/DPH

- In Great Britain, since World War II, vocational guidance for school children has beeb recognized as very important and has been recognized as very important and has been developed systematically. Nowadays responsibility for career guidance is shared between schools, many of which allocate one or more teachers part time to this function, and the career officers working in collaboration with them. Career officers are appointed by local education authorities which are empowered to provide a careers guidance and placing service for children and school leavers as well as for students in further education and teacher training. Young people are free to seek advice from the local authority careers service or from the Employment Service of the Department of Employment. PH

High School

In the U.S.A., a school intermediate between an elementary school and a college. 1824

■ The public school is the American co-educational institution providing compulsory, free secondary education for all the children of the nation. It makes no distinction between either the intellectual capacities of its pupils or the financial means of their parents. Education here follows after attendance at the elementary school. There are two types of high school: one begins in the ninth grade and ends in the twelfth, thus it comprises only four years; the other, more usual, from begins in the seventh grade and ends in the twelfth grade, thus it comprises six years (it can also be extended to include the thirteenth and fourteenth grade). The second type is more usual in urban areas. It is divided into the junior high school (grades 7 to 9) and the senior high school (grades 10 to 12 or 10 to 14).

A public high school which offers educational facilities for all the youth of a town, city or district has become known as a "comprehensive" high school *(Comprehensive School*)*.

There are two other types of high school: (1) the "specialized", also called vocational high school which provides primarily vocational education; (2) that high school which admits pupils on a selective basis and offers an academic curriculum.

The American high school has a place in the historical evolution of the country since it corresponds to the American ideal of democratic education; it became conspicuous in the colonial period and found expression in the revolutionary generation. Indeed, Jefferson proposed "a system of education which shall reach every description of citizen from the richest to the poorest". The American *Frontier** and the pioneer movement contributed to deepen this concept of equality.

Historians date the high school as an institution from the Boston English Classical School of 1821, but it was only in the second half of the 19th century that it became widespread. As late as 1890 there were 2,526 high schools in an entire nation of 63 million inhabitants. Today there are more than 29,500 high schools in the United States, and 75 per cent. of all American young people graduate from high school. Until recently the U.S. high school was becoming a college preparatory institution for the majority. Since 1974 the proportion of graduates going on to college has dropped. Average years of school completed has remained stable at 12.3 years for some time. A high school graduate is usually 17 or 18 years old.

In American popular opinion the high school is generally regarded as "society's organized effort to educate its adolescents". American society in general has refused to confine secondary education to intellectual growth, thus orienting the high school away from the European pattern and towards the youth's adjustment to the world in which he lives. Great emphasis is therefore placed on student government and student activities.

The high school has also been one of the most important instruments in the making of a new nation out of immigrants from Europe, Africa and Asia. The American high school aims at turning out not only Americans, but Americans who feel at home in any section of society. According to James B. Conant, this type of school is typical of American public education, since it came into being because of American devotion to the ideals of equality of opportunity and equality of status *(Melting Pot* and Immigration*).* Americans have now come to believe that a high school diploma is an important credential for every citizen. They have broadened their notions of what constitutes a high school education and, over the years, worked to offer the opportunity of a high school education to all persons. Yet there are still dropouts, and a feeling of disenchantment with high school is articulated by many students. Clearly the high school as the institution which integrates all persons into the mainstream of society remains an unrealized ideal.

Since no general federal legislation for education exists the evolution and organization of the high school depends on the states' administrations and to a large extent on the local school boards. Indeed, Professor Conant, in 1959, addressed his report on "The American High School Today" to the school board members and the school administrators. Within the high school of today all the varied patterns of educational organization and of curriculum are to be found although some common traits can be distinguished.

The curriculum is generally determined by three main objectives: (1) to provide a general education for all future citizens; (2) to provide elective courses for those who wish to take up a job immediately after graduation; (3) to provide satisfactory programmes for those who - after graduation - intend to continue their studies in colleges. It is stressed that to maintain individual freedom of choice each youth must be free to select his vocational goals and to pursue a high school programme leading to them.

Although local influences are considerable it can be said that most schools require all students to take a minimum number of general courses and guide them in choosing their electives. English is everywhere compulsory. Compulsory courses of a similar nature amount to approximately 25 per cent. of the whole curriculum. Social studies, encompassing history, geography, and particularly citizenship, are among the principal courses. In addition courses in mathematics and natural sciences appear as compulsory subjects, but only for the students of the first two grades. In the following grades these subjects are then offered as electives in a very great variety of choices. Physical training or gymnastics are generally compulsory. All the other subjects are elective, particularly languages, which were very widely neglected for a long time but the study of which is now strongly encouraged. The practice still prevails that languages are offered in courses limited in duration from two to four years, but they are now taught in a very progressive manner in which use is made of audio-visual aids and language laboratories. Recent court decisions and federal legislation have required that bilingual education be provided for those whose native language is not English.

Students who want to enter academic careers take the courses required of all students, the courses required for the particular curriculum they choose, and a few special electives. If a student loses interest in the curriculum he has chosen or discovers that his abilities lie in another field he may transfer to a different curriculum. The choice of electives offered to the students is on the whole as broad as can be imagined. Furthermore it can be enlarged at any time according to the wishes of the local school board, which is made up of lay persons. The prevailing tendency within the high school of today is to educate the able student. Thus a recent increase in the use of tests has been stimulated by legislation providing federal assistance to states which offer extensive programmes needed to identify the gifted and the talented. Subsidies to the states out of federal funds were further increased under the *National Defense*

*Education Act** of 1958 which was to promote the teaching of foreign languages as well as mathematics and sciences in the American high schools. This opened the way for further federal support for vocational education in 1961, education for poor children in 1965 and aid for handicapped students in the 1970s.

The past few years, however, may be considered as a period of unusually significant ferment in reassessing the status and need of secondary education in the United States. Strong trends seem to develop for fundamental reform and renewal . In order to clarify the contemporary problems five national commissions and panels have taken place in order to analyze the needs, identify the conditions and find effective ways of meeting the challenges of the last quarter of the 20th century. Different reports agree that "authentic learning can take place in a wide variety of settings, many of them remote from the schoolhouse... They recognize that a variety of other institutions and agencies are also involved in educating and socializing youth and propose moving a substantial portion of learning opportunities outside the school building."

P H/D P H

Ivy League

Popular name for a group of colleges or universities in the north-eastern United States, widely regarded as high in academic and social prestige.

■ Ivy: here referring to the prevalence of ivy-covered buildings on the campuses of the older U.S. colleges.

The term "Ivy League" refers to certain outstanding American institutions of higher learning which, with one exception, were founded during the colonial period of American history. The Ivy League originated when these institutions formed a group for athletic purposes. They are located in the eastern region of the United States, half of them in the States which are known as *New England*"*.

There are eight universities which belong to the Ivy League group:

Harvard University, Cambridge/Mass., which was founded as Harvard College in 1636 and was renamed Harvard University in 1869.

Yale University, New Haven/Conn., founded as Yale College in 1701, the name being officially changed to Yale University in 1887.

Princeton University, Princeton/N.J., founded as the College of New Jersey in 1746 and renamed Princeton University in 1896.

Columbia University, New York/N.Y., founded as King's College in 1754, named Columbia College in 1784 and Columbia University in 1912.

The University of Pennsylvania, Philadelphia/Pa., founded as the College and Academy of Philadelphia in 1740, renamed The University of Pennsylvania in 1791 (not to be confused with Pennsylvania State University).

Brown University, Providence, R.I., founded as Rhode Island College in 1764 and renamed Brown University in 1804.

Dartmouth College, Hanover/N.H., founded in 1769.

Cornell University, Ithaca/N.Y., founded in 1865.

Harvard University, the oldest institution of higher learning in the United States, was named "Harvard College" in honour of John Harvard, a *Puritan** minister from England, who emigrated to America after having been granted the Bachelor's and Master's Degrees from Emmanuel College, Cambridge/England. He bequeathed the major part of his property to the newly established "schoale or colledge" at Cambridge/Mass. (formerly named Newetowne).

The spirit of the founders of Harvard which was deeply rooted in their religious belief can be ascertained from the words carved on the college gates: "After God had carried us safe to New-England, and we had builded our houses, provided necessaries for our liveli-hood, rear'd convenient places for God's worship and settled the Civil Government; One of the next things we longed for, and looked after was to advance Learning and perpetuate it to Posterity; dreading to leave an illiterate Ministry to the Churches, when our present Minister shall lie in the Dust".

Throughout its existence Harvard has produced cultural and intellectual leaders. In the field of letters men such as Ralph Waldo Emerson, Henry Thoreau, James Russell Lowell, Henry Wadsworth Longfellow and Henry Adams were among its alumni as were the eminent 20th century men Robert Frost and T. S. Eliot. In the field of pure and applied sciences Harvard became one of the foremost institutions, astronomy, geology and chemistry having been taught there almost from the beginning. The Harvard School of Medicine was opened at Boston in 1782. Further *Graduate** schools of law, divinity (although theology had been taught from the foundation of Harvard College) followed at the turn of the 18th century. Thus Harvard College increasingly grew to the scope of a university in the modern sense of the word.

It is noteworthy that as early as 1882 Radcliffe College – one of the earliest *Colleges** for women – was established as an independent affiliate of Harvard.

In 1908 Harvard University opened its famous graduate School of Business Administration *(Management Education*)*.

Six presidents of the United States were educated at Harvard, among them Theodore Roosevelt, Franklin D. Roosevelt, and John F. Kennedy.

The foundation of Yale College in 1701 at Killingworth and Saybrook, Conn., resulted from the 17th century controversy within the Congregational Church between the adherents of pure Calvinism and those Puritans who were inclined to a more tolerant religious attitude. The former founded Yale College as a truer "school of prophets" and chose the Rev. Abraham Pierson as the first Rector of the College (the rector being the equivalent of the president of Harvard College). In 1716 Yale College was moved to New Haven, Conn. Yale College owes its name to Elihu Yale, a native of Boston and governor of Ft. St. George, Madras, India, who sent a large cargo of gifts to provide for a new college building.

In 1802 chairs in chemistry, mineralogy, and geology were established at Yale College, the first of their kind in the United States. Yale College had long since been non-sectarian when it was named Yale University in 1887. In 1933 a number of residential colleges were established for undergraduate students. Financed by large gifts made by a Yale graduate, they were modelled on the pattern of the residential colleges of *Oxford and Cambridge**.

William Howard Taft, 27th President of the United States (1908-12), was a graduate of Yale and Professor of Constitutional Law at Yale University from 1913 to 1921.

Princeton University, although nominally non-sectarian, was founded by *Presbyterians** and was for long under the sway of the church. Its foundation was made possible by large private funds which also provided for the cost of Nassau Hall, then the largest building on an American campus. One of the characteristic features of Princeton is student self-government by an honour system under which undergraduates participate in the administration of university discipline.

James Madison, 4th President of the United States (1808-16), and Woodrow Wilson, 28th President of the United States (1912-20), who proposed the famous "Fourteen Points" after World War I, both graduated from Princeton University. Wilson was a professor at Princeton from 1890 to 1902 and President of Princeton from 1902 to 1910.

Columbia University was founded under a grant by George II (hence the first name King's College). Although it was an Episcopal institution its charter provided that the governors should not "exclude any person of any religious denomination whatever from equal liberty and advantage of education or from any of the degrees, liberties, privileges, benefits, or immunities of the said college on account of his particular tenets in matter of religion" *(Religious Test*)*. Today Columbia University is a huge and very complex institution. It comprises *Liberal Arts** colleges for men and women as well as graduate schools in many areas of knowledge such as medicine, law, engineering, political science, natural science, architecture, international affairs, etc. It carries out a large programme of *University Extension**. Many other institutions such as the College of Pharmacy and the New York College for the Training of Teachers are affiliated with Columbia University.

The University of Pennsylvania was initially opened as an academy in 1751 with Benjamin Franklin as the first president of the Board of Trustees, and in 1755 it was converted into the College and Academy of Philadelphia. In 1765 the first medical school of North America was founded as a part of the existing institution. After it had been state-supported and state-controlled for some years it became a privately endowed and controlled institution, although today it is granted some states aid. William H. Harrison, 9th President of the United States (1840-41), was a graduate of the University of Pennsylvania.

Brown University was founded under the sponsorship of the *Baptists** but from its very beginning in 1764 it was an institution characterized by religious freedom. Its foundation as college of Rhode Island calls to mind that Providence, R.I., had been founded as a refuge for the victims of religious persecution by Roger Williams in 1636 *(New England*)*. The charter of Brown University provided that "all the members hereof shall forever enjoy full, free, absolute, and uninterrupted liberty of conscience". In honour of Nicholas Brown, a citizen of Providence, who made large benefactions to the college, its name was changed to Brown University in 1804.

Dartmouth College was founded by Royal Charter of George III as a liberal arts college for men. Despite its associated graduate schools, Dartmouth College has remained primarily an undergraduate liberal arts college. Its library, however, is the largest undergraduate library of the United States.

Cornell University was founded in 1865 as a *Land-Grant College** under the provisions of the Morill Act of 1862. Cornell University was designed by its founder Ezra Cornell as "an institution where any person can find instruction in any study". He made a gift of $ 800,000 and 200 acres of land to the new institution, the charter of which provided that besides agricultural research as specified under the Morrill Act "such other branches of science and knowledge may be embraced in the plan of instruction and investigation pertaining to the University as the trustees may deem useful and proper". The counterparts for the higher education of women are colleges such as Bryn Mawr, Vassar, Smith.

Today the term "Ivy League" is used not only to refer specifically to one or more of the above universities, but also as a general adjective to describe the style, manners, dress, and social standard usually associated with their graduates *(Establishment*)*. I Fr

Land-Grant College

■ Land Grant: (chiefly U.S.: the name given to a portion of land in the occupation of specified persons, 1719) a grant of public land by the Federal Government for various purposes such as the foundation of agricultural colleges.

Until a considerable time after the Civil War educational subsidies by the Federal Government to the states took the form of land grants. In the course of time the Federal Government has given public land totalling approximately 145,000,000 acres to the states for this purpose. (As to the term "public land" see *Conservation of Land*.)* The proceeds from the sale of the land were used to meet the cost of founding and maintaining educational institutions.

The Land-Grant Act, introduced by Senator Morill (hence also called Morill Act) and passed by Congress in July 1862, enabled the Federal Government to assign public land to the states with the sole intention of thereby endowing colleges of agriculture and mechanical arts. Through the second Morrill Act 1890 Congress began to make regular appropriations for the further support of these institutions. Under the provision of the Morrill Acts 68 land-grant colleges have been established.

This federal aid for furthering agricultural education has proved very fruitful; owing to their work in scientific agronomy the so-called land-grant colleges have exercised a tremendous influence upon the agricultural development of the country (see *Agrarian Revolution** and *Agricultural Relief*)*. Most land-grant colleges have developed in the course of time into universities furnishing a full range of liberal and professional studies in addition to the agricultural and mechanical task with which they were originally charged. Today the best land-grant universities (e.g. Cornell University cf. *Ivy League*)* rank with the finest institutions of higher education in the United States.

P H/D P H

Liberal Arts

The studies . . . that are presumed to provide chiefly general knowledge and to develop the general intellectual capabilities (as reason or judgement) as opposed to professional, vocational or technical studies. M. E.

The Shorter Oxford English Dictionary defines "liberal" as originally "the epithet of those 'arts' or 'sciences' that were 'worthy of a free man'." The "liberal arts" were deemed to be seven in number, and it was on these that medieval educational systems were based. The subjects of study were: grammar, rhetoric, and logic (these three forming the "trivium"), and arithmetic, music, geometry, and astronomy (forming the "quadrivium"). It will be seen that, in contrast to the so-called "fine arts" (from French: "Beaux arts", the arts dealing with the beautiful, chiefly sculpture and painting) which are cultivated more for their own sake and the aesthetic pleasure they afford, the liberal arts are subjects of practical value, in that they promote freedom of expression in language (grammar), speech (rhetoric), and reasoning (logic and mathematics), as well as the studies which help man to acquire a better understanding of his physical, social and cultural environment. It is in this sense that the word "arts" is to be understood in the terms "Faculty of Arts", "Bachelor of Arts" and "Master of Arts", widely used still in British and American *Universities** *(Graduate*)*. But whilst the basic conception remains unchanged – that of enabling men to appreciate their environment more fully – the subjects denoted by the term "arts" are no longer identical with the seven ancient arts.

In a modern university the term "arts" is applied to subjects such as languages, philosophy, history, literature, and sometimes pure (i.e. abstract) science. Closely allied to the phrase "liberal arts" is the term "humanities", which also refers to those fields of study which are primarily of cultural value, but which includes more especially the study of Latin and Greek literature. At the Scottish universities "humanity" is the recognized appellation for the course in Latin language and literature.

In this age of ever-increasing specialization the need has been felt, particularly by institutes of technology and technical *Colleges**, to make some attempt to restore the balance, principally by giving scientists and technologists some instruction in "arts" subjects. Consequently some of them have set up departments which provide scientists with courses in languages, literature, history, philosophy and similar subjects. Some other educational institutions likewise offer introductory science courses for the benefit of arts students.

J L F

London University

● Long before the 19th century some writers had been referring to England's "three famous *Universities** of *Oxford, Cambridge** and London". While there were certain academic institutions in London before the 19th century – the *Inns of Court** and the Divinity Schools at Westminster and St. Paul's had been in existence since the Middle Ages – there was no university in the accepted sense of the word, for the teaching bodies such as those already mentioned lacked the unity under a common government which for us is one of the essential features of a university. In the Middle Ages Paris, too, had been graced by the presence of a number of scholastic institutions; but there they had later developed into a university. It is therefore rather surprising that London, which after all was the largest city in the world in the 19th century, had to wait until well on into that century before it could boast of a university as we understand it.

Since 1581 it had been necessary for those wishing to gain admission to Oxford or Cambridge to subscribe to the teachings of the *Established Church**; these *Religious Tests** were upheld until their abolition by the University Tests Act of 1871. Meanwhile those holding *Nonconformist** views naturally resented their exclusion from higher education, and a group of them took positive action by founding a university of their own. On April 30th, 1827 in London the foundation stone of what is now known as University College was laid. Two years later a rival group of Anglicans and Tories retaliated by founding King's College, whose Royal Charter of Incorporation stated that it should be "a College in which instruction in the doctrines and duties of Christianity as taught by the Church of England should be forever combined with other branches of useful education". Despite the use of the term *College** the London foundations bear little resemblance to the colleges of Oxford and Cambridge; they were, in fact, strongly influenced by the German conception of a university.

In the meantime many other colleges have come into being. At first teaching was confined to the colleges themselves, while a separate body called the University of London was set up and entrusted with the work of conducting examinations and also with the conferment of degrees. At the turn of the century the University was reconstituted, making it a teaching body composed of the various colleges or "Schools of the University", but the original foundations nevertheless still enjoy a certain measure of autonomy. Over the past 150 years the University has seen rapid expansion, both in the number and size of the constituent colleges and teaching institutions and in the numbers of students admitted. That student numbers here far exceed those at any other British university is attributable on the one hand to the University's many world-famous institutions (such as the Imperial College of Science and Technology, the London School of Economics and Political Science, the School of Oriental and African Studies, and Guy's Hospital Medical School), and on the other, of course, to the unrivalled amenities afforded by the capital. For the session 1975-76 no fewer than 43,959 internal students were enrolled. To these must be added another 27,470 students taking *External Degrees** (i.e. degrees awarded by London University to students studying privately or working at other educational institutions throughout Britain and the Commonwealth for which London University acts as the examining body). It is interesting to note that with the decision of the University Senate and Convocation in 1878 to make every degree, honour and prize awarded by the University accessible to both sexes on equal terms London became the first university in Britain to admit women to degrees. J L F

Management Education

■ Management education as a special field of postgraduate studies was first introduced in the United States. In 1908 the University of Harvard established the School of Business Administration *(Ivy League*)*. Its students are postgraduates of one of the traditional faculties – mostly the economics or the social science faculties – who have also acquired some experience in a special line of business, thus qualifying not only as postgraduate but also as "postexperience" students. Harvard Business School was designed as a training centre for top management. Although a school for postgraduate studies and economic research, it has always closely co-operated with business, and thus tried to bridge the gap between academic studies and professional experience. Based on the idea of "active learning", which calls to mind the principle of "learning by doing" as developed by John Dewey, Harvard Business School introduced the "case-method" as a special feature of its curriculum. In 1929 the first "casebook" was published which is well known even today. The "case-method" takes into account the fact that top management is confronted with the need to make important decisions and that this requires special skill and knowledge. Analysis of current business cases to be solved by team work can go a long way towards giving managers the opportunity of developing wide experience and knowledge. Such team work is of special importance because it is a typical phenomenon of managerial strategy in modern industry. Harvard Business School has gained a world wide reputation and many offshoots have been established not only in the United States but on the Continent, especially in France, Switzerland and in the United Kingdom.

- Britain was particularly interested in the management education which Harvard University pioneered. Since amateurism, is definitely out of date, the business-school-trained professional has become the model for modern industry. He is expected to promote productivity and to increase economic growth. As a result of the Robbins Report on Higher Education (1963) and the proposal of a private *Committee** under Lord Franks, two postgraduate business schools were established in 1964; the London Graduate School of Business Studies, associated with the London School of Business Studies, and the Manchester Business School. Furthermore, management education on higher level outside the university is offered by the polytechnics. These are national institutions of higher learning which provide courses of study on a wide range of subjects mostly on advanced level.

Additionally, about 75 colleges offer business courses of all kinds on very different levels. They lead to a Diploma in management studies or – as far as the polytechnics are concerned - to the Master's Degree in Business Studies conferred by the Council for National Academic Awards.

For information on business studies the British Institute of Management (BIM) was founded as an independent, non-profitmaking institution in 1974.

The expansion of business studies in Britain during the seventies is sometimes called an "explosion in management education". But in the report "Management Education in the 1970s" Professor H. Rose points out that post-graduate courses have to be tripled to meet the need for well-trained professional managers in Britain.

On the other hand the value of academic management education has sometimes been questioned. In this connection it has been emphasized that efficient management does not only depend on knowledge but on attitude and personal abilities and that initiative and enterprise can hardly be stimulated by academic studies. To cope with the often unpleasant realities of business life above all experience is needed. In the Mant Report on post-experience management education (1970) the British Institute of Management (BIM) therefore stressed the importance of in-company training and recommended to transmit "classroom learning to the workplace". I Fr

National Defense Education Act (N.D.E.A.)

■ This American law was signed by President Eisenhower on September 2nd, 1958, after the launching of the first "Sputnik" on the part of the U.S.S.R. The Federal Government was enabled by it to spend millions of dollars in promoting educational activities in the elementary and secondary schools throughout the country, "to correct as rapidly as possible the existing imbalances in our educational programs which have led to an insufficient proportion of our population educated in science, mathematics, and modern foreign languages and trained in technology".

Included in the provisions for the enactment were funds for student loans, for aid to candidates for teacher education, purchase of equipment for science and foreign languages and facilities for the expansion of guidance services. The Education Bill of 1961 extended the National Defense Education Act; it provided a two-year extension of Federal Aid for "impacted" school areas. The Elementary and Secondary Education Act of 1965 meant a real breakthrough in that it authorized the Federal Government to spend $ 1,300 million on public school education. Between 1965 and 1975 more than $ 17,000 million were expended under the Elementary and Secondary Education Act (ESEA). Prior to the enactment of the National Defense Education Act, Federal funds were confined primarily to vocational education and a few aspects of higher education. Today, Federal funds are available in vastly greater amounts at every level of education, from pre-school to post-graduate level.

The principal educational legislation enacted by Congress after the passing of the National Defense Education Act 1958 includes the Economic Opportunity Act 1964; the *Civil Rights** Act 1964; the Elementary and Secondary Education Act 1965; the Higher Education Act 1965; the Adult Education Act 1966 (Amendments to E.S.E.A.); the Bi-lingual Education Act 1967 (part of E.S.E.A.); the Education Professions Development Act 1967; the Vocational Education Act Amendments 1968; the Juvenile Delinquency and Control Act 1968; the Emergency School Aid Act 1972; the Education Amendments of 1972 and 1974; and the Education Appropriations Act 1972. – These Acts were intended to meet national and social needs. For example, the Economic Opportunity Act 1964 included "Head Start", an educational programme for poor children, the Higher Education Act 1965 included grants for post-secondary students and provided funds for the strengthening of community service programmes of colleges and universities; the financial assistance provided by the Emergency School Aid Act 1972 was meant to contribute to the elimination of minority group segregation and discrimination in elementary and secondary schools. P H/D P H

National Education Association (N.E.A.)

■ This association is the largest and most important national organization of teachers, administrators, and others engaged in educational work or interested in its advancement, with a membership of more than 1.687 million members by August 1977. It was founded in 1857 as the National Teachers Association and chartered by Congress in 1906. Its general aim is to promote the welfare and professional status of teachers in the United States. Within the organization and affiliated to it are thirty and more departmental groups representing the special interests of teachers. Perhaps the two most influential of these are the American Association of School Administrators and the Department of Classroom Teachers.

Since 1922, a research division has been active in investigating such professional problems as teacher tenure, the teacher's financial position, the improvement of social studies, and many others. During the 1950s, 1960s and 1970s special units, both ad hoc and permanent, have been formed to deal with such problems as the improved use of new methods and new types of equipment; increased understanding of the social role of education; ways and means of improving education for highly talented, less able, and other special categories of pupils; audio-visual media; teaching machines and programmed learning. The Association publishes the "Today's Education" which is mailed to all its members, while many other publications are prepared by the N.E.A. during the course of a year.

In addition to the N.E.A., there are professional educational associations in each of the 50 states. They have purposes similar to that of the national organization and work with problems of school legislation within the states.

It is important to note the growth, especially in large cities, of the American Federation of Teachers (A.F.T.) within the A.F.L.-C.I.O. (*Trade (Labor)*

*Unions**). Not only is the A.F.T. important in its own right, with a membership of about 450,000 in 1975, but it also urges the N.E.A. to more aggressive negotiating methods with school authorities. The difference between the strikes called by the A.F.T. and the "professional sanctions" invoked by the N.E.A. is often only slight. However, the A.F.T. is more concerned with the employer-employee relationship than the N.E.A., while the N.E.A. stresses professional development, research, and attempts to influence national legislation. The two associations, though now becoming more competitive, appear to move toward ultimate merger. P H/D P H

National Union of Teachers (N.U.T.)

● The National Union of Teachers (N.U.T.) is the largest educational association in England and Wales. It comprises teachers on all school levels, from kindergarten to university, and has been affiliated to the Trades Union Congress since 1970. It was founded in 1870 and, in the course of the second half of the 20th century, has become an organization with about 294,000 members in 1977.

It has retained its original character as a union of local organizations. Its controlling body is the annual conference of approximately 2,000 delegates, regularly held at Easter. Its executive body consists of 40 members directing a large professional and clerical staff. The aims pursued by the N.U.T. are as follows: to associate and unite the teachers of England and Wales, to provide means for co-operation, manifestations of collective opinions upon matters of education, and to secure the establishment of an efficient national system of education.

In order to realize its aims the N.U.T. renders a number of services vital to the teaching profession by working for a general level of salaries and adequate pensions, giving legal advice, issuing insurance, maintaining a lending library, supplying educational information, publishing a periodical "The Teacher" and issuing miscellaneous reports. Through its manifold activities the N.U.T. exercises a considerable influence in the broadening and improving of educational opportunities for all types of pupils in England and Wales.

Whereas the N.U.T., making no distinction of either sex or academic status or professional status, has always had the interests of both men and women teachers as its prime concern, there was a group of male teachers believing that there should be an organization looking after the interests of male teachers. They formed a splinter group from the N.U.T., which became known as the National Association of Schoolmasters (N.A.S.). It then attempted to sponsor a woman's teachers' organization called the Union of Women Teachers. But with the passage of the Sex Discrimination Act in Britain, they have had to agree to merge with the women organization to provide a joint body called the National Association of Schoolmasters/Union of Women Teachers. This joint body is now the second largest professional organization.

An organization of particular importance in British educational development is "The Joint Four", e.g. the Joint Committee of four Associations: Head Masters' Association (HMA), Association of Head Mistresses (AHM), Association of Assistant Mistresses (AAM), Assistant Masters' Association (AMA). These four Associations established the Joint Four in 1919, and they have built up a tradition of co-operation and joint action, with a combined membership of the four Associations of approximately

85,000. Membership is not confined to grammar schools, but comprises members in secondary schools of all kinds.

An association established for the special purpose of defending the interests of the head teachers of maintained primary and *Secondary Modern Schools** constitutes the National Association of Head Teachers (N.A.H.T.). P H

New University

● The term designates the group of British universities of the 1960s which were planned in line with the recommendations of the Robbins Report (Report of the Committee on Higher Education under the Chairmanship of Lord Robbins, 1963). These institutions are known as "New Universities" because they are modelled after a new concept. They have had full university status, i.e. the right to confer degrees, from their beginnings. All other universities, except *Oxford and Cambridge**, had been founded as university colleges and at first depended on *London University** for the supervision of academic standards and the conferment of degrees *(Red-Brick University*)*.

The university of Keele does not – stricktly speaking – belong to this group because it was still founded as "University College of North Staffordshire" in 1949. But it was Keele with Lord Lindsay as its Vice-Chancellor who pioneered the New Universities. He succeeded in acquiring the necessary funds for what was then considered a new experiment: a university college entitled to grant its own bachelor's degrees without interference from London University. In 1962 the University College of Staffordshire was granted full university status which meant that it was authorized to confer even higher degrees *(Graduate*)*. It is now named the University of Keele. It is strictly residential, i.e. all students have to live in the college. It has extended the normal three years' undergraduate course by an obligatory "foundation year" which is supposed to provide a broad general education for the undergraduates.

The big upsurge in the demand for higher education after World War II which Lord Robbins called an "Educational Revolution" made it clear that the foundation of further universities was going to be needed. Between 1961 and 1965 seven English universities were established: University of Sussex in Brighton (1961), York (1963), East Anglia in Norwich (1963), Essex in Colchester (1964), Lancaster (1964), Kent in Canterbury (1965), and Warwick in Coventry (1965). The University of Surrey at Guildford received its charter in 1966. The New Universities were expected to experiment with the contents and organization of undergraduate courses and they have done so, as is best to be seen from Sussex University, the "oldest" of the New Universities. It is not by chance that Sussex University became one of the most attractive of the New Universities and as early as 1964 achieved over a thousand students. Located near the seaside and not too far from London, it is set in beautiful surroundings. Its modern quadrangle was designed by Sir Basil Spence who also designed the famous new Cathedral of Coventry. The educational programmes based on "schools of studies" such as European studies, Anglo-American studies, African studies enable students and the members of the academic staff to overcome the narrow boundaries of the traditional faculties and departments. It is intended to train specialists in interrelated studies focused on one main subject and irrespective of faculty limits. Most of the other New Universities are following the pattern of Sussex but are sometimes influenced by environmental or local traditions. The new Scottish universities are: Strathclyde, 1966, Heriot-Watt (Edinburgh), 1966, Stirling, 1967, and Dundee, (independent of St. Andrews), 1967. In Northern Ireland the New University of Ulster at Coleraine was founded in 1965. Mostly non-residential and non-collegiate, the New Universities lay stress on the tutorial system *(Tutor*)* and retain the traditional lecturer-student ratio of 1 to 8. Many young fellows from Oxford and Cambridge have been willing to take up posts at the New Universities. Although these universities are excellent places of higher learning, the question has been raised whether the creation of small new universities is the proper way for expansion to take place if the problem of cost is taken into consideration. The British system of higher learning has always been the most expensive (in relation to places available) in the Western World. Without doubt the multiplication of small universities, each providing its own libraries, laboratories and other expensive equipment is a much more expensive method of expansion than increasing the size of universities already existing.

Finally another group of New Universities must be mentioned. Following the Robbins Report the Government decided that the Colleges of Advanced Technology (C.A.T.s.), which were founded in 1957 to meet the steadily growing demand for technologists, should achieve university status. Prior to this decision serious discussions took place as to whether technological institutes ought to be integrated into existing universities or work as independent institutions outside the university though of university standard. Many experts, among them Lord Taylor, chairman of a committee on higher education appointed by the Labour Party in the early sixties, recommended a bilateral system consisting of universities in the proper sense of the word and the independent universities of advanced technology. The Government finally decided for the bilateral system *(College, Sandwich Courses*)*. In the meantime some former C.A.T.s have received their royal charter as universities, viz. Aston (Birmingham), Bath, Bradford, Brunel, Loughborough; and City (London) and Salford were granted university status. I Fr

Open University

- A university open to all. 1969.

In Britain it has long been possible to obtain a university degree without actually attending a university. Students registered at other types of educational institutions have been able to apply for the award of an *External Degree** of *London University**, and the establishment of the Council for National Academic Awards (C.N.A.A.) in 1964 represented another step towards making degrees more generally available. For more than a century the London External Degree has been available even to the person studying privately miles away from any college. But such private students received no tuition and precious little guidance from the University.

In May 1969, however, the Open University (O.U.) was established by Royal Charter. Its purpose was to provide instruction and an examination structure for people whose responsibilities at work or at home prevented them from taking full-time courses at other universities or colleges and for people studying privately who needed the close supervision and guidance London could not offer. The O.U. is, like others, autonomous and independent, awarding its own degrees and certificates. It is financed from fees and a grant from the Department of Education and Science. From its headquarters in

Milton Keynes, Buckinghamshire, it organizes a large number of courses which are taught by methods which have attracted the attention of educationists in many countries. The basis is a correspondence course supplemented by an integrated scheme of television and VHF radio broadcasts. When necessary, students may hire tape-recorders and kits of scientific equipment appropriate to their course. Residential summer courses and evening or weekend tutorials conducted at 260 regional study centres are also arranged. No formal qualifications are required of the students though there is a selection procedure. In January 1971, 24,000 students embarked on foundation courses in arts *(Liberal Arts*)*, social sciences, mathematics and science, and in 1972 about 20,000 students enrolled for these and a further foundation course in technology. There were approx. 65,000 students in 1977. The undergraduate programme continues to expand and postgraduate study will also be introduced. In addition, so-called "post-experience courses" have been available since 1973 for people with some years of working experience who wish to develop their skills in their present field of specialization or who need to acquire basic knowledge of a new subject in an age in which one period of specialized training is not necessarily adequate for a whole life-time. A typical "post-experience course" is that on Electronics. It comprises 17 correspondence units, 17 television and five radio programmes, 12 written assignments to test the student's progress, a week-long residential course and several Saturday tutorials.

The Open University has aroused considerable interest in the United States. A major New York television network plans to broadcast Open University courses and many colleges and several universities have expressed an interest in using or adapting the course materials. To support and promote this interest the Open University maintains a permanent office in Washington (shortly to move to New York). J L F

Oxford and Cambridge (Oxbridge)

● The University of Oxford was not founded, but has developed from the twelfth century when lectures in academic subjects were first held in the town. In 1133 one Robert Pullen, an English scholar from Paris, began lecturing at Oxford, though the university was not referred to as a studium generale until 1163. However within the next century the town became an accepted centre of learning, as described in an appeal to the King in the 13th century as "schola secunda ecclesiae" – second to Paris. The *College** "University College" was founded in 1249, "Balliol College" c. 1263 and Merton College c. 1264. Medieval Oxford could boast such famous names as Roger Bacon, John Duns Scotus and John Wycliffe.

Throughout the 14th and 15th centuries a further seven colleges were founded and the independence of the university in relation to the town was strengthened by royal charters granted at this period. The conflict of interests between university and town – the so-called "town and gown" struggle - sometimes led to open strife between students and townspeople in the Middle Ages; in the Civil War the townsfolk supported *Parliament** while the University took the side of the King, indeed an anti-parliament newspaper Mercurius Anticus was published at Oriel College from 1643. In 1571 an act of Elizabeth I reorganized the universities and further measures taken in 1636 by the Chancellor Archbishop William Laud provided the official code of the university which lasted until 1858. The colleges gradually lost some of their autonomous rights and greater power was placed in the hands of "masters and scholars" to decide university policy. During the 18th century written examinations were introduced to replace the old formal oral examinations and in 1877 reforms were carried out which obliged the colleges to contribute more of their income, from rents, endowments, trusts, etc., to finance new projects, particularly the creation of a Natural Science Faculty. During the last century the number of students increased threefold from 244 in 1800 to 840 in 1900, while in 1971, 8,000 students, or undergraduates as they are called, studied in Oxford.

In 1900 less than 15 per cent. of the college *Fellows** were teaching science subjects, while in 1940 well over 20 per cent. were doing so. During this century there has been increasing interest in science in Oxford and the university possesses good and modern laboratory facilities, including a modern engineering laboratory.

Control over university policy is exercised by "Congregation", a committee of about 1,000 M.A.s, who have to consent to all changes in the university's regulations. It passes judgement on proposals made to it by the Hebdomadal Council, which consists of 5 ex-officio members and 18 elected M.A.s. The large number of M.A.s sitting on Congregation means that the university cannot exercise complete control over the affairs of the individual colleges, nor does it try to. The partial independence of the colleges is highly prized by members of the university and as a result of their endowments and often large incomes, the colleges maintain to this day a certain financial autonomy. The report of the Franks Commission, set up to reform the University of Oxford and its administration, was published in May 1966. It recommended an increase in the number of students from 9,300 to 13,000 in the next few years, greater emphasis on scientific subjects, and certain reforms in college and faculty organization. It is Oxford's attempt to maintain its prominent position amongst English universities, when so many new and exciting developments are taking place.

An Oxford undergraduate cannot matriculate, that is be formally admitted to the university, until he has gained admission to one of the 34 men's or 5 woman's colleges. He normally studies for nine terms (three years) and at the end of this time, in June, he is obliged to take "Schools" – the Final Examination of his faculty – for the degree of Bachelor of Arts (B.A.) or Bachelor of Science (B.Sc.).

Admission to a college is gained through competitive examinations held once or twice a year. They include written tests as well as one or more interviews, value being laid not only on the candidate's academic ability, but also on his ability to profit from the communal college life. Once admitted, he studies under the direction of a *Tutor**, usually a *Fellow** of his college; each college has a body of fellows, who instruct mainly students from their own college, but who also lecture within the framework of the University faculty. At present, owing to the large number of students, each undergraduate spends one, or at most two of his three years in college; the remaining terms he lives outside college.

Plans to admit women students to some of the men's colleges in both Oxford and Cambridge have met with some opposition. In 1974 however, the Oxford colleges Brasenose, Hertford, Jesus, St. Catherine's and Wadham accepted woman students, who have to compete with the men for their places, while of the Cambridge colleges, Clare, King's and Churchill are already mixed.

Founded probably by scholars who left Oxford in the twelfth century, Cambridge is first mentioned as a place of learning in the 13th century. The first college, Peterhouse, was not founded until 1284. In 1318 Cambridge was recognized by Pope John XXII as a studium generale *(Universities*)*. Clare College was founded in 1326 and within thirty years five new foundations were created. In 1570 the Statutes of Elizabeth I gave the heads of colleges more power; however in the next century the University was less reputed than Oxford, although Isaac Newton, Professor of Mathematics from 1673 to 1702, reflected the great interest in Natural Sciences that existed in Cambridge at that time. In 1850 the State intervened to assist in the development of the University and as a result the "Senate" – the body of Masters of Arts (M.A.s) – was given more power. Control of the University was placed, as at Oxford, more and more in the hands of the resident Senior Members. The "Senate" consisting of Doctors and masters of faculties elects the Chancellor and other officials, although Regent House wields the real power, consisting as it does of all members of "Senate" who are resident university members. There are twenty-seven Cambridge colleges, twenty-four for men and three for women, which are run on approximately the same lines as at Oxford. D H

Parent-Teachers' Association (P.T.A.)

■ The Parent-Teachers' Association, a non-commercial, nonpartisan organization, comprises thousands of voluntary associations each of them composed of parents of children and teachers of a school or a community, the purpose of which is to improve the effectiveness of the school as an educational and social unit and to care for the educational, social, and economic well-being of children. In this organization the need for effective co-operation between parents and teachers on problems of mutual concern is fully recognized. Various methods have been tried to solve the problems of parent-teacher relationship. The best known and most widespread method has been the organization of parent-teacher groups. The vast majority of these local associations are now affiliated to the National Congress of Parents and Teachers (N.C.P.T.). The objects of the N.C.P.T. are as follows: to promote the welfare of children in the home, school, church, and community, to raise the standard of home life, to secure adequate laws for the care and protection of children and youth, to bring the home and the school into closer relation so that parents and teachers may co-operate intelligently in the training of the child, to develop between educators and the general public such united efforts as will procure for every child the highest advantage in mental, physical, social and spiritual education.

The origin of this organization can be traced back to the first Congress of Mothers in Washington, D.C., 1897. In 1908, the name was changed to the National Congress of Mothers-and-Parent-Teacher Associations. A "Mothers Congress Magazine" first appeared in 1906; in 1934 its name was changed to "The National Parent-Teacher".

Since 1974 the journal has not been published, because of substantial losses of circulation and revenue. The P.T.A. now has chapters in only about a third of the 88,000 public schools. The membership in the P.T.A. has declined from over 12 million in 1963 to 6.4 million in 1977. The P.T.A. has problems convincing parents and teachers of its value because it has often done nothing, and in an effort to be non-political has refused to take stand on major issues.

Currently, P.T.A. is trying to regain its importance through a programme of political lobbying, and such widely publicized efforts of a campaign against violence in television programmes. However, the national P.T.A. has still kept largely clear of the country's most divisive educational issues: desegration busing programs and efforts to set minimum high school graduation standards.
P H/D P H

- In Great Britain most schools now have some form of Parent-Teacher Association, e.g. a school-based association of teachers and parents. Their purpose is to facilitate home/school contacts and to work for the benefit of the school, often by raising funds. The term is sometimes used for other groups, such as a Parents' Association or Guild, a Home and School Society, or any school-based group which seeks to involve the community in similar ways. There is no standard Association, but each one develops to suit the needs of a particular school. The National Confederation of Parent-Teacher Associations (N.C.P.T.A.) has been in existence for over 21 years and exists as an organisation to draw together all those interested in home/school co-operation. There are 3,000 member schools representing over 1,000 000 parents. The N.C.P.T.A. is recognized as the main British body concerned with home/school relations.
P H

Prefect

- In some English schools, one of the body of senior pupils to whom authority is delegated for the maintenance of order and discipline. 1629.

At Merton College, Oxford, in the 14th century a system was established under which older students were invited to watch over their juniors and to report to the Warden of the College on their morals and the progress in their studies. When William of Wykeham, Bishop of Winchester, founded his famous school, Winchester College, in the latter years of the 14th century a similar system of supervision was established there. Older boys of good repute were to superintend the studies of the younger pupils. The scheme was a success, and it soon came to be adopted elsewhere. The prefects soon had an important role to play in the life of the school. Arnold, the great 19th century headmaster of Rugby School, attached great importance to the influence of his prefects, feeling that the respect which the younger boys had for them could not fail to contribute substantially to a general raising of the tone of the school.

The prefectorial system is therefore now a long-established feature in most British *Public Schools** as well as in many state comprehensive and other types of secondary schools. A number of specially selected, responsible senior pupils are charged with the performance of certain duties, concerned principally with helping with the maintenance of discipline. They are often empowered to impose punishment for various misdemeanours. In return for assisting the teaching staff prefects are usually granted certain privileges, the precise nature of which, of course, depends upon individual circumstances. Properly organized, the prefect body is an asset to any school.

The prefectorial system has also been adopted by a number of private schools in America.
J L F

Preparatory School

A school the purpose of which is the preparation of pupils for the entrance to an English public school. In U.S.A. a school in which older boys are prepared for college. 1828.

● The preparatory schools (shortened form sometimes "prep") are independent schools which are established for the purpose of preparing boys aged from about 8 to 13 years for the entrance to a *Public School**. The preparatory schools maintain close links with one or more public schools to which most of their pupils intend to move on. Many of the preparatory schools are boarding schools but there are also a number of day preparatory schools.

Very few of the preparatory boarding schools are co-educational. Some schools modelled to some extent after the preparatory boarding schools for boys exist exclusively for girls.

Some of the preparatory schools are owned and managed by independent non-profit-making bodies, others are privately owned by persons or groups of persons who want to make a living.

■ There are also preparatory schools in the United States. In contrast to the British schools bearing this name they are not established to prepare children for the entrance to any kind of secondary school. They are privately owned schools operated primarily to prepare older boys for the entrance to college.

P H

Primary Education

● "Primary education" as a term was introduced in England and Wales by the Education Act of 1944. This Act abolished the former division of education between elementary schools (with a junior part up to 11 years and a senior part after 11) and secondary schools. Schools catering for children between the ages of 5 and 11 are now called primary schools, and all boys and girls reaching the age of 11 are expected to go on to a Secondary School. Thus the senior elementary schools have been integrated into secondary education.

Furthermore in accordance with the Act of 1944, free public primary education now covers all educational provisions for children of 11 years and under, including those below the compulsory school age of 5 years; compulsory education begins at five. Primary education is now divided into three categories:

(a) The nursery school, from 2 to 5, which children are not obliged to attend.
(b) The infant school, from 5 to 7. All boys and girls of 5 are expected to attend the infant schools. In exceptional cases, however, the children may be taught by private tutors.
(c) The junior school from 7 to 11. The usual age of transfer from primary to secondary schools is 11, but an increasing number of local authorities are establishing "first" schools for people aged 5-8 and "middle" schools covering various age ranges between 9 and 14. In Scotland, the primary schools take children from 5 to 12, normally having infant classes for children under 7.

The public primary school – including the nursery school, the infant school and the junior school – has to a great extent become the successor of the public elementary school, the name of which became obsolete by the Education Act of 1944. Public elementary education was introduced by the Education Act of 1870 which first made it obligatory that elementary schools were to be universally provided throughout the country. Before 1870 "education of the poor" was cared for in private schools, especially in so-called "charity schools" established under the auspices of the Society for Promoting Christian

Knowledge, which was founded at the end of the 17th century. Towards the end of the 18th century elementary education received a stimulus from the establishment and rapid development of Sunday schools in which children were taught, among other things, to read and write.

At the beginning of the 19th century two educational reformers, Joseph Lancaster, a zealous Quaker, and Dr. Andrew Bell, backed by the Anglicans, developed so-called "monitorial systems", in which the teacher, in face of hundreds of pupils, obtained help from the older pupils, the so-called "monitors". Two societies were established to promote the rival causes: "The Royal Lancastrian Association" (1810), later known as "The British and Foreign School Society", and "The National Society for the Education of the Poor in the Principles of the Established Church" (1811), until recently familiarly known as "The National Society". These two societies attempted to provide a kind of national system of elementary education on a voluntary basis. From 1833 onwards the state came to the aid of these societies with grants until finally the state recognized its duty of caring for elementary education. The resultant public elementary schools were administered by locally elected School Boards and were called Board Schools, as distinct from the Voluntary Schools. Thus from 1870 (Forster Act) onwards there were elementary schools of two types - board schools provided and maintained by the School Boards out of rates, fees and state grants, and voluntary schools provided and maintained by voluntary, mostly denominational bodies and aided out of public funds. Under the provisions of the Education Act of 1902 (Balfour Act) the functions of the School Boards were transferred to the Local Education Authorities of the county councils *(Local Government*)* which were charged with the maintenance of the board schools and had to provide new elementary schools as required. The Education Act of 1918 finally abolished fees in elementary schools. In 1944 there were approximately 20,000 elementary schools, which were now called primary schools, for pupils below the age of 11. In most primary schools today boys and girls are taught together.

In accordance with the Education Act of 1944 the first stage of primary education is the nursery school, from 2 to 5. There has been a nursery school movement since 1870. In the Education Act of 1918 nursery schools were officially recognized. The Education Act of 1944 states that all authorities must provide nursery schools for very young children, but were such facilities provided only for a small proportion of children.

In 1972 the Government announced a new expansion programme of nursery education by the education services. The aim of the expansion plan is that ultimately nursery education should become available without charge to those children aged 3 and 4 whose parents wish them to have. In 1974 there were 724 publicly maintained nursery schools in England, Scotland and Wales.

But apart from children only just under five, the proportion of children aged two to four who attend public sector schools remains low (the supply of places being still inadequate to meet the demand for them) though attendance, and particularly part-time attendance, has been increasing very rapidly in recent years. The good nursery school is first and foremost a source of education, its success depending on the ability of the teacher to create a living community in which the young children can develop their senses and their imagination.

In the new system of primary education the infant school, from 5 to 7, plays an important part. It goes back to an infant school founded in 1816 by Robert Owen, the great social reformer, who endowed it with two ideals: pleasant harmonious conditions and a life of happy activities. Accordingly it is now generally agreed that the keynote of the infant school is to be activity and experience in airy and spacious surroundings; it is considered to be entirely inappropriate to attempt to translate it into any rigid or logically ordered curriculum. The main idea is that the child's interest will emerge during play, and that is why "the play way" is regarded as so important. The curriculum normally includes: (a) natural activities, embracing physical training, open-air life, rest, and play; (b) expression training; comprising speech, dancing, singing, handwork, and drawing; (c) in the later age groups, formal instruction in the three Rs: reading, writing, arithmetic. The general idea, however, is that there should be little or no formal instruction before the age of 6 at the very earliest.

The main part of primary education is performed within the junior school, from 7 to 11. It is considered to be the vital stage in English education and is to be granted a sufficiency of teachers and decent, well-equipped premises. Much progress has been achieved in the last 25 years, lately in consequence of the recommendations of the Plowden Report "Children and their Primary Schools" 1967, including the establishment of "middle schools" and special help to "educational priority areas" in poorer neighbourhoods. Moreover new subjects and new teaching methods have been introduced. Instead of emphasizing the three Rs. primary education is seeking to awaken interest and create alertness by the stimulus of activity and experience. Religious teaching is inevitably a subject apart, predetermined by denominational and "agreed" syllabuses. The main spheres of the modern curriculum are: English, especially spoken English; physical education; handicraft; and music. Visual aids of various kinds are playing an increasing part in the daily round of the teacher. About nine out of ten schools can receive television, and almost all have radios. Training in handicraft leads to contact with the sciences, opens the windows to the realm of art, and encourages calculation and measurement in a natural way. It is generally considered more important to foster the child's native curiosity than to heap up information.

It is remarkable that the English way of *Streaming** the pupils, i.e. dividing them in A, B, C, and D streams according to their capacities, is playing a perceptible role in the junior schools. It is even usual to find this organization whenever the schools are large enough to allow it, and such is the case in the cities. In infant schools it is normally absent, but even there children between the ages of 6 and 7 may be separated into "fast" and "slow" classes. The application of the "intelligence quotient" has done much to foster this development. But in the last years there is a clearly observable trend to "destream", i.e. to reduce or modify "streaming" in such a way as to minimise its ill effects on children placed in a lower stream; at the same time an increased importance is attached to motivation. P H

Private University

■ The origins of American higher education date from the 17th and 18th centuries *(Universities*)*. All such institutions founded in colonial times were private and especially dependent on church sponsorship. Their existence was threatened when at the beginning of the 19th century the states tried to bring them under their control and management. But a most memorable decision of the Supreme Court (in 1819) against the attempt of the state of New Hampshire to make the Dartmouth College a state institution subject to state control guaranteed private ownership of institutions of higher learning against public encroachment, as well as the right of any individual or association with sufficient means to found a college and to obtain a state charter. From this time on private and public education began to go their separate ways. Whereas afterwards all the states went on to establish *State Universities**, the private institutions founded before the outbreak of the revolution have continued as such. By their side, in the course of the settlement of the Middle West and beyond, were erected numerous private denominational schools of higher learning on the pattern of Harvard, Yale, and Princeton. As a result of the civil War, however, many of the weaker institutions were eliminated in the Middle West and the South. In the second part of the 19th century, however, new private universities were founded, especially on the basis of endowments of wealthy men, e.g., Johns Hopkins University 1876, Stanford University, and University of Chicago 1890. In addition, Roman Catholics began to establish private institutions of higher learning in order to propagate their own faith and learning. Before the outbreak of the Civil War they had established 14 permanent colleges, e.g. St. Louis University, St. Louis, Mo. (1832) and the University of Notre Dame (1844) in South Bend, Ind. In this time, too, a number of colleges for women were founded. Whereas a majority of these institutions fell short of the established academic standards Vassar College, Poughkeepsie, N.,Y., (opened 1865) set high intellectual standards from the outset. In co-education Oberlin College, Oberlin, Ohio (1834) became a pioneer.

A particular trend of the 19th century was the establishment of specialized technological institutes, e.g. Massachusetts Institute of Technology (1861) at Cambridge, Mass., and California Institute of Technology (1891) at Pasadena, Calif.

Higher education for Negroes was advocated even before the emancipation. In 1854 the Pennsylvanian General Assembly sanctioned the establishment of Ashmun Institute which became Lincoln University, Pa., in 1866. This university was among the first to have an interracial faculty. After the Civil War the Negroes themselves organized various institutions of higher learning, and gained missionary support in the States of the North. Outstanding among them are: Fisk University (1866) at Nashville, Tenn., and Tuskegee Institute (1881) in Alabama. By the 1950s there were more than 50 Negro institutes which were privately maintained (junior colleges and teacher-training colleges included).

Private institutions of higher learning continue to slightly outnumber public colleges and universities, although they only enroll about one fifth of the nation's advanced students. They are characterized by an extraordinary heterogeneity in both their scholarly standards and their academic customs. One trait links all these institutions together: studies are divided into roughly standardized units or credit hours (about 45 lectures or class meetings per course of three credit hours) and 120 such credit hours are required for the B.A. or B.S. degree. But the comparability of such credit hours in different institutions remains problematic. P H/D P H

Progressive Education

■ The term "progressive education" assumed its present defined status when the Progressive Education Association was organized in 1918. Although it never attracted more than 1 per cent. of the nation's teachers, it was very active in the 1920s and 1930s. The Association was disbanded in 1956.

The origin of this movement can be traced back to Rousseau, Pestalozzi and their disciples. But progressive education as it is known nowadays is mostly an American product. Francis W. Parker (1837-1902) started actually teaching along this line, but John Dewey (1859-1952) furnished the philosophy on which progressive education flourished.

The main features of the progressive education movement are:

(1) The child is to be respected as a person. The area of the child's decision is to be extended as far and as quickly as possible.
(2) Since the child learns what he lives the school should aim at being a place where the best possibilities for a sensible life prevail, the kind of life conducive to building the character.
(3) Man can truly become man only in associated life, thus it becomes a social duty to help each child to attain a purposeful life within a social group.
(4) The progressive school therefore refuses the usual practice of putting first the acquisition of "subject-matter" in isolation from its application in life. It prefers to aim at the building of dynamic characters who will use their knowledge and skill for life's broader purposes.

From the second decade of the 20th century, the progressive education movement spread rapidly, especially in elementary schools and the teachers' colleges.

But while it is true that many of the ideas of the progressive education movement were widely adopted, many others were not. Changes in the economic situation, the onset of World War II, the changing demographic and social patterns of the United States, and, perhaps most important of all, the changing educational needs of the country, all took their toll. Many aspects of progressive education, in its Deweyan form, as well as in the modes represented by Kilpatrick, Bode, and others, were more suited to the needs of a rural society than to those of an urban, technological, complex one. Many of the tenets of progressive education have persisted, particularly the stress on humane understanding of self and environment, and depth of learning.

The most considerable of the new developments in American education, i.e. great curriculum reforms in science, mathematics, and foreign languages, take forms which many of the progressives would not like. The emphasis on structured learning *(National Defense Education Act*)* is absolutely opposed to progressive notions. Moreover it has been suggested that the discovery method of progressive education makes the acquisition of knowledge and skills increasingly difficult for the child with a low I.Q. because of the demands placed on his intelligence. Many of these children are said to learn much better where the teaching methods stress rote learning. On the other hand, the emphasis on discovery, on the use of theoretical learning to develop new conceptual understanding, and on the unique and too often unnoticed value of non-cognitive intelligence (creativity) and such ideas as the open school and team teaching show the continued vitality of some progressive innovations.

P H/D P H

Public School

In England orig. a grammar school endowed for the use or benefit of the public, and carried on under some kind of public management or control; often contrasted with a "private school". In modern use applied espec. to such of these as have developed into large boarding-schools, drawing from the well-to-do classes pupils who are prepared mainly for the ancient universities or for the public services and also to some large modern schools with similar aims. 1580. In Scotland, British colonies, and U.S.A.: A school provided at the public expense and managed by public authority, as part of a system of public (and usu. free) education. 1636.

• In England the term "public school" was applied originally to grammar schools endowed for the use of the lay public. Today the public schools are outstanding institutions, more or less independent, mainly boarding schools of the grammar school type, which prepare pupils for university studies and charge tuition and boarding fees. These fees range between £ 380 and £ 670 per term. The public schools include not only the schools which were founded four or more centuries ago, such as Eton, Harrow, Rugby, Westminster, and Winchester, but also schools of comparatively recent creation such as Cheltenham and Clifton.

The formal test of whether a school is entitled to describe itself as a Public School depends on the election of its headmaster as a member of the Headmasters' Conference (H.M.C.), founded in 1869, or of the Association of Governing Bodies of Public Schools (G.B.A.) which was founded in 1941. In the so-called Fleming Report "The Public Schools and the General Educational System" published in July 1942, the Public Schools are defined as "schools which are in membership of the Governing Bodies' Association or Headmasters' Conference". One of the main differences between the two organizations is the fact that H.M.C. admits only boys' schools whereas G.B.A. will admit schools for girls (including co-educational schools). There are some 270 public schools, about half of which are for girls.

Public schools have made a notable contribution to English education. They have always emphasized the importance of character-building and there the prefect and house systems were developed. It is through the prefect system that the day-to-day discipline is upheld largely by the pupils themselves. The public school is also characterized by a high staff-pupil ratio and a high proportion of pupils pursuing advanced studies. The usual age of entry to the public school is 13. This is different from the entry age of 11 to the state secondary schools; the leaving age is about 18. There are also some girls' schools modelled to a certain extent on the public school for boys. Formerly the public schools received no public aid, but today a number of them obtain "grants-in-aid" directly from the Department of Education and Science *(Statutory System*)* and are bound to offer a corresponding number of scholarships to gifted children who may transfer from the publicly maintained secondary schools. In this way the exclusiveness of the public schools has been broken to some extent. But as the public schools take between them only 4 or 5 per cent. of the nation's children in each age group, the view has still been expressed that they promote class distinction and thus help to create "two nations".

That is the reason why the Labour Government had intended to consider how the public schools might best be integrated into the statutory sytem of education. Supporters of the public schools counter that the increasing emphasis on high intellectual achievement has substantially modified the character of many of the public schools and that they continue to prepare responsible leaders for the nation. In 1965 a Public Schools Commission under Sir John Newsome was set up, this time "to advise on the best way of integrating the public schools with the state system of education". The Commission reported in 1968, with moderate recommendations: many boarding schools should offer at least half their places to financially assisted pupils who could benefit from boarding education; the public schools should accept more children from lower standards. About the main suggestion nothing whatever was done. At this time the public sector was already supporting the independent schools to the extent of some twenty thousand places either wholly or partly paid for. The future course of the public schools has yet to be determined. It is far from clear whether they can, in fact, be fully integrated into the national system.

In Scotland most of the schools supported from public funds are known as public schools to which everybody's children can go without tuition fees being charged. Only a few schools of the English type of public schools are to be found in Scotland and Northern Ireland. P H

■ An American public school is a tax supported, non-sectarian, co-educational, elementary or high school open to anyone, administered by public officials. There is no national system of public schools, though federal support is furnished for a variety of subjects. Local government units, with various degrees of supervision and assistance from the state, operate and support the free public schools. Although private schools exist in the United States, they do not play so important a role as the English public schools. P H/D P H

Red-Brick University

● Red-brick universities: sobriquet coined by a Liverpool professor writing under the pseudonym of Bruce Truscot in the book "Red-Brick University", 1943, and applied thereafter to those seats of learning conceived in the second half of the 19th and the first half of the 20th centuries as colleges, which later became university colleges and finally universities. The name refers primarily to the university buildings, which are constructed often of red bricks, but also characterizes the whole group as homogeneous.

The most significant feature of university development in England between 1850 and 1960 was the rise of the "modern" or red-brick universities in the new centres of population. Desire to promote higher education in the industrial areas stimulated both civic effort and private benefaction in the mid-19th century. All the new institutions of learning were, from their inception, created to fulfil local needs, interested in nearby industries and determined to place particular emphasis upon the study of scientific and technological subjects.

After 1889 a royal charter had to be granted to the separate foundations before they could be regarded as university colleges. These were organized like universities, performed work of a university calibre but were not permitted to confer their own degrees *(Universities*)*. Instead, students were awarded external degrees of *London University** which had been entrusted with the task of conducting the examinations for the university colleges, in the absence of anything in England approaching the "Staatsexamen" of German universities. The university colleges were then obliged to undergo a period of apprenticeship, in order to safeguard academic standards, before they were considered worthy of the status of an autonomous degree-conferring university.

The actual growth of the status of a university college and thence to a university was achieved in the early days by amalgamation. In this process Owens College in Manchester (founded 1851) was the progenitor. It was established to teach "such branches of learning and science as were then or might hereafter be usually taught in English universities". Owens College became a part of the newly created Victoria University of Manchester (1880) which in 1884 affiliated Liverpool University College (established 1881 by the citizens of Liverpool) and in 1887 the Yorkshire College, Leeds, which incorporated a medical school. Mark Firth, a Sheffield steel manufacturer, founded Firth College (1879) which united with the local medical and technical schools to form the university college in Sheffield (1897). Firth's interest had been awakened by the Cambridge extension lectures *(Extra-mural Work*)* held in Sheffield. Moreover, the university colleges at Bristol (1876), Nottingham (1881), Reading (1892), Exeter (1901) and Leicester (1918) all originated from extension lectures. Birmingham began, like the college at Leeds, as an exclusively scientific institution, the Mason College (1880). Southampton opened as the Hartley Institution (1862) and experienced chequered fortunes before becoming, 40 years later, Hartley University College. Hull, on the other hand, arrived fully fledged as a university college, thanks largely to a munificent donation of £ 250,000 by T.R. Ferens.

What commenced as the college movement yielded a rich harvest of red-brick universities in two main periods of the 20th century. The reaping began in Birmingham (1900) and continued when the federation of Manchester, Liverpool and Leeds came to an end. A royal charter made Victoria University independent in Manchester (1903) and in the same year separate university status was granted to Liverpool. Leeds received its charter in the following year (1904). Sheffield (1905), Bristol (1909) followed soon after, while Reading (1926) provided the stimulus to the movement between the two major periods. The second crop appeared after the second world war when the pattern of giving autonomous university status was extended to Nottingham (1948), Southampton (1952), Hull (1954), Exeter (1955) and Leicester (1957). A refreshing policy has been introduced since the publication of the Robbins Report (1963) whereby universities are established from the outset with the right to grant students first and higher degrees *(New Universities*)*.

Each of the red-brick universities is the brain-child of a large industrial city and endowed by its citizens. Each is linked closely with the industries of its particular city. Each originally catered, though never exclusively, for local students and was non-residential, although halls of residence are a feature of all the red-bricks now. Each is completely free of *Religious Tests**, indeed, in some the teaching of religion was originally forbidden, although such no longer applies. Each has a strong scientific bias and the accent is placed, as ever, on academic achievement.

C C R

Sandwich Courses

- Sandwich: two slices of bread with a layer of any edible substance placed between them; also a confection of layers of sponge cake. So called after John Montague, Fourth Earl of Sandwich (1718-92), who once spent twenty-four hours at the gaming tables eating nothing but beef sandwiches.

Sandwich courses: courses in which periods of full-time employment in industry alternate with periods of full-time study. Between two "layers" of work in the factory appears the "substance" of study, or vice-versa – hence sandwich.

Sandwich courses are primarily designed for the comprehensive training of technologists. They usually last three to five years and consist of specially adapted periods of practical experience in industry which interchange every six months with periods of theoretical study at technical colleges or universities where the accent is placed on technology *(New University*)*. Sandwich courses are most popular at advanced levels and participants can obtain qualifications equivalent to honours degrees.

Many of the students availing themselves of the opportunities held out by sandwich courses are "industry-based". They are, from leaving school, employees of a firm which arranges supervised training for them in its own works and laboratories and sends them away to institutions of education which supply complementary studies. Most of these students receive salaries from their employers for the duration of the courses.

A growing number of students are "college-based" or "university-based". They proceed directly from school to either college or university which makes arrangements for them with a suitable firm where they receive their industrial training. Local education authorities grant them awards in the usual manner and even extend this policy to those students who are industry-based if the employers of the latter are reluctant to continue salaries during periods of study.

C C R

Scholarship

A sum of money or its equivalent offered to enable a student to pursue his studies at a school, college, or university. 1511.

Until the 20th century financial assistance for educational purposes was available to only a very small proportion of the population. But with the expansion of *Universities** the number of scholarships provided has increased greatly.

The term "scholarship" covers a wide range of awards. Some are designed to enable poor or perhaps specially gifted children to attend a certain school; most *Public Schools** award scholarships of this nature. Similar awards are open to the promising university student, enabling him to study at a particular *College** or to devote himself to a particular subject. Other awards may enable a *Graduate** to carry out research on a specific theme or help a highly qualified scholar to study abroad. Awards may be made by the state, by an institute of learning, whether school, college, or university, by a *Foundation**, an industrial organization, a public institution (e.g. the British Council), or even by private benefactors. Awards are sometimes made from funds raised by public subscription. One feature common to all scholarships is that they are all granted as a reward for meritorious work, usually on the basis of competitive examinations. Just as scholarships are of many types, so, too, they are distinguished by a bewildering variety of names – bursaries, exhibitions (usually of small value), fellowships (mainly for advanced study), postmasterships (at Merton College, Oxford), major scholarships, minor scholarships, studentships, to name but a few. Of importance, perhaps, are the terms "open scholarship" and "closed scholarship". By the former is meant that anyone may compete for the award in question, whereas in the case of the closed scholarship the candidate must first fulfil certain requirements stipulated by the awarding body. Typical requirements are that the candidate must have been born in a certain specified part of the country, or that his father must have been an Anglican clergyman, or that he attended a certain school. The justification of such stipulations has been a much debated question in recent years.

- In Britain it is part of the national educational policy that any child who shows that he or she has the ability to profit from an advanced course of study at a university or other similar establishment and who is accepted for admission to such a course shall not be prevented through lack of adequate financial means from pursuing his or her studies. Since 1962, Local Education Authorities have been obliged by the Education Act of 1962 to provide an adequate grant for any person accepted for admission to a university, should assistance be necessary. Over 90 per cent. of students in Britain now receive a grant from public or private funds. The amount of the award depends upon numerous factors, such as the place of study, duration and type of course, family circumstances, marital status, and private income.

■ In the United States a far higher percentage of the population reaches the university than is the case in Britain. There is therefore an even greater need for the provision of financial assistance to students. The facilities available in America are in many ways similar to those offered in Britain; in fact, many of them are modelled on British awards. But whereas in Britain a student's grant is comparatively generous (although the student himself will perhaps be the last person to agree with this), American awards often cover only tuition fees, so that many students are obliged to work for payment both during the vacations and in term-time in order to supplement their grants. In Britain students are generally not permitted to work during term-time and it is also discouraged during the vacations because these are intended primarily for study and rest.

In addition to scholarships provided by educational establishments, business, industry, and the governments of the individual American states, there exist in the United States several funds from which students may obtain loans at low interest rates with a long repayment period. Particular mention may be made of the vast resources which Congress set aside for this purpose in 1959. Whenever a similar loan scheme is suggested in Britain, the student organizations inveigh vehemently against it, claiming that the subsequent repayment of the loan would be an unfair burden to place on a young person's shoulders at the outset of his or her career. J L F

Secondary Education

- That part of the educational system which is between primary and further education (concerning mainly vocational training) or higher education (concerning mainly studies at university level).

The term refers to the education of all children which begins at the age of 11 and terminates at the age of 18 or 16 – the latter being the end of comulsory school attendance.

Before the beginning of the 20th century an education higher than elementary was the privelege of the upper classes. Social status and the parents' income decided whether a child was allowed to enjoy such education as offered by private institutions like *Public Schools** and *Grammar Schools**. These were financed by fees charged to the parents and by private endowments. Since both types of school placed stress on classical subjects and aimed at a gentleman-like general education, the barrier separating them was one of social distinction rather than of educational programme.

In the second half of the 19th century, however, rapidly spreading industrialisation gave rise to a growing demand for people who had acquired a higher education especially in the fields of science and technology. Ability, knowledge, and efficiency began to overcome the barriers of inherent class distinction, particularly when competitive examinations were introduced for admission to the Civil Service. Some local authorities set up higher grade elementary schools, partly secondary in character, and the Board of Trade (Science and Art Department) organised "science schools" which provided technical instruction. But this piecemeal development could not effectively fill the educational gap and the need for public provision of secondary education became pressing.

In 1902 publicly provided secondary education began under the Balfour Act – a real landmark in the history of secondary education. It abolished the former school boards and transferred responsibility for elementary and secondary schools to the Local Education Authorities (L.E.A.), newly established in the county and county borough councils. Subsequently, the L.E.A.'s founded a large number of secondary day schools providing secondary education at moderate charges which people of the middle classes could afford. From 1902 to 1918 the number of publicly assisted secondary schools increased twentifold. From 1907 onwards the Board of Education (established 1899) awarded grants to schools giving 25 per cent. of their places free of charge to talented children from elementary schools.

A turning point in educational development was the Education Act passed by the Coalition Government under Winston Churchill in 1944. It organized the whole system of public education in three progressive stages – primary, secondary and *further education**. Primary education now catered for children 5 to 11 years of age and secondary for those from 11 to 19 years.

The Act of 1944, which has become the legal basis of the whole educational system, thus abolished any overlaps between elementary (formely five to 14 years of age) and secondary education. Moreover, the Act made it the statutory duty of the L.E.A.'s "to secure that sufficient education throughout those three progressive stages shall be available . . . to afford for all pupils opportunities for education offering such variety of instruction and training as may be desirable in view of their different ages, abilities and aptitudes". Within one year the L.E.A's had to prepare and submit to the Minister of Education a "development plan" showing the action which should be taken for their area and giving particular proposals "as to the nature of education to be provided in the school". Following the recommendations of the Butler White Paper antecedent to the Act the majority of L.E.A's established a "tripartite system" of secondary education divided into Grammar School, Secondary Modern and Secondary Technical School. The idea was that the three kinds of school should have "parity of esteem". The educational reform was to accomplish equal educational opportunity for all children by providing "secondary education for all". This was the educational programme of the Labour party for many years.

The selection procedure allocating children to the different types of schools at the age of 11 has become known as the *eleven plus** examination. By the early 1960's, if not earlier, doubts had arisen as to whether "equality of educational opportunity" really had been provided by the education reform of 1944. With the decline of the number of secondary technical schools the "tripartite" system turned out to be only "bipartite" (grammar and secondary modern). There was never a genuine "parity of esteem"; on the contrary, a considerable status distinction separated and still separates the traditional grammar school from the secondary modern which furnishes a kind of all-round education for the less intelligent. As early as 1959 the Crowther Report "15 to 18" raised the question of abandoning the "11-plus", which indeed would require a new organisation of the educational system. "Once it is agreed . . . that it is wrong to label children for all time at eleven, the attempt to give mutually exclusive labels to the schools to which they go at that age, will have to be abandoned" (Crowther p. 23).

This reorganisation of secondary education began in earnest in the early 1960s with the widespread introduction of Comprehensive Schools wich demand no evidence of ability or aptitude for entry, and seek to mix streams within schools. A number of London Boroughs and Metropolitan Counties (in 1976: South Yorkshire and Tyne and Wear) have already done away entirely with selection at eleven or any other age. Of the 40 non-metropolitan counties in England and Wales only 5 have (by 1976) followed suit. Where selection remains, however, it is nonetheless being gradually phased out.

Comprehensive schools avoid the segregation of children at eleven and provide a very large number of courses for all or most of the children in their district. In 1970 approximately 32 per cent. of secondary school pupils in England and Wales attended Comprehensive Schools, 20 per cent. attended Grammar Schools, 46.5 per cent. attended Secondary Modern Schools and the remaining 1.5 per cent. attended secondary technical and other schools. By 1976 these figures had changed as follows: Comprehensive schools – 76.6 per cent., grammar schools – 8 per cent., secondary modern schools – 15 per cent., secondary technical schools 0.4 per cent.

One further quite recent development in secondary education should be mentioned: the raising of the school leaving age (ROSLA). In September 1972 the school leaving age was raised from 15 to 16 under the provisions of Section 35 of the 1944 Education Act. This measure noticeably increased the secondary school population and hence the demand for new schools. But with the financial crises of the mid 1970's and the resulting cut-backs in public expenditure particularly in the social services and education the majority of LEA's have not been in a position to expand their secondary education facilities.

In Scotland secondary education was legally based on the Education Act Scotland 1945 (consolidated in the Education Act Scotland 1962). Secondary education in Northern Ireland was established under the Education Act Northern Ireland, 1947. It is mainly in line with secondary education in England and Wales. Secondary schools of the comprehensive type have long been widespread in Scotland. In England a secondary education quite distinct from the publicly provided system was set up by the Public Schools (not to be confused with the public school system of Scotland).

■ For U.S.A. see *High School** I Fr/G W

Sixth Form

● The sixth form is the highest class in an English secondary school. It is a peculiarly English institution and its origins and ethos are to be found in the development of the English school. Originally the pupils of the first of these schools, Winchester, were divided into seven classes, but by the seventeenth century the last of these had disappeared and by the eighteenth century the highest form in most schools was called the sixth form. It has always been a section of the school in which students were prepared for university entrance, and for the most part still provides an academic education geared to the demands of the Advanced Level examination *(General Certificate of Education*)*. This differs radically from the German Abitur or the French Baccalaureat in being a subject examination, and entrance to a university is normally dependent on the achievement of satisfactory passes in two or three subjects. Pupils in the sixth form are thus aged between 16 and 19, and, although there is no formal entry requirement, they have usually passed the G.C.E. Ordinary level examination with some success (five subjects is normally the minimum) and are felt by the headmaster and staff to be capable of coping with the demands of the Advanced Level. Once in the sixth form, pupils specialize in two, three, or four subjects, either in the arts or sciences - possible combinations would be for example: English, French, History; Mathematics, Physics, Chemistry; Geography, Economics, History; Biology, Zoology, Mathematics. Because of the specialization groups of pupils are small, relations with the staff are more informal, and the sixth former is usually allowed a certain amount of free time within school hours in which to do his work. Sixth formers are often given small administrative and regulatory tasks within the school and certain rooms are reserved for them. The average stay in the sixth form is two years but certain pupils, especially those who are attempting to gain a place at Oxford or Cambridge, may stay on for a further year, and sixth formers are differentiated by being known as, first year (or lower) sixth, second year (or upper) sixth, and third year sixth. In Scotland the curriculum is far less specialised than in the rest of Britain and the Scottish universities have different entrance requirements.

Until the 1944 Education Act the sixth form was the preserve of the grammar schools. Nowadays, however, secondary modern and *comprehensive schools** often offer a sixth-form education and as Advanced Level passes are now demanded for most white-collar jobs, it is considered that up to 30 per cent. of children could benefit from such an extension of their education. *Grammar school** sixth forms have in any case more than trebled in size in the last two decades and in some cases one-third of the pupils in a school are in the sixth. The influx of new sixth formers not intending to go to university is bringing a further increase, and the nature of the sixth form is thus now changing considerably. The rapid growth in numbers has also made obvious the uneconomic size of most sixth form groups in any particular school and one response to this problem has been the sixth form college, of which some fifty are at present in operation or planned. Sixth form courses are also now offered by colleges of further education. G R C

State University

■ An American state university is an institution of higher learning controlled either as a whole or in part by the government which bears the cost of its maintenance. Each of the 50 American states maintains and controls one or more universities, but there is no national or federal university. The idea of a national university, once greatly fostered by George Washington, was never realized.

Although the first universities which were controlled by the state or received state assistance had been founded already in the last decades of the 18th

century (University of Georgia, 1785, University of Carolina, 1789, University 4
of Vermont, 1791), the foundation of the majority of state universities took place during the 19th century. Until the Civil War there were 21 state universities. The establishment of state universities corresponds to the democratic dream of public education for all from the elementary school to the highest level. The democratic concept of higher education demands that education must be open to everybody who can profit by it and that the states are obliged to furnish adequate facilities. A number of these state institutions applied themselves particularly to the needs of farmers, businessmen, and technicians.

At the beginning of the 19th century the trend towards state interference in the field of higher education induced various state governments to seek control of hitherto private colleges *(Private University*)*. But they only succeeded in part because of a Supreme Court decision which protected the private institutions from state interference. As a result the states began to establish universities on their own initiative.

The next stage in the development of state universities was the aid of land-grants from the Federal Government. Most of the 21 state universities founded before the Civil War had already been aided to a certain degree by grants of land from the Federal Government as was the case in Ohio, Michigan and Kansas. The Morrill Act of 1862 placed large grants of land at the disposal of states in order to encourage the establishment of agricultural and mechanical colleges which were intended to meet the needs of the frontier states for agricultural and mechanical education and research. *(Land-Grant College*.)* This resulted in the foundation of a great number of state colleges (first only for agriculture and mechanics, later with a gradually increasing range of courses) which were milestones in the development of higher education, especially in the Middle West and in the western states. A number of the state colleges established in this way later achieved the full status of universities or were incorporated into newly established state universities, as was the case in Maine, Illinois, and California.

An outstanding characteristic of the state universities is the wide range of instruction offered by them. Most of them comprise a large number of institutions of higher learning situated at various places throughout the state. The State University of New York, founded in 1948, for instance, comprises 31 branch institutes at different places in the state. Likewise, the State University of California comprises 10 campuses in Berkeley, Los Angeles, San Francisco, Santa Barbara, etc., and a great number of scientific laboratories, observatories, agricultural experiment stations, etc., which are dispersed over the whole state.

A typical state university is likely to place at the disposal of its students a college of liberal arts, schools of sciences, agriculture, engineering, commerce, education, music, medicine, etc. It often expands its courses to include accounting, husbandry, economics, etc. A large proportion of the activities of the state universities is devoted to research work in the pure and applied sciences, the humanities and the social studies.

The faculties (in the United States "faculty" is also employed to designate the members of the academic staff) vary in number from 100 to more than 2,000. The faculties play a vital part in the educational policy of the university since they determine the courses offered and the degrees granted.

The control of the state universities is in the hands of a board of trustees or regents whose members are appointed or elected. One of the principal functions of the board of control is the selection of the executive officers of the university, the president or the chancellor. As a rule the president is a faculty member of the university, but many men who have been prominent in public life as businessmen, politicians, or military leaders, are also chosen. One of the problems has been to keep the control free of pressure groups and partisan action. New organisational patterns are emerging that give students and faculty a share through direct involvement in the decision making process that governs the operation of colleges and universities. Sometimes they are members of the board.

In the state universities, as in all the American universities, the principle of "academic freedom" is recognized. Faculty members have the right to speak freely on all matters and to engage freely in research work, regardless of the implications for society and state. This right is ardently defended by most of the faculties. But in political, economic, and religious matters difficulties sometimes arise in consequence of this tradition. While not legally required, about one third of all high-school graduates take college entrance tests each year. Most graduates from accredited high schools can be admitted to their state university if they prove to have followed a reasonable programme of education in high school.

While attending state universities a large number of students are granted scholarships or contribute to the cost of their education by part-time employment. P H/D H

Statutory (State) System

- Adj. statutory: of or relating to statutes; enacted, created or regulated by statute.

Unlike independent schools which are owned and managed without public support by independent non-profit-making bodies or individual proprietors, the statutory system, as designed by the Education Act of 1944, comprises all schools, primary, secondary or further in character, which are supported or maintained by public funds. The amount of financial support determines to what extent public authorities are entitled to interfere with the management of the school. But it is to be noted, that, in general, public interference in the internal affairs of school management is much more limited in Britain than it is in continental countries. Until 1976 there were three kinds of schools fully operational in the statutory system:

1. The county schools (called council schools until 1944).
2. The voluntary schools.
3. The direct-grant schools.

In 1976 a phasing out of the grammar schools within the direct-grant category was begun, but county schools, voluntary schools and other types of direct-grant school remain as before.

County schools are provided by Local Education Authorities (L.E.A.s), i.e. their full costs fall on public funds. Attendance at county schools is free of charge. Books and equipment are likewise supplied free.

Voluntary schools have been provided by voluntary bodies, mostly denominational, but since 1944 they have also been maintained by Local Education Authorities. Voluntary schools fall into three groups: controlled, aided, and special agreement. In controlled schools the L.E.A. meets all running costs and the costs of building work, and nominates two-thirds of the governing body of the school; the rest are nominated by the voluntary body. In aided schools the running costs are borne by the L.E.A. while the costs of building work are met by the school. Special agreement schools are those where the L.E.A. may contribute to the costs of repair to an existing voluntary school, or to the construction of a new school building. As the name implies, such work is carried out by special agreement between the L.E.A. and the school concerned. The majority of the voluntary schools are Anglican schools but there are also approximately 2,000 Roman Catholic schools and a smaller number run by other denominations such as Quakers and Methodists. More than 10,000 voluntary schools are maintained by the L.E.A.s, which amounts to one-third of all maintained schools, this being a tribute to the important role which the churches have played in the history of education. It ought to be borne in mind that the nonconformists as well as the adherents of the Established Church were among the first to promote the education of children of the "labouring poor" *(Primary Education*).*

No fees are charged for voluntary schools if they are maintained out of Local Government funds. In voluntary schools of all kinds there is, of course, opportunity for denominational instruction.

Although the L.E.A.s spend the major part of public funds in education, they have, in fact, but little control over school management, for the responsibility for the school curriculum rests solely on the headmaster and the teachers of the school.

Since 1976 there have been significant changes in the situation as far as direct-grant schools are concerned. In 1975 the Department of Education and Science issued to all direct-grant schools Circular 7/75 giving instructions on the phasing out of direct-grant grammar schools. The regulations governing this phasing out were contained in the Cessation of Grant Regulations issued in 1976 by the Department. Under them the direct-grant grammar schools were given the option of seeking application to the state system as comprehensive schools or of becoming fully independent. By the beginning of 1976 about one-third of these schools had said they intended to seek entry to the state system. For all direct-grant grammar schools, however, the direct grant will cease when the last intake of pupils (1976) has completed its schooling (1983/84). It should be pointed out, though, that a change of government to one more sympathetic to the direct-grant schools could well slow down or even reverse the process of phasing out. Besides the direct-grant grammar schools there is a small number of direct-grant nursery and other schools. These schools charge fees but are obliged to offer 25 per cent. of all their places free. These places are awarded and financed by the L.E.A.s. A further 25 per cent. of the places in direct-grant schools is put at the disposal of local authorities, if required. As noted above, the direct-grant grammar schools formed the greater part of this category, and it is true to say that they were and are privileged in comparison with the grammar and comprehensive schools maintained by local authorities. It is this thinking that has been behind their phasing-out.

I Fr/G W

Streaming

● "Streaming" refers to the practice in many English schools of classifying children in streams according to their intelligence. This is in addition to the normal practice of classifying children according to age, and the new intake in a primary school, for instance, might well be divided into three classes 1A, 1B, 1C. Streaming is widespread at the primary school level and exists in various forms in *Grammar**, Secondary Modern, and Secondary Technical Schools.

Although the term "streaming" is of very recent origin, the practice was first recommended in the Hadow Report in 1926. Eleven years later a Board of Education Handbook of Suggestions for Teachers specifically suggests classification by "streams" in primary schools. Few schools were in fact "streamed" before 1939, but after the war the 1944 Education Act and the ending of war-time restrictions brought a rapid decline in the number of all-age schools and a correspondingly rapid increase in separate primary schools. These new primary schools contained sufficient classrooms to operate a streaming system. The actual term "streaming" first appears in articles and theses published in the mid-1950s.

Most children in Britain are graded into streams before they leave primary school at the age of eleven and the method used may be one of the following or any combination of them: (1) The opinion of the headmaster and his staff. (2) Tests in reading, arithmetic, and English set by the school. (3) The same tests together with an intelligence test set by an external body and therefore likely to give more objective results. Most schools, however, prefer to use tests of their own devising.

Recent research shows 80 per cent. of the staff in English primary schools to be in favour of the system, many of them seeing it as a perfectly natural element in a competitive and selective educational system which differentiates between Oxbridge and the other universities, between honours and ordinary degree (see *Graduates*)*, between grammar and secondary modern schools, etc.

The advantages claimed for streaming are that it makes the best use of available teaching resources and facilities and that the element of competition, which it actively fosters, speeds the progress of the more gifted children, relieves the strain on the less gifted, and makes teaching as a whole easier. Opponents of streaming (and thus proponents of the *Comprehensive School*)* contend that it favours the intelligent child unduly, that the competitive atmosphere means that the children never learn to help each other, and that those in the "C" stream rapidly become apathetic. A further disadvantage lies in the fact that the various streams may have slightly different syllabuses making transfer from one stream to another difficult and thus handicapping the late-developer. On the surface something like streaming exists in comprehensive schools, but, whereas streaming segregates children according to a somewhat arbitrarily obtained intelligence factor, comprehensive schools try to provide a wide variety of courses to suit the particular aptitude and inclination of the individual child.

Leaving aside academic considerations the major objection to streaming is a social one. Statistics show that a disproportionate number of children from middle class homes are to be found in the higher grades and the lower are filled mainly with children from working class homes. Streaming thus acts as a form of social as well as academic selection.

The only other countries in the world with streamed schools are those of Scandinavia and even here it is now being abandoned. Russia abolished it in 1936 and there is no primary school streaming on the continent. G R C

■ Streaming has become frequent at the senior level of the larger high schools in the United States. An increasing number of schools have provided for the academically talented. Wherever streaming is practised, children are classified in courses designated, e.g., as English A, B, and C; or Mathematics Honors Advanced Placement, Mathematics. Streaming is used with extreme caution in the U.S.A. to avoid the impression of discrimination. H H

Students' Union

Union society: a general club or debating society usually open to all members or all undergraduates of the university.

● At *Oxford and Cambridge** the "Union" is the name of the official debating society. The Unions of both universities enjoy an enviable reputation and often attract speakers of considerable eminence. The Union Debates are sometimes broadcast by the B.B.C. To become President of either Union is considered a great distinction.

At the other universities the Unions bear little resemblance to those at Oxbridge. In Britain it is recognized that a student does not go up to university merely to cram his head with learning he obtains from books; he should also take part in *Extra-curricular Activities** which, through bringing him into contact with other people, broaden his mind and enlarge the compass of his interests. It is the task of the Students' Union (or Union of Students, Union Society, or Guild of Students, to mention some variant terms) to provide the basis for this by sponsoring events of a social, cultural, or sporting nature. In general terms the purpose of the Union is "to promote and protect the interests of its members" (as the constitution of at least one of them proclaims). For the individual full-time student membership of the Union is obligatory, and the annual membership fee (which is normally paid by the body which awards the student his grant or *Scholarship**) usually runs to the order of several pounds. Even the smallest Union will therefore have several thousand pounds at its disposal every year, and the money is put to the provision of the facilities regarded as necessary to the students' well-being. These include, besides the provision of inexpensive meals and often of other subsidized services such as laundering, shoe-repairing and hair-dressing, recreational facilities of all types. To the Union are affiliated the many student clubs and societies to be found at every university and college; these cater for all conceivable interests, ranging from religious and political associations down to folk-dancing and cheese-tasting clubs, societies for bridge players and groups for communicants with the spirit world. Affiliation to the Union is a necessity if a society is to obtain a grant from Union founds towards defraying the expenses of guest speakers or the cost of equipment or excursion.

Another extremely important function of the Union is to represent the general student body in policy discussions with the university or college authorities. Most Unions are affiliated to the National Union of Students (N.U.S.), a central organization which looks after students' interests, particularly when matters such as grants are under discussion at national or local government level.

Each Union is run by a committee elected by the whole student body. The students elected to represent their fellows are often those who are would-be politicans and who enjoy the interminable deliberations of the committees and the subcommittees it sets up to deal with specific problems. The student body at large is usually apathetic to Union affairs and is perfectly happy to accept passively the benefits the Union affords. The Union is largely autonomous, but the actual degree of freedom from direction by the university authorities that it enjoys varies from institution to institution.

The term "Union" often also denotes the building in which the Union committee has its offices, and where refectories, bars and lounges are to be found, and most of the Union's activities take place. J L F

■ In the United States the Students' Union – mostly called College Union or Student Center – came into being during the last decade of the 19th century. Houston Hall at the University of Pennsylvania, which is the oldest College Union, was founded in 1896. During the last three decades the union movement has steadily grown. The clubhouse of the union is a centre of social and recreational life for all students – whether they may be members of *Fraternities** and *Sororities** or not – as well as for the faculties and the members of the administrative staff. Guests are also admitted. A great number of the college unions are members of the Association of College Unions founded in 1914. I Fr

Teacher Training

● In England teacher training developed rather late. For centuries teaching was considered an unattractive occupation. It was only in the early 19th century that the first training schools for monitors to do work in elementary education were established by private societies and by the church. The government finally took interest in these efforts and provided financial assistance. By the end of the first quarter of the 20th century approximately 50 voluntary training centres with a training period of two years were in operation, supplying trained teachers for elementary schools.

From 1893 onwards universities began to establish grant-aided departments for the training of elementary school teachers. The Education Act of 1902 empowered local authorities to establish and maintain training colleges for teachers. In 1955 there were 154 training colleges and 23 university departments of education in England and Wales. After the Second World War a committee with Sir Arnold McNair as chairman was appointed by the government to study the problem of teacher education. It recommended that each training centre should be affiliated to a university through an institute of education and by 1957 all training colleges were affiliated to universities.

Until 1975 the majority of teachers in England qualified by taking a three-year course at one of some 150 colleges of education so as to obtain a teacher's certificate. Since 1970 professional training for newly qualified people with degrees and ertain other specialist qualifications (who before then were entitled to teach without further training) has become mandatory for all school teachers except, temporarily, mathematics and science teachers in secondary schools. Such courses were at colleges of education and in university education departments.

Since August 1975, a basic reorganisation of the system of teacher training in England has been started. All higher and further education outside the universities including teacher training is being assimilated into a common system under the control of local education authorities. A number of the existing colleges have been merged either with each other or with other colleges of further education to form "liberal arts" colleges; some are to discontinue completely the initial training of teachers. As the first move towards a wholly graduate profession, three- and four-year degree courses incorporating educational studies are being developed, although the three-year certificate course will also be maintained as long as they are needed.

Moreover the education departments, universities, local authorities and other bodies provide a variety of short in-service training courses for practising teachers.

In Scotland the situations is different. There all teachers in education authority schools and grant-aided schools must be registered with the General Teaching Council for Scotland. Courses in colleges of education lead to the award of a Teaching Qualification (Primary Education) or a Teaching Qualification (Secondary Education). Graduates and holders of specialist diplomas undergo a one-year course; courses in practical and aesthetic subjects for non-graduates extend to two, three or four years. For primary teaching the course extends to one year for graduates and three for non-graduates. Most Scottish colleges of education also offer four-year courses leading to the degree of Bachelor of Education. P H

■ In the United States teacher training also began in the first half of the 19th century. In 1839 the first "state normal school" for the training of teachers was established in Massachusetts. By 1890 practically every state had one or more of these schools. The state normal schools which extended their courses from two to three or four years changed their names into "teachers' colleges". There developed a tendency towards teacher colleges which place more emphasis on basic subjects and devote less time to teaching methods. Thus an increasing number of teacher colleges have dropped the word "teacher" from their title and are now known as "state colleges". The general trend is towards a four-year pre-service collegiate training for both elementary and secondary teachers, with a fifth year which may be added leading to the Master's degree in Arts or Education.

Concurrently most universities have established programmes in teacher preparation which meet certification requirements. They have given particular attention to the teachers for the high schools. By 1950 most four-year colleges and universities had departments or schools of education. Nowadays a great variety of institutions participate in the preparation of students for the teaching profession: the teachers colleges, public and private colleges and universities, professional and technical schools, and the junior colleges. Usually the training for elementary school teachers emphasizes courses in methods of teaching, whereas the prospective high school teacher is encouraged to specialize in a particular subject. The baby boom at the end of World War II contributed to the growth in the number of children attending schools. This created a severe teacher shortage. The 1960s produced a new and large crop of teachers. The shortage has since abated, especially on the elementary school level. Meanwhile, with the number of teachers increasing, elementary school enrolment declining, the supply-demand situation has become reversed. There are hundreds of thousands more teachers available in 1978 than are needed. Enrolments in teacher education are declining. Public school teachers in the 1970s, according to a study by the National Education Association, are better prepared academically than those who taught in previous decades. Only three per cent. of the teachers in 1971 did not have a Bachelor's degree, as compared with 15 per cent. in 1961. In 1971 more than 27 per cent. of the teachers held a Master's degree, as compared with 23 per cent. in 1961. In general, teachers in the 1970s are younger, better educated and less experienced. They are less likely to have graduated from a teacher's college, more likely to be university educated. Teachers continue to participate in further education, though most federal and state grants and scholarships have ceased. Between 1970 and 1972, for instance, 61 per cent. of teachers earned a mean of 14 semester hours of college credit beyond the bachelor's degree, six teachers in ten participated in workshops sponsored by their school systems, and six per cent. of teachers, in 1971, had had a sabbatical leave for study, travel or other purposes at some time since fall 1968. In order to improve teacher education, there is now spreading a movement toward what is called "competence based teacher education" (CBTE) stressing as basic reference criteria knowledge, performance, and consequences, instead of judging prospecting teachers by their grades in courses and examinations. P H/D P H

Tutor

● A graduate (most often a fellow of a college) to whom the special supervision of an undergraduate (called his pupil) is assigned. 1610.

The tutorial system was first introduced in *Oxford and Cambridge**, but has been adopted by most British universities. In tutorials the pupil is usually alone with his tutor and is expected to present and discuss written work which he has prepared. In this way a friendly and yet academically stimulating relationship is often created between the tutor and his pupil.

At universities where the Oxbridge ideal of individual tuition is not practicable, as for instance at *London University**, it is usual for some instruction to be given by means of "tutorial groups". Meeting usually weekly or fortnightly a staff member and a small group of students (two or three, or perhaps six or seven) will discuss in detail particular aspects of the subjects dealt with in the more formal lecture courses. As well as being academically beneficial to the students it affords them a valuable opportunity to become better acquainted with their teachers.

Further, it is usual for each member of the teaching staff to be asked by the Head of his Department to give friendly advice and assistance to any student in the Department who should ask for it. The students are encouraged to discuss their problems, not only of a general academic nature but also personal ones, with their "personal tutor", and so there is no reason why, even in a large university, a student should feel "lost". Similar arrangements are usual in student hostels or "Halls of Residence". J L F

Universities

ME. Adoption of Latin universitas; Anglo-French université: a corporation or community, formed on Latin universus. As the designation of a whole body, community, or guild of masters and scholars, the full phrase was universitas magistrorum et scholarium.

In modern use "university" means an institution of higher teaching and learning which provides facilities for research work and is entitled to grant academic degrees. In the 12th century, however, when the first continental universities sprang up from the medieval cathedral schools, esp. from the famous cathedral school of Notre Dame at Paris – this being the original germ from which the University of Paris has grown – the equivalent term for our "university" was "studium generale" – a term pointing to the fact that the courses of study consisting of the Seven *Liberal Arts**, law, theology, and medicine were open to everybody wishing to attend these courses, regardless of his social status, nationality, or religion. As distinguished from "studium generale" the early "universitas" was but an association of teachers (later also of students), i.e. a guild or corporation for which at that time the term "universitas" was generally in use no matter whether associations of scholars or those of craftsmen were concerned. Centuries passed before the term "studium generale" was gradually replaced by "Universitas" (university) in the modern sense of the word.

● After the Norman Conquest not only the French language but also the French way of thinking found its way into Britain. As a consequence many young Englishmen went to Paris, which was the focus of intellectual life at that time. Coming back to their native country they formed the core from which the first English universities grew up: Oxford (first mentioned in 1163) and Cambridge (first mentioned in 1209). But whereas Paris University of today shows little resemblance to the institution from which it developed in the Middle Ages, *Oxford and Cambridge** have preserved without a break those features handed down to the present from its medieval pattern. One of their predominant features is the common life of teachers and students in hall, chapel, and chamber, deeply rooted in the corporate life of the Middle Ages and up to the present representing an essential criterion of the medieval "universitas magistrorum et scholarium" *(Oxford and Cambridge*; College*)*.

The Scottish University of St. Andrews, founded in 1411 (united with the University College of Dundee in 1897), was established as a collegiate university after the pattern of Oxford and Cambridge. Yet it is important to note that today the colleges of St. Andrews are no longer residential colleges like those of Oxford and Cambridge but serve specific academic purposes. St. Mary's College, for instance, houses the faculty of Divinity, St. Salvator's College that of Arts and Science. The further Scottish universities, Aberdeen (founded 1494), Glasgow (1450), Edinburgh (1583), Strathclyde (1966), Heriot-Watt (1966), Stirling (1967), and Dundee (independent of St. Andrews 1967), are non-collegiate and non-residential.

In England Oxford and Cambridge remained the only institutions of higher education for more than 600 years; a fact the more amazing because the Reformation *(Established Church*)* destroyed the spiritual unity of the nation; for the adherents of the Anglican Church were allowed to matriculate into Oxford and Cambridge while *Puritans**, *Jews** and *Roman Catholics** were excluded from these institutions by the Test Act of 1673 *(Religious Test*)*. But with the rise of Methodism during the 18th century the number of *Nonconformists** greatly increased and many of them acquired fame and fortune through the *Industrial Revolution**. The pressure of this growing number of influential nonconformists on public opinion finally led to the foundation of the University of London. The new university, intended to effect a separation between religion and education, started with the opening of University College as a private institution in 1827-28; the Royal charter was granted to the new University as a degree-conferring board in 1836. This development was subject to various changes *(London University*)*. From the very beginning London University acted as examining and degree-conferring board for the whole Empire and for the numerous university colleges in Britain which came into being during the 19th century. These colleges which had all reached full university status in the meantime were known as provincial or civic colleges (or universities respectively) and were also called "red-bricks" because they were mainly built of bricks. With the exception of Durham and

Newcastle upon Tyne, which as collegiate universities take an exceptional position within that group, all "red-bricks" are non-collegiate; in the 19th century their students were mainly residents of the surrounding industrial areas *(Red-Brick University*)*.

A further group of British universities are those established or planned in line with the Robbins Report (Report of the Committee appointed by the Prime Minister under the Chairmanship of Lord Robbins, 1963). These New Universities (sometimes called "concrete universities" because they are mainly built of concrete and glass) are mostly non-residential but lay emphasis on the tutorial system *(Tutor*)*. A characteristic feature is their organization in schools of study. *(New University*.)*

Furthermore it is to be noted that in order to meet the growing demand for technologists the Government decided in 1965 that the Colleges of Advanced Technology (C.A.T.s) were to achieve full university status as independent institutions of higher learning outside the university *(College*)*.

Although these different groups of British universities are in themselves quite distinct there are some features which they have in common: (1) British universities are independent. Although today they are all – even Oxford and Cambridge – publicly supported (about 75 per cent. of their incomes come out of public funds), there is no interference by the Department of Education and Science with the curriculum, or with the academic staff, the administering body, or with the employment of public funds within the quinquennial budget. The funds are distributed to the universities by the *University Grants Committee**. The U.G.C. is a body appointed by the Secretary of State concerned, which acts as a link between the Government and the Universities. (2) The traditional relation of 8 students to 1 member of the academic staff, which is considered the standard ratio for British universities, guarantees a contact between students and the academic staff which is much closer than that prevailing at Continental or American Universities. (3) Students wishing to obtain a academic degree are not allowed to change university during their undergraduate studies. This also helps to create a better connection between teachers and students. In 1974-75 the number of full-time students at British universities amounted to 773,000. These figures do not include the growing number of students of advanced studies pursued outside the university (espec. in the field of technology, business and art). Where these courses reach university level, even though the institutions which offer them have no university status, these students can be awarded *External Degrees**.

Entry to all universities in England, and to a certain number in Scotland, Northern Ireland and Wales, is organized through the Universities Central Council on Admissions (U.C.C.A.). Candidates list five universities and courses, in order of preference and these, together with a confidential report from the headmaster, are sent by the school to the U.C.C.A. headquarters, who forward applications to the universities concerned, and who inform the candidate of any places he is offered.

■ The first English settlers coming to the American colonies from across the Atlantic Ocean brought with them the idea of the great educational institutions Oxford and Cambridge. Thus the earliest American schools of higher education – Harvard (1636), William and Mary (1693), Yale (1701), New Jersey (now Princeton University, 1746), King's College (now Columbia University, 1754), Philadelphia (1755), Queen's College (1766), and Dartmouth College (1770), all of them older than the American nation – had in common that their characteristic features largely resembled those of Oxford and Cambridge.

It was the custom to use the term "college" for those early American institutions of higher learning because at that time they chiefly consisted of the historic "college of liberal arts" *(College** and *Liberal Arts**). In the course of time, however, those colleges have expanded horizontally, to include a great number of professional and vocational schools, and vertically, to include also postgraduate studies and research work. In this way most of the early "colledges" have grown up into the large and very complex organization which, today, we call the American university.

A number of eastern universities and colleges have become outstanding examples of American institutions of higher education. Among them are Harvard and Yale and some other institutions belonging to the group of *Ivy League.**

When the westward movement pushed the American *Frontier** into the wilderness new schools or colleges became necessary. Although cultural affairs were under the jurisdiction of the state concerned, the Federal Government helped to establish new institutions by munificent land grants to the states to enable them to create a new type of college, the so-called *Land-Grant College** which became a prominent feature of higher education in the United States. In the meantime, many land-grant colleges have reached the status of state universities. Since the middle of the present century the state universities, originally considered as inferior to "private" universities, have gained increasing influence in the life of the nation, which has become manifest in the quality of their teaching staff, the number of students, and the courses provided *(State University**).

Today many American institutions of higher learning, above all the famous graduate schools, are supported out of state or federal funds. Nevertheless, the majority of American universities and colleges are to be considered as private institutions, for they were founded and are still being financed by private groups such as religious denominations, industrial organizations, or individuals who, having amassed large fortunes, can afford to give munificent endowments for educational purposes *(Foundation**). Founded for widely varying purposes they are of very different standards *(Accreditation**). Famous graduate schools like Emory (1836), John Hopkins (1876), Chicago (1890), and Brandeis University, Boston/Mass. (1948) belong to this group just as much as many liberal arts colleges offering but a general education, and many schools for advanced training *Private University**).

Finally, it may be mentioned that in the United States there is a tendency to expand the activities and organizations of some big universities on an unprecedented scale which is already beyond the idea of a university in the original sense of the word as a community of teachers and students for the purpose of higher learning and research work. To quote only two examples: the State University of California and the State University of New York (SNNY), with about 100,000 students each, have hardly any resemblance to that original idea of a "universitas magistrorum et scholarium". Although it seems to be an exaggeration to call California State University a "multiversity" instead of a "university" as did one of its former presidents when speaking about future university life in the United States, this strange new term might nevertheless suggest a trend of future development which cannot be foreseen in the present day.

I Fr

University Grants Committee (U.G.C.)

● In modern Britain the *Universities** could not exist without state support. Today they receive from government sources a very large proportion of the money they need to enable them to carry out their work. The assessment of the financial requirements of the universities and the distribution of the funds provided by the state are the responsibility of the University Grants Committee, or, as it is often called, the U.G.C.

The 19th century saw rapid advances in the fields of science and technology, and the British Government realized that if the country was to maintain its position in the modern world it was its duty to foster the teaching of science. In 1889 *Parliament** voted to pay each year for five years the sum of £ 15,000 to aid the then twelve university colleges in England and Scotland; at the end of that period the question of the distribution of the money was to be reviewed, this being the origin of what still today is known as the quinquennial system. In 1919 the committee charged with making proposals for the distribution of the money was reconstituted and named the University Grants Committee.

At first its principal purpose was "to enquire into the financial needs of university education" and to advise the Government on these matters. However, in 1946 the scope of its work was extended to embrace the preparation and execution of plans for university development with regard to national needs.

British universities, although heavily state-supported, are free from all direction by the Department of Education and Science or any other government department or body. Until fairly recently the U.G.C. was similarly independent of government control, but it is now answerable to the Department of Education and Science. The U.G.C. is, however, not appointed by the minister responsible for educational affairs but by the Chancellor of the Exchequer. The Comptroller and Auditor General has access to the Committee's books but cannot question its academic policies. At present the U.G.C. has nineteen members, all, with the exception of the Chairman, part-time. The majority of these come from the universities, the remainder have had wide experience of other forms of education or industry. They deal directly with the universities, being responsible for visiting well over forty institutions, trying to ascertain the proper amount of financial assistance each should receive. Until recently funds were alloted for a five-year period, which greatly assisted forward planning, but the present economic crisis and the high rate of inflation have led to what, it is hoped, will be only temporary abandonment of the quinquennial system. It should perhaps be pointed out that the U.G.C. is not responsible for the award of student grants or *scholarships**. The Government instituted this system because it realized that if the universities were not permitted to apply the state's grants as they themselves thought fit, there would be a danger that their efficiency as teaching and research establishments could be impaired. The universities for their part recognize the value of this privilege and are deeply conscious of the great burden of responsibility which it necessarily entails, and strive to repay this gift of freedom by accepting the challenge and giving responsible service to the community. J L F

PART V
Religion

Anglican Communion
Baptist
Congregationalist
Convocation
Established Church
Freedom of Religion
General Synod
High Church
Jew
Low Church
Lutheran
Methodist
Mormon
Nonconformist
Presbyterian
Puritan
Quaker
Religious Test
Roman Catholic
Social Gospel
Thirty-Nine Articles
Unitarian

Anglican Communion

- A body of churches including the Church of England and those churches that hold essentially the same faith, order and worship with it and are therefore in communion with each other.

The term Anglican Communion is used to denote those churches scattered all over the world whose faith and teachings are basically the same as those of the Anglican mother church, the Church of England. Within Britain itself there are, besides this, the *Established Church** in England, three other Anglican churches, namely, the unestablished churches of Ireland, Wales and Scotland. Elsewhere in the world Anglican churches are found wherever Englishmen have gone, as traders, settlers or missionaries. The Anglican form of worship is naturally encountered chiefly in the countries of the British Commonwealth (e.g. Australia, New Zealand) or of the former British Empire (e.g. South Africa). But it is also represented in many other parts of the world, including China, Japan and the Middle East, where, for instance, there are five dioceses under the jurisdiction of the Anglican Archbishop in Jerusalem. A particularly important member of the Communion is the Protestant Episcopal Church in the U.S.A. with 109 dioceses, including a number of missionary dioceses in South America. With the exception of a number of overseas dioceses under the jurisdiction of the Archbishop of Canterbury all the constituent churches enjoy a greater or smaller degree of autonomy. Altogether the Anglican Communion comprises 27 Churches organised in 385 dioceses with a membership totalling over 65 millions.

Whilst the various churches are not subject to the dictates of the mother church they are linked to it through a bond of loyalty. This feeling of unity is furthered by the periodical conference of Anglican bishops. Known as the Lambeth Conference, this meeting, presided over by the Archbishop of Canterbury as primus inter pares, has as its purpose the unofficial consultation of the church leaders. The first conference of its kind was held at Lambeth, the official residence of the Archbishop of Canterbury, in 1867 and has been taking place ever since at approximately ten-year intervals, the most recent being held in Canterbury in 1978. Whilst the Conference exercises no official executive authority the fruits of its discussions on doctrine and policy are widely studied and enjoy great prestige, not only within the Anglican Communion itself but also amongst other Christian churches. The 1968 Conference recommended that an "Anglican Consultative" Council be set up. This body, which meets every second year, has an important liaison role between the member churches of the Communion and with other, non-Anglican churches. J L F

Baptist

A person of Protestant belief holding that baptism ought to be administered only to believers and by immersion; at first called by opponents Anabaptists. 1654.

The Baptist Churches owe their name to the practice of baptising adult believers only. Yet this is by no means the only, or even the most essential characteristic of the Baptist faith. Most important to them is the idea of a community based on individual religious experience and the stress placed on the teachings of the Bible as a sufficient guide in faith and life. They reject all ecclesiastical tradition, emphasize the independence of each congregation

(Congregationalist)* and, believing in the "priesthood of all believers", refuse to acknowledge any form of "priestly caste". They refer to a Baptist minister only as being "recognized", not "ordained". They demand freedom of religious practice and thus reject every form of connection between Church and State.

The principles of the Baptists and the conservative character of their biblical views are perfectly matched by their unrelenting, indeed *"Puritan"**, attitude towards daily life. This attitude still prevails especially among the Baptists in England; American Baptists nowadays seem to be comparatively more liberal-minded. Yet it seems to be the very intensity of the Baptists in maintaining their position which, in Britain, has saved them from the heavy losses in membership suffered by all the other Free Churches in recent times, and which, in the U.S.A., has gained for them a very definite lead among Protestant denominations.

● The Baptist Churches are among the oldest churches of British historic Dissent. Two main streams of Baptism had their origins in early 17th century England. In 1609 John Smyth, an Anglican clergyman who had become a Puritan and later a Separatist *(Puritan*)*, fled to Holland and set up a church in Amsterdam based on the idea of baptism upon personal profession of faith. A group of his followers returned to England in 1612 and founded the first Baptist community in London. By 1660 there were more than a hundred sister churches in all parts of England. Their members became known as the General Baptists.

The second main stream of Baptism rose about 1640 in London through secession from a Church of Congregational Separatists *(Congregationalist*)*. This group was strictly Calvinist in doctrine and maintained that the atonement of Christ was only for those predestined to be saved. They were called the Particular (sometimes also the Primitive) Baptists.

Both groups suffered severely under religious persecution after the Restoration (1660), and although their lot was improved through the Toleration Act in 1689, it took them a long time to overcome the effects of persecution *(Religious Test*)*. The *Methodist** revival eventually inspired them with new evangelistic zeal. In 1770 a New Connection was formed among the General Baptists, and in 1813 the Particular Baptists joined the majority of Baptist associations in the Baptist Union. In 1891 both groups merged, a Baptist Union of Great Britain and Ireland being formed with associated, though separately organized, Baptist Unions in Scotland and Wales. An important step was the foundation of a first Baptist Missionary Society as early as 1792 which became the nucleus of the later world-wide missionary activity of the Baptist Churches. The Baptist Union had some 187,000 members in 1975.

J L F

■ Like most other churches stemming from English Puritanism, the Baptists achieved their present striking importance in world-Protestantism mainly through their transplantation to North America. In the course of the emigration of persecuted Dissenters, Roger Williams (ca. 1603-83), one of the great spiritual forefathers of the present United States *(New England*, Freedom of Religion*)*, came to America in 1631. After having been banished from Massachusetts for his insistence on religious tolerance, he founded Providence, Rhode Island, in 1636 as a homestead for his persecuted fellow-believers. In 1639 he had himself baptized by a layman, whom he baptized in return, and founded the First Baptist Church of Providence, the oldest Baptist Church in the United States.

The American Baptists experienced their greatest upswing after the beginning of the great revival movements in the U.S.A., the Great Awakening (about 1740) in which one of the founders of Methodism, George Whitefield, played a leading role, and later the Great Revival (from about 1800 onwards). Henceforth, the Baptist Churches took over a leading role among the Protestant denominations of North America.

Both Baptists and Methodists have instilled new life into American Protestantism; however, there are striking differences in membership. In contrast to the American Methodists' strong middle-class tendencies, the Baptists recruit their members mainly from the lower and lower-middle classes. Statistics on church membership in the U.S.A. in the second quarter of the 20th century throw a revealing light both on the role of Baptism among the Protestant denominations of the U.S.A. and also on certain sociological aspects of the much-discussed American religious revival of recent decades, which, although not restricted to a certain social class, was at least largely determined by the strong emotional appeal to the masses exerted by such men as the Baptist preacher Billy Graham.

In spite of the Baptist Churches' basic *Abolitionist** attitude the American Baptist churches became divided on the slavery issue. In 1845 a Southern Baptist Convention was formed which still exists side by side with the Northern (now American) Baptist Convention. The Civil War led to the formation of two separate all-black Baptist Churches, the National Baptist Convention, U.S.A., and the National Baptist Convention of America, which still today, with currently about ten million members, lead a strong and independent existence. Segregation, though legally abolished by the Supreme Court in 1954, continues to manifest itself in the form of discriminatory acts and attitudes, even in the Church.

The Baptists are the numerically strongest of American Protestant denominations, comprising more than 27 million members. The continuing strength of their affiliations rests on their use of mass media and mass evangelism *(Freedom of Religion*).* E V/P v T

Congregationalist

Congregation: A body of persons assembled for religious worship. Congregationalist, an adherent of the Congregationalist church polity; a member of the Congregational Church; an Independent.

The Congregational churches have their roots in the English Reformation. Although the name "Congregational" was not generally adopted until after 1640, the *Puritan** Separatists of the Reformation – later also called "Brownists" or "Independents" – can be regarded as the direct ancestors of the later Congregationalists. With their decentralized form of Calvinism they became one of the three main strands of English Dissent, the other two being represented by the *Presbyterian** Churches, which had a centralized form of church order, and by the *Baptist** Churches.

The name "Congregationalist" refers to the practice of meeting in local congregations. The Congregationalists emphasized the full autonomy of each of these congregations, which they conceived as local congregations of the church universal, headed by Christ alone. They rejected any form of hierarchy, whether episcopal or presbyterian, and regarded "independency" as the ideal form of Christian democracy, based on the teachings of the Bible and on the idea of the priesthood of all believers.

● The Puritans of the English Reformation did not originally aim at separation from the Established Church but rather at reform from within. A number of them, however, felt impelled by their conscience to introduce separate worship. They were called "separatists" and the new groups they formed were called "gathered churches". The first great leader of the separatist movement was Robert Browne (1550-1633), whose "Treatise of Reformation without Tarying for Anie" became one of the basic documents of Congregationalism. Persecution forced a number of separatists to go into exile in Holland. In 1620 a group of them, wishing to preserve their mother tongue for their children and to withdraw from the unrest in the land, left Holland and then sailed from Plymouth on the *"Mayflower"** to found a new colony on the American continent.

Congregationalism in England had its great periods during the Civil War and even more during the Commonwealth when after a short time of Presbyterian establishment Oliver Cromwell made Independency – as Congregationalism was then called – the leading religious force in the country. After the Restoration Congregationalists suffered persecution like all the other churches of Dissent. The persecution was ended by the Toleration Act (1689), but Congregationalists, like all nonconformists, still had to contend with severe restrictions, such as exclusion from the civil service and from the *Universities**. The latter discrimination had the positive result of leading them to establish a number of Dissenting Academies which have had a great influence on the cultural life of England.

The Congregationalist emphasis on "voluntary fellowship" which has always gone hand in hand with the principle of independence, has for a long time led the Congregational churches to seek closer contacts with the other churches of their order and, more generally, with other "reformed" churches. In 1831 most of the English Congregational churches joined in a Congregational Union of England and Wales. Through this union Congregationalism has assumed more and more the character of a "Church" as represented by the more hierarchical and connexional types of denomination. In 1945 the English Congregational churches began to discuss a plan for union with the Presbyterian Church of England. This union was established in October 1972. The new church is called the United Reformed Church. The combined membership is about 250,000, with more than 2,500 congregations. J L F

■ In the United States the origins of Congregationalism go back to the earliest days of colonial settlement. The Pilgrim Fathers *(Mayflower Compact*)*, who were English separatists from Holland, were followed by a Puritan group which had fled from persecution in England and landed at Massachusetts Bay where they established settlements in and around Boston from 1629 onwards. These Puritans likewise introduced Congregationalism as their church polity in the new world. Congregationalism and Presbyterianism were the two major religious forces through which *New England** was to become the nucleus of political and cultural development in the United States. Up to the present day the members of both denominations belong to the best educated groups of society. There have always been close contacts between the Congregational churches of England and America, since even into the 20th century Congregationalism was primarily an Anglo-American form of Christian adherence.

The strong ecumenical trend in Congregationalism with its attractive church polity has led to various plans of union with other churches. Thus in 1957 the

"Congregational Christian Churches" in the United States merged with the "Evangelical and Reformed Church" into a new denomination (1,2 million members) known as the "United Church of Christ". E V/P v T 5

The Christian Churches in Britain and U.S.A. (in outline)

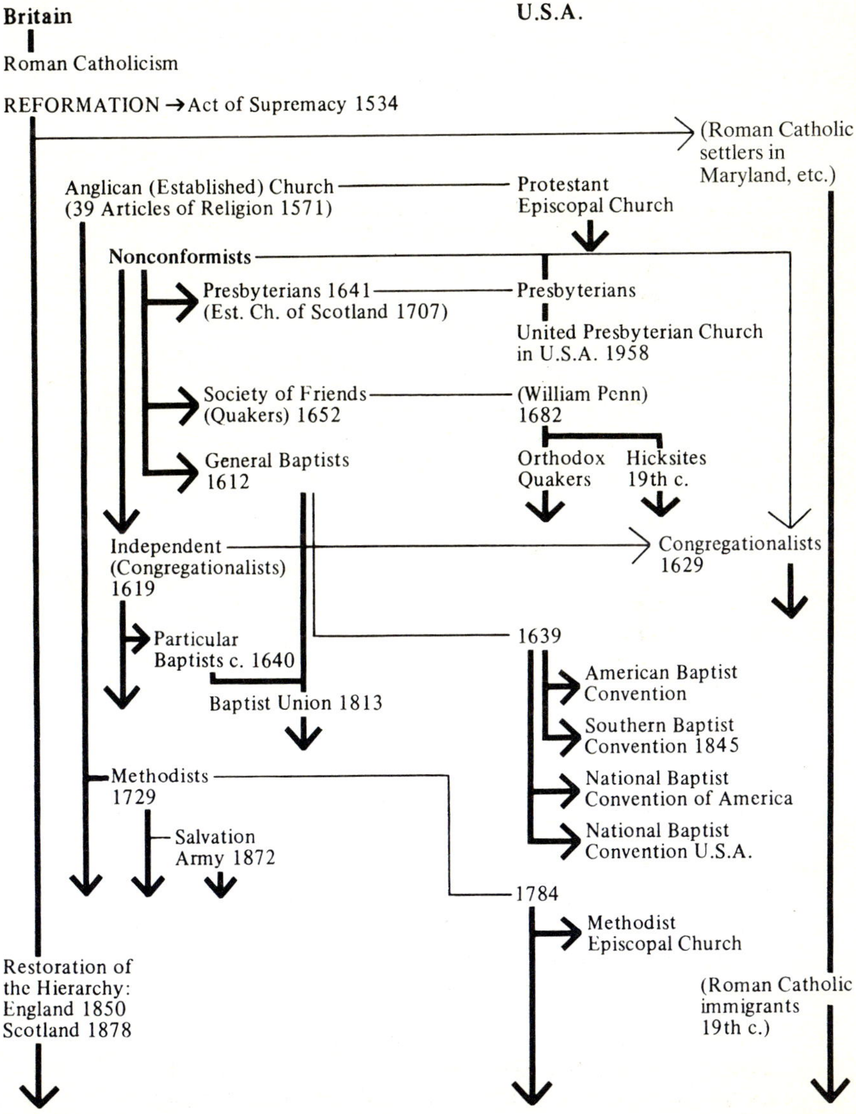

Convocation

- With special reference to the Church of England the term Convocation is applied to each of the two assemblies of representatives of the clergy whose purpose is to consult on church affairs. One Convocation is headed by the Archbishop of Canterbury, the "Primate of All England", the other by the Archbishop of York, the "Primate of England". They are constituted by parliamentary statute. Each assembly has two Houses, the Upper House consisting of the Diocesan and Suffragan Bishops of the province (Canterbury 35, York 17), and the Lower House consisting of the representatives of the rest of the clergy (Canterbury 171, York 80.) Nowadays Convocation is mainly a deliberative body; it has no power to enforce its resolutions. Each Convocation meets at the most three times a year. J L F

Established Church

- A church that is recognized by law as the official church of a nation.

  Establishment implies that there is some definite and distinctive relation between the civil authority of the state and a particular religious society and that this relation is not shared by any other of the religious societies found in the country concerned. Establishment does not imply any particular form of relationship between Church and State; it merely means that some kind of relation exists. An established church enjoys a privileged position, but in return, of course, it has obligations towards the State.

  In Great Britain two established churches are found, one in England, the other in Scotland. In England is the Church of England or Anglican Church, the mother church of the *Anglican Communion** of churches, which enjoys this status. It cannot be said that the establishment of the church in England dates from any particular year, for throughout history Church and State have co-operated closely. They have grown up side by side. However, certain events have helped to place the relation between the two on a firmer foundation. The first of these was when the English church became a national church as a result of King Henry VIII's repudiation of the authority of the Pope in England. By the Act of Supremacy (1534) the King became "the only supreme head in earth of the Church of England". Under Queen Elizabeth I the established church took on a more Protestant character, which it still retains today. Nevertheless many of its teachings and forms have been inherited directly from the medieval church, and so its claim that it is both reformed and catholic has some measure of justification. A formal statement of its doctrines was made in 1571 in the *Thirty-nine Articles** of Religion. Although the wording of these was deliberately left vague in the hope that they would be generally acceptable disputes soon arose, there being in particular a strong demand for a greater departure from the old Roman Catholic dogma and ritual. Because they desired what they considered a purer form of worship the adherents of such views became known as *Puritans** and later, because they refused to conform to the principles and practices of the established church as laid down in the 39 Articles of Religion and the Book of Common Prayer (first issued in 1549), they were called "*Nonconformists**. The churches founded by these are non-established. The position of the established church in England today is that, in law, it is under the control of the state. It is governed by a hierarchy of bishops (hence it is sometimes called the Protestant Episcopal Church), and, nominally at least, these bishops are appointed by the monarch. Changes in its ritual which is contained in the Book of Common Prayer are subject to approval by Parliament. But this legal control is exercised in close cooperation and sympathy with the church authorities, so that to a great extent the church is free to think and act it as pleases, though this does not prevent occasional agitation in favour of disestablishment. It is important to note that, whilst this is a state church, it is not maintained by the state. No church tax is payable in Britain. The church relies on contributions from the parishes and the income from property and investments.

In Scotland the church established by law is the Church of Scotland. In the 16th century the Scottish Parliament changed the state religion to Protestantism, and subsequently the presbyterian form of government was adopted. This meant a more complete break with the traditions of the Roman Catholic church than was experienced in the Church of England. Whereas the Church of England is governed by a hierarchy of bishops, the ministers of the Church of Scotland are all of equal status. The position of the Scottish church was first defined in law in 1707 and its constitution was restated in the Church of Scotland Act of 1921. It has been said to be the ideal model of a free church in a free state, for, though established within the framework of the state, it is, unlike the Church of England, not subject to state control. The state has, for instance, no say in matters of church legislation. In Scotland, therefore, establishment has no practical importance.

The United States of America have no established church. Here the legal position of a Christian church is simply that of a voluntary organization under the ordinary law of the land.*(Freedom of Religion*).* J L F

Freedom of Religion

■ The American *Bill of Rights** (1791) opens with the following words: "Congress shall make no law respecting an establishment of religion, or prohibiting the free exercise thereof . . ." *(Religious Test*)*. Article One of the Bill of Rights thus legally defines what has been from the early days of American settlement the chief characteristic of the American religious scene: the separation of church and state and the freedom of the people to practise whatever religion they choose.

In order to understand the full meaning of the term "separation of church and state" it is necessary to realize that it implies more than just the contrast to an *"Established church"** in the British sense. It is true that opposition to the idea of a state church lay at the root of religious development in the United States. The first settlers were English *Nonconformists* (Puritan, Mayflower Compact, New England*)* who left their country because they refused to conform to the Established Church. Yet the severe "theocratic" regime which the first Calvinist-Puritan settlers established in Boston was as far from the idea of "religious freedom" as had been the ecclesiastical establishment back home. It was only when Roger Williams *(Baptist*)* fled from Massachusetts to found Providence in Rhode Island as a community based on religious tolerance that the idea of "freedom of religion" first gained ground on the American continent.

The American religious scene today is characterized by a denominational pluralism unequalled in any other nation of the world. Religious freedom in the American sense means not only that there is no establishment to which people are expected to conform, it also means that people are not even expected to conform to any historically or numerically predominant church or denomination. Immigrants to the United States, though supposed to adjust themselves politically and culturally, are not only free to retain their religious self-identification, they are indeed expected to do so. This acceptance of religious pluralism is by no means equivalent to religious indifference. Americans "believe in religion" in a way few other nations do, and the much-discussed "revival" which again and again has determined the American religious scene bears full witness to this fact. Yet they emphasize less a particular creed than the necessity of religious faith in general. The overall idea of American religion is that of a "religion of democracy" as an expression of the "American way of life", with strong emphasis on pragmatic thought, moral responsibility and social commitment.

This common faith which, as a sort of superstructure, bridges the denominational pluralism, seems to imply a sort of "religious *Melting Pot*"*. In fact, however, the American religious scene has rightly been described not as a "single melting pot" but as a "triple melting pot", consisting of three great religious communities, Protestants, *Roman Catholics**, and *Jews**. Realization of this division is indeed essential for an understanding of religion in America, for religious self-identification in terms of one of these three communities is regarded as a more or less unchangeable factor. People may move from one Protestant church to another, but they will rarely convert to another of the three great religious communities. For each of these has its own distinct cultural background and social character.

According to the 1976 Yearbook of American Churches there are at least 200 religious bodies in the United States. The following approximate figures of the largest of these churches are based on information from the World Almanac questionnaire and the 1976 Yearbook (some 1959 figures in brackets). Yet it should be noted, that these figures cannot fully reflect the religious adherence in terms of self-identification, for many more people regard themselves as belonging to a religious body than are listed on the membership rolls.

(1) Roman Catholics	48,900,000	(35,800,000)
(2) 20 Baptist Bodies	27,000,000	(19,700,000)
(3) 12 Methodist Bodies	12,800,000	(12,000,000)
(4) 4 Lutheran Bodies	8,600,000	(7,500,000)
(5) Eastern Orthodox Churches	4,200,000	(2,500,000)
(6) 8 Presbyterian Bodies	3,800,000	
(7) 3 Jewish Congregations	3,700,000	
(8) Protestant Episcopal Church	2,900,000	(2,900,000)
(9) Latter-Day Saints (Mormons)	2,800,000	(1,500,000)
(10) United Church of Christ (Congregational)	1,900,000	(2,200,000)
(11) Christian Church (Disciples of Christ)	1,300,000	
(12) 5 Societies of Friends (Quakers)	125,000	(106,000)

Apart from the great denominational families listed above, several other religious groups have acquired importance in the United States, thus, for instance, the Christian Science movement (founded in Boston in 1866), the Jehovah's Witnesses, the Pentecostal Assemblies, the Holiness Groups, the Mennonites, etc.

The entirely voluntary nature of church membership implies that churches receive no financial support from the state. There is no church tax, and for that reason the denominations are solely dependent on the funds raised by the members. A member usually pledges a certain amount of his income (e.g. a tithe = 10%).

Since 1950 most of the larger Protestant churches have joined the National Council of the Churches of Christ in the U.S.A. for interdenominational and ecumenical purposes. Several mergers have taken place among the major Protestant churches in the post-World War II era, while further plans for union remain bogged down in discussion. The mergers in the Protestant denominations have emphasized the Church's desire for unity, consolidation and ecumenical goals, at the expense, however, of denominational traditions and individuality.

Besides this tendency towards unity and ecumenicity in Protestantism, a variety of other religious trends and phenomena are discernible on the American religious scene.

Most characteristic of contemporary American church life is the Evangelical movement which, though based on 19th century revivalism *(Baptist*)*, has experienced a renewed upswing in recent years. Evangelicalism cuts across all denominational lines and today comprises an estimated 45.5 million followers. It includes a variety of Christians ranging from Roman Catholics and Episcopalians to Fundamentalists (believing in the "fundamental" concepts and in the "inerrancy" of the Bible) and Pentecostals (believing in "spirit-filled" experiences and divine "gifts" in the form of visions and speaking in tongues). Many Evangelicals believe in the sole authority of the Bible and in bringing the Gospel (Greek: evangelion) to their fellowmen. They also believe in a personal commitment to Christ, a spiritual encounter known as the "born-again" experience. The most pronounced spokesmen of the mass evangelism movement are the Baptist preacher Billy Graham and the Pentecostal evangelist Oral Roberts.

A striking phenomenon on the fringe of the American religious scene is the present preoccupation of many young people with new religions of heterogeneous origins, some of them based on eastern cults, mysticism and transcendentalism. A number of larger sects and groups of this kind, like the Church of Scientology, the Unification Church (Moon Sect), the Hare Krishna Sect, the Children of God (COG), the Transcendental Meditation movement (TM), the Divine Light Mission (DLM) and other similarly based groups have in the past years prospered considerably. In their emotional motivations some of these new religious activities of the young bear a certain resemblance to the revival movements of the past. Nevertheless, they represent a search for entirely new paths and for new alternatives to traditional religion. In this search the youthful "dissenters opt for mystery, seek community and embrace joy" (E.S. Gaustadt, p. 149, ref.lit.). However, in their desire to turn away from established religion, some of these groups are esoteric to the point of eccentricity.

E V/ P v T

General Synod

● The General Synod of the Church of England, set up in 1970 in succession to the National Assembly of the Church of England, is the principal legislative and administrative body of the *Established Church**. It is composed of three

Houses: Bishops (52 members), Clergy (251), and Laity (248). While the first two consist of the members of the *Convocations** of Canterbury and York the third is composed of lay men and women elected by local synods throughout the country. Meeting at least twice a year the Synod discusses, formulates and frames legislation on church affairs. Its legislative measures are then laid before Parliament for approval.

Besides being responsible for legislation the General Synod administers many aspects of the Church's work. It deals, for instance, with general education and the training of prospective clergymen. It is responsible for about 8,000 Church of England schools and a total of about 17 theological colleges and a number of teacher training colleges.

The General Assembly of the Church of Scotland, which meets annually, is the senior court of the established Church of Scotland. It consists of elected ministers and elders and is presided over by an elected Moderator who serves for one year. Since the Church of Scotland is free of parliamentary control the General Assembly's resolutions, unlike the measures of the General Synod of the Church of England, can be put into practice immediately. J L F

High Church

● A party within the Church of England holding opinions which give a high place to the authority and claims of the episcopate and the priesthood, the saving grace of the sacraments, and generally, to those points of doctrine, discipline and ritual by which the Anglican Church is distinguished from the Calvinistic and the Protestant Nonconformist churches. 1702.

The High Church movement was a natural reaction to the Evangelical tendencies of the *Low Church** party. Within the *Established Church** there had been an Anglo-Catholic party which, while denying the Pope any authority in England, wanted the Church of England to be regarded as a part of the great universal Christian Church of which the Roman Church was also part. Anglo-Catholic tendencies were given fresh impetus by the "Oxford Movement" (1833 onwards), so called because many of its outstanding figures were members of Oxford University. They had a great veneration for the past. They stressed the derivation of the priest's authority through the bishops from Christ's apostles. This emphasis on the historical origins of the ministry naturally led to a respectful attitude towards the Roman Catholic Church which, after all, had introduced the ministry to Britain. They revived many ritual practices which had been discontinued in the 16th century. Their celebration of High Mass, for instance, caught the imagination of many people who, finding the simple services of Low Church uninspiring, might otherwise have been converted to Roman Catholicism.

Between the two extremes represented by the High Church and Low Church parties there developed also a Broad Church movement whose adherents, particularly active during the second half of the 19th century, wished to take the doctrines of the Church of England in a broad, liberal sense, thus allowing wide limits to orthodoxy. They desired to comprehend the two extremes and consequently their way of thinking is charitable and tolerant. J L F

Jew

● Although the history of Jewish immigration into England goes back to the time of the Norman conquest, Jews had to go through many centuries of persecution and social discrimination before they were able to obtain the equality of status they have today. In 1290 all Jews were expelled from England by Edward I, and it was not until three and a half centuries later that they were allowed to return under the rule of Oliver Cromwell. Even then, however, they were tolerated only for their usefulness in the promotion of trade, and it was by a slow process lasting more than two centuries that they obtained political equality. In the first half of the 19th century it was still necessary for a Jew to sever his religious ties in order to attain a high position *(Religious Test*)*. Benjamin Disraeli (1804-81), the Conservative Prime Minister, would not have been able to rise so far if he had not dissociated himself from the synagogue. By the Jewish Relief Act of 1858 Jews were first admitted to appointments in the Civil Service, and in the same year a Jew first took his seat in the House of Commons. It was not until 1871, however, that university tests were abolished and Jews were given unrestricted access to the universities of Oxford and Cambridge. Since 1890 all offices have been open to Jews.

The present Anglo-Jewish community – represented by a Board of Deputies of British Jews, founded in 1760 – has considerably increased in number since 1933 and is today, with approximately 410 000 members, the third largest Jewish community in Europe. It is divided into two denominational sections, the Orthodox and the Reform. The Orthodox group comprises 90 per cent. of British Jewry. The Reform movement came into being in 1840.

■ Jewish immigration into the United States goes back to the early days of American history. The first Jews to settle there from 1654 onwards were for the greater part "Sephardic" – Spanish and Portuguese – Jews who had been expelled from the Iberian peninsula. They were orthodox Jews who established their synagogues according to the Sephardic rites and who retained Spanish as their ritual language. They desired to transplant their orthodox pattern from home and only when this proved impossible did they gradually begin to adapt themselves to the new conditions.

For the first two centuries immigration continued at a slow rate, and by 1820 there were still only 5,000 Jews in the United States, in a total population of 10,000,000. Most of these Jews had settled along the east coast, in New York, Newport, Philadelphia and Charleston, where they pursued occupations as merchants and financiers.

In the 1820s a second wave of Jewish immigration set in. Between 1820 and 1870 approximately 300,000 Jews arrived in the United States from Germany and central Europe. In contrast to the "native" Sephardim, these Jews were "Ashkenazim" (a Hebrew word for Jews from central and eastern Europe) and considered by the former to be "inferior". Integration between the two groups therefore proceeded only slowly, particularly as many of the German Jews considered themselves as Germans rather than as Jews and frequently joined in cultural and mutual benefit societies with Germans of different religious identification. The newcomers, however, showed a talent for adaptation to American conditions equal to that of the native Jews, and their dispersal over the whole of the United States made quick progress. So strong was the trend towards Americanization among the German Jews that – especially in the second generation – defections increased on an unprecedented scale. In order to counteract this development towards dissolution and a general weakening of the immigrant Jewish traditions, a strong reform movement came into being which aimed at adapting the Jewish religious pattern to American conditions, by suggesting revisions of the liturgy, replacing other languages by English and eliminating the segregation of women. Great synagogues like Emmanu-El in New York and Har Sinai in Baltimore adopted the reforms. Many other German synagogues followed, and those converted by the Reform movement came to comprise one of the three main denominations of present American Judaism, the other two being the Orthodox and the Conservatives. The Conservative wing has more traditional tendencies but is just as Americanized as the Reform movement.

By 1880 the flood of Jewish immigration from Eastern Europe brought about another turning point in the history of American Jewry. The 500,000 Jews who came in this wave were a distinct ethnic group with Yiddish as their common language. They streamed into cities where they lived in a type of voluntary ghetto and became industrial proletarians. This state, however, lasted only for one generation, for the new Jewish immigrants, too, had the ability to adapt themselves to the new circumstances. With great energy they educated their children and quickly improved their social standing. Yet the difference between the newcomers – generally called the "Russians" – and the older Jewish inhabitants – from then on generally called the "Germans" – was to remain so marked that up to the beginning of the 20th century a deep chasm existed inside American Jewry. The Yiddish-speaking Russian Jews for their part were divided into two considerably different ideological strands. While the greater part remained orthodox, a smaller group began to participate in the secular ideologies of the time, in labour radicalism as well as in the Zionist movement. Zionism, founded in 1898 by Th. Herzl, a Viennese journalist, was first considered with scepticism by the wealthier American Jews. Eventually, "Der Judenstaat" found wider support among American Jewry.

Since the beginning of the 20th century a rapprochement has taken place between the "Germans" and the "Russians". Today they have reached a certain degree of amalgamation and have since been united in their determination to engage in Jewish philanthropic enterprises. The American Jewish Joint Distribution Committee and the United Jewish Appeal (organized in 1940) became the two major fund-raising agencies which enabled American Jewry to render support to persecuted Jews overseas. With the emergence of the state of Israel in 1948 the American Jewish population found a symbol of Jewish identity. Furthermore, what closely united American Jewry was the necessity for common defence against repeated waves of anti-Semitism in the United States itself, which led to the creation of the Anti-Defamation League in 1913. There also exists a militant Jewish "defense" organization, the Jewish Defense League.

In the 1930s another wave of Jewish refugees from Germany, Austria and Czechoslovakia increased the American Jewish population. This increase also favoured the intellectual level of American Jewry. Many European-educated Jewish writers, artists, scientists and professionals, amongst them many who had already attained fame, now came to exert an influence on all spheres of intellectual life in the United States.

Jews have always been one of the most highly urbanized groups of the American population. Over 75 per cent. live in cities of half a million or more inhabitants, and Jews, for instance, make up one quarter of the population of New York. In education American Jews rank far above the national average. The proportion of Jews in college is twice that of the general U.S. population. And the proportion of Jews enrolled in graduate and professional schools is triple that for students in the general population.

Jews have always made large donations to institutions of higher learning and played an active part in the foundation of such institutions. Brandeis University (1948), among others, was a Jewish foundation. The contributions of American-Jewish writers – such as J. D. Salinger, Arthur Miller, Saul Bellow, Bernard Malamud etc. – to contemporary American literature are also worth mentioning.

In the political life of the country Jewish sympathies usually tend more to the Democratic Party, but in each of the past administrations Jews have held important positions.

Jews – though comprising only three per cent. of the American population – form one of the three main religious communities of the United States, side by side with Protestants and Catholics (Freedom of Religion). Yet the criteria of their "belonging" are more ethnic than religious. Less than 50 per cent. are formally affiliated with a synagogue; the others assert their Jewishness through their keeping up of Jewish traditions, their Jewish modes of life and belief and their commitment to Jewish associations and aims.

The fear that successful assimilation and Americanization threaten the continuity of American Judaism has in the past years led to a religious revival along more traditional lines. *(Freedom of Religion*.)* E V/ P v T

Low Church

● A party within the Church of England holding opinions which give a low place to the authority and claims of the episcopate and the priesthood, to the inherent grace of the sacraments, and to matters of ecclesiastical organization, thus differing little from the opinion held by Protestant Nonconformists. 1702.

When in the 18th century the *Methodists** attempted to infuse new life into the Church of England the church authorities disapproved of their methods but yet were impressed by their ardour. A number of Anglican clergy started an Evangelical revival within the *Established Church** itself which led to a simple, personal form of Christianity with no importance attached to tradition and ritual or to control through bishops. Those who share these tendencies have since become known as the Low Church party. A reaction to this is to be seen in the *"High Church"** movement. J L F

Lutheran

A follower of Martin Luther (1483-1546) or his religious teachings; a member of the branch of the Protestant Church adhering to Luther's views, generally known as the Lutheran Church. 1521.

■ In the history of the Christian Church in North America, the Lutheran Church, as one denominational group, offers a great variety of national origins. The Scandinavian and German Lutherans settled largely in states according to their national churches. A population census shows that Lutherans settled in Pennsylvania, New York, North & South Carolina, Virginia, Ohio, Indiana, Illinois, Wisconsin, Missouri, Minnesota, etc. They remained independent and fostered their European tongues and the churches of their origin (e.g. Swedish, Dutch, German, Danish, Finnish, Norwegian, Icelandic, etc.). This development indicated their desire to evade the Anglo-Saxon culture and language, while at the same time clinging to their traditions and festivities, their moral codes and their beliefs. This independence was marked by their founding additional local synods (churches), which was a Lutheran characteristic into the 20th century.

In 1638, at the instance of Gustavus Adolphus, the first Lutheran community was established by the Swedes at New Sweden, Delaware. In 1655 Peter Stuyvesant, governor of the Dutch Reformed settlement, eliminated the Lutheran Church at New Sweden. However, Dutch and German Lutherans, following their Reformed brethren, continued to arrive in America in the 17th century and settled in New England and the other eastern states.

In 1664 the British conquered New Amsterdam (New York City) and established their authority along the entire east coast. A more lenient policy was inaugurated and the immigration to the New World increased. With the growing number of Lutherans scattered over the colonies, the Pietists of the School of Halle (Spener, Francke) took the initiative early to send clergymen, particularly as William Penn appealed for Germans to settle in his state (Pennsylvania). The leading figure and organizer of American Lutheranism was Heinrich Melchior Mühlenberg (1711-87), who arrived in Philadelphia in 1742 and six years later established the first Lutheran synod.

In contrast to the radical Protestant leaders of the 17th century (e.g. Pilgrims, Puritans, early Baptists, etc.), the settlers of the 18th and 19th centuries came to America from economic and social motives rather than to gain "freedom of religion"*. Many immigrants were underprivileged, seeking a more favourable financial and social standing, or in fact evading the hazards of serving in the armies of their homeland.

The 19th century marked the greatest flood of German and Scandinavian Lutherans to the mid-western states. Here the ever-multiplying local synods were founded on national and theological grounds. At times Lutherans regarded their Church as superior to other Protestant denominations, considering themselves the established Church. With the approaching 400th anniversary of Luther's proclamation of his 95 theses, a serious effort towards union was projected for the year 1917. It was somewhat successful, for today there are primarily four major Lutheran Churches in North America: the Lutheran Church of America (3 million), the American Lutheran Church (2,5 million), the German Evangelical Lutheran Synod of Missouri, Ohio and other States (2,8 million) and the Wisconsin Evangelical Lutheran Synod (395,000).

In retrospect it might be noted that while the English-speaking denominations severed their ties with the English churches because of the Revolutionary War (1775-83), many Lutheran churches (esp. German) loosened their ties to their European mother countries on account of World War I.

● As for Lutherans in Great Britain, one may speak of a few scattered congregations, comprised largely of residents from the Continent and served by clergymen from their own countries. P v T

Methodist

Orig. a member of the Holy Club, established at Oxford in 1729 by John and Charles Wesley and others; later, any of those who sympathized with the evangelistic movement led by the Wesleys and George Whitefield. 1733.

● The role of Methodism in British church history is characterized by a dichotomy; on the one hand it is an offspring of the Anglican Church and never considered its ties with the mother church to be permanently severed and in fact seems about to renew them in the near future; on the other hand it has grown into one of the leading Free Churches of England and as such has become one of the largest and most influential Protestant churches.

The Methodist movement started as one of the great revival movements at the beginning of the 18th century. Its origins are inseparably connected with the name of one of its founders, John Wesley. An Anglican priest himself he certainly never aimed at rebellion against his Church. But living at a time of revolutionary changes in the social structure of his country *(Industrial Revolution*)* he soon became aware of the need for a new intensity of religious feeling, and of the necessity for the Church to keep pace with the new social developments in the country by building churches and sending more priests to the new, densely populated manufacturing areas. The lethargy of the *Established Church** in meeting these requirements and even more its rationalist attitude towards Christian faith eventually led John Wesley to act on his own by preaching in the fields and by ordaining lay preachers. The result was an open break with the Anglican Church. Four years after Wesley's death in 1791, the break became official and a separate Methodist Church was established, a church which, in spite of several inner schisms in the course of the 19th century gained decisive influence in the life of the British nation.

The name "Methodist" can be traced back to the time when Wesley was a member of a group of students at Oxford who, because of their striving for personal holiness and a more methodical life and because of the rigid discipline to which they submitted themselves in the "Holy Club", were given the nickname "the Methodists". But Methodism as we know it was born on May 24th, 1738, when Wesley, while studying Luther's preface to the Epistle to the Romans, had a "heart-warming" religious experience of such intensity that it has since been called his "evangelical conversion". So profound was the recovery of Luther's religious conviction and so far-reaching its consequences that there is certainly some justification for the claim that Martin Luther's chief contribution to English religion came not at the Reformation, but centuries later through the Methodist revival.

Methodism's doctrinal liberalism allows an exceptionally wide range of beliefs and stresses personal intensity of faith as well as the idea of the "warm fellowship" of all believers. Other characteristic features are first its thorough organization and centralization, the "circuit system" (so called because the 34 districts in England, headed by the Conference, the supreme Methodist body, are subdivided into circuits), and secondly the "itinerant system" of travelling preachers. Wesley himself built up a presbyterian system of church government, and by his own endless journeyings through the country set the example for the later characteristic figure of Methodism, the travelling preacher. Nowadays these ministers must travel widely in order to comply with their rota of preaching appointments – the "quarterly plan". In every church in their circuit they are assisted by "local preachers", ordained laymen and laywomen who, because of their occupations, are bound to the place where they live.

British Methodism nowadays seems to be faced with the same fundamental problems which confront the other Free Churches in Britain. The need for such churches has subsided and so has the stimulus. Methodism at one time identified its aims fully with those of the new working classes. Methodists played an active part in the development of British socialism. In the 19th century Methodists even took the lead in many activities of the newly founded Trade Unions, some of which were even organized under the name of "chapel", a name which still lingers. Even today British Trade Unionists call each other not "comrade" but "brother".

Towards the end of the last century Methodism was already losing its revolutionary zeal and becoming "respectable". A reaction to this development was the foundation in 1872 of the Salvation Army, whose leader William Booth, a former Methodist local preacher, had resigned from his ministry because he found it impossible to reconcile his passion for administering to the poor with the growing middle-class tendencies within the Methodist Church. Indeed the Salvation Army, in spite of military trimmings which strike the foreign observer in particular as slightly ridiculous, seems to be the group which has best preserved the passionate aims of early Methodism.

■ Two men have played a decisive role in the foundation and development of American Methodism: John Wesley and Francis Asbury. Wesley visited America early in his career and never lost interest in the development of his Society in America. He exerted great influence by ordaining laymen for office in the New World and supplied American Methodists with his "Twenty-four Articles of Religion", those of the *Thirty-nine Articles** which he considered to be in keeping with Methodist principles. In 1784 the first American Conference in Baltimore, which set up an independent American Methodist Church, accepted these Twenty-four Articles but added another one, "Of the Rulers of the United States of America". Despite Wesley's personal influence the new American Methodist Church had its own way on a very important matter: the title given to the Church was "The Methodist Episcopal Church" and the subsequent appointment of bishops was definitely against Wesley's will. It is strange that the question of episcopacy, which now forms one of the main obstacles to reunion between Anglicans and Methodists in England, had been settled by American Methodists along the lines of their mother church.

Francis Asbury, who went to America in 1771 as a young travelling preacher, determined the development of American Methodism for half a century. It was on his initiative that American Methodist preachers, instead of concentrating their efforts on the towns, followed the ever extending *Frontier**, and it is due to his example that the Methodist "circuit rider" became one of the formative influences of American civilization.

Just as the Methodist Church in England suffered several schisms in the course of the 19th century, which persisted until the final reunion of most of these groups in 1932, so the American Methodist Church became divided over the question of slavery. In 1844 its Southern bishops seceded and this division was sustained until 1939. As a result of the Civil War three powerful Negro Methodist Churches were established in the South and they have remained independent to the present day.

There is another significant parallel between British and American Methodism in the social sphere. In both countries Methodism has shown a growing tendency towards a status improvement. The American Methodist Church has clearly become a church of the middle class. Also Methodism has long since adopted a leading role in education. Methodists have played a part in the foundation of more than a third of all the universities and *Colleges** in the United States.

Methodism has always shown itself open to ecumenical thought in its consciousness of world-wide Christian fellowship, in its endeavours to form a greater unity among the different Christian Churches and in its world-wide missionary activity. The discussions concerning reunion between the Anglican and the Methodist Church in England and the merger of the Methodist Church with the Evangelical United Brethren in America are clear proof of this willingness.

E V/P v T

Mormon

The alleged author of the Book of Mormon. A member of the Church of Jesus Christ of Latter-day Saints founded in 1830 at Manchester, New York, by Joseph Smith. 1837.

■ For several reasons the "Mormons" are the most indigenous of all American religious groups: (1) The Book of Mormon traces the history of a tribe of Israel who escaped the Babylonians and sailed to South America there to become the forefathers of the Incas, Aztecs, and the North American Indians; it also tells of Christ's visit to the Americas. (2) They do not consider themselves as Protestants and, indeed, they have nothing in common with the traditional forms of Protestantism imported to America from Europe. (3) The Church of Latter-day Saints was founded at a time when a new revivalism, "an unusual excitement on the subject of religion" (Joseph Smith in his autobiographical account) was rife all over the United States. (4) The Mormons were frontiersmen, pioneers; they moved from New York to Ohio, Missouri, and Illinois, where they founded the town of Nauvoo (see below), and finally trekked across the continent (1846/47) to found Salt Lake City. The Mormon Trail, leading from Nauvoo via Fort Laramie to Salt Lake City, was one of the important routes to the West. In the wilderness, a thousand miles away from continuos civilization, they transformed the desert into cultivated land within a decade, built irrigation canals and ditches, set up a system of small farms intensely cultivated, and established a disciplined community life. This community life may not have been in conformity with established political and religious codes existing in the East of the United States, but it certainly was with the Declaration of Independence and Amendment I of the American constitution, which established the pursuit of happiness and the free exercise of religion as elementary rights in the United States. Polygamy was supported by the Bible (Isaiah IV,1), but, for pragmatic reasons, it was prohibited by church manifesto in 1890, whereupon statehood was granted to Utah in 1896.

Mormon social and religious government remains predominatly theocratic and is administered by a complex church hierarchy, in which practically only the prophet President of the Church gets revelations from God. – In their "Articles of Faith" the Mormons confess, among other things, that they believe in God, Jesus Christ, and the Holy Ghost; that men will be punished for their own sins and "not for Adam's transgressions"; that the first principles and ordinances of the Gospel are faith in Jesus Christ, repentance, baptism by immersion, and laying on of hands for the gift of the Holy Ghost; they believe the Bible and the Book of Mormon to be the word of God; they believe in "the gift of tongues, prophecy, revelations, visions, healing, interpretation of tongues, etc.", and they believe that Zion will be built on the American continent.

They are convinced that only the baptized will enter heaven, so they aim to baptize everyone, the living and the dead. In order to save, posthumously, as many of their ancestors as possible they established a genealogical library at

Salt Lake City, the greatest in the world. Their faith centres around marriage, the family, the upbringing of children, and man and wife are bound together with all their family for the whole of eternity.

Joseph Smith (1805-1844) was the founder of the Mormon faith. At the age of 15 he began having visions. One day, while he was in the woods to pray for guidance, he saw God and Jesus Christ in "a pillar of light exactly over my head". Three years later, he was visited by a personage who announced himself as Moroni, a resurrected being. Moroni showed him the hiding-place of a package of inscribed gold plates, together with a pair of magic stones which "God had prepared . . . for the purpose of translating the book". The resulting "Book of Mormon" (1830) gave the story of certain Lost Tribes of Israel (the Indians). In the Illinois town of Nauvoo, Smith and his followers sought to found a new Zion. They received a State charter giving them virtual autonomy. Converts poured in from abroad, and, by 1842, Nauvoo was the largest and the most prosperous town in Illinois. In 1843, Smith received the "revelation" sanctioning polygamy, long practiced by himself and his elders. This revelation split the Church. In the following year, in an attempt to suppress the monogamous dissidents, Smith, who was mayor of Nauvoo, overstepped his authority, was jailed for this, pulled out by a mob and lynched. The church leaders chose Brigham Young as his successor. After two years of retaliation and terror in western Illinois, he led most of the community to the Great Salt Lake, which at that time still belonged to Mexiko *(Louisiana Purchase*)*. He called the land Deseret, a word coined in the Book of Mormon, meaning the working bee (the beehive is still one of Utah's State symbols), but the name was changed in 1850, when Congress organized Deseret as Utah Territory and appointed Brigham Young territorial governor. Salt Lake City still is the centre of the Mormon faith. Its leaders claim that their missionaries, mostly young people who may be sent by the Church to any part of the world, usually on an 18-months mission, make a new convert every three minutes. The Church of Jesus Christ of Latter-day Saints has spread all over the world and has a membership of approximately three million. In 1978, President Kimball announced that he had received the revelation that "the promised day has come when every faithful, worthy man in the Church may receive the holy priesthood . . . without regard for race and colour". This admission of blacks to the Mormon priesthood is the most far-reaching modification of the Mormon Church during this century.

In 1852, the monogamous dissidents among the Mormons (see above) founded the "Reorganized Church of Jesus Christ of Latter-day Saints". Their headquarters are in Independence, Missouri. Their membership is about 160,000. Unlike the Utah church, the Reorganized Church has always admitted blacks into the priesthood.

● When Brigham Young visited Liverpool in 1839 he converted many English people to Mormonism and started the movement that resulted in bringing many English immigrants to America to strengthen the Mormon Church. By 1844, almost 4,000 of the 15,000 inhabitants of Nauvoo were immigrants from England.

The Mormons have missions covering the whole of the British Isles. It is estimated that about 1,600 Mormon missionaries are engaged in proselytizing activities at any one time, and although Mormonism is a very American faith, the Church has an estimated membership of over 100,000 in Britain and is growing there more rapidly than any other religious group. H H

Nonconformist

● Originally one who, while adhering to the doctrine of the Church of England, refused to conform to its discipline and practice. Later, a member of a religious body which is separated from the Church of England. 1619.

After the Church of England had been set up as the *Established Church** of the nation voices were soon to be heard protesting that the State should have no power to interfere in purely religious affairs because this restricted the freedom of the individual to worship as he thought best. Other Protestants declared themselves against the system of church government by bishops whose spiritual authority, the Church claimed, derived through an unbroken line of succession from Christ's apostles. By about 1625 there were three principal groups which did not conform to the Anglican way of thinking. Because these nonconformist sects broke away or "dissented" (hence the term Dissenters) from the state-controlled established church their movements later became known as Churches of Protestant Dissent or Free Churches.

At first used to denote the three earliest movements, the independents (or *Congregationalists*),* the *Baptists** and the *Presbyterians**, the term nonconformist later came to be applied to the so-called *Methodists**, too. With the Act of Uniformity of 1662, Nonconformism was consolidated. In due course a new spirit of tolerance helped to bring the established church and the various nonconformist movements closer together. An outstanding feature of recent years has been the growth of co-operation between the churches in the interests of Christian unity. This trend towards reconciliation is all the more desirable as the membership figures of nonconformist churches have been steadily falling since the beginning of the present century owing to a decline in working-class zeal and a swing towards Anglicanism.

These religious movements are, of course, represented in the United States, too. But here they cannot properly be termed nonconformist, since America has no established church to the doctrines of which they could fail to conform.

J L F

Presbyterian

Presbyter: "elder"; an elder in the early Christian Church; in the Presbyterian Church the name ascribed to an elected elder, a member of the Presbytery. Presbyterian: a member of the Presbyterian Church, which has a central, synodical structure; a Protestant associated with the tradition of the Scotsman John Knox and the Calvinist theology. 1644.

The Presbyterian Churches had their origin in the 16th century Reformation in England where they formed the most radical group of English dissent and aimed at thorough reforms along Calvinist lines *(Puritans*)*. Their leaders were strongly influenced by the continental reformers, particularly John Calvin of Geneva, and the Presbyterian Churches consequently regarded themselves as belonging to the family of Reformed Churches in the world. Their name "Presbyterian" referred to their form of church constitution; it claimed for its origin the Christian Church during apostolic times, which then became redefined during the Swiss Reformation. This constitution provided for centralized church government through a hierarchy of constituent bodies ranging from the local Session – an assembly consisting of elders presided over by the minister – to the Presbytery and the Synod and culminating in the General Assembly, the supreme church body on the national level. The

Presbyterian system was based on the Calvinist idea that there is no distinction between laity and clergy and the most concrete expression of this is the office of the "elder" who, as a layman, continues to earn his daily bread through his "calling" but who is at the same time ordained to spiritual office. The ministers are not a "sacred order" but simply a group of officeholders sharing their duties within the church with teachers, elders, and deacons.

● In the British Isles Presbyterianism owes its major significance mainly to the fact that the Church of Scotland is a Presbyterian church. With more than 1,220,000 members it comprises the overwhelming majority of the population and is in fact the *Established Church** of Scotland. Its rights were laid down in the Treaty of the Union in 1707 and to the present day the Sovereign has to take an oath to preserve this church. Its characteristically Calvinist autonomy is expressed in the "Articles Declaratory of the Constitution of the Church of Scotland in Matters Spiritual" which state that "the Church of Scotland . . . declares that it receives from its Head and from Him alone the right and power subject to no civil authority to legislate, and to adjudicate finally in all matters of doctrine, worship, government, and discipline in the Church".

In contrast to the Presbyterian Church in Scotland the English Presbyterian Church – with about 60.000 members – held only a minor place among the Free Churches in England. It was in England, however, in 1643, that the constitutional and doctrinal basis of Presbyterianism was laid down. At that time *Parliament**, then wholly under Presbyterian influence, summoned the Westminster Assembly of Divines as an advisory body on religious matters. The results of the Assembly were the Westminster Confession of Faith (1647) and other constitutional documents which have since been adopted by the Presbyterian Churches throughout the world. In Wales today we find the strange phenomenon of a strong Presbyterian Church originating not in 17th century ecclesiastical reform but in the *Methodist** revival movement of the 18th century. The Calvinist Methodist or Presbyterian Church of Wales has exerted great influence on the development of modern Wales. In October, 1972 the English Presbyterian Church merged with the *Congregational** Church to form the United Reformed Church.

In Northern Ireland the Presbyterian Church has – mainly through Scottish settlers – become the second strongest church with 30 per cent. of the population. The Roman Catholic Church has 34.9 per cent. In the bitter conflict between Protestant and Catholic Ulstermen since 1968 the officials of the Presbyterian Church have tried to moderate and to mediate.

■ The United Presbyterian Church in the U.S.A., formed in 1958 through a merger of two large Presbyterian Churches, is today one of the strongest Protestant denominations, with 4.9 million members. Presbyterian history in North America goes back the to early times of *Puritan** settlement in *New England**. At thc time of the Revolution (1775-83) the Presbyterian Church, since it had been based on democratic traditions from the outset, strongly supported the fight for independence by taking up John Locke's idea of the state as a "social contract"*(Mayflower Compact*)*.

American revivalism exerted some influence on the Presbyterian Churches, too. They were in fact the first to introduce the "camp meeting". However, they later abandoned it to the more emotionally determined *Baptists** and *Methodists**. On the whole the religious attitude of Presbyterianism was more dogmatic than emotional and thus not as close to revivalism. In social stratification the Presbyterian Churches in the U.S.A. are predominantly churches of the upper and upper-middle class, with a very high proportion of businessmen and the relatively largest number of *High School** graduates among all the Protestant Churches in the U.S.A.

Apart from the United Presbyterian Church in the U.S.A. (U.P.U.S.A.), formed in 1958, and a major "southern" Presbyterian Church, often called "Presbyterian Church U.S.", there exist a number of smaller Presbyterian Churches in the United States, among them three all-Negro Presbyterian Churches with about 90,000 members.

A notable event was the United Presbyterians' 177th General Assembly in May 1965 in Columbus, Ohio, where the majority of delegates voted to accept their first new creed since the Westminster Confession of 1647. The "Confession of 1967", as it was called after final approval by the next two assemblies, contained a contemporary statement stressing the need for the involvement of the Church in social and political issues. For "Christian renewal", the United Presbyterians say, "includes the right and duty of a living Church to restate its faith from time to time". E V/P v T

Puritan

(Originally) a member of that party of English Protestants who regarded the reformation of the Church under Elizabeth I as incomplete and called for its further "purification" from unscriptural and corrupt forms and ceremonies retained from the unreformed church. 1572.

● The term was first used in England in the late 1560s to denote a person who was not satisfied with the steps that had been taken to reform the English church. Under Henry VIII the monarch had replaced the Pope as the head of the church in England. Under Queen Elizabeth I the rejection of Roman Catholicism went even further and the Church of England developed a more pronounced tendency towards Protestantism. At first those with stronger Protestant leanings hoped and expected that Elizabeth would carry out a more radical reform. But they were disappointed. The Puritans did not desire to break away from the Church of England; they merely wished to see it purified of what they regarded as unscriptural practices and beliefs. For them the Bible was infallible, and they considered its teachings in every way sufficient. The church with its traditional doctrines, on the other hand, they held to be fallible and therefore unsatisfactory. They further objected to the Book of Common Prayer, seeing in its set prayers an obstacle to true worship. By 1625 the Puritans had produced three main types of free (i.e. non-established) churches: the Independent or *Congregationalist**, the *Baptist** and the *Presbyterian**. To these may be added the less numerous but more extreme Society of Friends *(Quakers*)* who denied the need for any Sacraments at all or for any official ministers. The Puritans were partly responsible for the English Civil War. Unable to get their way in religious policy they sided with Parliament against the Royalists and succeeded in overthrowing both the monarchy and the established church. After the Restoration of King Charles II in 1660, Puritan influence in politics remained. This way of thinking served as the foundation stone of the Whig Party, the forerunner of the modern *Liberal Party**.

■ Other puritans were meanwhile seeking another solution to their problems. In 1620 a group known as the Pilgrim Fathers set sail for America, and until a check was put on emigration by the outbreak of the Civil War in England in 1642 many others followed their example. They settled mainly Massachusetts and the surrounding colonies. It was not their intention to secede from the Church of England, but this was the inevitable result of divergent trends of thought and also the natural consequence of the geographical separation from the English homeland. The Congregational or Independent form of worship soon came to be adopted. Even into the 19th century the Puritans continued to be involved in religious strife because of their insistence on the absolute authority of the Bible, their belief in the necessity of uniformity and their conviction that toleration was evil.

Attitudes such as these, together with their disapproval of pleasurable excesses, earned the Puritans the reputation of being over-precise moralists. Particularly in America they were regarded as being intent on such matters as the *Prohibition** of alcohol and tobacco. As a result, Puritan has come to be applied, chiefly in ridicule, to someone who is, or is said to be, excessively strict and precise in religion and morals, condemning pleasures or indulgences which he regards as impure or corrupting. This may have cost the Puritans a large number of possible converts, but the fact remains that they have exerted a tremendous influence on the intellectual, cultural and political life of the United States. J L F

Quaker

One of a religious sect founded by George Fox about 1650, the members of which call themselves "Friends". The name Quaker was applied in derision by a judge to Fox, who bade the justice tremble at the word of the Lord. 1653.

The name "Quaker", first used with contempt by the enemies of this sect but soon accepted with pride by its members, evokes memories both of the group's passionate and ecstatic founders in the 17th century and of the world-wide social and charitable work performed by Quakers especially in post-war times.

The Quakers' original, and still official, name, "The Religious Society of Friends", on the other hand, characterizes an essential feature of their religious attitude. They, even more radically than other denominations stemming from historic Dissent, reject any hierarchical form of church organization as well as any credal definition and the use of sacraments in worship. The Friends' informal meetings are conspicuous by the absence of any service and by long periods of silence which are broken spontaneously by whoever has received the Spirit's inspiration. "That of God in every man" is a favourite Quaker phrase. They believe in the Light of Christ in any man and their religious belief finds expression in a grave and sober daily life, in the rejection of military service according to their pacifist principles, and in large-scale social and charitable work. For centuries they have been the leading protagonists in the struggle for social reform, and by their example have brought about improvements in the care of the aged and the poor, in prison conditions and in educational development. Their relief actions after the two world wars gained them world renown. The Society recently established a Chair of Peace Studies at the University of Bradford.

The name "Quaker" has thus become of outstanding importance not only in their orginal countries, England, Holland and America, but in the whole world, an importance quite disproportionate to the actual number of their fellowship (20,000 in Great Britain, 125,000 in the U.S.A., about 200,000 in the whole world).

● The Society of Friends was founded in 1652 by George Fox who radically opposed not only the *Established Church** but also any milder form of Dissent and who in spite of persecution moulded the principal Quaker attitudes of today. There is a strange contrast between the radical figure of the Quaker movement's founder and the modern image of the Quaker which, in England at least, is determined by personalities such as the chocolate magnates Cadbury, Fry and Rowntree, men who "may be said to have sweetened both diet and business relationships" (Dr. Horton Davies) but who, nevertheless, in their active struggle for social reform have upheld the early Quakers' traditions.

The greatest of Quaker educational reformers was Joseph Lancaster (1778-1838). His main concern was the education of the poor. He was instrumental in the founding of numerous schools in England and America, all of them run according to the monitorial system *(Primary Education*)*.

■ One of the outstanding figures of early Quaker days, William Penn, went to America. In order to help his persecuted fellow-believers he founded the colony of Pennsylvania in 1682 to which he gave a constitution based on religious tolerance. In accordance with his Quaker principles he was the first to succeed in the setting up of peaceful relations with the Indians. It is also noteworthy that William Penn, as a social philosopher, was committed to world peace. In a famous "Essay towards the Present and Future Peace of Europe" (1693) he anticipated the idea of some sort of a European federation. Quakers later also took an active part in American abolitionism *(Abolitionist*)*. John Woolman's two essays "Some Considerations on the Keeping of Negroes" (1754, 1766) were among the earliest American anti-slavery works.

In the 19th century the Quaker movement in the United States suffered a split when a more evangelical wing under the leadership of Elias Hicks seceded from the movement. Both forms of Quakerism, the Orthodox Quakers and the Hicksites, now exist side by side in America.

Quakerism with its basic principles of tolerance, individual freedom, and human dignity has in the course of centuries exerted a profound influence on American political thought (B. Franklin), on the development of art and literature (J. G. Whittier, Walt Whitman) and on social and educational progress.

In spite of the Quakers' being a relatively small denomination, their influence on present-day life in England and the United States is still very strong. Their attitude to modern problems is open-minded and pragmatic. They have shown considerable courage and independence in their criticism of aspects of modern life.

In 1947 the Society of Friends was awarded the Nobel Peace Prize in acknowledgement of its work for peace and for the relief of suffering.

E V/J L F

Religious Test

● An ordeal or oath required as proof of conformity with a set of beliefs. 1665.

Article 18 of the Universal Declaration of Human Rights (1948) lays down the principle of religious freedom for all men. In ideal circumstances no person shall be subject to any disability on religious grounds, and many modern states have gone a long way towards granting their citizens this fundamental freedom. Thus Article 6 of the *Constitution** of the United States of America proclaims that "no religious test shall be required as a qualification to any office or public trust under the United States". In present-day Britain freedom of conscience is enjoyed by all. The fact that the Sovereign, as Head of the *Established Church**, must be an Anglican and that the Lord Chancellor may not be a Roman Catholic can scarcely be regarded as an infringement of this basic human right.

For several centuries, however, religious freedom was not an accepted principle in Britain. After the establishment of the Anglican faith as the state religion in England life became fraught with danger for Catholic and Nonconformist alike. A long period of religious strife ensued, of which one of the more significant consequences was the emigration, particularly between 1620 and 1642, of considerable numbers of unhappy people of *Puritan** outlook – English colonists of the New World.

In both England and Scotland, indeed in Ireland, too, Acts of Parliament were passed imposing severe limitations on religious freedom. Among early Acts of especial importance were the Act of Supremacy (1534) (requiring recognition of the Sovereign as Head of the church) and the Acts of Uniformity (demanding uniform acceptance of the doctrines of the Established Church as outlined in the 39 Articles of Religion and the Book of Common Prayer). Later Acts imposed further restrictions. Particularly notorious was the Test Act of 1673. Any person desirous of obtaining a civil or military appointment was obliged to take the oath of supremacy and allegiance to the Crown, subscribe a declaration against the doctrine of transubstantiation and also promise to receive the sacrament within three months of taking office. The Act did not apply to peers, but in 1678 these, too. had certain obligations imposed upon them. Similar tests were required in Scotland. Already by an Act of 1567 everyone appointed to public office there had to subscribe to the Established Church of Scotland, and by 1700 all persons active in the field of education were being made to renounce popery.

The history of education in England likewise bears the scars of religious struggles. Interdenominational strife on the level of primary and secondary education, aggravated as it was by the enforcement of a policy of education for all, abated when a compromise solution, the "agreed syllabus" of religious instruction acceptable to everyone, was worked out between education authorities and representatives of the various religious denominations. At university level the problems were even more acute. Religious tests were imposed at the older institutions. At Oxford, for instance, prospective teachers and students had since 1581 been required to make a declaration that they recognized the supremacy of the Sovereign and that they accepted the Anglican doctrine as set out in the 39 Articles. The very fact that *Nonconformists** were excluded from the privilege of university education caused them to establish their own institution of a similar nature, a foundation which has since developed into *London University**.

The religious test was a pernicious institution, founded as it was on prejudice. Gradually a spirit of toleration grew up. Frequent amendments were made to the various Acts we have discussed and parts of them were repealed. Gradually Acts were passed guaranteeing religious liberty to the adherents of various denominations. 1689 saw the passing of the Toleration Act which granted freedom of worship to Nonconformists. Under George IV the obligation of actually receiving the sacrament as a qualification for public office was abolished. The repeal of the Test Act and the Corporation Act in 1828 relieved Protestant dissenters of their political disabilities and enabled them to obtain appointments in the Civil Service. Roman Catholics were granted similar rights in 1829, and the Jewish Relief Act was passed in 1858. Further restrictions were repealed by the Promissory Oaths Act of 1871 and the Statute Law Revision of 1863. In Scotland all tests were abolished with the passing of an Act of 1889. As for the universities, subscription to the teachings of the Church of England, all oaths concerning religious belief and obligatory attendance at public worship were abolished in 1871 when the University Tests Act became law.

With the abolition of the religious tests at the end of the 19th century Britain was at last beginning to recover its balance and to settle down after the upheavals of the Reformation and its aftermath. J L F

Roman Catholic

● In Britain today everyone is entitled to worship as he pleases. But this has not always been so. In the 16th century King Henry VIII overthrew the Papal authority and set himself up as the Head of the English Church. For all those who did not allow themselves to be guided by the teachings of the *Established Church** of England difficult times lay ahead, and this is particularly true of those who remained loyal Catholics. From time to time they had to suffer severe persecution, not only because they opposed the Established Church but also because they were considered politically dangerous – sometimes not without reason. In the days of Elizabeth I they were suspected of sympathizing with England's arch-enemy, Philip of Spain, and a few years later, it will be remembered, a ruthless group of Catholic reactionaries, among them Guy Fawkes, conspired to blow up King and Parliament. Such activities could lead to distrust of Roman Catholics in general, and it was only gradually that tolerance prevailed.

The many civil disabilities laid upon them were gradually removed by Acts of Parliament, among which one of especial importance was the Catholic Relief Act of 1829 which granted them political emancipation. In England a properly organized Catholic hierarchy was restored in 1850, in Scotland in 1878.

In 1840 there were about half a million Roman Catholics in England and Wales, but owing to the removal of restrictions, to a general revival of interest and particularly to a large influx of Irish labour there were already about 1,300,000 adherents by 1900. Since no person in Britain is ever required to disclose his religious denomination, it is not possible to give accurate membership figures for the various churches at the present time, but it is thought that there are now about six million Catholics in the United Kingdom, more than 10 per cent. of the population. In England and Wales, the Roman Church is headed by five archbishops (of Westminster, Cardiff, Birmingham, Liverpool, and Southwark); Scotland has two archbishops (of St. Andrews and Edinburgh, and Glasgow).

At his (or her) Coronation the monarch – as Head of the Established Church – swears to uphold the Protestant faith. Likewise the Lord Chancellor may not be a Roman Catholic. Otherwise there is no religious bar to the holding of any office. Catholics play important roles in all spheres of life, including the arts; two prominent Roman Catholic writers may be mentioned: Graham Greene and the late Evelyn Waugh. J L F

■ The Roman Catholic Church in America is by far the United States' largest single denomination, comprising as it does almost 49 million members. It constitutes one of the three great religious communities which together make up the American religious picture *(Freedom of Religion*)*. Yet it had to go a long way to reach its present position of power and influence. The origins of Catholicism in America were entirely different from those of Protestantism. While the Protestant Churches made a new start as religious movements on American soil, the Roman Catholic Church was initially a "foreign" church widely considered to be something strange and alien to early American life and as such exposed to much persecution during the colonial period. It was only after independence had been gained in 1776 that American Catholics were granted equality of status. Even then their position was to remain difficult for about another century. Some states upheld discriminatory laws, and a shortage of clergy as well as the overwhelming pressure of Protestantism widely regarded as the "more truly" American form of religion, led to many defections on the part of Catholic immigrants *(Establishment*)*.

The actual development of American Catholicism towards its present importance began only with the great Irish *Immigration** of the 19th century, although some Catholic centres – Maryland, New Orleans and New Mexico – had existed since the early days of American settlement, and there were also Roman Catholic communities where Spanish and French influence had been prevalent before the birth of the Thirteen Colonies. The result of the Irish immigration was not only a large-scale increase in Catholic Church membership in the U.S.A. and a definite leadership of the Irish element in the strengthening of American Catholicism, but indeed a profound change in the whole attitude of the Church towards American social reality. Due to the Irish influence the Roman Catholic Church in the United States became "Americanized". By fully adapting themselves to American conditions and yet passionately preserving their loyalty to their Church, the Irish set a pattern which was to be followed by the later waves of Catholic immigrants, such as those from Eastern Europe and the Mediterranean countries. Towards the end of the 19th century the American Catholic hierarchy was almost entirely of Irish descent. The advancement in the social status of Roman Catholic immigrants has led to marked shifts in the social stratification of American Catholicism, which is today no longer overwhelmingly the religion of the urban working people but has more and more members among the middle class, especially in business and in the professions. The result has been an increased influence of the Roman Catholics on the social, cultural and political life in the United States. A spectacular outcome of this development was the election of John F. Kennedy as the first Roman Catholic President of the United States.

A certain traditional "conservatism" was always characteristic of the American Catholic hierarchy. Yet since the Secon d Vatican Council (1962-65) the progressive wing has increasingly determined the policies and theology of the Church. In the years following the Vatican Council the comparatively monolithic world of U.S. Catholicism was shaken by severe crises, and it went through a period of turmoil and division. Catholic laymen as well as clergy were split on questions of church authority and freedom, of tradition and change. In 1968 the birth control encyclical aroused passionate protests and in the ensuing years led to an unprecedented number of defections. In recent years there have been signs that American Catholicism is adjusting itself to the new conditions and is finding a new balance, though somewhat more remote from Rome. The more liberal basis reached in the course of these turbulent years has brought the American Catholic Church closer to the Protestant churches. Intercommunion between Catholics and Protestants has become more common. 5

The American Catholic laity's revived interest in matters of their Church has made itself felt especially in the field of education. In a spirit of voluntarism Catholic parents have joined to save the parochial schools which were threatened during the crisis. This has contributed to the preservation of the American Catholic Church's outstanding achievements in the field of education (parochial schools, universities and other institutions on the collegiate level). E V/P v T

Thirty-Nine Articles

Summary of the basic doctrine of the Church of England. 1571.

● The Thirty-nine Articles have been called one of the pillars of the Anglican faith. It was essential for the Reformers both in England and on the Continent to define their opinions in some way and the corpus of the Thirty-nine Articles is just one of a number of Confessions issued by Protestants in the 16th century. These Articles were not the first statement of religious thought issued by the English church; they have, however, been the most far-reaching in their effects in that they have retained their validity to the present day. They were first submitted to the English clergy for discussion by Archbishop Parker, the then Archbishop of Canterbury, in 1563. Adopted in a somewhat revised form in 1571, they have since that time remained essentially unchanged. Their content and wording were strongly influenced by the Confession of Augsburg of 1530 and the Confession of Württemberg of 1552. As a document relating to the Reformation and defining the nature of the Anglican protest they are of course of intense historical interest. But more than that, they are of inestimable value in that they lay down the fundamental standard of the *Established Church** and also give practical advice to the Christian believer. They do not cover the whole field of Christian doctrine but confine themselves to those aspects which were controversial in the period of religious strife in which they were conceived. Broadly speaking, the first eight Articles deal with the fundamentals of the Christian faith and with the importance of the Holy Scriptures. Articles 9 to 18 are concerned with details of personal religion (such as the questions of original sin, free-will, justification, good works, and predestination), while the remainder deal with problems of corporate religion, touching on such matters as the Church and its authority, the ministry, use of the vernacular, the sacraments, marriage of the clergy, and the relations between Church and State. To define the exact nature of the form of Protestantism they profess is somewhat difficult, for while chiefly in the Lutheran tradition they also have a Calvinist tinge though they avoid the extremes of this doctrine.

In order to ensure uniformity of doctrine throughout the Established Church an Act of Parliament of 1571 made it compulsory for all clergy to accept and subscribe to the Articles. A declaration of subscription to them is still required today of a clergyman on appointment to a new living. There is no *Religious Test** for laymen. J L F

Social Gospel

A Christian movement awakening social concern and a feeling of justice in the United States in the last quarter of the 19th century. It was an attempt to apply the teachings of Jesus to social and industrial problems in the cities within a Puritan free enterprise system.

The Social Gospel was the response within American Protestantism to the dislocations and the injustices arising from economic and urban expansion. A distinctly American contribution to Christianity, its origins can be traced back to the industrialization following the Revolutionary War (1776-83). The movement ignited the need for reforms in the factories, for the improvement of the lot of the poor and of the unfortunate, and for the abolition of the slave trade. The Social Gospel movement received two major impulses from Europe. Christian Socialism and Fabian Socialism *(Labour Party*)* came from England, while from Germany Albrecht Ritschl and Adolph von Harnack, among others, influenced the American reformers, mostly Congregational and Episcopalian clergymen and theologians, who had studied at German universities.

A pioneer document in the Social Gospel movement was "Our Country" (1885) by the Congregational minister Josiah Strong. He established the theory that in the course of organic evolution industry would inevitably become more democratically organized. Other influential clergymen like Walter Rauschenbusch, O. B. Frothingham, George D. Herron, Francis G. Peabody and Albion W. Small preached the importance of a social consciousness ("The Sermon on the Mount is the science of society", Herron). In 1889, the Society of Christian Socialists was founded in Boston by a group of prominent clergymen – Washington Gladden, W. D. P. Bliss and others – and economists, among them Richard T. Ely, stating their belief that socialism was the logical development of Christianity and that the accumulation of wealth was not in conformity with the teachings of Jesus.

The Social Gospel was saturated with the concern of Christian liberalism and it questioned the organized selfishness of the American free enterprise system based on Puritan economic ethics. It had much in common with working men's organizations like the Knights of Labor *(Trade/Labour Unions*)*, political groups like the Populist Party *(Parties*)* and progressive politicians like Theodor Roosevelt (who demanded a "square deal" for labour, advocated "trust-busting", and denounced "malefactors of great wealth"). Those who preached the Social Gospel believed in social progress and the essential goodness of man. In 1908 "the social creed of the churches" was adopted by the Federal Council of the Churches in Christ in America. The abolition of child labour, better working conditions for men and women, and the right of every worker to a living wage were ideas later absorbed by organized labour in the 20th century, also embodied in the New Deal legislation of the 1930s.

The most important figure in the Social Gospel movement was Walter Rauschenbusch (1861-1918). He was born in Rochester, N. Y., the son of an immigrant missionary from Germany. He spent some high-school years in Germany. Then, as a German Baptist pastor of a congregation near New York's Hell's Kitchen (a hangout for gunmen and thieves), he saw the misery of human beings in "an endless procession of men 'out of work, out of clothes, out of shoes and out of hope'" (Ahlstrom, op. cit., Vol. 2, p. 269). Rauschenbusch's books, "Christianity and the Social Crisis" (1907) and "A Theology for the

Social Gospel" (1917) emphasize the Social Gospel of the "Kingdom of God on earth", "the social aims of Jesus", "the immense latent perfectability in human nature", etc. World War I drastically undermined his hopes for such a "Kingdom", when his "Theology" developed a "Kingdom of Evil" as well.

In 1930 the Social Gospel movement was revived by the Fellowship of Socialist Christians, with Reinhold Niebuhr (1892-1971) becoming the leading spokesman. Serving as a pastor in the automobile city of Detroit from 1914 to 1927, Niebuhr directed much of his efforts towards a democratic socialism and supported the labour unions in the struggle for their rights. In his work, "Moral Man and Immoral Society" (1932), he emphasizes the importance of social ethics and political realism for the Christian in his society. Niebuhr recognized the conflicting and irreconcilable strains in human nature – Christian idealism and political realism. Following World War II, he dropped much of his social radicalism and preached a conservative realism. In "Faith and History" (1949) he defended Christianity as the world view that best explains the heights and the barbarisms in human behaviour. Niebuhr's conviction is expressed in his famous prayer: "O God, give us serenity to accept what cannot be changed, courage to change what should be changed, and wisdom to distinguish the one from the other". H H/P v T

Unitarian

One who affirms the unipersonality of the Godhead, especially as opposed to an orthodox Trinitarian; a member of a Christian religious body or sect holding this doctrine. 1689.

The Unitarians owe their name to their rejection of the Trinitarian concept of Father, Son and Holy Spirit and to their central doctrine of the single personality of God, a doctrine which conceives Jesus Christ as the greatest of human beings.

Yet what the name "Unitarian" implies today is not so much the anti-Trinitarian conception but rather a fundamental principle of freedom of reason and conscience in the search for religious truth, a rejection of the limits set by state authority or denominational adherence, an openness to the findings of biblical criticism and scientific research and a profound interest in the understanding of other religions.

Unitarianism, although it did not originate in England or America, has the majority of its followers (160,000 compared to a total world membership of 250,000) in the Anglo-American world. And despite this relatively small number and despite its somewhat ambivalent character as a "sect", and yet as a religious group of exceptionally high social standing, it has exerted profound influence on religious thought in both countries.

● In England Unitarian, or anti-Trinitarian, thought began to spread at the time of the Reformation. Although Unitarians were excluded from the Toleration Act (1689), they exerted an influence on religious and intellectual life in England, which found its expression, for instance, in Deism and rational theology. From about the middle of the 19th century onwards Unitarianism, mainly under the influence of the English thinker James Martineau (1805-1900), began to take the undogmatic and liberal direction it has maintained to the present day. Unitarian communities are very independent and only loosely connected through organizations. None of these organizations engages in missionary work, but they are very active in the social field. Through their activities in the foundation of institutions of higher learning, such as divinity schools in Oxford, Manchester, and Wales, they have contributed considerably to theological development in England. It was only in 1928 that the various Unitarian movements in England joined to form a denomination, by setting up a General Assembly of Unitarian and Free Christian Churches.

■ In America Unitarianism first gained followers among the educated class of *New England** during the middle of the 18th century. Harvard College, which led in the intellectual life of the country *(Ivy League*)*, was the first to promote Unitarian thought, and Harvard Divinity School, founded in 1816, was Unitarian for the first decades of its existence until it became an unsectarian department of the University. The importance of Unitarianism for spiritual life in the U.S.A. becomes obvious from the fact that one of its greatest thinkers (William Ellery Channing; 1780-1842) was deeply influenced by Unitarian thought and gave American Unitarianism its direction. This direction has corresponded up to the present day entirely to the American attitude towards Christian faith – a faith based on reason and reality and deep concern for the social needs of the time.

In 1900 an "International Council of Unitarian and other Liberal Religious Thinkers and Workers" was established in Boston. In 1930 this organization changed its name to the "International Association for Liberal Christianity and Religious Freedom". Unitarians often sought contact with other denominations. Thus in 1953 they founded, together with the Universalist Church of America, the Council of Liberal Churches. E V

Select Bibliography

GOVERNMENT AND SOCIETY

Abercrombie D., 'RP and Local Accent' in *Studies in Phonetics and Linguistics,* London 1965

Abraham, L. A., and Hawtrey, S. C. *A Parliamentary Dictionary,* Butterworth 1970

Adams, G. B., *Constitutional History of England,* London 1963

Adrian, C., *State and Local Governments, McGrawHill 1967*

Allen, H. C., *'The Frontier Concept', in British Essays in American History,* New York 1957

Allsop, K., *The Bootleggers,* London 1970

Aptheker, H., (ed.), *A Documentary History of the Negro People in the United States,* New York 1965

Babcock, R. S., *State and Local Government and Politics,* 1962

Bagehot, W., *The English Constitution,* London 1964

Baltzell, E. Digby, *The Protestant Establisment, Aristocracy and Caste in America, New York 1964*

Banks, A., *(ed.), Political Handbook of the World,* New York 1976

Banner, L. W., *Women in Modern America, A Brief History,* Hartrace 1974

Barnouw, Erik, *A history of broadcasting in the States;* vol 1-A tower of Babel, to 1933, Oxford 1966

Becker, Carl, *The Declaracion of Independence, A Study in the History of Political Ideas,* New York 1953

Beckett, J. C., *The Making of Modern Ireland, 1903–1923,* London 1966

Beer, S. H., *The British Political System,* London 1974

Benemy, F. W. G, *The Elected Monarch: The Development of the Power of the Prime Minister,* Harap 1965

Bergman, P. M., *The chronological history of the Negro in America,* New York 1969

Beth, Loren P., *The Development of the American Constitution, 1877–1917,* Harper 1971

Beyne, v., Klaus, *Interessentengruppen in der Demokratie,* München 1969

Billigton, R. A., *Westward Expansion, A History of the American Frontier,* New York 1949

Birch, A. H., *The British System of Government,* Allen & Unwin 1967

Blake, Robert, *The Conservative Party from Peel to Churchill,* Eyre and Spottiswoode, London 1970

Blaustein, Zangrando, *Civil Rights and the American Negro,* Washington Square Press, New York 1968

Blondel, J., *Voters, Parties and Leaders, The Social Fabric of British Politics,* Harmondsworth 1976

Bolton, G. C., *The Passing of the Irish Act of Union,* A Study in Parlamentary Politics, Oxford 1966

Boorstein, D. J., *The Americans, The Colonial Experience,* New Jork 1958

Bracey, et al., *Black Nationalism in America,* 1969

Brawley, Benjamin, *A Social History of the American Negro,* New York 1946

Bremner, Robert H., *American Philanthrophy,* Chicago / London 1960

Briggs, Asa, *The History of Broadcasting in the United Kindom;* Vol l. The Birth of Broadcasting, Vol ll. The Golden Age of Wireless, Vol lll. The War of Words, Oxford University Press 1961/1965/1970

Broadcasting in the Seventies, BBC 1969

Bromhead, P.A., *Britain's Developing Constitution,* London 1974

Brown, C.L., *Manchild in the Promised Land,* New York 1965

Brown, D., *Bury my Heart at Wounded Knee,* New York 1970

Brown, R. G. S., *The Administrative Process in Britain,* Methuen 1970

Bryce, James, *The American Commonwealth,* vols 1–2, New York 1933

Butler, Lord, *The Conservatives,* London 1977

Butterworth, E., and Weir, D., *Social Problems of Modern Britain,* Bungay/Suffolk 1976

Cahill, Gilbert A., *The Great Reform Bill of 1832: Liberal or Conservative?* Farnborough 1969

Campion, G.F.M., *An Introduction to the Procedure of the House of Commons,* London 1958

Carroll, B.A. *Liberating Women's History, Theoretical and Critical Essays,* Chicago 1976

Census 1971, *Preliminary Report, England and Wales,* H. M. Stationery Office 1971

Census 1971, *Preliminary Report, Scotland,* H.M. Stationery Office 1971

Chadwick, N., *The Celts,* Harmondsworth 1971 (Penguin)

Chapman, B., *British Government Observed,* London 1963

Charles, J., *The Origins of the American Party System,* London 1969

The British Civil Service, Reference Paper R. 5599/67, Central Office of Information 1967

Clarke, J.H., (ed.), *Marcus Garvey and the Vision of Africa,* New York 1974

Clarke, John Joseph, *Outlines of Central Government* (including the judicial system of England), Pitman 1965

Clarke, John Joseph, *Outlines of Local Government of the United Kingdom,* Pitman 1969

Cobbett, William, ed., *Parliamentary History of England from the Norman Conquest in 1066 to the Year 1803,* London

Cocks, B., (ed.), *Treatise on the Law, Privileges, Procedings and Usage of Parliament,* 1964

Cohen Carl, *Civil disobedience: conscience, tactics, and the law,* Columbia University Press 1971

Cole, G.D.H., *A Short History of the British Working-Class Movement 1789–1947,* London 1948

(Conservative Party) *The Right Approach, A Statement of Conservative Aims,* London 1976

Coogan, Tim Pat, *The IRA,* Fontana 1971

Cordasco, F., *The Puerto Ricans: Migration and General Bibliography,* McGraw 1973

Cox, L., and J. H. *Reconstuction, The Negro and the New South,* New York 1973

Curtis, L.P., *Coercion and Conciliation in Ireland, 1880–1892. A Study in Conservative Unionism,* Princeton and London 1963

Daniels, R., *Concentration Camps USA: Japanese Americans and World War II,* Holt 1971

Dasent, A.J., *The Speaker of the House of Commons from the Earliest Times to the Present Day,* London 1911

Deakin, N., and Ungerson, C., *Leaving London, Planned Mobility and the Inner City,* London 1977

Deusen, G., *The Jackson Era: 1828–1848,* London 1969

Devolution: *The English Dimension,* H.M.S.O. 1976

Divine, R.A., (ed.), *American Foreign Police since 1945,* Chicago 1969

Disturbancs in Northern Ireland. Report of the Commission appointed by the Governor of Northern Ireland, Belfast 1969

Draper, Theodore, *The rediscovery of Black Nationalism,* Viking Press 1970

Drury, A., *Advise and Consent,* Doubleday 1959

Dumbauld, E., *The Constitution of the United States,* University of Oklahoma 1964

Du Bois, W.E.B., *The Souls of Black Folk,* Chicago 1903

Dunning, W.A., *Reconstruction, Political and Economic: 1865–1877,* London 1969

Dye, Th.R., *Who's Running America? Institutional Leadership in the United States,* Englewood Cliffs/N.J. 1976

Parliamentary Elections in Britain, Reference Paper R.5513/70, Central Office of Information 1970

Elton, G.R. *The Tudor Constitution, Documents and Commentary,* Cambridge 1972

Emery, Edwin, *The Press and America; an interpretative history of journalism,* Prentice 1962

Edwards, O. D., Evans, G., Rhys, I., and MacDiarmid, H., *Celtic Nationalism,* London 1968

Facts on File, Weekly World News Digest with cumulative index, New York

Filler, L. (ed.) *Abolition and Social Justice in the Era of Reform,* London 1973

Filler, L. H., *The Crusade against Slavery 1830/1860,* London 1969

Fishel, L. H., *The Black Americans,* Scott 1976

Franklin, John Hope, *From Slavery to freedom; a history of Negro Americans,* Knopf 1967

Franklyn, J., *The Cockney: A Survey of London Life and Language,* London 1953

Frazier, E. Franklin, *The Negro in the United States,* rev. ed., New York 1957

Garrett, J., *The Management of Government,* Harmondsworth 1972
Gimson, A. C., *An Introduction to the Pronuncation of English,* London 1970
Glazer, N., and Moynihan. D. P., *Beyond the Melting Pot: The Negroes, Puerto Ricans, Jews, Italians, and Irish of New York City,* Cambridge, Mass, 1963
Glessing, Robert J., *The underground press in America,* Indiana Univ. Press 1970
Graham, Hugh Davis, *The history of violence in America: historical and comparative perspectives,* New York 1969
Great Britain and the Colonies 1818–1865, ed. by A. G. L. Shaw, Methuen 1970
Griffith, Ernest S., *The American System of Government,* New York 1954
Handlin, Oscar, *The Uprooted: The Epic Story of the Migrations That Made the American People,* Boston 1973
Hanham, H. J., *The Nineteenth Century Constitution, Documents and Commentary,* Cambridge 1969
Hansen, M. L., *The Immigrant in American History,* Cambridge, Mass. 1969
Hansen, M. L., *The Atlantic Migration 1607–1860.* New York 1961
Hardie, F., *The Politicial Influence of the British Monarchy,* Batsford 1970
Harrington, M., *The Other America, Poverty in the United States,* Baltimore/Md. 1973
Hart, J. F., *Regions of the United States,* London 1973
Hartley, T. C., and Griffith, J. A. G., *Government and Law: An Introduction to the Working of the Constitution in Britain,* London 1975
Harvie, Chr., *Scotland and Nationalism, Scottish Society and Politics 1707–1977,* London 1977
Hayther, D., *The Labour Party, Crisis and Prospects,* Fabian tract, London 1977
Hibbert, Chr., *London: The Biography of a City,* New York 1970
Hill, Chr., *The Growth of Parliamentary Parties 1689–1742, London 1977*
Hofstadter, R., *Anti-intellectualism in American Life,* New York 1962
Hofstadter, R., *The Idea of a Party System, The Rise of Legimitate Opposition in the United States, 1780–1840,* Berkeley 1972
Hofstadter, R., et al., *The Structure of American History,* Englewood Cliffs, N.J., 1973
Holbo, P.S., *Isolationism and Interventionism 1932–1941,* Chicago 1967
Holt, J.C., *Magna Carta,* New York 1965
Hook, S., *American Freedom and American Anarchy,* New York 1969
Hoover, D. W., (ed.), *Understanding Negro History,* Chicago 1968
Hoskins, W. G., *Local History in England,* London 1972
Immigration and Race Relations, Fabian Society 1970
Ives, E. W., (ed.), *The English Revolution 1600–1660,* London 1968
Jackson, K.T., and Schultz, S.K., *Cities in American History,* New York 1972
Jackson, W. E., *Local Government in England and Wales,* Harmondsworth 1966 (Penguin)
Jacobs, J., *The Death and Life of Great American Cities,* New York 1961
James, J. L., *American Political Parties,* Plymouth 1971
Jennings, Sir Ivor, *The British Constitution,* Cambridge University Press 1966
Jennings, I., *Cabinet Government,* London 1965
Jennings, I., *Constitution Laws of the Commonwealth,* London 1957
Jennings, I., *The British Commonwealth of Nations,* London 1961
Jennings, I. *The Law and the Constitution,* London 1959
Jennings, Sir Ivor, *Party Politics,* Cambridge University Press 1960/62
Jennings, I., and Ritter, G.A.: *Das britische Regierungssystem,* Köln 1970
Jewell, R. E. C., *Central and Local Government,* Knight 1966
Johns, E. A., *The Social Structure of Modern Britain,* Pergamon 1966
Johnson, N., *In Search of the Constitution, Reflections on State and Society in Britain,* Oxford 1977
Jones, Maldwyn Allen, *American Immigration,* Chicago 1960
Jones, P.d'A., *The U.S.A., A History of its People and Society,* vol. I/II, Homewood/Ill. 1976
Katznelson, I., and Kesselman, M., *The Politics of Power, A Critical Introduction to American Government,* New York 1977
Kellas, J. G., *The Scottish Political System,* Cambridge 1975
Kelly, A. H., and Harbison, W. A., *The American Constitution; its origin and development,* Norton 1963
Kenyon, J. P., *The Stuart Constitution, Documents and Commentary,* Cambridge 1969

Key, Jr., V. O., *Politics, Paries and Pressure Groups,* New York 1967

King, Martin Luther, *Why We Can't Wait,* Signet Books 1964

Kluxen, Kurt, *Die Entstehung des englischen Parlamentarismus,* Stuttgart 1966

Koenig, Louis William, *The Chief Executive,* Harcourt 1975

Konvitz, Milton Ridvas, *Expanding liberties; freedom's gains in post-war America,* Viking 1966

Labour's Programme 1976, London 1976

Laundy, Philip, *The Office of Speaker,* Casell 1964

Le May, G. H. L., *British Government 1914–1953, Select Documents,* London 1955

Lens, S., *The Forging of the American Empire, A History of American Imperialism from the Revolution to Vietnam,* New York 1974

Loewenstein, K., *Staatsrecht und Staatspraxis von Grossbritanien,* 2 vols., Berlin, Heidelberg and New York 1967

Loewenstein K., *Der britische Parlamentarismus, Entstehung und Gestalt,* rohwolts deutsche enzyklopädie, No. 208, 1964

Loewenstein, K. *Verfassungsrecht und Verfassungspraxis der Vereinigten Staaten,* Berlin 1959

(Local Government) *The New Local Authorities, Management and Structure,* H. M. S. O. 1972

Lyons, F. S. L., *The Fall of Parnell 1890–91,* London 1962

McCaffrey, L. J., *The Irish Question 1800–1922,* Lexington 1968

Mackintosh, J. P., *The British Cabinet,* London 1977

Mackintosh, J., *'The Problems of the Labour Party', in The Political Quarterley,* Jan. 1972, London

Mackintosh, J. P., *The Devolution of Power,* Harmondworth 1968

Maitland, F. W., *Constitutional History of England,* Cambridge 1961

Malcolm X, The Autobiography of ..., New York 1964

Mathiot, A., *The British Political System,* London 1958

McDowell, R. B., *The Irish Administration 1801–1914,* London and Toronto 1964

McKelvey, B., *The City in American History,* London 1969

McKissick, Floyd, *Three Fifths of a Man,* Macmillan Co., New York 1969

McLuhan, M., *Understanding Media: The Extensions of Man,* New York 1964

Mansergh, N., *The Irish Question 1840–1921* London 1965

Martin, Kingsley, *Crown and the Establishment* London 1962

Merz, Charles, *The Dry Decade,* University of Washington Press 1970

Miller, Elizabeth W., *The Negro in America, a bibliography comp. for the American Academy of Arts and Sciences,* Harvard University Press 1970

Minogue, M., (ed.), *Documents on Contemporary British Government,* 2 vols., Cambridge 1977

Morison, S. E., *The Intellectual Life of Colonial New England,* New York 1956

Morris Alfred, *The Growth of Parliamentary Scrutiny by Committee,* A Symposium, London 1970

Morrison, Herbert, *Government and Parliament – a survey from the inside,* 1960

Mühlen, N., *Die Schwarzen Amerikaner, Anatomie einer Revolution,* Stuttgart 1964

Namier, L., *Monarchy and the Party System,* Oxford 1952

Newman, Edwin S., *Civil liberty and civil rights,* Oceana Publications 1970

Newspaper Press Directory, 1970 Annual, Benn 1971

Norman, E., *A History of Modern Ireland,* London 1971 (Penguin)

Norman, E., *The Irish,* Harmondsworth (Penguin)

(Northern Ireland) Sunday Times Insight Team, *Ulster,* Harmondsworth 1972

O'Brien, C. C., *Parnell and his Party, 1880–90,* Oxford 1964

O'Brien, Maire Cruise, *Conor Cruise O'Brien introduces Ireland,* London 1969

O'Farrel, P., *Ireland's English Question,* London 1971

Official Congressional Directory, US Printing Office, Washington/D.C., (annual)

O'Gorman, F., *The Rise of Party in England, The Rockingham Whigs 1760–1782,* London 1977

O'Neill, W., *The Woman Movement, Feminism,* London

Orange and Green, *A Quaker Study of Community Relations in Northern Ireland,* Sedbergh 1969

Parsons, Talcott, and Clark, Kenneth B., eds., *The Negro American,* Boston 1966
The Organisation of Political Parties in Britain, Reference Paper R.4769/69, Central Office of Information 1969
Partridge, E., *Slang To-day and Yesterday,* London 1950
Pelling, H., *Short History of the Labour Party,* London 1972
Pinkney, A., *Red, Black, and Green, Black Nationalism in the United States,* Cambridge Univerity Press 1976
Pitt, L., *We Americans,* 2 vols., Glenview/Ill. 1976
Pollard, A. F., *The Evolution of Parliament,* London 1926
Pomeroy, Earl S., *The Territories and the United States 1861–1890,* Unversity of Washington Press 1970
Ramelson, M., *The Petticoat Rebellion, A. Century of Struggle for Women's Rights,* Tiptree/Essex 1972
Reich, Ch. A. *The Greening of America,* New York 1971
Reid. J. M., *Scotland's Progress: The Survival of a Nation,* London 1971
Report of the Royal Relations Board for 1974, H. M. S. O. 1974
Report on the Royal Commission on the Constitution, The Kilbrandon Report, H. M. S. O. 1973
Riordon, W. L., *Plunkitt of Tammay Hall,* New York 1963
Rivers, William L., *The mass media and modern society,* Rinehart Press 1971
Roberts, Geoffrey K., *Political Parties and Pressure Groups in Britain,* Weidenfeld & Nicolson 1970
Robson, W. A., (ed.). *The Civil Service in Britain and France,* London 1956
Roland, C. P., *The Confederacy,* Chicago 1962
Rossiter, C., *The American Presidency,* New American Library 1960
Sampson, A., *The New Anatomy of Britain,* London 1971
Schultz, E. B., *American City Government,* Stackpole & Heck 1949
Sebeok, Th. A., *Native Languages of the Americas,* 2 vols., Indiana University 1976
Sherrill, R., *Why they call it Politics, A Guide to America's Government,* New York 1977
Sinclair, A., *Era of Excess: A Social History of the Prohibition Movement,* London 1969
Sivanandan, A., *Coloured immigrants in Britain,* Institute of Race Relations 1969
Smith, E. C., Barnes, W. R., and Smith, S., *The Constitution of the United States,* New York 1970
Soson, J. M., *The Opening of the West,* London 1969
Spencer, R. F., *The Native Americans, "The Urban Indians",* Harper and Row 1977
Stacey, F., *British Government 1966–1975,* Oxford 1975
Stacey, F., *A New Bill of Rights for Britain,* London 1973
Stampp, Kenneth Milton, *The era of reconstruction, 1865–1877, Knopf 1965*
Stenton, D. M., *The English Woman in History,* London 1972
Stephenson, Carl, and Marcham, F. G., *Sources of English Constitutional History, a Selection of Dokuments from A. D. 6000 to the Present,* New York 1973
Sternberger, Dolf, and Vogel, Bernhard, eds., *Die Wahl der Parlamente und anderer Staatsorgane,* Berlin 1969
Stewart, A. T. Q., *The Ulster Crisis,* London 1967
Strauss, E., *Irish Nationalism and British Democracy,* London 1951
Taylor. E., *The House of Commons at Work,* Harmondsworth 1971
Tebbel, J., *The Media in America. New York 1974*
Thomas, N., *The Welsh Extremist: A Culture in Crisis,* London 1971
Thornley, D., *Isaac Butt and Home Rule,* London 1964
Thornley, D., 'The Irish conservatives and home rule, 1869–73' in *Irish Historical Studies* (1958–59)
Trattner, W. J., *From Poor Law to Welfare State, A History of Social Welfare in America,* London 1974
Trim, J. L. M., 'English Standard Pronunciation' in *English Language Teaching,* 16, 1961
Tunnard, Chr., and Reed, H. H., *American Skylines, The Growth and Form of our Cities and Towns,* Boston/Mass. 1956
Turner, Frederick Jackson, *The frontier in American history,* Holt 1921
United States Government Organization Manual, (published annually), Washington. D.C.
Urban Deprivation, *Racial Unequality, and Social Policy:* A Report, H. M. S. O., 1977
Voegelin, C. F., and F. M., *Map of North American Indian Languages,* University of Washington Press 1944

Walker. Gordon,*The Cabinet,* London
Warner, S. B., *The Urban Wilderness: A History of the American City,* London 1973
Wheare, C. H., *Federal Government,* New York 1964
Wheare, K. G., *The Statute of Westminster and Dominion Status,* Oxford 1953
Wheare, K. G., *The Constitutional Structure of the Commonwealth,* Oxford 1960
White, Cynthia, *Women's Magazines 1963–1968,* Michael Joseph 1970
White, J., and Willett, R., *Slavery in the American South,* London 1970
White, Theodore H., *The Making of the President,* New York 1968
Williams, E. N., *The Eighteenth Century Constitution, Documents and Commentary,* Cambridge 1970
Wissler Clark, *Indians of the United States* Doubleday 1966

LAW

Abel-Smith, Brand Stevens, R., *In Search of Justice: Society and the Legal System,* London 1968
Abraham, H. J., *The Judicial Process,* London 1972
Berkowitz, D. S., and Thorne, S. E., *English Legal History, A Bibliographical and Reference Manual,* New York
Berman, H. J., (ed.), *Talks on American Law,* New York 1971
Bernstein, *Einführung in das Recht der USA,* 1972
Black, H. K. and Latham-Brown, D. J., *An Outline of English Law,* London 1966
Blumenwitz, *Einführung in das Anglo-Amerikanische Recht,* München 1971
Blom-Cooper, L., and Drewry, G., *Final Appeal: A Study of the House of Lords in its Judicial Capacity,* London 1972
Carr, R. K., *Supreme Court and Judicial Review,* Greenwood 1942
Farnsworth, E., *An Introduction to the Legal System of the USA,* New York 1963
Fulda, *Einführung in das Recht der USA,* Baden-Baden 1966
Geldart, W., prep. by Yardley, D. C. M., *Elements of English Law,* London 1966
Harding, A. A., *Social History of English Law,* London 1966
Henrich, Dieter, *Einführung in das englische Privatrecht,* 1971
Her Majesty's Stationery Office, *The English Legal System,* 1968
Her Majesty's Stationery Office, *Britain, An Official Handboock,* 1972
James, Ph. S., *Introduction of English Law,* London 1969
Levy, L. W., (ed.). *Judicial Review in The Supreme Court,* London 1969
McCloskey, R., *The American Supreme Court,* Chicago 1961
Milton, F., *The English Magistracy,* London 1967
Morrison, F. L., *Courts and the Political Process in England,* London 1973
Radbruch, G., *Der Geist des Englischen Rechts,* 1964
The United States Courts, US Printing Office, Washington/D.C. 1975
Walker and Walker, *The English Legal System,* 1970
Whitaker's Almanack 1972

ECONOMY AND SOCIAL SERVICES

Acriculture in Britain, London HMSO, 1971
Bain, G. S., *The Growth of White Collar Unionism,* Oxford 1970
Barbash, J., *American Unions: Structure, Government and Politics,* Random 1967
Benson, R. S., and Wolman, H., *Counterbudget: A Blueprint for Changing National Priorities,* New York 1971
Blake, G., *Lloyd's Register of Shipping 1760–1960,* London 1960
Britain and the European Community, London 1976

Brittan, S., *Steering the Economy – The Role of the Treasury,* London 1971
Brody, D., *The American Labor Movement,* London 1971
Burns, E. W., *Health Services for Tomorrow, Trends and Issues,* New York 1973
Börsen- und Wirtschaftshandbuch, Frankfurt am Main 1974–1977
Breckenfeld, G., *Columbia and the New Cities,* New York 1971
The Budget of the United States Government Fiscal Year 1972, Washington 1972
Britain, An Offical Handbook, London 1974–1977
Buchanan Report: Traffic in Towns, London 1963
Chickele, R., *Agricultural Policy: Farm programs and National Welfare,* Lincoln, Neb., 1964
Clegg, H. A., *The System of Industrial Relations in Great Britain,* London 1970
The Changing Structure of Agriculture, London, HMSO, 1970
Congress and the Nation, A Review of Government and Politics 1973–1976, Washington/D.C. 1977
Conkin, P. K., *The New Deal, Arlington Heights/Ill. 1975*
Co-operative Movement in Britain, London, COJ, 1970
Cullingworth, J. B., *English Housing Trends,* London 1965
A Decent Home, Report of the President's Committee on Urban Housing, Washington 1968
Doris, L., *The American Way in Taxation,* New York 1963
Economic Report of the President, Washington 1973–1977
Edwards, C. D., *Control of Cartels and Monopolies,* New York 1967
Elliott, J., *Conflict or Co-operation – The Growth of Industrial Democracy,* London 1975
Faulkner, H. U., *American Economic History,* New York 1960
Federal Reserve System, Board of Governors: Federal Reserve Bulletin, Washington/D.C. (monthly)
Galbraith, J. K., *The Great Crash 1929,* Boston, Mass. 1955
Geschäftsbericht der Deutschen Bundesbank, 1974–77
Ginzberg, E., and Solow, R. M., *The Great Society,* New York 1974
Grove, J. W., *Government and Industry in Britain,* London 1962
Harrod, R., *The British Economy,* New York 1963
Hartig, P., *England, Handbücher der Auslandskunde,* Ffm. 1971
Hartig, P., *Amerikakunde, Handbücher der Auslandskunde,* Ffm. 1966
Hartwell, R. M., *The Industrial Revolution and Economic Growth,* London 1971
Hooberman, B., *An Introduction to British Trade Unions,* London 1974
Housing in Britain, COI Ref. Pamphlet, London 1970
Industrial Democracy including supplementary evidence to the Bullock Committee, London 1977
International Monetary Fund, Balance of Payments Manual, 1966
Kameraman, S. B., and Kahn, A. J., *Social Services in the United States, Policies and Programs,* Philadelphia 1976
Kefauver, E., *In a few hands: Monopoly power in America,* New York 1965
Kershaw, J., *Government against Poverty,* Washington 1970
Kellett, R., *The Merchant Banking Arena,* Basingstoke 1967
Kemmerer & Kemmerer, *The ABC of the Federal Reserve System,* Harper 1950
Knauth, O. W., *Policy of the United States towards Industrial Monopoly,* New York 1968
Land Conservation in Britain, Ref. Paper COI, London 1970
Lenihan, J. M. A., and Fletcher, W. W., *Reclamation,* Glasgow 1976
Lent, H. B., *Agriculture USA: America's most basic industry,* New York 1968
Leuchtenburg, Y. U., *Franklin D. Roosevelt and the New Deal,* New York 1963
Levin, A., *Health Services: the local perspective,* New York
Litwack, L., *The American Labor Movement*
Marsh, D., *The Welfare State,* London 1970
Mathias, P., *The Retailing Revolution,* London 1971
McCarthy, W. E. J., *Trade Unions,* London 1972
McGuire/Pichler, *Inequality: The Poor and the Rich in America,* Belmont, Calif., 1969
National Association of Social Workers Encyclopedia of Social Work, Washington/D.C. 1973
National Institute of Economic and Social Research: Economic Review, London (quarterly)

Nevin and David, *The London Clearing Banks,* London 1971
The New Towns of Britain, London, HMSO, 1974
OECD Survey of Current Business, Paris 1971
The Pattern of British Exports, London, COJ, 1970
Pelling, H., *American Labor,* Chicago 1974
Pelling, H., *A History of British Trade Unionism,* Harmondsworth,1971
Poverty amid Plenty, The American Paradox, Report of the President's Commission on Income Maintenance Programs, Washington 1969
Preliminary Estimates of National Income and the World Monetary System, London 1977
Prest, A. R., and Coppock, D. J., *The UK Economy: A Manual of Applied Economics,* London 1975
Pringle, R., *Banking in Britain,* London 1975
Radcliffe Report of the Committee on the Working of the Monetary System, London 1959
Report of the Committee of Inquiry on Industrial Democracy, (Bullock Report), London 1977
Roads in England 1968–69, Report of the Ministry of Transport, London 1969
Robertson R. M., *History of American Economy,* New York 1968
The Regulation of Monopolies, Mergers and Restrictive Trade Practices, London, HMSO, 1971
Sayers, R. S., *Modern Banking,* Oxford 1967
Self Peter, *Cities in Flood, The Problems in Urban Growth,* London 1961
Simpson, B., *Labour and the Unions and the Party,* London 1973
Smith, W. F., *Housing: the social and economic elements,* Berkeley 1970
Sobey, F., *Changing Roles in Social Work Practice,* Philadelphia 1977
Social Security Bulletin, Washington/D.C. (monthly)
Social Security Handbook, Washington 1974
Social Security Program in the United States, Washington/D.C. 1973
Social Service Review, Chicago (quarterly)
Stevens, R., *American Medicine and the Public Interest,* New Haven 1971
Stevens, R., and R. *Welfare Medicine in America, a case study of medicaid,* New York 1974
Taylor, Ph. A. M., *The Industrial Revolution in Britain: Triumph or Disaster,* Farnborough 1970
Tivey, L. J., *Nationalisation in British Industry,* London 1966
Towards a comprehensive Health policy for the 1970s. A white paper, US Departement of Health, Education and Welfare 1971
Trevelyan, G. M. *English Social History,* London
TUC Collective Bargaining and the Social Contract, London 1975
TUC Guide to the Bullock Report on Industrial Democracy, London 1974
United Kingdom Balance of Payments 1971. London, HMSO, 1971
United States Departement of Health, Education, and Welfare, *Social Security Administration, Social security programs throughout the world, 1969,* U.S. Govt. Print. Off, 1969
US Department of Commerce Survey of Current Business, Washington / D. C. (monthly)
United States Government Manual 1977–1978, Washington/D.C. 1978
The United Kingdom and the European Communities, London, HMSO, 1971
Whitaker's Almanack, London 1977
Wigham, E. L., *Trade Unions,* Oxford 1968
Williams, G., *The Coming of the Welfare State,* London 1967
Wirtschaftsjahrbuch, München 1974–1977
World Almanack and Book of facts, New York 1977

EDUCATION

Adult Education in the United Kingdom. A Directory of Organizations, London annually
Alexander, W. M. (ed.). *The Changing High School Curriculum.* Readings, New York /2/ 1972

Allen, H. R., *Open Door to Learning. The Land-Grant System enters its Second Century,* Illinois 1963

Bailey, St. W., *Teacher Associations in American Education,* New York 1966

Balsdon, D., *Oxford Now and Then,* London 1970

Bamford, T. W., *Rise of the Public School,* London 1967

Baron, G., *Bibliographical Guide to the Educational System,* London 1965

Barzun, J., *The American University. How it runs, Where it is going,* New York

Bell, R., et al., (ed.). *Education in Great Britain and Ireland,* Open University Set Book, London 1973

Birenbaum, W. M., *Overlive Power, Poverty, and the University,* New York 1969

Blackie, J., *Inside the Primary School,* London 1967

Boyson, Rh., *The Crisis in Education,* London 1957

Bristow, A., *Inside the Colleges of Further Education,* London HMSO, 1970

Brown, B. F., *The Nongraded High School,* New York 1965

Brown, B. F., et al., *The Reform of Secondary Education,* New York 1973

Burnet, J. F., (ed.),*The Public and Preparatory School Year Book,* London 1971

Calthrop, K. and Owens, G. (eds.), *Teachers for Tomorrow,* London 1971

Cane, B. S., *Research into Teacher Education,* London 1968

The Certificate of Secondary Education: Some Suggestions for Teachers and Examiners, London, HMSO, 1963

Committee on National Program Priorities in Teacher Education, *The Power of Competency-based Teacher Education,* Boston 1973

Conant, J. B., *The Comprehensive High School. A second report to interested citizens,* New York 1967

Conant, J. B., *The Citadel of Learning. An Old Tradition in a New World,* New Haven 1956

Conant, J. B., *The Education of American Teachers,* New York 1963

Conant, J. B., *Shaping Educational Policy,* New York 1964

Cordasco, F., *A Brief History of Education,* Totowa/N.J. 1976

Cremin, L. A., *American Education, The Colonial Experience 1607–1783,* New York 1970

Cressman, E. R., *Public Education in America,* New York 1956

Dainville, F. de, *La naissance de l'humanisme moderne,* Paris 1940

Dancy, J., *The Public Schools and the Future,* London 1963

Demerath. N. J., Stephens, R. W. and Taylor, R. R., *Power, Presidents, and Professors,* New York 1967

Dewey, J., *Experience and Education,* New York 1958

Dillenbeck, D. D. et al. (eds.), *The College Hand Book,* New York 1969

Doddor, S., *Teaching as a Profession,* Columbus, Ohio 1968

Dunkin, M. J., *The Study of Teaching,* New York 1974

The Education Authorities Directory and Annual, Merstham, Surrey, annually

(Education) *A Compilation of Federal Education Laws (as amended through Dec. 31, 1974),* US Government Printing Office, Washington/D.C. 1975

Eurich, A. C., *Reforming American Education,* New York 1969

Fields, R. R., *The Community College Movement,* New York 1962

Fine, B., *The Modern Family Guide to Education,* New York 1962

Fellowships in the Arts and Sciences, New York, 6th Edition, 1966/67

Foley, J. A. and Foley, R. R., *The College Scene. Students tell it like it is,* New York 1969

Gardner, B., *The Public Schools,* London 1973

Goodland, J. I. and Anderson, R., *The Nongraded Elementary School,* New York 1963

Graham, Gr., *The Public School in the American Community,* New York 1963

Hasley, A. H. and Trow, M., *The British Academics,* London 1971

Halstead, D. K., *Statewide Planning in Higher Education,* Washington/ D.C. 1974

Handlin, O., *John Dewey's Challenge to Education,* New York 1959

Haslam, K. R., *Learning in the Primary School,* London 1971

Heath, G. L., *The New Teacher,* New York 1973

Hilliard F. H. (ed.), *Teaching the Teachers, Trends in Teacher Education,* London 1971

Hoopes, R.(ed.), *State Universities and Colleges. A Guide to Prospective Students,* Washington D.C. 1962

Howarth T. E. B., *Culture, Anarchy and the Puplic Schools,* London 1969

Howson, G. (ed.), *Children at School, Primary Education in Britain Today,* London 1969
Jackson, Ph. W., *Life in Classroom,* New York 1968
Kalton, G., *The Puplic Schools,* London 1966
Karcher, W., *Studenten an privaten Universitäten. Zum Verfassungsrecht der USA,* Stuttgart 1971
Kelly, T., *History of Adult Education in Great Britain,* Liverpool 1970
Kinney, L. B., *Certification in Education,* New York 1964
Knowles, M. S., *The Adult Educational Movement in USA,* New York 1962
Landy, E. and Perry, P. A. (eds.), *Guidance in American Education – Background and Prospects,* Cambridge, Mass., 1964
Lawlor, J., *The New University,* London 1968
Lee, J. M., *Elementary Education Today and Tomorrow,* Boston, second edition 1972
Lee, J. M. and Lee, D. M., *The Child and His Curriculum,* New York 1972
Logan, Sir Douglas, *The University of London. An Intoduction,* London 1971
Lowe, J., *Adult Education in England and Wales,* London 1970
MacLure, J. S., *Education Documents England and Wales, 1816 to the present day,* London 1973
Masters, Ph. L., *Preparatory Schools Today. Some Facts and Inferences,* London 1966
Mayhew, L. B., *The Carnegie Commission on Higher Education,* San Francisco 1973
McConnell, T. R., *A General Pattern for American Public Higher Education,* New York 1962
Meiklejohn, A., *The Liberal College,* Boston 1920
Moore, E. C., *The History of Instruction,* 2 vols, New York 1938
Morison, R. S. (ed.), *The Contemporary University: USA,* Boston 1966
Mountford, Sir James, *British Universities,* London 1966
Neuhoff, K., *Amerikanische Stiftungen,* Baden-Baden 1968
The Open University, *Report of the Planning Committee,* London, HMSO, 1969
Orme, N., *English Schools in the Middle Ages,* London 1973
Pashely, B. W., *University Extension Reconsidered,* Leicester 1968
Perkin, H. J., *New Universities in England,* Paris 1969
Perry, W., *Open University, A Personal Account by the First Chancellor,* Walton Hall 1976
Peters, R. (ed.), *Perspectives on Plowden,* London 1969
Petersen, R. and W., *University Adult Education. A Guide to Policy,* New York 1960
Plowden Report, Children and Their Primary Schools, London 1967 2 volumes
Public Schools Commission, First Report, London, 1968, Second Report, Vol 1 London 1970
Provision for Adult Education, London 1970
Raybould, S. G., *University Extra-Mural Education in England 1945–62,* London 1964
Reimann, H., *Höhere Schule und Hochschule in den USA,* Weinheim 1970
Report by the Principal (of the University of London) on the Work of the University during the Year 1971–72, London 1972
Report on the Future of the External System, University of London 1972
Rickover, H. G., *American Education a National Failure,* New York 1963
Robbins Report: Higher Education, London 1963
Ryan, K., (ed.), *Yearbook on Teacher Education,* Chicago 1975
Sadler, J. E., *Concept in Primary Education,* London 1974
Sanford, N. (ed.), *The American College,* New York 1962
Scottish Education Department, *Primary Education in Scotland,* Edinburgh 1965
Schultz, Th., *Land-Grant Colleges: an Outsider's View,* Washington D.C. 1962
Select Committee on Education and Science, *Report on Teacher Training,* London 1970, 6 volumes
Semmelroth, K., *Die Gründung der Universität London und ihre historischen Voraussetzungen, unter besonderer Berücksichtigung des deutschen Einflusses,* Münster 1937
Silbermann, Ch. E., *Crisis in the Schoolroom,* New York 1970
Shepard, D. A., *Liberal Education in an Industrial Society,* New York 1957
Statistics of Education, 3: Further Education, London, HMSO, 1971

Statistics of Education, 5: Finance and Awards, London, HMSO, 1970
(Statistics) *The Condition of Education, A Statistical Report on the Condition of American Education,* Washington/D.C. 1975
Sufrin, S. Ch., *Administering the National Defense Education Act,* Syracuse, New York 1963
Taylor, Ph. H., et. al., *The English Sixth Form – a case study in curriculum research,* London and Boston 1974
Taylor, W., *Society and the Education of Teachers,* London 1969
UGC – The University Grants Commitee, London, HMSO, 1970
University Grants Commitee. Annual Survey, London, HMSO, annually
U.S. Departement of Health, Education and Welfare; Office of Education, *Elementary School Administration and Organisation,* Washington D.C. 1961
U.S. Department of Health, Education and Welfare: *Progress of Education in the United States of America: 1972–73 and 1973–74,* Washington/D.C. 1975
Wrenn, C. G., *The Counselor in a Changing World,* Washington D.C. 1962

RELIGION

Albright, R. W., *A History of the Protestant Episocal Church,* New York 1964
Ahlstrom, S. E., *A Religious History of the American People,* New York 1974
Atkinson, J. and Hughes, P. E., *Anglicanism and the Roman Church,* London 1964
Baker, F., *John Wesley and the Church of England,* London 1970
The Baptist Handbook, London, annually
Bicknell, E. J., *A Theological Introduction to the Thirty-nine Articles of the Church of England,* (3rd ed.), London 1955
Bolam, C. G., et al., *The English Presbyterians,* London 1972
Bossy, J., *The English Catholic Community 1570–1850,* London 1975
Brayshaw, A. N., *The Quakers: Their Story and Message,* London 1953
Brilioth, Y. T., *The Anglican Revival,* London 1925
Buchanan, C. O., (and others), *Growing into Union. Proposals for forming a united Church in England,* London 1970
Bucke, E. S.(ed.), *The History of American Methodism,* Nashville 1964
Chadwick, O., *The Victorian Church,* 2 vols, London 1966–70
The Church of England Year Boock, London, annually
Crockford's Clerical Directory, London, annually
Davies, H., The English Free Churches, London 1963
Davies, R. E., *Methodism,* Harmondsworth 1963
Fairweather, E. R. (ed.), *The Oxford Movement,* Oxford 1964
Fishman, P., *The Jews in the United States,* New York 1974
Garbett, C. F., *The Church of England today,* London 1953
Garbett, C. F., *The Church and State in England,* London 1950
Gaustad, E. S., *Dissent in American Religion,* Chicago 1973
Gorman, G. H., *Introducing Quakers,* London 1969
Gray, G. F. S., *The Anglican Communion,* London 1958
Greeley, A. M., *The Denominational Society,* Glenview/Ill. 1972
Green, R. W., *Protestantism and Capitalism: The Weber Thesis and its Critics,* Farnborough 1959
Hales, E. E. Y., *The Catholic Church in the Modern World,* Toronto 1958
Haller, W., *Liberty and Reformation in the Puritan Revolution,* New York 1955
Handy, R. D., *A History of the Churches in the United States and Canada,* Oxford 1977
Henriques, U. R. Q., *Religious Toleration in England 1787–1833,* London 1961
Henson, H. H., *Puritanism in England,* London 1912
Herberg, W., *Protestant, Catholic, Jew,* Boston, Mass, 1962
Hill, Ch., *Puritanism and Revolution,* London 1965
Hudson, W. S., *American Protestantism,* Chicago 1966

Hudson, W. S., *Religion in America,* New York 1965
Hughes, P., *The Reformation in England,* London 1963
Jordon, W. K., *The Development of Religious Toleration in England from the Beginning of the Reformation to the Death of Queen Elizabeth,* London 1932
Lamont, W. M., *Godly Rule: Politics and Religion, 1603–60,* London 1969
Loukes, H., *The Quaker Contribution,* London 1965
Marlowe, J., *The Puritan Tradition in English Life,* London 1956
Miller, P., *Errand into the Wilderness,* New York 1964
Miller, P. and Johnson, Th. H., *The Puritans,* New York 1963
Moorman, J. R. H., *A History of the Church in England,* London 1973
Murray, A. V., *The State and the Church in a Free Society,* Cambridge 1958
Murray, J. C., *The Problem of Religious Freedom,* London 1965
Neill, S. C., *Anglicanism* (3rd ed.), Harmondsworth 1965
New, J. F. H., *Anglican and Puritan,* London 1964
Nicholls, D., *Church and State in Britain since 1820,* London 1967
Payne, E. A., *The Free Church Tradition in the Life of England,* 3rd edition, London 1951
Robinson, H. W., *The Life and Faith of the Baptists,* London 1946
Simpson, A., *Puritanism in Old and New England,* Chicago 1955
Slack, K., *The British Churches Today,* London 1961
Stocker, A. P., *Church and State in the United States,* 1950
Stromberg, R. N., *Religious Liberalism in Eighteenth-century England,* Oxford 1954
Till, B., *The Churches Search for Unity,* Harmondsworth 1972
Torbet, R. G., *A History of the Baptist,* Philadelphia 1952
Wand, J. C., *Anglicanism in History and Today,* London 1961
Watkin, E. I., *Roman Catholicism in England from the Reformation to 1950,* Oxford 1957
Wertenbaker, J., *The Puritan Oligarchy,* London 1947
Winthrop, S. H., *Religions in America,* New York 1965

INDEX

APPENDIX

Acts of Parliament